Neuroscience and Behavioral Health

Neuroscience and Behavioral Health

Edited by **Vin Lopez**

Willford Press
New York

Published by Willford Press,
118-35 Queens Blvd., Suite 400,
Forest Hills, NY 11375, USA
www.willfordpress.com

Neuroscience and Behavioral Health
Edited by Vin Lopez

International Standard Book Number: 978-1-68285-199-9 (Hardback)

Printed in China.

Contents

Preface

This book aims to provide a comprehensive insight into the interdisciplinary fields of neuroscience and behavioral health. This book is compiled in such a manner, that it will provide an in-depth overview of the various aspects of neuroscience, neuropsychology and cognitive neuroscience. The various advancements in the field of behavioral health and neuroscience are glanced at and their applications as well as ramifications are examined in great detail. In this book, using case studies and examples, constant effort has been made to make the understanding of the difficult concepts as easy and informative as possible, for the readers.

Significant researches are present in this book. Intensive efforts have been employed by authors to make this book an outstanding discourse. This book contains the enlightening chapters which have been written on the basis of significant researches done by the experts.

Finally, I would also like to thank all the members involved in this book for being a team and meeting all the deadlines for the submission of their respective works. I would also like to thank my friends and family for being supportive in my efforts.

Editor

1

Health status and modeling of rural aged population of Kushtia District in Bangladesh

Rafiqul Islam*, Mosharaf Hossain and Moshiur Rahman

Department of Population Science and HRD, University of Rajshahi, Rajshahi-6205, Bangladesh.

Aged population is an emerging issue in Bangladesh. It is a frightening problem of rural area in Bangladesh as well as a national problem. It has many socio-economic effects on national development. So, the aim of this study is to identify the determinants of health status of aged population in Kumarkhali Thana of Kushtia District in Bangladesh. Furthermore, an effort has been made here to fit mathematical model for aged population due to ages. For this, a total number of 250 rural aged populations have been interviewed through a structured questionnaire by purposive sampling technique. In this study, logistic regression model and polynomial model are applied. In logistic analysis, it is indicated that the respondent's sex, type of family, occupation of the family head and suffering any diseases have significant effects for taking treatment on aged population. It is seen that age associated with aged population follow third degree polynomial model explaining more than 99% coefficient of determination.

Key words: Aged population, socio-economic variables, logistic regression analysis, polynomial model, Bangladesh.

INTRODUCTION

Aged population is defined as the group of population who belong to the age group of 60 years and more (BAG, 2003). Furthermore, population ageing is defined as an increase in the proportion of population, which is elderly. It is a product of history, individual experiences and social forces (Morgan and Kunkel, 2001). Aged population in Bangladesh is viewed as natural outcome of demographic transition from high fertility and mortality to low fertility and mortality. Until the year 1961, the sequence of high birth rate followed by high death rate kept the proportion of population aged 60 years and above at a low level. In the years, steady decline in birth rate accelerated the ageing process. It is likely to reach 9.1% in 2010 (Hossain, 1996) and in terms absolute number aged person would be 13.3 million in 2010. Between 1997 and 2010, the share of the population under fifteen years is expected to decline by about 19% under the assumption of replacement level fertility; whilst the share of elderly population during the same period will increase by about 50%. Similarly, the share of the working age population will increase by about 38%. The process of aging is expected to accelerate in the coming decades, mainly because the large cohorts born in 1950s and 1960s respectively will be joining the ranks of 60 years and beyond during this period. The decline in mortality, particularly at young ages, also means that a higher proportion of the large cohorts will survive to old age (Kabir, 2005). Aged population creates problems in every sector. In economic area, it creates problems on pension scheme, savings, retirement, employment etc. In political area, it is retards to change leadership. Since many years ago aged people are a social problem in developed countries but it is now-a-days a new problem in developing countries. In Bangladesh, the statistical data represent that from the year 1974 - 2001 the number of aged population has increased from 1.38 million to 6.05 million and at present 7.59 million of the total population are aged (BBS, 2003). It is expected that the number of aged people will be 7.2% of the total population by 2021 years (Kabir and Humayan, 1994). About 5.052 million aged people are living in rural areas in Bangladesh and among them 2.305 million are aged women (BBS, 2000). Aged people of rural area in Bangladesh are suffering from mental torture, permanent illness and physically depression (Cain, 1991). Abedin (1998) studied socio-economic and psychophysical conditions of the aged

*Corresponding author. E-mail: rafique_pops@yahoo.com.

population in which the study was based on 424 aged persons of whom 219 are in rural area and 205 are in urban area. In which it was investigated that most of the aged population, in particular, rural aged people were belonging to a low incoming group and the overall economic condition of aged people was not encouraging. Therefore, the fundamental objectives of the present work are addressed in the following:

1.) To identify the determinants of health status of aged population in rural area of Kumarkhali Thana of Kushtia District, Bangladesh.
2.) To build up mathematical model to aged population, and to apply cross-validity prediction power (CVPP) and F-test to this model to verify the validity of the model.

SOURCES OF DATA

In this study, a total number of 250 aged populations were questioned during the survey period in 2008. The respondents were randomly interviewed by some selected questions from several villages in the rural areas of Kumarkhali Thana of Kushtia District, Bangladesh by purposive sampling technique. Various socio-economic and demographic variables were considered at time of data collection.

METHODS

Logistic regression model

Logistic regression is a form of regression, which is used when the dependent is a dichotomy and the independents are of any type. In logistic analysis, aged people taking treatment is considered as dependent variable where respondent's age group, education, sex, religion, type of family, condition of house, occupation of the family head, sanitation, income and suffering for diseases are treated as independent variables. This technique expresses a qualitative dependent variable as a function of several independent variables, both qualitative and quantitative. The dependent variable is considered for this model is categorized in the following:

$$Y_i = \begin{cases} 1, & \text{if taking treatment} \\ 0, & \text{otherwise} \end{cases}, \quad i = 1, 2, 3, \ldots, n.$$

The results of logistic model are demonstrated in Table 2.

Smoothing of age data

If the aged population by ages is plotted in the graph paper then it is found that there exist some distortions in the data. Therefore, an adjustment is important and needed to minimize these unpredicted distortions before going to fit the model to this data set. In consequence, a modification is made here using the Package Minitab Release 12.1 by the most latest smoothing technique"4253H, twice" (Velleman, 1980). After that, the smoothed data are used to fit model for aged population and these observed, smoothed and predicted data is launched in Table 3.

Model fitting

Using the scattered plot of aged population by age group in years (Figures 1), it is observed that aged population can be fitted by polynomial model with respect to different ages. Therefore, an nth degree polynomial model is considered and the form of the model is

$$y = a_0 + \sum_{i=1}^{n} a_i x^i + u;$$

Where, x is the mean value of the age group; y is aged population; a_0 is the constant; a_i is the coefficient of x^i (i =1, 2, 3, ..., n) and u is the stochastic error term of the model. Here, a suitable n is chosen for which the error sum of square is least amount.

Model accuracy test

The cross validity prediction power (CVPP) is applied to evaluate the accurateness and reliability of the model. The arithmetical formula for CVPP is precised by

$$\rho_{cv}^2 = 1 - \frac{(n-1)(n-2)(n+1)}{n(n-k-1)(n-k-2)}(1-R^2).$$

Here, n is the number of classes, k is the number of explanatory variables in the fitted model and the cross-validated R is the correlation between observed and predicted values of the dependent variable (Stevens, 1996). The shrinkage and contraction of the model is the positive value of $\lambda = (\rho_{cv}^2 - R^2)$; where ρ_{cv}^2 is CVPP & R^2 is the coefficient of determination of the model. $1-\lambda$ is the stability of R^2 of the model. Closer the value of λ to zero, the better is the prediction. The estimated CVPP related to their R^2 and information on model fittings are presented in the result and discussion section. CVPP was employed as model validation or accuracy test by Islam (2003 and 2005) and Islam et al. (2003 and 2005).

F-test

To measure the overall significance of the fitted model as well as the significance of R^2, the F-test is employed at this juncture (Gujarati, 1998).

RESULTS

Percentage distribution of aged population

The distribution and percentage distribution of aged population based on socio-demographic as well as health related characteristics of this study are demonstrated in Table 1. These characteristics are, in brief and are explained in the discussion part of this paper.

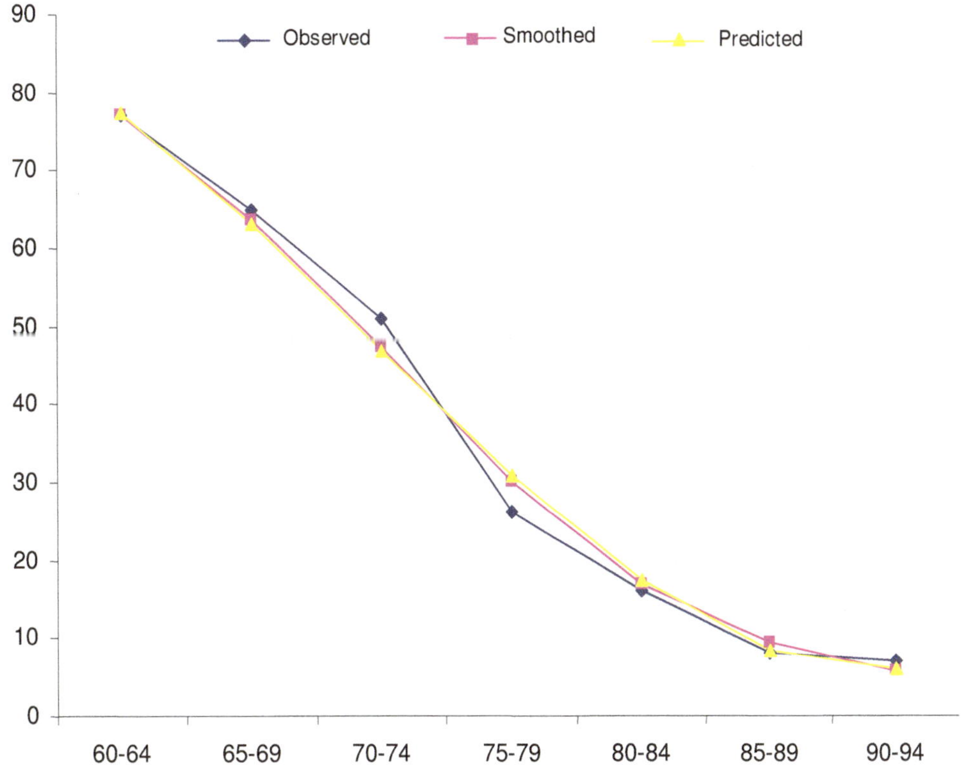

Figure 1. Observed, smoothed and predicted aged population of Bangladesh. X axis is age group and Y axis indicates population.

Determinant of health status of the aged population using logistic regression model

Results of the logistic regression model, where treatment is taken as dependent variable and age, education, sex, type of family, structure of house, sanitation facilities, family head occupation, monthly income and suffer any disease are considered as independent variables, are presented in Table 2 and findings are discussed in the discussion section.

Results of modeling fitting

The results of model fitting, that is, observed, predicted and residual are shown in Table 3 and the graph of observed, smoothed and predicted by age group is depicted in Figure 1 and the findings of model fitting are described in discussion section.

DISCUSSION

It is observed that most of the respondents are falling in the age group of 60-69 years, which is 56.8% and rest of the respondent is 43.2% in the age group 70 years and over. Education is the single most important indicator of the socioeconomic status of an individual, which affects almost all aspects of human life, including demographic health behavior. Usually an educated person lives a better life than an illiterate person. It is obvious that 40% of the respondents have no education and 60% respondents are educated. In our present study, the information suggests that 77.2% respondents are engaged in agriculture and 22.8% are engaged others occupation such as business, service, job etc. Religion is a very important characteristic in relation to the aging of person particularly for Islamic believes. It is an important community characteristic. Majority people of Bangladesh are Muslim. Also other people are Hindu, Buddha, and Christian. In this paper, 94.4% respondents belong to Muslims community and only 5.6% belong to Hindu community. Healthy and comfortable residence is essential for sound, body and mind. Unhealthy house is responsible for health hazard and diseases, so it is an important factor for human being. The information suggests that most of the house are tin which is 82.8 and 17.2% are others house such as katcha, boom house etc. The overall observations indicate that maximum of the respondents come from lower economic level. An unhygienic environment is enormously important causes of bad health of aged people. Aged population would be free from environmental hazards if the sanitary condition of a locality is better. The overall sanitation arrangements

Table 1. Percentage distribution of population according to selected characteristics.

Characteristic	Observed	Percentage
Age group		
60 - 69	142	56.8
70+	108	43.2
Education	100	40.0
Illiterate	150	60.0
Literate		
Sex	114	45.6
Male	136	54.4
Female		
Religion	236	94.4
Muslim	14	5.6
Non-Muslim		
Type of family	71	28.4
Unit	179	71.6
Joint		
Condition of houses	207	82.8
Tin	43	17.2
Others		
Occupation	193	77.2
Agriculture	57	22.8
Others		
Sanitation	185	74.0
No	65	26.0
Yes		
Income	50	20.0
<3000	189	75.6
3000-9900	11	4.4
10000+		
Suffering from diseases	7	2.8
No	243	97.2
Yes		

of the respondents are not so good in this study because it is seen that 26% are hygienic and 74% are unhygienic. Majorities (71.2%) are living in joint family and rest of them is living in unit family.

In logistic model, sex, type of family, structure of house, family head's occupation and suffers any diseases are found as significant variable. It is found that aged people who lived in a joint family had taken 3.577 times more treatment than that of unit family. Female respondents have taken treatment 3.237 times more than the male respondents. Aged people who are engaged in agricultural sector taking treatment 0.393 times less than others occupation. Other independent variables such as age group, education, religion, sanitation, house conditions and income are statistically insignificant.

The polynomial model is assumed for age associated with aged population of Bangladesh and the fitted model is:

Table 2. Logistic regression estimates of the effects of different selected characteristics on taking treatment

Characteristic	Co-efficient (β)	Odds ratio
Age group		
60 - 69 (r.c)	…	1.000
70+	0.795	2.215
Education		
Illiterate (r.c)	…	1.000
Literate	-0.047	0.954
Sex		
Male (r.c)	…	1.000
Female	1.175^{**}	3.237
Religion		
Muslim (r.c)	…	1.000
Non-Muslim	-0.557	.573
Type of family		
Unit (r.c)	…	1.000
Joint	1.274^{*}	3.577
Condition of houses		
Tin (r.c)	…	1.000
Others	0.844	2.325
Occupation		
Agriculture (r.c)	…	1.00
Others	-0.934^{***}	0.393
Sanitation		
No (r.c)	…	1.000
Yes	0.484	1.622
Income		
<3000 (r.c)	…	1.000
3000-9900	-0.826	0.438
10000+	-0.957	0.384
Suffering from diseases		
No (r.c)	…	1.000
Yes	3.741^{*}	42.154
Constant	-5.330^{*}	0.005

*Significance at 0.01 **Significance at 0.05 ***Significance at 0.10 r.c = Reference category.

Table 3. The observed and fitted aged population by age group.

Age group (x)	Mid value of x	Observed	Smoothed	Predicted	Residual
60 - 64	62.5	77	77.00	77.26	-0.26
65 - 69	67.5	65	63.56	63.12	0.44
70 - 74	72.5	51	47.34	46.91	0.43
75 - 79	77.5	26	30.02	30.86	-0.84
80 - 84	82.5	16	16.73	17.21	-0.48
85 - 89	87.5	8	9.36	8.20	1.16
90 - 94	92.5	7	5.61	6.05	-0.44

$y = -832.998 + 43.24692x - 0.64528x^2 + 0.002982x^3$

t (3)	-3.407	4.49330	-5.15490	5.541437
p-level	.042	.02057	.01415	.011585

Providing $R^2 = 0.99936$, $\rho^2_{cv} = 0.996343$, shrinkage coefficient = 0.003017143, F-test = 1561.5. This is the third degree polynomial model, that is, cubic polynomial model. From these statistics, it is seen that the shrinkage coefficient is very small. Hence, it is concluded that the model is better fit.

CONCLUSION AND RECOMMENDATIONS

In this study, majorities (71.2%) are living in joint family and rest of them is living in unit family. The overall observations indicate that maximum of the respondents come from lower economic level. The information suggests that most of the house are tin which is 82.8 and 17.2% are others house such as kacha, boom etc. In logistic analysis, it is showed that aged people lived in a joint family had taken 3.577 times more treatment than that of unit family. Female respondents have taken treatment 3.237 times higher than the male respondents. Aged people population who engaged agriculture they have taken 0.393 times less treatment than others occupation. It is observed that third degree polynomial model is fitted to aged population relating to age of Bangladesh.

The findings of this study may have some policy implications that would help the planners and policy makers of the Government to take necessary steps in identifying necessary conditions of the aged population. The following recommendations should be suggested for policy implications:

(1) The government should take proper steps to enhance the care giving capacity of family through appropriate programs. The traditional joint family system should be strengthened as well as encouraged in order to provide basic needs and psychosocial support to the aged people.
(2) Government should boost more economic security (like pension, medical allowance, recreational facility etc.) for geriatrics. The government be supposed to take essential steps for the welfare of the aged by taking mass education programs and awakening the people about the duty towards aged people. Government and NGOs have to build care and available recreational facilities for the aged people.
(3) Access to treatment facilities should be available and inexpensive for aged people and special emphasis on care of geriatrics should be taken every health centers, medical colleges and community clinics in both rural and urban areas. Government should provide latrine in low-priced rate to improve health and sanitation facility and necessary curriculum should be included in the national text.

REFERENCES

Abedin S (1998). Ageing in Bangladesh: Issues and Challenges, Report No. 23, under CPD-UNFPA. Program on Population and Sustainable development, Centre for Policy Dialogue.

Bangladesh Association of Gerontology (BAG) (2003). The Elderly Contemporary Issues, Dahka, Bangladesh.

BBS (2000). Statistical Pocketbook of Bangladesh. Ministry of Planning, Dahka, Bangladesh.

Bangladesh Bureau of Statistics (BBS) (2003). Population Census 2001, National Report, Government of the People's Republic of Bangladesh, Dhaka.

Cain MT (1991). The Activities of the Rural Elderly in Rural Bangladesh. Population Studies.

Gujarati DN, Damodar N (1998). Basic Econometrics, Third Edition, McGraw Hill, Inc., New York.

Hossain MS (1996). Population Growth and Structure 1961-2010. Dhaka, Bangladesh Bureau of Statistics (BBS).

Islam R (2003). Modeling of Demographic Parameters of Bangladesh- An Empirical Forecasting, Unpublished PhD. Thesis, Rajshahi University.

Islam R, Nurul MD, Ali MD, Ayub MD, Mostofa G (2003). Construction of Male Life Table from Female Widowed Information of Bangladesh, Inter. J. Stat. Sci. Dept. of Statistics, University of Rajshahi, Bangladesh 2: 69-82.

Islam R (2005). Construction of Female Life Table from Male Widowed Information of Bangladesh, Pakistan J. Stat. 21(3): 275-284.

Islam R, Islam Md, Nurul MD, Ali M, Korban M, Nazrul I, Mondal Md, Nazrul I (2005). Indirect Estimation and Mathematical Modeling of Some Demographic Parameters of Bangladesh, The Oriental Anthropologist 5(2): 163 - 171.

Kabir M, Humayun K (1994). Local Level Policy Development to Deal with the Consequences of Population Aging in Bangladesh. ESCAP, UN New York Asian Population Studies Series. Bangladesh. CPD,

Morgan L, Kunkel S (2001). Ageing the social context, Pine Forge press, California, USA.

Stevens J (1996). Applied Multivariate Statistics for the Social Sciences, Third Edition, Lawrence Erlbaum Associates, Inc., Publishers, New Jersey. Velleman PF (1980). Definition and Comparison of Robust Nonlinear Data Smoothing Algorithms J. Am. Stati. Assoc. 75(371): 609-615.

2

Analysis of combined anti-tuberculous drug induced neurotoxicity in the cerebral cortex of adult wistar rats by immunohistochemistry

Fakoya Francis Adelade[1,2]*, Osoniyi Omolaja[3] and Obuotor Efere Martins[3]

[1]Department of Anatomy and Cell Biology, Faculty of Basic Medical Sciences, Obafemi Awolowo University, Ile-Ife, Nigeria.
[2]Department of Anatomical Sciences, St. George's University School of Medicine, True Blue, St. George's Grenada, The Caribbean.
[3]Department of Biochemistry, Faculty of Science, Obafemi Awolowo University, Ile-Ife, Nigeria

Combined Isoniazid (INH) and Rifampicin administration still remain as two of the main drugs of choice in the treatment regimes of tuberculosis (TB) world wide, particularly in Africa, where tuberculosis incidence rates are among the highest in the world. This study evaluated the effects of chronic administration of combined Isoniazid/Rifampicin on the cerebral cortex of the adult rats by immunohistochemistry. Adult wistar rats (average weight of 220 g) maintained under standard laboratory conditions were randomly grouped into treatment and control (n = 10). The treatment group A received combined INH + Rifampicin (50 mg/kg each, i.p) while the control group B received normal saline (0.5 ml, i.p.) only; daily at 1600 h for 15 days. Animals were sacrificed by cervical dislocation for whole brain weight determination (n = 6) and by whole body perfusion following anaesthesia for neurohistology and immunohistochemistry (n = 4) from each group. Coronal samples of the frontoparietal cortex were taken from each hemisphere and processed routinely for paraffin embedding followed by Nissl staining of 6 µm thick sections. 30 µm thick sections were cryo-sectioned at -23°C, after cryoprotection in 30% sucrose/phosphate buffered saline (PBS) from the remaining samples and reacted for flourescent glial fibrillary acidic protein (GFAP) immunoreactivity and terminal deoxynucleotidyl transferase dUTP nick end labeling (TUNEL) method for the detection of apoptosis. The treatment group showed highly reactive intracortical and subpial GFAP positive astrocytes, mostly localized as clusters, compared to the control; GFAP immunostaining intensity was quantified using Adobe Photoshop Element 6.0. Cerebral cortical lamina was well preserved in both groups, while neuronal pyknotism were not observed in the treatment group, compared to the controls. The treatment group showed intense darkly stained discrete cells, positive for the TUNEL signals. These microanatomical and microchemical changes suggest neurotoxicity of these drugs, which though was not overt clinically.

Key words: Tuberculosis, anti-tuberculous drugs, neurotoxicity, quantitative immunocytochemistry, adobe photoshop elements, astrogliosis, apoptosis, cerebral cortex, isoniazid, rifampicin.

INTRODUCTION

The global burden of disease caused by tuberculosis (TB) was estimated in 2011 to be at 8.7 million incidence cases and 12 million prevalent cases (WHO, 2012). TB, a disease of poverty, is contagious and air borne, affecting mostly young adults in their productive years and ranks as the second leading cause of death from an infectious disease worldwide, after the human immunodeficiency virus (HIV). With a reported estimate of 8.7 million new cases of TB (13% co-infected with HIV), 1.4 million people die from TB, including almost one million deaths among HIV-negative individuals and 0.43 million among people who were HIV-positive (WHO, 2012). This is a slight reduction from the reported figures of new cases of TB in 2009 (WHO, 2010a) but the impact of HIV infection on mortality is still on the increase (WHO, 2012) and is one of the top killers of women, with 300,000 deaths among HIV-negative women and 200,000 deaths among HIV-positive women in 2011. This is despite the availability of treatment that will cure most cases of TB. Short-course regimens of first-line drugs that can cure around 90% of cases have been available since the 1980s (WHO, 2003; ATS, 2003).

While efforts are being made on the progress towards global targets for reductions in TB cases and deaths (Raviglione, 2006; WHO, 2003, 2012), with a mortality rate decreased by 36% since 1990 and the world appears to be on track to achieving the global target of a 50% reduction by 2015, the global burden of TB remains enormous, being highest in Asia and Africa 59 and 26%, respectively (WHO, 2012). Almost 80% of TB cases among people living with HIV reside in Africa. TB incidence rates in Africa are among the highest in the world (Raviglione et al., 1995; Dye et al., 1999, WHO, 2009, 2010a) and these rates have increased steadily over the past two decades as a result of the HIV epidemic (Cantwell and Binkin, 1996; Raviglione, 2006), the strongest known risk factor for the progression from tuberculosis infection to disease (Rieder, 1999), increasing susceptibility to primary tuberculosis and reactivation of latent tuberculous infection, thus increasing tuberculosis incidence directly (Harries, 1990; Perriens et al., 1991; De Cock et al., 1992; Range et al., 2001; WHO 2012).

Worldwide, 3.7% of new cases and 20% of previously treated cases were estimated to have multi-drug resistant tuberculosis (MDR-TB) (WHO, 2012; Connell et al., 2011). India, China, the Russian Federation and South Africa have almost 60% of the world's cases of MDR-TB. The highest proportions of TB patients with MDR-TB are in Eastern Europe and central Asia (WHO, 2012).

Current treatment of TB is usually the combination of isoniazid (INH) and rifampicin, which are given for at least six months, along with pyrazinamide and ethambutol (or streptomycin), which are used only in the first two months (WHO, 2003, 2010b, 2012; ATS, 2003). This treatment regime is referred to as short-course chemotherapy (Addington, 1979; Jawetz, 1987; NIAID, 1999; WHO, 2010b) and its success has been demonstrated through the Directly observed treatment short course (DOTs) and "Stop TB Strategy (WHO, 2010a; 2012). Major progress in global TB control followed the widespread implementation of the DOTS strategy (Raviglione and Uplekar, 2006; WHO, 2003, 2006).

Antituberculous drugs are generally safe but can occasionally be associated with life-threatening complications, since there has been sporadic reports of cases of neurotoxicity following use of the drug in the initiation of antituberculous therapy (Bharat et al., 2003), and as a preventive therapy (Martinjak-Dvorsek et al., 2000). INH is one of the anti-tuberculosis drugs widely prescribed for patients since the early 1950s. It is relatively nontoxic but some patients develop peripheral neuropathy attributed to a disturbance of vitamin B_6 metabolism. The incidence of acute isoniazid (INH)-related poisonings has increased, with parenteral pyridoxine as the antidote for INH-induced seizures (Romero and Kuczler, 1998; Santucci et al., 1999; Citak et al., 2002; Desai and Agarwal, 2004). While some isoniazid metabolites are hepatotoxic, little is known about their neurotoxic property (Sanfeliu et al., 1999; Kass and Shandera, 2010).

This study is an immunohistochemical evaluation of the cerebral cortex for microchemical and structural anomalies that could possibly underlie the adverse effects of chronic administration of combined INH and rifampicin.

MATERIALS AND METHODS

Adult wistar rats (*Rattus norvegicus*) of either sex (average weight 220 g) used for the experiment were maintained under standard laboratory conditions, fed with standard mouse chow (Ladokun Feeds, Ibadan, Nigeria) and provided with water *ad libitum.* All experimental protocols and animal use and care were approved by the University Research and Ethical Committees. The animals were randomly assigned into two groups (n = 10). Group (A) received a combined dose of 50 mg/kg body weight of INH and Rifampicin (Smithkline-Beecham, Nigeria) administered intraperitoneally (i.p.) daily at 1600 h for 15 days while group B received an equal volume of normal saline (i.p.). A pair-fed group (C) (n = 7) was included to control for the stress of chronic i.p. administration, and received food and water *ad libitum.* Feeding patterns and animal body weights of all groups were monitored throughout the experiment. All animals were monitored closely for clinical signs of neurotoxicity (generalized weakness, ataxia and paralysis of the limbs). At the end of administration, animals were sacrificed by cervical dislocation (n = 6) from Groups A and B; and (n = 4) from Group C and the whole brain was quickly removed, dried with Whatman filter paper No. 1 and weighed. The remaining animals were anaesthetized by an overdose of pentothal intraperitoneally, whole-body perfused under gravity, first with normal saline, followed by 10% formol calcium fixative.

The brains were removed and a 6 mm coronal sample of the frontoparietal cortex (para central sulcus) was taken from each hemisphere under stereoscopic dissection and further fixed in the same fixative for 4 h. Specimens of samples were processed routinely for paraffin embedding and 6 µm thick sections cut on a sliding microtome (Histoslide 2000, Hamburg, Germany), mounted unto slides and left overnight at 37°C in the incubator (for good adherence to the frost slides). The remaining samples were cryosectioned (Fibrigol cryocut) at -23°C, after cryoprotection in 30% sucrose/PBS and 30 µm thick sections were then cut, stored in wells containing 1 ml of acidic phosphate buffered saline (PBS) at 2 to 8°C before immunohistochemistry.

NISSL staining

Slides of paraffin sections were dewaxed and rehydrated according to standard protocol and stained in 2% cresyl violet solution (Nissl stain) for 5 to 10 min, rinsed briefly in distilled water and then dehydrated with ascending grades of alcohol, cleared in xylene and mounted using Canada balsam and cover slipped.

GFAP immunohistochemistry

Sections were washed thrice for 5 min in tris buffered saline (TBS) (pH 7.4), then blocked in 2% bovine serum with 5% normal goat serum (NGS) for one hour at room temperature. Incubation was done with Cy3-coupled-monoclonal anti-GFAP-antibody [Sigma (1:500)] in blocking solution for 2 h at room temperature. Sections were again washed thrice for 5 min in TBS (pH 7.4) and mounted on gelatinized slides and air dried overnight.

Tunel reaction

Apoptosis of nuclei were assessed by *in situ* terminal deoxynucleotidyl transferase (TdT)-mediated deoxyuridine triphosphate (dUTP)-biotin nick-end labeling (TUNEL) of DNA strand breaks using the *in situ* cell death detection, POD kit, for immunohistochemical detection of apoptosis (Roche Diagnostics, Mannheim, Germany). Sections were transferred unto slides through 0.2 M PBS, pH 7.4, and allowed to air-dry overnight. The following day, they were washed in PBS for 30 min. To block endogenous peroxidase activity and improve cell permeability, sections were rinsed with PBS and incubated with blocking solution (3% H_2O_2 in methanol) for 10 min at room temperature, then rinsed in PBS and incubated in permeabilisation solution for 2 min on ice (4°C). Labeling was done by rinsing sections in PBS twice, the area around the section dried with filter paper and 50 µl TUNEL reaction mixture was added onto the section, cover slip applied (to avoid evaporative loss and ensure homogenous spread of the mixture) and then incubated in a humidified chamber for 60 min at 37°C. For positive control, sections of rat ileum were incubated simultaneously without the enzyme in the reaction mixture. Sections were rinsed with PBS thrice. The areas around sections were dried again for signal conversion and analysis. 50 µl of converter-POD was added onto the section, cover slip applied (to avoid evaporative loss and ensure homogenous spread of the mixture) and then incubated in a humidified chamber for 30 min at 37°C, then rinsed thrice with PBS. A 50 to 100 µl sigma-3,3′-diaminobenzidine (DAB) substrate solution was added to sections and incubated for 10 min at room temperature, rinsed thrice with PBS and counter stained in nissl stain, dehydrated, cleared and mounted in entellan.

Image analysis

Sections were examined using Axioplan-2 epiflourescence photomicroscope (Carl Zeiss, Germany), with a Sony 3-CCD video camera (Tokyo, Japan) connected to a Compaq computer that has the AxioVision 3.0-Rel. software for digital image analysis. Images were opened in Adobe Photoshop (version 6; Adobe Systems, San Jose, CA) and stored in a TIFF file format on the hard drive. Photomicrographs were produced from the grabbed frames and printed on Hp premium photo glossy paper using an Hp 5700 DeskJet printer.

Quantification of immunocytochemical staining

For the entire study, the camera had its auto mode turned off and manual controls were used to adjust the image intensity which was kept at an identical level during the entire study. All images obtained from treatment and control groups were at the same level of magnification. Five fields were chosen so as to best reflect the overall immunostaining of the reactivity on the entire slide. The digitized images were stored on an external data storage device (IOGEAR 2.5" eSATA 3Gbps/USB 2.0 Combo ION™ External Hard Drive) until required.

The procedure for determination of immunostaining intensity and the technique of selection of similar features on a digitized immunohistochemical image has previously been described in detail (Lehr et al., 1996, 1997, 1999). The software used in this study was Adobe Photoshop Elements, version 6.0 (20070910.r.377499). Briefly, using the magic wand tool in the tool menu of Photoshop Elements 6.0, the cursor was placed on a GFAP-positive astrocyte. The tolerance level of the magic wand tool was adjusted so that the entire astrocyte was selected. Using the similar command in the select menu, all immunostained astrocytes were automatically selected. Subsequently, the image was transformed to 8-bit grayscale. An optical density plot of the selected area was generated using the histogram tool in the window menu. The mean staining intensity (in arbitrary units, AU) was recorded. Following this, the background was selected using the inverse tool in the select menu, and immunostaining was quantified using the histogram tool in the window menu. Immunostaining intensity was calculated as the difference between astrocytic immunostaining and background immunostaining and was designated as immunocytochemical index with arbitrary units (AU). The quantification of immunostaining data is presented in Figure 4.

Statistical analysis

The data were analyzed using the computerized statistical package 'Statistica 5.0'. The mean and standard error of mean (SEM) values for each group was determined. The means were compared by analysis of variance at a level of significance of 95 and 99%. However, the immunocytochemical index is unitless and hence values are therefore reported as energy units per pixel (eu/pix). In all instances, data are expressed as the means ± SEM.

RESULTS

Administration of combined INH/rifampicin did not affect the appetite of the animals and no clinical signs of neurotoxicity were observed, while there was no significant difference in the mean absolute and relative brain weights of the treatment group compared to the control ($p > 0.05$). Values were mean + SEM (Figure 1). The results showed no significant changes on the body weights of the animals throughout the duration of the experiment.

Combined INH and rifampicin induced highly reactive intracortical GFAP positive astrocytes, localized in clusters in the cerebral cortex (Figure 2a and c), while the control animals showed uniform distribution of GFAP signals across the cortex (Figure 2b and d). Astrocytes were intensely and brilliantly florescent, robust with short and heavy branching limbs (Figure 2c) compared to the slender, long and fewer branches seen in the control group (Figure 2d). The pial and subpial regions demonstrated GFAP positive reactions in both treatment (Figure 3a and b) and control groups (Figure 3c and d),

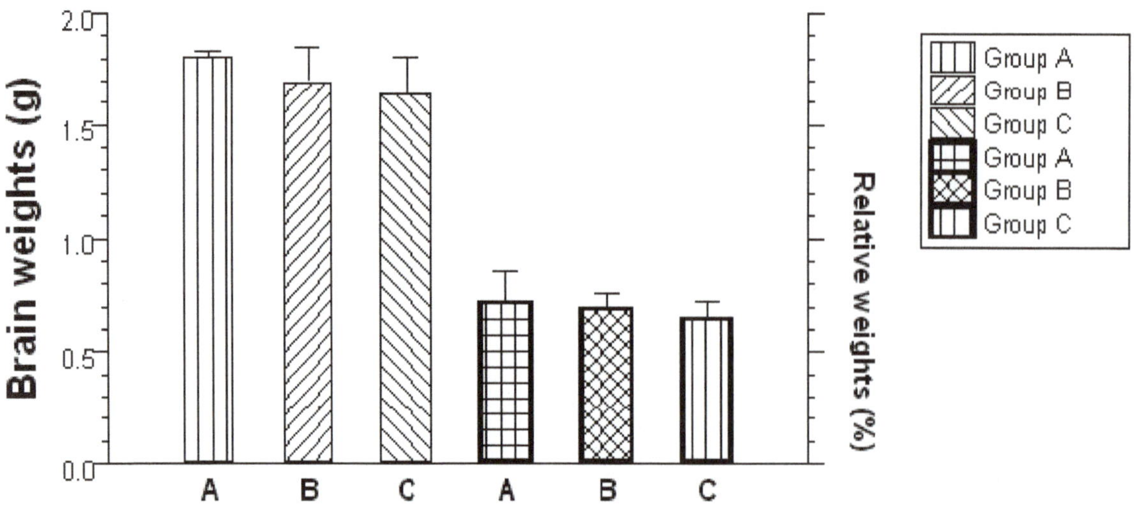

Figure 1. Mean absolute and relative brain weights of rats administered combined INH/rifampicin. Values are mean ± SEM ($p > 0.5$) [A and B: (n = 6); C: (n = 4)].

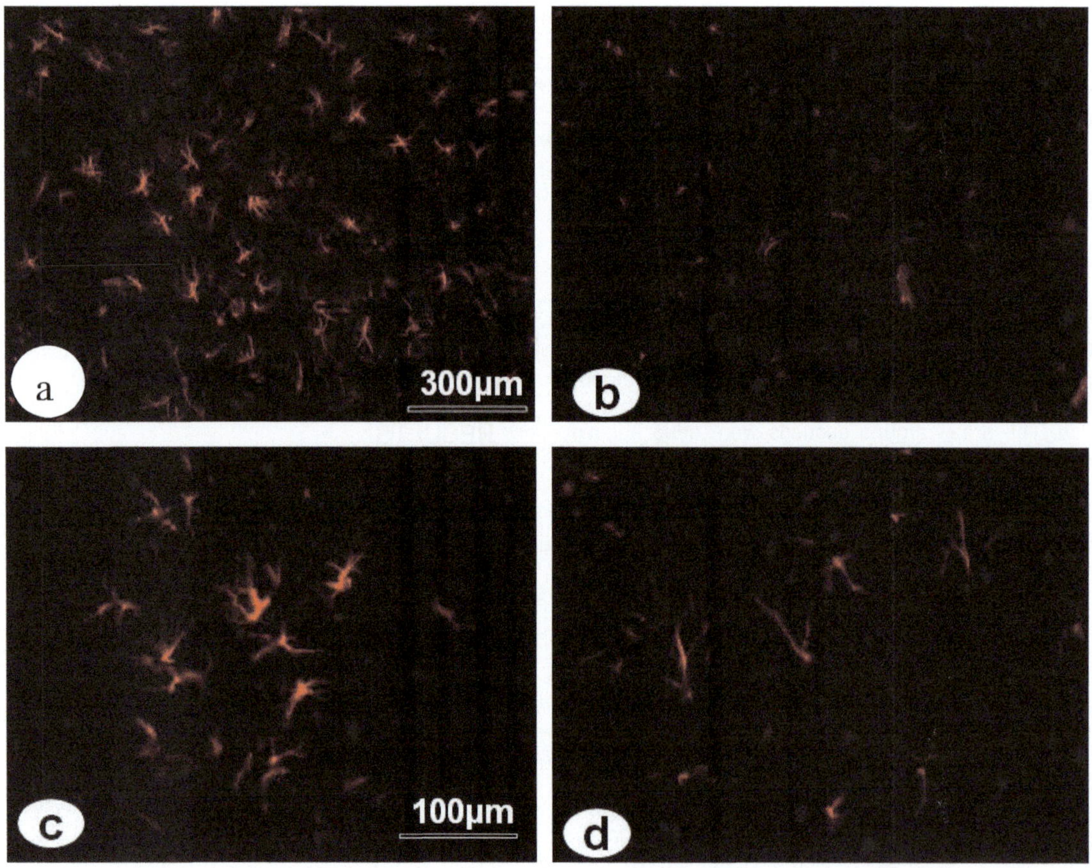

Figure 2. GFAP Immunohistochemistry of the cerebral cortex showing reactive astrocytosis in the treatment group (a, c) compared to control group (b, d). Bars: [a, b - 300 μm; c, d – 100 μm].

with the treatment group being slightly more reactive than the control group. The quantification of immunostaining intensity of GFAP immunoreactivity revealed significantly higher intensity over the entire cerebral cortex in the

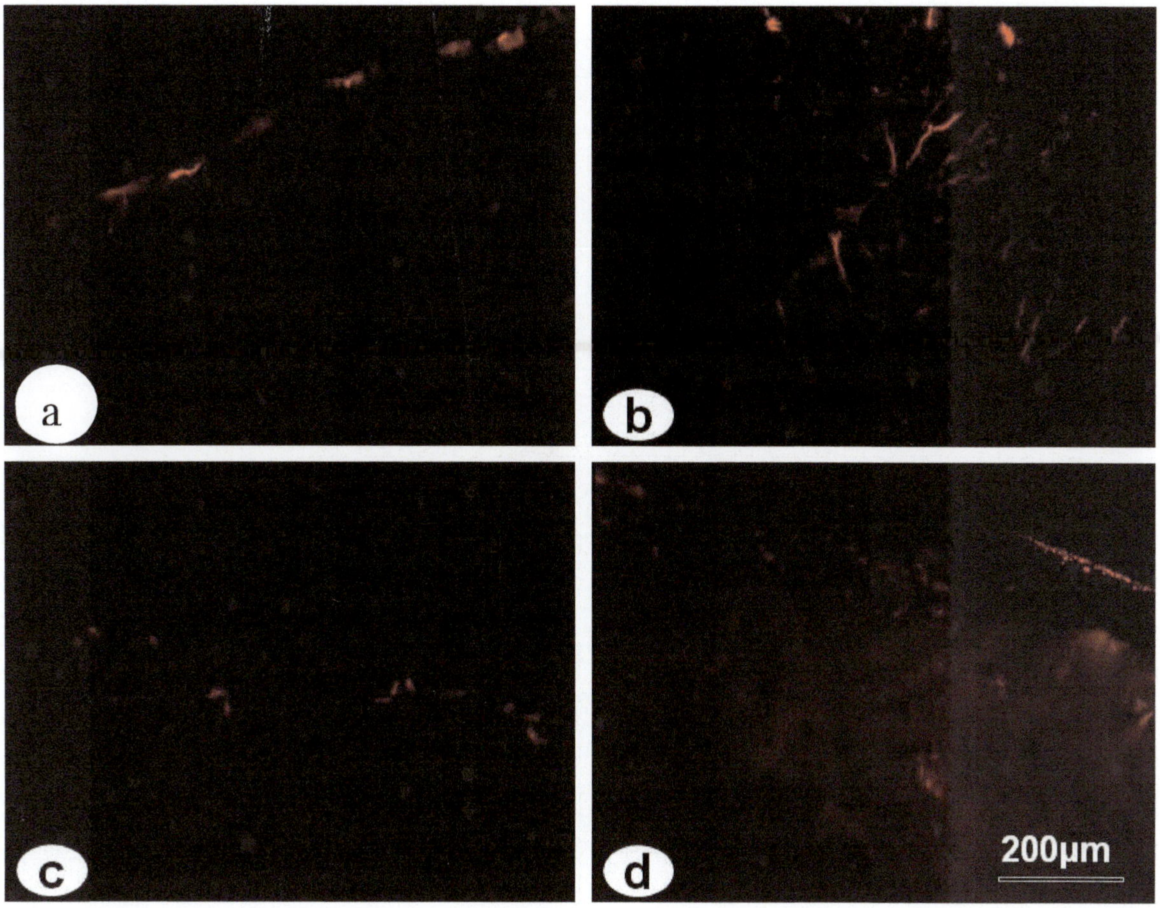

Figure 3. GFAP Immunohistochemistry of pial and subpial regions of the cerebral cortex showing significant immunostaining in the treatment group (a, b) compared to control group (c, d), respectively. Bar: 200 µm.

treatment group compared to the controls, even though slightly less in the pial region (Figure 4)

Nissl staining revealed an even distribution of the cortical lamina layers in all groups (Figure 5a and b). There were close apposition of densely stained 'peanut-shaped' bodies to neurons in the treatment group (Figure 5c) in contrast to the control (Figure 5d). Most of these bodies appear granulated. Neither cortical lamina distortion nor neuronal pyknotism were observed in the groups (Figure 5a and b).

TUNEL reaction revealed numerous intensely stained dark-brown cells of varying sizes, generalized over the cortex (Figure 6a) in the treatment group. No predilection for particular lamina in the treatment group. The control group showed few slightly stained cells positive for the TUNEL reaction (Figure 6b). The positive control was negative for the reaction.

DISCUSSION

The first line drugs in the treatment of TB remains isoniazid, rifampicin and ethambutol in Africa, Asia and parts of Latin America, where TB as a chronic inflammatory condition is still very prevalent, with increase in incidence due to the human immune deficiency virus/acquired immune deficiency syndrome (HIV/AIDs) scourge (WHO, 2012). Since the organism (*Mycobacterium tuberculosis*) (been intracellular and exhibiting long periods of metabolic inactivity) tends to develop resistance to any one drug, the combination drug treatment is employed (Addington, 1979; Dutt and Stead, 1982; Jawetz, 1987). The results of this study showed no clinical signs of neurotoxicity or changes in body weight or feeding pattern following chronic administration of combined isoniazid and rifampicin. Absolute and relative brain weight differences were not statistically significant.

Pyridine-4-carboxy hydrazide (isonicotinyl hydrazide; isoniazid - INH), the hydrazide of isonicotinic acid, (MW 137) is a simple molecule freely soluble in water, that has been used in the treatment of TB for over six decades, while rifampicin was introduced in 1963 (Connell et al., 2011). Neurotoxic effects of INH were reported since the early 1950s, with complications of peripheral neuritis,

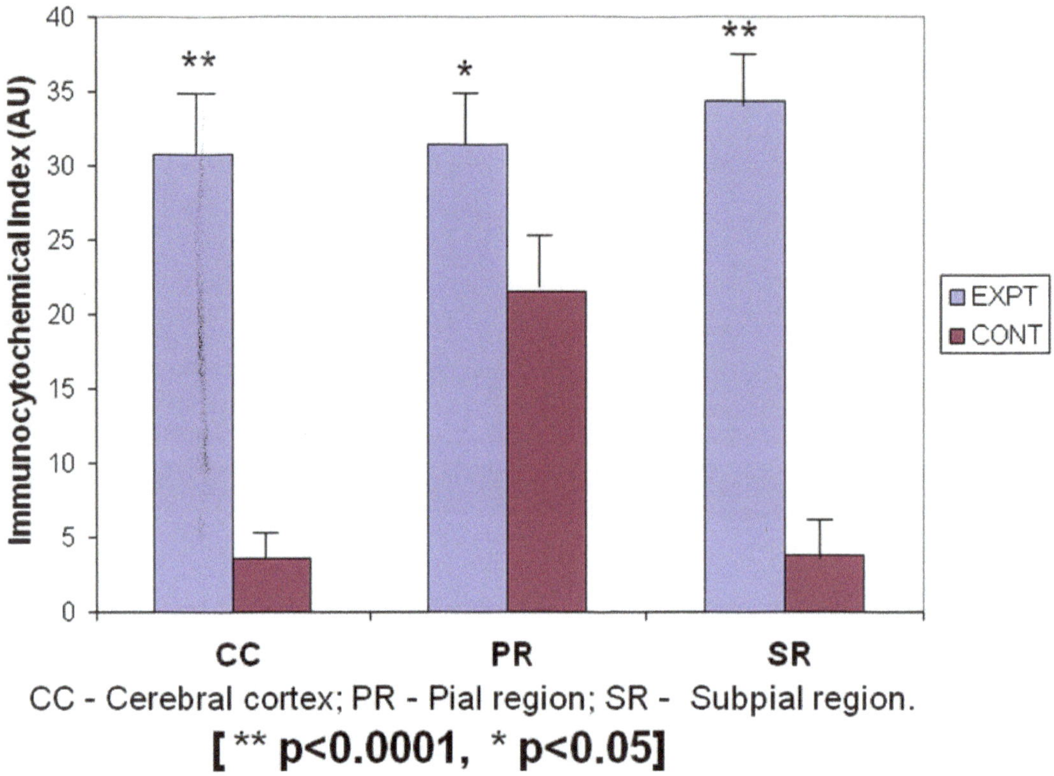

Figure 4. Quantification of GFAP immunoreactivity in the cerebral cortex (CC), pial region (PR) and subpial regions (SR) of the treatment and control groups compared.

convulsions, optic atrophy with blindness, and major psychoses being major features in up to 5% of patients (BMJ, 1958). Similar neurotoxic features have also been reported in animal studies (BMJ, 1958). Acute isoniazid intoxication is characterized by symptoms of vomiting, rapid onset of seizures, with or without fever particularly in children (Shah et al., 1995), metabolic acidosis (Koster et al., 1985) and prolonged obtundation (Citak et al., 2002). Isoniazid is also reported to be toxic to the optic nerve (Thomas, 1994; Desai and Agarwal, 2004), creating a mild sensory polyneuropathy and a bilateral retrobulbar neuritis which can progress to a severe optic atrophy (Leppert and Waespe, 1988) and acute cerebellar dysfunction (Blumberg and Gil, 1990). These complications have been attributed to a relative pyridoxine deficiency which can be prevented by administration of pyridoxine (Byrd et al., 1979; Lewin, 1996; Citak et al., 2002).

Our study showed that combined INH/rifampcin administration for 15 days in adult wistar rats produced astrocytic aggregation and hyperactivity in the cerebral cortex. Astrocytes are major neuronal supports that react to brain assault by aggregating, becoming enlarged in what is referred to as astrogliosis or so-called "reactive gliosis," a reaction with specific structural and functional characteristics (Pekny and Nilsson, 2005; Raivich et al., 1999; McGraw et al., 2001; Tacconi, 1998; Hatten et al., 1991). The marked immunostaining intensity of reactive astrogliosis was quantified using the Adobe Photoshop Element 6.0 as previously described by Lehr et al. (1996, 1997). This technique was found to be highly discriminatory and easy to establish. Once the chromogen is selected, quantification is accomplished using the histogram command in the window menu. The histogram is used to analyze the image's tonal distribution which is shown as the distribution of an image's pixel values in a bar chart. The information derivable from the histogram display include mean (represents the average intensity value), standard deviation (SD) (represents how widely intensity values vary), median (shows the middle value in the range of intensity values), pixels (represents the total number of pixels used to calculate the histogram) (Adobe Help resource Center). The slight elevation of glial fibrillary acidic protein expression in astrocytes of superficial glial limiting membrane in the treatment group usually is a response to sustained injury, which is supported by the presence of large number of apoptotic processes taking place in the cortex. A double labeling for TUNEL reaction and GFAP reactivity would precisely confirm whether astrocytes were also undergoing apoptosis.

Sanfeliu et al. (1999) showed that in cultures studies

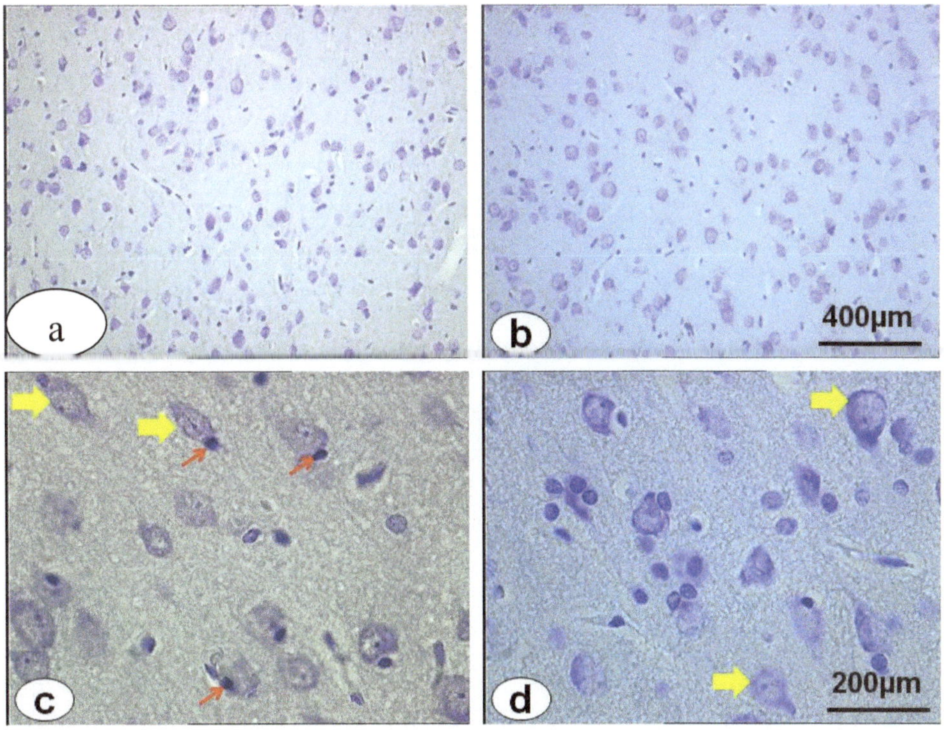

Figure 5. Effects of Combined INH/rifampicin administration on the cerebral cortex of the treatment group (a, c) compared to control (b, d) Nissl stain; [Red arrows – "peanut bodies"; yellow arrows – pyramidal neurons]. Bars: [a, b – 400 μm; c, d – 200 μm].

of mouse dorsal root ganglion (DRG) neurons and N18D3 mouse hybrid neurons, isoniazid did not cause neurotoxicity at exposures up to 7 days and hydrazine was found to be the most toxic metabolite with LC_{50} values of 2.7 and 0.3 mM after 7 days of exposure to DRG neurons and N18D3 hybrid neurons, respectively. This is supported by our findings of microstructural and microchemical anomalies after 15 days of administration of INH/rifampicin. Since 1952, when the drug was first introduced, multiple INH metabolites have been identified, including hydrazine (HZ), isonicotinic acid (INA), ammonia, the acetylated derivative N(1)-acetyl-N(2)-isonicotinylhydrazide (AcINH), hydrazones with pyruvic and ketoglutaric acids (INH-PA and INH-KA, respectively), monoacetylhydrazine (AcHZ), diacetylhydrazine (DiAcHZ), and oxidizing free radicals (Preziosi, 2007). Their formation is the result of hydrolysis (INA, HZ), cytochrome P450 (CYP)-dependent oxidation (HZ, NH(3), oxidizing free radicals), and N-acetyltransferase (NAT) activity (AcINH, AcHZ, DiAcHZ).

Doubts remain about isonicotinamide (INAAM) as an INH metabolite in mammals (Preziosi, 2007). Sanfeliu et al. (1999) suggested that metabolites including acetylisoniazid, acetylhydrazine, diacetylhydrazine and isonicotinic acid had moderate to minor neurotoxic effects on N18D3 hybrid neurons. However, pyridoxine, which is used in clinical practice to prevent or ameliorate the isoniazid-induced neuropathy (Santucci et al., 1999; Citak et al., 2002), did not consistently reverse the neurotoxicity of any of the metabolites in the cell cultures. Pyridoxine itself was found to be neurotoxic both in DRG neurons and N18D3 hybrid neurons, in agreement with human peripheral sensory neuropathy caused by prolonged overdosage (Sanfeliu et al., 1999). Pyridoxine (vitamin B6) is a co-factor in many enzymatic pathways involved in amino acid metabolism; the main biologically active form is pyridoxal 5-phosphate (Lheureux et al., 2005). The enzymes catalase and superoxide dismutase and the antioxidant agent selenium were reported to show some protection against hydrazine neurotoxicity, suggesting an involvement of the generation of reactive oxygen species in the pathogenesis of isoniazid neuropathy.

Astrogliosis, characterized by the enhanced expression of GFAP, represents a remarkably homotypic response of astrocytes to all types of injuries of the central nervous system (CNS), including injuries to the developing CNS. As such, astrocytes serve as microsensors of the injured microenvironment regardless of their location in the CNS. The diversity of insults that engender astrogliosis and the brain-wide nature of the astrocytic response suggest that common injury factors serve as the trigger of this cellular reaction. Reactive gliosis traditionally has been examined qualitatively by immunohistochemistry of GFAP (O'Callaghan, 1994), and the prominent theme that has

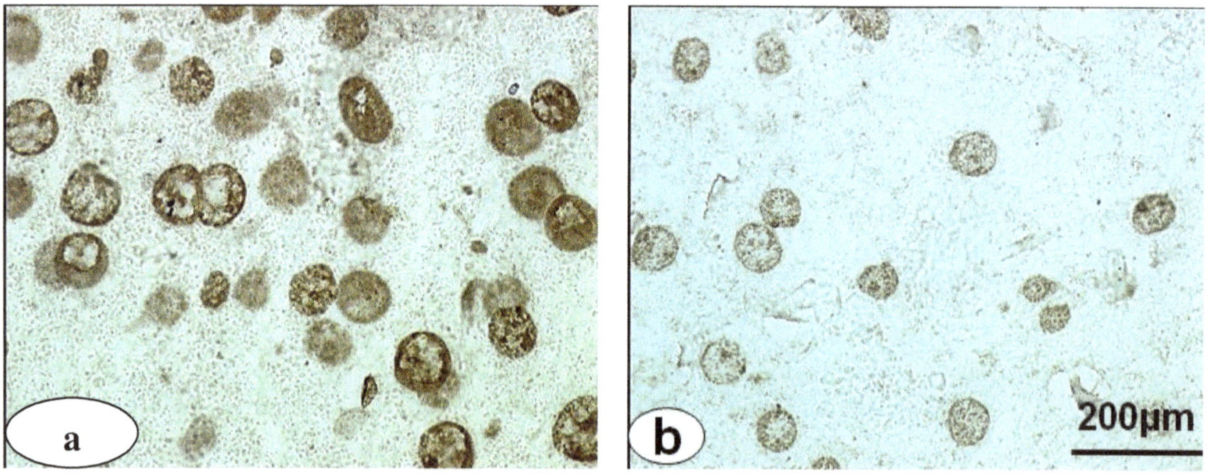

Figure 6. Effects of combined INH/rifampicin administration on the cerebral cortex of the treatment group (a) and control group (b) TUNEL reaction. Bar: 200 µm.

emerged in recent years is that proinflammatory cytokines and chemokines serve as a stimulus for induction of astrogliosis (Little and O'Callagha, 2001).

The numerous TUNEL positive cells are a strong indication of an active programmed cell death induced by the combined drug administration in the treatment group. With no particular predilection for any cortical lamina, it was unlikely however that all the apoptotic cells were neurons only. A double labeling for TUNEL reaction and GFAP reactivity would precisely confirm the involvement of astrocytes undergoing apoptosis. The cortical lamina was well preserved in all groups. The presence of few stained TUNEL positive cells in the control groups is an indication of lack of foolproof of the method. Apoptosis has been observed in a myriad of physiological and pathophysiological conditions (Kerr et al., 1972; Hengartner, 1998; Barinaga, 1998) including normal development, morphogenesis, disease conditions and degenerative disorders. However, Gal et al. (2000) has demonstrated TUNEL positivity of non-apoptotic fixed cells elicited by proteases, and was detected in both formaldehyde- and ethanol-fixed specimens in agarose-embedded fixed cells, and in chromatin spreads.

By urea-agarose gel electrophoresis, the average single-strand size of the DNA molecules carrying the free ends was found between 50 and 250 kb. They suggested that s=s discontinuities preexisting in the fixed normal cells are unmasked by protease treatment eliciting TUNEL positivity (Gal et al., 2000). While this study confirms that chronic administration of combined INH/rifampicin induces microchemical neurotoxicity in the cerebral cortex of wistar rats, how this plays out clinically is not yet known. There is a need to examine these agents in animal models of the disease and for longer periods to determine the manifestations of these microchemical changes observed within just two weeks of administration. When these agents are used for long periods in the treatment of TB, it is imperative that users are monitored closely for any manifestation, even after the medications has been discontinued.

Although most physicians are aware of INH hepatotoxicity, acute INH poisoning and its treatment are not well recognized. INH is increasingly being used to control the spread of tuberculosis, and health providers should be aware and alert with heightened suspicious index for its potential toxic effects. Given the prolonged and occasionally arduous nature of anti-tuberculous treatment for patients, we face an increasing incidence of multi-drug-resistant tuberculosis (MDR-TB), defined as infection with *M. tuberculosis* that is resistant to both rifampicin and isoniazid. Resistance to multiple anti-tuberculous drugs has arisen for a number of reasons; however, it can be argued that the principle reasons for these are the indiscriminate or poorly managed use of antibiotics, coupled with a lack of drug susceptibility testing in regions where it is most needed (Conde et al., 2009; Hall et al., 2009).

There is therefore a challenge not only to find new drugs to treat increasingly drug-resistant TB but also to find drugs that will allow shorter treatment courses and less complication. Second-line agents are used in cases of intolerance or some other contraindication to the firstline antituberculosis agents (rifampin, isoniazid, pyrazinamide, and ethambutol) and consist of cycloserine, ethionamide, *p*- minosalicylic acid (PAS), capreomycin, and the aminoglycosides. Fluoroquinolones are recommended as second-line agents but are being tested in multicenter trials as first-line agents (Hall et al., 2009). Several clinical trials are testing the possibility of replacing isoniazid with moxifloxacin, in an attempt to reduce duration of therapy to 4 months (Hall et al., 2009; Connell et al., 2011).

With an average of about 3.2 million new TB cases, Africa accounts for a quarter of the global total, and has the highest incidence and prevalence rates of any region (WHO, 2010a, 2012). Thirteen of the 15 countries with the highest incidence rates in the world, and 9 of the 22 high burden countries (HBCs), are in Africa (WHO, 2012). Hence, it is important to evaluate the impact of these drugs on different parts of the brain to determine how it will affect users on the long term.

ACKNOWLEDGEMENTS

The authors thank Mr. Matthew Adebayo for technical assistance in tissue processing and Mr. Clement Ihyar for the animal studies. The Authors affirm that there is no conflict of interest associated with this work.

REFERENCES

Addington WW (1979). Treatment of pulmonary tuberculosis: Current options. Arch Intern Med 139:1391.

Adobe Help Resource center: http://help.adobe.com/en_US/PhotoshopElements/6.0/. Accessed on May 15th 2009.

ATS, American Thoracic Society (2003). Centers for Disease Control and Prevention, Infectious Diseases Society of America. Treatment of tuberculosis. MMWR Recomm. Rep 52:1–77. (Erratum in MMWR Recomm. Re. 53:1203.

Barinaga M (1998). Death by dozens of cuts. Science 280:32-34.

Bharat A, Vedkumar M, Subhash HS, Abraham OC, Mathai D (2003) Antituberculous therapy-induced toxicity. J Assoc. Physicians India 51:522-524

Blumberg EA, Gil RA (1990). Cerebellar syndrome caused by isoniazid. DICP 24:829-831

BMJ (1958) Neurotoxic Effects of Isoniazid. Br. Med. J. 1(5075):880-881.

Byrd RB, Horn BR, Solomon DA, Griggs GA (1979) Toxic effects of isoniazid in tuberculosis chemoprophylaxis. Role of biochemical monitoring in 1,000 patients. JAMA 241:1239-1241

Cantwell MF, Binkin NJ (1996). Tuberculosis in sub-Saharan Africa: a regional assessment of the impact of the human immuno-412 deficiency virus and National Tuberculosis Control Program quality. Tuberc. Lung Dis. 77: 220–225

Citak A, Kaya O, Ucsel R, Karabocuoglu M, Uzel N (2002). Acute isoniazid neurotoxicity in childhood. Turk. J. Pediatr. 44:54-57

Conde MB, Efron A, Loredo C, De Souza GR, Graça NP, Cezar MC, Ram M, Chaudhary MA, Bishai WR, Kritski AL, Chaisson RE (2009). Moxifloxacin versus ethambutol in the initial treatment of tuberculosis: a doubleblind, randomised, controlled phase II trial. Lancet 373:1183–1189

Connell DW, Berry M, Cooke G, Kon OM (2011) Update on tuberculosis: TB in the early 21st century. Eur. Respir. Rev. 20:71–84

De Cock KM, Soro B, Coulibaly IM, Lucas SB (1992). Tuberculosis and HIV infection in Sub-Saharan Africa. JAMA 268:1581–1587

Desai VA, Agarwal SB (2004). Isoniazid Toxicity. J. Indian Acad. Clin. Med. 5:83-5

Dutt AK, Stead WW (1982). Present chemotherapy for tuberculosis. J. Infect. Dis. 146:698

Dye C, Scheele S, Dolin P, Pathania V, Raviglione MC, WHO Global Surveillance and Monitoring Project (1999). Global burden of tuberculosis: estimated incidence, prevalence, and mortality by country. JAMA 282:677–686

Gál I, Varga T, Szilágyi I, Balázs M, Schlammadinger J, Szabó G, Jr (2000). Protease-elicited TUNEL Positivity of Non-apoptotic Fixed Cells. J. Histochem. Cytochem. 48:963–969.

Hall RG, Leff RD, Gumbo T (2009). Treatment of Active Pulmonary Tuberculosis in Adults: Current Standards and Recent Advances. Pharmacotherapy 29:1468–1481.

Harries AD (1990) Tuberculosis and human immunodeficiency virus infection in developing countries. Lancet 335: 387–390

Hatten ME, Liem RK, Shelanski ML, Mason CA (1991). Astroglia in CNS injury. Glia 4:233-43.

Hengartner M (1998). Apoptosis. Death by crowd control. Science 281:1298-1299.

Jawetz E (1987). Antimycobacterial drugs. In: Katzung BG (ed.), Basic and Clinical Pharmacology. Appleton and Lange, California. pp. 135-139.

Kass JS, Shandera WX (2010). Nervous system effects of antituberculosis therapy. CNS Drugs 24:655-67.

Kerr JF, Wyllie AH, Currie AR (1972) Apoptosis: a basic biological phenomenon with wide-ranging implications in tissue kinetics. Br. J. Cancer 26:239-257.

Koster D, Dode U, Weber HP, Musch E (1985). Acute isoniazid poisoning. Anasth. Intensivther Notfallmed 20:32-4.

Lehr HA, Hansen KD, Coltrera MD, Russ JC, Gown AM (1996). Photoshop-based image analysis for the semiautomated assessment of Ki-67-defined proliferative activity in the routine diagnosis of breast cancer. Appl. Immunohistochem 4:117-127.

Lehr HA, Mankoff DA, Corwin D, Santeursanio G, Gown AM (1997). Application of Photoshop-based image analysis to quantification of hormone receptor expression in breast cancer. J. Histochem. Cytochem. 45:1559-1565.

Lehr HA, van der Loos CM, Teeling P, Gown AM (1999). Complete chromogen separation and analysis in double immunohistochemical stains using Photoshop-based image analysis. J. Histochem. Cytochem. 47:119-125.

Leppert D, Waespe W (1988) Neurotoxicity of antituberculous drugs in a patient without active tuberculosis. Ital. J. Neurol. Sci. 9:31-34.

Lewin PK. (1996) Isoniazid Neurotoxicity. Pediatrics 5:782-783.

Lheureux P, Penaloza A, Gris M (2005). Pyridoxine in clinical toxicology: a review. Eur. J. Emerg. Med. 12:78-85.

Little AR, O'Callagha JP (2001) Astrogliosis in the adult and developing CNS: is there a role for proinflammatory cytokines? Neurotoxicology 22:607-18.

Martinjak-Dvorsek I, Gorjup V, Horvat M, Noc M (2000) Acute isoniazid neurotoxicity during preventive therapy. Crit Care Med. 28:567-568

McGraw J, Hiebert GW, Steeves JD (2001). Modulating astrogliosis after neurotrauma. J. Neurosci. Res. 63:109-115.

O'Callaghan JP (1994). Biochemical analysis of glial fibrillary acidic protein as a quantitative approach to neurotoxicity assessment: advantages, disadvantages and application to the assessment of NMDA receptor antagonist-induced neurotoxicity. Psychopharmacol. Bull. 30:549-554.

Pekny M, Nilsson M (2005). Astrocyte activation and reactive gliosis. Glia 4:427-434.

Perriens JH, Mukadi Y, Nunn P (1991). Tuberculosis and HIV infection: implications for Africa. AIDS 43:127–133.

Preziosi P (2007). Isoniazid: metabolic aspects and toxicological correlates. Curr. Drug Metab. 8:839-51.

Raivich G, Jones LL, Werner A, Bluthmann H, Doetschmann T, Kreutzberg GW (1999). Molecular signals for glial activation: pro- and anti-inflammatory cytokines in the injured brain. Acta Neurochir Suppl. 73:21-30.

Range N, Ipuge YA, O'Brien RJ, Egwaga SM, Mfinanga SG, Chonde TM, Mukadi YD, Borgdorff MW (2001). Trend in HIV prevalence among tuberculosis patients in Tanzania, 1991-1998. Int. J. Tuberc. Lung Dis. 5:405-412.

Raviglione MC (2006). The Global Plan to Stop TB, 2006–2015. Int. J. Tuberc. Lung Dis 10: 238–239.

Raviglione MC, Snider DE, Kochi A (1995) Global epidemiology of tuberculosis. Morbidity and mortality of a worldwide epidemic. JAMA 273:220–226.

Raviglione MC, Uplekar MW (2006) WHO's new stop TB strategy. Lancet 367:952–955.

Rieder H L (1999). Epidemiologic basis of tuberculosis control. International Union Against Tuberculosis and Lung Disease, Paris.

Romero JA, Kuczler FJ (1998). Isoniazid overdose: recognition and management. Am. Fam. Physician 57:749-752.

Sanfeliu C, Wright JM, Kim SU (1999). Neurotoxicity of isoniazid and its metabolites in cultures of mouse dorsal root ganglion neurons and

hybrid neuronal cell line. Neurotoxicology 20:935-44.
Santucci KA, Shah BR, Linakis JG (1999). Acute isoniazid exposures and antidote availability. Pediatr. Emerg. Care 15:99-101.
Shah BR, Santucci K, Sinert R, Steiner P (1995). Acute isoniazid neurotoxicity in an urban hospital. Pediatrics 95:700-4.
Tacconi MT (1998) Neuronal death: is there a role for astrocytes? Neurochem. Res. 23:759-65
Thomas RJ (1994). Neurotoxicity of antibacterial therapy. South Med. J. 87:869-74
WHO, World Health Organisation (2003). Treatment of tuberculosis: guidelines for national programmes, 3rd ed. World Health Organization (WHO/CDS/TB/2003.313), Geneva.
WHO (2006). The global plan to stop TB, 2006–2015. World Health Organization, Geneva. (WHO/HTM/STB/2006.35).
WHO, World Health Organisation (2009). Global Tuberculosis Control 2009 – Epidemiology, Strategy, Financing. Global Tuberculosis Control 2009 – A Short Update to the 2009 report; World Health Organization, Geneva.
WHO, World Health Organisation (2010a). Report Global Tuberculosis Control (2010) Fifteen annual report. World Health Organization, Geneva.
WHO, World Health Organisation (2010b). Treatment of tuberculosis: Guidelines – 4th ed. Geneva, World Health Organization, 2010 WHO/HTM/TB/2009.420.
WHO, World Health Organisation (2012). Global tuberculosis report 2012. Geneva, World Health Organization. WHO/HTM/TB/2012.6.

Cognitive estimation in patients with Alzheimer's disease and schizophrenia

Siamak Khodarahimi[1]* and Ali Rasti[2]

[1]Islamic Azad University-Eghlid Branch, Iran.
[2]Islamic Azad University-Arsanjan Branch, Iran.

The purpose of this research was to examine the role of cognitive estimation in patients with schizophrenia and Alzheimer disease (AD), and also to investigate the role of gender and levels of education in the cognitive estimation. Participants were 43 patients with AD, schizophrenia and controls that were selected through matching sampling method in Iran. A demographic questionnaire and cognitive estimation test (CET) were used in this study. Resulting data demonstrated that patients with schizophrenia and AD had significantly higher size and quality underestimation than normal individuals and the control group had significantly higher size and time overestimation than patients with schizophrenia and AD. However, there weren't any significant group differences in weight under estimation and overestimation. Findings indicated that gender didn't have a significant effect in cognitive estimation and its dimensions. Nevertheless, the levels of education play significant roles in size underestimation, size overestimation, quality underestimation and time overestimation.

Key words: Cognitive estimation test (CET), schizophrenia, Alzheimer disease, gender, level of education.

INTRODUCTION

Cognitive estimation is an ability domain first proposed by Shallice and Evans (1978). This construct is typically assessed by posing questions for which the answers are not generally acquired through formal education and then to compare responses to estimations made by a normative sample. Cognitive estimation is an important task that people have to apply in their daily lives. For this task, person people often rely on several diverse mechanisms. For instance, numerical estimates can be directly retrieved from reconstructed memory (Friedman, 1993, 2004). In this manuscript, we will focus on the quantitative estimation: estimation from probabilistic information. To estimate a quantity of interest people usually rely on multiple information which is probabili-stically related to their required criterion in ongoing and working tasks. Overestimation is quite distance and higher from a real estimation while under estimation is somewhat close or smaller from a real object. For example, time as a dimension of cognitive estimation is a systematic tendency, an organization of mental representations and the way by which people give the order to their experiences (Michon and Jackson, 1985). The majority of the experimental work in the area of time perception has dealt with time estimation (Fraise, 1984), and the concept of time perspective (Decortis and Cacciabue, 1988; Marmaras et al., 1995; Zakay, 1990). However, people might show considerable differences in their efficiency with time. These differences and problems might result from their differences in a basic ability to perceive and estimate time (Wickens, 1992). Additionally, several factors such as gender, culture, and mental health have a direct influence on the participants' ability to estimate time (Block et al., 2000; Zakay, 1990). Likewise when people try to estimate a camel size or weight they could rely on information from many sources. Here, research indicated that size estimation is influenced by a few biological, educational and psychological intervention factors (Altabe and Thompson, 1990; Farrell et al., 2006; Rosen et al.,

*Corresponding author. E-mail: Khodarahimi@yahoo.com.

1995; Rosen et al., 1989). However, there are a variety of cognitive models that have been tendered to describe the cognitive processes caught up in quantitative estimations. These theories try to elucidate which information people rely on and how they use and integrate multiple pieces of information.

According to social judgment theory, human estimation comprising the cognitive one follows a linear additive strategy that can be apprehended by a regression model (Doherty and Brehmer, 1997). The linear additive approach infers that first; each cue is weighted according to its importance. Then, an estimate is procured by adding up the weighted cue values (Cooksey, 1996). Thus, optimal cue weights are building analytically by minimizing the squared deviation between the estimated quantity and the estimation (Cohen et al., 2003).

Exemplar models have been flourishing initially in modeling the cognitive process underlying categorizations (Nosofsky and Johansson, 2000). Due to this success, they recently have been pondered as models of estimations (Juslin, et al., 2003; Juslin et al., 2008). Exemplar models suppose that encountered objects are kept in memory and retrieved if a new object is evaluated. The estimation is grounded on a judgment of similarity between the object under evaluation and the exemplars put aside in memory. Consequently, the more similarity between an exemplar and the object under evaluation, there is the stronger the impact on the estimation of the requested task. The final estimate is given by the average of the criterion values of all stored exemplars, weighted by their similarities to the object under evaluation. Similarity is conceptualized as the cue or feature based and objects are described by their values on a list of features. Two objects are considered similar if their values on the features match. The features can differ in their importance for the similarity evaluation. For instance, when two objects are matching on all but one feature, they can still be considered as different if this cue is of central importance. Thus, the overall evaluation of similarity is reached by integrating all features based on the context model (Medin and Schaffer, 1978).

Heuristic models have been suggested as alternative models for explaining human estimation processes recently. In more complex decision situations, the simple heuristics were better suited to describe the behaviour than more complicated models based on optimization procedures (Bröder, 2000; Bröder and Schiffer, 2003; Rieskamp, 2006; Rieskamp and Otto, 2006). Hereby in many real-life situations, simple heuristics can predict human behaviour very well. For example, Hertwig et al., (1999) brought up a heuristic for estimation, which called the quick estimation. That is a non-compensatory model that does not merge information but bases its estimation on only one cue by sequentially searching through all available cues. Once a cue fulfils a previously set criterion, search is stopped and then an estimation is performed. However, there is no evidence that it can model human estimation processes successfully (Hausmann et al., 2007).

Brown and Siegler (1993) advocated a cognitive model of the quantitative estimation. They suggested two types of knowledge are necessary to make estimation. First, knowledge about the "mapping" properties of the objects is required. This knowledge reflects the ordinal relation among objects, that is, how high an object ranks on the criterion of interest, compared to the other objects. Secondly, knowledge about the "metric" properties of the criterion is necessary, such as the distribution, the mean, or the range. The mapping model describes how knowledge about the mapping properties of an object is linked to the metric properties of the criterion in the estimation process. During the first step, the mapping models use the cue information to capture the mapping properties of an object. Objects are grouped together according to their cue sums, inferring the ordinal relations of the objects from the number of positive cue values. Secondly, to represent the metric properties of the criterion, a typical criterion value is derived for each category by considering the criterion values of the objects falling into the same category.

Finally, based on a neuropsychological perspective, cognitive estimation is amongst the frontal lobe-associated functions and the neurological structures (Brand et al., 2003). Shallice and Evans (1978) have noted that patients with anterior brain lesions tend to make higher inaccurate and sometimes bizarre estimations. Coherent with the traditional view of executive dysfunction, Spencer and Johnson-Greene (2009) recognized that the assumption underlying the cognitive estimation tests are that there is a potential disconnection between an individual's fund of knowledge and their responses. They revealed that even if the causality of cerebral damage was not examined, it does not negate the finding that the CET was not differentially sensitive to executive dysfunction. However, estimations were found to be disturbed in patients with specific disorders or diseases that might be due to a deficiency in emotional processing or their deteriorated basic processes underlying all kinds of cognitive estimation tasks. Many investigations in this field suggest that time; size, quantity and weight estimations can play possible roles in patients with neurological and psychotic disorders. For example, the Alzheimer's disease (AD) patients showed significant deficits in cognitive estimation in all tested dimensions (Brand et al., 2002). It was documented that patients with AD perform worse on cognitive estimation than healthy controls (Brand et al., 2003a, b). Nevertheless, investigation of subjects with Parkinson's disease (Appollonio et al., 2003), frontote-mporal dementia (Mendez et al., 1998), and focal lesions (Taylor and O'Carroll, 1995) questioned the assumption that the cognitive estimation measures only evaluate frontal dysfunction. Alternatively, the study of time estimation in schizophrenia might reveal important information on the core cognitive disturbances of this disorder (Andreasen, 1999). This importance might arise from the involvement of key structures like the prefrontal cortex, thalamus, striatum and possibly the cerebellum (Gibbon et al., 1997).

Therefore, in spite of the aforementioned literature the complete and conclusive psychology of cognitive estimation in all dimensions has not been achieved properly. In sum, cognitive estimation is a type of problem solving ability and can be defined as a process of answer generation in which an exact answer is not readily available. Both semantic information and comparative strategies are used to generate an appropriate answer (Brand et al., 2002). According to aforesaid theories and literature cognitive estimation data could aid in differential diagnoses of patients with AD and schizophrenia from normal individuals but there is a lack of evidence for this area in Iran. This study proposed to investigate the influence of the estimates of size, weight, quantity and time in terms of the average error (accuracy) and the constant error (over and underestimation of the size, weight, quantity and time) in patients with AD, schizophrenia and in the control group; and then explore the differences between genders and the effects of levels of education concerning the size, weight, quality and time estimations. These would contribute to the further understanding of factors and variables involved in size, weight, quantity and time estimations, and thus help unravel this complex psychological puzzle. The first hypothesis of this study is that cognitive estimations (size, weight, quality and time) are differing among patients with AD, schizophrenia and the control group. The second hypothesis of this study is that gender and level of education play significant roles in cognitive estimations (size, weight, quality and time) among this sample.

MATERIALS AND METHODS

Participants

Participants included 43 patients with AD (N=12, F=5, M=7), schizophrenia (N=16, F=7, M=8) and control group (N=15, F=7, M=8) that were selected from Shiraz, Fars province, Iran. The control group screened for both Alzheimer's and schizophrenia diagnostic criteria by two professional specialists and after their approval, they recruited in this study. These samples were demographically comparable because all they matched with respect on their age and the level of education. The educational level of participants was assessed by asking them about their formal education in the national educational systems per years and their attained formal degrees. All patients recruited from outpatient departments. After informed consent was obtained, participants completed a demographic questionnaire with four inventories. For Alzheimer dementia patients, consent was acquired from a family member according to stately policies.

The demographic questionnaire contained age, gender and level of education. Then a cognitive estimation test (CET) was used for data collection on this issue. The CET is a 20-item test that was created by the authors in this study and measure four aspects of cognitive estimations with five estimation questions in each of these categories: Size, weight, quantity and time. This scale was founded on aforementioned theories and conceptualization models that involve dimensions of cognitive estimation across different situations in everyday life. All participants' replied to all items using three alternatives -1 (underestimation), 0 (accurate estimation) and +1 (overestimation). The CET reliability by Cronbach's alpha for all domains ranged from .63 to .86 in this study. According to the test-retest correlations provided by the authors the CET has a .86 correlation after one month interval. However, the construct validity of all domains was affirmed again by a few faculty staffs in psychology. When the CET concurrent validity was measured by the Biber cognitive estimation test (BCET; Bullard, Fein, Gleeson, Tischer, Mapou et al., 2004) its concurrent correlations were .72.

RESULTS AND DISCUSSION

To examine possible group differences in the first hypothesis one way analysis of variance (ANOVA) was conducted among the three groups with the group situation as between-subjects variables and all dimensions of CET as dependent variables. There are significant group differences in size underestimation (F2, 40=7.49, p=.002), size overestimation (F2, 40=19.72, p=.0001), quality underestimation (F2, 40=4.67, p=.01), and time overestimation (F2, 40=9.89, p=.0001). Posteriori following test for group differences by Duncan test indicated that patients with schizophrenia and AD had significantly higher size and quality underestimation than normal individuals. The control group had significantly higher size and time overestimation than patients with schizophrenia and AD. However, there aren't any significant group differences in weight under estimation and overestimation (Table 1). To examine the second hypothesis of this research study, a t-test for independent groups was conducted to evaluate the effects of gender and several ANOVAs were calculated for level of education differences in the cognitive estimations. Analysis rejected the effect of gender in the cognitive estimation. Findings indicated that levels of education play significant roles in size underestimation (F2, 39=4.15, p=.01), size overestimation (F2, 39=13.77, p=.0001), quality underestimation (F2, 39=3.57, p=.02) and time overestimation (F2, 39=2.89, p=.05). Posteriori following test for group differences by Duncan test indicated that individuals with elementary education had a significant lower size under estimation than those with secondary, high school and higher education but individuals with high school and higher education had significant size overestimation than other groups. Moreover, individuals with a higher education had significantly lower quality underestimation and higher time over-estimation than other groups. Additionally, to examine possible group, gender and levels of education differences and their interactions, a multivariate analysis of variance (MANOVA) conducted by

Table 1. The effects of cognitive estimation in different groups.

Dimension	Type of estimation	Groups						F	p
		Schizophrenia		Alzheimer disease		Normal			
		M	SD	M	SD	M	SD		
Size	Under	-20.25	10.06	-10.83	0.93	-0.93	0.88	70.36	0.002
	Over	0.68	10.07	10.50	10.31	30.13	0.91	190.72	0.0001
Weight	Under	-10.87	10.14	-20.58	10.62	-20.13	10.06	10.07	0.351
	Over	10.25	10.18	10.50	10.16	20.06	10.09	20.02	0.146
Quality	Under	-20.68	0.79	-30.58	0.99	-30.46	0.83	40.67	0.015
	Over	0.87	0.88	0.66	0.77	10.20	0.77	10.47	0.242
Time	Under	-0.87	0.80	-10.41	0.79	-0.86	0.51	20.52	0.093
	Over	20.00	0.81	20.25	0.62	30.40	10.18	90.89	0.0001

by group situation, gender, levels of education and their interactions as independents and the cognitive estimation and its four dimensions as dependent variables. An overall multivariate effect rejected the effects of gender, *Wilks' k* = .72; *F* (8, 24) = 1.14; *p*= .37, group status, *Wilks' k* = .41; *F* (16, 48) = 1.66; *p*= .08, levels of education, *Wilks' k* = .35; *F* (24, 70) = 1.24; *p*= .23, and their interactions in the cognitive estimation and its dimensions.

The results from this research in the first hypothesis demonstrated that patients with schizophrenia and AD had a significantly higher size and quality under-estimation than the normal individuals and control group had a significantly higher size and time overestimation than patients with schizophrenia and AD. However, there aren't any significant group differences in weight under estimation and overestimation. In line with previous literature, it seems that size estimation could be affected by three biological, educational and the psychological factors that including both psychological and neurological impairments (Altabe and Thompson, 1990; Farrell et al., 2006; Rosenet al., 1995; Rosen et al., 1989). This finding highlights the role of social judgment theory in cognitive estimation (Doherty and Brehmer, 1997).

It is possible both patients with schizophrenia and AD pursue underestimation strategy when they encounter different dimensions of estimation and this may result in cue's retrieval problems in their cognitive functioning in general. Therefore, there may be some correlation between memory difficulties and cognitive estimation in schizophrenia and AD, and this speculation is relatively supported by the exemplar models ((Nosofsky and Johansson, 2000; Juslin et al., 2003; Juslin et al., 2008). In contrast, heuristic models can simply predict the estimation strategy among healthy people (Bröder, 2000; Bröder and Schiffer, 2003; Rieskamp, 2006; Rieskamp and Otto, 2006). In addition, in concurrence with cognitive models it seems there is a different cognitive mapping and working mechanisms for knowledge attainment in normal individuals and patients with schizophrenia and AD (Brown and Siegler; 1993). The real explanation of these distinctions might needs to understand their neuropsychological underpinnings in schizophrenia and AD (Brand, Fujiwara, Kalbe, Steingass, Kessler et al, 2003; Shallice and Evans, 1978). Altogether cognitive estimation represents the personal knowledge procedures about the possible functionality of imaginative and non-compensatory problem solving skills that eventually will prevent the occurrence of executive dysfunction in normal individuals (Hausmann et al., 2007; Spencer and Johnson-Greene, 2009).

The results from this study in second hypothesis indicated that gender doesn't show a significant effect in cognitive estimation and its dimensions. However, the levels of education play a significant role in size under-estimation, size overestimation, quality underestimation and time overestimation. These are in contradiction with earlier literature, which supported the role of some cultural factor like gender in cognitive estimation (Block et al., 2000; Zakay, 1990).

Conclusion

In conclusion, the current research adds to the psychology literature because it explored the role of cognitive estimation in schizophrenia and AD as two deteriorating disorders with some shared neuropsychological impairment in the frontal lobe. Furthermore, this study rejected and confirmed the roles of gender and literacy in cognitive estimation respectively. Additionally, the results of the current study implicitly confirmed the roles of neuropsychological dysfunctions in cognitive estimation. However, this study limited because only was relied on data from the CET test in a clinical sample and control group. Further research may apply experimental and longitudinal designs for this purpose, and to examine this construct across different clinical samples with both psychological and neuropsychological instruments.

REFERENCES

Altabe M, Thompson JK (1996). Body image: A cognitive self-schema construct, Cognit. Ther. Res., 20: 173-195.
Andreasen NC (1999). A unitary model of schizophrenia: Bleuler's "fragmented phrene" as schizencephaly. Arch. Gen. Psychiatry, 56: 781–787.
Appollonio IM, Russo A, Isella V, Forapani E, Villa ML, Piolti R, Frattola L (2003) Cognitive [correction of cognitve] estimation: comparison of two tests in non-demented parkinsonian patients. Neurol. Sci., 24: 153–154.
Block RA, Hancock PA, Zakay D (2000). Sex differences in duration judgments: A meta-analytic review. Mem. Cogn., 28(8): 1333-1346.
Brand M, Fujiwara E, Kalbe E, Steingass HP, Kessler J, Markowitsch HJ (2003a). Cognitive estimation and affective judgments in alcoholic Korsakoff patients. J. Clin. Exp. Neuropsychol., 25(3): 324–334.
Brand M, Kalbe E, Kessler J (2002). Qualitative and quantitative differences in cognitive estimation of patients with probable Alzheimer's disease from healthy controls: What are the differences, Memory and Emotion, pp. 425-429.
Brand M, Kalbe E, Fujiwara E, Huber M, Markowitsch HJ (2003b). Cognitive estimation in patients with probable Alzheimer's disease and alcoholic Korsakoff patients. Neuropsychol., 41: 575–584.
Bröder A (2000). Assessing the empirical validity of the take-the-best heuristic as a model of human probabilistic inference. J. Exp. Psychol. Learn. Mem. Cogn., 26: 1332–1346.
Bröder A, Schiffer S (2003). Take the best versus simultaneous feature matching: Probabilistic inferences from memory and effects of representation format. J. Exp. Psychol. Gen., 132: 277–293.
Brown NR, Siegler RS (1993). Metrics and mappings: A framework for understanding real-world quantitative estimation. Psychol. Rev., 100: 511–534.
Bullard SE, Fein D, Gleeson MK, Tischer N, Mapou RL, Kaplan E (2004). The Biber Cognitive Estimation Test. Archives. Clin. Neuropsychol., 19(6): 835-846.
Cohen J, Cohen P, West SG, Aiken LS (2003). Applied multiple regression/correlation analysis for the behavioral sciences, 3rd ed. Hillsdale: Erlbaum.
Cooksey RW (1996). Judgment analysis: Theory, methods and applications. San Diego: Academic Press.
Decortis F, Cacciabue PC (1988). Temporal dimension in cognitive models. In E. W. Hagen (Ed.), Conference record for 1988 IEEE Fourth Conference on Human Factors and Power Plants. New York: Institute of Electrical and Electronic Engineers. pp. 279-284.
Doherty M, Brehmer B (1997).The paramorphic representation of clinical judgment: A thirty-year retrospective. Goldstein In WM, Hogarth RM (Eds.), Research on judgment and decision making: Currents, connections and controversies . Cambridge: Cambridge University Press. pp. 537–551
Farrell C, Shafran R, Lee M (2006). Empirically evaluated treatments for body image disturbance: A review. Eur. Eat. Disord. Rev., 14(5): 289-300.
Fraise P (1984). Perception and estimation of time. Ann. Rev. Psychol., 35: 1-36.
Friedman WJ (1993). Memory for the time of past events. Psychol. Bull., 113: 44–66.
Friedman WJ (2004). Time in autobiographical memory. Social Cogn., 22: 591–605.
Gibbon J, Malapani C, Dale CL, Gallistel C (1997). Toward a neurobiology of temporal cognition: advances and challenges. Curr. Opin. Neurobiol., 7: 170–184.
Hausmann D, Läge D, Pohl R, Bröder A (2007). Testing the QuickEst: No evidence for the Quick-Estimation heuristic. 19(3): 446-456.
Hertwig R, Hoffrage U, Martignon L (1999). Quick estimation: Letting the environment do the work. In G. Gigerenzer, P.M. Todd, & the ABC Research Group, Simple heuristics that make us smart. New York: Oxford University Press. pp. 209–234
Juslin P, Jones S, Olsson H, Winman A (2003). Cue abstraction and exemplar memory in categorization. J. Exp. Psychol. Learn. Mem. Cogn., 29: 924–941.
Juslin P, Karlsson L, Olsson H (2008). Information integration in multiple-cue judgment: A division-of-labor hypothesis. Cogn. Sci., 26: 563-607.
Marmaras N, Vassilakis P, Dounias G (1995). Factors affecting accuracy of producing time intervals. Percept. Motor Skills, 80: 1043-1056.
Medin DL, Schaffer MM (1978). Context theory of classification learning. Psychol. Rev., 85: 207–238.
Mendez MF, Doss RC, Cherrier MM (1998). Use of the cognitive estimations test to discriminate the front of temporal dementia from Alzheimer's disease. J. Geriatric. Psychiat. Neurolol., 11: 2–6.
Michon JA, Jackson JL (1985). In J. Michon and J. Jackson (Eds.), Time, mind, and behavior, pp.2-17. New York: Springer-Verlag.
Nosofsky RM, Johansen MK (2000). Exemplar-based accounts of "multiple system" phenomena in perceptual categorization. Psychonomic Bulletin. Rev., 7: 375–402.
Rieskamp J (2006). Perspectives of probabilistic inferences: Reinforcement learning and an adaptive network compared. J. Exp. Psychol. Learn. Mem. Cogn., 32: 1371-1384.
Rieskamp J, Otto EP (2006). SSL: A theory of how people learn to select strategies. General. J. Exp. Psychol., 135: 207–236.
Rosen JC, Orosan P, Reiter J (1995). Cognitive behavior therapy for negative body image in obese women. Behav. Ther., 26(1): 25-42.
Rosen JC, Saltzberg E, Srebnik D (1989). Cognitive behavior therapy for negative body image. Behav. Ther., 20(3): 393-404.
Shallice T, Evans ME (1978). The involvement of the frontal lobes in cognitive estimation. Cortex, 14: 294–303.
Spencer RJ, Johnson-Greene D (2009). The Cognitive Estimation Test (CET): Psychometric limitations in neuro rehabilitation populations. J. Clin. Exp. Neuropsychol., 31(3): 373–377.
Taylor R, O'Carroll R (1995). Cognitive estimation in neurological disorders. Br. J. Clin. Psycholol., 34: 223–228.
Wickens CD (1992). Engineering psychology and human performance. New York: Harper Collins.
Zakay D (1990). The evasive art of subjective time measurement: Some methodological dilemmas. In R. Block (Ed.), Cognitive models of psychological time. New Jersey: Lawrence Erlbaum, pp 59-84.

4

Intrauterine infection promotes brain region specific cytokine activation and hyperactivity in developing rat

Kedra Wallace[1]*, Jennifer Horgan[2] and William A Bennett[1]

[1]Department of Obstetrics and Gynecology, University of MS Medical Center, 2500 N. State St., Jackson, MS 39216, USA.
[2]Department of Pharmacology, University of MS Medical Center, 2500 N. State St., Jackson, MS 39216, USA.

Intrauterine infection during pregnancy is associated with premature birth, periventricular leukomalacia, early activation of the fetal immune system and poor neurodevelopmental outcomes. Previous clinical studies and studies with animal models have shown increased activation of the immune system evidenced by increased levels of inflammatory cytokines, white matter damage and delays in behavioral development. Animal models of intrauterine infection with consistent behavioral results, white matter damage and immune activation have been difficult to validate. Using a rodent model of intrauterine infection, we examined neurobehavioral development and locomotor development in the resulting pups, and measured inflammatory cytokines in the striatum, frontal cortex and cerebellum. Pregnant rats at gestational day 17 were inoculated with 1×10^5 colony forming units of *Escherichia coli* or 0.1 ml of saline. Intrauterine infection led to a significant increase in the expression of interleukin 1 β, interleukin-6 and tumor necrosis factor-α. *E. coli* injection increased walking, turning and overall motor activity in rats. In summary, the results of this study indicate that *E. coli* induced intrauterine infection resulted in neuroinflammation and led to hyperactivity in basic locomotion.

Key words: Intrauterine infection, *E. coli,* neurodevelopment behavior, immune activation.

INTRODUCTION

Intrauterine infection is a major risk factor for the development of neurodevelopmental brain damage (Dammann et al., 2002; Dammann and Leviton, 1998; Nelson and Willoughby, 2000; Yoon et al., 2000) and is associated with an increased risk of the development of motor impairments similar to those seen in cerebral palsy and periventricular leukomalacia (Bell and Hallenbeck, 2002; Dammann and Leviton, 1998; Wu and Colford, 2000; Yoon et al., 2003). White matter damage, astrocytosis and cytokine activation have been demonstrated in experimental models of intrauterine infection, all of which are capable of leading to delays in brain development (Bell and Hallenbeck, 2002; Cai et al., 2000; Debillon et al., 2000). Animal models of intrauterine infection have white matter lesions similar to those seen in children with cerebral palsy, and have delays in basic neurodevelopmental task (Poggi et al., 2005; Toso et al., 2005). These experimental models show that maternal or postnatal endotoxin exposure sensitizes the immature brain and increases cytokine levels, both of which can be detrimental to posture and motor development.

Endotoxin exposure is a common and powerful stimuli for inflammatory cytokine activation in the setting of intrauterine infection (Kadhim et al., 2001). Several studies looking at the incidence of *in utero* bacterial infections have also found an increased incidence in neurodevelopmental problems in these exposed infants (Schendel, 2001; Vigneswaran et al., 2004). In addition to these clinical studies, animal studies have shown that bacterial/endotoxin-induced intrauterine infection leads to an increase in inflammatory cytokines in both the uterine tissues and the fetal brain (Bell and Hallenbeck, 2002; Cai et al., 2000; Urakubo et al., 2001). *Escherichia coli* is a gram-negative bacterium, which is often found in the urinary tract leading to urinary tract infections. In the

*Corresponding author. E-mail: kwallace2@umc.edu.

setting of pregnancy, the bacteria can colonize in the uterine cavity and potentially the uterine tissues. Recent studies have shown that *E.coli* is one of the most common uropathogens, up to an incidence of 62.9% in pregnant women with infection, and that *E.coli* infection is strongly correlated with neonatal sepsis (Guiral et al., 2011; Kuhn et al., 2010; Rafal'skii et al., 2009). Even though *E.coli* is not the only bacteria associated with prenatal infection in humans, it has been isolated in 20 to 40% of prenatal infection related cerebral palsy cases (Mittendorf et al., 2001; Vigneswaran et al., 2004).

We recently reported that in a rodent model of intrauterine infection, developmental, cognitive and motor deficits are present in juvenile and adult offspring (Wallace et al., 2010a; Wallace et al., 2010b). In addition, white matter damage similar to that seen in periventricular leukomalacia is present, including astrocytosis, ventriculomegaly and changes in oligodendrocyte precursors and decreases in Purkinje cell density (Pang et al., 2005; Rodts-Palenik et al., 2004). Our goal in this study is to determine if intrauterine injection of *E. coli* alters postural and motor development in this rodent model of intrauterine infection, and if any changes are accompanied by increased cytokine production in the brain.

MATERIALS AND METHODS

Animal model

Twelve timed-pregnant Sprague Dawley rats (Harlan Sprague-Dawley, Indianapolis, IN) were obtained at gestational day (GD) 13. Food and water were available *ad libitum* and the colony was maintained in a 12:12 h light/dark schedule. On GD 17 dams were randomly assigned to either saline (n=6), or *E. coli* (ATCC #25922, Manassas, VA) (n=6). Animals were anesthetized and inoculated with 100 µl of sterile saline or 100 µl of 1×10^5 colony forming units of *E. coli* at the bifurcation of the uterine horns (Pang et al., 2005; Rodts-Palenik et al., 2004; Wallace et al., 2010a; Wallace et al., 2010b). Dams were maintained on a standard maintenance 8640 Teklad 22/5 rodent diet from Harlan for the length of the study. All animals were observed daily and allowed to deliver without any additional experimental manipulation and experiments were carried out with the approval of the institutional animal care and use committee of the University of MS Medical Center.

Behavioral testing

After delivery, rat pups (*E .coli* = 30; control = 30) were weighed and remained with dams for the length of the study. Locomotor testing (Altman and Sudarshan, 1975; Clarac et al., 2004) began at postnatal day (PND) PND 2 and ended at PND 12. Throughout this time rat pups were separated from dams for a period not exceeding one hour a day. All testing was done between 08:00 and 11:00 h in a room specialized for behavioral testing.

Locomotor testing was analyzed under the following parameters: (1) Crawling was indicated by paddling movements of the paws which results in the pup dragging or pulling itself. (2) Walking was defined as an advanced form of crawling in which the pup can move forward or backward without its' pelvis touching the floor. (3) Pivoting was indicated by the pup making broad swipes with the paws, producing a paddling motion which results in a turn. (4) Turning was defined as an advanced form of pivoting in which the pup can turn without its' pelvis touching the floor. (5) Head raise was indicated by the pup raising its head in a vertical motion with the nose pointing up. (6) Grooming was indicated by the pup licking its' paws or pawing its head.

For locomotor testing animals were placed individually in a clear cage and their movements were video-taped for 5 min. All cages were kept under an infrared light to insure that the animals would not lose any body heat while separated from their litter mates. Video tapes were viewed after testing, using a time-sampling method in which every 10 s the pups' activity was scored, for a total of 300 sc. Tape raters were blind to treatment and inter-rater reliability was r^2=0.91.

Homogenate preparation and ELISA

At PND 16 pups were sacrificed and the brains were extracted for cytokine analysis. The frontal cortex, striatum and cerebellum, were dissected, weighed and fast-froze with dry ice and stored at -80°C. To prepare tissue for biochemical analysis, tissue was crushed under liquid nitrogen using a mortar and pestle, followed by homogenization in ice-cold phosphate buffered saline containing a commercial mix of protease inhibitors (Roche Diagnostics, Indianapolis, IN). The homogenate was centrifuged at 4°C for 10 minutes at 1600 RPM. The supernatant was extracted and used for ELISA testing. Commercially available ELISA kits for tumor necrosis factor-α (TNF-α), interleukin-6 (IL-6) and interleukin 1β (IL-1β) (RnD Systems, Minneapolis, MN) were used to analyze the amount of cytokine expression for each region of interest and was carried out according to manufacturer's instructions. The immunoassay intra-assay coefficient of variation was less than 5% and the detection limits were 5 pg/ml, <5 pg/ml and 21 pg/ml, respectively. A commercially available BCA kit for total protein concentration (Pierce Chemical, Rockford, IL) was used to determine the total amount of protein in each sample. The total protein concentration was normalized for each brain region to the corresponding cytokine value.

Statistical analysis

Behavioral data was analyzed by RM-ANOVA using a general linear model created in SPSS version 14.0 for PC. Postnatal day was the repeated measure and prenatal treatment a fixed factor. Post-hoc analysis was done using Bonferroni method of analysis. To determine if intrauterine *E. coli* injection altered the appearance of any of the above behaviors (crawling, walking, etc.) Fisher's exact test using a two-tailed *p* value was used. Cytokine protein production in specific brain regions as measured by ELISAs were tested by ANOVA. Post-hoc analysis was performed by Bonferroni correction. P values < 0.05 were considered significant.

RESULTS

General newborn characteristics

All dams delivered between GD 21 to 22 and there were no statistically significant differences between survival rates in the *E .coli* group versus control (p = 0.087) or in birth weights (p=0.149) between the two groups. Surrogate dams were not used in this study, but dams in the saline groups had 1 to 2 pups taken away per litter to

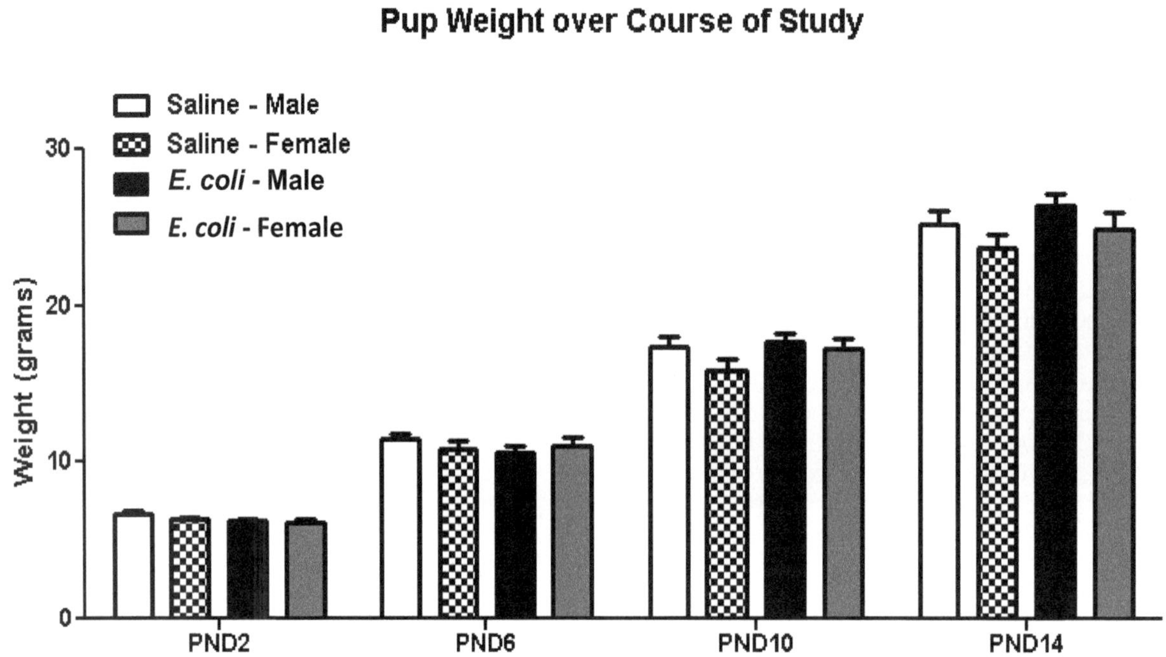

Figure 1. The effects of intrauterine infection on postnatal weight gain in pups from PNDs 2 to 14. There were no statistically significant (p=0.45) differences in postnatal weight gain between males and females within and between the groups. Data is represented as average weight (grams) ± S.E.M. recorded every 4 days. At each time point: saline males (n=16), saline females (n=14), *E. coli* males (n=13), *E. coli* females (n=17).

equalize litter sizes among treatment groups. There were no significant differences in pup weights ($p = 0.45$) among males or females within and between the treatment groups during the study (Figure 1).

Intrauterine infection leads to hyperactivity

Intrauterine infection did not have a gender specific effect on the development of locomotion, so all pups are reported together (saline males [n=16], saline females [n=14], *E. coli* males [n=13], *E. coli* females [n=17]; data not shown).

Intrauterine infection significantly reduced the total incidence of crawling ($p = 0.05$) and pivoting ($p = 0.05$; Figure 2A and B) while significantly increasing the incidence of walking ($p = 0.05$) and turning ($p = 0.05$) (Figure 2C and D) as compared to rat pups in the control group.

There was no significant difference in the incidence of head raises ($p = 0.319$) or grooming behavior ($p = 0.497$; data not shown) between the two groups.

There were no significant differences in the appearance of any locomotor behaviors between the two groups (Table 1).

To determine if the overall activity level of pups changed due to intrauterine infection, the total time spent moving was calculated. Intrauterine infection, significantly decreased the time spent active as compared to pups in the saline group on PND 2 ($p = 0.05$; Figure 3), while causing hyperactivity between PNDs 6, 9 to 11 as compared to pups in the saline group ($p < 0.01$; Figure 3).

Intrauterine infection leads to region specific increases in cytokine expression

As endotoxin administration increases the immune response, we set out to determine if fetal immune activation still persisted after the *in utero* insult. Intrauterine infection significantly increased IL-1β (15.86 ± 1.34 versus 7.26 ± 1.4 pg/ml; $p = 0.001$), TNF-α (40.94 ± 3.81 versus 17.38 ± 3.18 pg/ml; $p < 0.001$) and IL-6 (11.98 ± 2.27 versus 4.75 ± 1.15 pg/ml; $p = 0.008$) in the frontal cortex at PND 16 (Figure 4A) as compared to the saline group.

In the striatum intrauterine infection significantly increased IL-1β (6.48 ± 1.09 versus 3.36 ± 0.65 pg/ml; $p = 0.021$), TNF-α (10.18 ± 2.07 versus 3.62 ± 1.51 pg/ml; $p = 0.016$) and IL-6 (4.27 ± 0.19 versus 1.54 ± 0.63 pg/ml; $p = 0.001$) as compared to the saline group (Figure 4B). Intrauterine infection also significantly increased IL-1β (16.51 ± 2.56 versus 7.8 ± 1.19 pg/ml; $p = 0.005$), TNF-α (33.07 ± 3.95 versus 21.51 ± 1.34 pg/ml; $p = 0.010$) and IL-6 (10.14 ± 0.94 versus 3.31 ± 0.54 pg/ml; $p < 0.001$) in the cerebellum as compared to the saline group (Figure 4C).

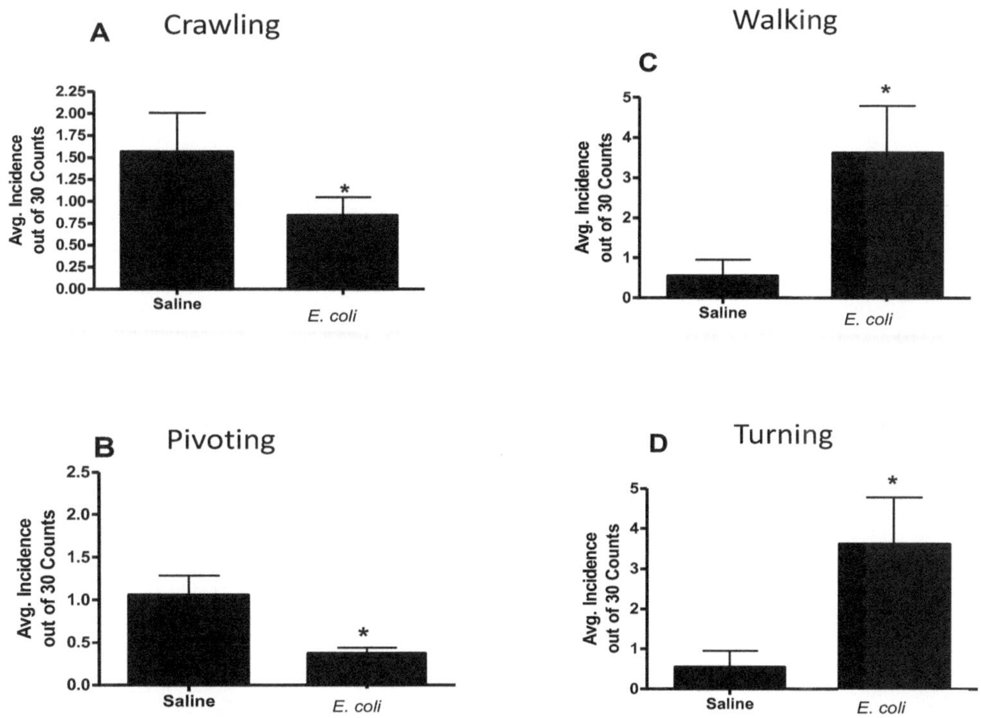

Figure 2. The effects of intrauterine infection on the development of locomotion in pups from PNDs 2 to12. Pups from the *E. coli* group demonstrated a statistically significant reduced incidence of crawling and pivoting and a statistically significant increased incidence of walking and turning as compared to the control group. These data represent an average of each form of locomotion over the indicated days. Each pup spent 5 min in a clear cage, in which their activity was recorded and scored at a later date. Every 10 s the action of locomotion was recorded, for a total recording of 30 incidents of movement. [A]Crawling, [B]Pivoting, [C]Walking, [D]Turning. Data is represented as average incidence of a behavior + S.E.M. There was no statistically significant treatment by postnatal day effect so the data was averaged for each day per treatment was analyzed using a student's *t*-test, and the data graphed as indicated in this figure. *Significantly different from corresponding saline group as indicated by two-way RM-ANOVA and post-hoc Bonferroni, corrected *t*-tests ($p < 0.01$). At each time point, saline n = 30 and *E. coli* n = 30.

Table 1. Appearance of basic locomotor skills in the development of walking.

Parameter	Saline n = 30 mean start date (range)	*E. coli* n = 3 mean start date (range)	P value
crawling	PND2 (2-12)	PND3 (3-12)	0.067
Walking	PND9 (9-12)	PND10 (9-12)	1.00
Pivoting	PND3 (2-12)	PND3 (2-12)	1.40
Turning	PND8 (8-12)	PND8 (7-12)	1.00
Head raise	PND2 (2-12)	PND2 (2-12)	1.40
Grooming	PND10 (10-12)	PND10 (10-12)	1.24

DISCUSSION

It is now well recognized that intrauterine infection can potentially lead to neurodevelopmental and neurological disorders through activation of the fetal immune system (Bell and Hallenbeck, 2002; Bell et al., 2004; Chew et al., 2006; Yoon et al., 2003). We have previously shown that *E. coli* induced intrauterine infection leads to white matter damage, astrogliosis, and increased IL-1β expression in the hippocampus and cerebellum (Rodts-Palenik et al., 2004; Wallace et al., 2010a; Wallace et al., 2010b). Furthermore, rat pups exposed *in utero* to *E. coli* have long-term sensorimotor, motor and cognitive deficits compared to rat pups from non-infected dams (Wallace,

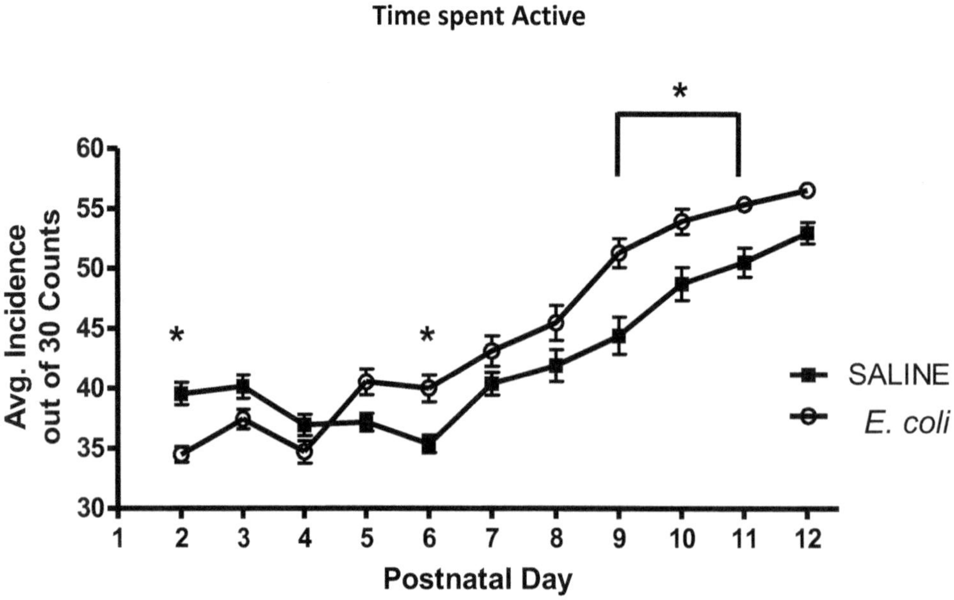

Figure 3. Intrauterine infection increases the total time spent active. *E. coli* induced-intrauterine infection increased the time spent active after PND 5, indicating that these pups were more hyperactive in comparison to pups in the saline group. Each pup spent 5 min in a clear cage from PN 2 to 12, in which their activity was recorded and scored at a later date. Every 10 s the mode of locomotion was recorded, for a total recording of 30 incidents of movement. The overall activity was assessed as the time spent motionless. Data is represented as average incidence of a motionless score + S.E.M. Significance by two way RM-ANOVA was set to $p < 0.05$. Post-hoc analysis with Bonferroni, corrected t-tests set to $p < 0.01$. *denotes days in which *E. coli* spent significantly less time motionless as compared to pups in the saline group. # denotes days in which *E.coli* spent significantly more time motionless as compared to pups in the saline group. At each time point, saline n = 30 and *E.coli* n = 30.

et al., 2010a; Wallace et al., 2010b). In the current study we demonstrate that intrauterine infection has a regional effect on cytokine activation which corresponds to increased motor activity.

The final output of locomotion depends on the development of the central nervous system and the muscular-skeletal framework. This phase of development starts during the embryological life and continues after birth (Kudo et al., 1991). In rodents there is a very precise onset of locomotive behaviors, thus making it easy to determine if prenatal or early age insults affect the onset and development of locomotor behaviors. Rat pups in the intrauterine infection group, had increased incidences of walking and turning over the observed periods of movement, and decreased incidences of crawling and pivoting. This corresponds to the overall increase in total activity seen after PND 6 which is indicative of an increase in motor activity. The significant increase in motor activity seen in this model implies that intrauterine infection does affect basic neural circuitry but not necessarily the ability to develop locomotion. Increases in pivoting are correlated with decreased striatal dopamine levels. Other investigators have found that endotoxin or pesticide administration elicits an inflammatory response in the nigrostriatal pathway capable of inducing behavioral changes (Choi et al., 2009; Lazarini et al., 2001). Furthermore, *in vivo* studies have shown that dopamine neurons and nigrostriatal development is compromised when the developing striatum was exposed to lipopolysaccharide (Snyder-Keller and Stark, 2008), suggesting that inflammation may indeed compromise motor behavior and may prove to be an important area of investigation in this model.

To determine if the changes in motor activity and development were accompanied by brain inflammation, we examined the frontal cortex, striatum and cerebellum for evidence of cytokine activation. *E. coli* injection significantly increased IL-6, IL-1β and TNF-α in all areas examined which is supported by several studies which have seen an inflammatory response due to endotoxin administration in the prenatal or early postnatal period (Bell and Hallenbeck, 2002; Bilbo et al., 2005; Cai et al., 2000). The frontal cortex is associated with the integration of voluntary motor activities, while the cerebellum is responsible for coordination, timing sequence and patterned activity of skilled or learned movements and the striatum helps integrate motor pathways (Adams and Victor, 1989; Kolb 1984; Konczak and Timmann, 2007). Despite the increase in inflame-mation in these regions, *E. coli* exposure did not affect

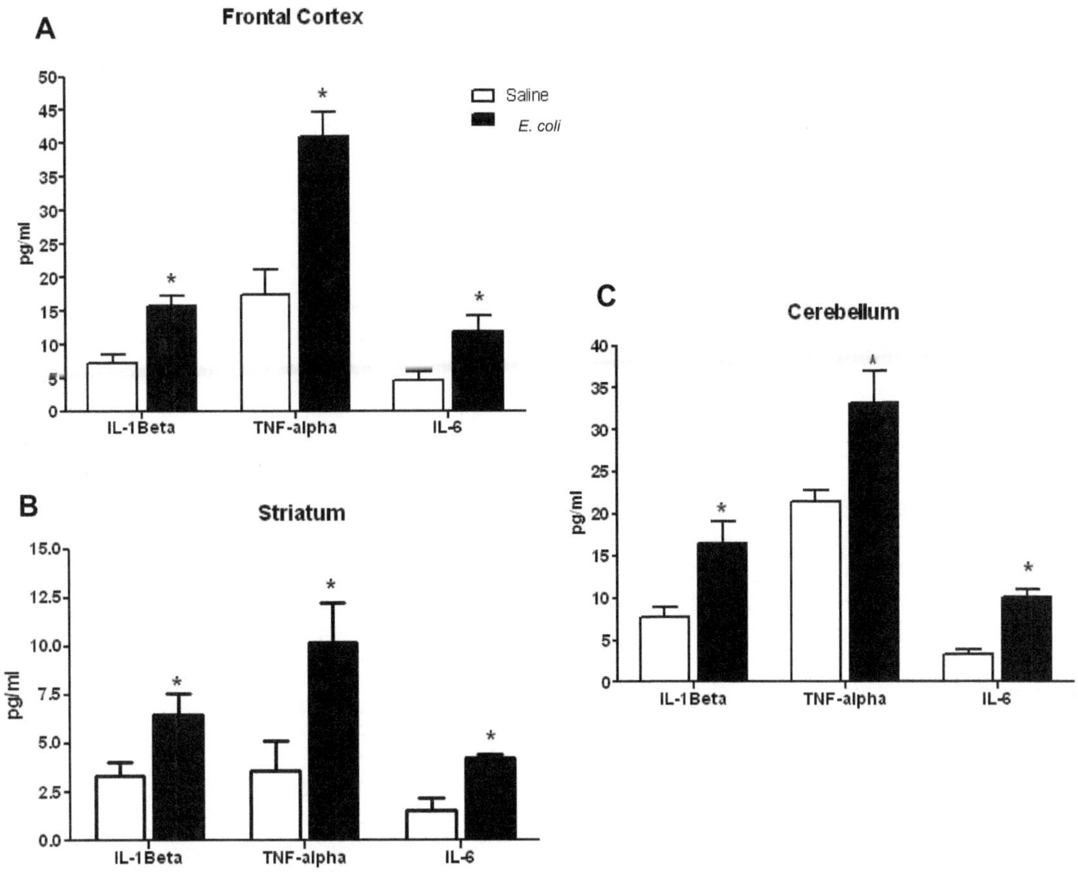

Figure 4. The effects of intrauterine infection on the inflammatory cytokine expression in the brain. IL-1Beta, IL-6 and TNF-alpha were significantly increased due to intrauterine injection of *E.coli* in all brain regions. Data is represented as mean + S.E.M. Data was analyzed using a student's t-test. *p < 0.05 significantly different as compared to corresponding saline group. Saline n = 15 and *E. coli* n = 15.

the pups' coordination or timing sequence of ambulatory skills. This would suggest that inflammation alone is not a causative factor for delays in basic ambulation.

Previous studies investigating the role of inflammatory cytokines on rodent behavior have shown that increased mRNA, plasma and neuronal levels of IL-6 are associated with animal models of autism and maternal immune infection (Pang et al., 2006; Parker-Athill and Tan, 2010; Wei et al., 2011). IL-6 plays a role in normal brain development, learning and memory through activation of the STAT (signal transducers and activators of transcription) pathway (Bauer et al., 2007; He et al., 2005). Through mechanisms that are not well understood, IL-6 can trigger the inflammatory cascade and lead to neuronal degeneration and lymphocyte migration thus leading to the development of behavioral abnormalities. IL-1β is capable of activating the hypothalamic-pituitary-adrenal axis and also works through activation of the STAT pathway. IL-1β is similar to IL-6 in that it also has a role in the normal development of the CNS, but can have long-term effects on developmental skills and cognition when activated above physiological levels (Giulian et al., 1988; Wallace et al., 2010a). TNF-α mediates and increases inflammatory cytokine activity similar to IL-1β. Several studies have also shown an immediate increase in TNF-α following intracerebral injections of lipopolysaccharide (LPS) (Cai et al., 2003; Gatti and Bartfai, 1993; Siren et al., 1992), which indicates that LPS is capable of increasing TNF-α production in the brain in response to either direct or indirect endotoxin exposure.

While there is converging evidence that there is a relationship between endotoxin infections during pregnancy and alterations in offspring behavior, the exact physiological mechanism linking the immune response to behavior is still unclear. Proinflammatory cytokines such as TNF-α, IL-1β and IL-6 act in a cascade-like fashion to induce each other and potentially affect the fetal brain when activated *in utero* (Dammann and Leviton, 1998; Luheshi, 1998), it is probable that the increase in inflammatory cytokines in the perinatal brain, is not the only factor leading to the altered behaviors in the offspring.

The peripheral immune system may also be activated, leading to further increases and activation of the inflammatory cascade. However, if this is possible it should be noted that the increase in inflammatory cytokines did not lead to sickness behavior, which is characteristic of high levels of inflammatory cytokines.

Elevations in inflammatory cytokines in rodents can lead to a set of behaviors, primarily weight loss and lethargy, termed sickness behavior (Konsman et al., 2002). In this study we did not use surrogate dams or monitor mothers for sickness behavior, but used the ability of the pup to gain weight as a main index of health (Jen et al., 1978). Although pup weight in the *E. coli* group was not significantly less than pups in the saline group, it is possible that there were some effects of sickness behavior among the dams (Figure 1). However due to the hyperactivity seen in the *E. coli* group it would appear as if these animals did not experience any malnourishment.

E. coli did not delay the development of walking but instead increased the activity of walking and turning. The lack of impairments in the development of locomotion as determined by postural assessments indicates that intrauterine infection did not appear to delay or impair any of the neuromuscular networks needed to have successful locomotion (Clarac et al., 2004). This is despite increasing cortical, striatal and cerebellar levels of inflammatory cytokines. Our group and others have shown that endotoxin and cytokine administration does impair cognitive and sensorimotor tasks, which suggest that more complex forms of behavior may be more sensitive to inflammation (Pang et al., 2006; Toso et al., 2005; Wallace et al., 2010a; Wallace et al., 2010b). Further studies are needed to fully elucidate the mechanism(s) by which neurochemical alterations and neuroinflammation may result in behavioral deficits.

ACKNOWLEDGEMENTS

We would like to thank Dr. Ian Paul for the use of his behavioral core facilities. This project was supported by funds from the OB/GYN Department at UMMC.

REFERENCES

Altman J, Sudarshan K (1975). Postnatal development of locomotion in the laboratory rat. Anim. Behav., 23: 869-920.

Bauer S (2007). The neuropoietic cytokine family in development, plasticity, disease and injury. Nat. Rev. Neurosci., 8: 221-232.

Bell M, Hallenbeck J (2002). Effects of Intrauterine inflammation on developing rat brain. J. Neurosci. Res., 70: 570-579.

Bell M (2004). Determining the fetal inflammatory response in an experimental model of intrauterine inflammation in rats. Pediatr. Res., 56: 541-546.

Bilbo S (2005). Neonatal infection induces memory impairments follwoing an immune challenge in adulthood. Behav. Neurosci., 119: 293-301.

Cai Z (2000). Cytokine induction in fetal rat brains and brain injury in neonatal rats after maternal lipopolysaccharide administration. Ped. Res., 47: 64-72.

Cai Z (2003). Differential roles of tumor necrosis factor-alpha and interleukin-1beta in lipopolysaccharide-induced brain injury in the neonatal rat. Brain Res., 975: 37-47.

Chew L (2006). Microglia and inflammation: impact on development and brain injuries. Mental Retardation. Dev. Disabil., 12: 105-112.

Choi D (2009). Striatal Neuroinflammation Promotes Parkinsonism in Rats. PLos ONE,. 4: 1-11.

Clarac F (2004). The maturation of locomotor networks. Progress in Brain Res., 143: 57-66.

Dammann O (2002). Perinatal Infection, fetal inflammatory response, white matter damage and cognitive limitations in children born preterm. Mental Retard. Dev. Disabil., 8: 46-50.

Dammann O, Leviton A (1998). Infection remote from the brain, neonatal white matter damage, and cerebral palsy in the preterm infant. Semin. Pediatr. Neurol., 5: 190-201.

Debillon T (2000). Intrauterine infection induces programmed cell death in rabbit periventricular white matter. Pediatr. Res., 47: 736-742.

Gatti S, Bartfai T (1993). Induction of tumor necrosis factor-alpha mRNA in the brain after peripheral endotoxin treatment: comparison with interleukin-1 family and interleukin-6. Brain Res., 624: 291-294.

Giulian D (1988). Interleukin-1 is an astroglial growth factor in the developing brain. J. Neurosci., 8: 709-714.

Guiral E (2011). Prevalence of Escherichia coli among samples collected from the genital tract in pregnant and nonpregnant women: relationship with virulence. FEMS Microbiol. Lett., 314: 170-173.

He F (2005). A positive autoregulatory loop of Jak-STAT signaling controls the onset of astrogliogenesis. Nat. Neurosci., 8: 616-625.

Jen K (1978). Effects of undernutrition and litter size on material variables and pup development. Dev. Psychobiol., 11: 279-287.

Kadhim H (2001). Inflammatory cytokines in the pathogenesis of periventricular leukomalacia. Neurology, 56: 1278-1284.

Kolb B (1984). Functions of the frontal cortex of the rat: A comparative review. Brain Res., 320: 65-98.

Konczak J, Timmann D (2007). The effect of damage to the cerebellum on sensorimotor and cognitive function in children and adolescents. Neurosci. Behav. Rev., doi:10.1016/jneubiorev.04.014.

Konsman J (2002). Cytokine-induced sickness behavior: mechanisms and implications. Trends Neurosci., 25: 154-159.

Kuhn P (2010). Incidence and distribution of pathogens in early-onset neonatal sepsis in the era of antenatal antibiotics. Paediatr. Perinatal. Epidemiol., 24: 479-487.

Lazarini C (2001). Effects of prenatal exposure to deltamethrin on forced swimming behavior, motor activity, and striatal dopamine levels in male and female rats. Neurotoxicol. Teratol., 23: 665-673.

Luheshi G (1998). Cytokines and fever: Mechansims and sites of action. Ann. Acad. Sci., 856: 83-89.

Mittendorf R (2001). The association of coagulase-negative staphylococci isolated from the chorioamnion at delivery and subsequent development of cerebral palsy. J. Perinatol., 21: 3-8.

Nelson K, Willoughby R (2000). Infection, inflammation and the risk of cerebral palsy. Curr. Opin. Neurol., 13: 133-139.

Pang Y (2006). Role of interleukin-6 in lipopolysaccharide-induced brain injury and behavioral dysfunction in neonatal rats. Neuroscience, 141: 745-755.

Pang Y (2005). Suppression of glial activation is involved in the protection of IL-10 on maternal *E. coli* induced neonatal white matter injury. Dev. Brain Res., 157: 141-149.

Parker-Athill E, Tan J (2010). Maternal immune activation and autism spectrum disorder: interleukin-6 signaling as a key mechanistic pathway. Neurosignals, 18: 113-128.

Poggi S (2005). No phenotype associated with established lipopolysaccharide model for cerebral palsy. Am. J. Obstet. Gynecol., 192: 727-733.

Rafal'skii V (2009). Present-day beta-lactame antibiotics in the treatment of urinary infections in pregnant women. Urologiia, 5: 14-18.

Rodts-Palenik S (2004). Maternal infection-induced white matter injury is reduced by treatment with interleukin-10. Am. J. Obstetr. Gynecol., 191: 1387-1392.

Schendel D (2001). Infection in pregnancy and cerebral palsy. J. Am. Med. Associ., 56: 105-108.

Siren A (1992). Release of proinflammatory and prothrombotic mediators in the brain and peripheral circulation in spontaneously hypertensive and normotensive Wistar-Kyoto rats. Stroke, 23: 1643-1651.

Snyder-Keller A, Stark P (2008). Prenatal inflammatory effects on nigrostriatal development in organotypic cultures. Brain Res., 1233: 160-167.

Toso L (2005). Inflammatory-mediated model of cerebral palsy with developmental sequelae. Am. J. Obstetr. Gynecol., 193: 933-941.

Urakubo A (2001). Prenatal exposure to maternal infection alters cytokine expression in the placenta, amniotic fluid, and fetal brain. Schizophrenia Res., 47: 27-36.

Vigneswaran R (2004). Cerebral palsy and placental infection: a case-cohort study. BMC Pregnancy Childbirth, 27: 1.

Wallace K (2010a). Interleukin-10/Cefriaxone prevents E.coli-induced delays in sensorimotor task learning and spatial memory in neonatal and adult Sprague Dawley rats. Brain Res. Bull., 81: 141-148.

Wallace K (2010b). Prenatal infection decreases calbindin, decreases Purkinje cell volume and density and produced long-term motor deficits in Sprague-Dawley rats. Dev. Neurosci., 32: 302-312.

Wei H (2011). IL-6 is increased in the cerebellum of the autistic brain and alters neural cell adhesion, migration and synapse formation. Journal of Neuroinflammation. 19: 1.

Wu Y, Colford J (2000). Chorioamnionitis as a risk factor for cerebral palsy. JAMA, 284: 1417-1424.

Yoon B (2003). Intrauterine Infection and the development of cerebral palsy. British. J. Obstetr. Gynecol., 20: 124-127.

Yoon B (2000). Fetal exposure to an intra-amniotic inflammation and the development of cerebral palsy at the age of three years. Am. J. Obstetr. Gynecol., 182: 675-681.

Predictors of burnout among community health personnel of primary care units in the Northern region of Thailand

Narongsak Noosorn[1]* and Rung Wongwat[2]

[1]Faculty of Public Health, Naresuan University, Mueang, Phitsanulok 65000, Thailand.
[2]Sukhothai Provincial Public Health Office, Mueang, Sukhothai 64000, Thailand.

The objectives of this research study were to study the predictors of burnout relationships between factors that contribute to burnout among health personnel in different Primary Care Units in the lower northern region of Thailand. The population consisted of 490 community health personnel. The questionnaire developed for this study was based on the Maslach Burnout Inventory. The data analysis was done for percentage, mean, standard deviation, Pearson Product Moment Correlation Coefficient and stepwise multiple regression analysis. The results showed that: workload, policy, income, equity, relationship with executives, the days of work overtime per month, relationship with colleagues, relationship with consumer were significant predictors which were accounted for the variance of burnout at 47.8% ($F = 19.137$, $P < 0.001$)

Key words: Burnout, health personnel, primary care unit.

INTRODUCTION

Burnout is a syndrome of emotional exhaustion, depersonalization, and reduced personal accomplishment that can occur among individuals who do "people work" of some kind (Maslach, 1982) and it is a process that begins with excessive and prolonged levels of job stress. The stress produces strain in the worker (feelings of tension, irritability and fatigue). The process is completed when the worker defensively copes with the job and becomes apathetic, cynical or rigid (Cherniss, 1980) Burnout is experienced by professionals who provide services and help to the public usually consist of those who deal with a great number of people all the time and sometime for a longer period of time. Such practices might lead to recurrence of physical and mental stress which can give rise to emotional depression, boredom, troubles in interpersonal relationships, and dissatisfaction with their daily responsibilities Maslach (2003). According to Sanguan (1999), burnout is detrimental to a single person, a group pf people, an organization, and society where one works or lives.Job stress is a great problem in developed countries of the world; it is increased due to additional reasons associated with economic crisis in the society. Health services and health workers are in particularly difficult conditions. Health workers are exposed to greater job stress, great sense of very high job responsibility and frequent overtime work (Nedic et al., 2002) The health professionals at risk include physicians, nurses, social workers, dentists, care providers in oncology and AIDS-patient care personnel, emergency service staff members, mental health workers, and speech and language pathologists, among others. Early identification of this emotional slippage is needed to prevent the depersonalization of the provider-patient relationship. Burnout is a health care professional's occupational disease which must be recognized early and treated (Felton, 1998). To work as a public health officer and be successful, one has to be tolerable, patient, merciful and morally/ethically conscious. In Thailand, the career status of public health workers has been overlooked since there is no legislation to clarify the status of public health profession. The legality of their practice has

*Corresponding author. E-mail: nnoosorn@yahoo.com.

always beena controversial issue raised by persons involved in someissues such as remuneration which is seen as relatively lower than other relevant professionals. Stress has been defined as an event which puts demands upon the organism and sets in motion a non-specific bodily response which leads to a variety of temporary or permanent physiological, psychological and structural changes (Onder et al., 2000). The various diseases arising out of stress are coronary heart disease, gastric ulcer, psychosexual disease, anxiety neurosis, etc. which can be controlled to a considerable extent through effective coping strategies (Winzelberg et al., 1999). Generally, public health officers face the stress from work, internal working environment, and external environment which gives rise to burnout which results in lowering the quality of their performance and the whole quality of public health profession in our country. So that, the researcher has been interested in exploring burnout and its causes suffered by public health officers in order to identify problems and guidelines for prevention of burnout and resolutions for reduction of burnout and also to provide information to those who are involved in this matter.

MATERIALS AND METHODS

Population and sample group selection

This descriptive and exploratory research was conducted among public health officers and community health personnel working in Phitsanulok, Phichit, Tak, Kamphaeng Phet, Phetchabun, Uttaradit Nakhonsawan and Sukhothai provinces; the lower northern region of Thailand. A total of 490 public health officers were selected by the multistage sampling method. The researcher selected three from nine provinces and selected one public health officer from every primary care unit in the three provinces: Phitsanulok, Sukhothai, and Phichit using convenience sampling method.

Instruments used for the study

1.) The instruments used for data collection were developed based on the measurement tool for burnout which was designed by Kitti (1998) and modified under the guidelines of survey form of burnout developed by using the Maslach Burnout Inventory (Maslach et al., 1996). The tools were separated into three parts as follows:

Part 1: Questionnaire on the status of public health officers which contained five checklists.
Part 2: Rating scale of measurement for working factors such as relationship with executives, relationship with colleagues, relationship with consumer, safety of work, policy, Income, Workload, Work stress, equity which were classified into five levels from 1 - 5.
Part 3: Rating scale of measurement for burnout which was classified into seven levels from 0 - 6. The measurement form for burnout was a tool for measurement of symptoms of burnout according to three elements. It contained 22 headings regarding emotional depression, defect in interpersonal relationship and attitude towards the outcome of operation. The score of burnout was classified into different levels. The researcher applied the criteria for classification of levels of burnout by Duke and Patricia (1995).

Data analysis

1.) Relationships between factors of personnel, the working condition and the burnout of the community health personnel by Pearson Product Moment Correlation Coefficient.
2.) Determine the added predictive validity of the burnout of the community health personnel by stepwise multiple regression analysis.

RESULTS

It was found that there were more females (67.8%) than males (32.2%) working as public health officers in different primary care units in the lower northern region of Thailand. Most of the public health officers had an age range of 31 to 40 years (42.7%) and followed by less than 30 years (32.4%). Most were married (57.9%). Most were Monthly income between 15,001 - 30,000 Bath per month (52.1%). Regarding work experience, most of the respondents had 11 - 20 years of work experience (54.1%) followed by less than 10 years (34.1%). The average of the patients treated a daily was 35.86 (S.D. = 12.53). The average of workload per week was 55.54 (S.D. = 11.64). The average of work overtime per month was 12 (S.D. = 3.75) (Table 1).

Regarding Correlation Matrix, the study showed that a positive relationship existed between the number of Patients treated a daily, Work overtime per month (days), relationship with executives, relationship with colleagues, relationship with consumer, safety of work, policy, Income, Workload, Work stress, equity and Burnout. A Pearson correlation coefficient between these variables revealed a significant positive relationship (r =.355, 167, 216, 258, 297, 367, 544, 273, 545, 447, 431 and $P < 0.01$) (Table 2).

And for the summary of the stepwise multiple regression for variables predicting burnout, the study showed that workload (W), policy (P), income (I), equity (E), relationship with executives (Re), the days of work overtime per month (Wm) and relationship with consumer (Rc) contributed significantly to R^2 and increased R^2 from .297 to .478 (Table 3). Therefore, the following regression model was established:

$$Y = 41.490 + .853\ W + 2.263\ P + -1.385\ I + 1.772\ E + -.572\ Re + .469\ Wm$$

DISCUSSION

The results of predictors of burnout among community health personnel of primary care units in the northern region of Thailand show that workload, policy, income, equity, relationship with executives, the days of work overtime per month, relationship with colleagues,

Table 1. General information.

General information	Number (n= 490)	Percent
Gender		
Male	158	32.2
Female	332	67.8
Age (years)		
< 31	159	32.4
31 - 40	209	42.7
41 - 50	98	20.0
> 50	24	4.9
Min = 19, Max = 59 , Mean = 38.54, S.D. = 1.64		
Status		
Single	190	38.8
Married	284	57.9
Divorced	16	3.3
Monthly income (Baht)		
< 15,000	187	38.1
15,001-30,000	255	52.1
> 30,001	48	9.80
Min = 7,250 , Max = 33,540 , Mean = 19,800.54, S.D. = 9001.584		
Work experience (years)		
1-10	167	34.1
11-20	265	54.1
>20	58	11.8
Min = 1, Max = 39 , Mean = 19.04, S.D. = 10.64		
Patients treated daily (persons)		
< 31	106	21.7
31- 60	244	49.8
61- 90	96	19.6
>90	44	8.9
Min = 20, Max = 50 , Mean = 35.86, S.D. = 12.53		
Workload per week (hours)		
< 41	49	10.0
41- 60	278	56.7
61- 80	90	18.4
> 80	73	14.9
Min = 40, Max = 82 , Mean = 55.54, S.D. = 11.64		
Work overtime per month (days)		
< 11	190	38.8
11- 20	282	57.5
> 20	18	3.7
Min = 7, Max = 30 , Mean = 12, S.D. = 3.75		

Table 2. Zero order correlation matrix for all variables in research question (N=490).

	x1	x2	x3	x4	x5	x6	x7	x8	x9	x10	x11	x12	x13	x14	x15	x16
x1	1	.924**	.985**	-.459**	-.416**	-.441**	.133*	.238**	-.150**	-0.072	-.222**	-.193**	-.119*	-0.024	.121*	-0.075
x2		1	.914**	-.362**	-.347**	-.350**	.112*	.155**	-0.088	0.006	-0.066	-.137**	-0.039	-0.004	.122*	0.006
x3			1	-.445**	-.402**	-.437**	.155**	.221**	-.150**	-0.071	-.238**	-.208**	-.134*	-0.064	.136**	-0.086
x4				1	.357**	0.05	-0.003	.144**	.306**	.208**	.402**	.172**	.525**	.354**	.131*	.355**
x5					1	.312**	-.173**	-.170**	0.002	-0.045	0.02	-0.011	0.059	-0.043	-0.089	0.079
x6						1	-0.005	-0.071	.208**	.203**	.137**	.108*	.131*	.130*	-0.013	.167**
x7							1	.766**	.510**	.219**	.336**	.321**	.377**	.415**	.692**	.216**
x8								1	.560**	.119*	.287**	.255**	.361**	.472**	.583**	.258**
x9									1	.356**	.620**	.532**	.587**	.628**	.469**	.297**
x10										1	.492**	.509**	.623**	.549**	.376**	.367**
x11											1	.645**	.740**	.692**	.418**	.544**
x12												1	.696**	.564**	.384**	.273**
x13													1	.755**	.472**	.545**
x14														1	.452**	.447**
x15															1	.431**)
x16																1

Note. X1 = age, X2= monthly in come, X3= work experience, X4= patients treated a daily (persons), X5= workload per week (hours), X6= work overtime per month (days), X7= relationship with executives, X8= relationship with colleagues, X9= relationship with consumer, X10= safety of work, X11= policy, X12=income, X13= workload, X14=work stress, X15= equity.

Table 3. Summary for stepwise multiple regression for variables predicting burnout among community health personnel of primary care units in the lower Northern region of Thailand.

Variable	B	SE B	β
Workload	.853	.142	.388**
Policy	2.263	.318	.443**
Income	-1.385	.282	-.275**
Equity	1.772	.288	.345**
Relationship with executives	-.572	.143	-.269**
The days of work overtime per month	.469	.125	.151**
Relationship with consumer	-.921	.237	-.231**
Relationship with colleagues	.467	.147	.206**

Note. R^2 = 0.478 for Step 8 **P < 0.01.

relationship with consumer were significant predictors which were accounted for the variance of burnout. The result of this research is in conformity with the study of a sense of responsibility in health personnel as a cause of work-related stress (Nedic et al., 2002) which has showed that, applying the scoring system it has been established that health workers are exposed to greater job stress, great sense of very high job responsibility and frequent overtime work ($p < 0.001$) and high sense of responsibility in health workers is a course of job stress. Comparing the effect of burnout with some demographic variables such as gender, it was found out that male and female public health officers are differently affected with regard to the three elements of burnout. In other words, gender has significant influence upon those three elements of burnout. The result of this research is in conformity with the study of Baylor College of Medicine (2003), which has shown that women experience more stress than their male counterparts especially if they have children at home. They tend to have internal stress when encountering external stressors. And it might be due to the fact that female public health officers have roles, duties, and responsibilities related to their positions and operations, hence are more likely to experience different levels of burnout than do male public health officers. However, too much stress adversely affects our health and well-being, job performance and behavior. Employment outside the home has not relieved women of responsibilities of childcare and housework. The number of mothers who work outside the home has increased steadily. Since working women have to perform the dual roles-domestic and occupational, it becomes necessary for them to know how to handle women to their best abilities. The stress of combining full-time employment with homemaking is not easy and balancing these two roles may be more difficult for some employed women than for others.

LIMITATIONS AND RECOMMENDATION

Due to time and financial constraints, this research study focused only on the lower northern region of Thailand. In view of the findings, the researcher recommends the following:

1.) The top public health executives or other policy-makers should seriously consider and implement measures for supporting the work of public health officers and help them to decrease their burnout levels.
2.) A building capacity program should be established for public health officers to enable them to deal with problems efficiently.
3.) Further researchers should be done nationwide to explore the extent to which other health professionals affected by burnout, and to design specific interventions in dealing with this problem.

Conclusion

This research study revealed that health professionals serving in the lower northern region of Thailand, face a high level burnout related different factors such as heavy workload, overtime work, the number of patients, colleagues, executives and so forth. By decreasing such factors contributing to burnout would considerably increase the well being of those employees, and eventually increase productivity.

REFERENCES

Baylor College of Medicine (2003). Women and stress: Successfully juggling your busy life, Office of Health Promotion.

Cherniss C (1980). Staff Burnout: Job Stress in the Human Services. Beverly Hills, California: Sage Publications p. 21.

Duke Patricia W (1995). Burnout Among Special Education Teachers and Former [Dissertation Abstracts] 55(10): 3051.

Felton JS (1998). Burnout as a clinical entity—its importance in health care workers Occupational Medicine 48: 237-250.

Kitti S (1988). Burnout and its causes occurred in the operation of teacher in the lower Northern region of Thailand [master's thesis]. Naresuan University, Thailand.

Maslach C (1982). Burnout-The Cost of Caring. Englewood Cliffs, New Jersey: Prentice-Hall p. 3.

Maslach C (2003). Job burnout: new direction in research and intervention. Current Directions in Psychol. Sci. 12: 189-192.

Maslach C, Jackson SE, Leiter MP (1996). The Maslach Burnout Inventory. (3rd ed.). Palo Alto, CA: Consulting Psychologists Press.

Nedic O, Jocic N, Filipovic D, Solak Z (2002). A sense of responsibility in health personnel as a cause of work-related stress, Med Pregl 2002 Mar-Apr; 55(3-4): 97-103.

Onder S, Cosar B, Oztaz, MO, Cadansayar S (2000). Stress and Skin Diseases in Musicians: Evaluation of the Beck Depression Scale, General Psychological Profile (The Brief Symptom Inventory), Beck Anxiety Scale and Stressful life events in Musicians. Biomedicine and Pharmacotherapy, 54, pp.258-262, Elsevier Science Ltd. Amsterdam, Netherlands. www.psychologygateway.com.

Sanguan L (1999). Job Burnout: Development, Definitions and Measurement. Songklanakarin J. Soc. Sci Hum. 5(2) May: 167-180.

Winzelberg J, Andrew, Frederic ML (1999). The effect of Meditation training in stress levels in Secondary School Teachers. Stress medicine, 15, pp.69-77, John Wiley & Sons, The Atrium, West Sussex, U.K.

6

Behavioural and haematological studies on effects of lycopene in Wistar rats subjected to psychological stress

Ogundeji, T.[1]*, Ayo J. O.[1], Aluwong T.[1] and Mohammed A.[2]

[1]Department of Veterinary Physiology, Faculty of Veterinary Medicine, Ahmadu Bello University, Zaria, Nigeria.
[2]Department of Human Physiology, Faculty of Human Medicine, Ahmadu Bello University, Zaria, Nigeria.

This study investigated the effects of prior lycopene supplementation on behaviour and haematology of Wistar rats subjected to psychological stress. Four groups of Wistar rats, each comprising seven animals were investigated: unstressed (U-Control), unstressed + lycopene (U+Lyco), stressed (S-Control) and stressed + lycopene (S+Lyco). Olive oil was given by oral gavage to each rat in the groups, either singly or mixed with 10 mg/kg lycopene daily for two weeks. S-Control and S+Lyco groups were subjected to psychological stress followed by behavioural assessment using excitability score test. Blood samples were collected after sacrificing the animals and then analyzed. Psychological stress increased ($P < 0.05$) erythrocyte malondialdehyde (MDA) concentration in Wistar rats. Lycopene significantly increased excitability scores and total blood plasma proteins, and decreased ($P > 0.05$) erythrocyte MDA concentration. In conclusion, antioxidant properties of lycopene may be attenuating the effects of psychological stress on excitability score and erythrocytes of Wistar rats.

Key words: excitability score, erythrocytes, total plasma proteins, fear stress, oxidative stress, antioxidant supplementation.

INTRODUCTION

Contextual fear conditioning is a useful behavioural paradigm that can evoke bio-behavioural changes in response to a psychological-based stressor (Sanders and Knoepfler, 2008). It involves placing a rodent into an apparatus and receives pairings of a phasic electrical shock to its feet. Subsequently, when tested in the original training context, the rat will display a natural defensive response termed freezing (Blanchard and Blanchard, 1969). The paradigm is associated with pro-long stimulation of the body stress response mechanism (Thompson et al., 2012) and may replicate the fear responses observed when an animal is exposed to psychological stressors such as novel task, environment or husbandry procedures. Such fear responses are capable of disrupting the body homeostatic mechanism which may lead to detrimental effects on animal well-being.

Adverse effects of psychological stressors such as fear on biological functions are well known (Thompson et al., 2012). Although physiological response to fear is beneficial when acute, it may be superimposed by excess free-radical production leading to detrimental effects on health (Shin and Liberzon, 2010). This is usually termed chronic stress and it occurs through persistent activation of limbic-hypothalamo-pituitary-adrenal axis and the secretion of stress hormones in the brain (Cordero et al., 2003; Grillon et al., 2007). Stress-related behavioural activities and haematological responses may be triggered for a long period by an exposure to psychological/ emotional stressor (Armario et al., 2008; Shin and Liberzon, 2010). Studies in man (Szanton et al., 2011) and domestic animals (Lay and Wilson, 2004; Minka and Ayo, 2008) have shown that psychological stress, acting singly or in combination with other factors, may induce adverse behavioural and/or haematological effects due to increased free-radical activity.

Antioxidant supplementation is useful in augmenting endogenous antioxidant capacity in animal (Tauler et al., 2006). Expanding the understanding of the biological role of antioxidant supplements is vital, particularly during stressful conditions. Lycopene is a potent dietary antioxidant supplement and previous studies have demonstrated the beneficial effects of prior lycopene supplementation (Djuric and Powell, 2001; Al-Jassabi, 2005), particularly during exposure to psychological stress (Ogundeji et al., 2012). Maintaining circulatory concentration level of lycopene may result in reduction in lipoperoxidation and other beneficial effects such as enhanced behavioural and haematological responses. The aim of the study was to investigate the protective role of prior lycopene supplementation on behavioural and haematological responses in Wistar rats subjected to psychological stress.

MATERIALS AND METHODS

Experimental animals, design and management

Twenty-eight adult, male, 10 to 14 week-old Wistar rats weighing 190 to 220 g were procured from the animal house of the National Institute of Trypanosomiasis Research, Kaduna, Nigeria. They were kept in the animal house of the Department of Veterinary Physiology, Ahmadu Bello University, Zaria at ambient temperature of 25 ± 0.8°C and a relative humidity of 86.14 ± 3.44%. The rats were housed seven animals per cage and on a 12 h light-dark cycle (light during 7:00 to 19:00 h). They had access to pellets made from grower's mash, maize bran and groundnut cake in the ratio of 4:2:1, and water was provided *ad libitum*. The rats were acclimatized to the experimental procedures for two weeks prior to the commencement of the experiment. They were randomly assigned to four groups, each comprising seven animals: unstressed control (U-Control), unstressed + lycopene (U+Lyco), stressed control (S-Control) and stressed + lycopene (S+Lyco). 10 mg lycopene in a gelatinous capsule (General Nutrition Corporation, Pittsburgh, U.S.A.) was reconstituted in olive oil (*Goya en espana*, S.A.U., Sevilla, Spain) to appropriate working concentration. Olive oil (1 ml/kg) was given by oral gavage to each rat in the groups, either singly or mixed with 10 mg/kg lycopene daily for two weeks (Djuric and Powell, 2001; Al-Jassabi, 2005).

U-Control and S-Control rats were administered olive oil only, while U+Lyco and S+Lyco rats were administered with lycopene lycopene mixed with olive oil. On days 13 and 14, S-Control and S+Lyco were subjected to psychological stress using the step-down inhibitory avoidance task. This is followed by behavioural assessment using the excitability score test on day 14, which was conducted in fully wake condition between the hour of 10:00 to 11:00 h. On the 15th day, that is 24 h after the psychological stress induction, each of the overnight-fasted rat was euthanized using light ether anaesthesia. After sacrificing the rats, blood samples were collected into heparinized sample bottles. The samples were analyzed for packed cell volume (PCV), haemoglobin (Hb) concentration, erythrocyte (RBC) count, total plasma proteins (TP), total leucocyte count (WBC), and erythrocyte malondialdehyde concentration (erythrocyte MDA). The study was approved by Ahmadu Bello University Animal Research Committee and in accordance with Guidelines for the Care and Use of Animals in Neuroscience and Behavioural Research.

Psychological stress induction

Psychological stress was induced using step-down inhibitory avoidance task that is based on contextual fear conditioning (Armario et al., 2008; Shin and Liberzon, 2010). The apparatus for the task is an acrylic chamber (40 × 25 × 25 cm), consisting of a floor made of parallel 2 mm calibre stainless steel bar, spaced 1 cm apart. An electric shock was delivered through the floor bars. Each rat was gently placed on the platform on day 13. Upon stepping down from the platform, the rat immediately received a single 80 volt foot shock. For rat that did not return to the platform, the foot shock was repeated every five seconds. Fear was considered to have been induced if the rat remained on the platform for more than two minutes. Subsequently, rats were returned to the home cage environment. Twenty-four hours later, on day 14, rats were re-exposed to this same apparatus in the absence of the foot shock, serving as a situational reminder. In this case, each rat was again placed gently on the platform until the rat voluntarily dropped down from the platform. Maximum period of staying on the platform before a rat was removed from the apparatus was two minutes.

Behavioural assessments

The behavioural response of each rat to handling was assessed using excitability score test (Adeiza and Minka, 2010; Ambali and Ayo, 2012). The test exploits the reaction of the animal to handling and on this basis, the level of response can be graded or scored. Briefly, each rat was held by the tail upside down and kept in such position for 30 s. The level of reaction of the animal was graded and scored as follows: (i) Score 1 (calm): Rat did not show any sign of wriggling and paw movement; (ii) Score 2 (occasional shakes): Rat responded through gentle wriggling and movement of forepaw; (ii) Score 3 (repeated shakes): Rat responded through stronger wriggling and movement of forepaw; (iv) Score 4 (violent shakes): Rat responded through vigorous wriggling, strong movement of fore- and hind limb as well as successfully climbing the tip of its tail.

Determination of haematological parameters

The PCV, Hb concentration, RBC count, WBC were determined as described by Schalm et al. (1975). The PCV was determined by microhaematocrit method and the Hb concentration by cyanomethaemoglobin method. RBC and WBC were determined by haemocytometeric method.

Determination of biochemical parameters

Erythrocyte MDA determination is a biochemical test with higher sensitivity in detection of haematological changes. To determine the MDA, heparinised blood sample (2.5 ml) obtained from each animal was centrifuged at 4,000 × g for 5 min and the plasma was seperated. Washing of erythrocytes three times in cold isotonic saline (0.9 % w/v) was done to obtain erythrocyte packets for the determination of MDA concentrations using Northwest Life Science Specialties (NWLSS^{TM}) Malondialdehyde assay kits (Northwest Life Science Specialties, Vancouver, WA 98662, USA). The principle of the method of determination was based on spectrophotometric measurement of the colour developed during reaction of thiobarbituric acid with malondialdehyde as described by Lykkesfeldt (2001). The blood plasma obtained was used to assay for total protein concentration. It was performed using hand-held refractometers (Eckersall, 2008).

Statistical analyses

Values obtained were expressed as mean ± standard error of mean (SEM). Excitability score data were analyzed by Student's *t*-test. Haematological and biochemical parameters data were analyzed by one-way analysis of variance (ANOVA), followed by Tukey's multiple comparison *post-hoc* test. The program used for the analysis was GraphPad Prism 4.0 version from GraphPad Software, San Diego, USA. Values of P < 0.05 were considered significant.

RESULTS

Effect of lycopene on behavioural response

Effects of lycopene on excitability score of each rat (on 14th day) are shown in Figure 1. None of the rats in the S+Lyco had excitability score of one (1), while 14.3 ± 0.7% of those in the S-Control had excitability score of one. Excitability score of two (2) was recorded in 57.1 ± 2.9% of the rats in S-Control, and the value was significantly (P < 0.001) higher than that of 42.9 ± 2.2% recorded for rats in the S+Lyco. 42.9 ± 2.2% of rats in the S+Lyco had excitability score of three (3), and the value was significantly (P < 0.001) higher than 14.3 ± 0.7% recorded in the S-Control.14.3 ± 0.7% of rats in each of the groups had excitability score of four (4).

Effect of lycopene on haematological parameters

There was no significant difference in PCV, Hb, RBC, WBC values, both between and within groups (Table 1).

Effect of lycopene on biochemical parameters

The MDA concentration in the erythrocytes of S-Control group was significantly (P < 0.01) higher than the unstressed group (that is, U-Control and U+Lyco). However, there was no significant difference between the values of erythrocyte MDA concentration recorded for U-Control, U+Lyco and S+Lyco groups (Figure 2). TP value was significantly (P < 0.05) increased in the S+Lyco group compared to that of S-Control. However, there was no significant difference between the TP values of U-Control and U+Lyco and when compared to the stressed group (Figure 3).

DISCUSSION

It is well known that psychological stressors can continuously activate the sympathetic nervous system to elicit stress response, consequently leading to increase free-radical production (Armario et al., 2008). In the present study, although there are no significant differences in the haematological parameters, a further analysis reveals that psychological stress impaired erythrocyte cell membrane integrity. This is evidenced by significant increase in erythrocyte MDA concentration in S-Control compared to that of U-Control. The effects of psycholo-gical stress on erythrocytes may have been indirectly mediated through the significant overlap existing among structures involved in the fear/ anxiety response and stress response in the brain, and corticotrophin releasing hormone is likely involved in the coordination of both limbic-hypothalamo-pituitary-adrenal (LHPA) axis activity and many fear/anxiety responses (Shin and Liberzon, 2010). Thus, this finding indicates that subjection to psy-chological stress triggered the stress response mecha-nism in the Wistar rats, thereby resulting in increased free-radical production.

Increased free-radical activities have been generally shown to decrease viability and integrity of nerve cells (Friedman, 2010). Earlier study by Ogundeji et al. (2012) has shown that lycopene exerts antioxidant effects by enhancing behavioural responses through de-creased brain free-radical activities. In the present study, none of the rats administered lycopene (that is, S+Lyco group) had excitability score of 1, instead majority obtained the score of 2 and 3, with greater percentage having score of 3. This finding indicates increased excitability. It implies that lycopene enhanced behavioural response, perhaps by activating the nervous system and facilitating transition from a state of depression to exci-tation through decreased free-radical activities. Ayo et al. (2006) made similar observation in goats administered ascorbic acids. Report has shown that positive beha-vioural response correlates with body activities leading to decreased free-radical production (Szanton et al., 2011).

The significant increase in TP value recorded for S+Lyco and the similarity in the values of erythrocyte

Table 1. Effects of lycopene supplementation on haematological parameters of Wistar rats (n = 5).

Parameter	U-Control	U+Lyco	S-Control	S+Lyco
PCV (%)	50.40±1.94	49.40±1.44	52.60±0.51	53.20±0.92
Hb (g/dl)	16.78±0.65	16.44±0.49	17.50±0.17	17.72±0.30
RBC ($\times10^{12}$/µl)	8.20±0.27	8.10±0.25	8.72±0.15	8.84±0.16
WBC ($\times10^{3}$/µl)	18.68±2.00	18.08±1.30	17.14±2.34	18.08±0.81
Neutrophils ($\times10^{3}$/µl)	19.60±4.10	20.60±2.50	20.00±0.84	23.80±3.25
Lymphocytes ($\times10^{3}$/µl)	81.80±5.52	76.20±3.28	73.80±1.32	78.20±3.26
Monocytes ($\times10^{3}$/µl)	0.00±0.00	1.20±0.49	2.00±0.55	1.80±0.49
Eosinophils ($\times10^{3}$/µl)	0.60±0.60	1.80±0.49	2.80±0.37	1.40±0.60
Band Neutrophils ($\times10^{3}$/µl)	0.00±0.00	0.80±0.37	1.40±0.40	1.00±0.45

U-Control = unstressed control; U+Lyco = Unstressed + Lycopene; S-Control = stressed control; S+Lyco = Stressed + Lycopene.

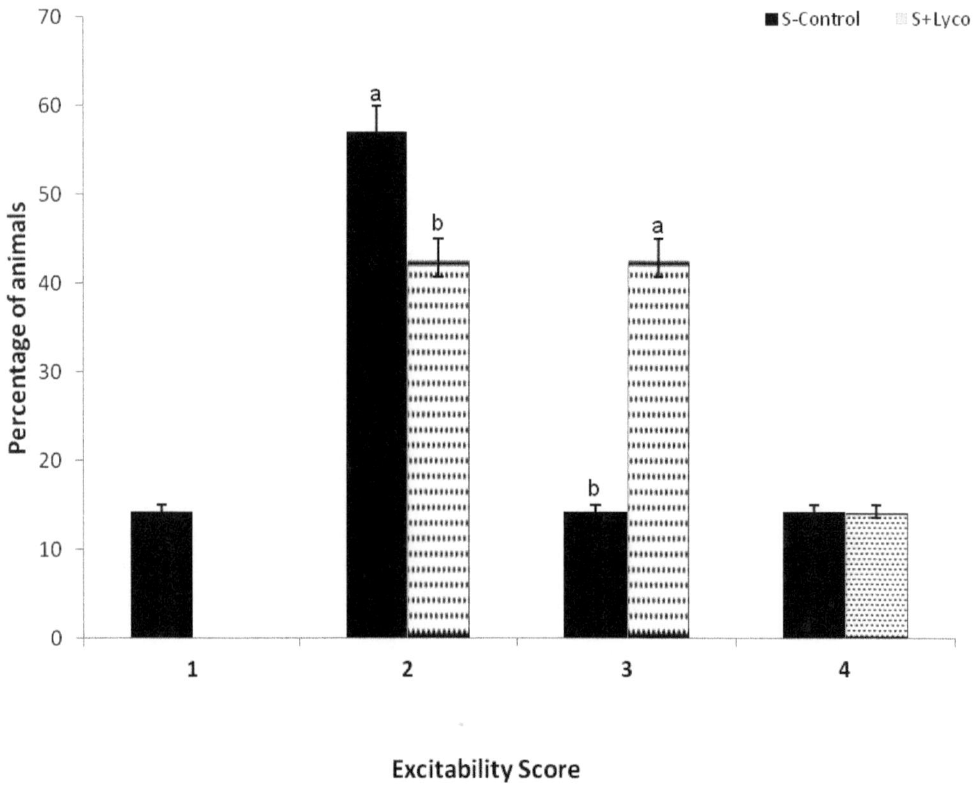

Figure 1. Effects of lycopene administration on excitability score in Wistar rats (n = 7). Mean values with different superscript letters are significantly (P < 0.001) different. Score 1: Calm; Score 2: Occasional Shakes; Score 3: Repeated Shakes; Score 4: Violent Shakes

MDA concentration recorded for S+Lyco and the unstressed group suggests that lycopene protected the erythrocytes from psychological stress-induced oxidative damage by increasing the total plasma protein concentration. This agrees with the reports that proteins, particularly albumin because of its large amount in plasma, exert antioxidant property in the body (Halliwell, 1988; Bourdon and Blache, 2001; Roche et al., 2008). Although the mechanism underlying its role in increased total protein concentration was not elucidated in the present study, preferential deposition of lycopene in organs such as liver may be implicated (Bramley, 2000). Protection of biomolecules such as serum lipoproteins from oxidative injury may be another mechanism of

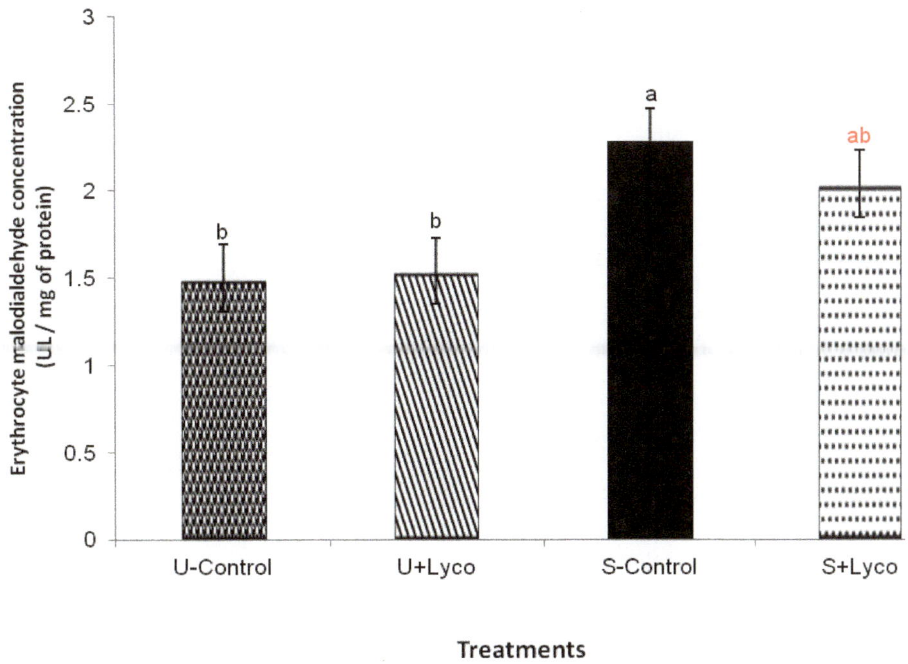

Figure 2. Effects of lycopene supplementation on erythrocyte malondialdehyde concentration of unstressed and stressed Wistar rats (n = 5).
[a,b]P-values with different superscript letters are significantly (P < 0.05) different. U-Control = unstressed control; U+Lyco = unstressed + Lycopene; S-Control = stressed control; S+Lyco = stressed + lycopene.

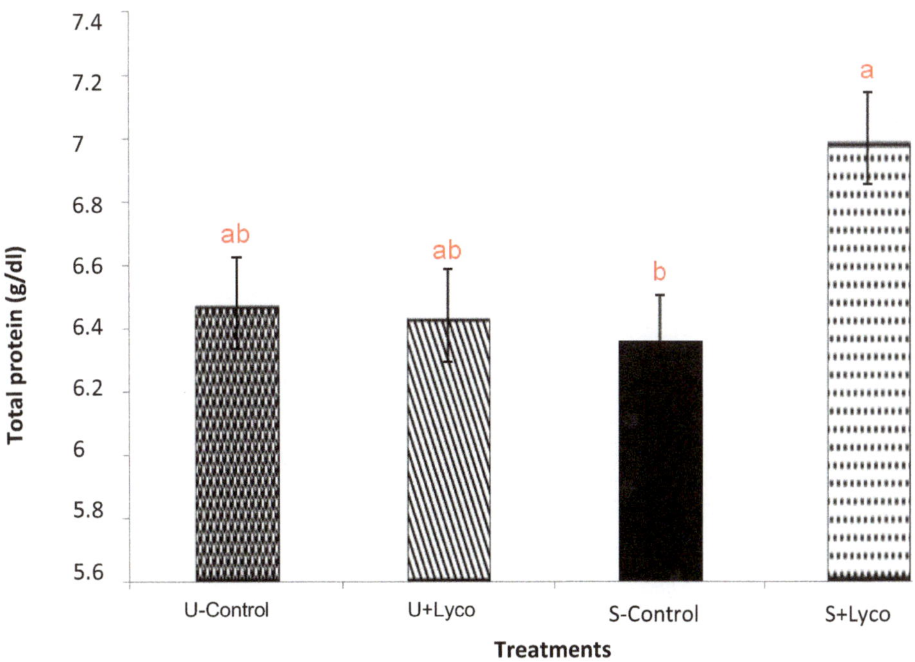

Figure 3. Effects of lycopene supplementation on total plasma protein concentration of unstressed and stressed Wistar rats (n = 5). [a,b]P-values with different superscript letters are significantly (P < 0.05) different. U-Control = unstressed control; U+Lyco = unstressed + lycopene; S-Control = stressed control; S+Lyco = stressed + lycopene.

lycopene action, although conclusive studies have not been shown (Rice-Evans et al., 1997; Bramley, 2000). Serum lipoproteins transport cholesterol to and fro the liver. Cholesterol is an important component of cell membrane and acts as free-radical scavenger. Relationships between serum lipid and erythrocyte membrane lipid show that the change in serum lipids may increase susceptibility of the erythrocytes to lipid peroxidation (Ulana et al., 1985; Clemens and Bursa-Zanetti, 1989). Alteration in the level of serum lipid may occur following oxidative damage to molecules such as serum lipoproteins due to increased free-radical activities.

Conclusion

Lycopene supplementation ameliorates the effects of psychological stress on behavioural response of Wistar rats, apparently through increasing the excitability scores thereby facilitating transition from a state of depression to excitation. Increased total plasma proteins in Wistar rats administered lycopene suggest antioxidant effects which may be reducing oxidative damage to erythrocytes. In conclusion, prior lycopene supplementation is beneficial in attenuating the effects of psychological stress in animals.

ACKNOWLEDGEMENT

Samuel Okey, Sheriff Isa, Eze Daniel, Joseph Bagi and Olu Ayegbusi are acknowledged for kindly assisting with technical support.

REFERENCES

Adeiza AA, Minka NS (2010). Neuromuscular behaviour of Wistar rats administered methanol extract of *Ximenia americana*. Arch. Appl. Sci. Res. 2(5):217-225.

Al-Jassabi S (2005). Biochemical studies on the role of lycopene in the protection of mice against microcystin toxicity. Chem. Ecol. 21(2):143-148.

Ambali SF, Ayo JO (2012). Vitamin C attenuates chronic chlorpyrifos-induced alteration of neurobehavioural parameters in Wistar rats. Toxicol. Int. 29(2):144-152.

Armario A, Escorihuela RM, Nadal R (2008). Long-term neuroendocrine and behavioural effects of a single exposure to stress in adult animal. Neurosci. Biobehav. Rev. 32:1121-35.

Ayo JO, Minka NS, Mamman M (2006). Excitability scores of goats administered ascorbic acid and transported during hot-dry conditions. J. Vet. Sci. 7(2):127-131.

Blanchard RJ, Blanchard DC (1969). Crouching as an index of fear. J. Comp. Physiol. Psychol. 67:370-375.

Bourdon E, Blache, D (2001). The importance of proteins in defence against oxidation. Antioxid. Redox Signal 3:293-311.

Bramley PM (2000). Is lycopene beneficial to human health? Phytochemistry 54:233-236.

Clemens MR, Bursa-Zanetti Z (1989). Lipid abnormalities and peroxidation of erythrocytes in nephrotic syndrome. Nephron 53:325-329.

Cordero MI, Venero C, Kruyt ND. Sandi C (2003). Prior exposure to a single stress session facilitates subsequent contextual fear conditioning in rats: evidence for a role of corticosterone. Horm. Behav. 44:338-45.

Djuric Z, Powell LC (2001). Antioxidant capacity of lycopene-containing food. Int. J. Food Sci. Nutr. 52:143-149.

Eckersall PD (2008). Proteins, Proteomics, and the Dysproteinemias. In: Kaneko JJ, Harvey JW, Bruss ML (Eds.), Veterinary Clinical Biochemistry of Domestic Animals, 6th ed. Elsevier Inc. pp.117-155.

Friedman J (2010). Why is the nervous system vulnerable to oxidative stress? In: Gadoth N, Gobel HH (Eds.), Oxidative Stress and Free Radical Damage in Neurobiology. Springer Science Business Media. pp. 20-21.

Grillon C, Duncko R, Covington MF, Kopperman L, Kling MA (2007). Acute stress potentiates anxiety in humans. Biol. Psychiatry 62:1183-1186.

Halliwell B (1988). Albumin: an important extracellular antioxidant? Biochem. Pharmacol. 37:569-571.

Lay Jr. DC, Wilson ME (2004). Considerations when using physiological data in assessing animal well-being. J. Anim. Vet. Adv. 3:613-625.

Lykkesfeldt J (2001). Determination of malondialdehyde as dithiobarbituricacid adduct in biological samples by HPLC with ultraviolet-visible spectrophotometry. Clin. Chem. 47:1725-27.

Minka NS, Ayo JO (2008). Haematology and behaviour of pullets transported by road and administered with ascorbic acid during the hot-dry season. Res. Vet. Sci. 85:389-393.

Ogundeji T, Ayo JO, Aluwong T, Mohammed A (2012). Lycopene enhanced behavioural and cognitive responses through decreased brain oxidative stress biomarker in Wistar rats subjected to psychological stress. J. Cell Anim. Biol. 6(16):233-240.

Rice-Evans CA, Sampson J, Bramley PM, Holloway DE (1997). Why do we expect carotenoids to be antioxidant *in vivo*? Free Rad. Res. 26:382-98.

Roche M, Rondeau P, Singh RN, Tarnus E, Bourdon E (2008). The antioxidant properties of serum albumin. FEBS Lett. 582:1783-1787.

Sanders BJ, Knoepfler J (2008). Neonatal handling increases cardiovascular reactivity to contextual fear conditioning in borderline hypersensitive rats (BHC). Physiol. Behav. 95(1-2):72-76.

Schalms OW, Jain NC, Carroll EJ (1975). Veterinary Haematology, 3rd ed. Lea and Ferbiger, Philidelphia.

Shin LM, Liberzon I (2010). The neurocircuitry of fear, stress, and anxiety disorders. Neuropsychopharmacology 35:169-191.

Szanton SL, Rifkin JM, Mohanty JG, Miller ER, Thorpe RJ, Nagababu E, Epek ES, Zonderman AB, Evans MK (2011). Racial discrimination is associated with a measure of red blood cell oxidative stress: A potential pathway for racial health disparities. Int. Soc. Behav. 19(4):489-495.

Tauler P, Aguilo A, Gimeno I, Fuentespina E, Tur JA, Pons A (2006). Response of blood cell antioxidant enzyme defences to antioxidant diet supplementation and to intense exercise. Eur. J. Nutr. 446(4):187-195.

Thompson RS, Strong PV, Fleshner M (2012). Physiological consequences of repeated exposures to conditioned fear. Behav. Sci. 2:57-78.

Ulana LB, Brewer GT, Hill GM (1985). Effects of dietary cholesterol on erythrocyte peroxidant stress *in vitro* and *in vivo*. Arch. Biochem. Biophys. 835: 434-440.

7

Polysomnographic differences between severe depression and schizophrenia

Ahmed Rady*, Adel Elsheshai, Osama Elkholy and Heba Abou el Wafa

Department of Psychiatry, Alexandria University, P. O. Box 518, Alexandria 21511, Egypt.

Certain subtypes of major depression, particularly if associated with severe psychomotor retardation or psychotic features, may be difficult to differentiate from schizophrenia due to overlapping symptoms. The aim of this study was to assess the potential role of polysomnography as a tool for differentiating between severe depression with or without psychotic features and schizophrenia. Forty patients aged 18 to 50 years were recruited, comprising 20 with severe depression and 20 with schizophrenia who had defaulted from follow-up visits and had been off their medications for over a week. Two successive overnight polysomnographic recordings were done for all patients. Rapid eye movement latency was 26 ± 6.9 minutes and 43.9 ± 16.9 min in patients with depression and schizophrenia, respectively, with a statistically significant difference between the groups (*P* < 0.006). Rapid eye movementintensity was 34 ± 14% in depressed patients and 21.4 ± 4.5% in patients with schizophrenia, again with a statistically significant difference between the groups (*P*<0.015). On the other hand, stage IV intensity was significantly (*P* < 0.03) lower in patients with schizophrenia (9 ± 7.9%) than in depressed patients (17.8 ± 9.2%). Polysomnographic parameters are different in schizophrenia and severe depression. Further research to assess cutoff scores for different polysomnographic parameters are needed to enable the utilization of polysomnography as a potential electrophysiologic tool for differentiating between these diagnoses.

Key words: Depression, schizophrenia, polysomnography, sleep, encephalography.

INTRODUCTION

Polysomnography helps in identifying encephalographic (EEG) sleep architecture in different mental disorders. Patients with schizophrenia tend to have shortened deep sleep and rapid eye movement (REM) latency (Cohrs, 2008; Benca et al., 1992; Yang and Winkelman, 2006). Whether sleep EEG is a trait or a marker of schizophrenia is unfortunately less clear. Some authors found consistent improvement in sleep continuity during neuroleptic treatment, with REM latency that increases with antipsychotics or, in other words, tends to normalize, while slow-wave deep sleep is more or less unchanged, questioning the later as a trait rather than a marker for schizophrenia (Goder et al., 2008; Maixner et al., 1997; Keshavan et al., 1996, 1995). On the other hand, major depression has been the subject of clinical research assessing polysomnographic analysis, and REM sleep as well as, non-REM sleep has been evoked by researchers. Shortened REM latency and ncreased REM intensity (percentage total sleep duration), as well as, shortened slow-wave sleep, have been reported by several authors, which are changes that may be in part attributable to endocrine rhythm disturbance (Germain et al., 2004; Armitage et al. 1999; Dew et al., 1996). Whether these polysomnographic changes represent

*Corresponding author. E-mail:dr_ahmed_rady@yahoo.fr.

Abbreviation: CGI-S, Clinical Global Impression of Severity; REM, rapid eye movement.

trait ora biological marker of depression has been questioned. The literature suggests correction with antidepressants, indicating a trait rather than a disease marker (Monteleone and Maj, 2008; Dew et al., 1996).

Severe major depression may present with symptoms overlapping with schizophrenia, for example, severe psychomotor retardation versus negative symptoms of schizophrenia. Both diagnoses may share psychotic features, whether they are delusions, hallucinations, or both. Our work focuses on polysomnography as a potential electrophysiological testing tool that may help in differentiating between schizophrenia and severe major depression.

MATERIALS AND METHODS

Twenty severely depressed patients and 20 patients with schizophrenia aged 18 to 50 years were randomly recruited from the outpatient service at Alexandria University Hospital from February to October, 2010. Only outpatients who had defaulted from follow-up visits and had been off their medications for over a week were included. All patients signed a consent form. The study was approved by the ethics committee at Alexandria Faculty of Medicine. Diagnosis was done by a structured clinical interview using DSM IV-TR (Diagnostic and Statistical Manual of Mental Disorders Fourth Edition Text Revision) diagnostic criteria (APA, 2004). Only patients scoring ≥ 4 on the Clinical Global Impression Scale for Severity (CGI-S) (Guy, 1976) and whose condition was stable enough to do polysomnography were recruited. Patients with mental retardation, as assessed by previous IQ testing available in records, or debilitating chronic physical illness were excluded. All participants were screened for drug abuse and alcohol before recruitment. Drug screening was done by urine strips for detecting opiates, THC, MDMA, Amphetamines, Benzodiazepines and Barbiturates. Those turning positive for any drug of abuse were excluded due to probable interference with hypnogram.

Sleep architecture study

Polysomnography consisted of simultaneous recording of multiple physiological parameters related to sleep and wakefulness. The software used for data acquisition was the Cadwell version 1.7. We monitored the following neurophysiologic channels:

1. Four EEG channels (central and occipital with an ear reference providing the best amplitude) to monitor sleep stage
2.Two electro-oculogram channels to monitor both horizontal and vertical eye movements (electrodes placed at the right and left outer canthi, one above and one below the horizontal eye axis)
3. One electromyography channel (usually chin or mentalis and/or submentalis) to record atonia during REM sleep.

Procedure

All patients underwent two successive overnight polysomnography recordings. Because the patients were in unfamiliar surroundings and we need them to sleep more naturally, the first recording session was necessary to make the patients familiar with their surroundings, to avoid the" first night effect". Sleep study was scored manually. Patients were off medication on both nights when polysomnography was performed. The scorer was blinded to the diagnosis of the patients. Sleep staging was done according to the Rechtschaffen and Kales staging system approved by the American Sleep Association. The patients also underwent overnight video-monitoring on both occasions.

Statistical methods

The data obtained were analyzed using the Statistical Package for Social Sciences version 13 (SPSS Inc, Chicago, IL). $P < 0.05$ was used as the cutoff value for statistical significance. Due to the small samples in each group ($n = 20$), we utilized the parametric Student's t - test for independent groups. For t - testing applied to sleep stage intensity; equal variance was assessed and confirmed before comparing frequencies.

RESULTS

The study included 20 patients with schizophrenia and 20 severely depressed patients all scoring ≥ 4 on the CGI-S. All had not been taking their medication for over one week before undergoing polysomnography. In the schizophrenia group, the mean duration off medication was 3 ± 0.2 weeks compared with 2 ± 0.4 weeks in the depression group.

Medications prescribed for the patients before they stopped taking them due to noncompliance, were as follows. In the schizophrenic group, four (20%) patients had been on haloperidol, 12 (60%) on risperidone, one (5%) on aripiprazole, and three (15%) on quetiapine.In the depression group, 13 (65%) were on sertraline, three (15%) were on amitriptyline, and four (20%) were on sertraline and haloperidol.

Duration of illness was not significantly different between the two groups (4.8 ± 2.01 years and 5.1 ± 2.83 years in the schizophrenic and depressed patients, respectively). Both groups were balanced in terms of age, gender distribution, and disease severity as assessed by the CGI-S scale (Table 1). Polysomnographic recordings show shorter REM latency and greater REM intensity in the depressed patients than in those with schizophrenia (Table 2). Intensity of the different non-REM phases in both groups shows decreased intensity of stage 4 in schizophrenic patients compared with depressed patients (Table 3). A sample hypnogram of a patient with schizophrenia is shown in (Figure 1a) and a depressed patient (Figure 1b).

DISCUSSION

Our study showed that severely depressed patients had increased REM sleep intensity and shorter REM latency than did patients with schizophrenia. On the other hand,

Table 1. Age, gender distribution, and duration and severity of illness.

Variable	Schizophrenic patients (n=20)	Depressed patients (n=20)	Statistical test
Gender	**{N(%)}**	**{N(%)}**	
Male	12 (60)	10 (50)	$X^2 = 0.52$
Female	8 (40)	10 (50)	
Age (years)	35.2 ± 8.01	36.9 ± 7.98	T = 0.67
Duration of illness (years)	4.8 ± 2.01	5.1 ± 2.83	T =1.6
CGI-S score	5.1 ± 0.55	4.6 ± 0.5	T = 0.89

*P < 0.05

Table 2. REM latency and intensity in schizophrenic and depressed groups.

Variable	Schizophrenic patients (n=20)	Depressed patients (n=20)	*T* - test
REM latency (min)	43.9 ± 16.9	26 ± 6	3.11 (*P* < 0.006)*
REM intensity (%)	21.4 ± 4.5	34 ± 14	2.7 (*P* < 0.015)*

*P < 0.05.

Table 3. Intensity of non-rapid eye movement phases in both groups.

Variable	Schizophrenic patients (n=20)	Depressed patients (n=20)	*T* - test
Phase 1	1.8 ± 1.7	3.8 ± 1.2	-3.03 (*P* < 0.007)*
Phase 2	38.8 ± 8.1	45 ± 7.4	-1.79
Phase 3	16.4 ± 5	12 ± 3.8	2.22 (*P* < 0.04)*
Phase 4	9 ± 7.9	17.8 ± 9.2	-2.29 (*P* < 0.03)*

*P < 0.05.

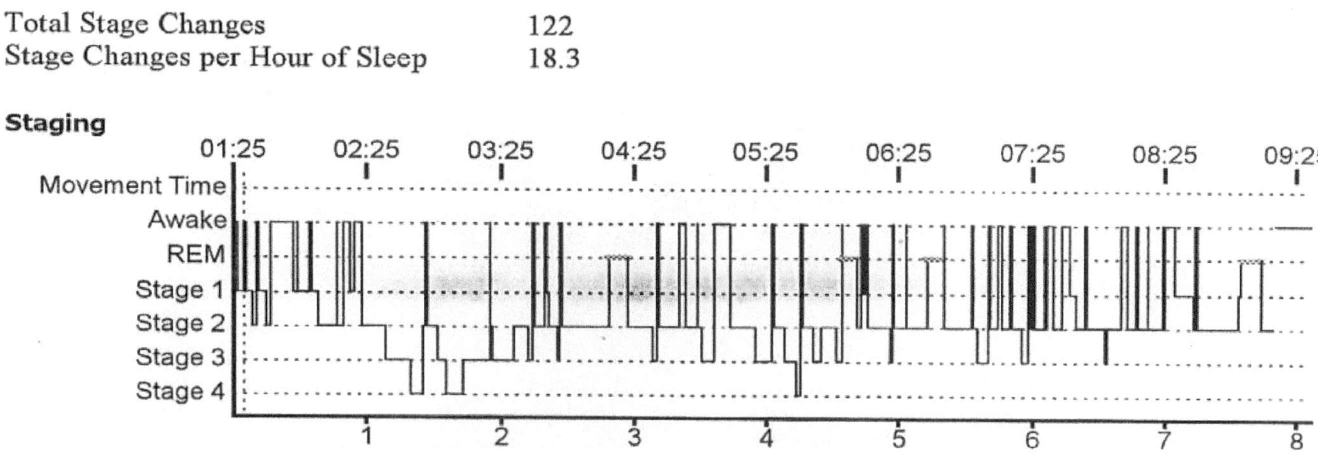

Figure 1a. Hypnogram from a schizophrenic patient.

patients with schizophrenia showed decreased intensity of phase 4 non-REM deep sleep than did depressed patients. Other authors have reported that changes in subjective sleep complaints are paralleled by EEG

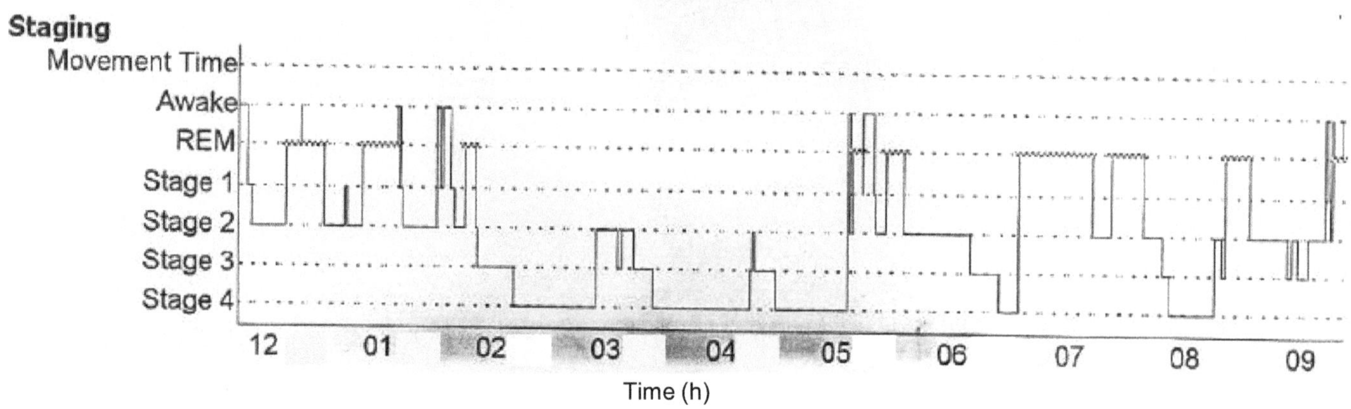

Figure 1b. Hypnogram from a depressed patient.

measures of sleep in patients with depression. These include increased sleep latency and decreased sleep continuity (Nofzinger et al., 1993; Monteleone and Maj, 2008). In terms of EEG sleep stages (that is, sleep architecture), depressed patients often show reduced stage 3 and 4 non-REM sleep, also known as slow-wave sleep because of the presence of slow delta activity on EEG during these stages. Several changes in REM sleep have also been noted. These include an increase in the amount of REM sleep, shortening of the time to onset of the first REM period of the night, shortened REM latency, and increased frequency of eye movements within an REM period (Nofzinger et al., 1993; Ivaneko et al., 2005).

Stressful life events also interact with EEG sleep. For instance, individuals who have severe stressful events preceding the onset of depression are less likely to have reduced REM latency than patients without such a stressor. Among older depressed patients, poor sleep is associated with a shorter episode duration, older age, greater medical burden, the presence of life stressors, and a lower level of perceived social support (Dew et al., 1996).

EEG sleep recordings aid our understanding of the neurobiology, longitudinal course, and treatment outcome in depression. Although, severely reduced REM latencies, phasic REM measures, and sleep continuity disturbances generally move towards control values after remission of depression, most sleep measures show a high correlation across the course of an episode (Monteleone and Maj, 2008; Rush et al., 1989).

Studies examining treatment-naïve patients with schizophrenia have shown no increases in REM sleep, so the increases in REM sleep observed in previously treated subjects may reflect the effects of medication withdrawal and/or changes related to the acute psychotic state. It is unlikely that the observed decreases in REM latency in some schizophrenia patients result from primary abnormalities in REM sleep (Benson, 2006; Keshavan et al., 1998).

Slow-wave sleep is of particular interest in schizophrenia because of the implications of the prefrontal cortex in this disorder and in generation of slow-wave sleep. Several studies have shown a reduction of slow-wave sleep in schizophrenic patients. Moreover, slow-wave sleep deficits have been seen in acute, chronic, and remitted states, as well as, in never-medicated, neuroleptic-treated, and unmedicated patients. However, not all studies show these deficits. Studies that have failed to find differences in slow-wave sleep have generally used conventional visual scoring (Keshavan et al., 1995; Benson, 1993).In fact, automated scoring of sleep stages may show different results based on the spectral analysis of EEG waves.

The polysomnographic patterns in schizophrenia and severe depression have been investigated by many authors, and our work is an attempt to replicate these and translate our findings to clinical application in terms of the potential differentiating diagnostic role of polysomnography when it comes to psychiatric disorders where clear diagnosis is problematic. Major depression, particularly when accompanied by severe psychomotor retardation or psychotic features overlapping with symptoms of schizophrenia, is a good example of a diagnostic dilemma.

Our study was limited by its small sample size. We recommend replication of our research in a larger population to allow more definitive conclusions. Another limitation of this research is the fact that the patients were not drug-naïve. Intake and withdrawal of different psychotropic agents may alter polysomnographic parameters. For example, antidepressants (except for mirtazapine) suppress REM sleep, and their withdrawal may lead to rebound REM. We recommend further polysomnographic studies in drug-naïve patients with schizophrenia and depression.

Conclusion

Depressed patients tend to show shortened REM latency and increased REM intensity, while patients with schizophrenia tend to have decreased intensity of phase 4 non-REM deep sleep. Further research to determine cutoff scores for different polysomnographic parameters is needed to enable the useof polysomnography as a potential electrophysiologic tool for differentiating between these two diagnoses.

REFERENCES

American Psychiatric Association (APA) (2004). Diagnostic and Statistical Manual of Mental Disorders. Fourth Edition Text Revision. Washington, DC: American Psychiatric Association.

Armitage R, Hoffmann RF, Rush AJ (1999). Biological rhythm disturbance in depression: Temporal coherence of ultradian sleep EEG rhythms. Psychol. Med., 29: 1435-1448.

Benca RM, Obermeyer WH, Thisted RA (1992). Sleep and psychiatric disorders: A meta-analysis. Arch. Gen. Psychiatr., 49: 651-668.

Benson KL (2006). Sleep in schizophrenia: impairments, correlates, and treatment. Psychiatr. Clin. North. Am., 29(4): 1033-1045.

Benson KL (1993). The effect of total sleep deprivation on slow wave recovery in schizophrenia. Sleep. Res., 22: 143.

Cohrs S, (2008). Sleep disturbances in patients with schizophrenia: impact and effect of antipsychotics. CNS Drugs, 22(11): 939-62.

Dew MA, Reynolds CF, Buysse DJ (1996). Electroencephalographic sleep profiles during depression. Effects of episode duration and other clinical and psychosocial factors in older adults. Arch. Gen. Psychiatr.., 53: 148-156.

Germain A, Nofzinger EA, Kupfer DJ (2004). Neurobiology of non-REM sleep in depression, further evidence of hypofrontality and dysregulation of thalamus. Am. J. Psychiatr., 161: 1856-1863.

Göder R, Fritzer G, Gottwald B, Lippmann B, Seeck-Hirschner M, Serafin I, Aldenhoff JB (2008). Effects of olanzapine on slow wave sleep, sleep spindles and sleep-related memory consolidation in schizophrenia. Pharmacopsychiatry, 41(3): 92-9.

Guy W (1976). ECDEU Assessment Manual for Psychopharmacology. Washington, DC: US Department of Health Education and Welfare.

Ivanenko A, Crabtree VM, Gozal D (2005). Sleep and depression in children and adolescents. Sleep. Med. Rev., 9(2): 115-129.

Keshavan MS, Reynolds CF, Miewald J (1995). Slow-wave sleep deficits and outcome in schizophrenia and schizoaffective disorder. Acta Psychiatr. Scand., 91: 289-292.

Keshavan MS, Reynolds CF, Miewald JM (1996). A longitudinal study of EEG sleep in schizophrenia. Psychiatr. Res., 59: 203-211.

Keshavan MS, Reynolds CF, Miewald MJ (1998). Delta sleep deficits in schizophrenia: Evidence from automated analyses of sleep data. Arch. Gen. Psychiatr., 55: 443-448.

Maixner S, Tandon R, Eiser A (1997). Effects of antipsychotic treatment on polysomnographic measures in schizophrenia: A replication and extension. Am. J. Psychiatr., 155: 1600-1602.

Monteleone P, Maj M (2008). Disturbed sleep as a core symptom of depression. Medicographia, 30: 17-23.

Nofzinger EA, Buysse DJ, Reynolds CF (1993). Sleep disorders related to another mental disorder (nonsubstance/primary): A DSM-IV literature review. J. Clin. Psychiatr., 54: 244-259.

Rush AJ, Giles DE, Jarrett RB (1989). Reduced REM latency predicts response to tricyclic medication in depressed outpatients. Biol. Psychiatr., 26: 61-72.

Yang C, Winkelman JW (2006). Clinical significance of sleep EEG abnormalities in chronic schizophrenia. Schizophr. Res., 82(2): 251-260.

Physical activities in patients with psychological disorders

Mahmoud Hakamizanjai[1], Abolfazele Ghoreyshi[2], Nooraddin Mosavinasab[3] and Davood Sohrabi[4*]

[1]Department of Physical Education, Zanjan University of Medical Sciences and Heath Service, Iran.
[2]Psychiatric Department, Zanjan University of Medical Sciences and Heath Service, Iran.
[3]Department of Social Medicine, Zanjan University of Medical Sciences and Heath Service, Iran.
[4]Department of Histology, Zanjan University of Medical Sciences and Heath Service, Iran.

Alterations in human life pattern in contemporary societies together with reduction of physical activities as well as increase in psychological disorders such as depression and anxiety endanger health of human beings. Regarding the positive effects physical activities on prevention, management and cure of psychological disorders, this study was conducted to investigate the status of sport and daily life as well as job-related physical activities in patients who referred to psychiatric centers. This study was a part of interdisciplinary research programme .The total population was 1500, the psychological part administered on 500 patients. The necessary data on physical activities of the patients were collected by means of a reliable and valid questionnaire and they were analyzed by statistical methods. The results showed that among different groups who referred to psychiatric centers, women, illiterate, low income groups and middle aged referred more than others. 97% of the patients did not exercise at all and 92% of them spent their leisure time in lying and sitting position or just sleeping. The results suggest that an active pattern of life be improved in the society to diminish the cases of psychological disorders.

Key words: Physical activities, psychic patients, Iran.

INTRODUCTION

Almost half of the population experience psychological disorders in the lifetime and cure expenditure of such diseases almost increase progressively. Typically cure and treatment system of a given society exposed to large number of psychological disorders will not be able to manage and cure all of them (Martinsen et al., 2000). The ancient philosophers and physicians have associated psychological disorders with the god's anger and dissatisfaction. But after renaissance and mainly after 17th century, awareness of human being on this subject has been increasing. Furthermore, human knowledge on various aspects of mental disorders, from pathology to management and medication has been improving as well (Hockenbury, 2004). The commonest psychological disorders such as anxiety and depression have been confirmed to be associated with low physical activity. During recent years a number of researches have been carried out on physical activities, anxiety and depression, which indicate that physical activities can have supportive role against depression in adults (Daumit et al., 2005). The findings of other study suggest that exercise may be effective in improving depressive state, hormonal response to stress and physiological fitness of adolescent females with depressive symptoms (Chanudda et al., 2006). In addition, other researches show that the quality of physical activities in psychologically acute disordered individuals is less than normal individuals. In a WHO report, low physical activity level is cited as one of the 22 fundamental factors threatening health of human being in the world. In fact, low physical activity level is considered as a major problem in developing and developed countries. The acquired data in different part of the world reveals that low level physical activity range varies from 60 to 80%. Due to social and biological differences, women suffer from depression and stress twice more than men (World Health Organization, 2003). The mental

*Corresponding author. E-mail: sohrabidavood@yahoo.com.

health pattern in Iran is similar to the western countries, but it seems that the prevalence of psychiatric disorders in Iran may be lower than these countries. It is estimated that at least about 7 millions of Iranian population suffer from one or more of the psychiatric disorders. It shows the importance of the role of the psychiatric disorders in providing preventive and management programs in Iran. According to the reports of ministry of health, the frequency of these disorders in Iran is 21% in population over 15 years old. In Iran 28% of women and 13% of men suffer from psychological disorders. The prevalence of depression in population over 15 years old is 34% in Zanjan city, 44% women have depression which is the highest in the country. For the points mentioned above, the focus of this study is to investigate the status of sport, daily life and job-related physical activities in patients referring to psychiatric centers.

MATERIALS AND METHODS

This study is a descriptive one which was performed on 500 patients who referred to either private or governmental psychiatric centers of Zanjan city in 2004. In private cure centers through a previous coordination with physicians, all patients were introduced by assistants to the trained interrogators in the physician's office.

In the case of psychologically sick who had been hospitalized, again after making necessary coordinations with the head of the hospital, the patients were interviewed and the interrogator obtained necessary data either directly from the patients or their attendants such as their children, siblings or the others who had thorough knowledge of the patients physical, job, daily and sport related physical activities. All the data were registered on the basis of patients' claims.

The instrument of collecting and measuring data was International Physical Activity Questionnaire (IPAQ) together with comments of medical experts inside the country. The testing of questionnaire reliability was performed by estimating a Cronbach alpha coefficient, which varied from 0.80 to 0.97 for different scales of questionnaire designed for patients.

This questionnaire included 56 questions in four parts. The first section had 12 questions containing general data such as age, sex, education level and income level, place of residence, place of birth and the frequency of their reference to treatment centers. The disease was diagnosed on the basis of the claim made by the visiting physician.

The second part of the questionnaire embodied 8 questions related to the amount of daily life-related physical activities in morning time, after waking up, the quality of daily conveyance, the quality and quantity of using stairs in house, the type of physical activities in leisure time, the severity of daily physical activities, etc.

Thirteen questions in the third section of the questionnaire hold job-related physical activities such as nature of job, its duration, quality of physical tiredness at work-place and severity of job related physical activities. The fourth part of questionnaire had 23 questions related to formal or informal sport-related physical activities. The questions of this part were designed so that quantity of sport-related physical activities in formal category (under supervision of a coach) and informal one (without a coach) were investigated and described.

The main variables under consideration throughout this study have been sport, job and daily life-related physical activities of patients who referred to psychological cure wards. The questionnaires were filled in with observance of ethical consideration in consideration in physician office or private and government clinics by trained interrogators. All questionnaires were filled out by interrogators and then were looked over by principal members of this research and all necessary revisions carried out for the purpose of improvement of the study throughout trial and performance stage. For the purpose of data analysis the collected data related to physical activities of patients were encoded first and then were saved in SPSS by research operator and analyzed by using tables, charts, central indices and their frequency. Excel and Minitab were also used for some measurements as well as for compound and comparative ranking.

RESULTS

Of 500 patients under investigation, more than 70% had behavioral disorders of anxiety and depression. The mean of the patient's age was 33. The most frequent age group was 21 to 40 years old (56%).

Prevalence of psychological disorders such as depression and anxiety in women (67%) was twice more than men (33%). Prevalence of psychological disorders in organic psychosis and personality disorders in women and men were almost identical while disorders such as substance abuse was more in women compared to men. About 50% of patients in our study were illiterate or had primary school education and 42% of them had guidance school or secondary education. On the basis of income, 75% of the patients had low income and only 2% of them had high income.

Accordingly, residents of urban areas (83%) referred to cure center more than residents of villages (17%). Among these patients 86% of them did not have any morning time physical activities such as running and bicycling. Only 40% of these patients used walking as a means of their daily transportation and the rest used vehicles. Almost 6% of them claimed to have physical and sport exercise in their leisure time. In contrast, ~28% spent their time in domestic works and ~66% spent their time in sitting, lying position while watching TV, getting together and the like or just spent their free time sleeping (Figure 1).

Among various jobs, housewives comprised the most frequent referents (Figure 2).

The vehicle of transportation in 83% of the patients from home to work-place and vice-versa was motorcycles but the rest were unemployed, sixty six percent of these patients did not use stairs at their work place. The most active part of their body at work was their hands (82%). According to claims made by patients, job-related physical activity in 41% of them was average. Nineteen percent had trivial physical activities and only 19% had been considerably active. However, 82% of them did not felt tiredness at their work place.

Questions on the status of formal and informal sport-related physical activities among these patients revealed that 94% of them did not perform such activities under supervision of a coach (Figure 3).

Sports of interest to only a few of them who had sport-

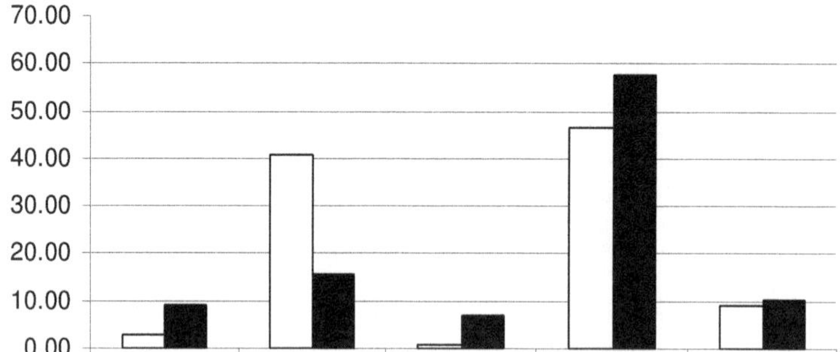

	Sport activites	Homeworks	gardening	Sitting lying position	sleeping
□ Women	2.81	40.87	0.98	46.35	8.99
■ Men	9.12	15.81	7.07	57.59	10.40

Figure 1. Comparison of the quality of physical activities of psychologically disorderd patients in their free time.

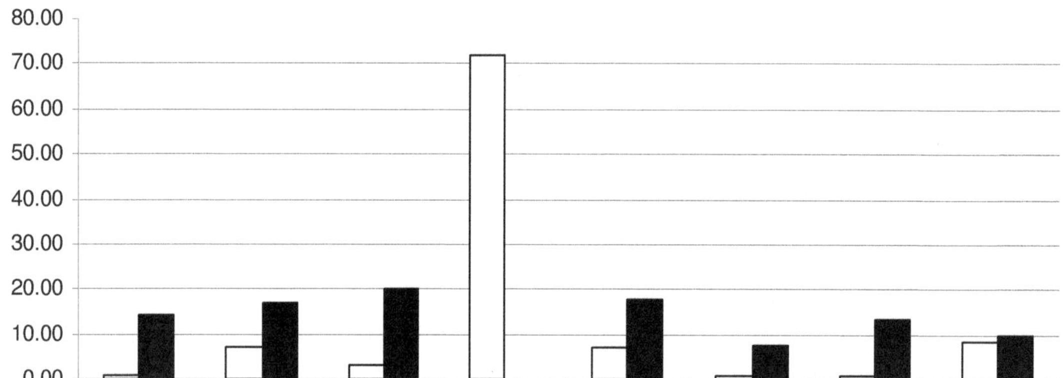

	Worker	Clerk	Free	Houswife	Unemployed	Retired	Farmer	Student
□ Women	0.83	7.22	3.33	71.81	6.94	0.69	0.83	8.33
■ Men	14.17	17.19	19.95	0.00	17.85	7.61	13.39	9.84

Figure 2. Comparison of the jobs of psychologically disorderd patients in Zanjan.

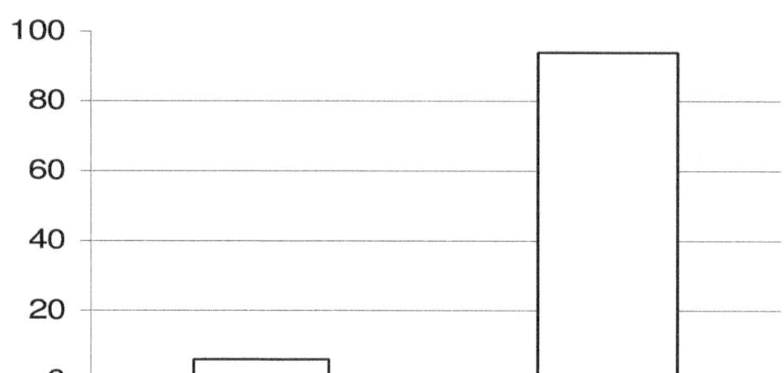

	Yes	**No**
□ **Series1**	**5.88**	**94.12**

Do you have any formal sport-related physical activites ?

Figure 3. Comparison of the quality of formal sport-related physical activities (with a coach) in psychologically disordered patients in Zanjan.

related physical activities were body building, football, judo, karate, taekwondo and swimming (6%).

The mean of the duration of formal sport related physical activities in these patients has been 2 month. Their participation level in sport competition at school level was 3% and at province level was 1%. At time of their reference to cure centers 3% had continued their sport-related physical exercises. On the other hand, 97% had not been exercising or had already stopped.

Considering informal sport-related physical activities people do in park, or nature, this research indicated that 89% of them did not perform any kind of exercise to be considered as sport and finally the left 11% were interacted in individual and team sport. The mean of each session of the exercise has been 7 min. Sport and exercise schedule of 86% of the patients was disorganized, whereas 12% of them had regular exercise. The mean of total time of informal exercise was 7 months. Among 11% of these who exercised, 6% informed that they were continuing their informal exercises, yet 94% of patients stated they did not have sport related physical activities.

DISCUSSION

The patients with psychological disorders experience a life with disability and low quality. Psychological disorders affect social and family relations. Many studies have revealed that physical activities reduce diseases such as chronic heart disease, muscular, skeletal, psychological disorders as well as cancers. Some researchers have found inverse relationship between physical activities and psychological disorders (Goodwin, 2003; Paffenbarger and Leung, 1994; Camacho, 1991; Farmer, 1998). Moreover, many investigators have found positive association between physical activities and improvement of psychological status (Lennox et al., 1990; Cooper Patrick et al., 1997). In spite of all the effort throughout this research, scarce data is available on quality and quantity of physical activities of patients and a number of patients either emphasize the effect of physical activities on their well being or talk on role of low level of physical activity. The result of this study indicates that 94% of psychological patients did not perform any sort of sport-related physical activities. Moreover, 66% spent their free time in sitting or lying position. The low physical activity status in the patients in this study exceeded that of normal individuals. A research in Canada reports that the amount of low physical activities in women in their free time was 68% and in men 56% (Weyer, 1992). Another research in Taiwan shows that physical activities in their free time has been 30% (Koezuka et al., 2006). Though majority of physicians recommend that daily walking or bicycling for 30 min can reduce chronic heart diseases, type II diabetes, psychological disorders and osteoporosis but in the USA only 1 out of 4 has proper physical activities in leisure time (Battling et al., 2005). Our research suggests that 88% of patients had jobs with low physical activity such as housewifery, official work and studies. We have found higher percentage of patients with low physical activity level as compared to the WHO report and other similar reports (60 to 80%). Furthermore, depression is one of the widespread disorders in the middle-aged women and is relevant to decrease in their capacities and to their weight gain (Pignone et al., 2002; Miranda and Green, 1999; Myers et al., 2002). The outcome of this investigation asserts that psychological disorders, especially depression, in women (67%) were twice as compared to that in men (33%). The findings are in accord with WHO research report undertaken in USA (Bromberger, 2004) and also with reports of ministry of health in Iran. The number of referents in 21 to 40 years old was more than other age groups. These findings are in agreement with reports of ministry of health in Iran concerning development of psychological disorders in age group over 15 years old. However the results assert the findings of faculty of medicine in Harvard university that consider the age of 11 as the start point for stress and the age of 30 for initiation of behavioral disorders 24. It seems that in many countries these ages are mostly exposed to psychological disorders. Participants of this research were almost illiterate or had low level of education and were unemployed or had low income. The study advocate the study conducted in Brazil in the USA in which illiteracy and poverty are considered as threatening factors of health (Regier et al., 1993; Kessler et al., 2005).

Conclusion

The various researches carried out on the relationship of low physical activity with psychological disorders, especially anxiety and depression, it seems that the quantity of physical activities in psychologically sick people has been lower than ordinary individuals. On the other hand, activity level has been in women, illiterate, people with low income and middle-aged compared to the other people. The findings of this investigation suggest to prevent economical and humanistic damages of psychological diseases especially anxiety and depression in society. It is essential that sport, daily life and job-related physical activities among women, illiterate, low income groups and middle-aged receive priority in health and sport related programs. Sports like physical activity is another important parameter in addition to education and income to reduce psychological disorders.

REFERENCES

Bromberger JT, Harlow S,Avis N, Kravitz HM, Cordal A (2004). Racial/ethnic differences in the prevalence of depressive symptoms among middle-aged women: the study of women's health across the nation (SWAN), Am. J. Public Health 90: 1378–1385.

Camacho TC, Robert RE, Lazarus NB (1991). Physical activity and depression—Evidence from the Alameda County Study. Am. J. Epidemiol. 134: 220–231.

Chanudda N, Nobuyuki M, Anek S, Suwanna J, Hiroichi Y, Mikio A, Kazuhisa M (2006). Effects of physical exercise on depression, neuroendocrine stress hormones and physiological fitness in adolescent females with depressive symptoms . Eur. J. Public Health. 16(2): 179-184.

Cooper Patrick L, Ford DE, Mead LA, Chang PP, Klag MJ (1997). Exercise and depression in midlife: a prospective study. Am. J. Public Health. 87: 670–673.

Daumit GL, Goldberg RW, Anthony C, Dickerson F, Brown CH, Kreyenbuhl J, Wohlheiter K, Dixon LB (2005). Physical activity patterns in adults with severe mental illness. J. Nerv. Ment. Dis. 193: 641-646.

Farmer ME, Locke BZ, Moscicki EK (1998). Physical activity and depressive symptoms, The NHANES-I epidemiologic follow-up-study. Am. J. Epidemiol. 128: 1340–1351.

Fenton Battling (2005). American's Epidemic of Physical Inactivity, Building More Walkable, Livable Communities, J. Nutr. Educ. Behav. 37: 115-120.

Goodwin RD (2003). Association between physical activity and mental disorders among adults in the United States. Prev. Med. 36: 698–703.

Hockenbury H (2004). Discovering Psychology. Worth Publishers. p. 20.

Kessler RC, Berglund P, Demler O, Jin R, Walters EE (2005). Lifetime prevalence and age-of onset distributions of DSM-IV disorders in the national co morbidity survey replication. Arch. Gen. Psychiatry. 62: 593-602.

Koezuka N, Malcolm K, Kenneth R, Edward M, Adlaf M, Dwyer JG (2006). The Relationship between Sedentary Activities and Physical Inactivity among Adolescents, Results from the Canadian Community Health Survey. J. Adolescent Health. 39: 515-522.

Lennox SS, Bedell JR, Ston AA (1990).The effect of exercise on normal mood. J. Psychosom. Res.1990; 34: 629–636.

Martinsen EW, Psykiatrisk K, Sentralsjukehuseti SF (2000) Physical activity for mental health, Tidsskr Nor Laegeforen. p. 120.

Miranda J. Green BL (1999). The need for mental health services research focusing on poor young women. J. Ment. Health Policy Econ. 2: 73–80.

Myers HF, Lesser I, Rodriguez N (2002). Ethnic differences in clinical presentation of depression in adult women. Cultur. Div. Ethnic. Minor Psychol. 8: 138–156.

Paffenbarger RS, Leung LR (1994). Physical activity and personal characteristics associated with depression and suicide in American-college men. Acta. Psychiatr. Scand. 89: 16–22.

Pignone MP, Gaynes BN, Rushron JL , Burchell CM, Orlean CM, Mulrow CD (2002). Screening for depression in adults: a summary of the evidence for the US Preventive Task Force, Ann. Int. Med. 120: 765–776.

Regier DA, Narrow WE, Rae DS (1993). The facto mental and addictive disorders service system. Epidemiologic Catchment Area prospective 1-year prevalence rates of disorders and services. Arch. Gen. Psychiatry. 50: 85-94.

Weyer S (1992). Physical inactivity and depression in the community—Evidence from the upper Bavarian field-study. Int. J. Sports Med. 13: 492–496.

World Health Organization (2003). Noncommunicable diseases and mental health: noncommunicable diseases prevention and health promotion Acceptabl from URL: http://www.who.int/topics/physical_activity/en/.

Suppression of exploration and locomotion in adult Wistar rats following quinine administration

Ajibade A. J.[1]*, Adenowo T. K.[2], Akintunde O. W.[1], Fakunle P. B.[1], Oyewo O. O.[1] Ashamu E. A.[1] and Onaolapo A. Y.[1]

[1]Department Anatomy, Ladoke Akintola University of Technology Ogbomoso, Nigeria.
[2]Department of Anatomy, Bowen University, Iwo, Nigeria.

The effect of quinine commonly used for the treatment of chloroquine resistant cases and cerebral malaria on exploration in Wistar rats was investigated. Adult male rats (n= 27), weighing between 150 and 190 g were randomly selected into two treatments groups (n=9) and control (n=9). Each control rat in Group I received intramuscularly injection of physiological saline. The rats in Group II were injected intramuscularly with quinine, 20 mg/kg for a starting dose, followed by 10 mg/kg 8 hourly for 7 days. The Group III rats received the same treatment as Group II, but were subjected to a withdrawal period of one week after the treatment. The exploration and locomotion of treated rats were significantly suppressed ($P < 0.05$) by quinine. The frequency of line crossing reduced significantly from 30.8 ± 5.7 in Group I to 2.2 ± 0.93 in Group II and 2.5 ± 1.1 in Group III rats. The frequency of hinding also reduced significantly from 7.4 ± 1.3 in group I to 0.7 ± 0.4 in Group II and 0.9 ± 0.3 in Group III. The marked decrease observed in exploratory activities in the treated groups might be the consequence of degeneration of cerebellar cortex.

Key words: Quinine, locomotion, exploration, suppression, Wistar rats.

INTRODUCTION

Malaria was a global epidemic disease causing great havoc in several countries, claiming a heavy toll of human lives and eluding an effective cure from eminent physicians during the seventeenth century (Elimear et al., 2003) Although a variety of drug formulations have been developed for used in the treatment of malaria over the years, quinine dihydrochloride appears to be among the spectrum of drugs still being preferred for the treatment of malaria especially in poor countries (Editorial., 2003).

The use of quinine in the treatment of malaria is particularly significant because extracts from the bark of 'quinquina' (cinchona) tree were the most widely used preparations for treating malaria between 1600 and 1800s, thus making them the first chemical compounds, used successfully to treat an infectious disease (Elimear et al., 2003). Quinine is used today as chemotherapy for malaria especially in chloroquine resistant cases and cerebral malaria (White and Warrell, 1983). Quinine is said to be more toxic than chloroquine (Kakkilaya, 2002). It was also found to cross the blood brain barrier thus, affecting the central nervous system (Kenmochi and Eggerment, 1997).

The cerebellum is vulnerable to damage from a variety of sources such as developmental defects, degenerative diseases infectious processes, chronic alcoholism, trauma, toxic and metabolic effects (West, 1995).

Ataxia and other gait disturbances had been reported to be due to the effects of such drugs as antibiotics, chloroquinine, quinine and guanidine (Eisenhauer and Murphy, 1998). Quinine sulphate had been observed to cause peripheral ototoxic and central effects on the central nervous system (Kenmochi and Eggermont, 1997). Cerebellar injuries also results from toxins, and autoantibodies, structural lesions and inherited cerebellar degeneration (Timothy, 2003).

The cerebellum is largely involved in co-ordination of equilibrium, posture and muscle tone necessary for smooth, co-ordinated motor activities (West, 1995). Any degeneration or distortion of the cerebellar cortical layers many impair cerebellar functions. This paper reports the exploration and locomotor activities in Wistar rats

*Corresponding author. E-mail: adeshinaajibade@yahoo.co.uk.

following experimental quinine administration.

In view of several reported cases of cerebellar pathologies following toxins and drugs. It became necessary to appraise the effects of quinine on explorations and locomotion in Wistar rats.

MATERIALS AND METHODS

Twenty-seven mature male albino rats of Wistar strain, weighing between 150 and 190 g were used for this study. The rats were fed daily with normal rats pellets purchased form Ladokun feeds (Ibadan, Nigeria) and water was given to the animals *ad libitum.* All the rats were carefully assessed, screened and confirmed to be healthy during the period of acclimatization.

Rats were randomly selected into three groups in relation to their weights. Each group contained nine rats. Group I served as the control and received intramuscularly injection of physiological saline of the same quantity as contained in the experimental doses. Groups II and III served as the treated groups. 300 mg/ml of the liquid quinine contained in the ampoule was used for the present study. Group II rats were injected intramuscularly with liquid quinine dihydrochloride; 20 mg/kg body weight for a starting dose, followed by 10 mg/kg 8 hourly for 7 days (Kakkilaya, 2002). Group III received the same treatment as Group II. However, they were subjected to post-treatment withdrawal period of one week to determine possible withdrawal effects on them before they were sacrificed by cervical dislocation.

The open field test was conducted following the methods of Brown et al. (1999), during the period of acclimatization and each day of the treatment period and at the end of one week withdrawal period.

Apparatus

The open field apparatus was constructed with plywood and measured 72 × 72 cm with 36 cm walls. The walls and floor were both white. Blue lines were drawn on the floor with a marker and were visible through the clear plexi-glass floor. The lines divided the floor into sixteen 18×18 cm squares. A central square of equal size was drawn in the middle of the open field (18 × 18 cm), (Brown et al., 1999).

Rats were taken from their home cages and placed randomly into one of the four corners of the open field, facing the centre and allowed to explore the apparatus for 5 min. After the 5 min test, the rats were returned to their home cages and the open field was cleaned with 70% ethyl alcohol and permitted to dry between test. The behaviours scored following the methods of Brown et al. (1999) which include:

1. Line crossing: Frequency with which rats crossed one of the grid lines with all four limbs.
2. Rearing: Frequency with which the rats stood on their hind legs in the open field.
3. Rearing against a wall: Frequency with which the rats stood on their hind legs while the forelimbs rested against the wall of the open field.
4. Hinding; the sum of the 2nd and 3rd behaviour.
5. Locomotor activity refers to the movement from one location to another. Locomotion is one of the most important components of exploration.
6. Exploration refers to all activities concerned with gathering information about the environment. Locomotor activity and exploratory behaviors such as rearing and rearing against a wall are components of exploration and are associated with behavioral activities in rats.

The animals were treated in accordance with the "Guide for the Care and Use of Laboratory Animals" prepared by the National Academy of Sciences and published by the National Institute of Health (1985).

Statistical analysis of the data obtained was performed using analysis of variance and student's t-test (Araoye, 2003). Experimental data were presented as mean and standard error of mean (Mean ± SEM). Values of probability ($P < 0.05$) were taken to be statistically significant.

RESULTS

Table 1 shows the mean ± SEM of the frequency of line crossing and body weights of the rats at the Acclimatization period and the End of the Study Periods.

Figure 1 similarity, shows the pattern of changes in the frequency of line crossing of treated and control rats during those periods. The frequency of line crossing in control rats did not increase significantly from the beginning of the treatment to the end of the treatment, while the frequency of line crossing decreased significantly from the beginning of the treatment to the end of the treatment ($P < 0.05$) in quinine treated rats. The frequency of line crossing in treated rats was significantly reduced throughout the treatment period compared with control rat (Figure 1).

However, the frequency of line crossing in Group III treated rats did not decrease significantly at the end of one week withdrawal period, while in control rats, the frequency increases significantly during that same period (Table 1 and Figure 1).

Table 2 shows the mean ± SEM of the frequency of hinding of the rats at the Acclimatization Period and the End of the study periods. Figure 2, shows the pattern of changes in frequency of hinding of rats in treated and control rats. The frequency of hinding in control rats did not decrease significantly from the beginning of the treatment to the end of the treatment, while the frequency of hinding decreased significantly from the beginning of the treatment to the end of the treatment ($P < 0.05$). The frequency of hinding in quinine–treated rats was signifycantly reduced throughout the treatment period compared with control rats (Figure 2). However, the frequency of hinding in control rats and Group III treated rats did not decrease significantly at the end of one week withdrawal period (Table 2 and Figure 2).

Table 3 shows that the population and diameters of Purkinje cells in the cerebellar cortex of the treated rats were significantly reduced ($P < 0.05$) compared with the control.

DISCUSSION

The cerebellum is largely involved in co-ordination, persons whose cerebellum does not work well are generally clumsy and unsteady (Timothy, 2003). The

Table 1. Mean ± SEM of the frequency of line crossing and body weights of the rats at the acclimatization period and the end of the study periods.

Group	n	No of lines crossed in 5 min before the treatment	No of Lines crossed in 5 min during the treatment	n	No of lines crossed after withdrawal period	Initial body weight (g)	Final body weight (g)
I	9	30.0 ± 7.1	30.8 ± 5.7	4	50.5 ± 2.4	148.0 ± 5.5	178.5 ± 8.2
II	9	48.5 ± 5.9	2.2 ± 0.93 *	-	-	149.6 ± 6.5	173.2 ± 4.7
III	9	43.0 ± 6.0	2.5 ± 1.1 *	9	2.1 ± 1.2 *	149.5 ± 4.6	171.3 ± 4.4

*($P < 0.05$) Significant difference when compared with control using the t-test.

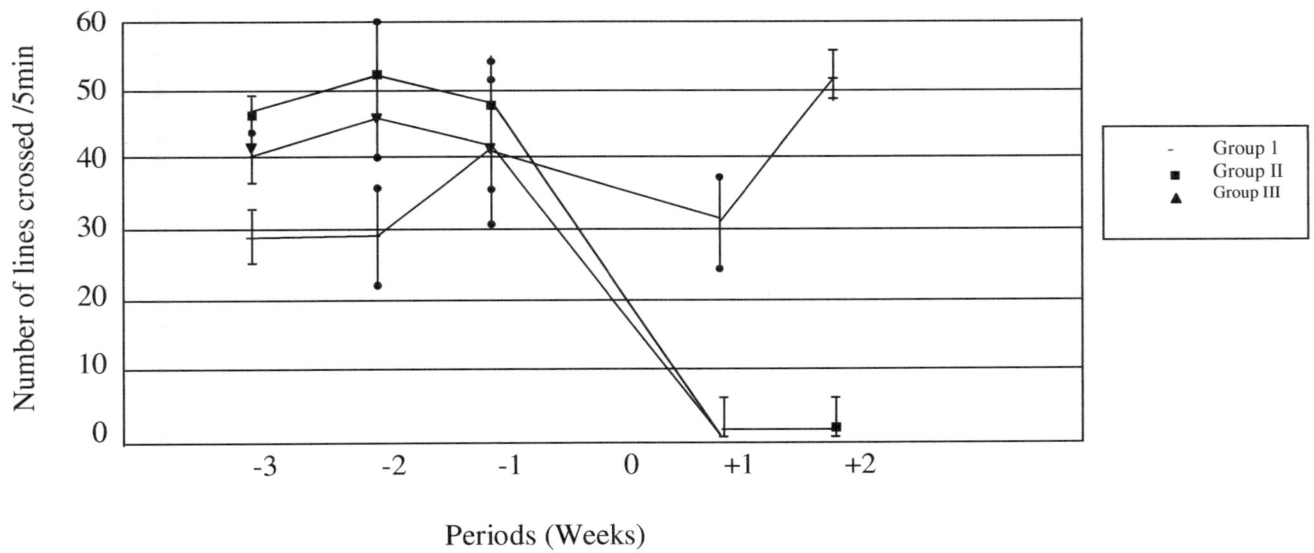

Figure 1. Graphs showing the frequency of line crossing in the animals from the acclimatization period to the end of the study.

cerebellum functions as a comparator and co-ordinator in that, it compares movement intention with performance and co-ordinates equilibrium, posture and muscle tone necessary for smooth, coordinated motor activities (West, 1995).

The open field test provides simultaneous measures of locomotion, exploration and anxiety, the frequency of line crossing and the frequency of rearing are usually used as measures of locomotor activity, these are also measures of exploration and anxiety of these rats (Walsh and Cummins,1976). The open field test (OFT) is a common measure of exploratory behavior and general activity in both mice and rats, where both the quality and quantity of the activity can be measured. The most basic and common outcome of interest is "movement"; however, this can be influenced by motor output, exploratory drive, freezing or other fear-related behavior, sickness, relative time in circadian cycle, among many other variables (Toddy et al., 2008). Distance moved, time spent moving, rearing, and change in activity over time are among many measures that can be tabulated and reported. Some outcomes, particularly defecation, center time and activity within the first 5 min, likely gauge some aspects of emotionality including anxiety. The OFT is also

Table 2. Mean ± SEM of the frequency of hindings of the rats at the acclimatization period and the end of the study periods.

Group	n	Values during acclimatization. No of times in 5 min	Values at the end of treatment. No of times in 5 min	n	During one week possible self cure period
I	9	8.7 ± 2.8	7.4 ± 1.3	4	7.6 ± 1.11
II	9	18.0 ± 3.8	0.7 ± 0.4 *	-	-
III	9	14.6 ± 3.8	0.9 ± 0.3 *	9	0.7 ± 0.2 *

*($P < 0.05$) Significant difference when compared with control using the t-test.

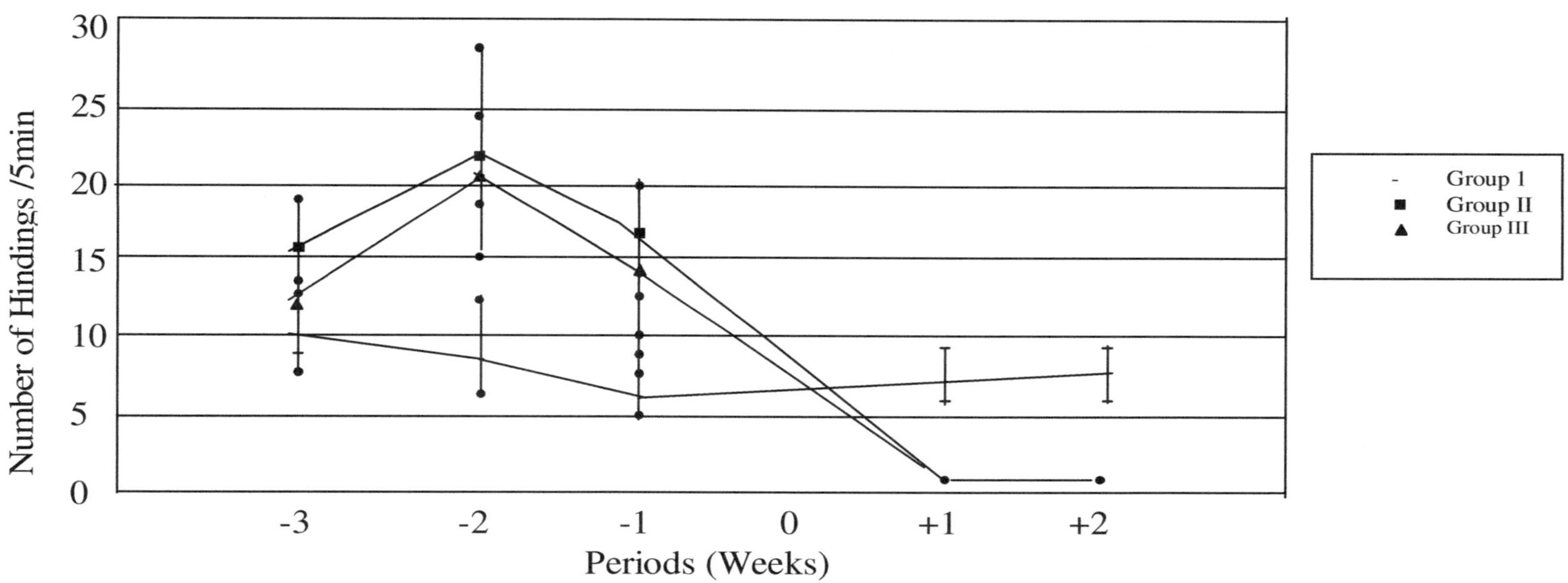

Figure 2. Graphs showing the frequency of hindings in the animals from the acclimatization period to the end of the study.

Table 3. Mean values of Purkinje cell population and transverse diameters of Purkinje cells in the cerebellar cortex of Wistar rats following quinine administration.

Group	Population of Purkinje cells (cells/mm^2) (Mean ± SEM)	Diameters of Purkinje cells (µm) (Mean ± SEM)
I	363 ± 5.2	1.20 ±0.02
II	239 ± 9.5$^+$	1.09 ±0.01$^+$
III	220 ± 6.6$^+$	0.75±0.03$^{+\ a}$

+ Significant difference when compared with control using t-test ($P < 0.05$). [a]Significant difference when compared with group II using t-test ($P < 0.05$).

commonly used as a mechanism to assess the sedative, toxic, or stimulant effects of compounds. Thus, the OFT measures a number of facets of behavior beyond simple locomotion. As such, the test has a number of uses and is included in almost every thorough analysis of rodent behavior (Todd et al., 2008).

A high frequency of these behaviours indicated an increase in locomotion and exploration of the animals. Repeated exposure to the open field apparatus result in time dependent changes in behaviours (Choleris, 2001). The assessment of open field locomotor activities of these rats before and following treatment is very significant in relation to cerebellar functions. Carrey et al. (2000) employed the open field test to assess the locomotor and exploratory behaviour of prepubertal mice following chronic methyl phenidate administration. Increased post weaning open field rearing activity was observed in rats following treatment with a toxic dye, Allura red AC (Vorhees et al., 1983).

Similarly, Benesova et al. (2001) have reported that the pattern of behavioural and neuroendocrine deviations in adult rats was dependent on the ontogenic stage exposed to drug insult. They recorded a depression of open field motor activity (from open field test) and emotional reactivity, as well as higher pituitary weight following treatment with idomethacin.

Effects of some central nervous system stimulants on exploration and locomotive activity have been reported (Agarwal, 1995). CNS stimulants such as Amphetamine, Leptazol, Picrotoxin, strychnine and Nikethamide have been reported to significantly suppressed the open field exploration and locomotor activity in mice treated with these stimulant drugs. Conversely, caffeine was known to increase locomotor activity in mice treated with the drug. Da Cunha et al. (1992), reported a decreased exploratory activity in rats treated with flumazenil, a benzodiazepine receptor antagonist. The open field locomotor activities of adult Wistar rats have been adversely affected following monosodium glutamate administration (Eweka and Om'Iniabohs, 2008).

In this study, quinine significantly decreased line crossing and hinding which constitute exploratory behaviour. Direct deficits in open field exploratory behaviour following quinine administration manifested as a suppression of open field locomotor activity. The decreased locomotor activity of the treated animals compared with control, might be partly due to neurotoxic effect of quinine on neuronal cells of the cerebellar cortex and the associated neurotransmitter substances. The neurotoxic effects of the quinine on the cerebellar cortex of these rats that were subjected to open field which resulted in cerebellar cortical degeneration had already been reported in (Ajibade et al., 2006). The marked suppression of exploration and locomotion is probably a consequence of neuronal degeneration in the cerebellar cortex which might have affected the integrity of the neuronal cells in the cerebellar cortex. Table 3 similarly, shows degeneration and massive loss of purkinje cells which are the principal neurons in the cerebellum were observed in the cerebellar cortex of these rats subjected to open field test, following quinine administration (Ajibade et al., 2008). The significantly reduced population and transverse diameters of the purkinje cells (principal cells of the cerebellum) in the treated rats might have resulted from neuronal degeneration following the neurotoxic effects of quinine. The activities of the various neurotransmitters associated with the neurons in the cerebellar cortex might also be altered by the toxic effect of quinine which may be a contributing factor to a suppressed exploration and locomotion.

The result of the open field locomotor activity in the present study is consistent with the findings of some investigators that recorded suppression of exploration and locomotor activity in the open field following drug administration. The significantly reduced exploratory activities in the treated rats may be the consequence of neuronal degeneration and loss in the cerebellum which might have consequently impaired cerebellar functions that partly manifested as suppressed exploratory activities in the treated rats.

It is possible that quinine had an irreversible effect on the locomotor and exploratory activities in Wistar rats which brought irreversible effects on exploration as observed in rats which were subjected to one week withdrawal period.

CONCLUSION AND RECOMMENDATION

The study concludes that the administration of quinine at

20 mg/kg body weight start followed by 10 mg/kg body weight to adult Wistar rats results in reduced locomotor and exploratory activities in Wistar rats. This study clinically implies the need for consultation and prescription before use and the need for adequate rest while on quinine therapy. The intake of glucose may be beneficial during quinine therapy. It is recommended that further studies aimed at corroborating these findings particularly on the biochemical and haematological parameters be carried out.

This study further revealed that consumption of MSG affects the locomotor activities in the adult Wistar rats. The line crossing, walling, hinding and grooming of the locomotor activities of the treated group in the open field test were significantly affected as compared to the control group.

The open field test (OFT) is a common measure of exploratory behavior and general activity in both mice and rats, where both the quality and quantity of the activity can be measured. The most basic and common outcome of interest is “movement”; however, this can be influenced by motor output, exploratory drive, freezing or other fear-related behavior, sickness, relative time in circadian cycle, among many other variables. Distance moved, time spent moving, rearing, and change in activity over time are among many measures that can be tabulated and reported. Some outcomes, particularly defecation, center time, and activity within the first 5 minutes, likely gauge some aspects of emotionality including anxiety. The OFT is also commonly used as a mechanism to assess the sedative, toxic, or stimulant effects of compounds. Thus, the OFT measures a number of facets of behavior beyond simple locomotion. As such, the test has a number of uses and is included in almost every thorough analysis of rodent behavior.

ACKNOWLEDGMENT

The authors wish to express their profound gratitude to the technical staff of the Anatomy and Cell Biology Department, Obafemi Awolowo University Ile-Ife, Nigeria for their support in the execution of this study.

REFERENCES

Agarwal AK (1995). Suppression of exploration and locomotion by central nervous system stimulants. Indian J. Pharmacol., 27: 178-182.

Ajibade AJ, Adenowo TK, Fajemilehin MF, Caton-Martins EA, Omotoso EO (2006). Some Histological Obervations on the Cerebellar Cortex of Adult Wistar rats following quinine administration. Sci. Focus, 11(2): 97-100.

Ajibade AJ, Adenowo TK, Fajemilehin ME, Caxton – Martins EA, Ekpo OE (2008). Effects of quinine administration on the population and transverse diameter of purkinje cells in the cerebellar cortex of adult Wistar rats. West Afr. J. Med., 27(1): 340-311.

Araoye MO (2003). Data Processing and Analysis Research Methodology with Statistics for Health and Social Sciences 1st edition pp. 183-219.

Benesova O, Tejkalova H, Kristofikova Z, Husek P, Nedvidkova J Yamamotova A (2001). Brainmaldevelopment and neurobehavioural deviations in adult rats treated neonatally with indomethacin, Pub Med. European. Neuro. Psychopharmacol., 5: 367-373.

Brown RE, Corey SC, Moore AK (1999). Differences in measures of exploration and fear in MHC cogenic C57 BL / 6J and B6 – H – 2K – mice behaviour. Genetics, 26: 263-271.

Carrey N, McFadyen MP, Brown RE (2000). Effects of chronic methyl phenidate administration on the locomotor and exploration behaviour of prepubertal mice. J. Child. Adolescent. Psychopharmacol., 10: 277-286.

Choleris EG, Thomas AW, Kavaliers M, Prato FS (2001). A detailed ethological analysis of the mosue open field test: effects of diazepam, chlordiazepoxide and an extremely low frequency pulse maynetiz field. Neuroscice. Biobehav. Rev., 25: 235-260.

Da Cunha C, Wolfman C, Levi destein M, Ruschel AC, Izquierdo I, Medina JH (1992). Antigenic effects of the infraamydala injection of Flumazenil, a benzodiazepine receptor antagonist. Functional Neurol., 5: 491-491.

Editorial (2000). Malaria Eradication and the Roll Back malaria campaign. Pharmanews 25(5): 3; Pharmanews Ltd Nigeria.

Eisenhauer LA, Murphy MA (1998). Drug therapy and physical assessment in pharmacotherapeutics and Advanced Nursing practice. NY: Mc Grand Hill, pp. 1-2.

Elimear B, Deasy J, Ruairi A, Mc Commack RR, Hawa V, Philip W (2003). Antimalarial Drugs from Nature. Trinity Student. Med. J., 3: 19.

Kakkilaya BS (2002). Quinine. Kakkilaya's malaria Website at malaria site.com., pp. 1-2.

Kenmochi M, Eggermont JJ (1997). Salicylate and quinine affect the central nervous system. Hearing Res., 113: 110-116.

National Institute of Health Guide for the Care and use of Laboratory Animals (1985). DHEW Publication (NIH), revised, Office of Science and Health Reports, DRR/NIH, Bethseda, USA.

Timothy CH (2003). Cerebellar Disorders. File HA. Disorders. Htm. Ataxia society www.ataxiaorg, pp. 1-414.

Vorhees CV, Butcher RE, Brunner RL, Wooten V, Sobotka JJ (1983). Developmental Toxicol and Psychotoxicity of FD and C red dye No. 40 (Allura red AC) in rats. Pub. Med. Toxicol., 28(3): 207-217.

Walsh RN, Cummins RA (1976). The Open Field Test. A critical review. Psychological Bulletin, 83: 482-504.

West JR (1995). The cerebellum: Neuroscience in medicine, edited by conn, P.N.J.B Lippincott Company Philadelphia. Chapter 12: 124-224.

White NJ, Warrell DA (1983). Chemical management of chloroquine – resistant plasmodium Falciparum malaria in South-East Asia. Trop. Doct., 13: 153-158.

NutriSim© protects against hippocampal neuronal damage induced by ischemia-reperfusion in Mongolian gerbils *(Meriones unguiculatus)*: Morphological and biochemical approach

Rolando Romero Dávalos[1], P. Fermín Pacheco-Moisés[2*], Armida Miranda-Riestra[3], Carmen Barajas-Martínez[2], Ariana Navarro-Meléndez[2], Sergio Rodríguez-Reynoso[4], Irma E. Velázquez-Brizuela[5], J. A. Cruz-Ramos[3] and Genaro Gabriel Ortiz[3]

[1]Laboratorios BioSim©; Área de Desarrollo e Investigación Científica, México.
[2]Departamento de Química, Centro Universitario de Ciencias Exactas e Ingenierías. Universidad de Guadalajara. Guadalajara, Jalisco, México.
[3]Laboratorio de Estrés Oxidativo, División de Neurociencias,Centro de Investigación Biomédica de Occidente, Instituto Mexicano del Seguro Social, Guadalajara, Jalisco, México.
[4]División de Investigación Quirúrgica, Centro de Investigación Biomédica de Occidente, Instituto Mexicano del Seguro Social, Guadalajara, Jalisco, México.
[5]OPD Instituto Jalisciense de Cancerología, Guadalajara, Jalisco, México.

Mongolian gerbil model has been extensively used for the study of neuroprotective drugs since transient bilateral common carotid artery occlusion induces neuronal cell death to selectively vulnerable regions, including the CA1 sector of the hippocampus. Oxidative stress is strongly involved in this phenomenon. NutriSim© a nutritive supplement has been used empirically in the treatment of several degenerative disorders. Therefore in the present work we studied the ability of NutriSim© to protect against brain damage induced by ischemia-reperfusion in Mongolian gerbils. Brain damage was monitored by histological analysis of CA1 region and quantitative determinations of lipoperoxides, nitric oxide catabolites (nitrates/nitrites) and Glutathione peroxidase enzyme (GPx) activity. We found that a single dose of NutriSim© reduces hippocampal neuronal death in the CA1 of the hippocampus and attenuates increases in lipid peroxidation products (malondialdehyde and 4-hydroxyalkenals), nitric oxide catabolites (nitrates/nitrites) and GPx activity. These results suggest that neuroprotective effects of NutriSim© are partly attributed to its antioxidant action.

Key words: NutriSim©, hippocampus, ischemia-reperfusion.

INTRODUCTION

Cerebrovascular diseases, including stroke, are associated with high mortality worldwide and ischemic stroke accounts for about 88 percent of all strokes. The most important etiologies of ischemic stroke include large-artery atherosclerosis, cardioembolism and cerebral small-vessel disease (Rosamond et al., 2008).

*Corresponding author. E-mail: ferminpacheco@hotmail.com.

The brain represents a structure extremely sensitive to hypoxia and the Mongolian gerbil (*Meriones unguiculatus)* has been widely used as a model for investigating the cerebral consequences of ischemia because of its unusual cerebral circulation which lacks connections between the carotid and vertebrobasilar circulations, therefore there is an incomplete arterial circle and the temporary bilateral occlusion of common carotid arteries provides a simple and reproducible approach to transient brain ischemia. A transient carotid occlusion for 5 min induces delayed neuronal death in the hippocampal

CA1 region (Kirino, 1982). This experimental model represents human stroke conditions due, for example, to atherosclerotic involvement of the common carotid arteries, respiratory arrest and cardiac arrest (Adams et al., 1993).

Reactive oxygen species (ROS) and nitric oxide ($NO^•$) also participate in the pathogenesis of cerebral injury induced by ischemia and reperfusion and oxygen free radicals are elevated during cerebral ischemia and reperfusion because of the failure of metabolic reactions (Fujimura et al., 2005; Moro et al., 2005). Activation of nitric oxide synthase leads to excess production of $NO^•$. High concentrations of $NO^•$ are toxic and interact with superoxide radical ($O2^•$) to produce the highly toxic peroxynitrite anion (ONOO–) (Traystman, 1991). These radicals react with intracellular proteins, lipids, sugars and nucleotides and impair the normal function and physiology of cells. Antioxidant defences including free radical scavengers and antioxidative enzymes are considered as the most effective means at attenuating the tissue injury induced by ischemia and reperfusion (Papadopoulos et al., 1998).

NutriSim© is a nutritional supplement that contains arginine, lysine, choline, ammonium chloride, calcium and magnesium. It is used empirically for several degenerative diseases. Using the gerbil model, it has been found that a single dose of NutriSim©, 30 min prior the ischemic treatment reduces significantly the brain edema (Miranda-Riestra, 2004).

Therefore to elucidate its possible mechanism of action we investigated the effect of NutriSim© on hippocampal delayed neuronal death and some markers of oxidative stress after transient cerebral ischemia.

MATERIALS AND METHODS

Animal model

180 adult male Mongolian gerbils weighing 90 - 100 g were maintained on a 12 h/ 12 h light/dark cycle at 22ºC and given access to food (Chow Purina) and water *ad libitum*. All animal experiments were approved by the ethical committee (Mexico) and were conformed to international guidelines on the ethical use of animals. Animals were randomly assigned into two groups: I) 120 animals for the biochemical determinations and II) 60 animals for the morphological evaluation. These groups in turn were subdivided evenly into five subgroups: subgroup 1, for control non-treated; subgroup 2, for sham operated; subgroup 3, underwent the surgical procedure of ischemia and reperfusion; subgroup 4, was intraperitoneally (i.p.) injected with a single dose of NutriSim© (10 µl/100 g of body weight) 30 minutes before ischemia; subgroup 5, was a non-ischemic group receiving a single dose of NutriSim© (10 µl/100 g of body weight).

Experimental procedures

Animals were anesthetized with droperidol (2.5 mg/Kg subcutaneous) and ketamine (50 mg/kg intramuscular). Bilateral common carotid arteries were dissected and occluded with atrau-matic microaneurism clips (Roboz Surgical Instruments, Rockville, MD). Occlusion was induced for 5 min to produce transient global ischemia of the forebrain. In sham-operated animals, both common carotids were exposed but not occluded. After removal of the clips, restoration of blood flow was verified by direct observation through a microscope. The surgical incision was sutured and disinfected and animals were returned to their cages. The body temperature (37 ± 0.5°C) was maintained with a heating blanket before, during the surgery and after the surgery until the animals fully recovered from anaesthesia.

Eight animals were killed at 90 min, 120 min and 7 days following the reperfusion insult. After decapitation, hippocampi were dissected and homogenized separately in ice-cold 20 mM tris (hydroxymethyl) aminomethane buffer (pH 7.4), 0.25 M sucrose, 10 mM KCl, 1 mM EDTA, 1 mM EGTA and 1 mM dithiothreitol with a polytron like stirrer. Homogenates were centrifuged at 15,000 g for 15 min at 4ºC and the supernatant was collected and immediately assayed for biochemical determinations. Biochemical and histological data were obtained by two independent investigators who were unaware of the treatment protocol.

Histological analysis

Sixty animals were re-anesthetized using the same protocol as previously described and perfused transcardially with 0.1 M phosphate-buffered saline (PBS, pH 7.4) followed by 4% paraformaldehyde in 0.1 M PB (pH 7.4) at 90 min, 120 min and 7 days after ischemia-reperfusion treatment.

Brains were removed and postfixed in the same fixative for more than 12 hours, processed and embedded in paraffin wax. Then, 5 m thick paraffin cross sections containing hippocampal tissue were mounted on slides and stained with haematoxylin and eosin. Microscopy was conducted on a Zeiss Axioscop (Goettingen, Germany) and images were captured and processed by a Spot CCD camera.

Lipid peroxidation

Lipid peroxidation products were assayed using a Kit from Oxford Biomedical Research Incorporated. (product No. FR 12). The Kit contains a chromogenic reagent (N-methyl-2-phenylindole) which reacts with the lipid peroxidation products malonaldehyde (MDA) and 4-Hydroxyalkenals (4-OHA) at 45ºC yielding a stable chromophore with maximal absorbance at a wavelength of 586 nm (Esterbauer and Cheeseman, 1990). Results are expressed as nmol MDA+4-OHA $(\text{mg protein})^{-1}$.

Nitric oxide catabolites (nitrates/nitrites)

Nitric oxide release was determined spectrophotometrically by measuring the accumulation of its stable degradation products, nitrite and nitrate. Quantification of these metabolites was done using a commercial package (Calbiochem Nitric Oxide Assay Kit, colorimetric 482650). Briefly, nitrate to nitrite conversion was done using nitrate reductase. Total nitrite is then determined spectrophotometrically by using the Griess reaction (Griess, 1864).

Determination of glutathione peroxidase activity

The protocol used was a modification of the method described previously (Jaskot et al., 1983). Briefly, homogenized hippocampi were centrifuged at 15,000 x*g* for 15 min at 4ºC and the supernatant was decanted and re-centrifuged at 100 000˙*xg* for 60 min at 4ºC. This supernatant was diluted 1:2 times with 50 µmol/L of potassium chloride (pH 7.6). Glutathione peroxidase (GPx) was measured by a coupled reaction with glutathione reductase (GRd) using cumene hydroperoxide as substrate and measuring the decrease in the NADPH absorbance at 340 nm. The product of GPx, GSSG, acts as a substrate for GRd. The primary role of GRd is to replenish the levels of GSH that have been oxidized by free radicals. The GRd activity was measured by following the decrease in absorbance of the reaction mixture at 340 nm as NADPH is converted to NADP in the presence of GSSG. This activity was referred to as micromoles of oxidized NADPH/min/mg of protein (oxidized NADPH μM min/mg protein).

Determination of Protein

Proteins were determined by the microassay procedure using the Bio-Rad Protein Assay Kit (Bio-Rad Laboratories, Hercules CA).

Statistical evaluation

All values reported are expressed as mean ± standard error. Statistical significance of differences among groups was tested by one-way analysis of variance (ANOVA), followed by multiple comparisons between each group and control or other groups using Dunnett's multiple comparison test. $P \leq 0.05$ was considered significant.

RESULTS

Histological analysis

Normal structure of hippocampal pyramidal neurons are shown in Figures 1a and b (for control non-treated and non-ischemic group receiving a single dose of NutriSim©, respectively). Macroscopically, at 90 and 120 min after ischemia the brains showed edema and widespread congestion, including NutriSim© treated groups. However, brain edema was reduced when NutriSim© was applied prior ischemia-reperfusion treatment. Sagittal section at the median eminence region was not altered macroscopically, in all groups. At day 7 after ischemia we did not observe any alteration both general and within the brain (data not shown).

Microscopic examination of CA1 region of hippocampus exhibited increased degenerative changes at different time after ischemia-reperfusion: hyperchromasia, widening of Virchow-Robin spaces, swelling of the nucleus and cellular shrinkage (Figures 1a - e). Furthermore, neuronphagia, astroglial aggregates and neuronal cell death were evident at 120 min and 7 days after ischemia-reperfusion (Figures 1d and e, respectively). Interestingly, we observed a protective effect of NutriSim©, that is, hyperchromasia and astroglial aggregates were still evident, but minor compared with the ischemia-reperfusion control group (Figures 1f and g). In addition, delayed neuronal death, at 7 days of ischemia-reperfusion was reduced by NutriSim© (Figure 1h).

Biochemical analysis

To explore if the neuroprotective effect of NutriSim© was

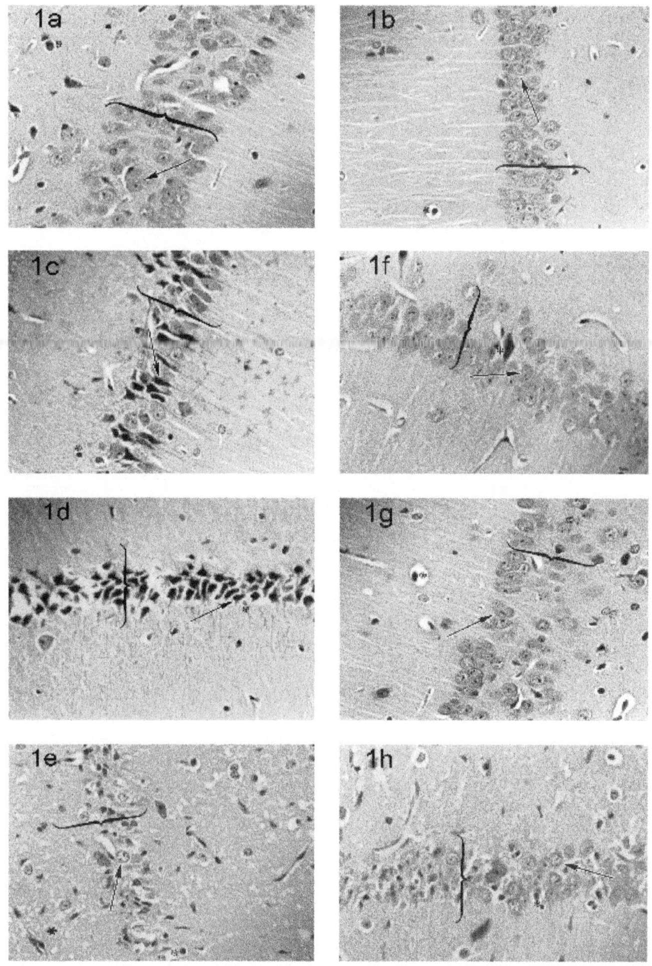

Figure 1. Representative light micrographs of the CA1 sector region of dorsal hippocampus of Mongolian gerbils. Control without ischemia (1a), control with NutriSim© (1b). Ischemia-reperfusion groups, at 90 min (1c), 120 min (1d) and 7 days (1e). NutriSim© plus ischemia groups, at 90 min (1f), 120 min (1g) and 7 days (1h). (Curly bracket, CA1 region; arrow, neurons).

mediated by a possible antioxidant action, we measured oxidative stress markers in hippocampi homogenates. As shown in Figures 2 and 3, respectively a basal level of lipid peroxidation products (malondialdehyde and 4-hydroxyalkenals) and nitric oxide catabolites (nitrates/nitrites) were detected in hippocampi from control, ischemia and NutriSim© treated gerbils. A minor increment in lipid peroxidation products (Figure 2) and nitric oxide catabolites (Figure 3) were detected in sham-operated animals, but there was a significant increase in lipid oxidation products in hippocampi isolated from gerbils subjected to the treatment of ischemia-reperfusion from 90 and 120 min. Interestingly, a single dose of NutriSim©, 30 minutes before the ischemia treatment attenuate the increase in lipid oxidation products and nitric oxide catabolites, quantified to 90 and 120 min after reperfusion. At 7 days after treatment, there was not a statistically significant change between treatments, but

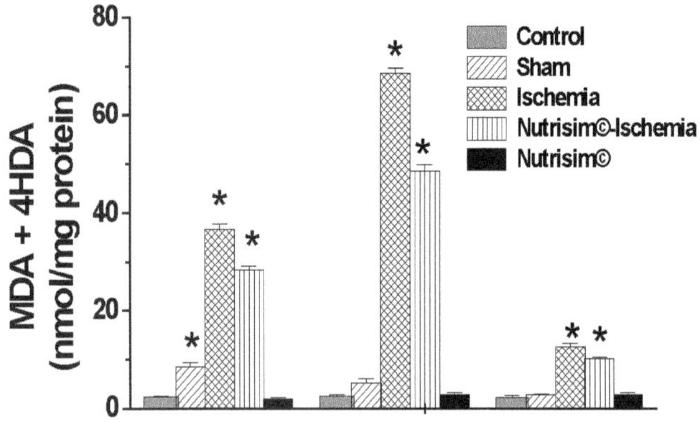

Figure 2. Lipid peroxidation products (malondialdehyde and 4-hydroxyalkenals) in hippocampi from the indicated gerbils groups at 90 min, 120 min and 7 days after reperfusion. Asterisks indicate a significant difference from the ischemia-reperfusion group ($P < 0.05$). The bar indicates the mean ± S.E.

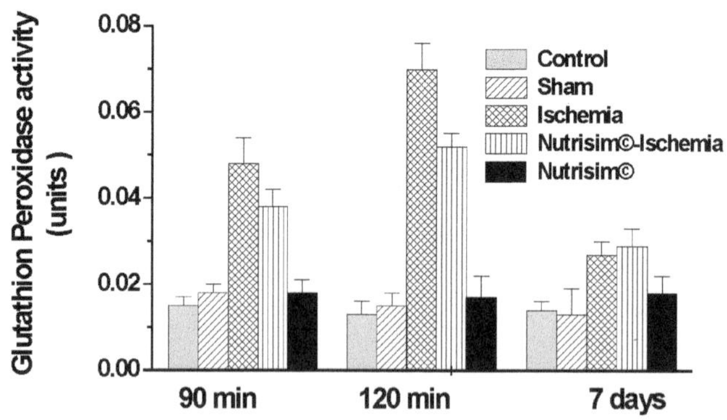

Figure 4. Glutathione peroxidase activity in hippocampi from the indicated gerbils groups at 90 min, 120 min and 7 days after reperfusion. Asterisks indicate a significant difference from the ischemia-reperfusion group ($P < 0.05$). The bar indicates the mean ± S.E.

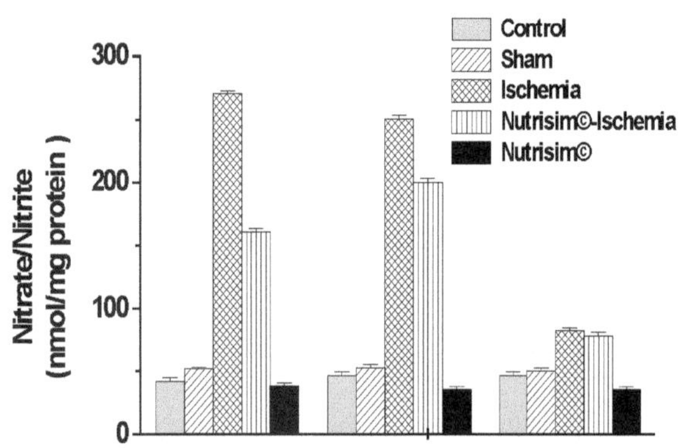

Figure 3. Nitric oxide catabolites in hippocampi from the indicated gerbils groups at 90 min, 120 min and 7 days after reperfusion. Asterisks indicate a significant difference from the ischemia-reperfusion group ($P < 0.05$). The bar indicates the mean ± S.E.

the trend is similar to previous experiments.

Figure 4 shows that the enzyme GPx activity was increased significantly in hippocampi from gerbils subjected to ischemia and reperfusion with respect to the hippocampi from groups control, sham operated and NutriSim© (single dose). In contrast, Figure 4 also shows that a single dose of NutriSim© before ischemia prevents partially the increase in glutathione peroxidase activity. Interestingly, that enzymatic activity was diminished 7 days after treatment in the groups subjected to ischemia.

DISCUSSION

The present work demonstrates that intraperitoneal injection of NutriSim© 30 minutes prior to forebrain ischemia in gerbils is neuroprotective under the conditions of bilateral carotid occlusion assayed. These data implicated that NutriSim© is capable of passing the brain-blood barrier and exerting neuroprotective effect in the CA1 region of the hippocampus. The results demonstrated that NutriSim© inhibited the production of lipid peroxidetion and nitric oxide catabolites and also diminishes the glutathione peroxidase activity. The net effect may be the reduction in oxidative stress. In addition NutriSim© reduces cortical neuron injury induced by ischemia-reperfusion.

NutriSim© contains arginine, lysine, choline, ammonium chloride, calcium and magnesium. Its components could exert some important functions as described below. L-arginine (L-arg), a semi-essential amino acid, depending on its metabolic pathway, becomes very essential in stress situations such as heatstroke, burns, sepsis, trauma and wound healing (Chatterjee, 2006; Tong et al., 2004). Additionally, it has been demonstrate that L-arg diminishes lipid peroxidation in patients with diabetes mellitus (Lubec et al., 1997) and has promising results during treatment of cardiovascular diseases including atherosclerosis, hypertension, angina pectoris, hyperlipidemia, and some kidney disorders, (Clarkson et al., 1996). Arginine affects cellular defense function, presumably by means of inducible nitric oxide synthetase (iNOS) mediated NO formation. These effects of arginine on cellular defense function led to its inclusion into current concepts of immune enhancing formulas to reduce the incidence of infectious morbidity and mortality in immune compromised patients). Arginine is used as a supplement in the treatment of arterial heart disease (Fisman et al., 1999; Wu and Meininger, 2000).

Lysine is an essential amino acid. This means that it must be obtained through the diet in adequate quantities to meet the body needs. Lysine is required in the body for the manufacture of carnitine, which is an amino acid used for the proper metabolism of fats Lysine deficiency can interfere with carnitine synthesis and have adverse impact upon fat metabolism to energy (Viviani et al., 1966).

Choline a precursor of brain phospholipids and the neurotransmitter acetylcholine is an essential nutrient (Sheard and Zeisel, 1996) and has a neuroprotective effect in situations of hypoxia and ischemia in animal models (De Bruin et al., 2003). Interestingly, cytidine 5' diphosphocholine, a choline precursor has a protective effect in patients with an acute cerebral infarction (Tazaki et al., 1988). On the other hand, calcium and magnesium are essential minerals that are needed for a broad variety of physiological functions, for instance an increased magnesium supply, however, might contribute to a risk reduction towards various diseases as for example coronary artery disease or osteoporosis (Vorman, 2003). At this time, it is not known if the whole mixture of NutriSim© or a specific component is the responsible for its effects. However the effects found in this work warrants further investigation.

REFERENCES

Adams Jr. HP, Bendixen BH, Kappelle LJ, Biller J, B. Love B, Gordon DL Marsh EE (1993). Classification of subtype of acute ischemic stroke. Definitions for use in a multicenter clinical trial. TOAST. Trial of Org 10172 in acute stroke treatment. Stroke 24: 35-41.

Chatterjee S, Premachandran S, Bagewadikar RS (2006). Arginine metabolic pathways determine its therapeutic benefit in experimental heatstroke: role of Th1/Th2 cytokine balance. Nitric Oxide 15: 408-416.

Clarkson P, Adams MR, Powe AJ, Donald AE, McCredie R, Robinson J, McCarthy SN, Keech A, Celermajer DS, Deanfield JE (1996). Oral l-Arginine improves endothelium dependent dilation in hypercholesteromic young adults. J. Clin. Invest. 97: 1989-1994.

De Bruin NMWJ, Kiliaan AJ, De Wilde MC, Broersen LM (2003). Combined uridine and choline administration improves cognitive deficits in spontaneously hypertensive rats. Neurobiol. Learning Mem. 80: 63-79.

Esterbauer HK, Cheeseman H (1990). Determination of aldehydic lipid peroxidation products: malonadehyde and 4-hidroxynonenal. Meth. Enzymol. 186: 407-421.

Fisman EZ, Tenenbaum A, Shapira I, Pines A, Motro M (1999). The nitric oxide pathway: is L-arginine a gate to the new millennium medicine? A meta-analysis of L-arginine effects. J. Med. 30: 131-148.

Fujimura M, Tominaga T, Chan PH (2005). Neuroprotective effect of an antioxidant in ischemic brain injury: involvement of neuronal apoptosis. Neurocrit. Care 2: 59-66.

Griess JP (1864). On a new series of bodies in which nitrogen is substituted for hydrogen. Phil. Trans. R.S (Lond.) 154: 667-731.

Jaskot RH, Charlet EG, Grose EC, Grady MA, Raycroft JH (1983). An automated analysis of glutathione peroxidase, S-transferase, and reductase activity in animal tissue. J. Anal. Toxico. 7: 86-88.

Kirino T (1982). Delayed neuronal death in the gerbil hippocampus following ischemia. Brain Res. 239: 57-69.

Lubec B, Hayn M, Kitzmuller E, Vierhapper H, Lubec G (1997). L-arginine reduces lipid peroxidation in patients with diabetes mellitus. Free Radic. Biol. Med. 22: 355–357.

Miranda-Riestra A (2004). Estudio bioquímico del efecto protector del NutriSim© en cerebros de mongolian gerbils (*Meriones unguiculatus*) sometidos a isquemia-reperfusi6n Thesis. Universidad de Guadalajara. México.

Moro MA, Almeida A, Bolanos JP, Lizasoain I (2005). Mitochondrial respiratory chain and free radical generation in stroke. Free Rad. Biol. Med. 39: 1291-1304.

Papadopoulos MC, Koumenis IL, Xu L, Giffard RG (1998). Potentiation of murine astrocyte antioxidant defence by bcl-2: protection in part reflects elevated glutathione levels. Eur. J. Neurosci. 10: 1252-1260.

Rosamond W, Flegal K, Furie K, Go A, Greenlund K, Haase N, Hailpern SM, Ho M, Howard V, Kissela B, Kittner S, Lloyd-Jones D, McDermott M, Meigs J, Moy C, Nichol G, O'Donnell C, Roger V, Sorlie P, Steinberger J, Thom T, Wilson M, Hong Y (2008). Heart Disease and Stroke Statistics_2008 Update: A Report From the American Heart Association Statistics Committee and Stroke Statistics Subcommittee. Circulation 117: e25-e146.

Sheard NF, Zeisel SH (1989). Choline: An essential dietary nutrient? Nutrition 5: 1-5.

Tazaki YF, Sakai E, Otomo F, Kutsuzawa T, Kameyama M, Omae T, Fujishima M, Sakuma A (1988). Treatment of acute cerebral infarction with a choline precursor in a multicenter double-blind placebo-controlled study. Stroke 19: 211–216.

Tong BC, Barbul A (2004) Cellular and physiological effects of arginine. Mini-Rev. Med. Chem. 4: 823-832.

Traystman RJ, Kirsch JR, Koehler RC (1991). Oxygen radical mechanisms of brain injury following ischemia and reperfusion, J. App. Physiol. 71: 1185-1195.

Viviani R, Sechi AM, Lenaz G (1966). Lipid metabolism in fatty liver of lysine- and threonine-deficient rats. J: Lipid Res. 7: 473-478.

Vormann J (2003). Magnesium: nutrition and metabolism. Mol. Asp. Med. 24, 27-37.

Wu G, Meininger CJ (2000). Arginine nutrition and cardiovascular function. J. Nutr. 11: 2626-2629.

Public perception of epilepsy: A survey from the rural population in Northeastern Thailand

Jiamjit Saengsuwan[1], Suwanna Boonyaleepan[1], Jitpinan Srijakkot[1], Kittisak Sawanyawisuth[2], Somsak Tiamkao[2]* N. Auevitchayapat[3], S. Arunpongpaisal[3], A. Chaiyakum[3], S. Jitpimolmard[3], S. Lertsinudom[3], W. Phuttharak[3], K. Phunikhom[3], Tiamkao Si[3], and S. Vannaprasaht[3]

[1]Faculty of Nursing, Khon Kaen University, Khon Kaen, 40002, Thailand.
[2]Department of Medicine, Faculty of Medicine, Khon Kaen University, Khon Kaen, 40002, Thailand.
[3]Srinagarind Epilepsy Research Group, Srinagarind, Thailand.

We conducted a survey to assess public awareness and attitudes towards epilepsy in five provinces of the Northeastern Thailand. A cross-sectional survey was conducted by using a face-to-face interview. There were 964 subjects who were randomly selected by a multistage sampling with a response rate of 86.9% (831 participants). There were 449 (60.0%), 102 (12.3%) and 127 (15.3%) participants who had heard of epilepsy, known someone with epilepsy, and witnessed a seizure, respectively. About 80 and 99% of the participants did not know the causes and types of epilepsy, respectively. More than half of the participants (58%) believed that epilepsy cannot be cured. The negative attitude rate ranged between 8 - 90%. The highest item was "persons with epilepsy cannot live in the society like other people." Age, gender, income, and provinces were significantly correlated with the negative attitudes. Six out of the ten questions regarding attitude toward epilepsy were significant correlated with knowledge. In conclusion, public perception of epilepsy is lacked and needs attention. Knowledge particularly regarding causes of epilepsy and attitudes toward epilepsy are closely related. Public education intervention is suggested to improve public attitudes of epilepsy.

Key words: Epilepsy, knowledge, attitudes, correlation.

INTRODUCTION

Although knowledge, attitude and beliefs towards epilepsy have improved in most countries, there is still misperception about the disorder (Austin et al., 2002). Living in the society is more challenging than epilepsy itself (Austin et al., 2002). Fear and misunderstanding of epilepsy may lead to social stigma resulting social discrimination particularly in teenagers.

In Thailand, despite 1 - 2% of the population have epilepsy; it remains a mysterious disorder shrouded in myths and misunderstanding for most people. Persons with epilepsy face many interpersonal, emotional and social difficulties as in other countries. The rural areas of the Northeastern, Thailand have unique cultures and tradition. In addition, beliefs and thoughts of people might be different from other areas in Thailand and the world. We therefore performed a survey to study the public knowledge and attitude towards epilepsy in these particular areas.

*Corresponding author. E-mail : somtia@kku.ac.th.

MATERIALS AND METHODS

A cross sectional survey was conducted in 5 rural areas of 5 provinces in the Northeastern Thailand including Udon Thani, Khon Kaen, Chaiyaphum, Kalasin, and Maha Sarakham. A structural questionnaire was used to assess the public knowledge and attitude towards epilepsy.

Instrumentation

The questionnaire was derived from literature reviews (Austin et al.,

2002; Bener et al., 1998; Daoud et al., 2007; Demirci et al., 2007; Diamantopoulos et al., 2006; Fong and Hung, 2002; Hills and MacKenzie, 2002; Tuan et al., 2007) and some questions related to local belief were added. It assessed participants' demographic data, epilepsy familiarity, knowledge, and attitude. Epilepsy familiarity consisted of three questions including; "Have you heard of epilepsy?", "Do you know someone with epilepsy?", and "Have you ever witnessed a seizure?". There were 14 questions regarding knowledge of epilepsy concerning causes, treatments, and precipitation factors of epilepsy. In addition, 10 questions were asked about participants' attitude towards epilepsy. All questions regarding knowledge and attitude had two options; yes or no.

Study population

The questionnaire was administered to 964 persons by multistage random sampling from September to November 2005. All participants were older than 18 years and gave an informed consent. This survey was a face-to-face interview at the participant's home. Ample time was allowed for completion of the questionnaire and the average time taken for a single interview ranged from 15 - 20 min.

Data analysis

Analysis of the data was executed with descriptive statistics, and chi-square test with the STATA (version 9). Epilepsy familiarity, knowledge, and attitude data were correlated with demographic data. In addition, the association between knowledge and attitude was also performed. A probability value of less than 0.05 was considered significant.

RESULTS

In this study a total of 831 subjects (86.9%) participated and completed the interview. The demographic data was presented in Table 1. The mean age (range) of subjects was 46.23 years (18 - 85). The majorities of the respondents were women (73%), had the education level of primary school (77.2%), and was farmers or employee (65%). The rest were businessman, government officials, retired, and students. The family income of ≤36,000, 36,001 - 100,000, >100,000 baht/year were categorized as low, average, and high income, respectively. There were 73.4% of participants with middle or high family income (Table 1).

Table 1. General characteristics of study subjects (Total subjects = 831).

Characteristics	N (%)
Age (years)	
< 40	273 (32.9)
40 - 49	222 (26.7)
50 - 59	197 (23.7)
≥ 60	139 (16.7)
Gender	
Male	221 (27.0)
Female	610 (73.0)
Education	
Primary school or lower	641 (77.2)
Secondary school or higher	190 (22.8)
Occupation	
Unemployed	101 (12.0)
Farmers or employee	539 (65.0)
Others	191 (23.0)
Provinces	
Udon Thani	101 (12.1)
Khon Kaen	303 (36.5)
Chaiyaphum	122 (14.7)
Kalasin	131 (15.8)
Maha Sarakham	174 (20.9)
Family income	
Low	221 (26.6)
Middle	301 (36.2)
High	309 (37.2)

Note: Low, middle, and high family income defined by total family income equal, respectively

Epilepsy familiarity

There were 449 (60.0%), 102 (12.3%), and 127 (15.3%) partici-pants who had heard of epilepsy, known someone with epilepsy, and witnessed a seizure, respectively. The sources of epilepsy knowledge were from health care personnels (35%), friends (31%), television (24%), books or magazines (10%), and radio (0.4%).

There were significant differences in numbers of participants who had heard of epilepsy by provinces ($p = 0.001$), occupation ($p = 0.018$), and family income ($p = 0.041$). Gender and provincial differences were significantly correlated with variables "knows someone who had epilepsy" and "has witnessed a seizure" (Table 2). In addition, the oldest age group was more likely than other age groups to know someone with epilepsy ($p = 0.038$) and farmers or employees had significantly witnessed a seizure.

Knowledge about epilepsy

The knowledge about epilepsy was divided into four aspects as follows: causes, types, treatments, and precipitating factors (Table 3).

Causes of epilepsy: Almost 80% of the participants reported that they did not know what causes epilepsy. However, about 50% of participants believed that epilepsy is a brain disorder (Table 3). Participants with higher education or average income, and those who know someone with epilepsy were significantly associated with

Table 2. Significant factors correlated with epilepsy familiarity.

Variables	N (%)	p value
Had heard of epilepsy		
Provinces		0.001
Udon Thani	58 (54.7)	
Khon Kaen	188 (62.1)	
Chaiyaphum	90 (73.8)	
Kalasin	64 (48.9)	
Maha Sarakham	99 (56.9)	
Occupation		0.018
Unemployed	44 (43.6)	
Farmer or employee	338 (62.7)	
Others	106 (55.5)	
Family income		0.041
Low	120 (54.3)	
Middle	178 (59.1)	
High	201 (65.1)	
Knows someone with epilepsy		
Gender		<0.001
Male	12 (5.4)	
Female	90 (14.8)	
Age (years)		0.038
< 40	25 (9.2)	
40-49	32 (14.4)	
50-59	20 (10.1)	
≥ 60	25 (17.9)	
Provinces		<0.001
Udon Thani	12 (11.9)	
Khon Kaen	26 (8.6)	
Chaiyaphum	34 (27.9)	
Kalasin	14 (10.7)	
Maha Sarakham	16 (9.2)	
Has witnessed a seizure		
Gender		0.01
Male	22 (10.0)	
Female	105 (17.2)	
Occupation		0.03
Unemployed	15 (14.9)	
Farmer or employee	94 (17.4)	
Others	18 (9.4)	
Provinces		<0.001
Udon Thani	12 (11.9)	
Khon Kaen	17 (5.6)	
Chaiyaphum	54 (44.3)	
Kalasin	25 (19.1)	
Maha Sarakham	19 (10.9)	

this response (p value = 0.001, <0.001 and = 0.001 respectively). Similarly, 54.9% of participants answered that epilepsy is a psychiatric disorder. This response was correlated with unemployment (p = 0.019). Participants with older age, lower education level, and low family income significantly thought that epilepsy is an infectious disease item (p = 0.003, 0.039 and 0.004 respectively). About 20 and 40% of participants believed that epilepsy is from evil or due to eating pork, respectively. The beliefs of evil or eating pork as causes of epilepsy were associated with unfamiliarity of epilepsy (p < 0.001 and p = 0.004). Approximately 43% of participants believed that epilepsy is an inherited disease. Though this belief had no association with any demographic variables, all other items regarding causes of epilepsy were found to be different among provinces.

Types of epilepsy: Almost all of participants (99%) declared that they were not able to identify type of epilepsy. In addition, 82% of participants perceived that epilepsy has only one type, which is generalized tonic-clonic seizure.

Treatments of epilepsy: More than half of the participants (58%) believed that epilepsy cannot be cured. This belief was associated with lower education level and unemployed status (p = 0.040, 0.032, respecttively). Similarly, 56% of the participants responded that persons with epilepsy have to take antiepileptic medication lifelong. About one-fifth of the participant believed that epilepsy can be treated by a spiritual healer. Participants who believed that persons with epilepsy need to take medication forever or epilepsy can be treated by a spiritual healer were also heard about epilepsy (p < 0.001). The numbers of participants who responded to three questions regarding treatment of epilepsy were significantly different by participants' provinces (p < 0.001 for questions "epilepsy cannot be cured" and "person with epilepsy have to take antiepileptic medication lifelong" and p = 0.043 for question "epilepsy can be treated by a spiritual healer")

Precipitating factors: The three most common beliefs that precipitated seizure attacks were mental stress, hard-working job, and alcohol (Table 3). The participants who were unfamiliar with epilepsy significantly responded that sleep deprivation, alcohol consumption, and hard-working job were precipitating factors (p value = 0.001, 0.02 and 0.017 respectively). The participants with high family income also believed that alcohol consumption is a precipitating factor (p = 0.003). Farmers and employees reported that hard-working job is a significant precipitating factor for seizure attack (p = 0.049). Older age, low family income, and unfamiliarity with epilepsy were significantly associated with sexual activities as a precipitating factor for seizure (p value = 0.048, 0.007, and <0.001, respectively). Even though mental stress as a precipitating factor for seizure attack had the highest percentage, it was not correlated with any demographic variables.

Table 3. Responses regarding epilepsy knowledge in three aspects among 831 participants.

Questions	Yes, N (%)	No, N (%)
Causes		
Epilepsy is a brain disorder	435 (52.4)	396 (47.6)
Epilepsy is a psychiatric disorder	457 (54.9)	374 (45.1)
Epilepsy is an inherited disorder	361 (43.4)	470 (56.6)
Epilepsy is an infectious disease	199 (23.9)	632 (76.1)
Epilepsy is caused by an evil	167 (19.9)	664 (80.1)
Epilepsy is transmitted by eating pork	324 (38.9)	507 (61.1)
Treatment		
Epilepsy can be cured	345 (41.5)	486 (58.5)
Persons with epilepsy need to take antiepileptic medications lifelong		
Epilepsy can be treated by a spiritual healer	466 (56.0)	365 (43.9)
What is/are precipitating factor (s) of epilepsy?	167 (20.1)	664 (79.9)
Sleep deprivation	458 (55.1)	373 (44.9)
Mental stress	564 (67.9)	267 (32.1)
Alcohol	513 (61.7)	318 (38.3)
Hard-working job	531 (63.9)	300 (36.1)
Sexual activity	242 (29.1)	589 (70.9)

Attitude towards epilepsy

The negative attitude rate ranged between 8 - 90% (Table 4). The highest item was "persons with epilepsy cannot live in the society like other people". The second highest item was "epilepsy is a form of insanity" that was significantly related with lower education level ($p = 0.011$). Participants who had lower income and never known persons with epilepsy were significantly related to the thought that persons with epilepsy have lower IQ (p value = 0.011, and 0.042, respectively). Nearly one third would not employ persons with epilepsy and this attitude was associated with the male sex ($p = 0.017$), high family income ($p = 0.003$) and provincial differences ($p < 0.001$). More than 20% of respondents would not allow their son/daughter to marry an epileptic person and recommend children with epilepsy to study in a selected school. These two rejections were associated with unfamiliarity with epilepsy and provincial factor, respectively ($p < 0.001$, = 0.035, respectively). The participants who would not allow their children to play with an epileptic person were found 12.9% and related to older age ($p = 0.003$) and low family income ($p = 0.014$).

The association of attitude and knowledge of epilepsy

The significant association of attitude and knowledge of epilepsy were shown in Table 5. Knowledge about causes of epilepsy was more related to attitude than other categories of knowledge; one item in treatment and another item in precipitating category. The rejection of allowing their children to play or get married with persons with epilepsy was related to the perception that epilepsy is a psychiatric disorder or infectious disease. The epilepsy attitude of employed persons was also significantly correlated with knowledge regarding causes of epilepsy.

DISCUSSION

Cross-cultural studies have shown that there is limited data on knowledge of epilepsy and the attitudes towards epilepsy can be varied (Gajjar et al., 2000; Lee et al., 2001). Some beliefs such as epilepsy are a neurological disease can lead to stigmatizing (Fatovic-Ferencic and Durrigi, 2001). Even though knowledge and attitudes have improved worldwide, there are differences among countries (Daoud et al., 2007).

Previous reports showed that knowledge about epilepsy was associated with age and education (Bener et al., 1998; Choi-Kwon et al., 2004; Kobau and Price, 2003). The level of knowledge regarding epilepsy was still inadequate even in medical students and teachers (Tiamkao et al., 2005; Tiamkao et al., 2007). We found differences among the provinces with respect to epilepsy familiarity, knowledge and attitudes. Moreover, knowledge regarding causes of epilepsy has drastically correlated with attitudes (Table 5).

Even though all study sites were in the Northeast, Thailand, there were significant differences in all three aspects of epilepsy familiarity by study provinces (Table 2). Regarding knowledge of epilepsy, only about half of participants answered the questions correctly in all categories (Table 3). Factors that correlated with knowledge

Table 4. Responses regarding epilepsy attitude among 831 participants, ordered by the most negative attitude item (bold numbers).

Questions	Yes, N (%)	No, N (%)
Do you think persons with epilepsy can live in the society like other people?	83 (10.0)	748 (90.0)
Do you think epilepsy is a form of insanity?	396 (47.7)	435 (59.3)
Is an average IQ of persons with epilepsy lower than normal population?	343 (41.3)	488 (58.7)
Do you agree that persons with epilepsy are dangerous persons?	338 (40.7)	493 (59.3)
Can women with epilepsy have their own children?	552 (66.5)	279 (33.5)
Do you think persons with epilepsy should be employed in the same jobs as other people?	571 (68.7)	260 (31.3)
Would you object to your son/daughter marrying a person who sometimes has seizure attack?	236 (28.4)	595 (71.6)
Should children with epilepsy study in a special school?	196 (23.6)	635 (76.4)
Would you object to your child playing with a person with epilepsy?	107 (12.9)	724 (87.1)
If you or your family members have epilepsy, would you tell others?	765 (92.1)	66 (7.9)

Table 5. The significant correlation between attitude and knowledge among 831 participants.

Attitudes	p value
Would you object to your child playing with a person with epilepsy?	
Epilepsy is a psychiatric disorder	0.006
Epilepsy is an infectious disease	<0.001
Sexual activity is a precipitating factor of epilepsy	0.002
Would you object to your son/daughter marrying a person who sometimes has seizure attack?	
Epilepsy is a psychiatric disorder	0.008
Epilepsy is an infectious disease	<0.001
Sexual activity is a precipitating factor of epilepsy	<0.001
Should children with epilepsy study in a special school?	
Epilepsy is an inherited disorder	0.002
Epilepsy is caused by an evil	0.005
Epilepsy is transmitted by eating pork	0.005
Is an average IQ of persons with epilepsy lower than normal population?	
Epilepsy is an infectious disease	0.009
Epilepsy can be cured	0.037
Sexual activity is a precipitating factor of epilepsy	0.002
Do you think epilepsy is a form of insanity?	
Epilepsy is a brain disorder	0.005
Epilepsy is an inherited disorder	<0.001
Epilepsy is caused by an evil	<0.001
Epilepsy is transmitted by eating pork	<0.001
Epilepsy can be cured	0.021
Do you think persons with epilepsy should be employed in the same jobs as other people?	
Epilepsy is a brain disorder	0.002
Epilepsy is a psychiatric disorder	0.004
Epilepsy is caused by an evil	0.001
Epilepsy is transmitted by eating pork	0.001
Sexual activity is a precipitating factor of epilepsy	<0.001

ledge of epilepsy were age, education level, family income, epilepsy familiarity, and provincial differences. Generally, the knowledge level in our participants was lower than other reports from Asian countries (Bener et al., 1998; Choi-Kwon et al., 2004; Chung et al., 1995; Daoud et al., 2007; Demirci et al., 2007). Even though factors that correlated to knowledge of epilepsy were quite similar to previous reports, we added that living are living areas were also associated knowledge level.

Regarding attitudes towards epilepsy, 90% of participants believed that persons with epilepsy cannot live in the society like healthy people do. This attitude implied that epilepsy is a serious disease. While 9.3% of participants in Jordan reported that persons with epilepsy were insane (Daoud et al., 2007), the number in our study was surprisingly high at 45%. Gender, age, family income, epilepsy familiarity, and provinces were associated with the negative attitudes towards epilepsy. Compare to previous reports in Asia, our negative attitudes towards epilepsy rates were quite higher. This might be due to the sensitive personality of people in these areas.

Our analyses showed that participants' attitudes were significantly related to their knowledge about epilepsy; mostly causes of epilepsy. These findings may indicate that knowledge about causes of epilepsy is the main factor affecting participants' attitudes. Educational program, focusing on causes of epilepsy, may be helpful to improve public attitudes about epilepsy.

In conclusion, public perception of epilepsy is lacked and needs attention. Knowledge particularly regarding causes of epilepsy and attitudes toward epilepsy are closely related. Public education intervention is suggested to improve public attitudes of epilepsy.

REFERENCES

Austin JK, Shafer PO and Deering JB (2002). Epilepsy familiarity, knowledge, and perceptions of stigma: report from a survey of adolescents in the general population. Epilepsy. Behav. 3:368-375.

Bener A, al-Marzooqi FH, and Sztriha L (1998). Public awareness and attitudes towards epilepsy in the United Arab Emirates. Seizure. 7:219-222.

Choi-Kwon S, Park KA, Lee HJ, Park MS, Lee CH, Cheon SE, Youn MH, Lee SK, Chung CK (2004). Familiarity with, knowledge of, and attitudes toward epilepsy in residents of Seoul, South Korea. Acta. Neurol. Scand. 110:39–45.

Chung MY, Chang YC, Lai YH, Lai CW (1995). Survey of public awareness, understanding, and attitudes toward epilepsy in Taiwan. Epilepsia. 36:488-493.

Daoud A, Al-Safi S, Otoom S, Wahba L, Alkofahi A (2007). Public knowledge and attitudes towards epilepsy in Jordan. Seizure. 16:521-526.

Demirci S, Dönmez CM, Gündoğar D, Baydar CL (2007). Public awareness of, attitudes toward, and understanding of epilepsy in Isparta, Turkey. Epilepsy. Behav. 11:427-433.

Diamantopoulos N, Kaleyias J, Tzoufi M, Kotsalis C (2006). A Survey of Public Awareness, Understanding, and Attitudes toward Epilepsy in Greece. Epilepsia. 47:2154-2164.

Fatovic-Ferencic S, Durrigi MA (2001). The sacred disease and its patron saint. Epilepsy. Behav. 2:370-373.

Fong CY, Hung A. Public awareness, attitude, and understanding of epilepsy in Hong Kong Special Administrative Region, China (2002). Epilepsia. 43:311-316.

Gajjar M, Geva E, Humphries A, Peterson-Badali M, Otsubo H (2000). A. new scale to assess culture specific beliefs and attitudes about epilepsy. Epilepsy. Behav. 1:235-255.

Hills MD, MacKenzie HC (2002). New Zealand community attitudes toward people with epilepsy. Epilepsia. 43:1583-1589.

Kobau R, Price P (2003). Knowledge of epilepsy and familiarity with this disorder in the U.S. population: results from the 2002 Health Style Survey. Epilepsia. 44:1449-1454.

Lee TM, Yang SH, Ng PK (2001). Epilepsy in Chinese culture. Am. J. Chin. Med. 29:181–184.

Tiamkao S, Auevitchayapat N, Arunpongpaisal S, Chaiyakum A, Jitpimolmard S, Phuttharak W, Phunikhom K, Saengsuwan J, Saetang

S, Tiamkao S, Vannaprasaht S (2005). Knowledge of epilepsy among teachers in Khon Kaen Province, Thailand. J. Med. Assoc. Thai. 88:1802-1808.

Tiamkao S, Tiamkao S, Auevitchayapat N, Arunpongpaisal S, Chaiyakum A, Jitpimolmard S, Phuttharak W, Phunikhom K, Saengsuwan MJ, Vannaprasaht S (2007). Basic knowledge of epilepsy among medical students. J. Med. Assoc. Thai. 90:2271-2276.

Tuan NA, Cuong le Q, Allebeck P, Chuc NT, Tomson T (2007). Knowledge attitudes and practice toward epilepsy among adults in BaVi, Vietnam: first report from the population-based EPIBAVI study. Epilepsia. 8: 1914-1919

Gender variation in risk factors and clinical presentation of acute stroke, Northeastern Nigeria

Watila M. M.[1]*, Nyandaiti Y. W.[1], Bwala S. A.[1] and Ibrahim A.[2]

[1]University of Maiduguri Teaching hospital, P. M. B. 1414, Maiduguri, Borno State, Nigeria.
[2]Federal Medical Centre, Azare, Bauchi State, Nigeria.

Studies suggest that gender differences exist in patients with stroke. This study is aimed at determining the gender difference in risk factors and clinical presentation of acute stroke among male and female patients. This is a prospective study conducted at the University of Maiduguri Teaching Hospital (UMTH) from 2005 to 2009. All patients admitted through the accident and emergency unit or directly to neurology unit with clinical and radiological proven stroke were enrolled into the study after informed written or oral consent. History with emphasis on clinical presentation and neurological examination were conducted by the authors. The national institutes of health stroke scale (NIHSS) was administered to all enrollees. Ninety-one patients were enrolled for the study, 61 males (63%) and 30 females (37%). There was no significant difference in the mean age (p=0.823). Females were less likely to be formally educated (p=0.024). Females were more likely to be in coma at time of presentation (p=0.003), but there was no significant difference in weakness, facial paralysis, speech or swallowing difficulties, hemianopia, headache and vomiting. Lacunar strokes were more frequent in males (p=0.048). Females were less likely to smoke (p=0.046) or take alcohol (p=0.027). We found 6.67% of the females with eclampsia as the possible cause of stroke. Females had a higher NIHSS on discharge (p=0.047). This finding support gender-related difference in stroke. More research is required to assess gender differences in stroke mortality and morbidity.

Key words: Gender, stroke, risk factor, clinical presentation.

INTRODUCTION

Stroke is a common cause of morbidity and mortality worldwide (Hart et al., 1999). The incidence and mortality for stroke is higher in blacks (Ogun et al., 2005; Wahab et al., 2007; Ottenbacher et al., 2008) and the prevalence is increasing in sub-Saharan Africa (Danesi et al., 2007), due to increasing incidence of hypertension and poor management of cases (Osuntokun et al., 1987). Several studies have shown gender differences in risk factor profile (Di Carlo et al., 2003; Gargano et al., 2008; Holroyd-Leduc et al., 2000; Gall et al., 2010; Reeves et al., 2009; Worrall et al., 2002), and there is now increasing evidence that gender, not only influences stroke presentation and severity (Reid et al., 2008; Petrea et al., 2009), but also the choice and response to therapy (Di Carlo et al., 2003; Smith et al., 2009; Ayala et al., 2002; Kent et al., 2005; Howard et al., 2009; Turtzo and McCullough, 2008).

Studies have shown that females are less likely to be treated with thrombolytics (Gargano et al., 2008; Reeves et al., 2009; Sacco et al., 2009), and it has been recognized that the efficacy of intravenous thrombolysis may be higher in females than males (Sacco et al., 2009). Males have a higher incidence of strokes, but the absolute burden of stroke is greater in females, and is likely to rise (Turtzo and McCullough., 2008; Lewsey et

*Corresponding author. E-mail: watilamusa@yahoo.com. Tel:

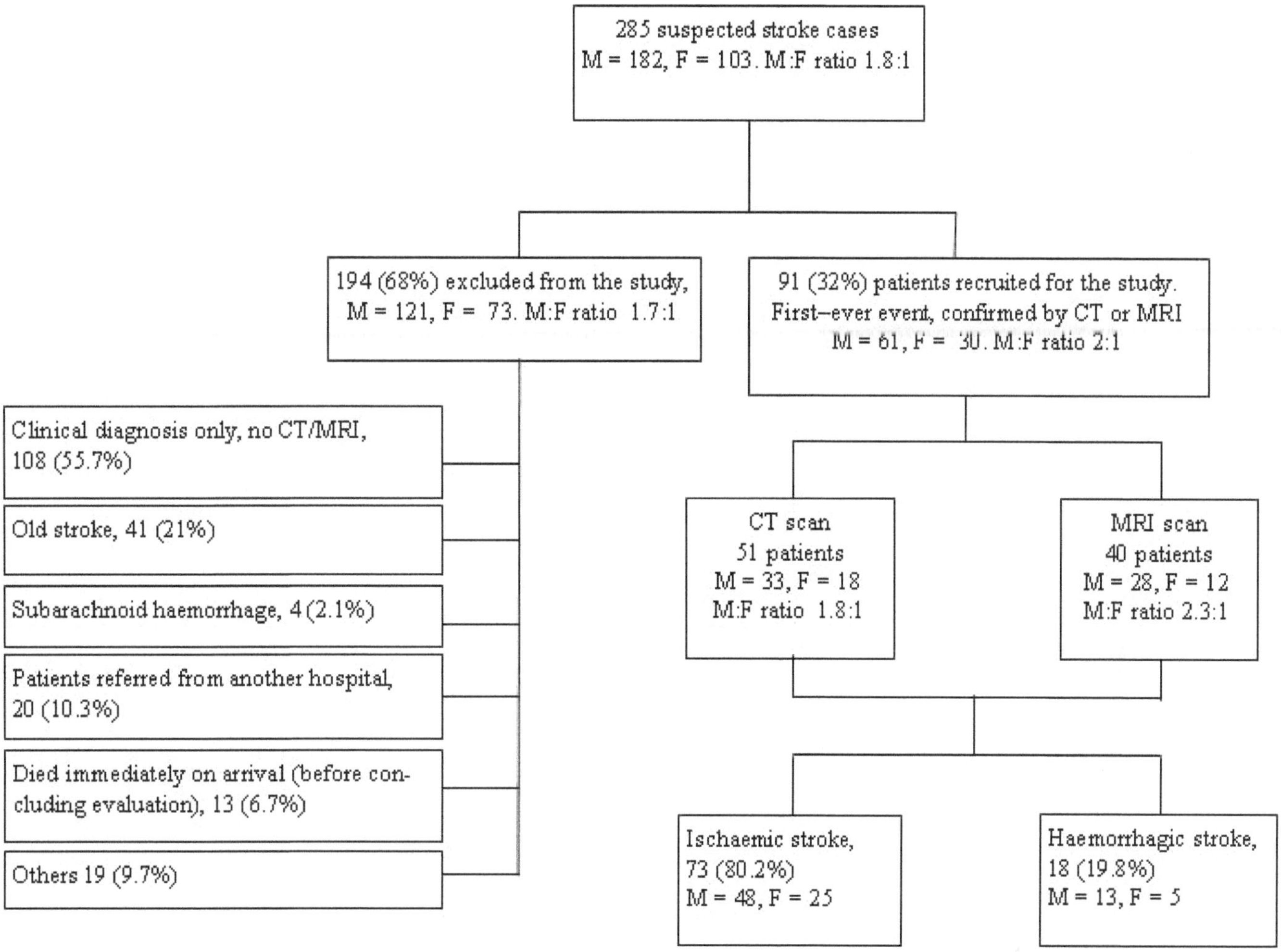

Figure 1. Inclusion and exclusion criteria, diagnosis and type of stroke.

al., 2009). The reasons for the gender differences is multifactorial and a subject for many researches (Turtzo and McCullough, 2008). In resource poor setting like ours, gender related issues in stroke have not been characterized, and appreciation of these differences will help in the management of women with stroke and improve their quality of life (Gargano et al., 2007). Based on the aforementioned observations, we sought to determine gender differences in risk factors and clinical presentation among our patients with acute stroke.

METHODS

The study was conducted at the University of Maiduguri Teaching Hospital (UMTH), a major referral center for North-eastern Nigeria, with about 600 beds. The study was conducted between January 2005 and December 2009. Those recruited for the study are patients with a diagnosis of acute stroke as defined by the WHO criteria (that is, rapidly developing clinical sign of focal and/or global disturbance of cerebral function, with symptoms lasting 24 h or longer or leading to death with no apparent cause other than of vascular origin) (WHO Monica project, 1988) and confirmed by brain computerized tomography (CT) or magnetic resonance imaging (MRI). A written or oral consent was administered to the patients or their next of kin. The consent form was interpreted into the local dialect for those who are not literate. Patients with subarachnoid haemorrhage, subdural haematoma, and past history of stroke were excluded from the study. Those also excluded were suspected stroke patients who had no brain CT or MRI, and those who died within 24 h of admission (Figure 1).

History and examination was conducted and documented in the UMTH stroke proforma which include the following: age, gender, educational level, risk factors such as, hypertension (current blood pressure values 140/95 mmHg or features of long standing hypertension), atrial fibrillation (AF), Transient Ischaemic Attack (TIA), diabetes mellitus (DM), smoking, alcohol consumption and a diagnosis of HIV infection; level of consciousness was evaluated by the Glasgow Coma Scale, a GCS $\leq$ 8 is taken as coma. Weakness, dysphasia, dysathria, hemianopia and swallowing were also assessed. Based on the CT or MRI, patients were grouped into haemorrhagic or ischaemic stroke. Ischaemic stroke subtype was further classified into Total anterior circulation stroke (TACS), Partial anterior circulation stroke (PACS), Posterior circulation stroke (POCS) and Lacunar stroke. Other necessary investigations were done to assess risk factors. The National Institutes of Health

Table 1. Comparison of demographic and clinical characteristics of subjects by sex.

	Females	Males	p-value
Demographic characteristic			
Total	30 (36.55%)	61(63.45%)	0.028*
Mean age	55.57 + 12.417	56.15 + 11.143	0.823
Median age	55 (35-80)	57 (24-80)	
Formal education †	4 (8.8%)	31 (33.18%)	0.024*
Stroke type			
Haemorrhagic	5(16.7%)	13 (21.3%)	0.812
Ischaemic	25 (83.3%)	48 (78.7%)	0.812
Clinical syndrome of Ischaemic stroke			
TACS	8 (32%)	14 (29.17%)	0.975
PACS	15 (60%)	25 (52.08%)	0.624
POCS	1(4%)	2 (4.17%)	1.000
Lacunar	1(4%)	7 (14.58%)	0.048*
Risk profile			
Hypertension	25 (83.33%)	49 (.80.33%)	0.953
Diabetes	2 (6.67%)	3 (4.91%)	1.000
TIA	2 (6.67%)	5 (8.20%)	1.000
Smoking	0 (0.0%)	10 (16.39)	0.046*
Alcohol	1 (3.33%)	15 (24.59%)	0.027*
HIV	1 (3.33%)	3 (4.91%)	1.000
Atrial fibrillation	2 (6.67%)	1(1.64%)	0.523
Antiphospholipid syndrome	1 (3.33%)	0 (0.0%)	0.725
Heart failure	1 (3.33%)	1 (1.64%)	1.000
Eclampsia	2 (6.67%)	-	-

TACS – total anterior circulation stroke, PACS-partial anterior circulation stroke, POCS – posterior circulation stroke, TIA – transient ischaemic attack. *p value ≤ 0.05 from student's t – test; † - have at least a secondary school education (about 12 years of formal education)

Stroke Scale (NIHSS) was used to assess stroke severity on admission and discharge. Duration of hospital stay was recorded only for those who survived till time of discharge. Death within 30 days attributable to the stroke was recorded from date of stroke admission. Student's t-test and the Z-test were used to assess continuous variables. All statistical data were analyzed using SPSS (version 16.1) software.

RESULTS

During the five year period 285 patients had a diagnosis of suspected stroke, 194 patients were excluded from the study as shown in Figure 1. Ninety-one patients were registered for the study. All recruited patients were blacks residing in Nigeria. There were 61 males (67%) and 30 females (33%), M:F ratio was 2:1. mean age 57.5 + 11.0 years for males and 55.3 + 11.0 years for females (p =0.823). Compared to males, females were less likely to be formally educated (at least a secondary school education) compared to males, 8.8% versus 33.2% (p=0.024). Table 1 shows stroke subtypes. There was no statistical difference in stroke subtype; as 25 females (83.3%) compared to 48 males (78.7%) had CT/MRI evidence of infarction (p=0.812), while 5 females (16.7%) compared to 13 males (21.3%) had haemorrhagic stroke (p=0.812). Apart from lacunar stroke that was more likely to occur in males (p=0.048), there was no major difference in clinical syndrome of ischaemic stroke.

Alcohol abuse (p=0.027) and smoking (p=0.046) were more frequent in males. No significant difference was observed for risk factors such as hypertension (p=0.953), diabetes mellitus (p=1.000), TIA (p=1.000), AF (0.523), human immunodeficiency (HIV) virus infection (p=1.000), antiphospholipid syndrome (p=0.725) and heart failure (p=1.000). About 6.7% of our pregnant female patients had eclampsia. Table 2 shows that females were more likely to be in coma compared to males (p=0.003). There was no major difference between gender regarding side of weakness, facial weakness, hemianopia, headache, vomiting, speech and swallowing problems. Males were

Table 2. Clinical state at time of presentation and stroke severity.

	Females	Males	p-value
Clinical state at presentation			
Right hemiparesis	15 (50.0%)	30 (49.2%)	1.000
Left hemiparesis	12 (40.1%)	26 (42.6%)	0.999
Facial weakness	22 (73.3%)	31 (50.8%)	0.068
Coma	9 (30.0%)	3 (4.92%)	0.003*
Headache	6 (20.0%)	10 (16.4%)	0.896
Vomiting	5 (16.7 %)	6 (9.8%)	0.544
Hemianopia	2 (6.7%)	4 (6.6%)	1.000
Aphasia	6 (53.3%)	32 (52.5%)	1.000
Dysarthria	4 (13.3%)	4 (6.6%)	0.505
Dysphagia	4 (13.3%)	8 (13.1%)	1.000
Mean SBP	148.47 + 29.143	158.10 + 37.941	0.225
min-max	(110-220)	(90-250)	
Mean DBP	90.47 + 18.320	100.05 + 22.631	0.047*
min-max	(60-130)	(40-150)	
Mean Random blood sugar (mmol/L)	6.274 + 2.4882	6.104 + 2.6922	0.772
Stroke severity			
NIHSS			
Admission	18.17 + 7.649	15.02+ 7.327	0.061
Discharge	16.96 + 15.961	10.86 + 12.310	0.047*
Duration of in-hospital stay	43.00 ± 33.1days	33.92 ± 27.3days	0.168
30-Day fatality	9(30.0%)	9(14.75%)	0.175

SBP – systolic blood pressure, DBP – diastolic blood pressure. NIHSS – national institutes of health stroke scale.
*p value $\leq$ 0.05 from student's t – test.

Table 3. Summary of significant differences.

Females>Males	Males>Females
Less likely to be Educated	Lacunar strokes
Coma on admission	Smoking
Higher NIHSS score on discharge	Alcohol
	Higher diastolic BP

NIHSS – National Institutes of Health Stroke Scale.

more likely to have a higher diastolic blood pressure (DBP) at presentation (p=0.047). There was no gender difference in mean admission random blood sugar (p=0.772). Compared to males, females had more severe stroke on discharge (NIHSS, p=0.047). There was no significant difference in duration of hospital stay, or 30-day case fatality. Summary of significant differences is shown in Table 3.

DISCUSSION AND CONCLUSION

This is the first study in Northeastern Nigeria to examine gender differences in stroke. The main findings in this study show that, females were slightly younger than males. Females were less likely to be educated, engage in smoking or consume alcohol. Females were more likely to be in coma, and have severe stroke on discharge. Our study showed no gender difference in other risk factors. Reports elsewhere have clearly shown significant differences in risk factors, hypertension is commoner in females in several studies ((Di Carlo et al., 2003; Gargano et al., 2008; Gall et al., 2010; Reeves et al., 2009; Worrall et al., 2002), but it is not universal (Hart et al., 1999). Atrial fibrillation (AF) is also commoner in females (Di Carlo et al., 2003; Gargano et al., 2008; Holroyd-Leduc et al., 2000). Males were more likely to have DM and heart disease (Holroyd-Leduc et al., 2000; Gall et al., 2010). We reported a higher mean diastolic blood pressure in males, despite the high prevalence of eclampsia in females; likely explanations may be that patients with eclampsia were more likely to receive aggressive antihypertensive treatment early on admission (Conde-Agudelo and Kafury-Goeta, 1998). The higher DBP may as well be due to the younger age of our patients, as males have a higher prevalence of hypertension at a much lower age (Andersen et al., 2010).

Our study shows that the proportion of our patients with DM and AF is low; this low prevalence is in conformity with a study in Mozambique (Damasceno et al., 2010). A study by Hajat et al. (2001) showed that blacks appear to suffer less from DM and AF. Recently, AF seem to be reducing in whites due to improved treatment of high blood pressure and use of anticoagulants (Lakshminarayan, 2006). We observed that alcohol consumption and smoking is commoner in males and is in accordance with the findings in other studies ((Di Carlo et al., 2003; Gargano et al., 2008; Gall et al., 2010; Worrall et al., 2002). Females in our environment are less likely to indulge in some of these social habits, as it is considered culturally unacceptable. Eclampsia is a unique risk factor in females and an important medical condition in sub-Saharan Africa because of poor maternal health care. Eclampsia is complicated by stroke in about 4.9% of patients ((Conde-Agudelo and Kafury-Goeta, 1998). With improved maternal health care the incidence of eclampsia could significantly reduce (Audu et al., 2002). Studies have reported that females were older, since they were more likely to survive into old age than males, an age where strokes are common (Smith et al., 2009; Stuart-Shor et al., 2009; Förster et al., 2009), but studies in Nigeria have reported a lower mean age for stroke both in males and females (Wahab et al., 2007; Bwala, 1989). After the age of 65 years, the prevalence of hypertension increases in females and levels of in males after that age (Andersen et al., 2010). The lower age of females in this study (though not statistically significant) should be interpreted with caution; unlike other studies where females were significantly older than males, it will be difficult to draw such conclusion in this study owing to the smaller number of female participants, lower life expectancy, high maternal mortality, and living in a community where females are less likely to seek medical attention due to socioeconomic reasons (Osuntokun et al., 1987; Kapral et al., 2002).

Our report shows that females were less formally educated and this may have a significant influence on stroke presentation in females. Level of education may affect employment and income, and this may invariably affect drug compliance and quality of care (Di Carlo et al., 2003). The study by Worral et al. (2002) showed that, females had a lower household income and thus influencing stroke presentation and care. This study showed that males were more likely to have lacunar strokes. Studies have reported that POCS is commoner in males and TACS was more common in females (Petrea et al., 2009; Smith et al., 2009). The explanation given was that, AF is commoner in females and hence a higher embolic phenomena (Howard et al., 2009), this may explain why females are more likely to have anterior circulation stroke. A different study by Förster et al. (2009) reported that, small embolic and lacunar stroke was commoner in males. AF is commoner in older females, but the females in our study are younger, and so we are not likely to get similar findings as aforestated.

Our study showed that females were more likely to be in coma at presentation compared to males; this is in keeping with other studies (Di Carlo et al., 2003; Gall et al., 2010). A study by Lisabeth et al. (2009) showed that, women were more likely to have a change in level of consciousness and may be attributable to; stroke severity, delays in seeking care, delays in prompt diagnosis and differences in access to acute stroke therapy. This study did not show any difference in clinical conditions such as headache, vomiting, speech and swallowing difficulties, and is congruent with other studies (Stuart-Shor et al., 2009; Barrett et al., 2007). Di Carlo et al. (2003) reported that, these symptoms were more in females since they were more likely to be in coma. In our study, females were more likely to have a higher NIHSS on discharge compared to males; a possible reason may be due to higher number of lacunar strokes occuring in males. Those with non-lacunar stroke are more likely to have a worse stroke and higher fatality rate compared to those with lacunar stroke (Sacco et al., 2006). Several studies indicate that females were more likely to have a severe stroke on admission and have worse outcomes after stroke (Lewsey et al., 2009; Shobha et al., 2010; Hill et al., 2006). Other reports have shown no difference in stroke severity (Petrea et al., 2009; Förster et al., 2009; Jongbloed, 1986). We reported no gender difference in the duration of hospital admission; this is in agreement with a study by Zhu et al. (2009).

Our study shows no gender difference in fatality, this is in keeping with some studies (Di Carlo et al., 2003; Forster et al., 2009), while other studies reported a higher mortality (Gall et al., 2010; Reeves et al., 2009). The difference in quality of care, increasing age and higher stroke severity were the explanation given for a higher mortality in females. Several studies have shown that gender influences response to therapy (Smith et al., 2009; Ayala et al., 2002; Kent et al., 2005; Howard et al., 2009; Turtzo and McCullough, 2008). A study by Sacco et al. (2009) showed that, primary prevention of stroke with aspirin was effective in females than males, as well as response to thrombolytics. Some of the limitations of our study include, a smaller sample size compared to other similar studies. This study did not take into account the effect of stroke treatment, especially gender differences in the use of thrombolytic agents for stroke treatment. We also did not assess long-term outcome. The absence of data on blood lipids is another limitation in this study.

In conclusion, we found that gender differences exist in our stroke patients. Females were more likely to be unconscious and have a worse stroke on discharge. They were less likely to be educated. Men were more likely to have lacunar stroke, and more likely to smoke and consume alcohol. These gender differences in risk profile should influence risk stratification and treatment. Our environment is a resource poor setting, it will be important to educate the populace on prevention of stroke.

REFERENCES

Andersen KK, Andersen ZJ, Olsen TS (2010) Age- and Gender-Specific Prevalence of Cardiovascular Risk Factors in 40 102 Patients With First-Ever Ischemic Stroke. A Nationwide Danish Study. Stroke, 41: 2768-2774.

Audu BM, Obed JY, Kyari O (2002). Review of factors predisposing to eclampsia and outcome. Trop. J. Obstetr. Gynaecol., 19: 23.

Ayala C, Croft JB, Greenlund KJ, Keenan NL, Donehoo RS, Malarcher AM, Mensah GA (2002). Sex Differences in US Mortality Rates for Stroke and Stroke Subtypes by Race/Ethnicity and Age, 1995-1998. Stroke, 33: 1197-1201.

Barrett KM, Brott TG, Brown RD Jr, Frankel MR, Worrall BB, Silliman SL (2007). Sex Differences in Stroke Severity, Symptoms, and Deficits after First-Ever Ischemic Stroke. J. Stroke Cerebrovasc. Dis., 16: 34-39.

Bwala SA (1989). Stroke in sub-Saharan Nigerian hospital: A retrospective study. Trop. Doctor, 19: 11-14.

Conde-Agudelo A, Kafury-Goeta AC (1998). Epidemiology of eclampsia in Colombia. Int. J. Gynaecol. Obstet., 61: 1-8.

Damasceno A, Gomes J, Azevedo A, Carrilho C, LoboV, Lopes H, Madede T, Pravinrai P, Silva-Matos C, Jalla S, Stewart S, Lunet N (2010). An Epidemiological Study of Stroke Hospitalizations in Maputo, Mozambique. High Burden of Disease in a Resource-Poor Country. Stroke, 41: 2463-2469.

Danesi M, Okubadejo N, Ojini F (2007). Prevalence of stroke in an urban mixed income community in Lagos, Nigeria. Neuroepidemiology, 28: 216- 223.

Di Carlo A, Lamassa M, Baldereschi M, Pracucci G, Basile AM, Wolfe CDA, Giroud M, Rudd A, Ghetti A, Inzitari D (2003). Outcome of Acute Stroke in Europe: Data from a Multicenter Multinational Sex Differences in the Clinical Presentation, Resource Use, and 3-Month Hospital-Based Registry. Stroke, 34: 1114-1119.

Förster A, Gass A, Kern R, Wolf ME, Ottomeyer C, Zohsel K, Hennerici M, Szabo K (2009). Gender Differences in Acute Ischemic Stroke: Etiology, Stroke Patterns and Response to Thrombolysis. Stroke, 40: 2428-2432.

Gall SL, DonnanG, Dewey HM, Macdonell R, Sturm J, Gilligan A, Srikanth V, Thrift AG (2010). Sex differences in presentation, severity, and management of stroke in a population-based study. Neurology, 74: 975-981

Gargano JW, Reeves MJ and for the Paul Coverdell National Acute Stroke Registry Michigan Prototype Investigators (2007). Sex Differences in Stroke Recovery and Stroke-Specific Quality of Life: Results From a Statewide Stroke Registry. Stroke, 38: 2541-2548.

Gargano JW, Wehner S, Reeves M (2008). Sex Differences in Acute Stroke Care in a Statewide Stroke Registry. Stroke, 39: 24-29.

Hajat C, Dundas R, Stewart JA, Lawrence E, Rudd AG, Howard R, Wolfe CDA (2001). Cerebrovascular Risk Factors and Stroke Subtypes Differences between Ethnic Groups. Stroke, 32: 37-42.

Hart CL, Hole DJ, Smith GD (1999). Risk factors and 20-year stroke mortality in men and women in the Renfrew/Paisley study in Scotland. Stroke, 30: 1999-2007.

Hill MD, Kent DM, Hinchey JA, RowleyH, Buchan MA, Wechsler LR, Higashida RT, Fischbein NJ, Dillon WP, Gent M, Firszt CM, Schulz GA, Furlan AJ (2006). On behalf of the PROACT-2 investigators. Sex based differences in the effect of intraarterial treatment of stroke. Analysis of the PROACT – 2 study. Stroke, 37: 2322-2325.

Holroyd-Leduc JM, Kapral MK, Austin PC, TuSex JV (2000). Differences and Similarities in the Management and Outcome of Stroke patients. Stroke, 31: 1833-1837.

Howard VJ, Voeks JH, Lutsep HL, Mackey A, Milot G, Sam AD II, Tom M, Hughes SE, Sheffet AJ, Longbottom M, Avery JB, Hobson RW II, Brott TG (2009). Does Sex Matter? Thirty-Day Stroke and Death Rates after Carotid Artery Stenting in Women Versus Men: Results From the Carotid Revascularization Endarterectomy Versus Stenting Trial (CREST) Lead-in Phase. Stroke, 40: 1140-1147.

Jongbloed L (1986). Prediction of function after stroke: a critical review. Stroke, 17: 765-776.

Kapral MK, Wang H, Mamdani M, Tu JV (2002). Effect of socioeconomic status on treatment and mortality after stroke. Stroke, 33: 268-275.

Kent DM, Price LL, Ringleb P, Hill MD, Selker HP (2005). Sex-based differences in response to recombinant tissue plasminogen activator in acute ischemic stroke: a pooled analysis of randomized clinical trials. Stroke, 36: 62-65.

Lakshminarayan K, Solid CA, Collins AJ, Anderson DC, Herzog CA (2006). Atrial fibrillation and stroke in the general Medicare population: a 10 year perspective (1992–2002). Stroke, 37: 1969-1974.

Lewsey JD, Gillies M, Jhund PS, Chalmers JWT, Redpath A, Briggs A, Walters M, Langhorne P, Capewell S, McMurray JJV, MacIntyre K (2009). Sex Differences in Incidence, Mortality, and Survival in Individuals With Stroke in Scotland, 1986 to 2005. Stroke, 40: 1038-1043.

Lisabeth LD, Brown DL, Hughes R, Majersik JJ, Morgenstern LB (2009). Acute Stroke Symptoms. Comparing Women and Men Stroke, 40: 2031-2036.

Ogun SA, Ojini FI, Ogungbo B, Kolapo KO, Danesi MA (2005). Stroke in South West Nigeria. A 10-year review. Stroke, 36: 1120-1122.

Osuntokun BO, Adeuja AOG, Schoeber BS, Bademosi O, Nottidge VA, Olumide AO, Ige O, Yaria F, Bolis CL (1987). Neurological disorders in Nigerian Africans; a community based study. Acta Neurol. Scand., 75: 13-21.

Ottenbacher KJ, Campbell J, Kuo Y-F, Deutch A, Ostir GV, Granger CV (2008). Racial and Ethnic Differences in Postacute Rehabilitation Outcomes after Stroke in the United States. Stroke, 39: 1514-1519.

Petrea RE, Beiser, AS, Seshadri S, Kelly-Hayes M, Kase CS, Wolf PA (2009). Gender Differences in Stroke Incidence and Poststroke Disability in the Framingham Heart Study. Stroke, 40: 1032-1037.

Reeves MJ, Fonarow GC, Zhao X, Smith EE, Schwamm LH (2009). Quality of Care in Women with Ischemic Stroke in the GWTG Program. Stroke, 40: 1127-1133.

Reid JM, Dai D, Gubitz GJ, Kapral MK, Christian C, Phillips SJ (2008). Gender Differences in Stroke Examined in a 10-Year Cohort of Patients Admitted to a Canadian Teaching Hospital. Stroke, 39: 1090-1095.

Sacco S, Cerone D, Carolei A (2009). Gender and stroke: acute phase treatment and prevention. Jan-Mar; Funct. Neurol., 24(1): 45-52.

Sacco S, Marini C, Totaro R, Russo T, Cerone D, Carolei A (2006). A population-based study of the incidence and prognosis of lacunar stroke. Neurology. May 9, 66(9): 1335-1338.

Shobha N, Sylaja PN, Kapral MK, Fang J, Hill MD (2010). Differences in stroke outcome based on sex. Neurology, 74: 767-771.

Smith DB, Murphy P, Santos P, Phillips M, Wilde M (2009). Gender Differences in the Colorado Stroke Registry. Stroke, 40: 1078-1081.

Stuart-Shor EM, Wellenius GA, Dellolacono DM, Mittleman MA (2009). Gender Differences in Presenting and Prodromal Stroke Symptoms. Stroke, 40: 1121-1126.

Turtzo LC, McCullough LD (2008). Sex Differences in Stroke. Cerebrovasc Dis., 26: 462-474.

Wahab KW, Sani MU, Samaila AA, Gbadamosi A, Olokoba AB (2007). Stroke at a tertiary medical institution in Northern Nigeria: Patient's profile and predictors of outcome. Sahel Med. J., 10: 6-10.

WHO Monica project, Principal investigators (1988). The World Health Organization Monica project (monitoring trends and determinants in cardiovascular disease) a major international collaboration. J. Clin. Epid., 41: 105-114.

Worrall BB, Johnston KC, Kongable G, Hung E, Richardson D, Gorelick PB (2002). Stroke Risk Factor Profiles in African American Women. An Interim Report from the African-American Antiplatelet Stroke Prevention Study. Stroke, 33: 913-919.

Zhu HF, Newcommon NN, Cooper ME, Green TL, Seal B, Klein G, Weir NU, Coutts SB, Watson T, Barber PA, Demchuk AM, Hill MD (2009). Impact of a Stroke Unit on Length of Hospital Stay and In-Hospital Case Fatality. Stroke, 40: 18-23.

Lead toxicity and some subsets of motor skill: Comparative evaluation of adult and prenatally exposed rats

P. D. Shallie[1]*, A. K. Adefule[1], H. B. Akpan[1], O. O. Olubiyi[2], P. B. Fakunle[3] and E. N. Adejumo[4]

[1]Department of Anatomy, Obafemi Awolowo College of Health Sciences Olabisi Onabanjo University, Ago-Iwoye, Ogun State, Nigeria.
[2]Department of Biochemistry, Obafemi Awolowo College of Health Sciences, Olabisi Onabanjo University, Ago-Iwoye. Ogun State, Nigeria.
[3]Department of Anatomy, Ladoke Akintola University, Ogbomosho, Oyo State, Nigeria.
[4]Department of Chemical Pathology, Obafemi Awolowo College of Health Sciences, Olabisi Onabanjo University, Ago-Iwoye, Ogun State, Nigeria.

Research has shown that even low levels of lead (Pb) exposure are dangerous. Thus, Pb exposure/toxicity continues to be a leading environmental health issue for children and women of childbearing age. A variety of toxic effects caused by Pb exposure during gestation and early childhood have been reported in both human and animal studies. Adult wistar rats of both sexes were used for this study. They were housed in individual improvised cages and were given food and water *ad libitum*. The animal room temperature was maintained at approximately 27°C with a 12 light/dark cycle. After the period of acclimatization, adult rats were randomly assigned into four groups of eight rats each (4 males and 4 females) viz; Adult exposed and control; prenatally exposed and control. The adult and prenatally groups received 2n mM lead acetate solution as sole drinking fluid for the duration of the experiment. The study showed significant ($p \leq 0.05$) results in pups negative geotaxis and cliff avoidance and sex by measure interaction response to weight changes in the adult groups, while the adult negative geotaxis, cliff avoidance, pups' righting reflex showed no significant value($p \geq 0.05$). The lead exposed group hastens the eruption of upper incisors and eye opening and delayed the ear unfolding. The present results suggest that the prenatal exposure to Pb, influences the rate of physical maturation and sensory motor reflexes in pups.

Key words: Lead acetate, toxicity, physical maturation, motor reflexes, anomalies.

INTRODUCTION

Research has shown that even low levels of lead (Pb) exposure are dangerous (Silergeld, 1990). Thus, Pb exposure/toxicity continues to be a leading environmental health issue for children and women of childbearing age (Mushak, 1992). A variety of toxic effects caused by Pb exposure during gestation and early childhood have been reported in both human and animal studies. Many neurological and behavioral anomalies have been attributed to pre- and post-natal Pb exposure, such as aggressiveness, decreased IQ, learning disabilities, hyperactivity, and impulsiveness, as well as aberrant neuromotor coordination function (Kishi et al., 1983; Needleman, 1987, 1993). In both humans and experimental animals, Pb readily crosses the placental-fetal barrier (Donald et al., 1986; Goyer, 1990; Lataillade et al., 1995), causing a direct relation between the Pb exposed mother and the possibility of irreversible developmental damage to her offspring.

Keller and Doherty (1980) reported that Pb-exposed mouse dams transmitted a significantly greater amount of Pb to their offspring through their milk than by *in utero*

*Corresponding author. Email: Shallie.philemon@yahoo.com.

exposure (transplacentally). Earlier studies in humans and experimental animals have shown that not only does Pb accumulate in the fetus from the second trimester onwards (Bhattacharayya, 1983), but during lactation, it is excreted into the milk, which continues the risk to nursing offspring (Namihira et al., 1993; Hallen et al., 1995a; b; 1996). The detrimental effects of Pb occur regardless of the developmental time exposure, although gestational exposure appears more sensitive to the Pb effects (Dearth et al., 2002). The developmental toxicity of lead has become a significant area of research since children are more sensitive than adults to learning impairment following low-level lead exposure (Davis and Svendsgaard, 1987). Regarding this point, animal and human studies have reached similar results, since behavioral effects induced by lead are seen in rats at approximately the same blood levels that cause deficits in humans (Davis et al., 1990; Annau, 1990; Needleman et al., 1990).

Administration of diets with a high lead content to rodents during suckling causes growth impairment, hema-tological alterations, breakdown of the blood-brain barrier, and higher pup mortality (McClain and Becker, 1972; Rosenblum and Johnson, 1968). Moreover, significant effects on neuromotor development of rats have also been described. Reiter and colleagues (Reiter et al., 1975) reported delay in development of righting reflex and eye opening in animals exposed to lead acetate in the drinking water through gestation and lactation. These data were confirmed by Luthman and colleagues (Luthman et al., 1992), who described delayed eye opening and impairment in negative geotaxis However, a statistically significant effect of lead treatment on body weight was evidenced in these studies. Since it is well known that undernutrition is causally related to neurobehavioral development retardation (Smart and Dobbing, 1971), it becomes difficult to attribute these deficits solely to lead exposure. Studies using milder forms of lead intoxication have revealed no differences in weight gain, but significant effects on adult rat behavior (Rodrigues et al., 1993; 1996). Therefore, in the present study we comparatively evaluated the effects of chronic lead exposure on adult and prenatal rats starting from day one of gestation to post natal day 30 on body weight and some subset of motor skills and physical maturation.

MATERIALS AND METHODS

Animal care

Adult wistar rats of both sexes were obtained from animal holding of the department of Anatomy, Olabisi Onabanjo University, and Remo campus, Ikenne, Ogun State, Nigeria. They were housed in individual standard cages. They were given food and water *ad libitum*. The animal room was maintained at approximately 22°C with relative humidity of between 40 - 60% a 12 h off light/dark cycle was maintained. The animal beddings were changed thrice weekly. The present study was approved by the Animal Ethics Committee of the Faculty of Basic Medical Sciences of the University in line with the National Animal Care Standard Operating Procedures.

Feed composition

Rats pellets was purchased from Grand Cereals and Oil mills limited depot, was given to the rat throughout the period of experiment *ad libitum*. The feed composition includes; crude protein - 14.50%, fat -7.00%, crude fibre - 7.20%, calcium - 0.80%, available phosphorus - 0.40%

Experimental design and duration

After the period of acclimatization, adult rats were randomly assigned into four groups of eight rats each (4 males and 4 females) viz; Adult exposed and control; prenatally exposed and control. The adult and prenatally groups received 2mM lead acetate solution as sole drinking fluid. The adult rats were exposed for a period of 4weeks. Prenatally rats were exposed rats were placed 1 male to 2 females in a cage containing wood shavings which was regularly replaced. After the confirmation of pregnancy they were separated into individual cages for a period of 21 - 22 days (gestation period). Reflex tests and observations of the maturation of physical characteristics (The date of appearance of ear unfolding, eruption of upper incisors and eye opening) were carried out daily at the appropriate ages by one experimenter that was not aware of the subject treatment in accordance with previous criteria (Kruck and Pycock, 1979; Lee, 1980; Kellog et al., 1980; Jett and Guilarte, 1995; Soufir, 1995. Testing was carried out between 9:00 and 11:00 am, and progress of the same individuals from each litter was followed throughout the experiment. Animals in the adult group were weighed every 3 days while Cliff avoidance was carried out every 5 days and Negative geotaxis every 3 days. Pups from this group were subjected to reflex analysis, observation of behavioral pattern and physical parameters at appropriate ages within 30 days of birth. These include body weight at postnatal day 0, 5, 10, 15, 20, 25, 30. Date of appearance of ear unfolding, eruption of upper incisors and eye opening was also observed. Reflexes assessed include Cliff avoidance, equilibration on 2 L beaker, Negative geotaxis and righting reflex

Sample collection and chemical analysis

After 4 weeks of administration, adult rats were deeply anaesthetized, while the Pups were sacrificed after postnatal day 30. Brain was dissected out and 5 g weight and 5 mm thick section of the prefrontal taken and homogenized. This was used for neurotransmitters assessment.

Reflex analyses

The reflex analyses assessed in the adult group are cliff avoidance every 5days, negative geotaxis every 3 days. Reflex analyses for the pups were taken at appropriate ages such as

(i) Righting reflex: Postnatal day 1 - 5
(ii) Equilibration on beaker rim: Postnatal day 19

Righting reflex

This was assessed by measuring the time required for the animal to turn ventrally after being placed in a dorsal position from postnatal day 1 - 5.

Table 1. Physical parameters evaluated with dates or percentage. Values shown are the group of mean ± SEM (n=5).

Variable	Control	Exposed
Percentage of stillbirth	0	16.13
Percentage of unilateral Amelia in pups	0	3.23
Date of eye opening	Postnatal day 17	Postnatal day 13
Date of ear unfolding	Postnatal day 3	Postnatal day 4
Date of eruption of upper incisors	Postnatal day 10	Postnatal day 8
Balance and movement along beaker rim	10.29% fell	18% fell
Lead serum level	19.60 ± 2.93	40.00 ± 2.86

Cliff avoidance

This was assessed by placing the animal on the edge of a bench with nose and forepaws just over the edge and the number of times the animal moves away in 3 consecutive 30 s trial recorded.

Negative geotaxis

This was measured by placing the rat on a slope with the head downward and scored 0, 1, 2, 3, and 4, if it turns to face up the slope 0, 45, 90, 135 and 180°, respectively, in a 90 s session while that of the adult treated group was measured by the time required for the animal to turn 180° that is, to hold the tail in a 30 s trial.

Equilibration on beaker rim

This was assessed by measuring the ability of the rat to balance on a 2 L beaker. Latency to escape the from the rim and percent of animals that fell from the rim was recorded

Statistical analysis

The statistical analysis were carried out by student't' test, $p \leq 0.05$ was considered significant. All the values are reported as Mean ± SEM. The diagrams were drawn using Microsoft excel 2007 version.

RESULTS

The average water consumption in the control group was 16 mls per day while the fluid consumed by the treated groups was 12 mls. Table 1 shows the developmental observations of the control and exposed groups. It follows that the mean number of pups at birth is not significantly ($p \geq 0.05$) different between the control and the treated, likewise the weight of pups from postnatal day 0 - 30. Other developmental observations include unilateral amelia in some exposed pups, hasten eye opening, eruption of upper incisors and delayed ear unfolding. Balance and movement along beaker rim also reveal a more coordinated movement among the pups of the control rat compared to the Pups from exposed group. Figure 1 reveals significant ($p < 0.05$) increase in weight in the male as compared to the female adult rats, while Figure 2 shows steady increase in weight between the control and exposed pups although not significant ($p \geq 0.05$).

The negative geotaxis in adult and pups are presented in Figure 3 and 4. The mean adult values between the control and the exposed was not significant ($p \geq 0.05$), while the mean values between the control and the exposed pups was significant ($p < 0.05$). Figure 5 and 6 presented significant ($p < 0.05$) percentage differential value between the control and exposed groups, in both the adult and pups that score 3 out of 3 in cliff avoidance test. The mean righting reflex values between the control and exposed pups are presented in Figure 7. Lead exposure increased the time for righting reflex when compared to the control. The mean level of acetylcholine was significantly ($p < 0.05$) reduced in the exposed group (Figure 8).

DISCUSSION

Administration of lead led to higher pup mortality in the present study, this observation is in agreement with previous studies Rosenblum et al., 1968; McClain et al., 1972 and as a result suggested a deleterious role of lead on developing embryo. Lead was also observed to be a teratogenic agent in the present study characterized by unilateral Amelia of the forelimb in the prenatally exposed pups of lead treated rats. Previous study reported congenital anomalies, such as failure of the ventral body wall to close along the midline and leg dysfunction, were observed in treated chicks (Yara et al., 2007). Lead treatment did not affect the number of living pups and body weight of adult and prenatally exposed pups at birth and weight gain, These results are consistent with previous research proving that no gross differential body weight difference in adults` rates in normal physiological state (Salinas and Huff, 2002; Cory-Slechta et al., 1989) or during pregnancy and suckling (Trombini et al., 2001). This implies that there is a balance between caloric intake and utilization of caloric in both groups (Figure 2). A significant sex by measure interaction response to weight changes was observed among the individual sexes (Figure 1) which supports previous research by

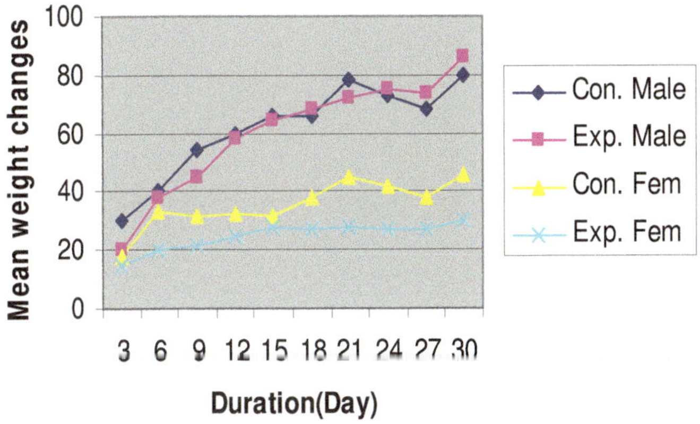

Figure 1. Mean weight changes in adult individual sexes. Values shown are the group of mean ± SEM (n = 5) $p \leq 0.05$ between the male and the female and $p \geq 0.05$ among the individual sexes.

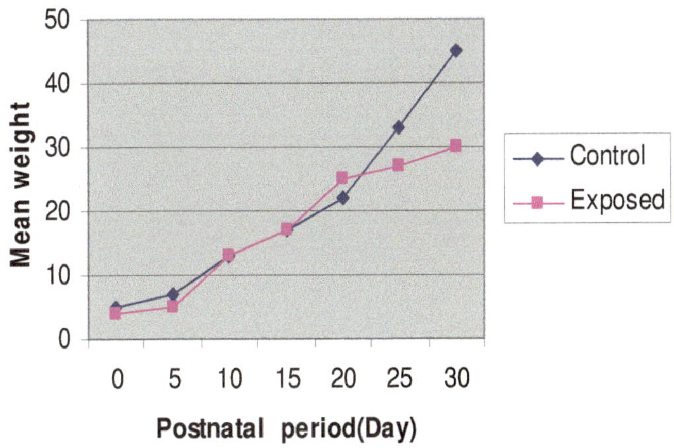

Figure 2. Mean weight of pups. Values shown are the group of mean ± SEM (n = 5) $p \geq 0.05$ between control and the exposed.

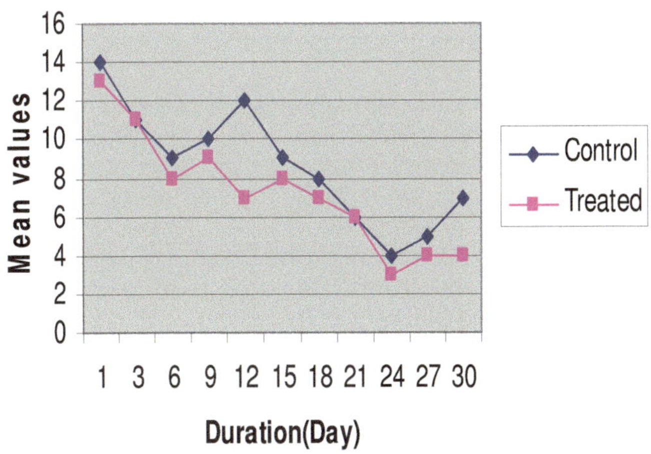

Figure 3. Mean negative geotaxis in adult Wistar rats. Values shown are the group of mean ± SEM (n = 5) $p \geq 0.05$ between the control and the treated.

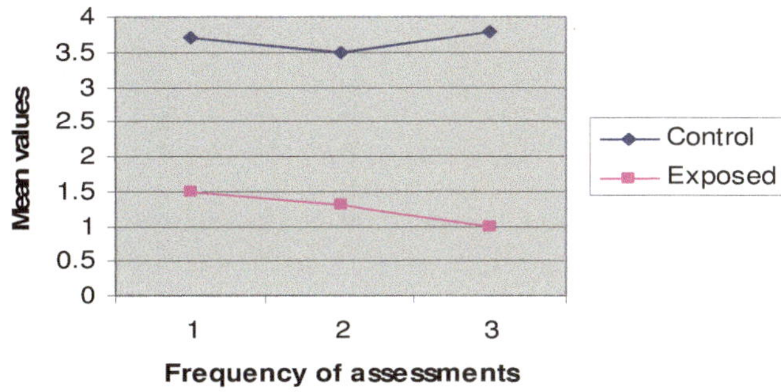

Figure 4. Mean negative geotaxis score in pups. Values shown are the group of mean ± SEM (n = 5) $p \geq 0.05$ between the control and exposed.

Mello et al., 1998 that males exhibit a higher weight gain curve compared to females therefore this method of lead intoxication does not affect weight gain, Rodrigues et al., 1993; Rodrigues et al., 1996. The differences in response to weight gain suggest that under the same environmental condition, males exhibit a significantly higher response to weight changes. The present results suggest that the prenatal exposure to Pb, influences the rate of physical maturation, sensory motor reflexes of the pups at different developmental stages. Abnormalities in response to teratogens may be due to several factors that causes alterations in normal cell metabolism, especially in enzymes and their substrates (Wilson, 1973), or due to combination of several factors (Coyle et al., 1976).

The motor reflexes evaluated in this study show significant decline in the mean values in pup's negative geotaxis, cliff avoidance and righting reflex while the adult values were insignificant (Figure 3 - 7). These results show that lead toxicity results in hypoactivity, which has been associated with lead intoxication in rats during the early postnatal period, resulting transient as well as persistent dysfunctions in exploratory behavior and motor skills. These observed actions of lead may be related to impaired maturation of sensitive brain regions which develop postnatally (Johan et al., 1992). Lead was reported to induce important deficits on motor behavior of chicks during the first postnatal week and such phenomena are related to lead deposition in the cerebellar tissue during embryonic development (Yara et al., 2007). Implicated in behavior process is ACh (Allikmets, 1974). Changes in the behavior due to toxicants are presumably due to alterations in the availability of neurotransmitters (Kruck and Pycok, 1979; Kellog et al., 1980; Lee, 1980). It is known that a major portion of brain cells (70%) of the closely related rats are formed after birth (Patel, 1983).

In this study a significant ($p < 0.05$) reduction in the level of ACh was detected in all lead exposed pups (Figure 8). This could possibly explain why the sensory motor reflexes of Pb exposed pups were compromised. Thus, lead could have produced developmental abnormalities in the brain as well as an alteration in the level

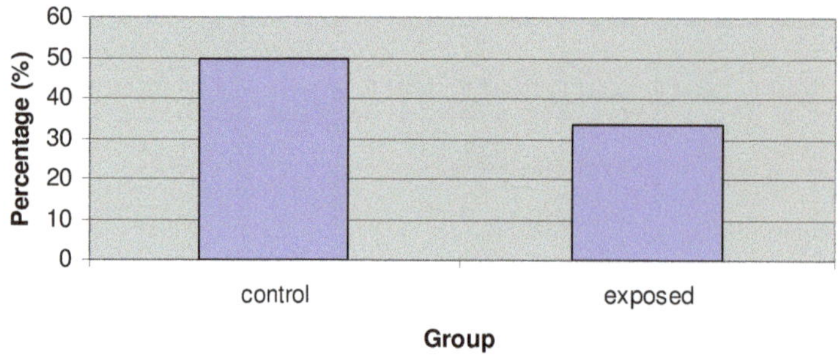

Figure 5. Percentage of adult rats that score 3 out of 3 during cliff avoidance. Values shown are the group of mean ± SEM (n = 5) $p \leq 0.05$ between the control and the exposed.

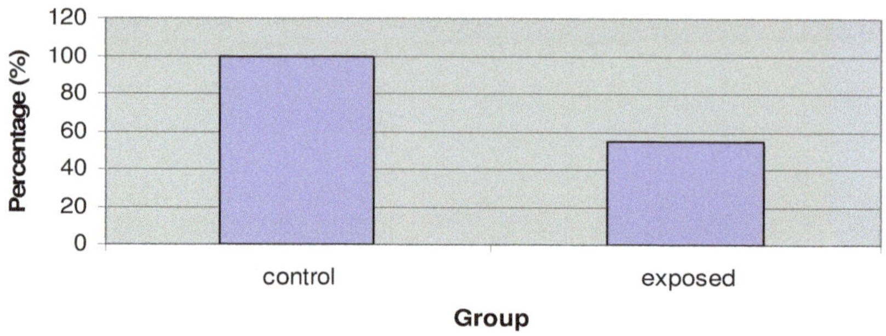

Figure 6. Percentage of pups that score 3 out of 3 during cliff avoidance. Values shown are the group of mean ± SEM (n = 5) $p \leq 0.05$ between the control and the exposed.

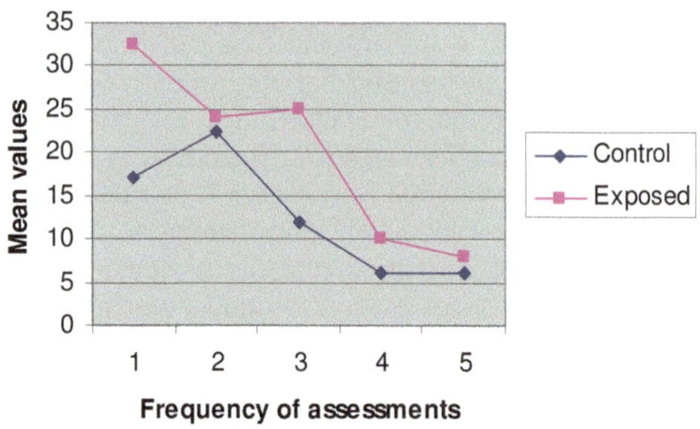

Figure 7. Mean righting reflex score in pups. Values shown are the group of mean ± SEM (n = 5) $p \leq 0.05$ between the control and the exposed.

level of ACh that might have brought about the observed effects on the motor reflexes of the developing pups in the present study. It has been reported that alterations in brain enzymes are among the factors responsible for disturbances in behavioral activities of affected animals (Branchey and Friedhoff, 1976; Kellog et al., 1980; Johnson et al., 1981; Ajarem and Ahmad, 1991). Analysis of other physical development parameters in the current study revealed that lead-treated animals presented accelerated eye opening, as also observed by Mello et al., 1998 and in animals subjected to prenatal methylmercury exposure without concomitant undernutrition (Vorhees, 1985), indicating a teratogenic role for lead acetate. The eruption of upper incisors appeared earlier in lead treated animals, while the appearance of ear unfolding was delayed. In contrast to the study, some previous studies (Reiter et al., 1975; Luthman et al., 1992; Mello et al., 1998) reported either a delayed or no difference between groups as regards eye opening in rats exposed to lead.

The present results strongly suggest that lead exposure *in utero* and via mother's milk tend to produced severe effect as compared to adult exposure. Lead produces it deleterious effects probably by causing oxidative stress which ultimately alters the cellular processes. Such effects might be affecting the overall morphological developments and sensory motor reflexes of the developing pups, and behavior of the young adult offspring. In conclusion, the present study demonstrated that lead acetate intoxication caused significant alterations in the development of rats. The majority of the observed alterations pointed to an advance in the day of appearance in physical maturation and decline in some reflexes, Therefore, the lead-induced developmental alterations in rats observed here are important in terms of searching for

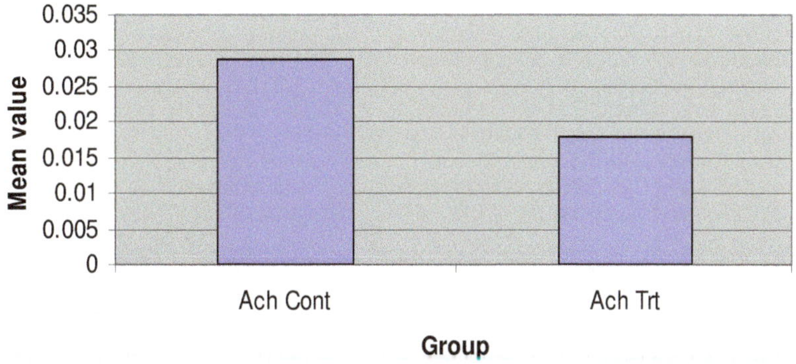

Figure 8. Mean value of a acetylcholine in the prefrontal cortex of prenatally lead exposed pups. Values shown are the group of mean ± SEM (n = 5) p ≤ 0.05 between the control and the treated.

similar developmental alterations in human beings exposed to lead.

REFERENCES

Ajarem JS, Ahmad M (1991). Behavioural and biochemical consequences of perinatal exposure of mice to instant coffee: a correlative evaluation. Pharmacol.Biochem. Behav., 40: 847-852.

Allikmets LH (1974). Cholinergic mechanisms in aggressive behavior. Med. Biol., 52: 19–30.

Annau Z (1990). Behavioral toxicology and risk assessment. Neurotoxicol. Teratol., 12: 547-551.

Bhattacharayya MH (1983). Bioavailability of orally administered cadmium and lead to the mother, fetus, and neonate during pregnancy and lactation. Sci. Total Environ., 28: 327–342.

Branchey L, Friedhoff AJ (1976). Biochemical and behavioural changes in rats exposed to ethanol in utero. Ann. N.Y.Acad. Sci., 273: 328-330.

Cory-Slechta DA, Weiss B, Cox C (1989). Tissue distribution of Pb in adult vs. old rats: A pilot study. Toxicol., 59: 139-150.

Coyle I, Wayner MJ, Singer C (1976). Behavioural teratogenesis: A critical evaluation. Pharmacol. Biochem. Behav., 4: 191-200.

Davis JM, Svendsgaard DJ (1987). Lead and child development. Nature, 329: 297-300.

Dearth RK, Hiney JK, Srivastava V, Burdick SB, Bratton GR, Dees WL (2002). Effects of lead (Pb) exposure during gestation and lactation on female pubertal development in the rat. Reprod. Toxicol., 16: 343–352.

Donald JM, Cutler MG, Moore MR (1986). Effects of lead in the laboratory mouse. I. Influence of pregnancy upon absorption, retention, and tissue distributuion of radiolabelled lead. Environ. Res., 41: 420–431.

Goyer RA (1990). Transplacental transport of lead. Environ.Health Perspect. 89: 101—105.

Guilarte TR, Miceli RC, Jett DA (1995). Biochemical evidence of an interaction of lead at the zinc allosteric sites of the NMDA receptor complex: effects of neuronal development. Neurotoxicol., 16: 63-72.

Hallen PI, Jonsson S, Karlsson MO, Oskarsson A (1996). Toxicokinetics of lead in lactating and nonlactating mice. Toxicol. Appl. Pharmacol., 136: 342 –347.

Hallen PI, Jorhem L, Lagerkvist B, Oskarsson A (1995b). Lead levels in human milk and blood. Sci.Total Environ. 166: 149–155.

Hallen PI, Jorhem L, Oskarsson A (1995a). Placental and lactational transfer of lead in rats: a study of the lactational process and effects on offspring. Arch. Toxicol., 69: 596–602.

Jett DA, Guilarte TR (1995). Developmental lead exposure alters N-methyl-D-aspartate and muscarinic cholinergic receptors in the rat hippocampus, an autoradiographic study. Neurotoxicol, 16: 7-18.

Johan L, Agneta O, Lars O, Barry H (1992). Postnatal lead exposure affects motor skills and exploratory behavior in rats. Environ Res., 58(1-2): 236-252.

Johnson JWC, Mitzner W, Beck JC, London WI, Sly DL, Lee PA, Khonzami VA, Calvalieri RL (1981). Longterm effects of betamethasone on fetal development. Am. J. Obstet. Gynecol., 141: 1053-1064.

Kellog C, Tervo D, Ison J, Parisi T, Miller RK (1980). Prenatal exposure to diazepam alters behavioral development in rats. Science 207: 205-207.

Kishi R, Ikeda T, Miyake H, Uchino E, Tsuzuki T Inoue K (1983). Effects of low lead exposure on neurobehavioral function in the rat. Arch. Environ. Health, 38: 25–33. NOT CITED

Kruck ZL, Pycock CJ (1979). Neurotransmitters and Drugs. Croom-Helm, London.

Lataillade GP, Thoreux-Manlay A, Coffigny H, Masse R, Soufir JC (1995). Reproductive toxicity of chronic lead exposure in male and female mice. Hum. Exp. Toxicol., 14: 872–878.

Lee ML (1980). Aminoacidopathy and mental retardation and other developmental disabilities. In: McCormack, M.K. (ed.). Marcel Dekker, New York, pp. 135-150.

Livesey DJ, Livesey RGD, Barrett J, Spickett TJ (1986). Lead retention in blood and brain after preweaning low-level lead exposure in the rat. Pharmacol. Biochem. Behav., 25: 1089-1094.

Luthman J, Oskarsson A, Olson L, Hoffer B (1992). Postnatal lead exposure affects motor skills and exploratory behavior in rats. Environ. Res., 58: 236-252.

McClain RM, Becker BA (1972). Effects of organolead compounds on rat embryonic and fetal development. Toxicol. Appl. Pharmacol., 21: 265-274.

Mello CF, Kraemaer CK, Filipin A, Morsch VM, Rodrigues ALS, Martins AF Rubin MA (1998). Effect of Lead Acetate on Neurobehaviuoral Development of Rats Brazillian J. Med. Bio. Res., 31(7): 943-950.

Mushak P (1992). Defining lead as the premier environmental health issue for children in America: Effect of prenatal lead in the cross-fostered mice offspring criteria and their quantitative application. Environ. Res., 59 : 281–309.

Namihira D, Saldivar L, Pustilnik N, Carreon GJ, Salinas ME (1993). Lead in human blood and milk from nursing women living near a smelter in Mexico City. J. Toxicol. Environ. Health, 38(3): 225–232.

Needleman HL (1987). Low level lead exposure in the fetus and young child. Neurotoxicol., 8: 389–393.

Needleman HL (1993). The current status of childhood low-level lead toxicity. Neurotoxicol., 14: 161–166.

Needleman HL, Schell AS, Bellinger D, Leviton A and Allred EA (1990). The long-term effects of exposure to low levels of lead in childhood. New Engl. J. Med., 322: 83-88.

Patel AJ (1983). Undernutrition and brain development. Trends Nat.

Sci., 6: 151-154.
Reiter LW, Anderson GE, Laskey JW, Cahill DF (1975). Developmental and behavioral changes in the rat during chronic exposure to lead. Environmental Health Perspectives, 12: 119-123.
Rodrigues ALS, Rocha MA, Souza DA, Mello CF (1996). Effect of Perinatal lead exposure on rat beahaviour in Open Field and Two way Avoidance Tasks. Pharmacol. Toxicol., 79: 150-156
Rodrigues ALS, Rubin MA, Souza DO, Mello CF (1993). Lead exposure and latent learning ability of adult female rats. Behav. Neu. Biol., 60: 274-279.
Rosenblum WI, Johnson MG (1968). Neuropathologic changes produced in suckling mice by adding lead to the maternal diet. Arch. Pathol., 85: 640-648.
Salinas JA, Huff NC (2002). Lead and spatial vs. cued open field performance. Neurotoxicol. Teratol., 24: 551-557.
Smart JL, Dobbing J (1971). Vulnerability of developing brain. II. Effects of early nutritional deprivation on reflex ontogeny and development of behavior in the rat. Brain. Res., 28: 85-95.
Soufir JC (1995).Reproductive toxicity of chronic lead exposure in male and female mice. Hum. Exp. Toxicol., 14: 872-878.
Trombini TV, Pedroso CG, Ponce D, Almeida AA, Godinho AF (2001). Developmental lead exposure in rats: Is a behavioural sequel extended at F2 generation. Pharmacol. Biochem. Behav., 68: 743-751.
Vorhees CV (1985). Behavioral effects of prenatal methylmercury in rats: A parallel trial to the collaborative behavioral teratology study. Behav. Toxicol. Teratol., 7: 717-725.
Wilson JG (1973). Mechanisms of teratogenesis. Am. J. Psychiatry 136: 129-132.
Yara MRM, Lilianna BDR, Márcia CC, Karoline KMF, Evelise MN, (2007). Behavioral impairments related to lead-induced developmental neurotoxicity in chicks. Arch. Toxicol., 82(7): 445-45.

Laterality of voluntary motor tasks: Are basketing, targeting, and peg-moving performance asymmetric?

Yalçin Yetkin[1]* and Koksal Erman[2]

[1]Department of Physiology, Medical Faculty, Yüzüncü Yil University, 65 200, Van, Turkey.
[2]Department of Biology, Science Faculty, Atatürk University, 25 240, Erzurum, Turkey.

The principal objective of this work is to investigate the relationship between lateral functions of the brain and morphology of the hands, eyes and feet. The study was carried out with 233 volunteers within the age range of 18 to 27 years. Out of the total number of participants, 208 (94%) of them were right-handed and the remaining 13 (6%) were left-handed. The participants were divided into two groups and assessed by twenty items. First ten (Q1) and second ten (Q2) items were taken from Edinburg Handedness Inventory (EHI) and the Yetkin Laterality Questionnaire (YLQ). The degree of hand preference was determined by Geshwind scores (GSs). Q1 was used to assess only hand preference, while Q2 was used for laterality of the one side of the body from eye to foot. Statistically, non-significant (p>0.05) difference (3%) was observed between the Q1 (63%) and Q2 (60%). Breadths and lengths of the hands were measured across 2 to 5 metacarpal region, from peripheral line on the wrist to middle fingertip. While the difference between the breadths of right and left hand was significant (p<0.05), the difference between the lengths of hand was non-significant (p> 0.05). The breadths and lengths of the feet were also measured in the same way. Subjects performed three different voluntary motor activities, such as basketing (throwing basketball: BT), aiming at (targeting: TT) and peg moving tasks (PMT) with their right and left hands in turn to perform the tasks, respectively. In the BT and TT tasks, the difference between the right and left hand performance was non-significant (p>0.05), though, the difference was significant (p<0.05) for PMT. The findings suggest that both the proximity of the hand preferences and the difference of the hand sizes could be the results of the hemispheric dominance in the brain. In this study, it was found that there was a significant difference for left- versus right- hand breadths and left and right-hand motor performances which is shown to be both morphological and functional in asymmetry.

Key words: Laterality, hand preference, basketing, targeting, peg-moving, motor performances, brain asymmetry, human.

INTRODUCTION

Most of the studies on the functional asymmetries are recent, although the first observation of the brain asymmetry is that of Broca (1861) (Yetkin, 2001). Since the first evidence of the functional asymmetry was first implied by Broca, the left hemispheres are important for fine control of motor skills in distal extremities (Mohr, 1976; Purves et al., 2001). The pioneering works of Broca (1861) and Wernicke (1874), and later Geshwind (1965) and Sperry (1974) clearly established the differences in hemispheric functions (Hellige, 1990). Handedness is also first and fore most an example of the advantage of having a specialized function on one side of the brain (Geshwind, 1967; Bakan, 1975; Wilson, 1998). Hand preferences and brain asymmetry are commonly assumed to be unique in both human (Corballis, 2009) and non-human species (Glick and Shapiro, 1985). Every morning, even before individuals were out of bed, their hands come to life, goading their weak and helpless body into the day (Wilson, 1998).

In the hemispheric dominance, the left cerebral hemisphere is closely related to complex motor control; some non-language motor skills are tightly associated

*Corresponding author. E-mail: yyetkin@yyu.edu.tr

with the brain functions. Brain organization for such functions is rather different in left- and right-handed individuals, as well as between men and women (Kimura, 1993). Kimura's (1996) latest studies have also shown that there are important differences in the way the brain is organized between one person and another. These differences may underlie some of our unique talents. In the book "Hand und Wort", written by André Leroi-Gourhan (1988), bilateral symmetry and the relationship between hand and external and internal-world has been narrated successfully. Some motor asymmetry methods have also been described by Kimura (2011). One of the most remarkable features of complex functions is the ability to use the hands with elaborate skill (Vogan and Tabin, 1999). This emerges clearly when using hands in daily activities. Moreover, the sizes of the two hands are most probably different. This difference may come from either laterality or from using one hand more often than the other. People can actually compare each of their hands to verify this difference. The hand of the human being also has a long history since the beginning of the human civilization on its social interaction and attention (Young, 1983).

Both biologically and physiologically, the left and right hemispheres undertake different functions (Geshwind and Galaburda, 1984, 1987). Thus, asymmetry arises functionally and anatomically. In biology, symmetry is a definition that denotes the arrangement of the body parts of a living being in a particular order, according to the line dividing the body in two similar parts, in respect to dimension, shape and position on both sides. In addition, symmetry is an important feature of the body in biological systems maintaining a physical quantity such as the protection of energy and balance of the body (Yetkin, 1993). The left hemisphere seems to be heavier and denser than the right hemisphere of the brain (Yetkin, 2002a). The left hemisphere is dominant with respect to the control of the right side (Rothwell, 1994) of the body. In humans, approximately 90 to 95% of the general population is shown to be right-handed, that is, they prefer their right hand for intricate, complex acts, and are more skillful with it (Annet, 1985, 1996; Tan, 1993a; Yetkin, 1993; Adams et al., 1997).

However, the right hemisphere seems to be more voluminous than the left hemisphere. The dominancy of right hemisphere is about 5 to 10% (Geschwind, 1971; Tan and Kutlu, 1992; Yetkin, 2002b). In right-handed people, left and right hemispheric dominance are 96 and 4%, respectively (Wada et al., 1975; Kupfermann, 1999). Having individuals answer a series of questions about preferred manual behaviors such as "which hand do you use to write, to throw a ball, to brush your teeth?" were used to assess handedness. In the same way, laterality of the feet and eyes can be assessed with questions such as "which foot do you use to kick a ball?" or "which foot do you use to play hopscotch?" and "which eye do you use to look in a microscope?" Each answer is given a value, which then provides a quantitative measure of the inclination toward right- or left-handedness (Coren, 1992; Davidson and Hugdal, 1995). For the relationship among human hand preferences (Annet, 1972; Tan, 1988, 1993b), hand sizes (Yetkin, 1995, 2002a) and voluntary motor skills (Tan, 1992; Yetkin, 2002b), a few modeling studies addressing these questions are available. Anthropologists have estimated the incidence of handedness in ancient cultures (Tattersall, 1995) by examining artifacts. Based on this evidence, humans have been mostly right-handed as far back as can be ascertained. Handedness is not peculiar only to humans; many studies have demonstrated paw preference in animals, at least in some ways, similar to human handedness (Purves et al., 2004). The present study focused on the effect of using the dominant hand during daily activities on its anatomical sizes and functional preferences (Long, 1981). Size differences of hands and feet as related to the laterality are in part, the results of changes of the activity of preferable hand and foot in daily life. The genetic information is increasingly considered in functional rather than structural terms, but time to time, the structural phenomena remain predominant in humans (Reeves, 2000). The genetic program which directs their development is also proving to be complex. Trying to understand how it works is keeping researchers busy (Cohn, 2002). Several mechanisms could be responsible for the differences evident of hand and foot sizes, as well as their preferences (Adams et al., 1997; Purves at al., 2001).

For the lateral function, it has been suggested that it is important to motor, mental, emotional, perceptual and cognitive functions. The physiology of the human hand pushes currently on emotional interests in the research of motor functions. Although the fine manual motor skills are complex, researches provide important improvement in the understanding of the interested mechanisms (Wiesendanger and Nirkko, 2001). In this paper, the necessity of the bimanual coordination and adaptation of the hand in observation of the subjects were investigated. For this purpose, this study aims to assess the breadth and length of the hand and foot in relation to their lateral functions with a metric dimension in both the right and left hands and feet of men and women subjects. Inquiries were also made for learning, to confirm if there are differences between the dimensions of left and right hands and feet sizes as morphologic asymmetry. On the other hand, the velocity of the hand using PMT was studied by inserting nails into a hole on a table having a hundred holes. Details of this are discussed subsequently.

METHODS

Subjects

The present study was carried out with young volunteer students (N=233) whose age range is from 19 to 27 years (mean 22±2 years). The participants were the students in Biology and Nursing Sciences of Atatürk University in Erzurum, Turkey. None of them had a history of neurological and psychological disorders. They were also in healthy condition and neither of them had tissue damage nor defect on their hands and feet. They were divided into two groups: the first group included 22 subjects and the second group included 211 subjects (Table 1).

Assessing of hand preferences and laterality degrees

Hand preference and laterality of the participants was assessed by means of twenty item questionnaire with two groups (Yetkin, 2001). The first group with ten items (Q1=G1) was taken from Edinburg Handedness Inventory (EHI; Oldfield, 1971) and translated for the Turkish population by Tan (1988) and Yetkin (1993). Respondents were asked to indicate which hand they used in "writing", "drawing", "throwing", or "using scissors", "toothbrush", "knife", "spoon", "broom (upper hand)" "striking a match" and "removing a lid". The second group of Handedness Inventory with ten items (Q2=G2) was developed by Yetkin (YLQ/I: 1993, 1995, 2001) to assess the whole lateralization degree of one side of the body. Respondents were also asked to indicate which hand, foot and eye they used in "looking through a microscope", "passing a thread through a needle", "kicking a ball", "aiming at (with hand, finger and eye)", "shaking hand and saluting", "sewing", "holding a saw", "throwing a hammer", "carrying a suitcase", and "playing hop-scotch". These two questionnaires have been composed by Yetkin (1993) in his studies. Thus, a new questionnaire with twenty questions has been created to assess the whole laterality. For every two groups, the columns of the questionnaires were scored as "+10 (always right hand: AR-H)", "+5 (usually right hand: UR_H)", "zero point (either hand/or side: EH-S)", "-5 (usually left hand: UL-H)", and "-10 (always left hand: AL-H)". The Composed Handedness Inventory (CHI) was administered to a sample of 233 students, comprising 90 (40.4%) men and 143 (59.6%) women in different disciplines of the university. Before given a task, all subjects took composed Handedness Inventory in Turkish translation by Tan (1988) and Yetkin (1993, 2003). The first part of the questionnaire (Q1) included ten items taken from EHI, and the second part (Q2) included ten items taken from YLQ. A different composed questionnaire was used for the assessment of the laterality (Steenhuis and Bryden, 1989). Respondents were asked to indicate which hand they would use in daily activities. Subjects were also tested for the actions related to the questions. Before the voluntary tasks, the laterality degrees were assessed by Geshwind scores (GSs), and and then the planned voluntary actions were shown to the subjects to familiarize them with the actions before they perform them. While the first group of actions (Q1) was directly related to the hand preferences, the second group of actions (Q2) was related to the laterality of the other parts of the body, including eye, hand and foot preferences. After the assessment of the preferences, GSs were used for laterality degrees.

Left (LH) - right hand (RH) and left (LF) - right foot (RF) sizes

The anthropometric measurements of the dimensions of hands and feet were made by using a sensible electronic compass (±0.01 mm). The subjects were seated on a comfortable chair similar to an armchair for watching TV. The right and left arms were set at the upper side of the supporting winds of the armchair as to wrist of the hands. Thus, their feet and hands were free and without suppression. The muscles of the hands and feet were kept on their special position and tension. The palm of the hand was faced in a similar manner to the flat surface and the foot was in the normal upright position. Then, the breath and lengths of the right (RH) and left hands (LH), and right (RF) and left foot (LF) were measured by sliding compass.

The breadth of the hands

The hand characteristics of palm breadth and distal point of the middle finger were measured from 233 subjects that performed activities like throwing basketball, targeting and peg-moving task. To measure the breadth, the hands were kept free on the position as parallel to the ground with the fingers closed side by side except the thumb being 45° apart from the others. The inter-metacarpal line from 2nd to 5th metacarpus was measured as breadth of the hand (Figure 1).

The measurement of the length of the hands

The length of the left and right hands were measured while the palm of the hand was kept on the position which could be seen. The length of the hand was measured from transfer carpal ligament (Tcl), which lies between interstyloid on the surface of the wrist, to the middle fingertip. The line between antero-brachial fascia (Anbf) and Tcl can be seen on the skin surface of the wrists (Figure 2).

The measurement of the breath of the feet

The breath of the feet was measured while the subjects were on the sitting position. The distance between the first and fifth metatarsals was taken as foot breath (Figure 3a).

The length of the feet

In the same way, the length between the skin surface of the calcanei and the fingertip of the foot's thumb was taken as foot length (Figure 3b).

Motor tasks: Basketball, targeting and peg-moving (inserting a nail in a hole)

The functional apparatus that was developed by Yetkin (1995) for some voluntary tasks was used in the present study. The features of the apparatus have been described and calculated in previous studies (Yetkin, 1995, 2002b).

Basketing (throwing basketball) task (BT)

The subjects performed basketball actions at the basket set (Yetkin, 1995). The action of basketball was repeated a hundred times. They threw a special rubber ball of 7 cm diameter by using their left and/or right hands from a distance of 3 m into a basket that is 25 cm in diameter and placed 160 cm above ground on a board of 100 × 100 cm in dimensions. At the end of these trials, the basketing performances of the subjects were recorded in percentage (Table 1).

Targeting /or aiming at (TT task)

The set of targeting task was also developed by Yetkin (1995). The participants walked from a 3 m distance toward a board to touch target point placed on the board that was 75 × 75 cm in dimensions. They were asked to use their index fingers to touch the target point that was 157.5 cm high from the ground, perform targeting task hundred times with their right and left hands, respectively, and the targeting performance was determined in percentage (Table 1).

Peg-moving task (PMT)/ or Sarah-peg works

This activity is related to inserting pegs (nails) in holes. The set contained 100 holes (20 × 5 holes) on a board. The subjects were required to insert 100 pegs into the holes. The time spent for this

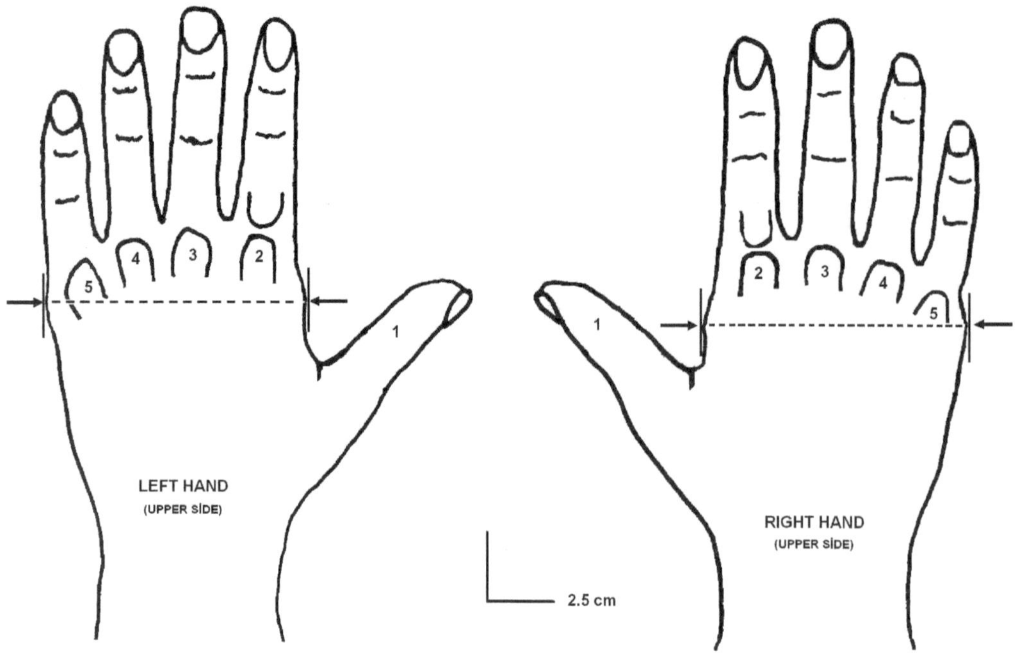

Figure 1. The reference points for measurement of the breadth of the left- and right hands. The longest line was measured on the palm from the 2nd to the 5th metacarpi as the breath of the hands. The arrows indicate the widest points of the right and left hands on the palm.

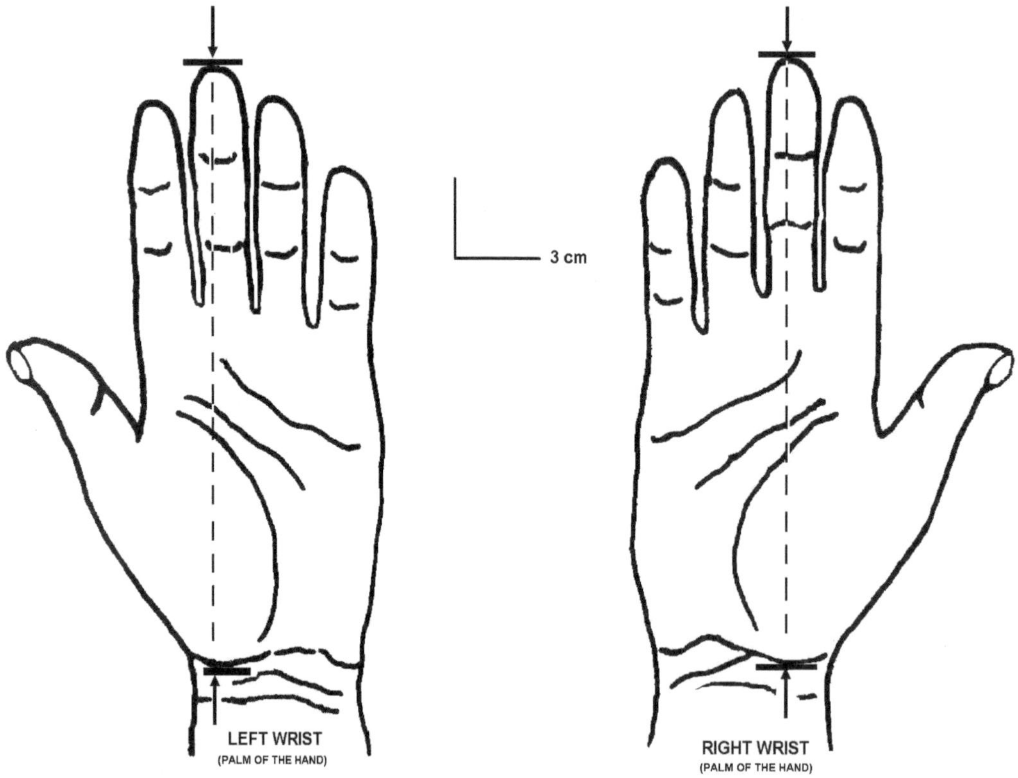

Figure 2. The reference points for the measurement of the lengths of the left- and right hands. To determine the hand lengths, the longest line from Tcl on the skin surface of the wrist to the middle fingertip was measured. The arrows indicate the longest points between Tcl and middle fingertip of the right and left hands.

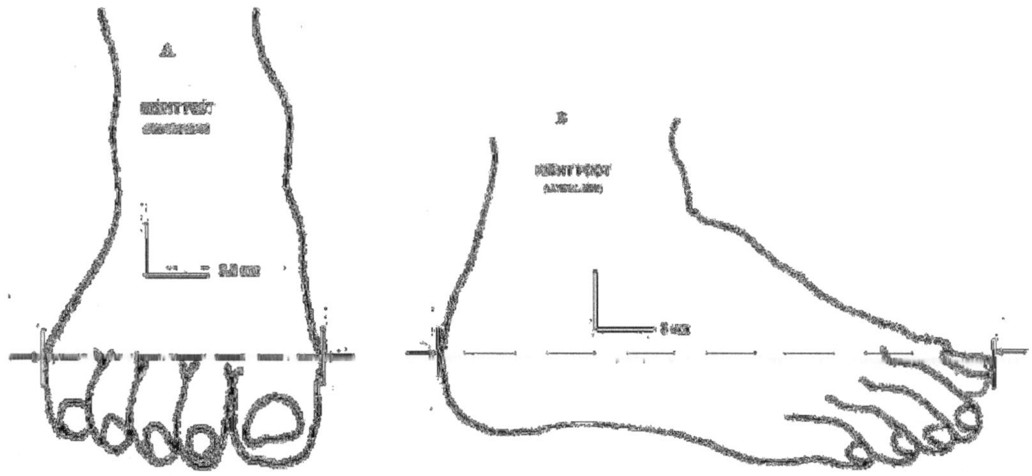

Figure 3. The points of the measurement of foot breadth (A) and foot length (B). The arrows indicate the longest and widest points of right foot. While the line between the first and fifth metatarsals was measured as the breadth of the foot, the length of the foot was measured by taking the distance between the skin surface of the calcanei and fingertip of the thump.

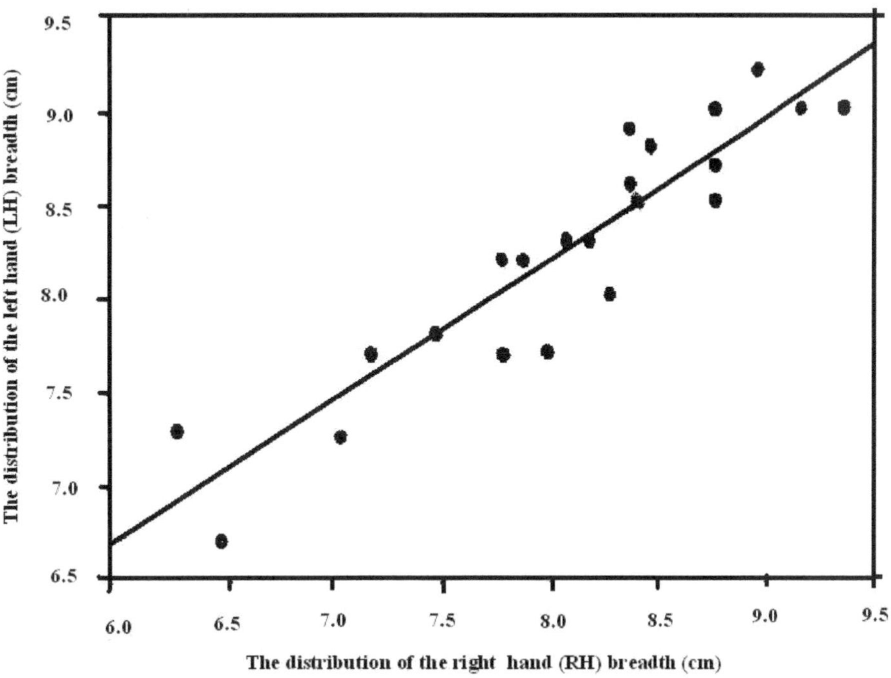

Figure 4. The results of the breadth of the left and right hands observed from left- and right-handers. There is a positive linear correlation between the right and left hand breadth (cm) of the subjects (n= 22, n=221) as a morphological features. Statistical results*:* t=1.95; $p<0.05$; Se = 0.133; r =0.921; r^2 = 0.8582; Cor = 0.913.

task was measured by mechanical and electronic devices (Yetkin, 2002b). The peg-moving performances of the subjects were assessed by a chronometer and recorded (Table 1).

Statistical analysis and descriptive statistics

The data obtained were summarized as means ± standard deviation. In the statistical analysis of the results, student's *t*-test, and SPSS for windows 10.0 were used. The data recorded from volunteers were averaged and then analyzed for correlation using the two-sample t-test and ANOVA. The student's test was used to compare male and female subjects, and left and right hand usage. The distribution of GSs for hand preferences was analyzed in percentage. T-test was used to disclose the distribution of hand preferences and hand performances. In addition, the differences

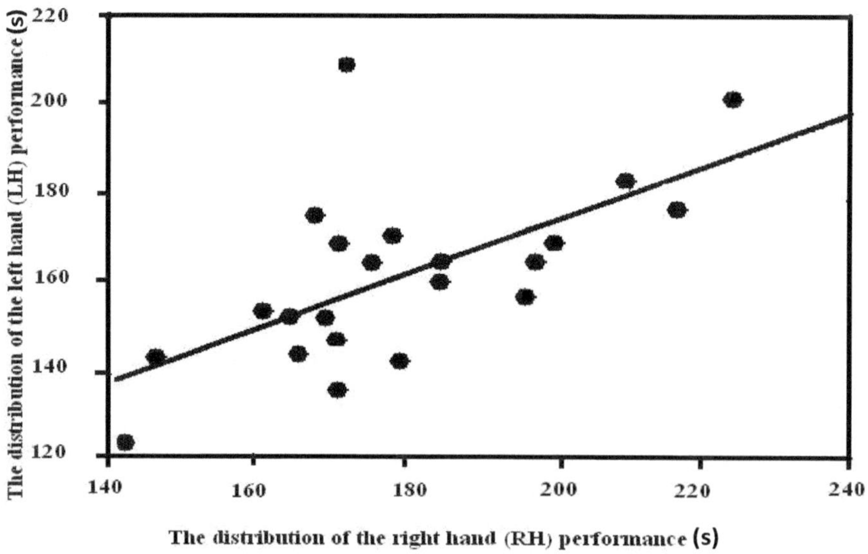

Figure 5. The results of the left and right hand performances obtained from peg moving task in left and right-handers. There is a positive linear correlation between the right and left hand performance recorded from peg-moving task (s) (inserting a nail in a hole). Statistical results: $t = -4.74$; $p<0.005$; $SE = 4.40$; $r = 0.651$; $r^2 = 0.4238$; Cor = 0.630.

Table 1. Geschwind scores (GSs) of hand preference assessing from Q1 and Q2 points,and Targeting (TT: 100 times), Basketball (BT: 100 times), and Peg Moving Tasks (PMT: 100 nails in a hole -second) performances.

Sexuality (M & W)	Geschwind score (GS: %)		Targeting task (TT: 100 times)		Basketing task (BT: 100 times)		Peg-moving task (PMT: sec./100)	
	Q1	Q2	RH	LH	RH	LH	RH	LH
1.M	55	65	100	100	60	30	122, 60	141,60
2.W	80	65	100	100	0	0	168, 50	171,50
3.W	40	40	20	40	10	20	142, 00	180,00
4.W	60	35	40	60	30	40	152, 00	165, 00
5.W	60	60	80	100	30	20	182, 80	210, 40
6.W	55	45	80	60	20	50	202, 30	224, 70
7.W	60	75	100	80	20	20	165, 00	185, 20
8.M	10	60	100	60	30	10	141, 40	146, 00
9.M	80	80	60	0	30	30	177, 30	217, 30
10.M	40	30	10	80	50	40	152, 40	169, 30
11.M	80	80	20	40	40	20	164, 30	176, 00
12.M	95	70	20	40	40	30	170, 80	178,70
13.M	85	80	100	100	40	20	135.10	170, 00
14.M	60	70	100	100	30	40	157, 00	197, 00
15.M	80	40	100	100	60	40	165, 00	198, 00
16.M	75	55	100	100	40	20	143, 40	165, 80
17.M	75	55	100	100	30	50	160, 00	185, 00
18.W	85	80	60	80	30	10	147, 00	171, 00
19.M	85	100	100	100	30	20	168, 40	200, 60
20.W	85	65	100	100	20	10	175, 00	168, 00
*21.W**	*-55*	*-25*	*60*	*80*	*50*	*70*	*210, 00*	*172, 00*
22.M	95	90	100	100	60	70	153.20	160, 80
Arithmetic's means	63, 00	60, 00	79.10	78.20	34.10	30.00	161, 63	179,67
Difference	3.00	%	0.90		4.10		18.04	
Min.	10	30	10	0	0	0	122, 60	141, 60
Max.	95	100	100	100	60	70	210, 00	217, 30

Abbreviations: Q1: the first group of the questions, Q2: the second group of the questions, TT: targeting Task, BT: Basketing task, PMT: peg-moving task, RH: right-hand, LH: left-hand, GS: Geschwind Score, M: men, W: women.

between Q1 and Q2 group questions related to the left- and right hand preferences during voluntary skills was compared according to GSs. The statistical results are shown in the study's tables and figures.

RESULTS

The main goals of the present study were to evaluate the relationship between differences of lateralization in the human brain derived from asymmetric function and from voluntary motor tasks involving basketing, targeting and peg-moving tasks.

This study was performed to assess the possible impact of changes in the morphometry of hand and foot sizes arisen by dominant hemisphere and laterality. In the present study, some important results were indicated as related to laterality, especially the relationship between anatomical and functional asymmetry. However, an exploratory study was conducted by Reio et al. (2004). The present work also aims to add to an understanding of hemispheric lateralization by examining the relationships between functional laterality (handedness, eyedness and footedness) and anatomical differences.

The results of the statistical analysis of data showed that most of the subjects tend to use the right hand. The assessment of the hand preferences and the relationship between the two question groups named Q1 and Q2 (Yetkin, 2001) were indicated by GSs. The Q1 by EHI deals only with hand preferences, and the Q2 by YLQ contains the questions related to one side of the body from eye to foot preferences. To assess the relationship between hand, eye and foot preferences, the scores obtained from the first and second group was compared by using t-test. Thus, the hand preferences indicated by Oldfield's (1971) questionnaire and other lateral preferences, such as eye, feet and finger preferences, indicated by Yetkin's questionnaire, were compared.

Analysis of hand preferences

In order to attain the goal of this study, important results have been obtained by statistical analyses according to the data of the present research. In the small population of 22 subjects, 21 of them were found to be right-handed, corresponding to approximately 95%, while one subject was left-handed, corresponding to 5%. In the larger population (n=221), 208 subjects were right-handed, corresponding to approximately 94%, while 13 of them were left-handed, corresponding to approximately 6%. The percentage of the left-handedness was found to be slightly higher in the second population than in the first population (Table 1).

On the other hand, the mean laterality degrees in right-handers were found to be 63 and 60% for Q1 and Q2, respectively. For the left-hander who was the only left-handed person in the population, however, the mean laterality degrees were found to be -55 and -25% for Q1 and Q2, respectively.

Morphological asymmetry of the hands and feet

From the perspective of biomechanical anatomy, the hand is an integral part of the entire arm, and it has a crane-like structure suspended from the neck and upper chest (Wilson, 1998). In the same manner, the foot is an integral part of the entire leg that keeps the body at upright position; it has a carrier-like structure connected to the body by the pelvis and hip joint. The difference between the sizes of the left and right hands and feet were found (Table 2) as discussed thus.

Breadth and length of the hands

The longest line was measured on the palm from the 2nd to the 5th metacarpi as the breath of the hands (Figure 1). The arrows indicate the widest points of the right and left hands on the palm. The breadth of the hands was measured by compass (±0.01) across inter-metacarpal line.

The thumb was positioned at 45° apart from the other fingers during the measurement. The difference between the right and left hand breadth was found to be significant ($p<0.05$, Table 3). In the females, the difference between right and left hand breadth 'd' was also found to be significant ($p<0.05$) as shown in Table 4.

To determine the hand lengths, the longest line from Tcl on the skin surface of the wrist to the middle fingertip was measured. The arrows indicate the longest points between Tcl and middle fingertip of the right and left hands.

The difference between right and left hand lengths was found to be insignificant (Table 3), and there was no difference between the sexes and the left and right-handed subjects ($p>0.5$; Table 5).

Hand breadths and lengths were recorded from the second group with 221 subjects, 208 of which were right-handed and 13 of which were left-handed. In the first group which comprised 22 subjects, 21 of them were right-handed and one of them was left-handed. The statistical result was found in values of $t=1.95$; $p<0.05$; Se = 0.133; $r=0.921$; $r^2 = 0.8582$; Cor= 0.913 between left and right breadths. The difference between the right and left hand breadth in females was statistically significant ($p<0.05$) both in the small (n=22) and large (n=211) groups (Figure 4). However, the difference between the hand widths of the right- and left-handers was found to be insignificant (Table 3). In the same way, the difference between the right- and left-hand lengths was also insignificant in both females and males, and there was no significant relationship between hand lengths of the right- and left-handed subjects, statistically (Tables 4 and 5).

Breath and length of feet

While the line between the first and fifth metatarsals was measured as the breadth of the foot, the length of the foot was measured by taking the distance between the skin

Table 2. Hand- breadth (B) and length (L) of the right- (RH) and left-handed (LH) subjects.

Sex (M and W)	Hand preference	Right hand (RH)		Left hand (LH)	
	RH/ LH	RH-B	RH-L	LH-B	LH-L
1.M	RH	8.70	19.40	8.80	19.30
2.W	RH	7.80	18.60	7.50	18.00
3.W	RH	8.20	20.50	7.80	20.10
4.W	RH	8.00	18.90	8.30	19.00
5.W	RH	8.90	18.90	8.40	18.00
6.W	RH	8.30	18.30	8.10	18.50
7.W	RH	7.30	17.50	7.30	17.50
8.M	RH	9.20	21.20	9.00	20.60
9.M	RH	8.30	19.50	8.10	19.50
10.M	RH	8.60	20.20	8.40	20.10
11.M	RH	8.20	18.00	7.90	18.30
12.M	RH	7.70	19.50	7.80	19.50
13.M	RH	9.00	21.00	9.20	21.00
14.M	RH	8.80	22.00	8.50	21.80
15.M	RH	8.50	20.00	8.80	20.30
16.M	RH	8.30	19.50	8.20	18.50
17.M	RH	9.00	20.00	8.80	20.40
18.W	RH	7.70	18.50	7.20	18.30
19.M	RH	8.30	19.50	8.20	19.20
20.W	RH	6.70	18.00	6.50	17.00
*21.W**	*LH*	*7.70*	*18.50*	*8.00*	*18.50*
22.M	RH	9.00	21.00	9.40	18.40
Means	21 RH, 1 LH	8.30	18.90	8.20	18.40

(*) Left handed; B: breadth; L: Length; RH: right hand; LH: Left hand; M: men; W: women.

Table 3. The mean values and results of the data in the total sample by the t-test in SPSS-Windows.

Preference	Mean*	Cor.	Sd.	Se.	t-value	df	p-value	r	(+, -)
Geschwind scores (%)									
Q1	62.9545	0.801	33.369	7.114	0.750	21	>0.463		(-)
Q2	59.7727		26.208	5.588					
Breadth(cm)									
RH-B	8.2818	0.913	0.624	0.133	1.950	21	<0.05	0.921	(+)
LH-B	8.1455		0.179	0.166					
Length (cm)									
RH-L	19.3955	0.939	1.289	0.275	0.630	21	>0.538		(-)
LH-L	19.3364		1.221	0.260					
Targeting (100 times)									
RH-TT	79.0909	0.743	29.906	6.356	0.200	21	>0.840		(-)
LH-TB	78.1818		28.223	6.017					
Basketball (100 times)									
RH-BT	34.0909	0.559	15.632	3.333	1.180	21	>0.250		(-)
LH-BT	30.0000		18.516	3.948					
Peg moving (100 nails)									
RH-PMT	161. 6136	0.630	20.603	4.393	-4.74	21	<0.005	0.651	(+)
LH-PMT	179. 7745		21.550	4.510					

Cor=correlation; sd=standard deviation; Se=standard error; df=degree of freedom; (*)=statistically; (**)=(+) significant and, (-) in-significant statistically.

Table 4. The relationship between the right- and left-hand breadths (B) from right- (RH) and left-handed (LH) men (M) and women (W).

Hand (cm)	Mean (Q1, Q2)	t-value	p-value	Sd (Q1)	Sd (Q2)	df	(+, -)
Total population							
RH-B	8.422	1.67	>.1	0.70	0.71	420	(-)
LH-B	8.309						
Men							
RH-B	8.950	1.47	>1.4	0.50	0.50	200	(-)
LH-B	8.845						
Women							
RH-B	7. 940	1.96	<. 05	0.45	0.47	218	(+)
LH-B	7. 817						
Right-handed							
RH-B	8.436	1.86	>.07	0.68	0.70	396	(-)
LH-B	8.307						
Left-handed							
RH-B	8.196	-0.388	>.7	0.92	0.82	22	(-)
LH-B	8.333						

Q1= first ten questions; Q2=second ten questions; B=breadths; RH= right-handedness; LH=left-handedness; M=men; W=Women; Sd=standard deviation; df=degree of freedom; (+, -)* = significant (+) and in-significant (-) statistically.

surface of the calcanei and the fingertip of the thumb. The difference between the left and right foot lengths was also insignificant in the general population, as well as between males and females, and between right- and left-handed groups (Tables 6 and 7). Foot breadths and lengths were recorded from the second group. The difference between the right- and left-foot widths was found as statistically insignificant (P>0.05, Table 6), that is why we have no expected correlation between the data. The differences observed from the general population and between males and females for the left and right foot width were also not significant. Similarly, the differences between the right and left foot lengths were found as statistically insignificant (Table 7).

Functional asymmetry

By means of the anatomical structure of the hand, we are able to hammer nails or insert nails into a hole or use a pencil; this is an indication of our laterality. The perspective of physiological and functional anatomy suggests that some parts of the brain regulate the hand function.

The problem of understanding what the hand is becomes infinitely more complicated if we try to account for differences in the way people use their hands, or if we try to understand how individuals acquire skill in the use of their hands (Wilson, 1998). The differences between the left- and right hand performances are as given thus.

Targeting (aiming at) performance

Volunteers in the present study performed the TT a hundred times. However, the action of targeting in previous studies was done for ten times (Yetkin, 1995, 2002b). In this study, there was no significant difference between the right and left performance (p>0.8, Table 1). This result supports our hypothesis on biological evolution of the symmetry. The mean success rate of the targeting performance was approximately 79.10 and 78.20% for the right and left hand respectively.

Basketing (throwing basketball) performance

Subjects performed the BT a hundred times. The mean values of the success rate in the BT were 34.10 and 30.00% for right and left hand performance respectively. The difference between left and right hand preference in the basketball task was not statistically significant (p>0.3). However, there are some studies which indicated that the left hand performance is better than the right hand performance in voluntary motor tasks (Tan, 1989; Parlow, 1990). As it is shown in Table 3, the mean success of the BT was lower than the mean success of the TT.

Table 5. The relationship between the right- and left-hand lengths (L) from right- (RH) and left-handed (LH) men (M) and women (W).

Hand (cm)	Mean (Q1, Q2)	t-value	p-value	Sd (Q1)	Sd (Q2)	df	(+, -)
Total population							
RH-L	18.066	0.87	>0.40	2.415	1.242	420	(-)
LH-L	17.906						
Men							
RH-L	19.087	1.11	>0.27	3.081	1.055	200	(-)
LH-L	18.727						
Women							
RH-L	17.129	-0.17	>0.90	0.820	0.863	218	(-)
LH-L	17.148						
Right-handed							
RH-L	18.093	0.906	>0.37	2.460	1.232	396	(-)
LH-L	17.917						
Left-handed							
RH-L	17.617	-0.135	>0.90	1.452	1.428	22	(-)
LH-L	17.696						

Q1= first ten questions (EHI); Q2= second ten questions (YLQ); B= breadths; RH= right-handedness; LH = left-handedness; M= men; W= Women; Sd= standard deviation; df= degree of freedom; (+, -)* = significant (+) and in-significant (-) statistically.

Table 6. The relationship between the right- (RF) and left–foot (LF) breadths (B) from right- and left handed subjects.

Foot (cm)	Mean (Q1, Q2)	t-value	p-value	Sd (Q1)	Sd (Q2)	df	(+, -)*
Total population							
RF-B	9.607	0.459	>0.65	0.965	0.959	420	(-)
LF-B	9.564						
Men							
RF-B	10.285	0.346	>0.73	0.810	0.757	200	(-)
LF-B	10.247						
Women							
RF-B	8.984	0.560	>0.58	0.613	0.644	218	(-)
LF-B	8.936						
Right-handed							
RF-B	9.626	0.453	>0.65	0.970	0.960	396	(-)
LF-B	9.582						
Left-handed							
RF-B	9.300	0.080	>0.94	0.858	0.917	22	(-)
LF-B	9.270						

RF= right foot; LF= left foot; B= breadth of foot; (*) significant (+), un-significant (-).

Table 7. The relationship between the right- (RF) and left–foot (LF) *lengths (L)* obtained from the left- and right handed subjects.

Foot (cm)	Mean (Q1, Q2)	t-value	p-value	Sd (Q1)	Sd (Q2)	df	(+,-)*
Total population							
RF-L	24.653	0.114	> 0.90	2.103	2.092	420	(-)
LF-L	24.676						
Men							
RF-L	26.183	-0.383	>0.70	1.670	1.523	200	(-)
LF-L	26.270						
Women							
RF-L	23.248	0.200	>0.85	1.340	1.340	218	(-)
LF-L	23.213						
Right-handed							
RF-L	24.683	-0.131	>0.90	2.115	2.101	396	(-)
LF-L	24.710						
Left-handed							
RF-L	24.163	0.064	>0.95	1.893	1.940	22	(-)
LF-L	24.710						

RF= right foot; LF= left foot; L= length of foot; (*) significant (+), un-significant (-).

Table 8. A comparison between the Q1 and Q2 and functional motor task of right and left handers.

Parameter	Pair	Mean	Standard deviation	Standard error of mean	Min.	Max.
Geshwind scores (%)	Q1	62.95	33.37	7.11	-55.00	95.00
	Q2	59.77	26.21	5.59	-25.00	100.00
Targeting (100 times)	RH-TT	79.09	29.91	6.38	20.00	100.00
	LH-TT	78.18	28.22	6.02	0.00	100.00
Basketing (100times)	RH-BT	34.09	15.63	3.33	0.00	60.00
	LH-BT	30.00	18.52	3.95	0.00	70.00
Peg-moving task (s/100 peg)	RH-PMT	161.61	20.60	4.39	122.60	210.00
	LH-PMT	179.72	21.18	4.52	141.60	224.70

Table 9. Paired comparison for Q1 versus Q2.

Pair	Paired differences			t	df	P value
	Mean	Std. deviation	Std. error mean			
Q1 - Q2	3.18182	19.97293	4.25824	0.747	21	0.463

Difference between two means is not significant.

Table 10. Paired comparison for RH-TT versus LH-TT.

Pair	Paired differences			t	df	P value
	Mean	Std. deviation	Std. error mean			
RH-TT - LH-TT	0.90909	20.91003	4.45803	0.204	21	0.840

Difference between two means is not significant.

Table 11. Paired comparison for basketing task (RH-BT versus LH-BT).

Pair	Paired differences			t	df	P value
	Mean	Std. deviation	Std. error mean			
RH-BT - LH-BT	4.09091	16.23022	3.46029	1.182	21	0.250

Difference between two means is not significant.

Table 12. Paired comparison for RH-PMT versus LH-PMT.

Pair	Paired differences			t	df	P value
	Mean	Std. deviation	Std. error mean			
RH-PMT - LH-PMT	-18.10909	17.91958	3.82047	-4.740	21	0.000

Difference between two means is significant (P<0.001).

Peg-moving (Sarah-peg works) performance

In PMT, performance of the right hand was found to be better than that of the left hand. The mean values were 161.6136 and 179.7745 s for the right and left hand, respectively. The difference was about 18 s. The difference between the right and left hand performance was significant (t = -4.74; p<0.005; SE =4.40; r =0.651; r^2= 0.4238; Cor = 0.630). The results are shown in Table 3 and Figure 5.

Comparison between the Q1 and Q2 and the functional motor task of a right and left hander: The results of the descriptive statistics

Descriptive statistics of Geshwind scores and functional motor task of the right and left handed subjects were assessed separately (Table 8 to 12). According to the laterality, the mean Geshwind scores were found as 62.95 and 59.77% for Q1 and Q2 respectively. The difference between Q1 and Q2 was about 3.18% mathematically. The targeting (100 times) task for RH-TT (79.09 times) and LH-TT (78.18 times) were rather close to each other.

There was no significant difference, mathematically. Basketing (100 times) task was found for RH-BT (34.0 times) and LH-BT (30.00 times). The mean difference was found to be 4%. However, the difference in the peg-moving task (s/100 pegs) was RH-PMT (161.61) and LH-PMT (179.72) separately.

According to the paired comparison for Q1 versus Q2, the difference between the two means (3.18%) was not significant (p> 0.05). The paired comparison for RH-BT versus LH-BT of basketing task was found to be 4.09091, and the difference between the two means was not significant (p>0.05). According to the paired comparison for RH-PMT versus LH-PMT, the difference (-18.10909) between the two means was significant (P<0.001). Also, a paired comparison was done for RH-TT versus LH-TT, and the difference (0.90909) between the two means was not significant (p>0.05).

DISCUSSION

In the present study, firstly, the constructional, biomechanical and functional characteristics of the hands and feet were investigated after which a comparison was made for them. This study presents the application and observational data that suggest possible effect of functional asymmetries on morphological and anatomical differences of the hands and feet. In humans, handedness is thought to be related to the hemispheric processing of specific aspects of language, including speech (Redmond and Lamperez, 2004). The development of the lateralized functions have also been assessed as being important to cognitive, emotional, perceptual, social, and motor skills (Young, 1983).

A number of studies have recently been carried out in animals as it was in humans; paw preferences (Tan et al., 1991; Tan, 1993b; Yetkin, 2001) and physical properties in cats are closely related to the measurements of hand

and foot sizes in human. There is a harmonic relation between the use of the hand and brain functions as evolutionary phenomena (Niebauer et al., 2004). In the anthropologic process, the brain develops a device and the hand is used to make it. Then, the brain is used to make more developing devices. Thus, a harmonic relation was set between the hand and the brain. Presumably, people may have heard that the two distinct hemispheres of the brain have different capabilities. For example, the sensory control from the left side of the body is sent to the right hemisphere of the brain, and the sensory control from the right side of the body is sent to the left hemisphere of the brain. Likewise, the control of the right arm and leg is sent to the left hemisphere, and the control of the left arm and leg is sent to the right hemisphere. The left hemisphere is said to deal with language and analytical thought, while the right hemisphere is said to deal with spatial relations and creativity (Kimura, 1996).

Broca (1861) showed that asymmetry was a hallmark, and that symmetry increased as asymmetry went down the phylogenetic scale in biological evolution (Yetkin, 2002a). In the light of this opinion, the female's brain is more symmetrical than that of the male, and children show more symmetry than adults (Finger, 1994). Appropriate differences in motor functions between the left and right hemispheres have always been discussed to find a structural correlation for the functional asymmetry. An anatomical difference between hemispheres was identified about four decades ago (Geschwind, 1965; Geschwind and Levitsky, 1968). The superior aspect of the temporal lobe known as the planum temporale was significantly found to be larger on the left than on the right side (David and Hugdal, 1995, Westbury et al., 1999; Williams, 2001).

The hypothesis stipulates that one of the organs, which are symmetric in biologic systems, can develop more than the other ones, if it works much more than the other ones (Darwin, 1871).

The purpose of this work is to develop a method of using a maximal forced laterality maneuver for the study of morphologic and functional asymmetry induced by hand usage. For this goal, the results and findings were discussed in the light of anthropological and evolutionary, biomechanical and physiological, and neurobehavioral and developmental perspectives (Wilson, 1998). To our knowledge, this work is the first study that is conducted to examine the relationship between hand preferences and hand and foot sizes. The relationship between the functional asymmetry and the sizes of the body parts such as hand, foot and brain would be an evidence for the reason of the morphological asymmetry. However, the reason for the asymmetry is still not a completely clarified concept. Hence, the main purpose of this study is to determine the morphological asymmetry of the hands and feet as preferences. The hand plays an important role in daily life (Napier, 1956). There is a close relationship between the function of the brain and the preference of the hand and foot (Glick and Shapiro, 1985; Previc 1991; Yetkin, 1993). It is known that this is a result of the fact that psycho-motor setting up of one hand is more effective than that of the other. A hand preferred for a particular action can be superior to the other in the realization of that action.

A considerable amount of articles is already available on the hand preference (Annett, 1970a; Oldfield, 1971; Phillips, 1986; Knecht et al., 2000), and the functional and morphological asymmetry (Yetkin, 1992) observed in common daily activities of human kind. However, new research areas have recently emerged on the laterality of the voluntary motor skills, such as targeting, basketball and peg moving task (Tan, 1992; Yetkin, 1995), and hand and foot sizes related to the functional asymmetry. These preferences and handedness are generated by the central nervous system (CNS) (Hammond, 1990). The present paper has concentrated upon the questions of which hand, foot and eye do humans use to perform their daily activities (Annett, 1972; Yetkin, 1993), how many papers have been published on the plasticity of the functional and morphological asymmetry (Annett and Kilshaw, 1983; Kilshaw and Annett, 1983; Lewis, 1989; Tan, 1989, 1994a; Tan and Kutlu, 1992) and how many of them affect conduction velocity related to hand usage in humans' daily activities. Humans are able to learn a remarkable array of skilled motor tasks and perform them with such proficiency that movements become almost automatic (Lisberger, 1988).

Anthropologic studies (Tattersall, 1998) show graphic representation of the hand which has been found on the walls of the cave of Pech Menle (Kapandji, 1981; Jordan, 1999). After humans were able to walk in an upright position on hind extremities, they began to use the hands freely in daily activities. Thus, the anatomical and functional asymmetry of the hands emerged depending on the hand used. Moreover, there is a principle in biology; if one of the symmetric organs in an organism would be used in daily activities more than the other one (Annett, 1981), it can be denser than the other (Yetkin, 1993). Our findings also support the morphological asymmetry between left and right hands as related to their lateral performance.

The hand is also a sensory organ by way of manufacturing and carrying more specialized tools (Annett, 1970b; Marzke, 1997). For this, the body and hand complement each other. On the other hand, according to Immanuel Kant, the hand is also outside of the human brain: humans can interact with the world and make tools to easy their life (Young, 1983).

Morphological asymmetry

Study of the embryology of the hand is of utmost interest on the studies of the hand. It helps in understanding a lot of unexpected aspects of the anatomy of the hand. The hand sizes begin to assume adult features at 13 to 14 years of age. The phalangeal epiphyses become wider than the shaft. The carpal bone attains their mature size. At the age of 16 to 18 years, all phalange epiphyses unite with the shafts. The radial epiphysis reaches its mature size and unites with the shaft. The ulnar epiphysis also unites with the shaft (Tubiana, 1981a). The hand lies flat on a smooth area and the pronated forearm lies in a posterior-anterior way. The hand is stretched out with the thumb held wide apart, and the vertical beam is classically countered below the midpoint of the interstyloid line. For special examination of the hands (or fingers), the beam was focused more distally on the head of the third metacarpal (Tubiana, 1981b). Foot preferences are also considered as an evidence for anatomical and functional asymmetry. In some behaviors, however, motor functions seem to be similar in the dominant and non-dominant leg in apparently healthy young adult men and women (McCurdy and Langford, 2005).

In the present study, the difference between the right and left hand breadth was found to be statistically significant ($p<0.05$) for both the first small group ($n=22$) and the second large ($n=211$) group (Figure 4) in females. However, the difference between the right and left hand breadth was found to be statistically insignificant ($p>0.1$) in males. The difference of the right and left hand lengths was also found to be statistically insignificant in both males and females. Similarly, there were insignificant relationships between the hand lengths of right and left-handed males and females.

The differences between the right and left foot breadth and lengths were found to be insignificant in males and females and right and left handed subjects. Hand and foot measurements are not common practices in radiology except in trauma or congenital defect of the hands and foots. Several comprehensive studies have been made at different ages on hand sizes in both sexes.

There is a difference between the brain of men and women as to which part of the left hemisphere is responsible for speech and hand movements. There are two major areas devoted to speech, one in the frontal lobe, and the other at the back, where the temporal and parietal lobes meet. In women, the frontal region is more important than the area at the back; so, problems with speaking are more likely to happen if the front part of the left hemisphere is damaged. In men, the areas contribute more equally, but if anything, the back part, especially the parietal region, is more important (Kimura, 1996).

Functional asymmetry

The hand is characterized greatly with prehensile capabilities, such as pincer-like movements, wrapping-around, the use of gravity in conjunction with placement of the hand in hook-like position and the use of palmar plateau for grasping (Tubiana, 1981), and different free flexor movement of the fingers. One of the aims of the present study was to investigate the effect of hand preference on morphological and anatomical differences. In this study, discussions on some motor tasks are further given (Winter, 1990). The results are discussed in terms of implications for voluntary tasks about differences in left- and right-handed persons. A similar study was made on the drawing performance of the children (Vlachos and Bonoti, 2004; Long, 1981).

Targeting (aiming at) performance

The differences between the left and right hand performance observed in voluntary motor tasks, including basketball (mean performance of 3.9%) and targeting (mean performance of 90%), were found to be statistically non-significant ($p>0.05$). These results can also be described as biological phenomena. If the hands can be used freely without depending on a tool, it seems to be that the degree of laterality for hand preferences goes toward symmetry. In addition, one side of the body is used together with a hand for motor tasks. As it is known, brain hemispheres control both sides of the body reciprocally. It shows that there is a close affinity between the brain hemispheres functionally. The results of a study conducted by Simon-Thomas et al. (2005) suggest that emotional responses facilitated the right hemisphere processing during higher cognitive task performance. However, the left hemisphere controls the motor performance. This means that motor performance is more effective on morphological asymmetry than on cognitive performance.

With targeting and basketball performances, despite the fact that objects looked larger in the right eye of right-eye dominant subjects and in the left eye of left-eye dominant subjects (McManus and Tomlinson, 2004), an investigation has also been performed on the lateral side of the body from eye to foot. On the other hand, there were few studies on 'aiming at' in adults in the preferred and non-preferred hands in right handed adults (Barral and Debu, 2004). The results obtained from targeting in this study support those results. Volunteers conducted the performance of TT a hundred times. In some previous studies, however, the action of targeting was provided for ten times (Yetkin, 1995, 2002b). In this work, there was no remarkable difference (about 1 point) between right and left performance, and this difference was also non-significant ($p>0.8$; Table 1). This result supports our hypothesis which stipulates that symmetry is a biological process related to evolution.

The mean success of the targeting performance was approximately 79.10 and 78.20% for right and left hand respectively. However, the mean targeting performance was found to be higher (78.65%) than basketball performance (32.05%), but the difference between the left and right hand performance was statistically insignificant. In these actions, subjects experienced their right and left hand separately for a hundred times to perform the targeting and basketball tasks.

The subjects used their index finger together with the left and right eye during targeting. The index finger can assume the various degrees of skills needed for adjusted movement levels without involving other fingers (Oldfield, 1971; Kilbreath and Gandavia, 1994; Yetkin, 1995).

Basketing (throwing basketball) performance

Subjects conducted the basketball task a hundred times. The mean values were 34.10 and 30.00% for right and left hand performance, respectively. The difference between left and right hand performance for basketball was 4 point, which was non-significant ($p>0.3$). However, there are some studies which indicate that the performance of the left hand is better than that of the right hand for voluntary motor tasks (Tan, 1989; Parlow, 1990). As shown in Table 3, the mean success of the BT was lower than that of the TT.

Peg-moving task / Sarah-peg work performance

There are different studies on the peg-moving task (Suguieda et al., 2008) and there are different peg-boards for this task. A new peg-board developed by Yetkin was used in this study which has a hundred holes, whereas the peg-board used in previous studies that were conducted recently had 25 holes (Tan and Kutlu, 1992). The time required for the PMT on the board with 25 holes was too short for the exact difference to emerge between the right and left hand performance, although, the subjects might spend too much time for the difference between the right and left hand performance to emerge on a board with hundred holes.

In PMT, the mean of the right hand performance was found to be better than that of the left hand performance. The performance was 161.61 and 179.78 s for the right and left hand, respectively, and a difference of 18 s was significant ($t= -4.74$; $p<0.005$; $r=0.651$). The results are shown in Table 3, and the linear correlation between left-right hand performances for PMT is shown in Figure 5. The difference between right- and left- hand for PMT was about 18 s. This is a big difference. It shows that the right hand which was used for PMT was more conducive than the left hand.

Sex differences

When the results obtained from men and women were compared, the relation between them was found to be statistically significant. Although the main purpose of the present study was not to compare the differences between the sexes, this characteristic was appraised in this report.

Finally, if the studies related to functional and morphological asymmetry are based on biological principles depending on the brain functions, the mechanisms of both symmetry and asymmetry can be better understood. Biological principles of physiological functions, such as motor skills, learning, memory, motor and mental developments (Eccless, 1989) in human beings can be discussed on the right basis.

Conclusions

In conclusion, it was found that there was a significant relation ($p<0.05$) between right and left hand breaths in women (Table 4). The mean breath of the right hand was larger than that of the left hand in all subjects (Table 3). This is a wonderful sample for anatomical asymmetry. These results show that there is an anatomical asymmetry between the left and right hand widths, which could depend on their usage. Similarly, there was a significant difference between the left and right hand performance for PMT that could be related to hand preference. This is also a wonderful sample of functional asymmetry depending on hand performance. These findings support our opinion on laterality and its reason during the evolutionary process (Parsons et al., 1998; Corballis et al., 2000). Results of this study explain the effects of the morphological and anatomical differences of functional asymmetries of the brain hemispheres. These findings also support our opinion related to the evolution of symmetry as a biological phenomenon.

REFERENCES

Adams RD, Victor M, Ropper AH (1997). Principles of Neurology, 6th edition. McGraw-Hill Inc, New York. pp. 275-350.

Annett M (1970a). The growth of manual preference and speed. Br. J. Psychol. 61:545-558.

Annett M (1970b). A classification of hand preference by association analysis. Br. J. Psychol., 61: 303-321.

Annett M (1972). The distribution of manual asymmetry. Br. J. Psychol. 63:343-358.

Annett M (1981). The right-shift theory of handedness and developmental language problems. Bull. Orton Soc. 31:103-121.

Annett M, Kilshaw D (1983). Right and left hand skill II. Right and left hand skills- II. Estimating the parameters of distribution of L-R differences in males and females. Br. J. Psychol. 74:269-83.

Annett M (1985). Left, Right, Hand and Brain: right shift theory. Lawrence Erlbaum Associates Ltd., London.

Annett M (1996). In defense of the right shift theory. Perceptual Motor Skill 82:115–137.

Bakan P (1975). Are left- hander brain damaged? Neuroscientists 67:2000-2002.

Barral J, Debû B (2004). Aiming in adults: Sex and laterality effects. Laterality 9(3):299 – 312.

Broca P (1861). Portée de la parole:Ramolisement Chronique et Destruction Partielle du Lobe Anterieur Gauche du Cerveau. Paris Bull. Soc. Anthropol. pp. 2-4.

Cohn MJ (2002). Giving limbs a hand. Nature 406:953-54.

Corballis PM, Funnell MG, Gazzaniga MS (2000). An evolutionary perspective on hemispheric asymmetries. Brain Cognit. 43:112-117.

Corballis MC (2009). The evolution and genetics of cerebral asymmetry.

Philosophical Transactions of the Royal Society B: Biol. Sci. 364(1519):867–87.
Coren S (1992). The left-hander Syndrome. The course and consequences of left- handedness. Free Press, New York.
Davidson R, Hugdahl K (1995). Brain Asymmetry. In: R Davidson and K. Hugdahl (Eds.), The Asymmetrical Brain. MIT Press, Cambridge, Massachusetts.
Eccles J (1989). Evolution of the Brain. Routledge, New York.
Finger S (1994). Origins of Neuroscience: A History of Explorations into Brain Functions. Oxford University Press Inc., New York.
Geshwind N (1965). Disconnection syndromes in animals and man, Part I and II. Brain 88:237-294.
Geshwind N (1967). Wernicke's contribution to the study of aphasia. Cortex 3:449-450.
Geschwind N (1971). Aphasia. N. Engl. J. Med. 284:654-656.
Geshwind N, Galaburda A (1984). Cerebral Dominance: The Biological Foundation. Harvard University Press, Cambridge, Massachusetts.
Geshwind N, Galaburda A (1987). Cerebral lateralization: Biological Mechanisms, Association and Pathology. MIT Press, Cambridge.
Geshwind N, Levitsky W (1968). Human brain: Left-right asymmetries in temporal speech region. Sci. 161:186-187.
Glick SD, Shapiro RM (1985). Cerebral Lateralization in Nonhuman Species. New York: Academic Press.
Hammond GE (1990). Cerebral Control of Speech and Limb Movements. The University of Western Australia, Nedlands, Australia.
Hellige OB (1990). Hemispheric asymmetry. Psychology 41:51-80.
Jordan P (1999). Neanderthal: Neanderthal man and the Story of Human Origins. Sutton Publishing, New York.
Kapandji IA (1981). The Hand, Part III. In: R Tubiana (ed.), The hand in art. WB Saunders, Philadelphia. Chapter 64, pp. 715-722
Kilbreath S, Gandavia S (1994). Limited Independent Flexion of the Thumb and Fingers in Human Subjects. Br. J. Physiol. 3:484-97.
Kilshaw D, Annett M (1983). Right and left hand skill I. Effect of age, sex and hand preference showing superior skill in left-handers. Br. J. Psychol. 74:25-68.
Kimura D (1993). Neuromotor mechanisms in human communication. Oxford University Press, New York.
Kimura D (1996). Understanding the Human Brain In: Cox J (Ed.), Children's Britannica. Encyclopedia Britannica Inc., London. pp. 136-141.
Kimura D (2001). From ear to brain. Brain Cogn. 76(2):214-7.
Knecht S, Dröger B, Deppe M, Bobe L, Lohmann H, Flöel A, Ringelstein EB, Henningseen H (2000). Handedness and hemispheric language dominance in healthy humans. Brain 123:2512–18.
Kupfermann I (1999). Localization of Higher Cognitive and Affective Functions. The Association Cortices. In: Kandel ER, Schwartz JH (Eds.) Jessell TM, Principle of Neural Science. Elsevier, New York. pp. 515-38.
Leroi-Gourhan A (1988). Hand and Worth (La geste at la parole): Die Evolution von Technik, Sprache und Kunst. Suhrkamp Taschenbuhch, Germany. pp. 42-80.
Lewis OJ (1989). Functional Morphology of the Evolving Hand and Foot. Clarendon Press, Oxford.
Lisberger SG (1988). The neural basis for motor learning in the vestibule-ocular reflex in Monkeys. Trends Neurosci. 11(4):147-148.
Long C (1981). Electromyographic Studies of Hand Function. In: Tubiana R (ed.), The Hand; Part III, VI. W. B. Saunders, Philadelphia. Chapter 64.
Marzke M (1997). Precision Grips, Hand Morphology and Tools. Am. J. Phys. Anthropol. 102:91-110.
McCurdy K, Langford G (2005). Comparison of unilateral squat strength between the dominant and non-dominant leg in men and women. J Sports Sci. Med. 4:153 – 159.
McManus IC, Tomlinson J (2004). Objects look different sizes in the right and left eyes. Laterality 9(3):245–265.
Mohr JP (1976). Broca's area and Broca's aphasia. In: Whitaker HA and Whitaker H (eds.), Studies in Neurolinguistic. MIT Press, New York. pp. 201-235.
Napier J (1956). The prehensile Movements of the Human Hand. J. Bone Joint Surg. 4:902-13.
Niebauer CL, Christman SD, Reid SA, Garvey KJ (2004). Interhemisfepheric interaction and beliefs on our origin: degree of handedness predicts beliefs in Creationism versus evolution. Laterality 9(4):433 – 447.
Oldfield RC (1971). The Assessment and Analysis of Handedness: The Edinburgh Inventory. Neurophysiology 9:97-113.
Parsons LM, Gabrieli JDE, Phelps EA, Gazzaniga MS (1998). Cerebrally lateralized mental representations of hand shape and movement. J. Neurosci. 18:6539-6548.
Phillips C (1986). Movements of the hand. Liverpool University Press, Liverpool England.
Previc HF (1991). A general theory concerning the prenatal origins of cerebral lateralization in human. Psychol. Rev. 98:298-334.
Purves D, Augustine GJ, Fitzpatrick D, Katz C, LaMantia AS, McNamara JO, Williams SM (2001). Neuroscience: Language and Lateralization, 2nd edition. Sinauer Associates, Sunderland, Massachusetts. Chapter 27.
Purves D, Augustine G, Fitzpatric D, Katz LC, La MAS, McNamara JO, Redmond JC, Lamperez A (2004). Leading limb preference during brachiation in the gibbon family member, *Hylobates syndactylus* (siamangs): A study of the effects of singing on lateralization. Laterality 9(4):382-396.
Reeves RH (2000). Recounting a genetic story. Nature 405: 283–284.
Reio TG, Czarnolewski M, Eliot J (2004). Handedness and spatial ability: Differential patterns of relationships. Laterality 9(3):339–358.
Rothwell J (1994). Control of Human Voluntary Movement. Chapman and Hall, New York.
Simon-Thomas ER, Role KO, Knight RT (2005). Behavioral and Electrophysiological Evidence of a Right Hemisphere Bias for the Influence of Negative Emotion on Higher Cognition. J. Cognit. Neurosci. 17(3):518–529.
Sperry RW (1974). Lateral specialization in the surgically separated hemispheres. In: Schmidt FO and Worden FG (eds.), Neuroscience; 3rd Study Program. MIT Press, Cambridge, Massachusetts. pp. 5–19.
Steenhuis R, Bryden MP (1989). Different Dimensions of Hand Preference that relate to Skilled and Unskilled Activities. Cortex 25:289-304.
Suguieda DY, Nunes G, de Oliveira SB, Dellatolas G, da Paz AC, Braga LW (2008). Computerized procedure for analyzing hand kinematics with a peg-moving task (Sarah-Pegworks). Behav. Res. Methods 40(2):503–11.
Tan U (1988). The distribution of hand preference in normal men and women. Int. J. Neurosci. 41:35-55.
Tan U (1989). Manual proficiency in Cattle's intelligence test in left-handed male and female subjects. Int. J. Neurosci. 44:17-26.
Tan Ü, Kara I, Kutlu N (1991). The effect of the testosterone on paw preference in adult cats. Int. J. Neurosci. 56:187-191.
Tan U, Kutlu N (1992). Right and left hand skill in relation to cerebral lateralization in right handed male subjects: The prominent role of the right brain in the right handedness. Int. J. Neurosci. 64:125-138.
Tan U (1993a). Normal distribution of hand preference and its bimodality. Int. J. Neurosci. 68:61-65.
Tan U (1993b). Distribution of paw preference in mongrel and tortoise-shell cats and the relation of hemispheric weight to paw preference: Sexual dimorphism in paw use and its relation to hemispheric weight. Int. J. Neurosci. 70:199-212.
Tattersall I (1995). The Fossil Trail: How We Know What We Think We know about Human Evolution. Oxford University Press, New York.
Tattersall I (1998). Becoming Human: Evolution and Human Uniqueness. Hardcourt Brace and Co., New York.
Tubiana R (1981). Architecture and Functions of the Hand. In: Tubiana R (ed.), The Hand I. WB Saunders, and Philadelphia.
Tubiana R (1981). The Hand I. WB Saunders, Philadelphia. pp. 493-498.
Vlachos F, Bonoti F (2004). Left- and right-handed children's drawing performance: Is there any difference? Laterality 9(4):397- 409.
Vogan KJ, Tabin CJ (1999). A new spin on handedness asymmetry. Nature 397:295-298.
Wada JA, Clarke R, Hamm A (1975). Cerebral hemispheric asymmetry in humans: cortical speech zones in 100 adult and 100 infant brains. Arch. Neurology 32:239-246.
Wernicke K (1874). Der Aphasische Symptomkomplex. Braslau, Kohn and Weigert. In: English Translation by GH Eggert Wernicke's Works

on Aphasia, A Source Book and Review (1977). The Hague, Moulon.
Westbury CF, Zatorre RJ, Evans AC (1999). Quantifying variability in planum temporale: A probability map. Cerebral cortex 9:392–405.
Wiesendanger M, Nirkko A (2001). Hand und Hirn: Forschung-Lehre. Publication DPG 16:7-13.
Williams SM (2001). Language and Lateralization. In: Purves D, Augustine GJ, Fitzpatrick D, Katz LC, LaMantia AS, McNamara JO, Williams SM (eds.), Neuroscience, 2nd edition. Sinauer Associates, Sunderland, Massachusetts.
Wilson FR (1998). The Hand. Pantheon Books, New York. pp. 56-127.
Winter DA (1990). Biomechanics and motor control of human movement (2nd Ed.). Wiley & Sons, New York.
Yetkin Y (1993). The examination of preferences related to using of right or left hand, foot and eye. Trends J. Med. Sci. 19:133-142.
Yetkin Y (1995). Laterality during voluntary tasks of young males and females. Trends J. Med. Sci. 23:129-134.
Yetkin Y (2001). Do environmental and hereditary factors affect the psychophysiology and Left-right shift in left-handers? Int. J. Neurosci. 110:109-34.
Yetkin Y (2002a). Physical properties of the cerebral hemispheres and paw preferences in Mongrel cats: sex-related differences. Int. J. Neurosci. 112:239-262.
Yetkin Y (2002b). A comparison related to the laterality of the voluntary motor performance such as basketing, targeting and peg-moving. Anadolu Univ. J. Sci. Technol. 3:31-40.
Young G (1983). Manual Specialization and the Developing Brain. Academic press, New York.

15

Meningiomas: Quality of life before and after surgery

Camila Batista dos Santos[1]*, Maria Fernanda Gouveia da Silva[2] and Paulo Henrique Pires de Aguiar[1]

[1]Hospital das Clínicas's - Department of Neurology of São Paulo Medical School (HC-FMUSP), Brazil.
[2]Hospital das Clínicas's Development and Qualification Center (HC-FMUSP), São Paulo, Brazil.

Evaluation of the quality of life before and after the development at three, six and twelve months intervals from meningioma resection was considered. A prospective study was carried out with 29 patients carrying benign meningioma, whose ages ranged from 28 to 76 years old. In order to evaluate the quality of life, two instruments were used: the Nottingham Health Profile (NHP) and the Innsbruck Health Dimensions Questionnaire for Neurosurgical Patients (IHD-NS). Meaningful differences were found between the NHP and the IHD-NS total score, when comparing the evaluations before and after intervention. A significant improvement in pain, emotional reaction, physical ability, sleepiness, communication, physical condition, independence and the psychological condition domains was noticed. It was possible to observe that patients who had meningiomas in the left hemisphere have shown higher symptomatology, but those were also the ones who have shown significant reduction of the symptoms after the surgical intervention. Patients who undertook surgical intervention for the meningioma resection presented a significant improvement in their quality of life. A meaningful improvement took place up to the first three months. There was then a tendency to stabilize between three to six months (because of a rise in the Emotional Reactions Domain) and thereafter there was a reduction in new symptom taking place up to twelve months from intervention. Taking this study into to consideration it seems beneficial to recommend psychotherapy intervention after three months from surgery.

Key words: Quality of life, intracranial tumor, meningioma, psychology.

INTRODUCTION

Over the last decades we have observed a growing interest in Quality of Life (QOL), to evaluate not only the effectiveness and efficiency, but also the impact of certain treatments, and the physical and psychosocial impact that these diseases exert on people.

Meningiomas are extra-axial meninges tumors, with a slow growth rate, and most of them are benign. They are most often diagnosed in female patients, with ages ranging from 20 to 60 years old (Black, 1993). They may be symptomatic or asymptomatic, depending on their location, size and degree of cerebral edema. When symptomatic they can cause motor deficits, aphasia, visual loss, seizures, intracranial hypertension, and cognitive deficits, amongst others (Santana et al., 2002; Figueiredo et al., 1998). Treatment for the meningioma is surgical, whereas the approach and extension of the resection depends on the tumor´s location. After surgical treatment, studies point out that the patient lives between 8 to 10 years more (Chan and Thompson, 1984;

*Corresponding author. E-mail: camilabsantos@gmail.com.

Mirimanoff et al., 1985; Simpson, 1957), and the QOL improves (Arienta et al., 1992; Chan and Thompson, 1984; Hernández and Rodriguez, 2004; Kalkanis et al., 2000; Mohsenipour et al., 2001; Neil-Dwyer et al., 2000; Sachenheimer et al., 1992; Yamashiro et al., 2007) and the death rate ranges from 7 to 14% in different levels (Rachlin and Roseblum, 1991).

The concept of QOL is diverse and complex as it involves objective and subjective aspects, being physical, social and emotional. Authors state that QOL "is not only the level of function but also the level of satisfaction within this" (Chibnall and Talt, 1990). It would be a "multidimensional construct that reflects the individual's daily function ability, social support, emotional understanding and lack of psychological discomfort" (Mcdonough et al., 1996). An important definition in literature about the term, points to the term QOL as the "state of well-being that includes the ability to perform daily activities and the satisfaction performances and control of the disease and / or treatment of related symptoms (Gotay and Moore, 1992).

Numerous studies indicate that factors such as age (Sachsenheimer and Bimmler, 1992), size, location (Kozler et al., 2007; Salo et al., 2002), histology, excision grade and the pre-operative condition (Chan and Thompson, 1984), are all matters of great importance when considering the QOL together with the period the patient lives after meningioma surgery. It is also shown that modifications in physical conditions, energy level (Mohsenipour et al., 2001), depressive symptoms and behavioral disturbances (Mohsenipour et al., 2001; Sachsenheimer and Bimmler, 1992; Wertenbroek et al., 2006) may occur, however the surgical intervention does not have a negative impact on the QOL, even in asymptomatic patients, as long as there are no complications during surgery (Yamashiro et al., 2007). As an element of interference in the QOL evaluation, authors refer to the presence of other diseases and the senescence effects (Mohsenipour et al., 2001).

Most studies in literature that evaluate the QOL are based on clinical observation and indices (Karnofsky et al., 1948). There are few studies that use specific scales for assessing the QOL and no studies of prospective evaluation where the patient was evaluated before surgery and systematically reassessed after the procedure.

The current study aimed the thorough verification of the QOL in patients with meningiomas before and after surgical procedure. Neurosurgical studies indicate an improvement in clinical symptoms after intervention and therefore report improvement in QOL, based on professional evaluation. However, the concept of QOL encompasses not only issues related to the disease but also subjective aspects, those related to the perception of the person in relation to his/her current state (Schiestel and Ryan, 2009). Therefore, this study aims to understand the QOL in its broadest sense, at different times of patient treatment and with specific instruments for such evaluation.

PATIENTS AND METHODS

104 cases of supratentorial meningiomas were surgically treated between 2005 and 2009. The main approaches for tentorial meningiomas were parietooccipital, and temporal craniotomies, and for parasagital and convexity, the craniotomy was performed in the high point were the tumor is placed and the craniotomy is accomplished surrounding the complete border of tumor and dural tail. For left ventriclular tumor the approach is parieto coccipital avoiding deep speech areas and in the right side is temporal through the middle and superior girus.

For the present study 29 voluntary patients of both genders were selected and operated on during the period between 2005 and 2009 (17 women – 59% and 12 men – 41%), whose ages ranged from 28 to 76 years old, amongst them were 14 up to 55 years old (48%) and 15 being 55 years old or more (52%). As to their educational level, 17 patients had up to 8 years of study (59%) and 12 patients more than 8 years of study (41%).

These patients were surgically treated (22 patients with Complete Resection – 76% and 7 patients with Partial Resection – 24%) and in all cases anatomopathological examination showed meningioma grade 1 (WHO, 1993). They were all supratentorial, 16 patients on the right side (55%) and 13 on the left side (45%).

Patients that presented meningiomas grade 2 and 3 (WHO, 1993), infratentorials, neurofibromatosis, intra-axial tumors, recidivism, co morbidities that affected the encephalon and a history of depression and high scores in the HAD (Botega et al., 1995) diagnosis aid rate for depression and anxiety, were excluded from the sample. Patients that showed lighter symptoms of depression stayed in the study.

In order to investigate the patients` symptoms and thus their QOL, four prospective evaluations were made, before surgery, after three months (to minimize the impact of secondary alterations to immediate postsurgical) and six to twelve months from intervention. The data collection was kept at the Tumor Group's outpatient clinic, at the Department of Neurology of the São Paulo Medical School Teaching Hospital -, from 2006 to 2009. All patients have signed a Free Informed Term of Consent (FITC).

The choice of instruments was based on the article "Quality of Life in Patients after meningioma resection," published by Mohsenipour et al. (2001) in which the author developed an assessment tool for neurosurgical patients QOL. With the objective of using the Innsbruck Health Dimensions Questionnaire for Neurosurgical Patients (IHD-NS) and of adapting a cultural change for the Brazilian population, we chose to use the Nottingham Health Profile (NHP), as a tool for general assessment of QOL, as this showed good correlation with the instrument IHD-NS. The following instruments were applied:

- Nottingham Health Profile (NHP) (Teixeira-Samela et al., 2004) – generic instrument to appraise the QOL, which provides a simple means to measure the individuals` physical, social and emotional health. This is a tool adapted for the Brazilian population. It´s development is based on the classification of disability as described by the World Health Organization (WHO) and is considered to be clinically valid in distinguishing patients with different levels of dysfunction and to detect significant changes in the patients health overtime.

Table 1. Average and standard deviation in the four moments of the NHP Total Score.

	Before	3 months	6 months	12 months	Friedman (p)
Average	9.07	5.66	5.14	4.07	
Standard deviation	9.01	5.68	5.40	4.53	0.00003 *
N	29	29	29	29	

Table 2. Average and standard deviation in the four moments of the IHD-NS Total Score.

	Before	3 months	6 months	12 months	Friedman (p)
Average	11.66	8.52	7.24	6.76	
Standard deviation	5.31	5.06	5.16	5.06	<0.0001 *
N	29	29	29	29	

-Questionário de Dimensões de Saúde para Pacientes Neurocirúrgicos de Innsbruck DSI – NC (Santos et al., 2008) (Innsbruck Health Dimensions Questionnaire for Neurosurgical Patients IHD-NS, Mohsenipour et al., 2001) – instrument developed to evaluate neurosurgical patients quality of life. This is composed of aspects, physical, social and emotional. The trans-cultural instrument proved to have quality, consistency and to be trustworthy in the Portuguese version and included a high agreement índex with no erratic items in its composition (Santos et al., 2008).

Both questionnaires were conducted by the author seeking to minimize the impact of lower school education and the question of misunderstandings. It is worth emphasizing that the patients QOL is directly related to the presence and severity of symptoms, therefore, the more severe the symptoms are, the worse the QOL is and a reduction in the symptoms will indicate an improvement in the QOL.

For statistical analysis the non-parametric Friedman tests were applied, to compare moments; and Mann-Whitney tests to compare groups. The level of significance was 5%.

RESULTS

QOL analysis before and after surgery through NHP and IHD-NS, indicated the following results:

As regards education and sex no significant differences were observed. As to age both groups presented significant improvement DSI(NC), however only the group up to 55 years showed significant improvement in PSN. The group 55 years up had a tendency to improve. When analyzing the QOL and the tumor location, significant differences are not noticeable; however we realize that patients with meningioma on the left hemisphere present more symptoms, although they seem to show a more intense improvement than the patients with meningioma on the right hemisphere in one of the scales (NHP). Concerning the resection grade, it was not established as being relevant.

Differences between the groups (total and partial resection)

We noticed that patients who were submitted to a total resection presented a solid improvement of their QOL, dissimilar to the partial resection group.

After studying the total scores of both scales, that represent the individual QOL, gathering all the domains evaluated from NHP and from IHD-NS, relevant differences were noticed when taking into account the patients` development before and after surgery. Through multi comparisons it was observed that the QOL improves significantly after surgery, that is to say, in the first three months, and continues to improve after six months from intervention (Tables 1 and 2).

When analyzing the patients evolution, comparing the before, and the after three, six and twelve months evaluations, in the domains that compose the NHP scale (Table 3), we observe a statistically meaningful improvement in the following domains: pain, emotional reaction, sleepiness and physical abilities. We do not notice relevant differences in energy level and social isolation domains.

In the IHD-NS scale (Table 4), the communication, physical condition, independence and psychological condition domains, presented statistically meaningful improvement. Relevant differences were not evident in the autonomic nervous system function nor in the social isolation domain.

DISCUSSION

Few studies are presented in the literature relating to

Table 3. Average and standard deviation in the four moments of the NHP Domains.

	Before	3 months	6 months	12 months	Friedman (p)
NHP – Energy Level Domain					
Average	0.48	0.45	0.52	0.41	
Standard deviation	0.74	0.83	0.91	0.82	0.7212
NHP – Pain domain					
Average	1.90	1.24	0.66	0.38	
Standard deviation	2.64	1.92	1.42	0.94	0.0001 *
NHP – Emotional reactions domain					
Average	2.90	1.62	2.10	1.55	
Standard deviation	2.27	1.82	2.30	1.84	0.0005 *
NHP – Sleepiness domain					
Average	1.07	0.38	0.28	0.45	
Standard deviation	1.58	0.82	0.75	0.83	0.0014 *
NHP – Social isolation domain					
Average	1.24	0.86	0.90	0.76	
Standard deviation	1.86	1.13	1.40	1.27	0.1849
NHP – Physical abilities domain					
Average	1.48	1.10	0.69	0.52	
Standard deviation	3.02	1.54	1.20	1.06	0.0050 *

Individual analysis of each NHP domain shows significant improvement of the symptoms in Pain, Emotional Reactions, Sleepiness and Physical Abilities, pre-surgical, 3 months, 6 months and 12 months after surgery evaluations are compared.

people with meningiomas and QOL and the methodology used to measure the quality of life, without classifying the periods of the evaluation and the Karnofsky (Karnofsky et al., 1948) index used as an evaluation system, disabled greater correlations within this study.

Elements such as, the presence of other diseases and the senescence process effects, pointed out by Mohsenipour et al. (2001), were also difficult to isolate in our results, as the QOL instruments do not allow the distinction from the presented disease.

Though the sample size does not allow further analysis concerning location, we may compare the before and after surgery QOL with the meningioma side. In spite of the fact that we do not find relevant differences in either scale, we noticed that patients with meningioma on the left hemisphere presented larger symptomatology, which means, a worsening of QOL as opposed to patients with meningioma on the right hemisphere. This difference is related to the fact that the meningioma is possibly in contact with noble areas of the brain, the language area for instance, causing a worse QOL due to a greater impact in the patients' interpersonal relations and daily routine (Kozler et al., 2007). We also observed that patients with meningiomas on the left hemisphere seem to present a larger reduction of the symptoms after surgery, probably because of the removal of the tumor that was having an impact against the noble areas causing more intense symptoms. The meningioma location is a matter of greater importance for the QOL study and must be better explored in ulterior studies, as stated in the Chan and Tompson's study (Chan and Thompson, 1984).

As to the meningioma resection grade, meaningful differences were not noticed between the groups (Partial and Total Resection), however, it was observed that those who have a total resection presented a significant improvement in their QOL, dissimilar to the partial resection group. Probably the group with partial resection did not show significant improvement as they continues to present lesions and taking into consideration that the instruments evaluated the QOL and relate to the persons perception of him/herself and their actual condition, we

Table 4. Average and standard deviation in the four moments of the IHD-NS Domains.

	Before	3 months	6 months	12 months	Friedman (p)
IHD-NS – communication domain					
Average	2.00	1.52	1.41	1.24	
Standard deviation	0.93	0.91	1.05	0.95	0.0008 *
IHD-NS – Physical condition domain					
Average	3.07	1.41	1.48	1.55	
Standard deviation	2.37	1.59	1.70	2.03	0.0005 *
IHD-NS –Autonomic nervous system function domain					
Average	0.66	0.55	0.45	0.45	
Standard deviation	0.67	0.69	0.63	0.51	0.3203
IHD-NS – Independence domain					
Average	1.93	1.86	1.38	1.34	
Standard deviation	1.16	1.33	0.94	0.94	0.0330 *
IHD-NS – Psychological condition domain					
Average	2.76	2.07	1.76	1.52	
Standard deviation	2.01	2.07	1.92	1.66	0.0025 *
IHD-NS –Social isolation domain					
Average	0.90	1.00	0.72	0.66	
Standard deviation	1.23	1.10	1.25	1.01	0.2320

Individual analysis of each IHD-NS domain shows significant improvement of the symptoms in Communication, Physical Condition, Independence and Psychological Condition, pre-surgical, 3 months, 6 months and 12 months after surgery evaluations are compared.

can also consider the impact of emotional questions and reactions to the fact that they continue to present a tumor or rather, the situation has not been fully resolved and fails in the expectation of a total solution after surgical intervention.

When analyzing patients general QOL in both instruments general (NHP) and specific (IHD-NS), gathering every domain in its composition, we verified that patients submitted to a surgical intervention for meningioma removal presented relevant improvement of QOL as a whole (Figures 1 and 2). These discoveries are strengthened by studies found in literature, which point out meaningful symptom reduction (Sachsenheimer and Bimmler, 1992) and QOL improvement (Arienta et al., 1992; Kalkanis et al., 2000; Miao et al., 2010) after meningioma surgery.

It is also noted in the scale total score analysis, that greater symptoms reduction takes place up to the first three months, between three and six months the situation tends to settle and then new symptom reductions occur up to twelve months (Figures 1 and 2).

From the qualitative point of view, during the six months surgery interval, it may be observed that the majority of the patients referred to an important improvement after surgery, but that some difficulties remained and they were still not able to resume their normal activities. These comments make us consider that these patients have great expectations about the surgery, believing it to be complete banishment of the symptoms, and the important improvement after the procedure reinforces these expectations. Nonetheless, when noticing that some difficulties and/or symptoms remain, these patients become saddened and discouraged and their symptoms end up having an influence on their perception of the general situation, since the QOL gathers factors such as: perception, satisfaction and well-being (Chibnall and Tait, 1990; Gotay and Moore, 1992; Guiteras and Bayés, 1993).

The intenseness of the emotional difficulties after six months surgery, was evident in the Emotional Reactions Domain from NHP scale (things are getting me down, depressing me/ I forgot how to have fun/ I feel extremely annoyed/ the days seem too long/ I am losing my temper easily lately/ I feel like losing control/ the concerns are keeping me up all night/ I feel life is not worth living/ I wake up feeling depressed), and where the symptoms

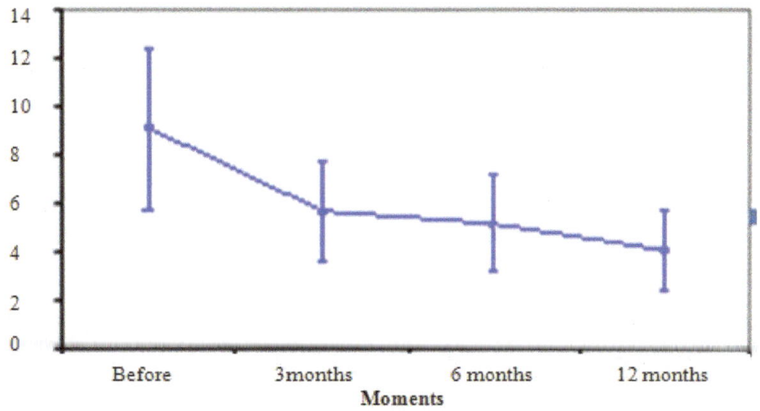

Figure 1. Analysis of the four moments in the NHP Total Score (before and after three, six and twelve months from surgery). Analyzing NHP total score in relation to QOL, comprising all the domains evaluated, significant differences have been observed in regards to its development at the four moments: pre-surgical, 3 months, 6 months and 12 months after surgery (Table 1 and Figure 1).

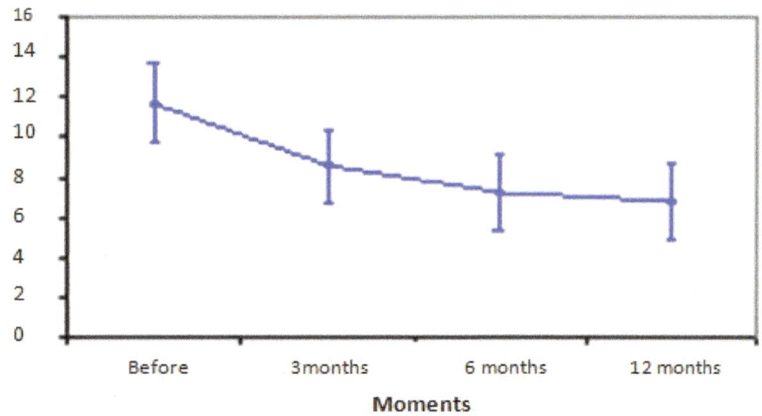

Figure 2. Analysis of the four moments in the IHD-NS Total Score (before and after three, six e twelve months from surgery). Analyzing IHD-NS total score in relation to QOL, comprising all the domains evaluated, significant differences have been observed in regards to its development at the four moments: pre-surgical, 3 months, 6 months and 12 months after surgery (Table 2 and Figure 2).

get considerably higher (Table 3). The symptoms possibly show an affect on the Energy Level domain (I get tired all the time/ everything demands too much effort / I get powerless easily) (Table 3) and, therefore, the instrument global score, justifying the tendency to stabilize the situation between three and six months after the meningioma resection (Figure 1). It seems relevant to consider a psychotherapeutic intervention hypothesis after three months from surgery, aiming to prevent emotional and effective changes, and regular evaluations of these symptoms to, if it is necessary to undergo medical treatment. High depressive symptomatology was encountered by Sachsenheimer and Bimmler (1992), before as well as after surgical intervention.

It is noteworthy that between six and twelve months a new reduction of the symptoms took place, possibly linked to the acceptance of some pre-existing difficulties, as observed in interviews (Figure 1).

These findings were not noted in the psychological areas of IHD-NS probably due to the fact that although the instruments are composed of similar domains, they are designed for different questions in relation to the emotional state.

When comparing the QOL before surgery with the NHP twelve months evaluation, we notice meaningful improvement, in total score (Table 1) that reflects global

QOL, as well as, in the domains (Pain, Emotional reaction, Sleepiness and Physical Abilities). As the first post-surgical evaluation was performed after three months of the intervention it was not possible to observe the impact of the surgery or side effects such as craniotomy pain or peri-incisional edema. There was an observed improvement in the Pain domain at the three month evaluation but this was probably related to the removal of the tumor. Evidence of significant improvements were also observed in Social Interaction and Energy Level domains. The improvement was less evident in the Energy Level domain (Table 3). Mohsenipour et al. (2001) also testified to variances in this domain.

However, in the specific instrument IHD-NS, we verified meaningful improvement in the total score (Table 2) and in the communication, physical condition, independence and the Psychological Condition dimensions when comparing the before and after twelve months from surgical intervention evaluations. A tendency for improvement was observed after the meningioma removal only in Social Isolation and Autonomic Nervous System Function domains (Table 4). This study displayed different results from those reported by Mohsenipour et al. (2001) that evidence was restricted to severe damage in Physical Condition domain.

Conclusion

The present study allowed us to conclude that patients who undergo surgical intervention for the resection of meningiomas presented meaningful improvement in their QOL. It is also noticed that the QOL improvement, that is, symptom reduction, takes place more intensively up to three months after surgery, between three and six months the situation tends to settle and a new reduction takes place up to twelve months.

The stabilized situation at six months seems to be linked to emotional and effective aspects, as well as to symptoms that arise in the Emotional Reaction domain, making it relevant to consider a psychotherapeutic intervention. Hypothesis after three months from surgery, aim to prevent emotional and affective changes, and regular evaluation of these symptoms, if necessary, to undergo medical treatment. After twelve months from the meningioma removal the patients meaningfully improved in the Pain, Emotional Reactions, Sleepiness, Physical Abilities, Communication, Physical Condition, Independence and Psychological Condition dimensions. In the remaining dimensions (Autonomic Nervous System, Function, Energy Level, Isolation and Social Interaction) we observe a tendency, thought not significant, to reduce symptoms (QOL improvement).

Studies that specifically look at the emotional aspect with prospective evaluations could better elaborate this question – as well as conducting evaluations both pre and post psychotherapeutic and/or drug therapy to verify the importance of a specific treatment over a period of time to improve the QOL of patients during their recovery.

This study featured were limited due to the size of the sample, this made it difficult for a more specific analysis concerning factors such as age, level of school education, size of tumor, grade of edema, resection grade and meningiomas location. Even so, it was possible to observe that patients who had meningiomas in the left hemisphere show higher symptomatology, but those were also the ones who have shown significant reduction of the symptoms after the surgical intervention.

The presence of co-morbidities possibly interfered in the results obtained in this work, since the QOL instruments do not allow the distinction from existing diseases.

REFERENCES

Arienta C, Caroli M, Balbi S (1992). Intracranial meningiomas in patients over 70 years old. Follow-up in operated and inoperable cases. Aging (Milano), 4: 29-33.

Black PM (1993). Meningiomas. Neurosurgery, 32: 643-657.

Botega NJ, Bio MR, Zomignani MA, Garcia C Jr, Pereira WAB (1995). Mood disorders in hospital and the validation of the measurement of the (HAD) scale, anxiety and depression. Rev. Saúde Pública, 29(5): 355-363.

Chan RC, Thompson GB (1984). Morbidity, mortality, and the QOL following surgery for intracranial meningiomas. A retrospective study in 257 cases. J. Neurosurg., 60: 52-60.

Chibnall JR, Tait RC (1990). The quality of life scale: A preliminary study with chronic pain patients. Psychol. Health, 4: 283-292.

Figueiredo EG, Aguiar PH, Córdoba BF (1998). Meningiomas supratentoriais: diagnosis, surgical results and complications. Arq Neuro-Psiquiatr., 56: 429-35.

Gotay CC, Moore TD (1992). Assessing QOL in head and neck cancer. Qual. Life Res., 1: 5-17.

Guiteras AF, Bayés R (1993). Desarrolo de un instrumento para la medida de calidad de vida en enfermedades crónicas. In: Forns M, Anguera MT, organizadores. Aportaciones recientes a la evaluación psicologica. Barcelona: Universitas, pp. 175-195.

Hernández EG, Rodriguez MR (2004). Meningiomas Intercranial evolution in patients treated in INNN. Av. Med. Cuba, 11(40): 10-11.

Kalkanis SN, Quiñones-Hinojosa A, Buzney E, Ribaudo HJ, Black PM (2000). Quality of life following surgery for intracranial meningiomas at Brigham and Women's Hospital: a study of 164 patients using a modification of the functional assessment of cancer therapy-brain questionnaire. J. Neurooncol., 48: 233-241.

Karnofsky DA, Abelmann WH, Craver LF, Burchenall JF (1948). The use of nitrogen mustard in the palliative treatment of cancer with particular reference to bronchogenic carcinoma. Cancer, 1: 634-656.

Kozler P, Benes V, Netuka D, Kramár F, Charvat F (2007). Preoperative neuro-image findings as a predictor of postoperative neurological deficit in intracranial meningiomas. Zentralbl Neurochir., 68(4): 190-194.

McDonough EM, Varvares MA, Dunphy FR, Dunleavy T, Dunphy CH, Boyd JH (1996). Changes in quality of life resulted in a population of patients treated for squamous cell carcinoma of the head and neck. Head Neck, 18: 487-493.

Miao Y, Lu X, Qiu Y, Lin Y (2010). A multivariate analysis of prognostic factors for health-related quality of life in patients with surgically

managed meningioma. J. Clin. Neurosci., 17(4): 446-449.
Mirimanoff RO, Dosoretz DE, Linggood RM, Ojemann R, Martuza R (1985). Meningioma: Analysis of recurrence and progression following neurosurgical resection. J. Neurosurg., 62: 18-24.
Mohsenipour I, Deusch E, Gabl M, Hofer M, Twerdy K (2001). Quality of Life In Patients After Meningioma Resection. Acta Neurochir. (Wien), 143: 547-553.
Neil-Dwyer G, Lang DA, Davis A (2000). Outcome from complex neurosurgery: an evidence based approach. Acta Neurochir (Wien), 142: 367-371.
Rachlin JR, Roseblum ML (1991). Etiology and biology of meningiomas. In : Al-Mefty O (ed). Meningiomas. Nova York: Raven Press, pp. 22-37.
Sachenheimer W, Piotrowski W, Bimmler T (1992). Quality of life in patients with intracranial tumors on the basis of Karnofsky's performance status. J. Neurooncol., 13: 177-181.
Sachsenheimer W, Bimmler T (1992). Assessment of quality of survival in patients with surgically treated meningioma. Neurochirurgia (Stuttg), 35: 133-136.
Salo J, Niemelä A, Joukamaa M, Koivukangas J (2002). The effect of brain tumor laterality on patients' perceived quality of life. J. Neurol. Neurosurg. Psychiat., 72(3): 373-377.
Santana Jr PA, Marie SKN, Aguiar PHP (2002). Molecular Biology of meningiomas: Many unknown factors remain to be clarified. J. Bras. Neurocirurg., 13: 81-86.
Santos CB, Carvalho SCA, Silva MFG, Fuentes D, Santana PA, Furlan AB, Aguiar PHP (2008). Cross-cultural Adaptation of Innsbruck Health Dimensions Questionnaire for Neurosurgical Patients (IHD-NS). Arq Neuropsiquiatr., 66(3-B): 698-701.
Schiestel C, Ryan D (2009). Quality of life in patients with meningiomas: the true meaning of "benign". Front Biosci. (Elite Ed), 1: 488-493.
Simpson D (1957). The reoccurrence of intracranial meningiomas after surgical treatment. J. Neurol. Neurosurg. Psychiat., 20: 22-39.
Teixeira-Samela LF, Magalhães LC, Souza AC, Lima MC, Lima RCM, Goulart F (2004). Adaption of a health profile Nottingham: A simple instrument to evaluate the QOL. Cad. Public Health, 20: 905-914.
Wertenbroek AA, Kuiters RR, de Bruijn SF, van Woerkom TC (2006). A meningioma resulting in drastic changes in behavior and life course. Ned Tijdschr Geneeskd, 150(50): 2733-2738.
WHO international histological classification of CNS tumors (1993). Springer, Berlin. Heidelberg. New York, Tokio.
Yamashiro S, Nishi T, Koga K, Kaji M, Goto T, Muta D, Fujioka S, Kuratsu J (2007). A self assessment of quality of life in patients who underwent surgery for asymptomatic Meningiomas. No Shinkei Geka, 35(12): 1149-1155.

Postoperative bilateral thalamic infarct: Rare but mortal neurologic complications of the coronary artery bypass graft surgery

Sureyya Talay, Derih Ay, Ozgur Dag, Mehmet Ali Kaygin and Bilgehan Erkut*

Department of Cardiovascular Surgery, Erzurum Regional Training and Research Hospital Erzurum, Turkey.

We report a case of an early postoperative major neurologic complication following coronary artery bypass graft operation with cardiopulmonary bypass. Computed tomography scanning at the first postoperative day of the head revealed a cerebral infarction in bilaterally thalamic location and mesecephalon with a surrounding edema of the tissue. Following the antiedematous therapy, computed tomography scanning was repeated at the fifth day of postoperation, while cerebral pathology was proved to persist at the twelfth day of postoperation. Patients' neurological status did not improve with medication and as such, worsened gradually. However, extubation was not possible during the intensive care unit follow-up period. Consequently, the patient died at the fifteenth day of post operation.

Key words: Bilateral thalamic infarct, myocardial revascularization/adverse effects, cerebrovascular accident, postoperative stroke, risk factors.

INTRODUCTION

Early postoperative complications of surgical revascularization of the heart may involve all organ systems including the heart, lungs, gastrointestinal tracts and nervous system by different degrees. Specific complications are generally rare, but can occur as a heart attack, death or stroke (Arthur et al., 1996). Neurological injury presents a wide perspective of the mental status which differs from minor neurocognitive disabilities to coma. Coronary artery bypass grafting (CABG) with cardiopulmonary bypass (CPB) technique is reported to be with a percentage of 3 to 5% for postoperative stroke in various publications. Postoperative stroke may result to a variety of operative sources (Anyanwu et al., 2007; Oliveira et al., 2008) and the ascending aorta is considered to be the main reason for mobile plaques and/or calcifications which can be affected by side clamps during proximal anastomosis and aortic cannulation. As such, emboli from this structure may lead to stroke postoperatively. This major and mortal neurologic complication produced a catastrophic clinical situation. In this case, the origin of emboli was unclear and we were unable to verify or exclude a certain determination. Nonetheless, this major neurologic complication is considered to be lethal by our experience.

*Corresponding author. E-mail: bilgehanerkut@yahoo.com.

Case report

We report a case of an early postoperative major neurologic complication following coronary artery bypass graft operation with CPB. In January 2010, a 47 year old male patient with a history of unstable angina pectoris was presented to the emergency department following hypertension episodes and nausea. He has a past medical history of hypertension, hyperlipidemia and tobacco smoking for 22 years. On physical examination, he was alert with a normal mental status. His arterial blood pressure was 170/90 mmHg with a sinus and his regular heart rate was between 100 and 110. His oral temperature was 38°C with oxygen saturation of 95% and his lungs and heart were clear to auscultation without murmurs. Neurological examination was also noted to be normal, whereas peripheral arterial pulses were palpable in all extremity areas. However, cervical murmur was not noted with carotid auscultation, in that the remainder of the physical examination was normal.

Laboratory examination was normal and the chest radiograph showed no abnormalities including aortic calcification. By the transthoracic echocardiogram, no aortic insufficiency and/or stenosis were observed and the left ventricular ejection fraction was 60% without any wall motion abnormality. As such, the coronary angiography demonstrated a critical stenosis for the left anterior descending artery, the high lateral branch of the circumflex coronary artery and the right coronary artery (Figure 1). However, there was no evidence suggestive of thrombus in the left ventricle, but a coronary arterial bypass grafting (CABG) was indicated after the presentation of the coronary lesions. Preoperatively, the patient was re-evaluated by the laboratory findings clinically, and it showed that there was no neurological pathology and laboratory examination.

After routine preoperative preparation, the patient was undertaken in a general anesthesia with central venous catheterization and arterial monitorization. Then, the left internal thoracic artery and right lower extremity great saphenous vein were harvested for grafts after sternotomy. Three reversed autogenous saphenous vein grafts were anastomosed to the right coronary artery distally, the second obtuse branches of the circumflex artery and to the diagonal artery distally which were followed by a left internal thoracic artery to the left anterior descending coronary anastomosis. The aortic x-clamp time was 62 min and the proximal anastomosis was performed with a single application of a side-biting aortic clamp. As such, the operation was closed with an uneventful routine. Upon returning from the operation room, the patient was noted to be hemodynamically stable for the early postoperative period without any hypotensive or tachycardia episodes and the evaluation of his postoperative vital signs was normal in the intubation period. The patient's pupil examination revealed a normal shape and size. Bilaterally, the pupils were constrictive to light on both direct and consensual response. Although a normal pupil examination was done, he did not have the normal extremity movement and the related awakening of the cerebral functions. Besides, there was no spontaneous eye opening. As a result of this pathological undesirable situation, the computed tomography (CT) was made. CT scanning revealed a cerebral infarction in bilaterally thalamic location and mesecephalon with surrounding edema of the tissue at the second postoperative day (Figure 2). The antiedematous therapy (deksametazon sodyum 4 mg, as 3x1 P.E) was started on the patient and the cerebral pathology was proved to persist at the twelfth day of postoperation. The patient's neurological status did not improve with medication and as such, worsened gradually. However, extubation was not possible during the intensive care unit follow-up period. As a result, the patient died at the fifteenth day of post operation.

Comment

CABG is one of the most frequently performed surgical procedures. The annual number of operations is approximately 800,000 worldwide. Parallel to the increased quantity of this operation, co-morbidities, mortalities and complications also enhance the number steadily. Early deaths after CABG operation were reported to be around 4 to 25% in heterogeneous groups. These premature deaths occur because of patient ages, severity and location of atherosclerosis in coronary system, chronic lung diseases, lower left ventricle function, ischemic mitral insufficiency, unstable angina pectoris, emergency cases and co-morbidities such as hypertension and diabetes (Arthur et al., 1996). Early postoperative complications of surgical revascularization of the heart may involve all the systems of the organ including the heart, lungs, gastrointestinal tracts and the nervous system by different degrees. Specific complications are generally rare, but can occur as an heart attack, death or stroke (Arthur et al., 1996; Anyanwu et al., 2007).

Stroke is defined as a focal or generalized cerebral dysfunction by vascular pathologies lasting more than 24 h. As clearly stated by the previous medical reports, one of the most devastating and catastrophic postoperative situation after CABG operation is neurologic injury (Anyanwu et al., 2007; Oliveira et al., 2008; Glance et al., 2007). The neurological injury presents a wide perspective of the mental status which differs from the minor neurocognitive disabilities to coma. CABG with cardiopulmonary bypass technique is reported to be with a percentage of 3 to 5% for postoperative stroke in various publications (Arthur et al., 1996; Anyanwu et al., 2007; Oliveira et al., 2008; Glance et al., 2007). Postoperative stroke may result to a variety of operative sources. Ascending aorta is considered to be the main reason for mobile plaques and/or calcifications which can be affected by side clamps during proximal anastomosis and aortic cannulation. Emboli from these structures may lead to stroke postoperatively (Ngaage et al., 2008). The neurological defects are also reported to be associated with the cardiopulmonary bypass circuit by lower intra-operative circulation pressures and micro and macro emboli which can be caused by gasses, foreign surface reactions and a wide variety of hematological factors such as platelet clots (Lev-Ran et al., 2005). Early postoperative arrhythmia and atrial fibrillation may be another reason for cardiac emboli in the central nervous system. On the other hand, concomitant cerebral and carotid system atherosclerosis enhances the postoperative rates of stroke (Manabe et al., 2002).

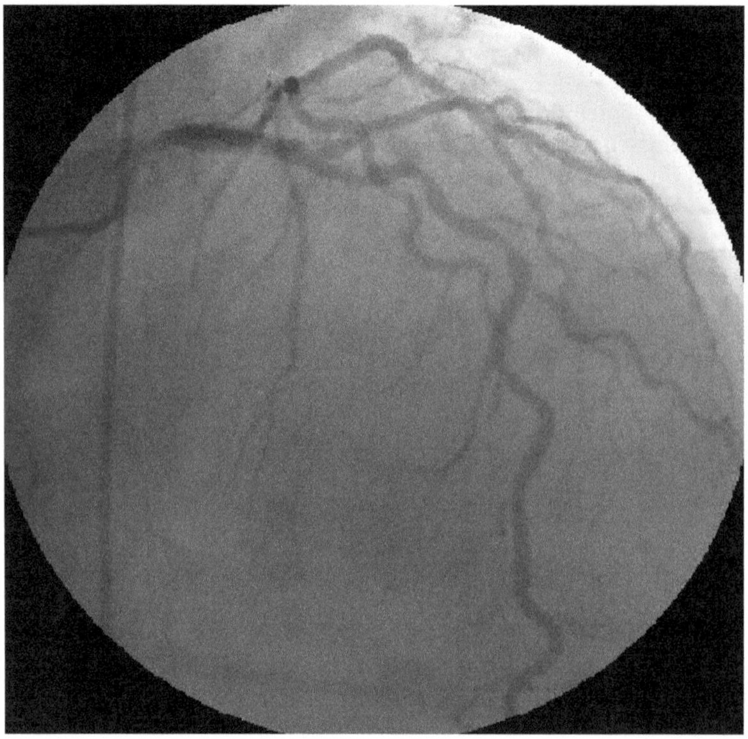

Figure 1. Preoperative coronary angiography with severe coronary stenosis.

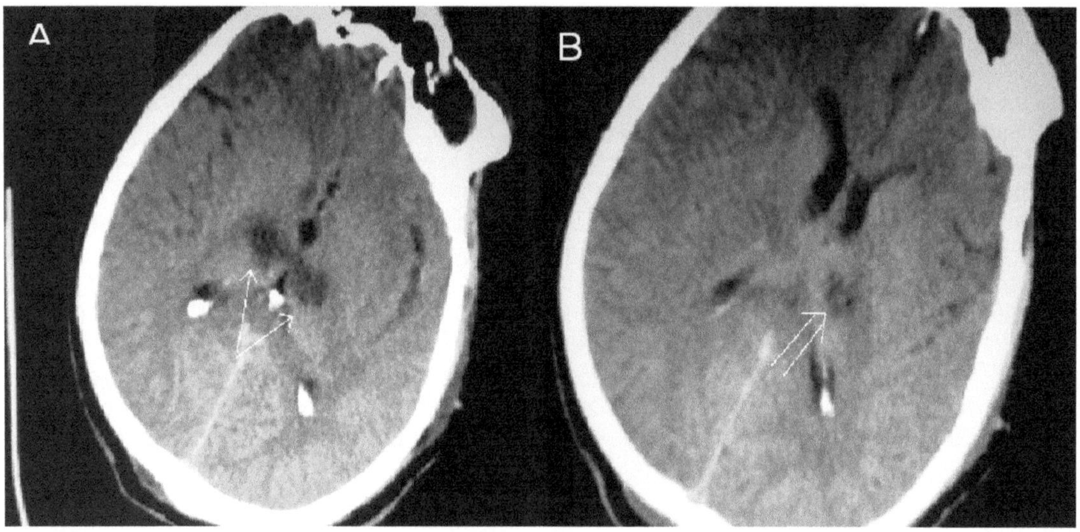

Figure 2. Postoperative CT demonstrating mesecephalic and bilateral thalamic infarction early at the fifth day.

Evaluations of the surgical technique of practice have been focused on the elimination of this neurological complication. Despite these efforts, elderly patients undergoing CABG operations are at higher risk of stroke depending on the facts of aorta calcifications and cerebral conditions. Almost every patient, over 75, presents a severe aortic atheroma by postmortem evaluations. In this case, it is the most frequent reason why emboli leads to cerebral infarctions (Patel et al., 2002). With regards to this view, the incidence of cerebral emboli may be reduced by avoiding any manipulations of the aorta as in no-touch aorta off-pump coronary surgery and MIDCAB operations.

Definition of the aortic atherosclerosis and the existing calcifications are advocated to be executed by preoperative trans-eosophageal echocardiography in the medical literature. In our opinion, this non-invasive imaging technique is definitively profitable, but administration difficulties may limit its practice especially for severe coronary atherosclerosis patients with unstable angina pectoris. Naresh et al. (2000) reported a significant reduction on postoperative stroke among cardiac surgery patients with preoperative trans-eosophageal echocardiographic evaluations and off-pump techniques. They underlined the rate of mobile atherosclerosis at the aorta in a rate of 2.84% for 3,660 patients and reported a stroke rate of 0.96%, which is considerably lower than other publications which indicate the beneficial sides of preoperative echocardiography. Additionally, among off-pump CABG patients, he reported a peri-operative stroke rate for 0%.

Conventional chest roentgenograms are another valuable preoperative evaluation technique for aortic calcifications. Findings on x-ray and intra-operative palpations may play a life-saving role on cannulation and anastomosis decisions. On the other hand, the carotid system Doppler ultrasonography may alert the surgeon against possible extra cerebral and extra cardiac sources of postoperative stroke. Postoperative stroke may occur because of focal or multi-focal and/or generalized cerebral infarctions. Several studies and medical reports (Stroobant et al., 2002) underline the possible reasons for peri-operative neurological deterioration; although postoperative cerebral lesion localizations still remain unclear. Directly, the localization of infarction is clearly the most significative factor of the patients' clinical outcome. Weinstein et al. (2001) reported their experience of perioperative stroke among CABG operations. He published the data of cerebral infarction localizations and its determinatives in a group of patients that consisted of 2,217 consecutive cases, while the stroke rate was reported in 51 cases (2.3%). Cerebral localizations were also classified as 21 left hemisphere, 10 right hemisphere, 7 bilateral, 1 brainstem, 7 lacunar and 5 indeterminative. Conclusively, he reported 75% (18 out of 24 patients) of the cases as left-sided. Contrary to common belief, stroke patients were observed to be younger than the non-stroke group (66.3 ± 10.52 versus 71.4 ± 8.47 years). Weinstein advocated a side-hole aortic cannula to reduce stroke rates eventually. In this present case report, an end-hole aortic cannulation was preferred, while in our case report, we specifically present a cerebral postoperative infarction which took place in the mesencephalon and bilateral thalamic region. This major and mortal neurologic complication produced a catastrophic clinical situation. In this case, the origin of emboli was unclear and we were not able to verify or exclude a certain determination. Nonetheless, this major neurologic complication is considered to be lethal by our experience.

REFERENCES

Anyanwu AC, Filsoufi F, Salzberg SP, Bronster DJ, Adams DH (2007). Epidemiology of stroke after cardiac surgery in current era. J. Thorac. Cardiovasc. Surg., 134: 1121-1127.

Arthur E, Baue MD (1996). Glenn's Thoracic and Cardiovascular Surgery, Sixth Edition. Appleton. And. Lange, pp. 2095-2099.

Glance LG, Osler TM, Mukamel DB, Dick AW (2007). Effect of complications on mortality after coronary artery bypass grafting surgery: Evidence from New York State. J. Thorac. Cardiovasc. Surg., 134: 53-58.

Lev-Ran O, Braunstein R, Sharony R, Kramer A, Paz Y, Mohr R, Uretzky G (2005). No-touch aorta off-pump coronary surgery: The effect on stroke. J. Thorac. Cardiovasc. Surg., 129: 307-313. 5.

Manabe S, Shimokawa T, Fukui T, Fumimoto K, Ozawa N, Seki H, Ikenaga S, Takannashi S (2002). Influence of carotid artery stenosis on stroke in patients undergoing off-pump coronary artery bypass grafting. Eur. J. Thorac. Surg., 21: 434-439.

Naresh T, Manisha M, Ravi RK, Anil M (2000). Reduced neurological injury during CABG in patients with mobile aortic atheromas: a five year follow-up study. Ann. Thorac. Surg., 70: 1558-1564.

Ngaage DL, Cowen ME, Griffin S, Guvendik L, Cale AR (2008). Early neurological complication after coronary artery bypasses grafting and valve surgery in octogenarians. Eur. J. Cardiothorac. Surg., 33: 653-659.

Oliveira DC, Ferro CR, Oliveira JB, Malta MM, Barros NP, Cano SJ, Martins SK, Souza LC, Jatene AD, Piegas LS (2008). Risk factors for stroke after coronary artery bypass grafting. Arq. Bras. Cardiol., 91: 213-216.

Patel NC, Deodhar AP, Grayson, Pullan M, Keenan DJM, Hasan R, Fabry BM (2002). Neurological outcomes in coronary surgery: İndependent effect of avoiding cardiopulmonary bypass. Ann. Thorac. Surg., 74: 400-406.

Stroobant N, Nooten GV, Belleghem YV, Vingerhoets G (2002). Short-term and long-term neurocognitive outcome in on-pump versus off-pump CABG. Eur. J. Thorac. Surg., 22: 559-564.

Weinstein G (2001). Left hemispheric strokes in coronary surgery: implications for end –hole aortic cannulas. Ann. Thorac. Surg., 71: 128-132.

17

Non-drug strategies in the management of depression: A comprehensive study of systematic review and meta-analysis of randomised controlled trials

Sameer Dhingra[1,2]* and Milind Parle[2]

[1]Institute of Pharmacy and Emerging Sciences, Baddi University of Emerging Sciences and Technology, Baddi, Himachal Pradesh, India.
[2]Pharmacology Division, Department of Pharmaceutical Sciences, Guru Jambheshwar University of Science and Technology, Hisar, Haryana, India.

Between 5 to 10% of the population experience depression at any time in any year, needing psychiatric or psychosocial intervention. The World Health Organization has reported that depression's financial burden globally ranked fourth in 2000, and will increase by 2020 to be the second most costly disease. This paper focus on the range of non-drug strategies available to patients, other than prescribed pharmacological treatments, which could be helpful in treating depression.

Key words: Systematic review, meta-analysis, depression, non-drug, psychological therapies, exercise and lifestyle interventions, complementary and alternative treatments.

INTRODUCTION

Depression is a global health problem. According to the World Health Organization, it affects about 121 million people worldwide, and those numbers are increasing. It is estimated to be the leading cause of mental disability worldwide and is predicted to be the 2nd leading cause of all health disability by 2020. Depressive disorders affect as many as 18.8 million American adults or about 9.5% of the U.S. population age 18 and older in any given year, according to the National Institute of Mental Health. Though the global estimates are not available, depression costs more than US$ 83 billion annually in medical treatment and lost productivity in work place to US economy, according to a published report (Michael, 2011).

The management of depression depends on its severity, and treatment includes non-pharmacological and pharmacological approaches or both. The non-pharmacological approaches play a significant role in the management of depression individually as well as in addition to pharmacological treatment. Sometimes, these are preferred over pharmacological approaches due to their non-harmful and non addictive effect. This paper identifies and examines the non-drug strategies for the management of depression. These include psychological therapies, exercise and lifestyle interventions, and complementary and alternative treatments. It also provides evidence based an assessment of these interventions for depression in adult population.

METHODS

This paper focus on systematic review and randomised controlled trial (RCT) evidence of effectiveness, with searches extended to identify observational studies only where appropriate. Therapies commonly available to patients without prescriptions were selected for inclusion. Studies were excluded where there was no formal diagnosis by International Classification of Disease (ICD) 9, ICD 10, Diagnostic Statistical Manual (DSM)-III or DSM-IV, or use of a recognized, validated and reliable measurement scale specifically for depressive symptoms. Further, the studies in patient groups with clear indicators of severe depression or with significant psychological and/or physical comorbidities were also excluded.

A systematic review of the literature was carried out using an unambiguous search strategy. Databases searched include: Pubmed, Medline, Embase, Cinahl, PsycINFO, AMED, and the Cochrane Library. The year range covered was 1998 to 2010 with

*Corresponding author. E-mail: sameerdhingra78@yahoo.com.

variations depending on topic. Internet searches were also carried out on various websites.

RESULTS

Results of the systematic review and meta-analysis of RCTs are broadly classified and detailed into psychological therapies, exercise and lifestyle interventions, and complementary and alternative treatments along with evidence based assessment of these interventions.

PSYCHOLOGICAL THERAPIES

Psychological therapies include a range of treatments that are usually based on a time-limited interpersonal relationship between the therapist and patient/client. The aim of the psychological therapies is to alleviate the symptoms of depression using a variety of techniques which put different emphasis on the past, present or future. These include:

Behavioural activation

Behavioral activation is a brief, structured, goal-focused therapeutic approach to treating acute depression that seeks to alleviate depression by promoting an individual's contact with sources of reward through increasing activation, improving problem solving, and decreasing avoidance and other barriers to activation (Dimidjian and Davis, 2009). A meta-analysis of 34 randomised controlled studies with 2055 participants found behavioural activation to be effective in reducing depressive symptoms in adults and older adults compared to treatment as usual and waiting list control, and as effective as cognitive therapy (Mazzucchelli et al., 2009). This is consistent with the conclusions of other studies incorporating behavioural activation therapy as part of a larger meta-analysis in adults and older patients (Cuijpers et al., 2006, 2007).

Cognitive behavioural therapy

Cognitive behavioural therapy (CBT) is a psycho-therapeutic approach, a talking therapy, which aims to solve problems concerning dysfunctional emotions, behaviors and cognitions through a goal-oriented, systematic procedure. The title is used in diverse ways to designate behavior therapy, cognitive therapy, and to refer to therapy based upon a combination of basic behavioral and cognitive research (Dimidjian and Davis, 2009). There is strong and consistent meta-analysis and systematic review evidence that CBT is more effective than either treatment as usual or waiting list control in the treatment of depression in adults and older adults and is at least as effective as antidepressant medication. For those studies where follow up was examined, CBT was at least as effective as antidepressant medication over six months to two years follow up. In some studies CBT was more effective than other psychological therapies whilst other studies suggest CBT has similar effectiveness to other systematic therapies such as psychodynamic therapy and interpersonal therapy (Cuijpers et al., 2006; Churchill et al., 2001; Hensley et al., 2004; Leichsenring, 2001; Mackin and Arean, 2005; Pinquart et al., 2006).

In an another systematic review, patients receiving individual CBT were more likely to improve and had fewer symptoms as follow up than patients receiving group CBT (Churchill et al., 2001). A systematic review of CBT in adults with major depressive disorder who had not responded to at least one course of antidepressant medication identified two studies providing adequate data for interpretation. Although there was benefit of CBT (15 to 30 sessions) in treatment-resistant depression, the evidence base is insufficient to support a recommendation in this patient group (McPherson et al., 2005).

Counselling

Counselling is the skilled and principled use of relationships which develop self knowledge, emotional acceptance and growth, and personal resources. The overall aim is to live more fully and satisfyingly. Counselling may be concerned with addressing and resolving specific problems, making decisions, coping with crises, working through inner feelings and inner conflict, or improving relationships with others. The counsellor's role is to facilitate the patient's work in ways that respect the patient's values, personal resources, and capacity for self determination (Michael and Gillian, 2001). In the literature the term 'counselling' encompasses a variety of approaches. An RCT compared GP treatment as usual with GP treatment as usual plus psychodynamic or cognitive behavioural counselling (average 6 sessions, range 1 to 16 sessions) in patients with depression. At 6, 12 and 36 months follow up there were no significant differences between the study groups in Beck Depression Inventory scores. Diagnostic selection criteria were unclear and there were variations in the counselling intervention (Simpson et al., 2000, 2003; Corney and Simpson, 2005).

Another RCT had patient preference arms and compared randomised antidepressant treatment with randomised counselling, preference antidepressant and preference counselling. The recommended number of counselling sessions was six. GPs were guided to prescribe one of three antidepressants (Bedi et al., 2000;

Chilvers et al., 2001). There was no clear superiority of any treatment approach at eight weeks. At 12 months follow up, generic counselling was as effective as antidepressants but antidepressants may result in more rapid recovery and are likely to be chosen by those who are more severely depressed.

Marital therapy

Marital therapy or couple-focused therapy has the twofold aim of modifying negative interaction patterns and increasing mutually supportive aspects of couple relationships, thus changing the interpersonal context linked to depression (Barbato and D'Avazo, 2007). A systematic review identified eight studies evaluating the effect of marital therapy on depression (Barbato and D'Avazo, 2007). A variety of treatment models were subsumed within the marital therapy approach, including CBT, emotion-focused, interpersonal and systemic therapy. A variety of control comparisons were used, including CBT, interpersonal therapy, drug therapy, combined individual and drug therapy and waiting list. Duration of treatment ranged from 10 to 20 weeks and follow up ranged from post-test to two years. Studies were characterized by small sample size, lack of intention to treat analysis and high numbers could not follow up. The review concluded there was no evidence to support marital therapy being any more or less effective than one to one therapies or drug therapy in the treatment of depression, even when associated with marital distress. In comparison to no/minimal treatment the outcome for depression was better in the marital therapy group, although this was based on only two small studies. Marital therapy should be considered where the current relationship is contributing to the depression, or where involvement of a partner is considered to be of potential therapeutic benefit.

Family therapy

Family therapy helps people in a close relationship to help each other. It enables family members to express and explore difficult thoughts and emotions safely, to understand each other's experiences and views, appreciate each other's needs, build on family strengths and make useful changes in their relationships and their lives (Allison et al., 2003). Studies of the effect of family therapy on depressive symptoms have been conducted in very specific patient populations and the results are not easily generalized. In one poor quality study, twelve sessions of cognitive behavioural family intervention were as effective as 12 sessions of behavioural family intervention in alleviating depressive symptoms in mothers who have a child with conduct disorder (Sanders and McFarland, 2000).

Hypnotherapy

Hypnotherapy is any therapeutic approach using hypnosis as a main technique, for example, to promote imaginal re-exposure or relaxation (Alladin and Alibhai, 2007). One RCT with methodological limitations found that CBT supplemented by hypnotherapy produced a significantly larger reduction in depressive symptoms than CBT alone. This effect was sustained at six and 12 month follows up. It is unclear whether the interventions were equivalent in terms of duration of therapy offered to patients (Alladin and Alibhai, 2007).

Interpersonal therapy

Interpersonal therapy (IPT) is a time-limited intervention, which aims to reduce symptoms by working on improving the quality of the patient's interpersonal relationships. IPT focuses on specific interpersonal problem areas such as grief, role transition and interpersonal disputes. A positive therapeutic alliance is encouraged and a range of therapeutic strategies are employed to encourage the open expression of affect and problem resolution. Patient literacy is not required (Stuart and Robertson, 2003). A systematic review examining achievement of complete remission in major depression found that IPT, CBT and medication were equally effective (Casacalenda et al., 2002). A further systematic review of nine studies reported consistent evidence that IPT, delivered according to the standard manual of over 12 to 20 sessions, is superior to placebo and similar in effectiveness to antidepressant medication (prescribed at therapeutic doses) and to CBT in patients with depression (de Mello et al., 2005). A subsequent RCT comparing IPT with CBT concluded that the therapies are equally effective for depression. For severe depression CBT showed slightly higher levels of symptom reduction at end of treatment than IPT (Luty et al., 2007).

Mindfulness based cognitive therapy

Mindfulness-based cognitive therapy is a brief group intervention that seeks to prevent depressive relapse by promoting mindful attention, acceptance, and skillful action to help individuals interrupt habitual cognitive and effective patterns associated with risk of relapse (Dimidjian and Davis, 2009). A systematic review identified two RCTs showing that mindfulness based cognitive therapy conducted in a group setting (8 x 2-2.5 h sessions) reduced relapse in chronic depression (three or more depressive episodes) by over 50% during a one year follow up period, compared to treatment as usual. There was no reduction in relapse for patients having experienced one or two episodes of depression (Coelho et al., 2007).

Music therapy

Music therapy is a therapeutic approach where music-making forms the primary basis for communication (Maratos et al., 2008). A Cochrane review of five small and diverse studies concluded that music therapy on its own or as an adjunct to psychological therapies, is acceptable to people with depression and is associated with improvements in mood. Due to less number of studies, it is not possible to be confident of its effectiveness (Maratos et al., 2008).

Problem solving therapy

Problem solving therapy (PST) is a brief focused psychological intervention that is delivered by an individual trained in problem solving approaches. These are often highly individualized and have a pragmatic focus, in which the professional and individual work through a series of defined steps to clarify the person's problems, desired goals, generate potential solutions and help to implement the chosen solution (Cuijpers et al., 2007). A well conducted meta-analysis of PST in depression found that, in general, PST was more effective than control interventions. There was significant variation in the outcome measures used and there was large heterogeneity. Overall effect size (ES) varied according to the type of analysis: ES = 0.34, when it was assumed that all interventions were equivalent (fixed effects model), ES = 0.83, when it was assumed the interventions differed in some way (random effects model). This indicates that PST has varying effects on depression and may be considered as a treatment option for patients with depression (Cuijpers et al., 2007).

Psychodynamic psychotherapy

Psychodynamic psychotherapy is based on psychodynamic theories of development and of the mind and includes attention to unconscious as well as conscious mental processes. The approach places emphasis on the importance of the therapeutic relationship, including transference and counter transference, are difficulties from the past and can be repeated in the therapeutic relationship as well as in current relationships and therefore understood and changed. The therapy involves both expressive and supportive elements. By allowing the patient to express thoughts and feelings freely in the sessions with the therapist the patient can become more objective and effect desired change (Leichsenring, 2001). A number of variants of psychodynamic psychotherapy are used in studies, making comparisons difficult. One systematic review identified six studies comparing short term psychodynamic psychotherapy with CBT for outpatients with major depression and found the two therapies to be equally effective in the treatment of depression, although results were considered to be preliminary due to the small number of trials (Leichsenring, 2001).

Reminiscence therapy

Reminiscence therapy involves a progressive return to an awareness of past experiences, both successful and unsuccessful, so that salient life experiences may be re-examined and re-integrated. The life review process gives older people opportunities to place their accomplishments in perspective, to resolve lingering conflicts, and to find new significance and meaning in their lives, thereby relieving the despair and depression that often accompany ageing (Watt and Cappeliez, 2000). Two studies of reminiscence therapy in older adults with depression were identified (Klausner et al., 1998; Watt and Cappeliez, 2000). Reminiscence therapy was compared with goal-focused psychotherapy and active socialization group as the control condition. Results were equivocal and studies were generally of poor methodological quality.

Art therapy

Art therapy is a form of psychotherapy that uses art media as its primary mode of communication (Shirley, 2001). No evidence specific to depression was identified on the use of art therapy.

Cognitive behavioural analysis system of psychotherapy

Cognitive behavioural analysis system of psychotherapy (CBASP) is an integrative model that combines behavioural, cognitive, psychodynamic and interpersonal procedures. It was developed specifically for treatment of chronic forms of depression and focuses primarily on helping the depressed person to understand how their behaviour can influence the outcome of problematic interpersonal situations. Specific examples of such situations, including the therapeutic relationship are analyzed in detail in order to improve interpersonal skills and teach more effective engagement with the social environment (McCullough, 2000). No evidence specific to depression was identified on the use CBASP therapy.

Cognitive analytic therapy

Cognitive analytic therapy is a brief integrative therapy comprising elements of cognitive behavioural and psychodynamic therapies in an active, structured and collaborative approach, based on written and diagrammatic reformulations of the presenting difficulty (Denman, 2001). No evidence specific to depression was identified on the use cognitive analytic therapy.

Eye movement desensitization and reprocessing

Eye movement desensitization and reprocessing (EMDR) therapy is used for post-traumatic conditions in which the client is asked to hold in mind the image of the trauma, a negative self cognition, negative emotions and related physical sensations. While doing so the client is instructed to move his or her eyes quickly and laterally back and forth. Other forms of left-right alternating stimulation (auditory) may be used. This procedure continues until desensitisation of troubling material is complete and positive self cognitions have replaced the previous negative self cognition (Shapiro, 2001). No evidence specific to depression was identified on the use EMDR therapy.

Neurolinguistic programming

Neurolinguistic programming (NLP) is a therapeutic technique to detect and re-program unconscious patterns of thought and behaviour in order to alter psychological responses (Lisa, 2008). No evidence specific to depression was identified on the use NLP therapy.

EXERCISE AND LIFE STYLE MODIFICATIONS

Exercise

Exercise is a subset of physical activity, which is any movement of the body that results in energy expenditure rising above resting level, and includes activities of daily living, domestic chores, gardening and walking. Exercise is undertaken to improve health or as part of sports or leisure time activities including swimming, jogging, brisk walking, going to the gym, tennis, football and cricket. Evidence from systematic reviews and meta-analyses consistently supports structured exercise in a range of environments; home, community, health care settings, leisure center etc. as an effective treatment in reducing symptoms of depression. Exercise (both aerobic, for example, Walking and jogging and anaerobic, for example, weight training) reduces depressive symptoms in patients with mild to moderate depression and is as effective as antidepressant medications. There is a large evidence base for aerobic exercise than for anaerobic exercise (Babyak et al., 2000; Blumenthal et al., 2007; Dunn et al., 2002, 2005; Mather et al., 2002; Nabkasorn et al., 2006; Singh et al., 2001).

A Cochrane review of 23 trials (n = 907) found a large and statistically significant clinical effect of exercise (measured post-treatment) when compared to no treatment or control intervention. Further, in comparisons of effectiveness with antidepressant medication and CBT there was no difference between exercise and the established interventions (Mead et al., 2008). The benefits of exercise have generally been shown to be independent of social group effect (Dunn et al., 2005).

Lifestyle modifications

No good quality evidence was identified on the effect of reducing alcohol consumption and caffeine intake on depressive symptoms.

COMPLEMENTARY AND ALTERNATIVE THERAPIES

Acupuncture

Acupuncture is a family of procedures involving the stimulation of anatomical locations on or in the skin by a variety of techniques. There are a number of different approaches to diagnosis and treatment in acupuncture that incorporate medical traditions from China, Japan, Korea, and other countries. Four good quality systematic reviews of poor quality RCTs of acupuncture in patients with depression were identified (Smith, 2005; Mukaino et al., 2005; Leo and Ligot, 2007; Hao et al., 2008). Results were inconclusive and studies had a number of methodological limitations.

Animal assisted therapy

Animal assisted therapy is a therapy that uses dogs or other pets to improve the physical and mental health of patients with certain acute or chronic diseases. There is evidence from one systematic review that the introduction of animal assisted activities may have beneficial effects on the severity of depressive symptoms in older people resident in nursing homes and psychiatric institutions. The degree to which the benefits found are a result of animal contact or human contact with the animal facilitator is unclear and requires further investigation (Souter and Miller, 2007).

Homeopathy

Homeopathy is a system of medicine which is based on treating the individual with highly diluted substances given mainly in tablet form, which trigger the body's natural system of healing. In a good quality systematic review only two RCTs were identified, one of poor quality and one in which only six patients completed the study. This review concluded that the evidence for the effectiveness of homeopathy in depression is limited due to lack of clinical trials of high quality (Pilkington et al., 2005).

Light therapy

Light therapy involves the therapeutic exposure to full-spectrum artificial light that simulates sunlight, used to treat various conditions such as seasonal affective disorder. A Cochrane review of light therapy for non-seasonal depression identified 20 RCTs comparing bright light with inactive placebo treatments for non-seasonal depression. The review found that bright light may confer modest benefits on severity of depression symptoms in the very early stages of treatment of people with depressive disorder in hospital and long term care settings (Tuunainen et al., 2004). A subsequent good quality systematic review reported that trials evaluating light therapy as a stand-alone intervention in non-seasonal depression had inconsistent results (Even et al., 2008).

Massage therapy

Massage therapy involves the manipulation of the soft tissues of the body - the muscles, tendons and ligaments. A systematic review of massage therapy for depression identified 17 RCTs (n = 786) from 246 retrieved references. All seventeen RCTs were of moderate quality and showed positive effect of massage therapy on depressed people with a mean quality score of 6.4 (SD = 0.85). Limitations of these RCTs were lack of standardized protocols of massage therapy, various depression rating scales, and ill-defined target populations (Hou et al., 2010).

Yoga

Yoga is an ancient system of breathing practices, physical exercises and postures, and meditation, intended to integrate the practitioner's body, mind, and spirit. A systematic review of five RCTs examined the effectiveness of different forms of yoga in patients with depression ranging in severity from mild to severe (Pilkington et al., 2005). All trials reported positive benefits of yoga interventions on the severity of self reported or assessor-rated symptoms of depression. Basic details of trial methodology were poorly reported and a meta-analysis was not attempted due to the diversity of outcome measures, absence of assessor blinding in all but one of the studies, and inadequate information on participant characteristics. There were no details on method of randomization, compliance or attrition rates.

Aromatherapy

Aromatherapy is a therapy based on the use of very concentrated "essential" oils from the flowers, leaves, bark, branches, rind or roots of plants with purported healing properties (van der Watt and Janca, 2008). No applicable evidence was identified on the use of aromatherapy as stand-alone treatment for patients with depression.

Emotional freedom technique

Emotional freedom technique is an emotional, needle-free version of acupuncture (Waite and Holder, 2003). No applicable evidence was identified on the use of emotional free technique as stand-alone treatment for patients with depression.

Reflexology

Reflexology involves massage of reflex areas found in the feet and the hands (Ernst, 2009). No applicable evidence was identified on the use of reflexology as stand-alone treatment for patients with depression.

Reiki

Reiki is hands-on alternative healing technique that involves the exchange of energy between practitioner and patient to restore mental, physical, emotional, and spiritual balance (Lee et al., 2008). No applicable evidence was identified on the use of Reiki as stand-alone treatment for patients with depression.

Tai chi chuan

Tai chi chuan is a Chinese exercise system that uses slow, smooth, body movements to achieve a state of relaxation of both body and mind (Wang et al., 2010). No applicable evidence was identified on the use of Tai chi chuan as stand-alone treatment for patients with depression.

Thought field therapy

Thought field therapy involves tapping with the fingers at meridian points on the upper body and hands (Callahan, 1995). No applicable evidence was identified on the use of thought field therapy as stand-alone treatment for patients with depression.

Conclusions

In the present review, a number of non-drug strategies available in the management of depression were identified and reviewed. Among psychological therapies, behavioural activation, individual CBT and IPT is recommended as a treatment option for patients with depression. Mindfulness based cognitive therapy in a group setting may be considered as a treatment option to reduce relapse in patients with depression who have had three or more episodes. Whereas, problem solving therapy and short term psychodynamic psychotherapy may be considered as a treatment option in depressed patients. Structured exercise may be considered as a treatment option for patients with depression. No applicable evidences were identified on which to base a recommendation for complementary and alternative therapies.

REFERENCES

Alladin A, Alibhai A (2007). Cognitive hypnotherapy for depression: An empirical investigation. Int. J. Clin. Exp. Hypn., 55: 147-66.

Allison S, Stacey K, Dadds V, Roeger L, Wood A, Martin G (2003). What the family brings: gathering evidence for strengths-based work. J. Fam. Ther., 25: 263-284.

Babyak M, Blumenthal JA, Herman S, Khatri P, Doraiswamy M, Moore K, Craighead WE, Baldewicz TT, Krishnan KR (2000). Exercise treatment for major depression: maintenance of therapeutic benefit at 10 months. Psychosom. Med., 62: 633-638.

Barbato A, D'Avazo B (2007). Marital therapy for depression (Cochrane Review). In: The Cochrane Library, London: Wiley, p. 4.

Bedi N, Chilvers C, Churchill R, Dewey M, Duggan C, Fielding K, Gretton V, Miller P, Harrison G, Lee A, Williams I (2000). Assessing effectiveness of treatment of depression in primary care: Partially randomised preference trial. Br. J. Psychiatry, 177: 312-318.

Blumenthal JA, Babyak MA, Doraiswamy PM, Watkins L, Hoffman BM, Barbour KA, Herman S, Craighead WE, Brosse AL, Waugh R, Hinderliter A, Sherwood A (2007). Exercise and pharmacotherapy in the treatment of major depressive disorder. Psychosom. Med., 69: 587-596.

Callahan R (1995). A thought field therapy (TFT) algorithm for trauma: A reproducible experiment in psychotherapy. Paper presented at the 105th Annual Convention of the American Psychological Association, New York, NY.

Casacalenda N, Perry JC, Looper K (2002). Remission in major depressive disorder: A comparison of pharmacotherapy, psychotherapy, and control conditions. Am. J. Psychiatry, 159: 1354-1360.

Chilvers C, Dewey M, Fielding K, Gretton V, Miller P, Palmer B, Weller D, Churchill R, Williams I, Bedi N, Duggan C, Lee A, Harrison G (2001). Antidepressant drugs and generic counselling for treatment of major depression in primary care: randomised trial with patient preference arms. BMJ., 322: 772-775.

Churchill R, Hunot V, Corney R, Knapp M, McGuire H, Tylee A, Wessely S (2001). A systematic review of controlled trials of the effectiveness and cost-effectiveness of brief psychological treatments for depression. Health Technol. Assess., 5: 1-173.

Coelho HF, Canter PH, Ernst E (2007). Mindfulness-based cognitive therapy: Evaluating current evidence and informing future research. J. Consult. Clin. Psychol., 75: 1000-1005.

Corney R, Simpson S (2005). Thirty-six month outcome data from a trial of counselling with chronically depressed patients in a general practice setting. Psychol. Psychother., 78: 127-138.

Cuijpers P, van Straten A, Smit F (2006). Psychological treatment of late-life depression: a meta-analysis of randomized controlled trials. Int. J. Geriatr. Psychiatry, 21: 1139-1149.

Cuijpers P, van Straten A, Warmerdam L (2007). Behavioral activation treatments of depression: A meta-analysis. Clin. Psychol. Rev., 27: 318-326.

Cuijpers P, van Straten A, Warmerdam L (2007). Problem solving therapies for depression: A meta-analysis. Eur. Psychiatry, 22: 9-15.

de Mello MF, de Jesus Mari J, Bacaltchuk J, Verdeli H, Neugebauer R (2005). A systematic review of research findings on the efficacy of interpersonal therapy for depressive disorders. Eur. Arch. Psychiatry Clin. Neurosci., 255: 75-82.

Denman C (2001). Cognitive–analytic therapy. Adv. Psychiatr. Treat., 7: 243-252.

Dimidjian S, Davis KJ (2009). Newer variations of cognitive-behavioral therapy: behavioral activation and mindfulness-based cognitive therapy. Curr. Psychiatry Rep., 11: 453-458.

Dunn AL, Trivedi MH, Kampert JB, Clark CG, Chambliss HO (2002). The DOSE study: a clinical trial to examine efficacy and dose response of exercise as treatment for depression. Control Clin. Trials, 23: 584-603.

Dunn AL, Trivedi MH, Kampert JB, Clark CG, Chambliss HO (2005). Exercise treatment for depression: efficacy and dose response. Am. J. Prev. Med., 28: 1-8.

Ernst E (2009). Is reflexology an effective intervention? A systematic review of randomised controlled trials. Med. J. Aust., 191: 263-266.

Even C, Schroder CM, Friedman S, Rouillon F (2008). Efficacy of light therapy in nonseasonal depression: A systematic review. J. Affect. Disord., 108: 11-23.

Hensley PL, Nadiga D, Uhlenhuth EH (2004). Long-term effectiveness of cognitive therapy in major depressive disorder. Depress. Anxiety, 20: 1-7.

Hou WH, Chiang PT, Hsu TY, Chiu SY, Yen YC (2010). Treatment effects of massage therapy in depressed people: a meta-analysis. J. Clin. Psychiatry, 71: 894-901.

Klausner EJ, Clarkin JF, Spielman L, Pupo C, Abrams R, Alexopoulos GS (1998). Late-life depression and functional disability: The role of goal-focused group psychotherapy. Int. J. Geriatr. Psychiatry, 13: 707-716.

Lee MS, Pittler MH, Ernst E (2008). Effects of Reiki in clinical practice: a systematic review of randomized clinical trials. Int. J. Clin. Pract., 62: 947-954.

Leichsenring F (2001). Comparative effects of short-term psychodynamic psychotherapy and cognitive-behavioral therapy in depression: a meta-analytic approach. Clin. Psychol. Rev., 21: 401-419.

Leo RJ, Ligot Jr JSA (2007). A systematic review of randomized controlled trials of acupuncture in the treatment of depression. J. Affect. Disord., 97: 13-22.

Lisa W (2008). Neurolinguistic psychotherapy: A postmodern perspective. 1st Ed. New York : Taylor and Francis e-library.

Luty SE, Carter JD, McKenzie JM, Rae AM, Frampton CMA, Mulder RT, Joyce PR (2007). Randomised controlled trial of interpersonal psychotherapy and cognitive-behavioural therapy for depression. Br. J. Psychiatry, 190: 496-502.

Mackin RS, Arean PA (2005). Evidence-based psychotherapeutic

interventions for geriatric depression. Psychiatr. Clin. North Am., 28: 805-820.
Maratos AS, Gold C, Wang X, Crawford MJ (2008). Music therapy for depression (Cochrane Review). In: The Cochrane Library, London: Wiley, p. 1.
Mather AS, Rodriguez C, Guthrie MF, McHarg AM, Reid IC, McMurdo ME (2002). Effects of exercise on depressive symptoms in older adults with poorly responsive depressive disorder: randomised controlled trial. Br. J. Psychiatry, 180: 411-415.
Mazzucchelli T, Kane R, Rees C (2009). Behavioral Activation Treatments for Depression in Adults: A Meta-analysis and Review. Clin. Psychol. Sci. Pract., 16: 383-411.
McCullough JP (2000). Treatment for Chronic Depression: Cognitive Behavioral Analysis System of Psychotherapy. New York, NY: Guilford Press.
McPherson S, Cairns P, Carlyle J, Shapiro DA, Richardson P, Taylor D (2005). The effectiveness of psychological treatments for treatment resistant depression: A systematic review. Acta Psychiatr. Scand., 111: 331-340.
Mead GE, Morley W, Campbel IP, Greig CA, McMurdo M, Lawlor DA (2008). Exercise for depression (Cochrane Review). In: The Cochrane Library, London:Wiley,. p. 4.
Michael B, Gillian EH (2001). Counselling and interpersonal therapies for depression: towards securing an evidence-base. Br. Med. Bull., 57: 115-132.
Michael L (2011). Depression Costs America as Much as the War in Afghanistan. http://www.associatedcontent.com/article/7945103/depression_costs_america_as_much_as_pg2.html?cat=72.
Mukaino Y, Park J, White A, Ernst E (2005). The effectiveness of acupuncture for depression - A systematic review of randomised controlled trials. Acupunct. Med., 23: 70-76.
Nabkasorn C, Miyai N, Sootmongkol A, Junprasert S, Yamamoto H, Arita M, Miyashita K (2006). Effects of physical exercise on depression, neuroendocrine stress hormones and physiological fitness in adolescent females with depressive symptoms. Eur. J. Public Health, 16: 179-184.
Pilkington K, Kirkwood G, Rampes H, Fisher P, Richardson J (2005). Homeopathy for depression: a systematic review of the research evidence. Homeopathy, 94: 153-163.
Pilkington K, Kirkwood G, Rampes H, Richardson J (2005). Yoga for depression: The research evidence. J. Affect. Disord., 89: 13-24.
Pinquart M, Duberstein PR, Lyness JM (2006). Treatments for Later-Life Depressive Conditions: A Meta-Analytic Comparison of Pharmacotherapy and Psychotherapy. Am. J. Psychiatry, 163: 1493-1501.
Sanders MR, McFarland M (2000). Treatment of depressed mothers with disruptive children: A controlled evaluation of cognitive behavioral family intervention. Behav. Ther., 31: 89-112.
Shapiro F (2001). Eye movement desensitization and reprocessing: Basic principles, protocols and procedures. 2nd Ed. New York: The Guilford Press.
Shirley R (2001). Art therapy with adolescents. West J. Med., 175: 54-57.
Simpson S, Corney R, Beecham J (2003). A randomized controlled trial to evaluate the effectiveness and cost-effectiveness of psychodynamic counselling for general practice patients with chronic depression. Psychol. Med., 33: 229-239.
Simpson S, Corney R, Fitzgerald P, Beecham J (2000). A randomised controlled trial to evaluate the effectiveness and cost-effectiveness of counselling patients with chronic depression. Health Technol. Assess., 4: 1-83.
Singh NA, Clements KM, Singh MA (2001). The efficacy of exercise as a long-term antidepressant in elderly subjects: a randomized, controlled trial. J. Gerontol. A Biol. Sci. Med. Sci., 56: 497-504.
Smith CA (2005). Acupuncture for depression (Cochrane Review). In: The Cochrane Library, Issue 2. London: Wiley.
Souter MA, Miller MD (2007). Do animal-assisted activities effectively treat depression? A meta-analysis. Anthrozoos, 20: 167-180.
Stuart S, Robertson M (2003). Interpersonal Psychotherapy: A Clinician's Guide. London, England: Edward Arnold.
Tuunainen A, Kripke D, Endo T (2004). Light therapy for nonseasonal depression (Cochrane Review). In: The Cochrane Library, London: Wiley, p. 2.
van der Watt G, Janca A (2008). Aromatherapy in nursing and mental health care. Contemp. Nurse., 30: 69-75.
Waite LW, Holder MD (2003). Assessment of the Emotional Freedom Technique: An Alternative Treatment for Fear. Sci. Rev. Mental Health Pract., 2: 20-26.
Wang C, Bannuru R, Ramel J, Kupelnick B, Scott T, Schmid CH (2010). Tai Chi on psychological well-being: systematic review and meta-analysis. BMC Complement. Altern. Med., 10: 23.
Watt LM, Cappeliez P (2000). Integrative and instrumental reminiscence therapies for depression in older adults: Intervention strategies and treatment effectiveness. Aging Ment. Health, 4: 166-177.

18

Recurrent giant malignant peripheral nerve sheath tumor of the scalp with intracranial extension

R .S. Jaggi[1*], S. Mehta[2] and S. Pasricha[3]

[1]Department of Neurosurgery, Rajiv Gandhi Cancer Institute and Research Centre, Sector V, Rohini, New Delhi, India.
[2]Department of Plastic surgery, Rajiv Gandhi Cancer Institute and Research Centre , Sector V, Rohini, New Delhi, India.
[3]Department of Pathology, Rajiv Gandhi Cancer Institute and Research Centre, Sector V, Rohini, New Delhi, India.

Malignant peripheral nerve sheath tumors (MPNSTs) are rare neoplasms, usually arising from somatic soft tissues or peripheral nerves. The incidence of MPNSTs is approximately 0.001% in the general population. MPNSTs are mainly located in the buttocks, thighs, brachial plexus, and paraspinal region. Scalp is an unusual and surgically challenging site of occurrence. We report a case of giant recurrent MPNST in the left fronto-parietal region, with intracranial extension, in a 58 year old female which was excised completely along with the involved overlying skin, and reconstruction was done for the bony and skin defect. She was given adjuvant radiotherapy. She is doing well after treatment and is in regular follow up. MPNST should be considered by neurosurgeons in the differential of an enlarging scalp soft-tissue lesion with bony and intracranial involvement. Scalp MPNSTs are mostly aggressive lesions, and multimodality approaches are necessary to optimize outcomes

Key words: Malignant peripheral nerve sheath tumors (MPNST), scalp, intracranial, surgery.

INTRODUCTION

Malignant peripheral nerve sheath tumors (MPNSTs) are rare neoplasms, usually arising from somatic soft tissues or peripheral nerves. The incidence of MPNSTs is approximately 0.001% in the general population (Al-Gahtamy et al., 2005). MPNSTs are mainly located in the buttocks, thighs, brachial plexus, and paraspinal region (Wanebo et al., 1993). To the best of our knowledge, only 3 cases of MPNSTs of the scalp with intracranial extension have been reported in the English literature (Garg et al., 2004; Ge et al., 2010; Kumar et al., 2007).

We report a case of giant recurrent MPNST in the left fronto-parietal region, with intracranial extension, in a 58 year old female which was excised completely along with the involved overlying skin and bony reconstruction was done for the bony defect.

CASE REPORT

A 58 year old female presented to us with progressive right sided weakness for the past 3 months along with a gradually increasing nodular swelling in the left parietal scalp. The patient was operated 22 years ago for the swelling at the same site with surgical excision, and bony removal and was advised adjuvant radiotherapy which the patient did not undergo. The details of the previous treatment including the biopsy report were not available to us. She remained asymptomatic for all these years till 3 months back when she started having the present problem. On examination, she was conscious, and oriented with normal higher mental functions. There was a right upper motor neuron type facial involvement. She had right hemiparesis with a power of 0/5 in the right upper limb and 2/5 in the right lower limb. Local examination revealed a 3 × 3 cm hard nodular swelling in the left parietal scalp with erythematous and indurated overlying skin, fixed to the underlying mass. There was a 5 × 5 cm sized bony defect in the left fronto-parietal region reaching midline, and previous surgical scar was healthy.

The brain magnetic resonance imaging (MRI) revealed a 7 × 6 × 6 cm sized extraxial lobulated mass lesion in the left fronto-parietal region, hypointense on T1 weighted images and hyperintense on T2 weighted images with

*Corresponding author. E-mail: rsjaggi2000@yahoo.com

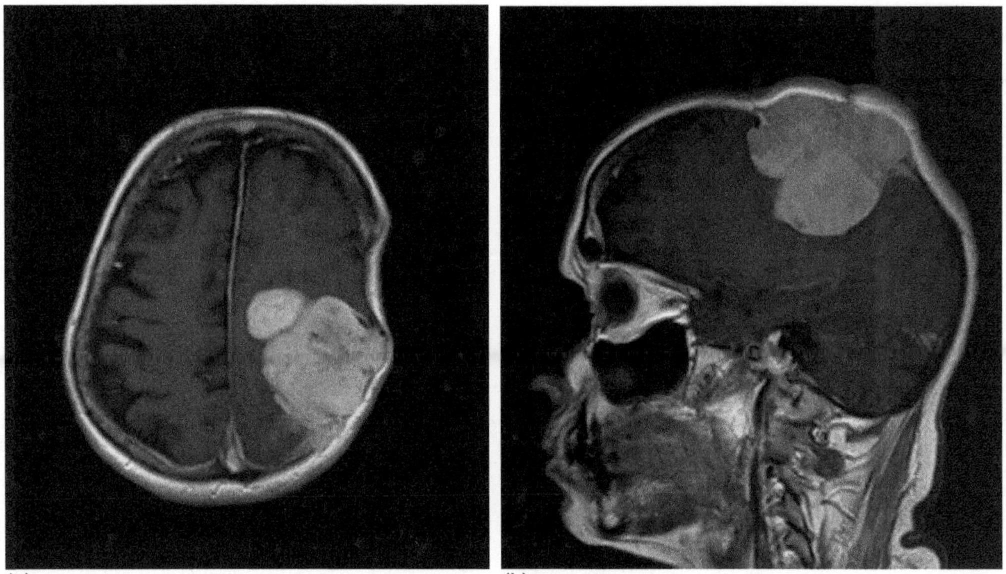

(a) (b)

Figure 1. (a) Preoperative MRI brain contrast enhanced T1 weighted axial image showing a large extra axial lobulated left fronto-parietal mass lesion compression the brain parenchyma with resultant mass effect. (b) Preoperative MRI brain contrast enhanced T1 weighted sagittal image showing a large extra axial lobulated left fronto-parietal mass lesion compression the brain parenchyma with resultant mass effect along with involved overlying skin.

homogenous enhancement on contrast administration, compressing the brain parenchyma and growing out of the bony defect involving the overlying skin (Figure 1; a and b). The patient was investigated for any lesion elsewhere in the body but none was found. The patient underwent exploration via previous scalp incision and complete surgical excision of the lesion, along with removal of overlying involved skin with cranioplasty for bony defect with methylmethacrylate and closure of the scalp defect with transpositioned scalp flap from right fronto-parietal region and split skin grafting.

Post-operative computated tomography (CT) head showed complete excision of the mass (Figure 2). The patient improved neurologically after surgery. The biopsy report showed proliferation of spindle cells with mild pleomorphism in interlacing fascicles, with alternating hypercellular and hypocellular areas (marbelized effect), with cartilaginous metaplasia and buckling of nuclei corresponding to schwannian differentiation. No significant mitoses or necrosis was seen. On immuno-histochemistry, the tumor cells were positive for vimentin and S-100, and negative for EMA, CK, CD34 and SMA, and a final diagnosis of MPNST was established (Figure 3). She was given adjuvant radiotherapy and has been in regular follow up for 2 months and is fine.

DISCUSSION

As defined by the World Health Organization, MPNSTs are malignant tumors arising from a peripheral nerve or showing a nerve sheath differentiation, with the exception of tumors originating from the epineurium or the peripheral nerve vasculature (Kumar et al., 2007). These tumors are treated as a subcategory of soft tissue sarcomas, in which they comprise 3 to 10% of all such tumors (Al-Gahtamy et al., 2005). MPNSTs are associated with genetic alterations such as NF1 loss of heterozygosity.

Approximately one-third of MPNSTs arise *de novo*, whereas the remainder represent a sarcomatous degeneration of a pre-existing plexiform neurofibroma in a neurofibromatosis I or non-neurofibromatosis I patient (World Health Organization, 2000). In present case, as the previous biopsy report was not available, we presume that it was a primary scalp MPNST involving the underlying bone which was excised 22 years ago and which recurred. There were no features of neurofibromatosis I in the present case. MPNSTs usually occur in the third to sixth decades of life and usually affect the medium and larger nerves. Tumor location has been found to be a strong prognostic factor with those in the thoracic and retroperitoneum having worse outcomes (Wanebo et al., 1993). Histopathologically, these are highly cellular tumors that characteristically show a fascicular pattern, spindle-shaped nuclei, and scant cytoplasm. The majority of tumors show geographic necrosis and mitotic activity. Most features were seen in this case, except for mitosis and necrosis.

Magnetic resonance imaging is the investigation of

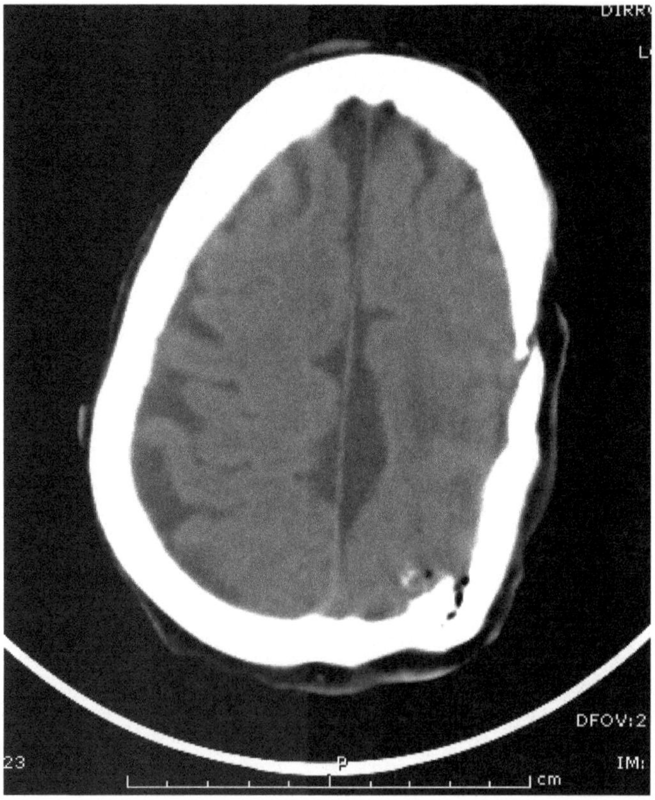

Figure 2. Postoperative contrast enhanced axial CT head image showing complete excision of the tumor and bony reconstruction.

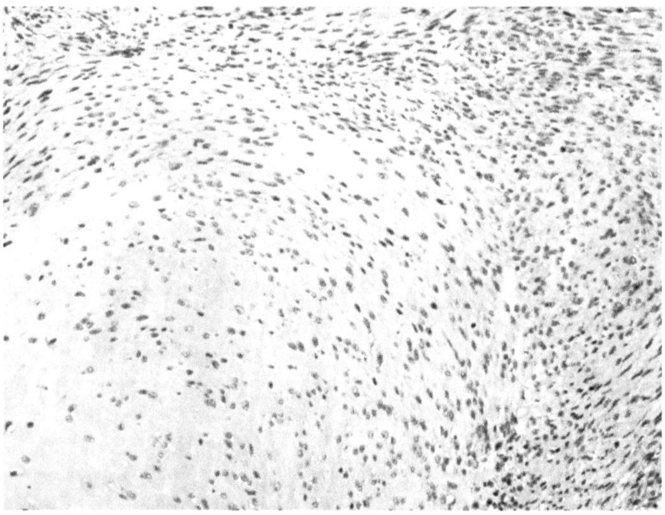

Figure 3. Microphotograph showing interlacing fascicles of spindle cells exhibiting minimal pleomorphism along with buckling of nuclei and cartilaginous metaplasia. (Hematoxylin and eosin, ×100).

choice because it reveals the nerve origin and the relationship to adjacent structures in most cases (Al-Gahtamy et al., 2005). The International Consensus Group has recommended that the current management of MPNST should be identical to that of any other soft tissue tumors. Adjuvant radiation therapy (RT) should be considered for all intermediate- and high-grade lesions, as well as low-grade tumors with positive margins and was given in this case as well (Angelov et al., 1998; Vege et al., 1994). Local recurrences have been reported to vary from 52 to 88.9% for different sites, whereas metastasis (mainly in the lungs and liver) ranged from 11.1 to 18%. The 5-year survival rate among patients with MPNSTs ranges from 30 to 50% (Angelov et al., 1998; Ferner and Gutmann., 2002; Vege et al., 1994). In this case, it recurred locally and there was no metastatic lesion elsewhere in the body.

In view of the high incidence of local recurrence in MPNSTs after surgery, adjuvant postoperative RT has been shown to improve local control. This could be explored further, especially in sites in which complete surgical resection may not always be feasible (for example, the scalp) with intracranial extension (Kumar et al., 2007; Wilson et al., 1994). With MPNSTs being relatively radioresistant, similar to soft tissue sarcomas, an attempt should always be made for near total surgical debulking of the tumors, and adjuvant postoperative RT could help to reduce the local recurrence.

Conclusion

MPNST should be considered by neurosurgeons in the differential of an enlarging scalp soft-tissue lesion with bony and intracranial involvement. Scalp MPNSTs are mostly aggressive lesions, and multimodality approaches are necessary to optimize outcomes

REFERENCES

Al-Gahtamy M, Midha R, Guha A, Jacobs WB (2005). Malignant peripheral nerve tumors, in Beyer MS, Prados MD: Textbook of Neuro-oncology. Elsevier Saunders, Philadelphia. pp. 564–571.

Angelov L, Davis A, O'Sullivan B, Bell R, Guha A (1998). Neurogenic sarcomas: Experience at the University of Toronto. Neurosurgery 43:56–65.

Ferner RE, Gutmann DH (2002). International consensus statement on malignant peripheral nerve sheath tumors in neurofibromatosis 1. Cancer Res. 62:1573–1577.

Garg A, Gupta V, Gaikwad SB, Mishra NK, Ojha BK, Chugh M, Sharma MC (2004).Scalp malignant peripheral nerve sheath tumor (MPNST) with bony involvement and new bone formation: Case report. Clin Neurol. Neurosurg. 106:340–344.

Ge P, Fu S, Lu L, Zhong Y, Qi B, Luo Y (2010). Diffuse scalp maliognant peripheral nerve sheath tumor with intracranial extension in a patient with neurofibromatosis type 1. J. Clin. Neurosci. 17(11):1443-4.

Kumar P, Jaiswal S, Agrawal T, Verma A, Datta NR (2007). Malignant peripheral nerve sheath tumor of occipital region. Neurosurgery 61(6):1334-5; Discussion E1335.

Wanebo JE, Malik JM, VandenBerg SR, Wanebo HJ, Driesen N, Persing JA (1993). Malignant peripheral nerve sheath tumors. A clinicopathological study of 28 cases. Cancer 71:1247–1253.

WWilson AN, Davis A, Bell RS, O'Sullivan B, Catton C, Madadi F, Kandel R, Fornasier VL (1994). Local control of soft tissue sarcoma of the extremity: The experience of a multidisciplinary sarcoma group

with definite surgery and radiotherapy. Eur. J. Cancer 30:746–751.
World Health Organization (2000). Pathology and Genetics of Tumors of the Nervous System. IARC Press, Lyon. pp. 169–171.
Vege DS, Chinoy RF, Ganesh B, Parikh (1994). Malignant peripheral nerve sheath tumors of the head and neck: A clinicopathological study. J. Surg. Oncol. 55:100–103.

Assessment of quality of life, stigma associated and self-management practices among patients suffering from epileptic seizures: A cross sectional study

Nitin Joseph*, Ananya Ray, Reshma B. K., Shruthi Bhat, Madhumitha Herady, Ashith Kumar and Shri Kiran K.

Department of Community Medicine, Kasturba Medical College, Mangalore, Manipal University, India.

Epileptic patients are often neglected in our society. This hospital based cross sectional study was done among epileptic patients in Mangalore city of south India in February 2011. Epileptic patients aged 7 or more were interviewed using a pretested semi-structured questionnaire. Standardised scales were used for assessing the quality of life (QOL), stigma and self-management practices of patients. Association of these parameters was done with various socio demographic factors of patients. Of the 56 patients, 55.4% patients had GTCS and 80.4% had multiple episodes of seizures. QOL and self-management practices were good in 44.6% and 71.4% patients, respectively. Self-management practices was found to significantly improve with age of patients (P=0.012). Educational status of patients was found to significantly improve their QOL and self-management practices (P=0.031). Stigmatization was reported by 66.1% patients and it was significantly more in patients in the age groups 30 to 50 years (P=0.043). Gender and occupation of patients was not significantly associated with any of the parameters. Self-management practices were good in most patients but this was not so with QOL or experience of stigma. These aspects could be improved by educating the people in order to generate greater social support for epileptic patients in future.

Key words: Epileptic seizures, quality of life, stigma, self-management practices.

INTRODUCTION

Epilepsy which means a tendency to have seizures is a common neurological condition, frequently associated with psychosocial difficulties (Baker, 2002). The occurrence of psychosocial problems related to epilepsy in certain situations could be even more troublesome than the effect of the seizure disorder themselves (Shibre et al., 2006). The fear of impending seizures among patients leads to a feeling of insecurity, which in turn adversely affects their healthy social development (Moffat et al., 2009a,b). They also experience a feeling of shame and guilt compared with individuals without epilepsy (Jacoby et al., 1996). People with epilepsy are thus prone to have poorer self-esteem, higher levels of anxiety and depression (Rodin, 1968). The diagnosis of epilepsy challenges their self-perception and causes concern about ability to function in normal social roles, such as getting a job or having a family (Scambler and Hopkins, 1990). Epilepsy causes serious problems among children too. Children with epilepsy have been found to be behaviorally disturbed and develop poorer academic attainment than children with diabetes or asthma (Austin et al., 1994).

Epilepsy is also a known stigmatizing condition. Due to its unpredictable nature society may fear dealing with someone who is having an epileptic seizure. Misconception about etiological factors, curability, cause and outcome are other factors which have contributed to the social stigma (Suurmeijer et al., 2001).

Because of its clinical uncertainty and its social meaning and consequent stigmatization, the impact of epilepsy on a person's quality of life (QOL) can be significant (Moffat et al., 2009a,b). Studies in Europe (Baker,

*Corresponding author. E-mail: drnitinjoseph@gmail.com

2002) and North America (Dilorio et al., 2003) suggest that the stigma of epilepsy is one of the most important negative influences on the quality of life of people with epilepsy. Paradoxically, this facet of epilepsy is rarely studied, especially in limited resource countries (Li and Sander, 2003), where the burden of epilepsy is higher. Of the 50 million people with epilepsy worldwide, around 80% reside in resource-poor countries, which are ill-equipped to tackle the enormous medical, social and economic challenges posed by epilepsy. The capability to identify people with epilepsy and provide cost-effective care is compromised by widespread poverty, illiteracy, inefficient and unevenly distributed health-care systems, and social stigma and misconceptions surrounding the disease. The high cost of treatment, lack of availability of antiepileptic drugs, side effects of medication and superstitious and cultural beliefs contribute to a large epilepsy treatment gap. A substantial proportion of the current burden of epilepsy in resource-poor countries could be minimized by educating the public about positive features of life with epilepsy. This will minimize the stigma associated with this disease. This together with improvement in self-management practices of epileptic patients will help in the betterment of their quality of life. There is thus a need of a comprehensive epilepsy care model which considers the marked heterogeneity of the disorder and its variable effects on the patient, family and community (Radhakrishnan, 2009).

We therefore conducted this study in an urban area where clinic and outreach services for treating people with epilepsy are well established with the main goal of assessing the quality of life of epileptic patients, their self-management practices, stigma experienced by them and to find out association of each of these with various socio demographic factors.

MATERIALS AND METHODS

This cross sectional study was done in various tertiary care hospitals in Mangalore, a coastal city of Karnataka state of south India in February 2011.

The ethical clearance for the conduct of this study was taken from the Institutional Ethics Committee. Permission to do the study in the hospital was taken from the respective medical super-intendents of these hospitals. Following this, epileptic out and in patients were approached and were taught about the importance of the study. All the patients who gave written informed consent for participation were enrolled in this study. In case of minors (aged less than 18 years) consent for participation was taken from their accompanying parents or guardians. Epileptic patients below the age of 7 years and those with mental handicap or with severe psychiatric disturbances were excluded from this study. A total of 56 such patients could be enrolled by convenient sampling over the data collection period. Each of the participants were interviewed using a pretested semi-structured questionnaire by a team of investigators. Information with respect to socio demographic profile of patients such as age, gender, marital status, occupation, educational status, family income and place of residence were recorded. For assessing quality of life, Quality of life in childhood epilepsy (QOLCE) (Sabaz et al., 2000), quality of life in epilepsy inventory for adolescents (Cramer et al., 1999) and QOLIE 31 for adults (Grudzinski et al., 1998) was used. For assessing stigma, explanatory model interview catalogue stigma scale was used (Weiss et al., 1992) and for assessing self management practices, epilepsy self management scale (Dilorio et al., 1994) was used. The questions in quality of life scale comprised of perception about seizures, feeling of loneliness or nervousness or tiredness due to the disease, adjustment with the disease, state of mental health, level of concentration with routine work and experience of side effects due to anti epileptic drugs (AED) therapy. The questions in stigma scale comprised of whether patient preferred secrecy about the disease, feeling of shame due to the disease, whether they attend social gatherings following diagnosis of being epileptic, whether they experienced avoidance or disrespect from peer groups and relatives and whether they had any problems in getting married or had experienced any discord in marital life. Good self-management practices include measures like taking medication on time, maintaining a record of seizure episodes, carrying an identity card, periodic consultation with treating doctor, adequacy of sleep, avoiding food substances and activities that may precipitate seizures and avoidance of dangerous works like cooking or swimming.

All the data collected were entered and analyzed using version 11.5 of the statistical package for social sciences software package (SPSS Inc., Chicago, IL) into categories and percentages. Chi-square was used for testing association and P value less than 0.05 was considered as statistically significant.

RESULTS

Of the 56 patients, most (46.5%) were of the age group 20 to 40 years. The mean age of all participants in this study was 30.95 ± 18.19 years. Majority was males (55.4%) and most of them were educated up to high school (25%). Most of the study participants were students (21.4%). Few of them (3.6%) were separated from their spouses because of epilepsy. The number of married individuals was 69.6% (Table 1). Out of the 44 patients who knew the type of seizures they developed, 24 (54.5%) said that it was of generalized tonic clonic type (GTCS), 16(36.4%) said it was partial seizures (simple/complex) while 4 (9.1%) said it was absence seizures.

Majority of patients 28 (50%) had 2 to 6 episodes of seizures followed by 11 (19.6%) with single episode followed by 10 (17.9%) with 12-24 episodes of seizures and lastly 7 (12.5%) with 6 to 12 episodes of seizures. Out of 56 epileptic patients 46 of them could recollect when they developed seizures for the first time. The mean age of first episode among these 46 epileptic patients was 25.3 ± 16.6 years (Table 2).

The quality of life was good in 25 (44.6%), average in 17 (30.4%) and was poor in 14(25%) of epileptic patients. Quality of life in patients was found to be significantly associated with educational status (P=0.031). Patients educated from pre degree and beyond were found to have a better quality of life than the rest. Quality of life was found to be better among patients aged between 40 to 50 years, males, among professionals and house wives. However these observations were not statistically significant (Table 3).

Stigmatization was reported by 37 (66.1%) patients in

Table 1. Socio demographic distribution of epileptic patients.

Age group	Number	%
7-10 years	8	14.3
10-20	8	14.3
20-30	16	28.6
30-40	10	17.9
40-50	4	7.1
50-60	6	10.7
>60	4	7.1
Gender		
Male	31	55.4
Female	25	44.6
Marital status		
Single	15	26.8
Married	39	69.6
Divorced	2	3.6
Educational status		
Illiterate	6	10.7
Primary school	11	21.4
Middle school	10	19.6
High school	14	25
PUC	8	14.3
Graduation & above	7	8.9
Occupation		
Professional	3	5.4
Semi-professional	4	7.1
Businessman	11	19.6
Skilled	10	17.9
Unskilled	10	17.9
Housewife	6	10.7
Student	12	21.4
Total	56	100

this study. Patients in the age group of 30 to 50 years reporting greater stigmatization than other age groups (P=0.043). Stigmatization was reported by more number of male patients, students and semi-professionals. However these observations were not statistically significant (Table 4).

Among the 56 patients, 40 (71.4%) had good, 8 (14.3%) had average and rest 8 (14.3%) had poor self-management practices. The quality of self-management practice was found to improve with age of the patients with best performance by patients aged between 40 to 50 years (P=0.012). Educational status was also found to significantly influence self-management practices with performance being better among those patients educated at least up to middle school (P=0.031). Good self-management practices were seen more among male patients, house wives and students. Professionals and semi-professionals had a greater percentage of poorer self-management practice as compared to others. However these observations were not statistically significant (Table 5).

Table 2. Distribution of patients based on age at first episode of developing seizures.

Age in years	Number	Percentage
7-10	7	12.5
10-20	16	28.7
20-30	11	19.7
30-40	3	5.3
40-50	3	5.3
50-60	3	5.3
>60	3	5.3
Total	46	100

DISCUSSION

People with epilepsy in developing countries are known to experience problems with marriage, education, social isolation and employment (Baker, 2002). This study analyses these aspects in a less prioritized disease, by health care providers, like epilepsy. In this study 4% participants were separated from their spouses because of seizures which were similar to other studies (Baker et al., 1997; Baker et al., 1997). The marriage rate of about 70% in this study was higher than that observed in a study done in Kanpur where it was only about 46% among epileptic patients (Agarwal et al., 2006).

Even though most participants (80.4%) had multiple episodes of seizures in this study none of them were unemployed because of their illness. However a European study reported unemployment rate of 23% among epileptic patients due to seizures (Baker et al., 1997).

Several other studies too reported unemployment among epileptic patients (Baker, 2002; Bahou et al., 2011; Fraser et al., 1983; Herodes et al., 2001; Kleinman et al., 1995). Unemployment and lower rates of marriage among epileptic patients leads to greater social isolation which will further depress the lives of these patients.

Commonest type of seizure was GTCS which was seen in more than half of the participants. This observation has also been supported by other studies (Baker et al., 1997; Bahou et al., 2011; Goodridge and Shorvon, 1983). Mean age of first episode of seizure in this study (25.3 years) was slightly higher than that observed in a Atlanta based study where it was 22 years (Dilorio et al., 2003).

The quality of life was found to be good only in 44.6% of patients. This was lesser than the findings of a Jordanian

Table 3. Association between age, gender, occupation and educational status with quality of life in epileptic patients.

Age group	Quality of life			
	Poor (%)	Average (%)	Good (%)	Total (%)
7-10 years	4 (50)	2 (25)	2 (25)	8
10-20	1 (12.5)	4 (50)	3 (37.5)	8
20-30	3 (18.8)	5 (31.2)	8 (50)	16
30-40	1 (10)	5 (50)	4 (40)	10
40-50	0 (0)	0 (0)	4 (100)	4
50-60	4 (66.7)	1 (16.7)	1 (16.7)	6
>60	1 (25)	0 (0)	3 (75)	4
			X^2=19.5, DF=12, P=0.076	
Gender				
Male	5(16.1)	10(32.3)	16(51.6)	31
Female	9(36)	7(28)	9(36)	25
			X^2=3.02, DF=2, P=0.22	
Occupation				
Professionals	1(33.3)	0 (0)	2 (66.7)	3
Semi-professionals	1 (25)	1 (25)	2 (50)	4
Businessman	3 (27.3)	3 (27.3)	5 (45.4)	11
Skilled	3 (30)	2 (20)	5 (50)	10
Unskilled	5 (50)	4 (40)	1 (10)	10
Housewife	1 (16.7)	1 (16.7)	4 (66.6)	6
Student	3 (25)	6 (50)	3 (25)	12
			X^2=10.4, DF=12, P=0.58	
Educational status				
Illiterate	4 (66.6)	1(16.7)	1 (16.7)	6
Primary school	8 (72.7)	1 (9.1)	2 (18.2)	11
Middle school	4 (40)	5 (50)	1 (10)	10
High school	2 (14.2)	6 (42.9)	6 (42.9)	14
P.U.C	1 (12.5)	2 (25)	5 (62.5)	8
Graduates	2 (28.6)	1 (14.3)	4 (57.1)	7
			X^2=19.8, DF=10, P=0.031	
Total	14	17	25	56

Table 4. Association between age, gender, occupation and educational status of patients with experience of stigmatization.

Age group	Stigmatization		
	Present (%)	Absent (%)	Total (%)
7-10 years	2 (25)	6 (75)	8
10-20	4 (50)	4 (50)	8
20-30	12 (75)	4 (25)	16
30-40	8 (88.9)	1 (11.1)	9
40-50	5 (100)	0 (0)	5
50-60	3 (50)	3 (50)	6
>60	3 (75)	1 (25)	4
Total	37	19	56
			X^2=13, DF=6, P=0.043
Gender			
Male	21 (67.7)	10 (32.3)	31

Table 4. Contd.

Female	16 (64)	9 (36)	25
			X^2=0.0864, DF=1, P=0.769
Occupation			
Professional	2 (66.7)	1 (33.3)	3
Semi-professional	3 (75)	1 (25)	4
Businessman	8 (72.7)	3 (27.3)	11
Skilled	7 (70)	3 (30)	10
Unskilled	5 (50)	5 (50)	10
Housewife	3 (50)	3 (50)	6
Student	9 (75)	3 (25)	12
			X^2=2.7, DF=6, P=0.846
Educational status			
Illiterate	2 (33.3)	4 (66.7)	6
Primary school	7 (63.6)	4 (36.4)	11
Middle school	8 (80)	2 (20)	10
High school	8 (57.1)	6 (42.9)	14
P.U.C	7 (87.5)	1 (12.5)	8
Graduation and above	5 (71.4)	2 (28.6)	7
			X^2=5.99, DF=5, P=0.307
Total	37	19	56

Table 5. Association of age, gender, occupation and educational status with quality of self-management practices among epileptic patients.

Age group	Self-management practices				
	Poor (%)	Average (%)	Good (%)	Total (%)	P value
7-10	5 (62.5)	0 (0)	3 (37.5)	8	
10-20	1 (12.5)	1 (12.5)	6 (75)	8	
20-30	2 (12.5)	2 (12.5)	12 (75)	16	
30-40	0 (0)	2 (22.2)	7 (77.8)	9	
40-50	0 (0)	0 (0)	4 (100)	4	
50-60	0 (0)	3 (42.9)	4 (57.1)	7	
>60	0 (0)	0 (0)	4 (100)	4	
				X^2=25.7, DF=12, P=0.012	
Gender					
Male	4 (12.5)	4 (12.5)	24 (75)	32	
Female	4 (16.7)	4 (16.7)	16 (66.7)	24	
				X^2=0.467, DF=2, P=0.792	
Occupation					
Professionals	1 (33.3)	1 (33.3)	1 (33.3)	3	
Semi-professionals	1 (25)	1 (25)	2 (50)	4	
Businessman	1 (9.1)	2 (18.2)	8 (72.7)	11	
Skilled	1 (10)	2 (20)	7 (70)	10	
Unskilled	2 (20)	1 (10)	7 (70)	10	
Housewife	0 (0)	0 (0)	6 (100)	6	
Student	2 (16.7)	1 (8.3)	9 (75)	12	
				X^2=6.85, DF=12, P=0.868	
Education					
Illiterate	1 (16.7)	2 (33.3)	3 (50)	6	
Primary school	5 (45.4)	3 (27.3)	3 (27.3)	11	

Table 5. Contd.

Middle school	1 (10)	0 (0)	9 (90)	10
High school	1 (7.1)	1 (7.1)	12 (85.8)	14
P.U.C	0 (0)	1 (12.5)	7 (87.5)	8
Graduates	0 (0)	1 (14.3)	6 (85.7)	7
				X^2=19.8, DF=10, P=0.031
Total	8	8	40	56

study which reported that 84% did not have any restriction of daily activities due to epilepsy and substantial proportions (range 52 to 88%) did not perceive any impact of epilepsy on the aspects of daily living (Bahou et al., 2011). Other studies have found that because of the clinical uncertainty and social meaning associated with this disease, the impact of epilepsy on a person's quality of life can be significant (Dilorio et al., 2003; Dilorio et al., 1994; Begley et al., 2010; Collings, 1990). The European study had reported that 44% of respondents worried a lot of possible side effects of their medication, 47% reported that it substantially affected their plans and ambitions for the future (Baker et al., 1997). Quality of life of patients in this study was found to significantly increase with educational status. This could be because well-educated patients are well aware of self-management practices and are better educated about the disease and also know that by being regular with treatment can avoid seizures and hence lead a normal life. Stigmatization was reported by about 66% of patients in this study. High rate of stigmatization was also reported by a European study where more than half of all epileptic patients (51%) experienced this sometime in their lives (Baker et al., 1997). The rate of stigmatization was found to be lesser in a Jordanian study where it was reported by 14% of patients (Bahou et al., 2011).

Epilepsy being a stigmatizing condition has also been reported in other studies as well (Jacoby et al., 2005; Ablon, 2002; Scambler and Hopkins, 1990).

Superstitious beliefs among people that evil spirits or curse God as the cause of seizures could be one reason for its presence in our society. Even educated people are found to stigmatize epileptic patients probably because these patients have a poor social life due to poor marriage and employment rates. Stigmatization could also arise because of their fear or helplessness in dealing with these patients during an epileptic attack.

Consequently an attitude of non-acceptance of self or reluctance in disclosing their disabilities to others has developed among epileptic patients as observed (Goodridge and Shorvon, 1983). The stigmatization due to epilepsy was significantly associated with age of patients. Patients in the age group of 30 to 40 years reported greater stigmatization than patients of other age groups. No association of stigma was seen with gender, occupation and educational status of participants. In a study done In Atlanta It was found that the perceived stigma was similar for men and women, ethnic groups and age groups. Here it was also observed that the participants reporting higher levels of perceived stigma also reported lower levels of self-efficacy to manage epilepsy; more negative outcome expectancies related to treatment and seizures and lower levels of medication management, medication adherence and patient satisfaction (Dilorio et al., 2003).

The social cause of epilepsy depends on economic and social factors, and, for this reason, the stigma can be heterogeneous and changeable (Kleinman et al., 1995). The perception of epilepsy is often negative, which impairs the patient's quality of life and reinforces the stigma (Scambler and Hopkins, 1990).

Studies have reported that prejudice and discrimination often have a greater impact on the daily lives of people with epilepsy than seizures (Suurmeijer et al., 2001; Fisher et al., 2000). In a Glasgow based study few children reported episodes of bullying, teasing or being laughed at because of their epilepsy. The study also reported that few epileptic children were not permitted by their teachers to join activities, however few others reported that teachers were helpful and supportive. These children also reported difficulty to concentrate during lectures more since epilepsy onset (Moffat et al., 2009a, b).

All children are likely to encounter issues and concerns during the course of their development, which are further complicated by the presence of epilepsy or other chronic illnesses of childhood. Hence stigma associated with epilepsy need to be eliminated by whatever possible means such as creating awareness among people for the betterment of plight of epileptic patients. Mass media campaigns should target these social segments to fight prejudice and improve society's acceptance of people with epilepsy (Fernandes et al., 2007).

Of late, positive attitude has been witnessed among epileptic patients in certain parts of the world. The Glasgow based study for example reported that few epileptic patients have decided to tell others about their illness so that they could feel safer if they had seizures (Moffat et al., 2009a,b).

Self-management practices are another area which has been found to be good in about 71% patients in this study. Significant association of this was seen with age of patients particularly of the age group 30 to 50 years. Self-management practice was also found to significantly increase with educational status of patients. However no significant association was seen between gender and occupational status of patients. Similar observation was made in a Texas based study where epileptic patients with higher levels of self-efficacy and social support also reported higher self-management ($P<0.01$) regardless of demographics, seizure frequency and socio-economic status ($P<0.05$). These findings provide little support for age, gender and socio economic status related disparities in self-management and suggest that the focus of strategies to improve self-management may be similar across diverse populations (Begley et al., 2010). Thus educating patients is all that is required to improve their self-management practices so as help them to cope up with epilepsy. The association of economic status with various parameters could not be studied as family income was not revealed by most participants.

Conclusion

Quality of life was significantly associated with educational status of patients. Poor quality of life being reported by more than half of patients indicates the importance of empowering people to adjust with epilepsy so that they can better accommodate their condition. Reducing side effects and achieving better control of seizures are also key to improving the quality of life of people with epilepsy, as is reducing the stigma and handicap associated with it. Stigmatization being reported by more than 65% of patients and being significantly more among patients in the age groups 30 to 50 years indicates the gravity of this issue. Stigma can be alleviated by better family and social support. For this, general public need to be educated so that they get the right perspective of this disease. They also need to be taught the required skills to help an epileptic patient during an attack. Self-management practices being good in more than 70% patients indicate that most patients know the dos and don'ts practices associated with epilepsy quite well. These beneficial practices were found to significantly improve with increasing age of patients and also were significantly associated with educational status of patients. Hence if quality of life of epileptic patients is improved and stigma associated minimized it will improve their self-esteem and help them lead a normal life like any other individuals.

ACKNOWLEDGEMENTS

The authors would like to thank Dr. Unnikrishnan Bhaskaran, HOD, Department of Community Medicine, KMC, Mangalore for his continued support throughout the study. We also thank authorities of the concerned hospitals and patients who participated in this study for their cooperation rendered to us during the period of data collection.

REFERENCES

Ablon J (2002). The nature of stigma and medical conditions. Epilepsy Behav., 3: 2-9.

Agarwal P, Mehndiratta MM, Antony AR, Kumar N, Dwivedi RN, Sharma P, Kumar S (2006). Epilepsy in India: nuptiality behaviour and fertility. Seizure, 15: 409-415.

Austin JK, Smith MS, Risinger MW, McNelis AM (1994). Childhood epilepsy and asthma: comparison of quality of life. Epilepsia, 35: 608-615.

Bahou YG, Jaber MS, Kasasbeh AS (2011). Quality of life in epilepsy at Jordan University Hospital. Neurosciences (Riyadh), 16: 18-23.

Baker G (2002). The psychosocial burden of epilepsy. Epilepsia, 43: 26-30.

Baker GA, Jacoby A, Buck D, Stalgis C, Monnet D (1997). Quality of Life of People with Epilepsy: A European Study. Epilepsia, 38:353-62.

Begley CE, Shegog R, Iyagba B, Chen V, Talluri K, Dubinsky S, Newmark M, Ojukwu N, Friedman D (2010). Socioeconomic status and self-management in epilepsy: comparison of diverse clinical populations in Houston, Texas. Epilepsy Behav., 19: 232-238.

Collings JA (1990). Psychosocial well-being and epilepsy: an empirical study. Epilepsia, 31: 418-426.

Cramer JA, Westbrook LE, Devinsky O, Perrine K, Glassman MB, Camfield C (1999). Development of the quality of life in epilepsy inventory for adolescents: the QOLIE-AD-48. Epilepsia, 40: 1114-1121.

Dilorio C, Faherty B, Manteuffel B (1994). Epilepsy self-management: partial replication and extension. Res. Nurs. Health, 17: 167-174.

Dilorio C, Osborne Shafer P, Letz R, Schomer DL, Yeager K (2003). The association of stigma with self-management and perceptions of health care among adults with epilepsy. Epilepsy Behav., 4: 259-267.

Fernandes PT, Salgado PC, Noronha AL, de Boer HM, Prilipko L, Sander JW, Li LM (2007). Epilepsy stigma perception in an urban area of a limited-resource country. Epilepsy Behav., 11: 25-32.

Fisher RS, Vickrey BG, Gibson P, Hermann B, Penovich P, Scherer A, Walker S (2000). The impact of epilepsy from the patient's perspective: I. Descriptions and subjective perceptions. Epilepsy Res., 41: 39-51.

Goodridge DM, Shorvon SD (1983). Epileptic seizures in a population of 6000. II: Treatment and prognosis. Br. Med. J. (Clin. Res. Ed.): 287: 645-647.

Grudzinski AN, Hakim Z, Coons SJ, Labiner DM (1998). Use of the QOLIE-31 in Routine Clinical Practice. J Epilepsy, 11: 34-47.

Jacoby A, Baker GA, Steen N, Potts P, Chadwick DW (1996). The clinical course of epilepsy and its psychosocial correlates: Findings from a UK community study. Epilepsia, 37: 148-161.

Jacoby A, Snape D, Baker GA (2005). Epilepsy and social identity: the stigma of a chronic neurological disorder. Lancet Neurol., 4: 171-178.

Kleinman A, Wang WZ, Li SC, Cheng XM, Dai XY, Li KT, Kleinman J (1995). The social course of epilepsy: chronic illness as social experience in interior China. Soc. Sci. Med., 40: 1319-1330.

Li LM, Sander JW (2003). National demonstration project on epilepsy in Brazil. Arq. Neuropsiquiatr., 61: 153-156.

Moffat C, Dorris L, Connor L, Espie CA (2009). The impact of childhood epilepsy on quality of life. A qualitative investigation using focus group methods to obtain children's perspectives on living with epilepsy. Epilepsy Behav., 14: 179-189.

Moffat C, Dorris L, Connor L, Espie CA (2009). The impact of childhood epilepsy on quality of life: A qualitative investigation using focus group methods to obtain children's perspectives on living with epilepsy. Epilepsy Behav., 14: 179-189.

Radhakrishnan K (2009). Challenges in the management of epilepsy in resource-poor countries. Nat. Rev. Neurol., 5: 323-330.

Rodin EA (1968). The prognosis of patients with epilepsy. Springfield: Charles Thomas.

Sabaz M, Cairns D, Lawson J, Nheu N, Bleasel A, Bye A (2000).

Validation of a new quality of life measure for children with epilepsy. Epilepsia, 41: 765-774.
Scambler G, Hopkins A (1990). Generating a model of epileptic stigma: the role of qualitative analysis. Soc Sci Med., 30: 1187-1194.
Shibre T, Alem A, Tekle-Haimanot R, Medhin G, Jacobsson L (2006). Perception of stigma in people with epilepsy and their relatives in Butajira, Ethiopia. Ethiop. J. Health Dev., 20:170-176.
Suurmeijer T, Reuvekamp MF, Aldenkamp BP (2001). Social functioning, psychological functioning and quality of life in epilepsy. Epilepsia, 42: 1160-1168.
Weiss MG, Doongaji DR, Siddhartha S, Wypij D, Pathare S, Bhatawdekar M, Bhave A, Sheth A, Fernandes R (1992). The Explanatory Model Interview Catalogue (EMIC). Contribution to cross-cultural research methods from a study of leprosy and mental health. Br. J. Psychiatry, 160: 819-830.

Relation between depression and Omega-3 fatty acids: A study in the Greek population

Archaniotis I. Vasilios[1], Wozniak Greta[2]*, Zoe Roupa[2], Mouzas D. Odysseas[3] and Constantinos Tsipras[4]

[1]Primary Health Care Course Program, Medical School, University of Thessaly, Mezourlo, Larissa, Greece.
[2]Department of Medicine, University of Thessaly, Mezourlo, Larissa, Greece.
[3]Department of Psychiatry, Medical School, University of Thessaly, Mezourlo, Larissa, Greece.
[4]Endocrinologist, Outwards Patients, Athens, Greece.

The role of essential fatty acids in the human body and especially the decreased levels of it in patients with depression is a domain of interest for many researchers. The aim of the present study is to investigate the correlation between consumption of food rich in omega-3 fatty acids and depressive symptoms in the general population at the area of Larissa, central Greece. The sample consisted of 300 individuals (mean age 41.01, 137 men (46%) and 163 women (54%), randomly selected by the method of stratified multistage sampling. The Food Frequency Questionnaire (FFQ) and the Beck Depression Inventory-II (BDI-II) were used in order to investigate the relationship between food consumption and depression. A statistically significant negative correlation was detected between fish consumption and score at the BDI-II (-0.451, p<0.01). As concern the kind of fish consumed by our sample, statistically significant negative correlation was also detected by Pearson's Correlation Test. Individuals with increased consumption of fatty fish (rich in omega-3 fatty acids) have reduced scores at the BDI-II (-0.453, p<0.01). The same statistical difference was found among the combined consumption of fish, seafood and food supplements (containing omega-3 fatty acids) and BDI-II score (-0.480, p<0.01). Finally, the combined consumption of fruit, vegetables and nuts was negatively correlated with BDI-II score (-0.260, p<0.01). The present study indicates that depressed mood in our sample is negatively associated with dietary intakes of food rich in omega-3 fatty acids. It is also clear that omega-3 fatty acids should be delivered in a dietary framework that includes and other important nutrients contained in fruits, vegetables and nuts.

Key words: Omega-3 fatty acids, eicosapentaenoic acid, docosahexaenoic acid, depression, nutrition, general population.

INTRODUCTION

An emerging research sector analyses the neurobehavioral aspects of omega-3 fatty acids (eicosapentaenoic acid, docosahexaenoic acid) and their important role in the function of the central nervous system. Many studies have reported a decrease in the levels of omega-3 fatty acids in patients with depression (Adams et al., 1996, Maes et al., 1998). Fish contain high concentrations of omega-3 polyunsaturated fatty acids, especially eicosapentaenoic acid (EPA) and docosahexaenoic acid (DHA). It has been suggested that the inadequate consumption of fish can increase the occurrence of depression, as EPA and DHA are crucial for the optimal function of neurons and come from the consumption of fish (Timonen et al., 2004).

Long chain omega-3 fatty acids are polyunsaturated fatty acids and have a vegetable or sea origin. As these important fatty acids cannot be created in the human

*Corresponding author. E-mail: greta@med.uth.gr.

body, they have to be taken in through dietary sources (Allport, 2006). Fish contain various quantities of omega-3 fatty acids, mainly eicosapentaenoic acid (EPA) and docosahexaenoic acid (DHA) (Sargent et al., 1996).

During last years, researchers have investigated the role of these important fatty acids in humans. In contrast with the healthy population, people suffering from depression have lower concentrations of omega-3 fatty acids in the plasma and the membranes of the erythrocytes (Adams et al., 1996, Peet et al., 1998, Maes et al., 1998). Furthermore, in another study it has been found that people suffering from depression have an increased ratio of omega-6/omega-3 fatty acids (Adams et al., 1996).

Mood disorders, including depression, are repeatable and possibly threatening for the patient's life. During the last 100 years, the age at which the depression symptoms occur has decreased and the general impact has increased in the western countries. For example, serious depression forms have an impact of 5% in the population of USA, while 20% of the population has milder forms. Furthermore, 2% of the population has bipolar disorder (Blazer, 2000). In contrast with the nutrition 50 years ago, today people consume 34% less vegetables and 66% less fish (Allport, 2006). Fish is the main source of omega-3 fatty acids, which are important for the good function of the brain (Allport, 2006).

The food impact on the psychological health can be direct and long lasting, because of the way in which the structure and the function of the brain is influenced (Bourre et al., 1991). Depression has been connected with the lower intake of omega-3 fatty acids, which results from the inadequate consumption of fish. The majority of people (66%), who report that they do not suffer from psychological disorders, consume fresh fruits and vegetables every day as well as fish. In contrast, fewer than 50% of those with psychological problems report a relative consumption (Silvers and Scott, 2002).

Despite the progress of medicine, a large percentage of patients with depression do not improve with the use of medical treatment (Kornstein and Schneider, 2001). Poor compliance, side effects and lack of desirable results are not uncommon during the treatment with antidepressants. The treatment with selective serotonin reuptake inhibitors (SSRI) results in the improvement only of the 50% of the patients, while 30% of the people suffering from depression stop the use of medication before the completion of six weeks (Anderson, 2000).Bearing in mind the above facts, we tried to investigate whether there is a significant relationship between consumption of food with high concentrations of omega-3 fatty acids and the occurrence of depression in representative population at the area of Larissa, Central Greece.

MATERIALS AND METHODS

Study population

This study was conducted in the general population at the area of Larissa, Central Greece (ages 18+) (Figure 1). The information, which came from the processing of the file of the statistical office for the population census during 2001, was used as a sampling frame (Larissa prefecture). The referral population of the study was 272.966 people for the year 2001. The size of the sample was n=300 individuals.

A random sample of 300 households was selected with a systematic cluster sampling method. Then, from each household an adult aged between 18 and 70 years old was selected at random for the interview, using the Kish selection grid. The final sample included 266 individuals from urban and semi-urban areas and 34 individuals from rural areas. The mean age of the participants was 41 years (SD ±11.9).

The sample consisted of 163 women (54%) and 137 men (46%). 203 of the participants were: married, 56 were single, 25 were divorced and 16 were widowed. The majority of the participants (143) had a secondary education, 170 had tertiary education and 50 people had primary education (mainly aged participants). Table 1 shows the demographic features of the sample.

Methodology

The collection of the data was done with the use of questionnaires in the residence of the participants. The questionnaires were completed in an average of 7 min. The study was conducted in the period of October 18th 2008 to February 1st 2009. Each participant completed two questionnaires: Food Frequency Questionnaire (FFQ) (adjusted to the needs of the study) and Beck Depression Inventory. The Beck Depression Inventory-II (Cronbach's index a=0.86) was used in the form of 'Which statement expresses the way you feel during the last two weeks, including this day'. The answer in each question is scored by Linkert system with 0, 1, 2, and 3. A total score of 0 to 9 does not indicate depression, a total score of 10 to 18 indicate mild depression, a total score of 19 to 29 indicates serious depression and a total score of 30 to 63 indicates major depression.

The Food Frequency Questionnaire (FFQ) was used in order to investigate the dietary habits (or styles) of our sample. FFQ includes 8 questions (adjusted to the needs of the study) with the following form: 'How often do you consume... what kind...' The answers, which have to do with the consumption of fish, seafood and red meat, are scored with the following way: 3 to 4 times a week (score 2), 2 times a week (score 1), once a week (score 0.8), 2 to 3 times a month (score 0.4), once a month (score 0.2). The answers that have to do with the type of fish, receive 1 to 0.2 points based on the concentration of the fish in omega-3 fatty acids. For example, salmon, which is a fish rich in omega-3 fatty acids, takes 1 point, while flounder, which has a poor concentration in omega-3 fatty acids, takes 0.2 points. The answers that have to do with the consumption of fruit, vegetables and nuts take the following points: 2 times a day (score 2), once a day (score 1), 3 to 4 times a week (score 0.8), 2 times a week (score 0.4), once a week (score 0.2).

Apart from the classic descriptive methods, the statistic analysis included the use of the parametric Pearson's Correlation Test, Kendall's Tau_b Test and Spearman's Test for the evaluation of the relation between depression and consumption of seafood, depression and the consumption of fish, depression and consumption of seafood, fish and nutritional supplements combined, depression and fish type, depression and consumption of red meat, depression and consumption of fruits, depression and consumption of vegetables, depression and consumption of nuts and depression and consumption of fruit, vegetables and nuts combined.

An impression of the linear regression that describes the above correlations was also made. The statistical analysis of the data was done with the use of SPSS program (version 16.0.1).

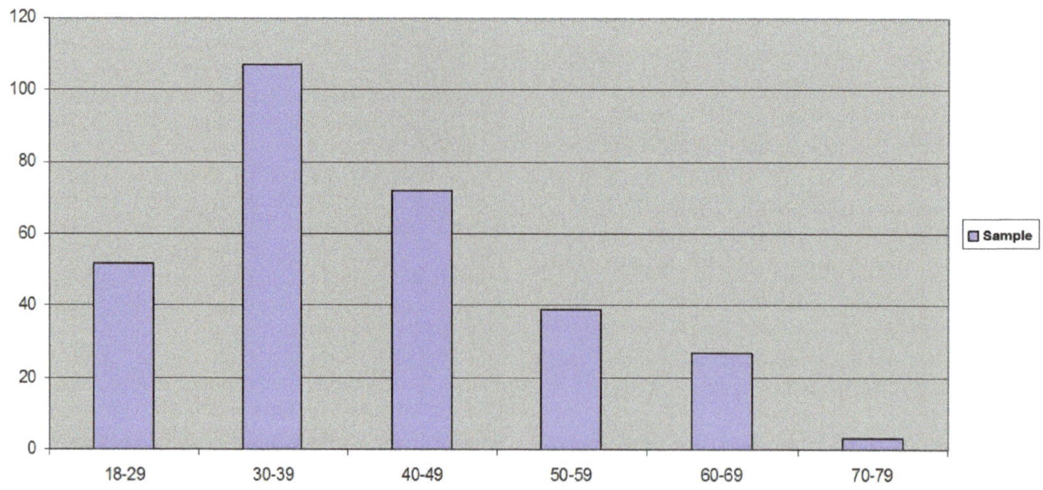

Figure 1. Age of sample.

Table 1. Dietary habits of participants in our study.

Variable	N	Minimum	Maximum	Mean	Std. deviation
Age	300	18.00	70.00	41.0133	11.98800
BDI-II Score	300	0.00	37.00	9.6100	6.83327
Fish Consumption	300	0.20	2.00	0.8853	0.47002
Kind of Fish	300	0.20	1.00	0.5976	0.17207
Seafood	300	0.20	2.00	0.5580	0.48520
Fish Seafood Suppl.	300	0.20	4.00	1.0937	0.74393
Nuts	300	0.20	2.00	0.6453	0.44113
Fruit	300	0.20	2.00	0.9287	0.54014
Vegetables	300	0.20	2.00	0.8960	0.49841
Fruit Veget. Nuts	300	0.20	5.00	2.4410	1.05422
Red Meat	300	0.20	2.00	1.2353	0.62454
Valid N (listwise)	300				

RESULTS

Dietary habits

Table 1 indicates the dietary habits of our sample. It is important to note that the mean value of the consumption of red meat was 1.2353, which means that a large percentage of the population consumes red meat with a high frequency (over 2 times a week). The mean value of the consumption of fish is 0.8853 (once per week). The consumption of fatty fish, which are rich in omega-3 fatty acid is medium with a mean value of 0.5976. The consumption of seafood is relatively low with a mean value of 0.5580 (average consumption of seafood 3 times a month). The consumption of fruit and vegetables is satisfactory with a mean value for the consumption of fruit of 0.9287, which means that the average of the sample consumes fruit once per day, and a mean value for vegetables of 0.8960 (average consumption of vegetables 3 to 4 times a week). The consumption of nuts is relatively low with a mean value of 0.6453 (average consumption of nuts 2 times per week) (Table 1).

Finally, the mean value of depression is 9.61, which is at the higher levels of the healthy spectrum in Beck Depression Inventory-II. Figure 2 shows the percentage of fish consumption by our sample. Twenty nine individuals report that they consume fish 3 to 4 times per week, 104 people report that they consume fish 2 times per week, 60 people report that they consume fish once per week, 57 people report that they consume fish 2 to 3 times a month and 50 people report that they consume fish one per month (Figure 2).

The percentage of seafood consumption in the sample is: 6% report that they consume seafood 3 to 4 times per week, 15% report that they consume seafood 2 times per week, 12% report that they consume seafood once per

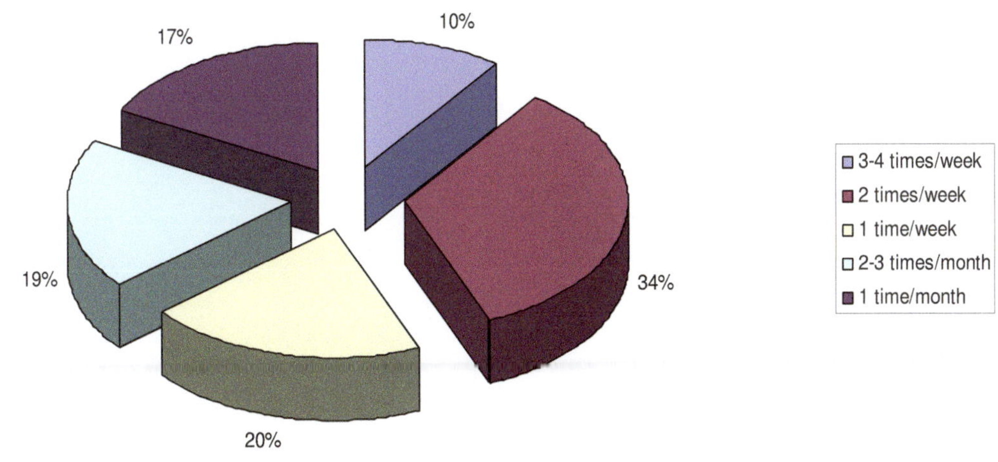

Figure 2. Fish consumption.

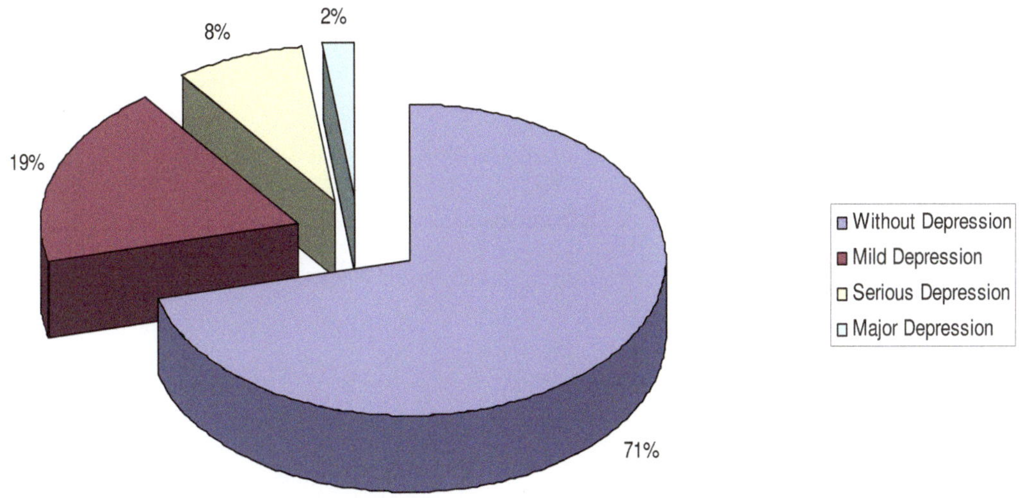

Figure 3. Beck Depression Inventory-II results.

week, 27% report that they consume seafood 2 to 3 times per month and 40% report that they consume seafood once per month. If we analyze the consumption of red meat in the sample we can see that 110 people report that they consume red meat 3 to 4 times per week (37%), 33% report that they consume red meat 2 times per week, 16% report that they consume red meat once per week, 7% report that they consume red meat 2 to 3 times per month and 7% report that they consume red meat once per month.

The consumption of fruit is considered satisfactory with a large proportion of the sample (32%) reporting that they consume fruit 3 to 4 times per week and 27% reporting that they consume fruit once a day. 13% of the sample report that they consume vegetables 2 times a day, 27% report that they consume vegetables once a day, 35% report that they consume vegetables 3 to 4 times per week, 16% report that they consume vegetables 2 times per week and 9% report that they consume vegetables once per week. The consumption of nuts is relatively low in the sample. 5% report that they consume nuts 2 times a day, 17% report that they consume nuts once a day, 30% report that they consume nuts 3 to 4 times per week, 15% report that they consume nuts 2 times per week and 33% report that they consume nuts once per week.

Depression

The majority of the sample (212 individuals, 71%) belongs in the healthy spectrum of Beck Depression Inventory-II. According to BDI-II results, 57 people (19%) suffer from mild depression. 25 people (8%) suffer from serious depression and 6 suffer (2%) from major depression (Figure 3).

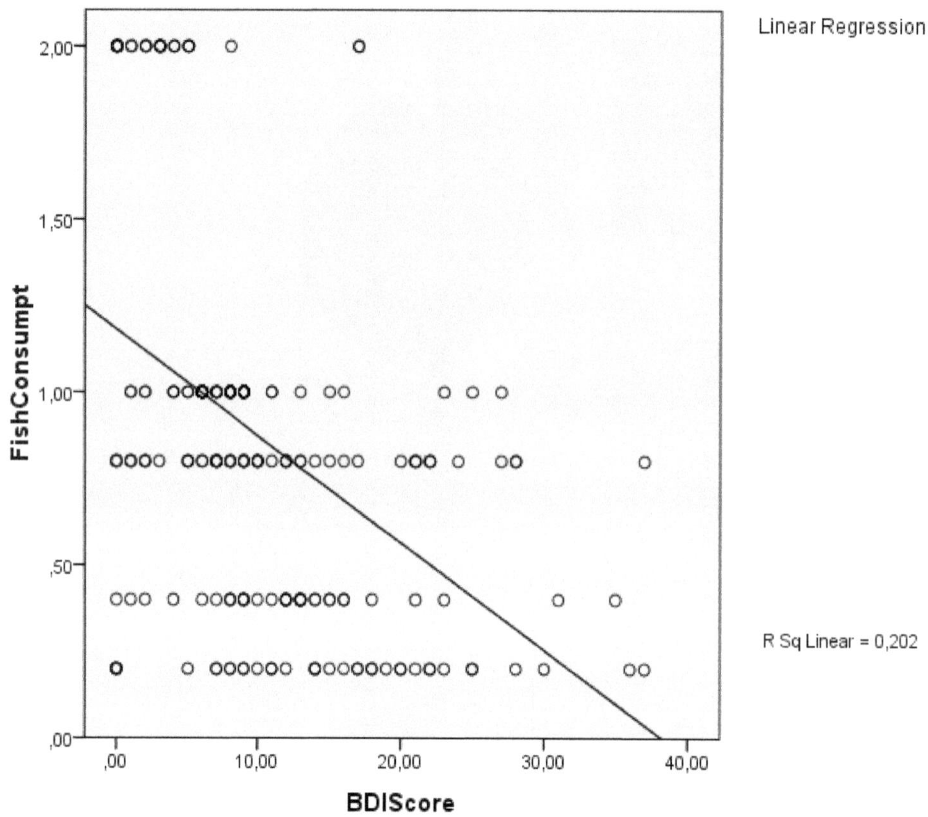

Figure 4. Linear regression line, which describes the relationship between the two variables (Beck Depression Inventory-II score and fish consumption).

Table 2. Beck Depression Inventory-II score and fish consumption correlations.

		BDI-II Score	Fish consumption
BDI-II Score	Pearson correlation	1,000	-.451**
	Sig. (2-tailed)		.000
	N	300,000	300
Fish consumption	Pearson correlation	-.451**	1,000
	Sig. (2-tailed)	.000	
	N	300	300,000

**. Correlation is significant at the 0.01 level (2-tailed).

Correlations

A correlation was found between the consumption of fish and depression. We noticed that when the consumption of fish increases, the levels of depression in BDI-II decrease (Figure 4). The result of Pearson's Correlation Test is -0.451 with $p<0.01$, the result of Kendall's Tau_b Test is -0.390 with $p<0.01$ and the result of Spearman's Rho is -0.469 with $p<0.01$ (Table 2). A very low negative correlation between the consumption of seafood and depression was found (practically there is no correlation). The result of Pearson's Correlation Test is -0.164 with $p<0.01$, the result of Kendall's Tau_b Test is -0.255 with $p<0.01$ and the result of Spearman's Rho test is -0.295 with $p<0.01$.

There is also a correlation between the type of fish, which was consumed by the sample and depression. We notice that as the consumption of fatty fish (rich in omega-3 fatty acids) is increased, the levels of depression in BDI-II decrease. The result of Pearson's

Table 3. Combined consumption of fish, seafood, supplements and Beck Depression Inventory-II score correlations.

		BDI-II Score	Fish seafood suppl.
BDI-II Score	Pearson Correlation	1,000	-,480**
	Sig. (2-tailed)		,000
	N	300,000	300
Fish seafood suppl.	Pearson Correlation	-,480**	1,000
	Sig. (2-tailed)	,000	
	N	300	300,000

**. Correlation is significant at the 0.01 level (2-tailed).

Correlation test is -0.453 with p<0.01, the result of Kendall's Tau_b Test is -0.405 with p<0.01) and the result of Spearman Rho test is -0.513 with p<0.01. Another correlation was found between the combined consumption of fish, seafood and nutritional supplements (which contain omega-3 fatty acids). The result of Pearson's Correlation Test is -0.480 with p<0.01, the result of Kendall's Tau_b Test is -0.475 with p<0.01 and the result of Spearman's Rho Test is -0,558 with p<0.01 (Table 3) Correlation between red meat consumption and depression was not found. The result of Pearson's Correlation Test is -0.059 with p=0.305, the result of Kendall's Tau_b Test is -0.027 with p=0.546 and the result of Spearman's Rho Test is -0.034 with p=0.557.

A correlation between the consumption of fruit, vegetables and nuts, and depression was found. The result of Pearson's Correlation Test for fruit was -0.193 with p<0.01, the result of Pearson's Correlation Test for vegetables was -0.183 with p<0.01 and the result of Pearson's Correlation Test for nuts was -0.193 with p<0.01. A correlation was found between the combined consumption of fruit, vegetables, nuts and depression. The result of Pearson's Correlation Test is -0.260 with p<0.01, the result of Kendall's Tau_b Test is -0.272 with p<0.01 and the result of Spearman's Rho Test is -0.326 with p<0.01.

DISCUSSION

Depression is a serious problem for the modern society and has an increasing impact on the western world. Bearing in mind the fact that it is underestimated for various reasons, for example the fact that it coexists with other diseases or with old age, it is not exaggerated to characterize it as one of the diseases of the future. The purpose of this study is to evaluate the relationship between dietary habits as far as the consumption of food rich in omega-3 fatty acids is concerned and depression in the general population at the area of Larissa, central Greece. Based on the results of BDI-II spectrum of depression, 19% of the people in the study (n=57) exhibit mild depression, 8% (n=25) exhibit serious depression and 2% (n=6) exhibit major depression. 10% (n=29) of the sample report that they consume fish 3 to 4 times per week, nearly the half (54%, n=164) report that they consume fish once or two times per week and 36% (n=107) report that they consume fish 2 to 3 times per month or less. The consumption of seafood is relatively low with the 67% of the sample consuming seafood 2 to 3 times per month or less. The consumption of red meat is very high with the 37% of the sample (n =110) consuming red meat 3 to 4 times per week and the 33% (n=100) consuming red meat 2 times per week. The consumption of fruit and vegetables is satisfactory with the 43% of the sample consuming fruit one time per day and the 40% of the sample consuming vegetables once per day.

The results show a negative correlation between the consumption of fish and depression in the population of the sample (300 individuals residing at the area of Larissa, central Greece). Important is also the relationship between the type of fish that is being consumed and depression. A negative correlation was found between the combined consumption of fish, seafood and nutritional supplements (which contain omega-3 fatty acids). This kind of relationship between the low consumption of fish and the high levels of depression has been reported in other studies as well (Silvers and Scott, 2002, Tanskanen et al., 2001, Timonen et al., 2004). Fish and seafood are the main source of omega-3 fatty acids in the human diet. Thus, a small consumption of fish may mean low intake of omega-3 fatty acids and increased danger of depression.

A correlation between the consumption of red meat and depression was not found (Pearson's Correlation Test = -0.059 with p=0.305). An insignificant negative correlation was found between the consumption of seafood and depression (practically there is no correlation). Finally, an insignificant negative correlation was found between the consumption of fruit, vegetables and dried fruit and depression, but the consumption of all the above in combination shows that there is a small negative correlation. A small number of studies (or research) depict the beneficial impact of folic acid, which is contained in fruit and vegetables, on depression and its potential to strengthen the effectiveness of antidepressants with the use of doses of 500 mg (Paul et al., 2004; Coppen and Bailey, 2000). We must note that folic acid is proven to increase the levels of omega-3 when it is administered as a nutritional supplement, while decreased omega-3 levels are noticed when there is inefficiency of folic acid (Pita and Delgado, 2000). Furthermore, a poor in folic acid diet can strengthen lipid peroxidation (Durand et al., 1996).

The study did not include structured diagnostic interviews, like the Structured Clinical Interview for DSM or the objective evaluation of depression symptoms. The use of this measure could probably strengthen the findings. The evaluation of fish consumption was done with the use of the Food Frequency Questionnaire, which is not a food-recording questionnaire, a fact that limits the research. However, the value for the use of a frequency questionnaire (FFQ) for the estimation of fish and seafood consumption in the everyday diet has been proven (Hu et al., 1999). Another limitation of this study is the relative small sample number. The present study is one of the very few that have been conducted in Greece and the results indicate that depression has a negative relationship with the dietary consumption of fish. It is clear that the intake of omega-3 fatty acids must be conducted in a way so as it will include other important nutrients.

Nutritional therapy, which is unregarded by the main stream of doctors, appears justified in psychiatry and neurology. While it is not essential for the professionals of mental health to be clinical nutritionists, the introduction of a diet rich in omega-3 fatty acids may be important for their patients. The basic conclusions, which must be taken into account, are two: a) A diet rich in omega-3 fatty acids may contribute in the decrease of the danger of depression and, b) the same diet can offer positive results in other situations (e.g. cardiovascular disorders), which may relate in a small or big degree to the occurrence of depression (e.g. a patient with coronary disease may present depression because of his fear for his health) (Holub, 2002).

REFERENCES

Adams PB, Lawson S, Sanigorski A, Sinclair AJ (1996). Arachidonic Acid to Eicosapentaenoic Acid Ratio in Blood Correlates Positively With Clinical Symptoms Of Depression. Lipids 31: 157-161.

Allport S (2006). The Queen Of Fats: Why Omega-3 Were Removed From Western Diet And What We Can Do To Replace Them. University Of California Press, Los Angeles, CA.

Anderson IM (2000). Selective Serotonin Reuptake Inhibitors versus Tricyclic Antidepressants: A Meta-Analysis of Efficacy and Tolerability. J. Affect. Disord., 58(1): 19-36.

Blazer DG (2000). Mood Disorders: Epidemiology. In Comprehensive Textbook of Psychiatry. Lippincott, Williams and Wilkens, New York, pp. 1298-1308.

Bourre JM, Dumont O, Piciotti M, Clément M, Chaudière J, Bonneil M, Nalbone G, Lafont H, Pascal G, Durand G (1991). Essentiality of omega-3 fatty acids for brain structure and function. In: Simopoulos AP, Kifer RR, Martin RE, Barlow SM, eds. Health effects of omega-3 polyunsaturated fatty acids in seafoods. Basel, Karger: World Rev Nutr Diet., 66: 103–17.

Coppen A, Bailey J (2000). Enhancement Of The Antidepressant Action Of Fluoxetine By Folic Acid: A Randomised, Placebo Controlled Trial. J. Affect. Disord., 60: 121-130.

Durand P, Prost M, Blache D (1996). Pro-Thrombotic Effects Of A Folic Acid Deficient Diet In Rat Platelets And Macrophages Related To Elevated Homocysteine And Decreased ω-3 Polyunsaturated Fatty Acids. Atherosclerosis. 121: 231-243.

Holub BJ (2002). Omega-3 Fatty Acids in Cardiovascular Care. CMAJ. 166:608-615.

Frank BH, Eric R, Stephanie AS, Diane F, Meir JS, Albert A, Laura S, Walter CW (1999). Reproducibility and Validity of Dietary Patterns Assessed with a Food-Frequency Questionnaire. Am. J. Clin. Nutr., 69:243-249.

Kornstein SG, Schneider RK (2001). Clinical Features of Treatment-Resistant Depression. J Clin. Psychiatry, 62:18-25.

Maes M, Christophe A, Delanghe J, Altamura C, Neels H, Meltzer HY (1999). Lowered Omega-3 Polyunsaturated Fatty Acids In The Serum Phospholipids And Cholesteryl Esters of Depressed Patients. Psychiatry Res., 85(3): 275-291.

Paul RT, McDonnell AP, Kelly CB (2004). Folic Acid: Neurochemistry, Metabolism and Relationship to Depression. Hum. Psychopharmacol., 19: 477-488.

Peet M, Murphy B, Shay J, Horrobin D (1998). Depletion of Omega-3 Fatty Acid Levels in Red Blood Cell Membranes of Depressive Patients. Biol. Psychiatry, 43:315-319.

Pita ML, Delgado MJ (2000). Folate Administration Increases ω-3 Polyunsaturated Fatty Acids in Rat Plasma and Tissue Lipids. Thromb Haemost, 84: 420-423.

Sargent JR, Bell MV, Bell JG, Henderson RJ, Tocher DR (1996). Origins and Functions of Ω-3 Polyunsaturated Fatty Acids in Marine Organisms. In Phospholipids: Characterisation, Metabolism And Novel Biological Applications. American Oil Chemists' Society Press, IL, pp. 248–257.

Silvers KM, Scott KM (2002). Fish Consumption And Self-Reported Physical And Mental Health Status. Pub. Health Nutr., 5: 427-431.

Tanskanen A, Hibbeln JR, Hintikka J, Haatainen K, Honkalampi K, Viinamaki H (2001). Fish consumption, depression, and suicidality in a general population. Arch. Gen. Psychiatry, 58:512-513.

Timonen M, Horrobin D, Jokelainena J, Laitinen J, Herva A, Räsänen P (2004). Fish Consumption and Depression: The Northern Finland 1966 Birth Cohort Study. J. Affect. Disord., 82: 447-452.

Physico-chemical assessment of sorghum brew adjunct and barley brew lager beer

Olu Malomo*, Ogunmoyela O. A. B., Oluwajoba S. O. and Daniel 'Toyosi

College of Food Science, Bells University of Technology, P.M.B. 1015, Ota, Ogun State, Nigeria.

The type of alcoholic beverage produced in any particular region or country almost entirely reflects the types of crop grown. Thus the cooler region of Europe, Scandinavia, Poland and Russia produces beer and lagers from barley (Palmer, 1992). In tropical Africa, alcoholic beverages especially beer have been brewed from micro-organisms especially fungi are to expect. It is necessary to treat harvested crop with fungicide to prevent spoilage (Gomez, 1992). Sorghum has a wide range of colors and sizes. The best known are the white (*farafara*), yellow (*kaura*) brown and the red types (Gomez, 1992). Although the red types are malted for traditional beer production, the white type is preferred for modern beer production (Palmer, 1992). The type and strain of yeast used in fermentation has a great influence on the taste and character of beer produced (Kunze, 1996). Apart from brewing, sorghum has been used extensively in food industries. Vitamin enriched sorghum based product are enjoying acceptance at institutional levels as mid shift drinks and high energy breakfast food (Aluko, 1989). Sorghum is also used in industrial production of cellulose, paper, starch, sugar and chemicals (Subramaniann et al., 1989). Other uses of sorghum include livestock feed production (Al- Hazzan et al., 1989). Sorghum as adjunct in beer production already has a widespread acceptance. However, the availability of the grain poses a great problem to the brewing industry. Sorghum is already a staple diet, so to make a substantial replacement for barley malt, huge quantities of adjunct will be required (Nweke, 1989).

Key words: Sorghum, beer, adjunct.

INTRODUCTION AND LITERATURE REVIEW

Alcoholic beverages which occur throughout the world in many forms and taste results from the action of microorganisms or enzymes on a wide range of agricultural products such as grapes, grains, and soybeans (Smith, 1996; Rose, 1989). Such biological action was associated with biochemical changes that gave rise to significant organoleptic improvements to the final products (Brill, 1981). These products which are more nutritious and more easily digestible are toxicologically and microbiologically safer (Smith, 1996).The process of fermenting raw materials is of wide diversity, using technology from the most primitive to the most advanced, achieving an outstanding range of sensory and textural quality in the final product (Rose, 1989). Alcoholic beverages and potable spirit industries represent one of the most economically stable sectors in the present day commerce. Materials for alcoholic beverages normally comprise either sugary material (fruit juice, plant sap) or starchy materials (grains or roots) which need to be hydrolyzed to simple sugar before fermentation. When these substrates are incubated with suitable microorganism and allowed to ferment, the end product is a liquid containing from a few percentages to about 16% alcohol with a slightly acidic pH.

The type of alcoholic beverage produced in any particular region or country almost entirely reflects the types of crop grown. Thus the cooler region of Europe, Scandinavia, Poland and Russia produces beer and lagers from barley (Palmer, 1992). In tropical Africa, alcoholic beverages especially beer have been brewed for generations with locally available cereals like sorghum, rice, maize and millet (Okafor, 1987).

Barley malt is also known to be rich in protein and

*Corresponding author. E-mail: oludaremalomo1951@yahoo.com

enzymes. It has a high ß- glucan and pentosan level when compared to local grains. The enzyme potential of barley malt is sufficient to catabolize additional starch (Kunze, 1996). Consequently, throughout the world, part of the malt, usually 15 to 20% is replaced by unmalted cereal. The unmalted cereal called adjunct was added to remove excess protein which could cause haziness in beer (Kunze, 1996).

Barley malt, whose diastatic power is higher than other cereals, has a high level of maltose producing ß-amylase which is the key enzyme in breaking down malt starch (Palmer, 1996). Due to economic reasons, cheap raw materials are used as adjunct as partial replacement for malt in wort production (Canales, 1979). In some African countries and in some parts of U.S.A, sorghum has been the grain of choice as adjunct in lager beer production, because is cheaper than barley (Okolo et al., 1995).

Sorghum is the fifth largest cereal produced in the world (KUnze, 1996). It is drought resistant and indigenous to Africa. It is a staple food rating third behind rice and wheat (Okolo et al., 1995). It belongs to the grass family, essentially adapted to the semi-arid regions of the world, where it is traditionally used as food, beverages and building materials (Gomez, 1992). Sorghum known as *Sorghum vulgaris* is an old crop with yet unknown genetic variability (Palmer, 1992). It is a dry land summer cereal cultivated in areas of rainfall of 400 and 750 mm and a temperature of 38 to 40°C (House, 1993). During germination, sorghum produced an enzyme, which breaks down the storage materials it contains. Since planting is during the raining season, contamination by microorganisms especially fungi are to be expected. It is necessary to treat harvested crop with fungicide to prevent spoilage (Gomez, 1992). Sorghum has a wide range of colors and sizes. The best known are the white (*farafara),* yellow (*kaura)* brown and the red types (Gomez, 1992). Although the red types are malted for traditional beer production, the white type is preferred for modern beer production (Palmer, 1992).

The type and strain of yeast used in fermentation has a great influence on the taste and character of beer produced (Kunze, 1996). Apart from brewing, sorghum has been used extensively in food industries. Vitamin enriched sorghum based product are enjoying acceptance at institutional levels as mid shift drinks and high energy breakfast food (Aluko, 1989). Sorghum is also used in industrial production of cellulose, paper, starch, sugar and chemicals (Subramanian et al., 1989). Other uses of sorghum include livestock feed, production (Al-Hazzan et al., 1989). Sorghum as adjunct in beer production already has a widespread acceptance. However, the availability of the grain poses a great problem to the brewing industry. Sorghum is already a staple diet, so to make a substantial replacement for barley malt, huge quantities of adjunct will be required (Nweke, 1989).

In brewing the basic principles remain the same over the centuries. This includes malting, mashing, boiling and fermentation (Kunze, 1996). During malting, the grains are allowed to steep in water for 48 to 72 h at 10 to 15°C. The grains are allowed to germinate. However, as soon as the enzymes are produced and before the young seedling can make an appreciable in road into the nutrient reserve of the grain, development of the seedling is halted by drying at a temperature which will not completely inactivate the enzymes.

These enzymes are reactivated during mashing to hydrolyze starch and protein and release nutrients for the nourishment of the yeast during fermentation (Okafor, 1987). After malting the grains are milled and mixed with water. The mash after several processes of brewing is filtered and boiled before fermentation. Wort is usually inoculated with the fermenting organism, yeast. The sugar in the wort is fermented by yeast to alcohol. For this purpose yeast specie such as *Saccharomyces carlsbergensis* are used. Selected strains are systematically isolated and grown (Pollock, 1981).

Yeast has a high vitamin and enzyme content. They are particularly rich in vitamins B_1 and B_6 (Smith, 1996). Yeast makes use of carbohydrates in two ways: by respiration and fermentation. During fermentation, the nitrogen content of the wort, formed as a result of protein hydrolysis should at least be 23 mg of free amino nitrogen to allow for proper yeast nutrition (Malomo, 1993). Yeast cells are usually ovoid or round in shape. They are non-motile cells measuring between 5×10^6 (5 nm) to 10×10^6 (10 nm) in diameter. They reproduced by budding and grow rapidly on a defined medium. They also have a well-developed genetic cycle (Pollock, 1981). Yeast cells are able to ferment the trisaccharide raffinose, made up of glucose, fructose, and galactose. When using an adjunct as a replacement for malt during brewing, it must be remembered that protein is deposited in the adjunct in a more stable form. The protein is degraded only to a slight extent, because of this adjunct mashes contain less molecular weight nitrogenous materials (alpha amino nitrogen) than malt mashes. Adjunct beer therefore always contains more polyphenols. It follows then that the higher the adjunct the less the nitrogenous compounds (Kunze, 1996).

MATERIALS AND METHODS

Raw materials used for brewing were collected from the warehouse of the International Breweries PLC Ilesa. Barley malt (*Hordeum distichon*) or (*Hordeum vulgare*) was the chief raw material used. Others include, raw sorghum (*S. vulgaris*) was used as adjunct, brewing water, yeast (*S. carlsbergensis*), hop, and other additives like Vitamin C (ascorbic acid), sulphuric acid, sodium hydroxide and calcium chloride. These additives are used to adjust the pH of wort, when and where necessary.

Sample collection

Pilsener barley malt (*H. disichon*) with moisture content of 4.55%, kernel weight of 330.4 g was used as the substrate in brewing. The barley was collected from the warehouse of Intrnational Breweries PLC, Ilesa. The yellow type raw sorghum (*S. vulgare*) with a moisture content of 6.15% and kernel weight of 350.5 g was used as adjunct. This was purchased from L.O. Omole and Sons store, Ilesa.

Brewing process

A laboratory manual Glasbaserei milling machine was used to reduce the particle sizes of the grains and also to expose the starch in the grains in readiness for enzymatic action during brewing. In 100% barley malt brew, 600 g of malted barley was weighed into a flask. In the case of other formulations, the following proportions were used; 90% barley: 10% sorghum = 540 g barley: 60 g sorghum. 80% barley: 20% sorghum = 480 g barley: 120 g sorghum. 70% barley: 30% sorghum = 420 g barley: 180 g sorghum. 60% barley: 40% sorghum = 360 g barley: 240 g sorghum.

Two 25 L capacity Carlsberg's flasks were used for fermentation. An electronic Julabo water bath was used to monitor the temperature of wort during brewing.

Procedure

Six hundred grams of malted barley was weighed and mashed with 1.5 L of water inside a 5.0 L conical flask. This mash was placed inside a water bath and the temperature was raised to between 50 and 55°C for about 20 min, to allow for optimum activity of the enzymes present in the malt. The temperature was later raised to 72°C for 45 min to terminate enzymatic activities. The mash was then allowed to rest for 45 min to allow the mash to undergo complete saccharification (Okafor, 1987).

Saccharification, which is the complete hydrolysis of starch to simple sugar is shown by a brown or colorless reaction with 2% iodine solutions (Brauhaase, 2000). After saccharification, the mash was filtered. The aqueous solution collected, that is, wort was boiled for 1 h. After boiling, the wort was allowed to cool and the following parameters were determined; pH, color, gravity and temperature. The cooled wort was transferred into the Carlsbergen's vessel and inoculated with the fermenting organism. The pitching wort was then kept in the refrigerating incubator at 6°C. With malt/ adjunct brew the gelatinized sorghum adjunct was added to the malt mash at 55°C. The enzyme in the barley malt also acted on the adjunct mash to hydrolyzed the gelatinized starch in the adjunct.

Fermenting organism

A genetically modified strain of *S. carlsbergensis* no. 01185, strain 370 from Horlunann, Hamburg, was used as the fermenting organism. The yeast used was obtained by the propagation of pure yeast culture in the Laboratory.

Yeast propagation

About 5 ml of sterile wort was poured into a test-tube, a loopful of yeast from PDA agar slant was used to inoculate the sterile wort and shaken vigorously. The test-tube was allowed to stand for 24 h. The inoculated wort was transferred into a 100 ml flask containing sterile wort and this was also allowed to stand for another 24 h. This was also transferred into another flask containing 250 ml of sterile wort and subsequently to 500 and 1000 ml sterile wort and each was allowed to stand for 24 h. At the end 1000 ml of fermenting wort was obtained and this was used as the inoculant for the fermentation process.

Fermentation

Wort collected after brewing was transferred into Carlsberg's vessels. About 150 ml of the propagated inoculant with a yeast count of about 22 million cells/ml was introduced into the fermenting vessels using an injection syringe. The flask was shaken vigorously and kept in the refrigerating incubator with an inserted thermometer to monitor the temperature. Fermentation was allowed to proceed for nine days and the pH, temperature, color, gravity, yeast count, attenuation, yeast viability and yeast consistency were monitored and determined daily.

pH determination

The pH was determined using a Jenway 3015 pH meter. Ten milliliter of fermenting wort was taken and the electrode of the pH meter was inserted into the wort sample. The reading on the screen of the pH meter was observed and recorded daily. The pH value of wort after brewing, that is, 1st day of fermentation is found in Table 1 (24 h after the addition of yeast).

Colour determination

The color of wort before and after fermentation was recorded. The wort sample was put in a color comparator (colorimeter). The color of the wort at 320 nm wavelength was measured with the color comparator and the values recorded. The color of wort before fermentation was recorded in Table 1.

Yeast viability and consistency

About 5 ml of fermenting wort was placed in a test-tube, two drops of methylene blue was added to the sample, the sample was vigorously shaken and one or two drops of the stained sample was placed on the haemocytometer, mounted on the microscope and observed. The dead cells which absorbed the stain and retained the blue stain of the methylene blue was expressed as the percentage of the living cells (Peppler, 1978). Yeast viability is calculated as follows:

$$\frac{\text{Total number of cells} - \text{Dead cells}}{\text{Total number of cells}} \times 100$$

Yeast consistency was carried out by placing about 20 ml of fermenting wort in a cuvette. The cuvette was placed in the chamber of a Heraeus Christ Labofuge centrifuge. The sample in the cuvette was spinned at 4000 rpm. After spinning, the supernatant was discarded and the compressed yeast was weighed and recorded. This experiment was carried out in duplicates and the result was calculated as follows (Rose, 1977):

$$\text{Tube 1} = \frac{e - a}{c - a} \times 100\%$$

$$\text{Tube 2} = \frac{f - b}{d - b} \times 100\%$$

Table 1. Gravity value, pH color, temperature and attenuation limit of substrate after brewing (24 h).

Malt /adjunct ratio	pH	Color (EBC)	Gravity (°P)	Temperature (°C)	Attenuation
100% Barley malt	4.98	5.25	11.0	10.5	2.0
90% barley: 10% sorghum	4.87	5.25	11.0	11.2	2.0
80% barley: 20% sorghum	4.48	5.75	11.2	10.8	2.0
70% barley: 30% sorghum	4.86	6.50	11.3	11.5	2.0
60% barley: 40% sorghum	5.00	7.00	11.5	13.2	2.0

Where: weight of tube 1 = a, weight of tube 2 = b, weight of tube 2 + fermenting wort = d, weight of tube 1 + fermenting wort = c, weight of tube 1 + compressed yeast = e, weight of tube 2 + compressed yeast = f.

Attenuation determination

The attenuation was calculated by expressing the final gravity as a percentage of the original gravity, that is:

$$\frac{Og - Fg}{Og} \times 100\%$$

After fermentation, the green beer was filtered to remove the yeast cells. The clear beer was then checked for final gravity, pH, color and alcohol. The alcohol content was determined using the Variag Hans Carl alcohol chart. On this chart, the original gravity (Og) and final gravity (Fg) of the beer was used to determine the specific gravity (Sg), real extract (Re), refractive index (RI) and alcohol content of the beer for each formulations (Kunze,1996) (Table 2).

RESULTS AND DISCUSSION

pH

In the different formulations, it was observed that pH was between 4.48 in 80% barley: 20% sorghum to 5.00 in 60% barley: 40% sorghum. These pH values still conform with the desired pH range of wort, which is between 4.0 and 5.4 (Kunze, 1996), Table 2 shows the pH values of the wort.

Colour (EBC –European brewery convention)

The color of the wort increased with increase in adjunct concentration from 5.25 in 100% barley malt wort to 7.00 in 60% barley: 40% sorghum adjunct (Table 1). This could be attributed to the color of raw sorghum used due to the presence and oxidation of polyphenols and melanoidin in the sorghum, though not toxic, but inimical to producing good beer (Brauhaase, 2000).

Gravity

The gravity of the wort increased with increase in the adjunct proportion (Table 2). This implies that sorghum adjuncts contain more fermentable sugar than barley malt due to the high starch content of sorghum. However very little of the soluble protein is contributed to the wort by sorghum (about 5% of their total protein) Brauhaase, 2000).

Temperature

The temperature of fermentation was maintained at between 10 to 13.3°C. This is to allow for initial vigorous fermentation. A low initiating temperature may lead to too sluggish fermentation due to cold shock that could be experienced by the yeast cells on pitching while a higher temperature would lead to too vigorous fermentation thereby producing unwanted by product, which could affect the quality of the final beer (Hough et al., 1977).

Attenuation

The attenuation values of all the formulations were recorded in Table 2. All values are within the specified limit (1.5 to 2.5). The essence of attenuation is to know at what value the primary fermentation, (verified using the saccharometer spindle) should be terminated so that enough extract will be available for secondary fermentation in the storage tanks. The attenuation values of all the formulation ranged between 2.0 to 2.4 as recorded in Table 2.

Brewing

During brewing process, it was observed that the brew with 40% sorghum adjunct took a longer period of time to saccharify (30 min) as compared to the brews with lower adjunct proportion (8 to 10 min). It was also observed that the filtration rate of the high adjunct proportion brew was slower than the other formulations. This could as a result of the endosperm hardness of the sorghum grains (Malomo, 1993).

Fermentation

During fermentation, the green beer in all the

Table 2. Parameters monitored during fermentation: temperature, pH, attenuation limit (apparent and deformed yeast).

Days of fermentation	Temperature					pH					Attenuation limit (fermented extract)					Deformed yeast				
	100	90:10	80:20	70:30	60:40	100	90:10	80::20	70::30	60:40	100	90:10	80:20	70:30	60:40	100	90:10	80:20	70:30	60:40
Day 1	13.5	12.0	10.2	12.6	10.8	4.98	4.96	4.43	4.86	5.00	2.0	2.0	2.4	2.0	2.0	-	-	-	-	-
Day 2	12.8	12.2	12.0	10.8	10.8	4.80	4.90	4.33	4.49	4.63	7.82	14.54	28.6	18.6	16.03	-	-	-	-	-
Day 3	10.8	12.6	11.9	10.8	11.4	4.51	4.64	4.21	4.35	4.20	12.73	21.81	32.14	34.5	33.0	-	-	-	-	-
Day 4	10.6	12.4	11.8	10.7	12.0	4.21	4.52	4.18	4.32	3.73	18.26	41.86	69.6	50.4	59.8	-	-	-	-	-
Day 5	10.4	11.4	11.6	10.6	10.2	4.10	4.40	4.02	4.44	3.70	34.78	45.4	79.5	60.17	70.4	-	-	-	-	-
Day 6	10.4	10.6	10.8	10.2	10.2	4.08	4.08	4.02	4.26	3.75	44.34	47.2	80.4	72.6	82.6	-	-	-	-	-
Day 7	9.0	10.0	8.6	8.6	10.0	4.06	4.06	4.00	4.30	3.76	63.47	782	81.25	77.9	84.3	-	-	-	-	-
Day 8	8.5	8.2	7.5	7.5	8.2	4.02	4.04	3.88	4.32	3.77	82.6	83.6	81.25	85.0	87.0	-	-	-	-	+
Day 9	6.2	6.5	5.0	6.8	5.0	4.0	4.0	3.80	4.15	3.72	84.34	89.0	82.14	89.3	89.56	-	-	-	-	+

formulations were covered with white layers of foam. As fermentation progressed, the bubbles became fluffy and form brown caps. The appearance of bubbles showed that fermentation was progressing favorably (Kunze, 1996). Towards the end of fermentation, the high crest of foam formed slowly collapsed and the foam appeared browner and the bubbles became less pronounced. This showed that fermentation process had slowed down, less carbon dioxide was been produced and fermentation was slowly going to an end (Kunze, 1996).

Gravity

The amount of fermentable sugars reduced as fermentation progressed. This is because the yeast cells utilized these sugars which were converted to ethyl alcohol and carbon dioxide. The gravity of wort dropped at almost 24 h during fermentation. This is because about 3% of the extract were fermented every 24 h (Brauhaase, 2000). The gravity fall corresponded with an increase in the yeast population. This is because yeast cells multiply when the nutrients were available in the medium. An increase in yeast population indicated that more yeast cells utilized the sugar in the wort more readily, thereby bringing down the gravity of the wort. The peak of the yeast population was recorded on the 4th day of fermentation in all cases of formulations except the 60:40% malt adjunct proportion. This inconsistency could be as a result of early depletion of the nutrients in the substrate. It is known that the higher the adjunct, proportion, the lower the availability of free amino nitrogen in the substrate. This is because the protein in the adjunct is deposited in the crude (unhydrolysed) form and so the amino acid in the form of α-amino nitrogen is not readily available for yeast nutrition (Kunze, 1996).

In all the other formulations, after the 4th day of fermentation, yeast population dropped gradually. The metabolic activity of the cells reduced drastically due to the depletion of nutrients in the medium, eventually resulting in the settling down of the yeast cells called yeast flocculation. However, further drop in gravity was observed until the gravity of the wort was between 1.2 to 2.0°P on the 9th day of fermentation (that is, the final gravity, FG). The original gravity of the wort (gravity on the first day of fermentation) ranged between 11.0 to 11.5° P. The extract fermented by the yeast cells was calculated using the formula shown as:

$$\frac{OG - FG}{OG} \times 100\%$$

Temperature

The temperature of the fermenting medium ranged between 10.2 to 13.2°C. The temperature of the fermenting wort was maintained at between 10.8 to 12.8°C. This was to allow the yeast cells to act at their optimum temperature. As yeast cells act well at this temperature range (Pollock, 1981). It should be noted that the temperature in the fermenting vessel was controlled by a cooling device (refrigerating incubator), because metabolic activity of yeast cells would lead to temperature increase inside the fermenting liquor, which would

Table 3. Original gravity, final gravity, specific gravity, real extract, refractive index, and alcohol of fermented extracts.

Proportions	Original gravity	Final gravity	Specific gravity	Real extract	Refractive index	Alcohol
100% Barley malt	11.5	2.0	1°°/602	3.84	36.5	3.95
90% Barley : 10% sorghum	11.0	1.8	1°°/702	3.95	36.45	3.61
80% Barley : 20 % sorghum	11.2	2.1	1°°/820	4.20	37.38	3.90
70% Barley : 30% sorghum	11.3	1.7	1°°/663	3.80	36.50	3.78
60% Barley : 40 % sorghum	11.5	1.5	1°°/585	3.75	36.35	3.90

lead to an increase in fermentation rates and therefore reduces fermentation period. The cumulative effect of this action is the production of unwanted by-products such as more diacetyl. The foam and colloidal stability of the beer may worsen. From the 6th day of fermentation, a drop in temperature was observed. This was because the metabolic activity of the yeast had greatly reduced. The low temperature observed also assisted in yeast flocculation (Kunze, 1996).

pH

The pH of the pitching wort ranged between 4.43 to 5.00 at Day 1.Ideally, the pH of any pitching wort is between 4.5 to 5.6 (Goldammer, 2002). As fermentation progressed, the pH decreased until the final day. The pH values ranged between 3.75 in 60: 40 malt/adjunct to 4.15 in 70:30 malt adjunct ratio. The reduction in pH values of the fermenting liquor could be as a result of the production of organic acids, uptake of ammonium ions, and the use of primary phosphate ions by the yeast (Kunze, 1996). A drastic fall in pH observed in the 60:40 malt/adjunct ratio s not desirable in the beer because it imparts acidic taste to the beer (Hough, 1977). This low pH value also affected the growth and performance of yeast cells in the fermenting wort. Generally speaking, the pH desired by any brewer is between 4.2 and 4.4 (Brauhaase, 2000).

The fluctuation in the pH in the fermenting wort on Days 5 and 7 of the 70:30 malt/adjunct ratio and in 60:40 malt/ adjunct ratio on Days 6, 7 and 8 could be as a result of yeast autolysis (Kunze, 1996). This results from the process of self digestion of the yeast cells when there is an early depletion of nutrients in the wort (Kunze, 1996).

Yeast count

Yeast count increased progressively in all generations as observed from Day 2 to 4 of fermentation. It followed a normal growth curve whereby growth increased exponentially after introducing a microbe into a nutrient until limiting growth factors bring it down (Pollock, 1981). In this fermentation, the yeast in the 60:40 malt/adjunct proportion was not consistent. The yeast dropped after Day 2 of fermentation. This could be due to the high percentage of adjunct and because of the low value of the free amino nitrogen in the wort, essential nutrient likes, amino acids, lysine, and nitrogen were not available for proper yeast nutrition and nourishment.

Alcohol content

The desired alcohol content of beer is generally 3.92 ± 0.08% (Pollock, 1981). All formulations however produced beer of desired alcohol level. Considering the high extract fermented in 60:40 malt/adjunct ratio (Table 3), it was expected that the alcohol content should be higher than other formulations (Table 3). This could be related to the fact that most of the available nutrients in the medium had been used up for yeast nutrition and nourishment rather than for alcohol production. Table 3 shows the original gravity, final gravity, specific gravity, real extract, refractive index and alcohol content of all the formulations.

Apparent attenuation (fermented (real extract)

Apparent attenuation is the total amount of fermented extract in the wort. From the experiment, it was observed that the highest quantity of fermentable extract was recorded in the 60:40 malt /adjunct formulation (89.5°P) while the least observed was recorded in 80:20 malt/adjunct (82.14°P). The high extract percentage used up by yeast in the 0:40 malt /adjunct formulation showed that most of the extract had been utilized by yeast during primary fermentation. This would undoubtedly have a negative effect on the secondary fermentation, which is the maturity stage of the beer (Anon, 1972). Table 3 shows the values of fermented extract for each formulation.

Conclusion

All proportions of malt/adjunct ratio produced beer of desirable physico chemical parameters; however, 60:40 malt adjunct ratio produced beer with low pH which could have deleterious effect on the beer and the yeast cells used in fermentation. The emergence of deformed yeast after fermentation showed that the 60:40 formulations did not contain enough nutrients for yeast nutrition and metabolism.

Since the aim of every brewing outfit is to be able to compete favorably in the highly competitive Nigerian beer market as well as to produce beer of optimum quality, it is advisable to stick to beer produced with malt /adjunct proportion of up to 70:30 malt /adjunct proportion whose yeast behavior can be scientifically predicted to avoid deleterious side effects like fusel oil production,that is, higher alcohols, acid, sulfide and other volatile compounds which could affect the quality of the beer. Also a good beer yeast is expected to be used up to 8 to 10 generations (Pollock, 1981). The emergence of deformed yeast in the 60:40 malt /adjunct ratio in the first generation showed that the yeast used might not be able to withstand the stress of long usage.

However the use of external enzymes like amylase, protease and filtrase could assist in bringing out optimum activity when using sorghum adjunct in a higher proportion as in 60:40 malt adjunct proportion. The use of higher percentage of adjunct should therefore be explored putting in consideration the use of external enzymes which although would give desired end product but will be more finance intensive.

REFERENCES

Al-Hazza N, Umunna N, Alawa JP (1989). Symposium,at the Intentional crop research institute for the semi-arid tropics (INCRISAT).

Aluko AO (1989). Cereal Science today. Rev. Biotechnol., 12: 259.

Anon NA (1972). Alcoholic Beverages. Academic Press.New York, pp. 139.

Brauhaase S (2000). Standard operating manual. General parameters in brewing, pp. 3-49.

Brill LW (1981). Cereal science today. Food Sci. Technol. Report, 3(7): 259.

Canales AM (1979). Unmalted grains in brewing science. Academic press, London, 1: 146-123.

Gomez MI (1992). Screening of sorghum for malting and use. Agriculture of sorghum symposium (SADCC/INCRISAT). Bulawayo. Zimbabwe.

Hough JS (1977). Development of brewing Analysis. A Historical review. The Institute of Brewing, London, p. 12.

Hough JS, Briggs DE, Stevens R (1977). Malting and Brewing Science. Chapman and Hall London.

House LR (1993). Agriculture of sorghum. Symposiumfor the International crop research institute for the semi- arid tropics. (SADCC/ICRISAT).

Kunze W (1996). Technology malting and brewing. VLB Germany. pp. 120-250, 253-259.

Malomo O (1993). Sorghum in lager beer production in Nigeria. Regional symposium on current progress in the processing and utilization of sorghum and other related cereals. Ouagadougou, Burkina Faso.

Nweke FI, Ibe DG (1989). Nigeria Agriculture and Brewing; A new symbiosis. Symposium for brewing industry, pp. 13-16.

Okafor N (1987). Industrial Microbiology. 1st edition University of Ife Press, pp. 174-182.

Okolo BN, Lewis IE (1995). Enhancement of amylolytic potentials of sorghum malt. J. Inst. Brew., 102: 267-274.

Palmer GH (1992). "Sorghum" The world class cereal; Symposium on science and technology, Belgium.

Pollock JRA (1981). Brewing science. Academic press New York and London, p. 2.

Rose AH (1989). The microbial production of food and drinks " The advent of genetic engineering and food Microbiology. A handbook of Microbiology, pp. 45-54.

Smith EY (1996). Introduction to Biotechnology. Academic press,New York, 1st Edition, pp. 185-186.

Subramanian V, Jambunathan R (1989). Industrial utilization of sorghum. Symposium on International crop research institute for the semi arid tropics (ICRISAT).

22

Psychiatric symptoms and disorders in seizure cases referred to psychiatric out-patient service

Shakya Dhana Ratna

Department of Psychiatry, B P Koirala Institute of Health Sciences, Nepal. E-mail: drdhanashakya@yahoo.com.

Epilepsy and seizure disorders affect more than 1% adult population. Associated psychiatric problems are reported to increase and worsen the morbidity. In Nepalese context of scant data, this study was conducted to sort-out psychiatric symptomatology and disorders among psychiatry out-patient seizure patients. This hospital-based descriptive study analyzed 100 consecutive seizure patients visiting a psychiatric out-patient service in a 1-year period. Seizure diagnosis was as per clinical evidence and electroencephalography (EEG) findings; psychiatric symptomatology was checked and rated with the help of 'Brief psychiatric rating scale' (BPRS) and psychiatric diagnoses were made according to 'International Classification of Diseases: ICD-10'. In this study, 51% subjects were male. Forty-two patients had family history of significant illness, including seizure in 15% and psychiatric illness in 19%. Forty five percent had ICD-10 diagnosis of 'mental and behavioural disorders' and all, including the ramaining 55% had significant psychopathology. Mood (mainly depression) and anxiety disorders were the most common psychiatric co-morbidities. The most common BPRS items (besides seizure and related) were: somatic, mood, psychotic, hostility and anxiety symptoms. Hence, seizure may manifest with various psychopathology mainly: somatic, mood, psychotic, hostility and anxiety besides seizure-related (for example disorientation and motor) symptoms. A number of psychiatric disorders, mainly depression co-occur in seizure.

Key words: Epilepsy, mental illness, psychiatric symptoms, seizure.

INTRODUCTION

Seizure disorder or epilepsy is one of the most common neuro-psychiatric disorders, affecting about 1% of population within the age of 20 years, and even more in some parts of the world (Hauser and Annegers, 1993). It is one of the largest neuro-psychiatric contributors of Global Burden of Disease by Disability Adjusted Life Year (DALY) (World Bank, 1993). It may be associated with a range of other disorders; those as a causative factor, and effect or manifestation of seizure itself (Mendez, 2009; Raghuthaman et al., 2005; Lishman, 1998; Engel et al., 1986). Depression (Ettinger et al., 2004; Kanner, 2003), anxiety, and psychotic disorders (Nadkarni et al., 2007) are frequently reported higher than among general population (de Araújo Filho et al., 2007). Seizure is associated also with various syndromes, as a manifestation of seizure itself or as induced by seizure, referred to as 'organic mental disorders', for example psychotic, mood, etc (World Health Organization, 1993; American Psychiatric Association, 2000). Profile of those associated disorders and psychopathology offer the insight into common etiological factors in a particular setting and manifest features, leading to better management and prevention strategies.

We have few local data from Nepal about this common but disabling illness, more so about its co-morbid psychiatric disorders and associated symptoms. Hence, we conducted this cross-sectional descriptive study in the Department of Psychiatry, B. P. Koirala Institute of Health Sciences (BPKIHS), Dharan, Nepal in 2006/2007 to sort-out psychiatric symptomatology and disorders among

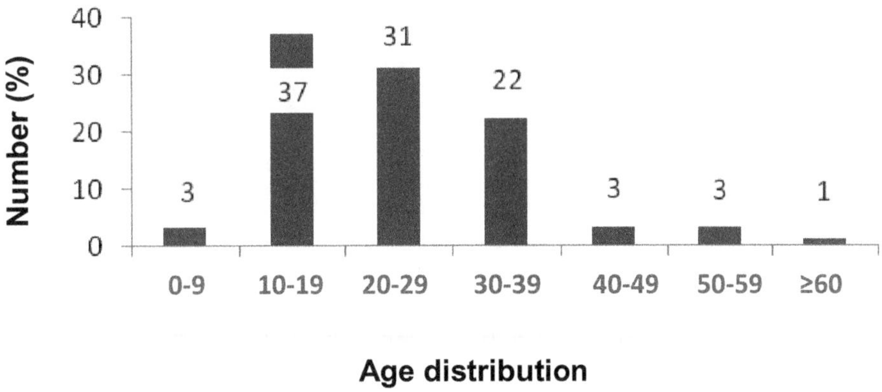

Figure 1. Age distribution.

seizure patients.

MATERIALS AND METHODS

This study, with purposive sampling, enrolled 100 consecutive seizure disorder (SD) patients clinically diagnosed or diagnosed with the help of electroencephalography (EEG), and associated with one or other clinically significant/manifest psychopathology for which they came in contact and consulted with the psychiatrist/investigator in the study period of 1 year duration from August, 2006 to July, 2007. Those patients who did not give consent and were severely medically unstable were excluded.

The number of subjects required that is, sample size was calculated by using the formula: $N = (1.96)^2 \times P \times (100 - P) / [P \times \beta]^2$. Where, N = number of sample, P = estimated prevalence and β = beta error, maximum permissible is 20%; the smaller the figure, the better is the power. We took 50% as the estimated prevalence of psychiatric co-morbidities because we came across the range of 30 to 60% for comorbid psychiatric disorder as a whole in literature (Mendez, 2009; Raghuthaman et al., 2005; Lishman, 1998). The subjects were those who had some psychiatric symptom and had come for psychiatric consultation and also because the objective was to study psychopathology profile too, besides the disorder. Hence, keeping the average for estimated prevalence, P as 50% and β error at 0.2, the calculated sample size was 96, and additional 4% subjects were taken for better representation. Hence, the sample size was taken to be 100. The initial concept was to enroll either minimum of 100 or a sizable number that could be enrolled in 1 year period, whichever would be greater and possible. The estimated sample size could be enrolled in more or less of the stipulated study period.

A brief explanation about the study was given and informed written consent was taken from the subject or significant others. Strict confidentiality of information was maintained. The socio-demographic profile and information about the illness (reason for referral, co-morbid conditions, and psychiatric diagnosis) were recorded on a Performa pre-designed for this study. The detailed psychiatric work-up and necessary investigations were done as per the indication, and their affordability and referrals were made to respective departments. The physical diagnoses were recorded as per the department from or to where the referrals were made. The final psychiatric diagnosis and co-morbidities were made according to the 'International Classification of Diseases-10' (ICD-10) (World Health Organization, 1993).

Psychiatric symptomatology were checked, studied and rated with the help of 'Brief psychiatric rating scales' (BPRS) (Overall and Gorham, 1962). This scale is physician rated and is one of the most researched instruments in psychiatry. The process of rating with this scale takes about 15 to 30 min. Reliability coefficients of 0.56 to 0.87 have been reported (Sajatovic and Ramirez, 2003). The rating scale was utilized in this study as a symptom check-list since it consists of a wide range of psychopathologies. The psychopathologies were rated on 1 to 7 point Likert scale, 1 being absent and 7 being extreme, by asking with patient or family member and by direct observation during the assessment by the investigator.

In this study, the score of 4 that is, moderate or more has been operationally defined as clinically significant for the item to be included as present. Data were entered into computer and analyzed using 'Statistical package for social studies' (SPSS 10) software.

RESULTS

Out of a total of 100 patients, 51 were male (with M: F ratio of almost 1: 1), 42% were married, 56% unmarried and 1% widow(er) and separated each. Average age of the subjects was 24.08 (range: 3, 60) years. Age group (10 to 19 years) constituted the largest proportion of 37%, followed by (20 to 29 years) 31% and (30 to 39 years) 22% (Figure 1). We had subjects of different caste/ethnic groups: 32% Mongol (Rai/ Limbu/ Tamang/ Magar/ Sherpa/ Gurung, etc.), 21% Brahmin, 16% Terai ethnic origin (Mandal, Raya, Jha, Yadav, Shah, Gupta, etc.), 12% Chhetri, 10% dalit/disadvantaged, 6% Newar and 3% Indian. Hindus were the most (78%), followed by Buddhists (12%), Muslims 2%, Christians and Kirat 4% each and 43% came from semi-urban, 29% urban, and 28% rural setting. We also had subjects of diverse professions: students (48%), homemakers (25%), laborers (9%), farmers (8%) and others. One fifth (20%) were illiterate and the subjects were relatively better educated

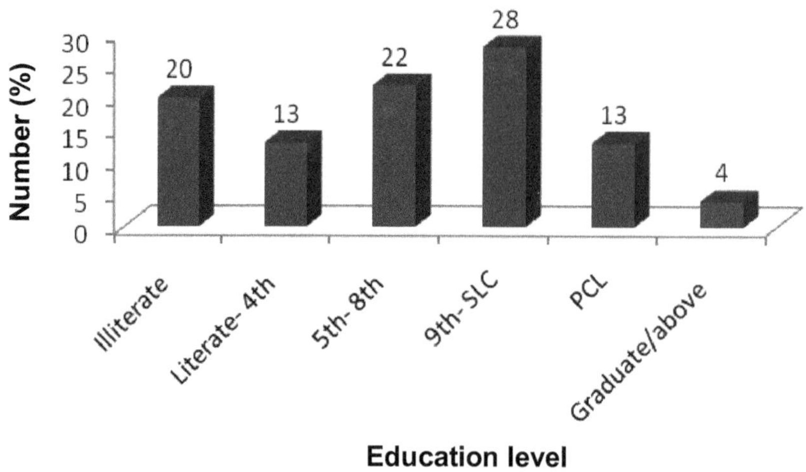

Figure 2. Educational level.

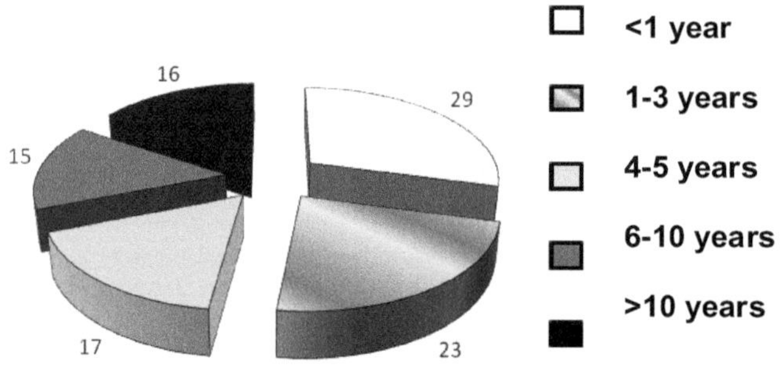

Figure 3. Total duration of seizure illness (%).

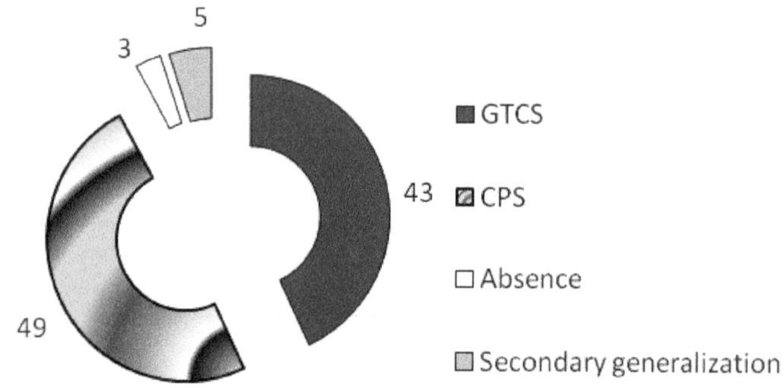

Figure 5. Types of seizure (%).

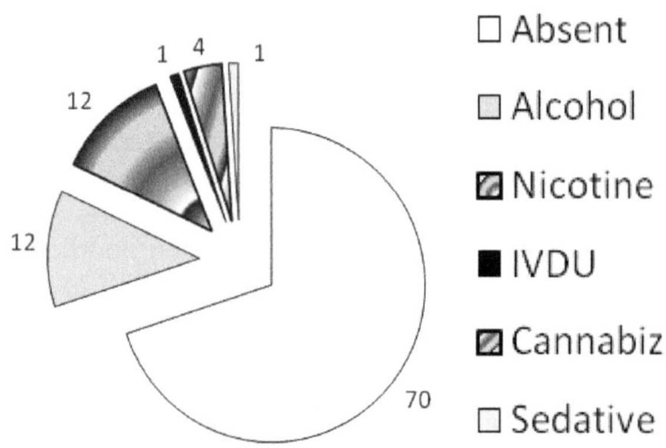

Figure 4. Current psychoactive substance usage (%).

better educated as a whole (Figure 2).

Most of the cases were brought or accompanied by family member for psychiatric consultation (Table 1). Almost all (96%) had sudden onset and 90% had episodic course of illness. About one third had illness of less than 1 year. More than two-third had seizure morbidity of 1 to 10 years (Figure 3). Nearly half of the total subjects (46%) reported some stressors preceding the seizure attacks. Relational and health related stressors were among the common ones (Table 2). The most common complaints were directly related to seizures, that is misrecognition and or unresponsiveness due to alteration of consciousness (89%). Other main symptoms were somatic or physical complaints (56%) and mood (43%) symptoms (Table 3).

One third of the subjects had a clinically significant illness in their past history, and more than two fifth (42%) had illness in their blood relatives, including 15% with seizure disorder (Table 4). One third (30%) of all seizure patients reported to abuse psycho-active substances (Figure 4). About one fourth of them had some personality traits and 4% had mental retardation which affected the clinical course of illness (Table 5). About half of these seizure subjects had complex partial seizures and 43% generalized tonic clonic seizures (Figure 5).

All subjects had one or other significant BPRS symptom item. Seizure related symptoms: loss of consciousness

Table 1. Sources of referral.

Source of referral	%
Family members	69
Internal Medicine	11
Emergency	4
Family medicine OPD	4
Pediatrics	3
Gynecology/Obstetric	1
Other health centre	1
Alternative medicine	1
Relatives/friends	3
Self	3

OPD: Out-patient department.

Table 2. Types of stressors#.

Stressor type	%
Relational	10
Relative away	4
Death of relative	3
Illness of relative	3
Study related	4
Physical illness/health	10
Environmental	3
Stopping treatment	4
Political/social conflict	8
Sleep disturbance	2

Table 3: Presenting complaints#.

Complaint	%
Misrecognition/ Unresponsive	89
Thought, speech	7
Substance use	3
Behavioral problem	29
Mood symptoms	43
Anxiety	20
Perceptual	16
Somatic/ physical symptoms	56
Self harm	4
Personality changes	3
Others	41
'Aunse purne' (cultural expression)	4

consciousness, abnormal body movements, and stereotypy/mannerism were the most common symptom items among BPRS psychopathology. Other common items were somatic concerns, hallucinatory behavior,

Table 4. Past and family history of illness#.

Illness in past	%
Absent	67
Seizure	9
Neurological	12
Other medical diseases	4
Psychiatric	10
Substance use disorder	1
Not available	2
Illness in family	
Absent	57
Seizure	15
Neurological	8
Other medical diseases	2
Psychiatric	19
Substance use disorder	4

Table 5. Pre-morbid temperament/ traits/ personality.

Personality trait	No. of cases (%)
Well adjusted	64
Cluster 'A'	3
Cluster 'B'	8
Cluster 'C'	12
Others	4
Not applicable	7
Low IQ	4

anxiety, depression and hostility (Table 6). Forty five percent fulfilled the ICD-10 criteria for a psychiatric disorder. The most common psychiatric diagnoses were mood (affective) disorders (23%) and anxiety neurosis (15%). Deliberate self harm was seen in 4%. Out of the total subjects, 55% had some clinically significant psychopathology which did not fulfill criteria for an ICD-10 diagnosis (Table 7). Migraine was the most common physical disease among these seizure cases (Table 8). The most common treatments included antiepileptic drugs. They required some sort of psycho-education, counseling or psychological intervention (Table 9).

DISCUSSION

Seizure disorder, including epilepsy, has the prevalence of about 1% of adult population (Hauser and Annegers, 1993) and is one of the most common and disabling

Table 6. Significant psychological symptoms of BPRS (with scores ≥ 4).

BPRS item	%
Somatic Concern	73
Anxiety	55
Emotional withdrawal	23
Concept disorganization	16
Guilt	8
Tension	39
Mannerism/posturing	69
Grandiosity	19
Depressed mood	42
Hostility	40
Suspiciousness	10
Hallucinatory behavior	56
Motor retardation	29
Uncooperativeness	23
Unusual thought content	8
Blunted affect	9
Excitement	37
Disorientation/derealization	89

neuro-psychiatric disorders (World Bank, 1993). It is basically the neuro-psychiatric manifestation of paroxysmal hyper-synchronous brain discharges (Mendez, 2009; Raghuthaman et al., 2005; Lishman, 1998). Different seizure or epilepsy types have various clinical features, for example alteration of consciousness (simple or complex) and convulsions (focal or generalized), as comprehensively classified by 'International League against Epilepsies' (1981) (Engel, 2001). Seizure is an important differential diagnosis in cases of episodic phenomena, with a mixture of neurological, somatic and psychiatric symptoms and seizure attack is sometimes precipitated by psycho-social stress, though to a less extent, as most of the mental disorders (Mendez, 2009; Raghuthaman et al., 2005).

Besides the psychiatric manifestations, seizure patients are reported to suffer more from various psychiatric problems than general population. Mood, anxiety and other neurotic (pseudo-seizures or dissociative), psychotic disorders, personality problems, mental retardation and cognitive changes, and suicide and self injurious behaviours are seen more among seizure cases (Mendez, 2009; Raghuthaman et al., 2005; Lishman, 1998). It is however, at times difficult to distinguish them as independent or secondary to seizure activity.

The co-morbid mental illness further worsens the quality of life of the patients. Hence, psychiatric manifesttations and associations in seizures or epilepsies deserve a particular attention. Timely identification and proper

Table 7. Psychiatric diagnosis#.

Diagnosis	%
ICD-10 diagnosis present	45
Delirium	1
Substance use (F10-F19)	7
Schizophrenia (F20-29)	4
Mood (affective) (F30-39)	23
Neurotic, Stress, anxiety (F40-49)	15
Mental retardation	4
ADHD	1
Intentional self harm	4
Significant mental symptom only	*55*

Table 8. Co-morbid physical diagnosis#.

Disease	%
Infection/malignancy	3
Thyroid/endocrine	3
Migraine	12
Head injury	2
Cardio-vascular	3
Vertigo	1

Table 9. Management strategies#.

Treatment modality	%
Antipsychotic	15
Benzodiazepines	23
Antidepressant	18
Carbamazepine	49
Sodium valproate	39
Other AED	26
Supplementation	25
Other/IV fluids	8
Counseling/psycho-education/psychological	78

Multiple response category: one respondent may have ≥ 1 responses.

proper management will enhance the better productivity and quality of life whereas seizure itself is reported under-diagnosed and under-treated (Eisenberg, 1997). More so because of prevalent myths and misconceptions about psychiatric illness, epileptics hesitate to seek help from mental health professionals even when they are in dire need.

There is a dearth of data about seizure, particularly about its psychiatric manifestations and associations in Nepalese context. We have to rely on our clinical

Observations (Shakya., 2012) and to make assumptions from the data of other parts of world. This study aimed to explore the associated psychopathology and psychiatric co-morbidities in seizure disorders. It was also anticipated that it would open avenues for the studies in other aspects of the disease; like psycho-social, community based prevalence, etiological aspect etc.

This is a hospital based cross sectional descriptive study in 100 consecutive seizure disorder cases, with some psychiatric complaints or symptoms hence, coming in contact with the investigator in the Department of Psychiatry, BPKIHS, Dharan, Nepal during the study period. It utilized the ICD-10 and BPRS as research tools, both being administered by clinician and widely validated across the world (Overall and Gorham, 1962; Sajatovic and Ramirez, 2003). For pre-morbid personality problem, the cluster concept of Diagnostic and statistical manual of mental disorders, fourth edition (DSM-IV) (American Psychiatric Association, 2000) was adopted for the sake of simple and comprehensive categorization. As both systems of classification of disorders have similar or equivalent categories to a great extent, this cluster concept would not make much difference.

Majority of the subjects were in the age range of 10 to 39 years. It is on the whole because child and adolescent patients usually visit the Department of Pediatrics and adult patients visit Department of Psychiatry and Internal Medicine in this institute. The 'male: female' ratio being more or less 1:1 is consistent with most of the studies (Hauser and Annegers, 1993; Mendez, 2009; Raghuthaman et al., 2005). Mere 20% illiterate subjects seeking help in this study, obviously less than the general population, reflects the fact that more illiterate people might have been suffering from seizures or epilepsies in community without treatment (Eisenberg, 1997).

Most of the cases in this study were brought by family members when the symptoms did not disappear with other measures, mainly traditional healing, or when they developed additional problems like psychiatric illness. They presented late to medical services; less than one third of the subjects had come to this service within 1 year of the onset of seizure morbidity, reflecting the sad reality about the under-diagnosis (Eisenberg, 1997). Majority had sudden onset and episodic course of illness. Nearly half of the total subjects recall some precipitating stressors for seizure attacks, relational and health related problems being the most common ones.

When they presented to the health service, seizure related symptoms like loss or alteration of consciousness, misrecognition and abnormal body movements (stereotypy/mannerism) were the most common symptom items among the BPRS psychopathology. Other frequent psychopathologies were somatic concerns (headache, body ache, etc), hallucinatory behavior, anxiety, depression and hostility. Though in general population also, depression and anxiety are the most common mental problems (Murray and Lopez, 1996), they are even more among these epileptic subjects. This fact has been replicated in the diagnostic profile of this study too, showing mood and anxiety as being the most common psychiatric co-morbidity, and in the BPRS scoring of associated or manifested psychopathology, showing somatic concerns, hallucinatory behavior, anxiety, depression and hostility as being other most common symptom items with scores 4 or more. Thirty percent re-vealed to use psycho-active substances currently, mainly alcohol and nicotine, which was less than in other general psychiatry patients' profile studies of this institute (Shakya et al., 2009), but clearly in excess to general population (Murray and Lopez, 1996).

One third of the subjects had some significant illness, mainly neuro-psychiatric illness in their past. More than two fifth (42%) of the subjects had family histories of significant illnesses. Fifteen percent of the subjects had some blood relatives with seizure which is similar to Western data (Mendez, 2009; Lishman, 1998).

In this hospital based study conducted in general psychiatry service setting, partial seizure (mainly complex) was the most common seizure type (49%), followed by generalized tonic clonic seizures (GTCS 43%). This is consistent with the fact about the prevalence of seizure types in adult population (Mendez, 2009; Raghuthaman et al., 2005). About one third had some personality traits significant enough to affect the clinical course of illness. People of all clusters were affected by seizures, though Cluster C traits were the most common. Mental retardation was present in 4 cases.

In seizure and epilepsy patients coming to this psychiatric service, 45% had psychiatric co-morbidities (ICD-10 diagnosis), mood and other neurotic/anxiety disorders being the most common as in Western/other studies (Mendez, 2009; Raghuthaman et al., 2005) and the remaining 55% had some significant mental symptoms, with the BPRS score 4 (moderate) or more but did not fulfill the ICD-10 criteria for any psychiatric disorder.

Suicide phenomena are relatively more in these seizure patients than in general population (Thapa and Carlough, 2000). The high rate may be because of the high co-morbidity and severe grading of psychopathology at the time of presentation. The suicide problem in this region needs validation with further community based studies.

As in other parts of the world, the Nepalese clinicians rely on various antiepileptic drugs like Carbamazepine, Sodium valproate and other anti-epileptic drugs. High psychiatric symptoms and co-morbidities were additional consideration during management of these cases; many of them needed benzodiazepines, anti-psychotics and antidepressants. Carbamazepine and Sodium valproate were over representing in this study, maybe because they were considered also for their mood stabilizing and other favorable effects besides antiepileptic property. Some forms of psychological interventions are complimentary to drug therapy, for example psycho-education.

Our study is biased in a way since it enrolled only those patients who had some manifest mental symptoms and came in contact with the investigator in Department of Psychiatry. Hence, this may not reveal the true prevalence rate but we believe that this study satisfactorily depicts the range of possible psychopathology and psychiatric disorders associated with seizure disorders and looking at the cause and effect relationship of psychiatric symptom/disorder and seizure is beyond the objective/scope of current study which might be the topic for further research here. These observations however corroborate that psychiatric affliction, association, manifestation or co-morbidity is common in seizure disorders and epilepsies from different standpoints: etiological, clinical manifestations, co-morbidities and management. Hence, collaboration among various departments is crucial and it increases the success rate of treatment. The seizure patients should also be aware about these facts and should not hesitate to seek psychiatric help when needed.

Conclusions

1. Seizure and epilepsy patients usually present late (after 1 year of seizure) to the psychiatric service when they also have other co-morbidity, other traditional measures do not work, they are severely affected (high BPRS scores) and have to be brought by family members.
2. Some of them have past history of illness, including neuro-psychiatric illness. Many of them have family history of illness, including some with seizure disorder or epilepsy.
3. These seizure patients present with various symptoms such as altered consciousness, stereotypy, other somatic complaints, anxiety, hallucinatory behavior, mood symptoms, etc.
4. Some of them use substances, including alcohol and nicotine, and also have some significant personality traits, mainly of cluster 'C'. A remarkable proportion of seizure patients presenting with some psychiatric symptoms fulfill the criteria for psychiatric disorders. Others with symptoms also have clinically significant ones. The most common psychiatric diagnosis was mood (affective) disorders, followed by neurotic, stress related and anxiety. A terrific number of them displayed deliberate self harm. Hence, seizure disorders have a wide range of psychiatric association as manifestation or co-morbidity.

REFERENCES

American Psychiatric Association (2000). Diagnostic and Statistical manual of Mental Disorders. 4th ed. Text rev. Washington, DC.

Commission on Classification and Terminology of the International League against Epilepsy (1981). Proposal for revised clinical and electroencephalographic classification of epileptic seizures. Epilepsia 22:489-501.

de Araújo Filho GM, Pascalicchio TF, da Silva Sousa PC, Lin K, Ferreira Guilhoto LM, Yacubian EM (2007). Psychiatric disorders in juvenile myoclonic epilepsy: a controlled study of 100 patients. Epilepsy Behav. 10(3):437-441.

Eisenberg L (1997). Socio-cultural perspectives. In: Engel J, Pedley TA (Eds.), Epilepsy: A comprehensive textbook. Lippincott-Raven Publishing, New York. pp. 41-6.

Engel J Jr. (2001). A proposed diagnostic scheme for people with epileptic seizures and with epilepsy: report of the ILAE Task Force on Classification and Terminology. Epilepsia 42:796-803.

Engel J Jr., Caldecott-Hazard S, Bandler R (1986). Neurobiology of behavior: anatomic and physiological implications related to epilepsy. Epilepsia 27(2):3-13.

Ettinger A, Reed M, Cramer J (2004). Epilepsy Impact Group. Depression comorbidity in community-based patients with epilepsy or asthma. Neurology 63:1008-1014.

Hauser WA, Annegers JF (1993). Epidemiology of epilepsy and unprovoked seizures in Rochester, Minnesota, 1935-1984. Epilepsia 34:453.

Kanner AM (2003). Depression in epilepsy: prevalence, clinical semiology, pathogenic mechanisms and treatment. Biol. Psychiatry 54:388-398. Abstract.

Lishman WA (1998). Epilepsy. In: Organic Psychiatry, 3rd ed. Blackwell Science. pp. 237-98.

Mendez MF (2009). Neuropsychiatric Aspects of Epilepsy. In: Sadock BJ, Sadock VA, Ruiz P (eds), Comprehensive Text Book of Psychiatry, 9th ed. Wolters Kluber/ Lippincott Williams & Wilkins, Philadelphia. pp. 451-62.

Murray CL, Lopez AD (1996). The Global Burden of Disease: a Comprehensive Assessment of Mortality and Disability from Diseases, Injuries, and Risk Factors in 1990 and Projected. Harvard University Press, Cambridge, Massachusetts.

Nadkarni S, Arnedo V, Devinsky O (2007). Psychosis in epilepsy patients. Epilepsia 48(9)17-9.

Overall JE, Gorham DR (1962). The Brief Psychiatric Rating Scale (BPRS). Psychol. Rep. 10:799-812.

Raghuthaman G, Jacob KS, Ranjith G (2005). Psychiatric aspects of epilepsy. In: Bhugra D, Ranjith G, Patel V (eds.), Handbook of Psychiatry- A South Asian Perspective. Byword Viva Publishers Pvt. Ltd. pp. 117-26.

Sajatovic M, Ramirez LF (2003). Brief Psychiatric Rating Scale (BPRS). In: Rating Scales in Mental Health. Panther Publishers Pvt Ltd, Bangalore. pp.130-33.

Shakya DR (2012). Depression in Seizure disorder- a case report. Health Renaiss. 10(1):59-61.

Shakya DR, Pandey AK, Shyangwa PM, Shakya R (2009). Psychiatric morbidity profiles of referred Psychiatry OPD patients in a general hospital. Indian Med. J. 103(12):407- 411.

Thapa B, Carlough MC (2000). Suicide incidence in the Lalitpur district of Central Nepal. Trop Doct. 30 (4):200-3.

The World Bank (1993). World development report- Investing in health (world development indicators). World Bank and Oxford University Press.

World Health Organization (1993). The ICD-10 Classification of Mental and Behavioral Disorders- Diagnostic Criteria for Research. WHO, Geneva.

Effects of methamphetamine on the hippocampus of rats: Behavioural and morphological approach

Ijomone Omamuyovwi M.*, Nwoha Polycarp U., Olaibi Olayemi K., Obi Augustine U. and Alese Magaret O.

Department of Anatomy and Cell Biology, Obafemi Awolowo University, Ile-Ife, Nigeria.

This investigation examined the effects of methamphetamine (METH) on performance of rats using the Morris water maze and on the morphology of the hippocampus. Twelve adult Wistar rats were used for this study. Animals were randomly assigned into two groups (A and B) of six each. Group A rats served as control and were given normal saline. Group B animals were given single administration of METH (10 mg/kg, i.p.). Animals were subjected to behavioural studies on the water maze prior to treatment. Three days following METH administration, animals were again subjected to behavioural studies, sacrificed, brain excised and processed histologically. Results showed high level of methamphetamine-induced stereotypic movement. There was no significant difference in behavioural performance of the rats on water maze prior to treatments, but group B rats showed significantly poor performance after treatment when compared to control (P<0.05). Histological analysis revealed extensive neuronal destruction of the pyramidal layer of the hippocampus following methamphetamine administration. In conclusion, this study has shown the neuro-destructive effects of METH on the hippocampus and such degenerating effects could affect the learning, memory and possibly spatial navigation ability of rats during the water maze task.

Key words: Methamphetamine, hippocampus, behavioural studies, Morris water maze.

INTRODUCTION

Methamphetamine (METH) is an amphetamine (AMPH) - like compound, whose abuse is a serious problem worldwide (Tatsua et al., 2007). There is extensive evidence that METH is neurotoxic in animal models, thus the concern for the increasing use of these drugs (Escubedo et al., 2005). AMPH and METH are potent central nervous system (CNS) stimulants with additional peripheral sympathomimetic effects. They have been used clinically in the treatment of obesity, minimal brain dysfunction, narcolepsy, depression and to counter fatigue. Following the acute administration of the AMPHs, there is an increase in blood pressure, heart rate, respiration, sweating and tremor. The behavioral manifestations include species specific stereotypic behavior, anorexia, sleeplessness, hyperexcitability, and hyperactivity (Kita et al., 2003). Though it is now established that METH induces neurotoxicity in animal models, the mechanism by which it does induce neurotoxicity is still quite complex. Increasing body of evidence has shown that METH-induced neurotoxicity is dependent upon the production of reactive species, irrespective of METH mode of entry into the neuron (Davidson et al., 2001; Escubedo et al., 2005). Three basic mechanisms have been identified by which METH administration could result in production of such species; (1) Dopamine (DA) release and subsequent enzymatic oxidation; (2) DA auto-oxidation and (3) mitochondrial disruption. Aberrant release of DA can also induce oxidative stress by excitatory amino acid (EAA) excitotoxicity through increased glutamate release. (Davidson et al., 2001; Pubill et al., 2002; Kita et al., 2003; Escubedo et al., 2005; Pubill et al., 2005; Tatsua et al., 2007). Much of the study on METH-induced neurotoxicity has been focused on the DA system and the striatum, but it has been shown that METH may cause

*Corresponding author. E-mail: godmamus@yahoo.com.

neurodegeneration in other parts of the brain including the parietal cortex, thalamus and hippocampus (Davidson et al., 2001; Nwoha et al., 2007).

The Morris water maze is one of the most widely used tasks in behavioral neuroscience for studying the psychological processes and neural mechanisms of spatial learning and memory, which are major functions of the hippocampus (Jarrard et al., 1984; Kesner et al., 1987). The water maze was developed by Richard Morris (Morris, 1981; Morris et al., 1982) and place navigation in the water maze is now often used as a general assay of cognitive function (Brandeis et al., 1989), for example for testing the impact of various disturbances of the nervous system (e.g. animal models of stroke (Nunn et al., 1994), aging (Gallagher and Rapp, 1997), neurodegenerative disease (Hsiao et al., 1996), or the potential impact of novel therapeutic drugs (D'Hooge and De Deyn, 2001). Most behavioral studies following administration of METH have shown hyper-locomotor and stereotypic behavior following METH administration. This study was however designed to investigate the effects of METH administration on learning and memory behavior. Though earlier studies have shown that neonatal exposure of rats to METH have deleterious effects on learning and memory when the rats become adults thus indicating negative effects of METH on the developing brain (Vorhees et al., 2000; Broening et al., 2001).

MATERIALS AND METHOD

Animals

Twelve adult male and female Wistar strain albino rats weighing between 150 and 200 g were used for this research. The rats were randomly assigned into two groups of six rats each (Groups A and B). Animals were housed in clean plastic cages under natural light and dark cycles at room temperature. Animals in all groups were fed normal laboratory chow *ad libitum* and allowed free access to water. All animals were handled in accordance with the guidelines for animal research as detailed in the NIH Guidelines for the Care and Use of Laboratory Animals (NIH Publication, 1985).

Animal treatment

Animals in group A which was administered normal saline only served as control animals. Animals in group B served as experimental animals and were administered single dose of METH (neurotoxin) dissolved in normal saline, at 10 mg/kg body weight, intraperitoneally. Animals were left for three days in their cages, following administration of neurotoxin to allow for effects of the drug on the hippocampus (Nwoha et al., 2007). METH was obtained from Sigma Chemicals, USA.

Morris water maze study

The Morris water maze was used to study behavioural differences in the animals. The Morris water maze is one of the most widely used tasks in behavioral neuroscience for studying the psychological processes and neural mechanisms of spatial learning and memory. The Morris water maze has advantages over conventional mazes such as the elimination of local cues, like scent traces, and the fact that there is no fixed escape formula. Animals, usually rats or mice, are placed in a large circular pool of water and required to escape from water onto a hidden platform whose location can normally be identified only using spatial memory.

The apparatus consists of a large circular pool (tank) about 6 ft in diameter and about 3 ft deep. The inside of the tank was painted white and the outside brown. It was filled up with tap water, measuring about 25°C. A platform of 24 cm high and 10 cm in diameter was placed at one quadrant of the pool. During training, it was exposed 1 inch above the water. This teaches the rat that there is a platform, and that it is the way to get out of the water. Later, after the animal is trained and ready for testing, the escape platform was 1 inch below the water, and the water was made opaque by adding milk. Training and testing was done across a single day. Behavioural study on the water maze was carried out before treatment with METH and three days after the rats were treated with METH, with a two weeks period between the pre-treatment study and post-treatment.

Each animal underwent three consecutive trials during training. During testing each animal underwent four sessions of three consecutive trials per session. All animals completed a session before another session is carried out. The latency (time taken to reach the platform) was recorded manually with a stopwatch. If the animal failed to climb onto the platform within 60 s, the trial was stopped and the animal was removed from the water and placed on the platform. The inter-trial interval was 10 s, the animal remaining on the platform during this period before beginning the new trial. At the end of the three trials, the animal was removed and placed under a lamp for warmth. The inter-session interval was 1 h. One probe trial was performed after testing on the same day, in which the platform is removed from the pool. The probe trial was performed to verify that the animal understands the location of the platform and the strategy that the animal follows when it discovers the platform is not there (Pierre and Debouzie, 2000). The number of times the animal crossed the position of the removed platform was counted as probe trial value.

Histological analysis

After undergoing the water maze testing on the third day following neurotoxin administration, animals were weighed. The animals were then sacrificed by cervical dislocation. The skulls were opened so that the whole brain can be excised. They were fixed in 10% formal calcium (pH 7.1), for twenty-four hours for histological procedures. Brains were routinely processed for paraffin wax embedding. Then, 6 µm thick paraffin cross sections containing hippocampal tissue were mounted on slides and stained using routine haematoxylin and eosin (Drury and Wallington, 1980) method. Microscopy was conducted on an Olympus microscope (Tokyo, Japan) and images were captured and processed by an attached eyepiece camera.

Statistical analysis

One-way ANOVA was used to analyze data obtained from behavioural studies. Primer for windows (McGraw-Hill, version 4.0.0.0) was the statistical package used to analyse data. Results are expressed as mean ± standard error of mean. $P<0.05$ was taken as accepted level of significant difference.

RESULTS

Physical observations

METH-induced stereotypic movements were observed in

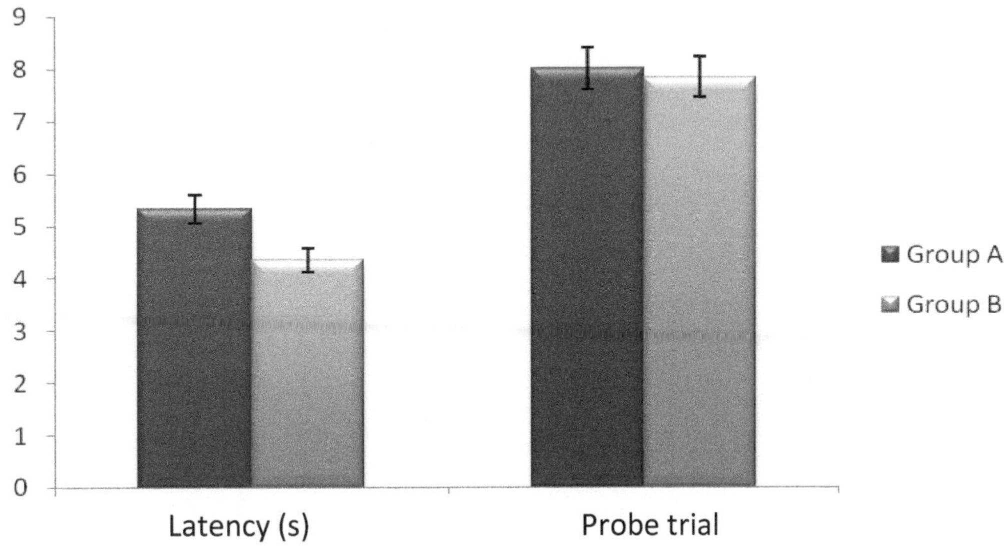

Figure 1. Pre-treatment behaviour of rats on the water maze. Each bar represents Mean ±SEM. * $P<0.05$ compared to control. n = 6.

all six animals treated with METH in Group B. The stereotypic movement observed included circling, nail and/ or wood-chip biting, sniffing, repetitive rearing, vigorous and compulsive grooming. The onset of this symptom was observed about 20 min following injection with METH in Group B rats. The symptom lasted for just 3 to 4 h in the rats except for two rats in Group B, where even on the third day following injection, circling and continuous sniffing were still observed for a few minutes. 24 h after METH administration, the rats in Group B showed signs of sluggishness and excessive sleeping. There was a reduction in these symptoms 48 h after METH administration. None of these symptoms were observed in Group A rats, as they received no METH.

Pre-treatment behavioural studies

As shown in Figure 1, there was no significant difference between control and treated groups, in the duration it took animals to locate the platform (latency) and the probe trial.

Post-treatment behavioural studies

Following treatment with METH (Figure 2), animals in Group B had significantly longer duration to locate the platform (latency) when compared to control group. Group B animals also had a significantly lower probe trial values when compared to control group, as the control animals crossed the position of the platform significantly more times than Group B animals in the probe trial.

H&E staining

The normal histology of the hippocampus for the control group showed three distinct layers as shown in Figure 3. They are stratum oriens, stratum pyramidale and stratum radiatum. In the control group (Figure 3a1 to a4), the cells were intact with well stained nuclei. The regions of the principal cell layer of the hippocampus proper (pyramidal layer) were also intact through CA1 to CA4 and well demonstrated in this group. The dentate gyrus (DG) was intact and well stained. Its principal cell layer, the granular layer was well demonstrated. As shown in Figure 3b1 to b4, the layers of the hippocampus were shown to have histological alteration in Group B (METH treated rats). The pyramidal layer of the hippocampus was observed with extensive vacuolations of the cells as compared to the control group, thus indicating neuronal cell death. Figures 3b1 to b4 shows that neuronal cell death was more in the CA1 and CA2 region than CA3. The cells of the CA4 region, the hilus of DG and granular cell layer of DG, were least affected. The stratum radiatum of treated group also shows extensive degeneration of neuronal fibres in the CA1 and CA2 regions (Figure 3b1 to b2) when compared with the control (Figure 3a1).

DISCUSSION

METH administration at low to high doses has been known to induce stereotypic movements in laboratory rats and mice (Kita et al., 1998; Canales and Graybiel, 2000; Escubedo et al., 2005; Tatsuta et al., 2007; Kristen et al., 2010). In the present study, METH-induced stereotypy was

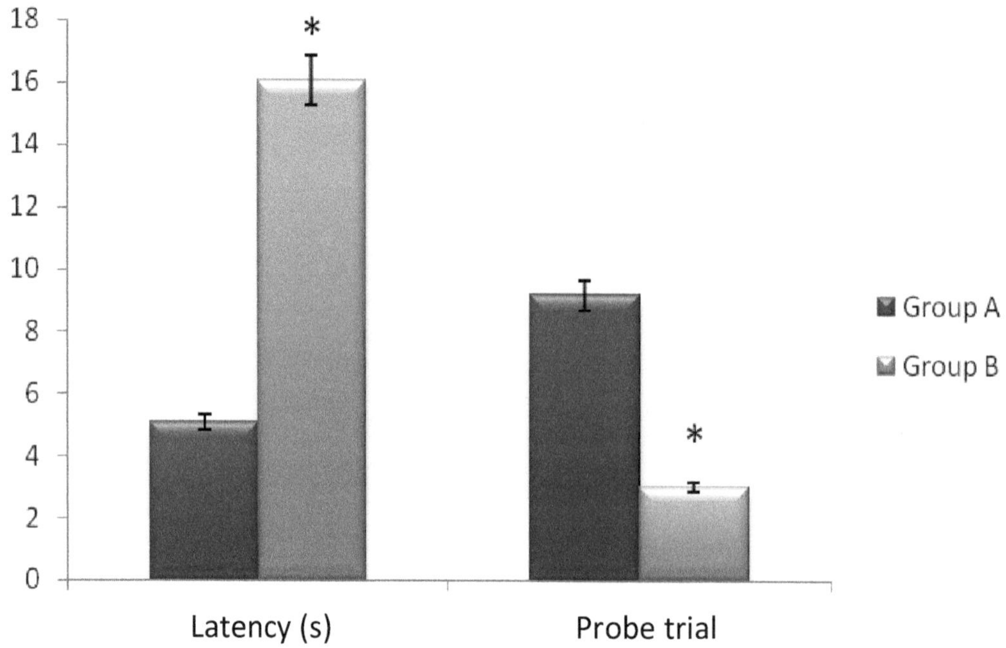

Figure 2. Post-treatment behaviour of rats on the water maze. Each bar represents Mean ±SEM. * $P<0.05$ compared to control. n = 6.

was observed in all animals following administration.

Stereotypy is defined as the development of abnormally repetitive motor actions that coincides with an inability to initiate normal adaptive responses (Canales and Graybiel, 2000; Kristen et al., 2010). Stereotypy is a cardinal feature of a broad range of neurologic and neuropsychiatric disorders and is a major component of the behavioral syndrome induced by psychomotor stimulant drugs (Canales and Graybiel, 2000) of which METH is one of such drugs. Motor stereotypies can be induced by dopaminergic stimulation of the striatum and can be abolished by intrastriatal blockade of dopaminergic transmission. Clinical evidence also implicates basal ganglia dysfunction in complex behavioral and cognitive stereotypies (Canales and Graybiel, 2000). Excessive sleeping is known to characterize METH withdrawal (McGregor et al., 2005) and this could possibly be the reason for this observed symptom a day following the single dose administration of METH.

Behavioural studies using the water maze showed that METH significantly affected the performance of Wistar rats on the maze. Animals administered with METH alone showed significantly longer latency and reduced number of times they located the platform during the probe trial after administration. This indicates poorer learning and memory capacity. This supports earlier evidence that showed METH negatively affects learning and memory as seen after neonatal exposure of rats to METH (Vorhees et al., 2000; Broening et al., 2001). The water maze is used to study the psychological processes and neural mechanisms of spatial learning and memory. The present behavioural studies have shown that METH negatively affects learning and memory and this indicates an injury to the hippocampus which is involved in spatial/relational memory (Jarrard et al., 1984; Kesner et al., 1987). The hippocampus of rats is now known to have some pyramidal neurons that help the animals navigate better through their environment as the firing of these cells indicates a specific location in the environment of the rats. These cells are called "place cells" and they probably help in the place navigation ability of rats which can now be studied in the water maze (Brandeis et al., 1989; Nakazawa et al., 2004). Extensive destruction of hippocampal pyramidal cells by METH would have affected the ability of exposed rats to correctly navigate in the maze and this could also have contributed to their poor performance on the maze.

Histological results of this study clearly support earlier reports that METH extensively destroys hippocampal neurons (Nwoha et al., 2007) and that METH induces neurotoxicity in the brain. High doses of METH disrupt blood brain barrier in the limbic regions producing extensive neuronal degeneration in the hippocampus, leading to learning and memory loss (Nwoha et al., 2007). Also METH, has been reported to induce neurotoxicity by generating reactive oxygen species (Kita et al., 2003; Escubedo et al.,2005) and these free radicals cause oxidative stress that result in brain neuronal damage (Anderson, 2004). Histological findings in this study showed higher destruction of cells in the CA1 and CA2 regions than the CA3 region of the pyramidal cell layer. The cells in the CA4 region, the hilus of the DG and

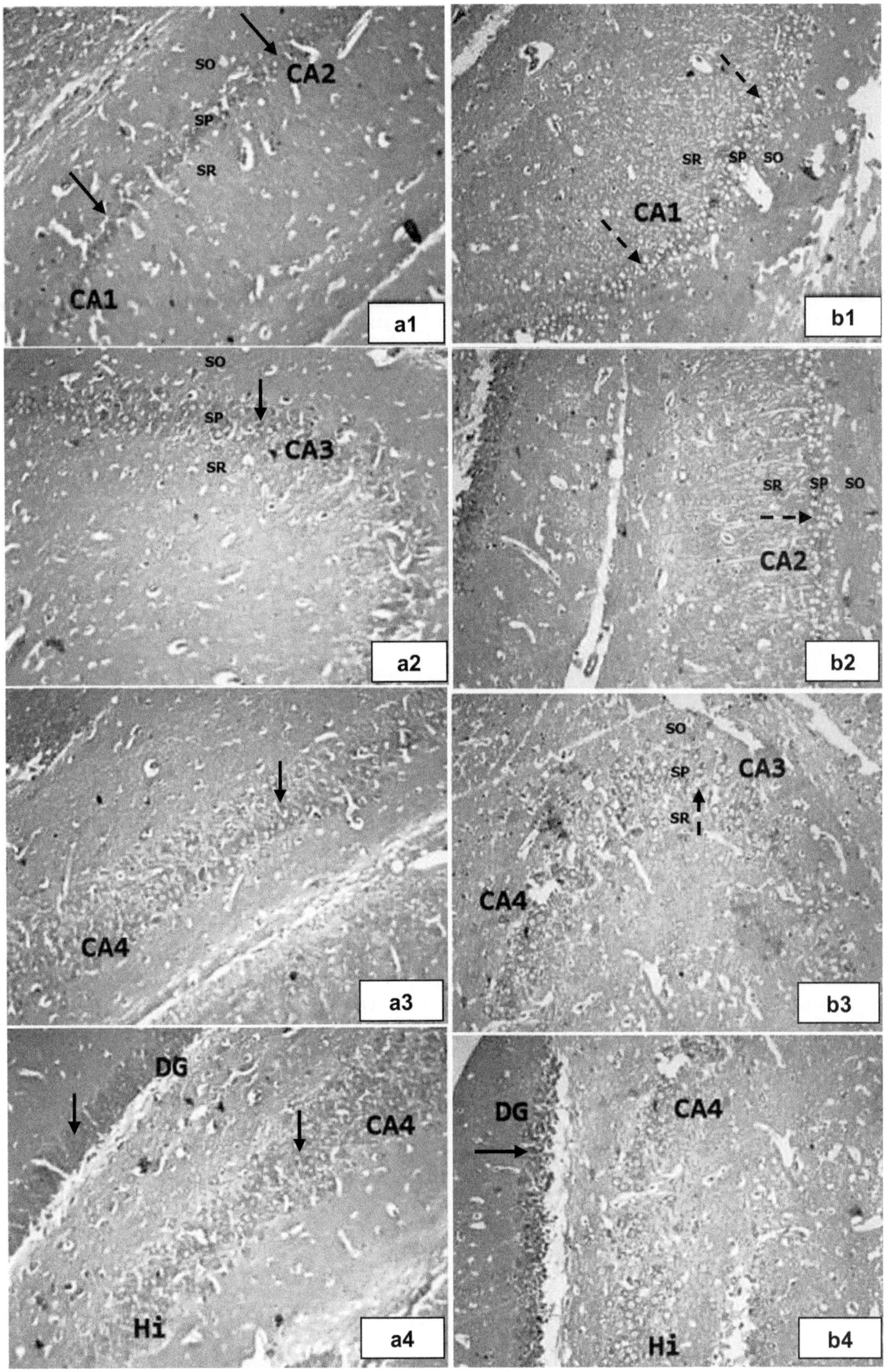

Figure 3. Light micrographs of different layers and parts hippocampus of control (a) and treated (b) rats. H&E ×100. CA, Cornu ammonis; DG, dentate gyrus; Hi, hilus of DG; SO, stratum oriens; SP, stratum pyramidale (Pyramidal layer); SR, stratum radiatum (Straight arrows- intact neurons; dashed arrows- vacuolations).

the DG, were least affected by the effect of METH.

In conclusion, this study has shown the neuro-destructive effects of METH on the hippocampus and that such degenerating effects could affect some behaviour such as learning, memory and possibly the spatial navigation ability of rats during the water maze task.

REFERENCES

Anderson JK (2004). Oxidative stress in neurodegeneration: cause or consequence? Nature Rev. Neurosci., 5: 18-25.

Brandeis R, Brandys Y, Yehuda S (1989). The use of the Morris Water Maze in the study of memory and learning. Int. J. Neurosci., 48(1-2): 29-69.

Broening HW, Morford LL, Inman-Wood SL, Fukumura M, Vorhees CV (2001). 3,4-Methylenedioxymethamphetamine (Ecstasy)-Induced Learning and Memory Impairments Depend on the Age of Exposure during Early Development. J. Neurosci., 21(9): 3228–3235.

Canales JJ, Graybiel AM (2000). A measure of striatal function predicts motor stereotypy. Nat. Neurosci., 3: 377–383.

Davidson C, Gow AJ, Lee TH, Ellinwood EH (2001). Methamphetamine neurotoxicity: necrotic and apoptotic mechanisms and relevance to human abuse and treatment. Brain Res. Rev., 36(1): 1–22.

D'Hooge R, De Deyn PP (2001). Applications of the Morris water maze in the study of learning and memory. Brain Res. Rev., 36(1): 60-90.

Drury RA, Wallington EA (1980). Carleton's Histological Techniques. 5th Ed. Oxford University Press, New York, p. 195.

Escubedo E, Chipana C, Pe´rez-Sa´nchez M, Camarasa J, Pubill D (2005). Methyllycaconitine Prevents Methamphetamine-Induced Effects in Mouse Striatum: Involvement of _7 Nicotinic Receptors. J. Pharm. Exp. Ther., 315(2): 658–667.

Gallagher M, Rapp PR (1997). The use of animal models to study the effects of aging on cognition. Ann. Rev. Psychol., 48: 339-370.

Hsiao K, Chapman P, Nilsen S, Eckman C, Harigaya Y, Younkin S, Yang F, Cole G (1996). Correlative memory deficits, A-beta elevation, and amyloid plaques in transgenic mice. Science, 274(5284): 99-102.

Jarrard LE, Okaichi H, Steward O, Goldschmidt RB (1984). The role of hippocampal connections in the performance of place and cue tasks: comparisons with damage to the hippocampus. Behav. Neurosci., 98: 946-954.

Kesner RP, Exans RB, Hunt MA (1987). Further evidence in support of the neurological basis of an attribute model of memory: role of hippocampus. Int. J. Neurosci., 21-22: 184-196.

Kita T, Shunchoru P, Masahiro T, Kaoru K, Wagner CG, Nakashima T (1998). Methamphetamine-induced neurotoxicity in BALB:c, DBA:2N and C57BL:6N mice. Neuropharmacology, 37: 1177–1184.

Kita T, Wagner CG, Nakashima T (2003). Current Research on Methamphetamine-Induced Neurotoxicity: Animal Models of Monoamine Disruption. J. Pharmacol. Sci., 92: 178–195.

Kristen AH, Erika SN, Yamiece EG (2010). Methamphetamine-induced stereotypy correlates negatively with patch-enhanced prodynorphin and arc mRNA expression in the rat caudate putamen: The role of mu opioid receptor activation. Pharmacol. Biochem. Behav., 95: 410–421.

McGregor C, Srisurapanont M, Jittiwutikarn J, Laobhripatr S, Wongtan T, White JM (2005). The nature, time course and severity of methamphetamine withdrawal. Addiction, 100(9): 1320–1329.

Morris RGM (1981). Spatial localisation does not depend on the presence of local cues. Learning and Motivation, 12: 239-260.

Morris RGM, Garrud P, Rawlins JN, O'Keefe J (1982). Place navigation impaired in rats with hippocampal lesions. Nature, 297(5868): 681-683.

Nakazawa K, Thomas JM, Matthew AW, Susumu T (2004). NMDA receptors,place cells and hippocampal spatial memory. Nature Rev. Neurosci., 5: 361-372.

National Institute of Health Guide for the Care and Use of Laboratory Animals (1985). DHEW Publication (NIH), revised, Office of Science and Health Reports, DRR/NIH, Bethseda, USA.

Nunn JA, LePeillet E, Netto CA, Hodges H, Gray JA, Meldrum BS (1994). Global ischaemia: hippocampal pathology and spatial deficits in the water maze. Behav. Brain Res., 62(1): 41-54.

Nwoha PU, Ojo GB, Ajayi SA, Ofusori DA, Oluwayinka OP, Odukoya SA, Falana BA (2007). Garcinia kola diet provides slight neuroprotection to mice hippocampal neurons against neurotoxin. J. Environ. Neurosci. Biomed., 1 (2): 125-136.

Pierre C, Debouzie A (2000). BALB:c mice are not so bad in the Morris water maze. Behav. Brain Res., 117: 115–118.

Pubill D, Carlos C, Camins A, Palla`s M, Camarasa J, Escubedo E (2005). Free radical production induced by methamphetamine in rat striatal synaptosomes. Toxicol. Appl. Pharmacol., 204: 57–68.

Pubill D, Verdaguer E, Sureda FX, Camins A, Palla`s M, Camarasa J, Escubedo E (2002). Carnosine prevents methamphetamine-induced gliosis but not dopamine terminal loss in rats. Euro. J. Pharmacol., 448: 165–168.

Tatsuta T, Kitanaka N, Kitanaka J, Morita YB, Takemura M (2007). Lack of effect of anticonvulsant topiramate on methamphetamine-induced stereotypy and rewarding property in mice. Pharmacol. Biochem. Behav., 87: 48–55.

Vorhees CV, Inman-Wood SL, Morford LL, Broening HW, Fukumura M, Moran MS (2000). Adult Learning Deficits after Neonatal Exposure to D-Methamphetamine: Selective Effects on Spatial Navigation and Memory. J. Neurosci., 20(12): 4732–4739.

24

Acute low dose monosodium glutamate retards novelty induced behaviours in male swiss albino mice

Onaolapo, Olakunle James[1]* and Onaolapo, Adejoke Yetunde[2]

[1]Department of Pharmacology, Faculty of Basic Medical Sciences, College of Health Sciences, Ladoke Akintola University, Ogbomoso Oyo State, Nigeria.
[2]Department of Human Anatomy, Faculty of Basic Medical Sciences, College of Health Sciences, Ladoke Akintola University, Ogbomoso, Oyo State, Nigeria.

The study investigated the effects of acute systemic administration of monosodium glutamate (MSG) on novelty induced behaviours in male albino mice. The aim was to provide information on the neurobehavioural effects of a single i.p.(intraperitoneal) injection of MSG. Forty male swiss albino mice (age, 6 to 8 weeks; mean weight, 22.5 ± 2.5 g) were divided into four treatment groups (n = 10). Novelty induced behaviours that is horizontal locomotion (line crossing), rearing and grooming was carried out after intraperitoneal injection of varying doses of MSG (0.5, 1.0 and 1.5 m/kg) or its vehicle (normal saline). Each parameter was measured over a thirty minute period of ten minute intervals. Statistical analysis was carried out using a one way ANOVA followed by the Student-Newman-Keul's test. Compared with the control mice, a single intraperitoneal injection of MSG significantly reduced locomotor and rearing activities as horizontal locomotion and rearing was found to be significantly lower at 1.5 mg/kg when compared to their respective controls; grooming showed an initial slight increase followed by a visual but progressive reduction. The study concluded that acute administration of monosodium glutamate has a retardant effect on novelty induced behaviors in male mice.

Key words: Monosodium glutamate, novelty induced behaviours.

INTRODUCTION

Monosodium glutamate (MSG) is one of the commonest food additives in the developed world and it is a commonly used flavour enhancer. MSG can be found in various concentrations in numerous food products (Walker and Lupien, 2000). MSG is a sodium salt of glutamic acid, a naturally occurring non-essential amino acid with trade names such as Ajinomoto, Vetsin, Ac'cent and Tasting Powder. It was once made predominantly from wheat gluten, but is now made mostly from bacterial fermentation (Leung et al., 2003).

MSG added to foods produces a flavouring function similar to the glutamate that occurs naturally in foods. It adds a fifth taste, called "umami", which is best described as a savoury, broth-like or meaty taste, although traditional East Asian cuisine had often used seaweed extract, which contains high concentrations of glutamic acid, it was not until 1907 that MSG was isolated by Kikunae Ikeda. It was subsequently patented by Ajinomoto Corporation of Japan in 1909. In its pure form, it appears as a white crystalline powder that, as a salt, dissociates into sodium cations and glutamate anions while dissolving (glutamate is the anionic form of glutamic acid) (Sano, 2009).

Glutamate is a naturally occurring amino acid that is one of the most abundant amino acids in the central nervous system (CNS). It exist in atypically high concentration in brain regions that are critical in the mediation of cognitive performance such as cerebral cortex, dentate gyrus of hippocampus and striatum (Park et al., 2000) indicating the amino acid plays an important role in higher cognitive functions including memory formation (Hlinák et al., 2005). Glutamate is the primary excitatory amino acid neurotransmitter in the human brain. It is important in synaptic plasticity, learning, and development (Maragakis and Rothstein, 2001). Over the last four decades, a direct correlation between the neuroexcitatory and neurotoxic properties of glutamate

*Corresponding author. E-mail: olakunleonaolapo@yahoo.co.uk.

has been linked to activation of excitatory amino acid receptors. This stimulation leads to an enzymatic cascade of events ultimately resulting in cell death (Maragakis and Rothstein, 2001).

MSG interacts with two main subtypes of membrane receptors, ionotropic and metabotropic coupled to ion channels and G proteins, respectively. The ionotropic receptors are further subdivided based on selective agonists into N-methyl-D-aspartate (NMDA), kainate and a-amino-3-hydroxy-5-methyl-4-isoxazolepropionate (AMPA) subtypes (Zomurski and Thio, 1992). Interactions of glutamate with its ionotropic, mainly NMDA, receptors have been found to lead to neurotoxic changes in some experimental situations by allowing excessive amounts of calcium to enter the neuron (Choi, 1985) Glutamate's activity at the synaptic cleft is carefully balanced by receptor inactivation and glutamate reuptake. When this balance is upset, excess glutamate can itself become neurotoxic (Maragakis and Rothstein, 2001).

The neurotoxic properties of glutamate were first demonstrated in 1957 by Lucas and Newhouse (Lucas and Newhouse, 1957) who showed that systemic administration of glutamate to infant mice caused retinal degeneration, following this discovery, a series of studies available now have demonstrated serious neurotoxicologic effects of MSG on animals at significantly high doses. Park and his colleagues in 2000 found that single intraperitoneal injection of 4.0 mg/g bodyweight of MSG caused significant damage to hypothalamic neurons in the arcuate nucleus and impaired memory retention in adult mice (Park et al., 2000). Gonzalez-Burgos et al. (2001) also found that subcutaneous administration of 4.0 mg/g bodyweight of MSG to male neonate rats induced excitotoxicity, leading to cell death in prefrontal cerebral cortex. Another study using also high dose glutamate (4.0 mg/g body weight) reported reactivity of astrocytes and glial cells in the fronto-parietal cortex, including hyperplasia and hypertrophy (Martinez- Contreras et al., 2002). While MSG's similarity to glutamate might be the reason for its neurotoxicity, it is important to note the extremely high dosage administered in these animal studies.

To cause neuronal damage in animals, MSG plasma level needed to be100 to 130 mumol/dl in neonates and >630 mumol/dl in adults (Ng, 2002), hence the choice of low doses in our study. Neurobehavioural effects of glutamate also at high doses have been studied with the respect to variables such as age, time course of administration and neurobehavioural models. Carter and Levesque (1979) studying the effects of MSG on neurobehaviour in rats described a significant decrease in open-field activity at the 2 mg/g MSG group, with the decreases seen in the 4 mg/g MSG group being only visual. In 1999, Dubovicky et al. investigated the effect of monosodium-L-glutamate (MSG) administration in the neonatal period on habituation of exploratory behavior related to gender differences, rats of both sexes received intraperitoneal injection of MSG (4 mg/g) or vehicle on postnatal days 2, 4, 6, 8 and 10 and then exposed to the open field apparatus on the 65th postnatal day for four consecutive days to test their habituation with respect to exploratory behaviour, compared to intact controls, there were no significant differences found in interrupted habituation, neither in males nor in females.

Hlinák et al. (2005) evaluated the long-term behavioral consequences of neonatal MSG treatment in rats. The pups received subcutaneous injections of MSG at 3 mg/g daily from postnatal day 5 to 12. Data from an automatic activity monitor showed that locomotion of MSG-treated females and males aged 56 and 84 days was significantly reduced. Beginning from postnatal day (PD 120), three different behavioral tests were performed, in the open field test; a significant decrease in the habituation rate was found in MSG-treated animals. Sex-dependent differences in behavioral performance were suggested in the open field and elevated plus maze tests. These findings although inconsistent with dubovisky's findings in 1999 buttresses the fact that rats showed behavioural changes to MSG administration at high doses irrespective of the presence of gross morphological changes. Kiss et al. (2007) studied the changes in open-field activity and novelty-seeking behavior in periadolescent rats neonatally treated with monosodium glutamate; newborn rats were treated with 4 mg/g MSG subcutaneously on postnatal days 1, 3, 5, 7 and 9. Open-field behavior was tested at 2, 3, 4, 6 and 8 weeks of age, they found that MSG administration led to only temporary increases in locomotor behavior, which was more pronounced during the first few postnatal weeks, followed by a subtle hypoactivity at 2 months of age. Novelty-seeking was tested in four 5 min trials at 3 weeks of age and the conclusion was that the behavioral pattern of MSG-treated rats was the opposite in all tested signs in the novelty exploration test compared to control pups.

Investigation of novelty-seeking behavior is of growing importance for its relationship with sensitivity to psychomotor stimulants (Kiss et al., 2007) and though a lot has been done studying the effects of MSG on novelty induced behaviours at high doses, in this present study we decided to evaluate the possible acute neurobehavioural effects of MSG (if any) at doses otherwise recognized as being within normal dietary allowances.

MATERIALS AND METHODS

Equipments and apparatus

Electronic precision balance, plastic animal cages, sterile disposable syringes (1, 5, and 10 ml) and needles, cotton wool, stop watch and open field box.

Reagents and drugs

99% monosodium glutamate (Ajinomoto brand) was purchased

from the open market, weighed and dissolved in measured volume of isotonic saline solution to get desired concentrations MSG at the varying doses (0.5, 1.0 and 1.5 mg/kg) was administered intraperitoneally using an insulin syringe. The selection of this doses was arbitrary although cognizance was given to the LD 50 (i.p) of monosodium glutamate in mice which is 6900 mg/g (Yanagisawa et al., 1961) and also to previous reports that had used much higher doses successfully (Park et al., 2000; Hlinák et al., 2005; Kiss et al., 2007).

Animals

Healthy adult male swiss albino mice purchased from the Empire Animal farms in Osogbo, Osun State, Nigeria were used (age in the range of six to eight weeks) with weight in the range of 20 to 25 g. After being weighed on an electronic scale, the animals were randomly divided into four treatment groups. The animals were housed in plastic cages measuring 16"x12"x10" (10 mice in each cage). All animals had free access to food and water *ad libitum.* They were maintained under standard laboratory conditions that is a well aerated room with alternating light and dark cycles of 12 h each and at room temperature of 25°C. The experimental protocol was approved by the Institutional Animal Ethics Committee (IAEC). All rules applying to animal safety and care were observed.

Method

The animals were randomly assigned into four groups. Group I (n=10) was the control group, they were administered equivalent volume of intraperitoneal injection of normal saline (0.01 ml/g). Group II, III and IV (n=10) received intraperitoneal injections of MSG at 0.5, 1.0 and 1.5 mg/kg respectively. Behavioral testing was commenced immediately after administering monosodium glutamate or its vehicle (normal saline).Thirty minute period of the following behavioral states; horizontal locomotion, rearing and grooming were observed and scored at 10 min interval. This was used to characterize behavioral changes in the mice when placed in the open field.

Behavioural tests: The behavioural tests were conducted in a large quite room between the hours of 8 a.m. and 5 p.m. Novelty induced behaviours were evaluated using the open field box. Behaviours were scored by the authors using a stop watch; all animals in a group were tested on the same day (10 animals per day). All events were observed manually.

The open field box: The open field box is a rectangular area composed of a hard floor measuring 36 x 36 x 26 cm and made of white painted wood. The floor was divided by permanent red markings into 16 equal squares at the bottom. Generally, spontaneous motor activity was monitored for 30 min in the open field as described by Ajayi and Ukponmwan (1994). After treatment as explained earlier, each mouse was introduced into the field and the total locomotion (number of floor units entered with all paws), rearing frequency (number of times the animal stood on its hind limbs or with its fore limbs against the walls of the observation box or free in the air) and frequency of grooming (number of body cleaning with paws, picking of the body and pubis with mouth and face washing actions) within each 10 min interval were recorded. The arena was cleaned with 70% alcohol to eliminate olfactory bias and the arena allowed to dry before introducing a fresh animal.

Statistical analysis

All behavioral data were analyzed using the one way analysis of variance (ANOVA) followed by post hoc tests (Student Newman Keul's) carried out to determine the source of a significant effect. Results are expressed as Mean ±S.E.M. $p<0.05$ was taken as accepted level of significant difference from control.

RESULTS

Effects of monosodium glutamate (0.5, 1.0 and 1.5 mg/Kg) on locomotor activity

Following thirty minutes of exposure in the open field, there was significant ($F (3, 39) = 3.94$, $p<0.05$) retardant effect on locomotor activity between the drug treated animals and vehicle treated animals at dose level of 1.5 mg/kg although this effect is seen also at dose levels of 0.5 and 1.0 mg/kg, respectively. It is however only visual as shown in Figure 1.

Effects of monosodium glutamate (0.5, 1.0 and 1.5 mg/Kg) on rearing activity

Following thirty minutes of exposure in the open field, there was significant ($F (3, 39) = 3.08$, $p<0.05$) retardant effect on rearing activity between the drug treated animals and vehicle treated animals at dose level of 1.5 mg/kg although this effect is seen also at dose levels of 0.5 and 1.0, respectively it is however, only visual (Figure 2).

Effects of monosodium glutamate (0.5, 1.0 and 1.5 mg/Kg) on grooming behaviour

Following thirty minutes of exposure in the open field, there was no significant ($F (3, 39) = 1.31$, $p = 0.285$) difference in grooming behaviour between the drug treated animals and vehicle treated animals at any of the dose levels. Visual increases in grooming behaviour were seen at all doses compared to control, although compared with the effect seen at the 0.5 mg/kg dose the responses seen at the 1.0 and 1.5 mg/kg doses were reduced as shown in Figure 3.

DISCUSSION

A number of studies in the past have been conducted to investigate the effects of glutamate administration on various body organs especially, the brain. This study however, tried to investigate the acute neurobehavioural effects of MSG using the open field. The study differs in at least one important aspect; lower doses of glutamate were used. It is already known that glutamate administered parentrally increases the brain free glutamate levels (Bogdanov et al., 1996), is neurotoxic at high concentrations and contributes to the developments of a number of neurodegenerative diseases (Narayanan et al., 2010). Our study investigated possible

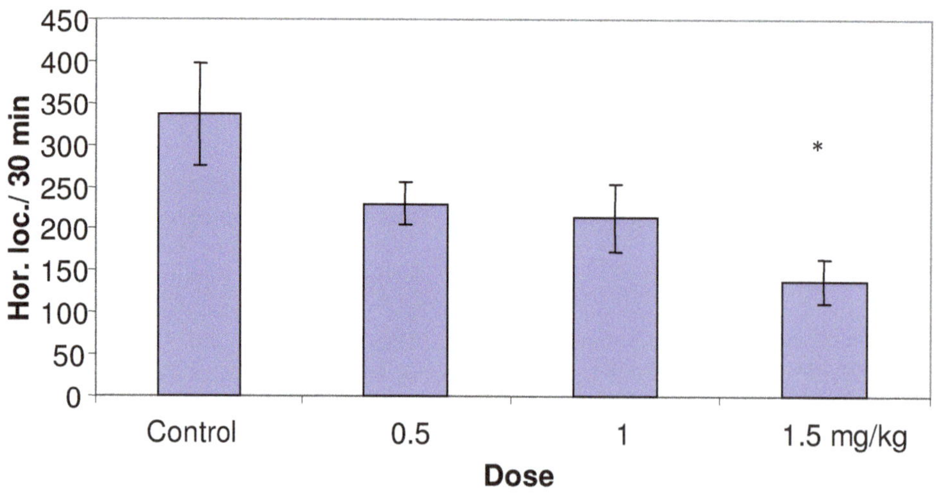

Figure 1. Effects of monosodium glutamate (0.5, 1.0 and 1.5 mg/kg i.p.) on horizontal locomotor activity in male mice over 30 min. Each bar represents, Mean ± S.E.M,* $p<0.05$ compared to control, n = 10.

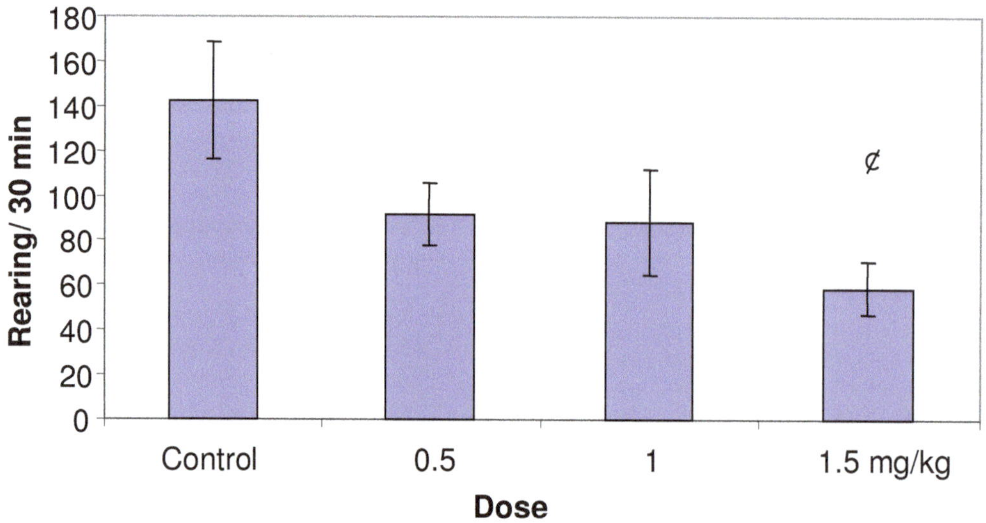

Figure 2. Effects of monosodium glutamate (0.5, 1.0 and 1.5 mg/kg i.p.) on rearing activity in male mice over 30 min. Each bar represents, Mean ± S.E.M, ¢ $p<0.05$ compared to control, n = 10.

neurobehavioural effects of MSG at dose levels otherwise accepted as being within normal limits with respect to a possible increase in brain free glutamate level, although we did not quantify level of free glutamate in the brain.

The data showed a reduction in horizontal and vertical locomotor (rearing) activity in the MSG treated at all dose groups during the open field tests. This effect of MSG on locomotion could be attributed to the modulatory effects of MSG on the hypothalamic brain regions. Reports suggest that activation of the rostro-caudal axis of the arcuate nucleus leads to their neurobehavioural reactions as seen in anxiety like behaviours in the elevated plus maze (Cortese and Phan, 2005) which we propose may be similar to the reactions seen here although studies that focus on the novelty induced behavioural effects of glutamate in adult animals do not appear to be common and results regarding changes of exploratory behaviour after neonatal MSG treatment are controversial (Dubovický et al., 1999). Some authors have described increased exploratory behaviour in mice (Dawson and Annau, 1983). However, Grimm and Frieder (1985) reported reduced exploratory behaviour, which is consistent with our findings.

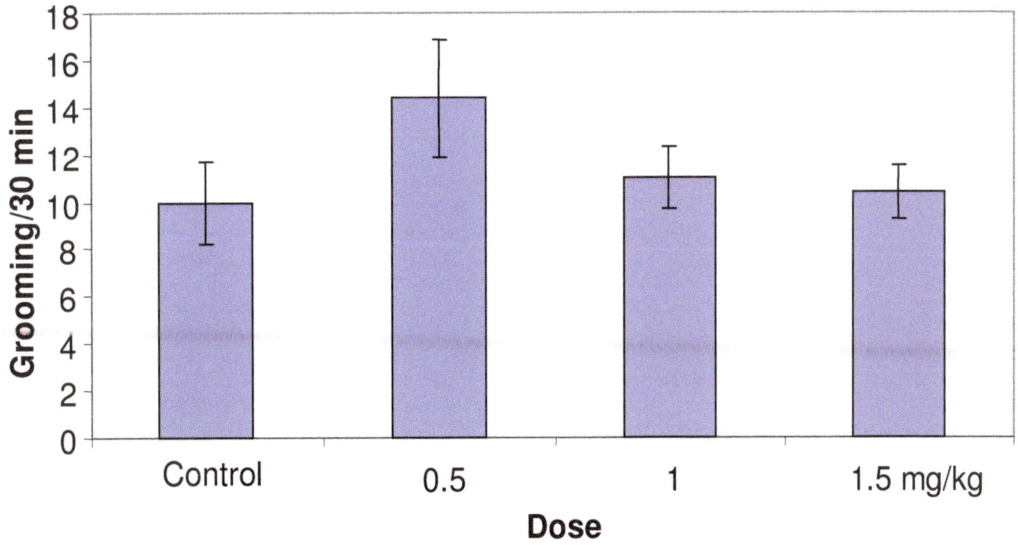

Figure 3. Effects of monosodium glutamate (0.5, 1.0 and 1.5 mg/kg i.p.) on grooming behaviour in male mice over 30 min. Each bar represents, Mean ± S.E.M, $p<0.05$ compared to control, n = 10.

It has been suggested that glutamate may play a more important role in general locomotion than previously thought. Glutamate is now known to exerts its actions in the brain by affecting the release of other neurotransmitters including monoamines and GABA (Cortese and Phan, 2005). Injection of glutamate antagonists had been shown to lead to induction of locomotion (Dalia et al., 1996) although this induction of locomotion was abolished by dopamine antagonists thereby suggesting that glutamate retards locomotion by interaction with dopamine. *In vivo* microdialysis experiments in awake, freely moving rats (Jedema and Moghddam, 1996, Takahata and Moghaddam, 1998) have demonstrated that both mild stress (that is handling) and intra-striatal infusion of AMPA/kainate agonists facilitate the presynaptic synthesis and release of dopamine in prefrontal cortex, while infusion of an NMDA agonist resulted in a trend toward a decrease in prefrontal cortical dopamine release (Jedema and Moghddam, 1996).

There was a visual increase in grooming activity at all doses studied although this increase was more marked at the lowest dose compared to the other doses, the increased grooming behaviour observed in a novel environment has been attributed to release of peptides derived from proopiomelanocortin (POMC), such as adrenocorticotropic hormone (ACTH), α-melanocyte-stimulating hormone (α-MSH), or β-endorphin, which themselves can elicit grooming (Dunn et al., 1985). This is because novelty-induced grooming is attenuated both by hypophysectomy and by antiserum to ACTH injected into the cerebral ventricles. Expression of grooming in rodents is also known to be dependent on dopamine (Cools et al., 1988). Dunn et al. (1985) reported that neonatal treatment with otherwise high doses of MSG did not alter grooming behavior in either home or novel environment in adult rats, there were also no differences between MSG and saline-treated rats in the grooming scores observed following graded doses of ACTH administered intracerebroventricularly, therefore the visual enhancement of grooming activity seen at 0.5 mg/kg and then suppression at other doses relative to the 0.5 mg/kg dose may suggests that acute glutamate administration initially enhanced and then suppressed dopaminergic transmission as well as the release of other peptides. Could the mild increase seen be a response to the novel environment? Or could this be due to stimulation of dopamine receptors by free glutamate or release of other peptides derived from proopiomelanocortin family? These are the questions we intend to answer in further experiments.

Conclusion

These results provide evidence for the involvement of glutamatergic input in the control of behaviours such as locomotion and grooming. We therefore suggest that more attention should be paid to studies that investigate effects of glutamate at doses that may not cause obvious structural brain damage but nevertheless may have important behavioral effects.

REFERENCES

Ajayi AA Ukponmwan OE (1994). Evidence of angiotensin 2 and endogenous opiod modulation of novelty induced rearing in the rat. Afr. J. Med. Med. Sci., 23: 287-290.

Bogdanov MB, Tjurmina OA, Wurtman RJ (1996). Consumption of a high dietary dose of monosodium glutamate fails to affect extracellular glutamate levels in the hypothalamic arcuate nucleus of adult rats Brain Research, 736(1-2): 76-81.

Carter LT, Levesque L (1979). Monosodium glutamate-induced changes of aggression and open-field activity in rats. Neurobehav. Toxicol., 1(4): 247-251.

Choi DW (1985). Glutamate neurotoxicity in cortical cell culture is calcium dependent. Nellrosci. Lerr., 58: 293-297.

Cools AR, Spruijt BM, Ellenbroek BA (1988). Role of central dopamine in ACTH induced grooming behavior in rats, Annals of the New York Academy of Sciences. Neural Mechanisms and Biological Significance of Grooming Behavior, 525: 338-349.

Cortese BM, Phan LK (2005). The Role of Glutamate in Anxiety and Related Disorders CNS. Spectr., 10(10): 820-830.

Dalia A, Uretsky NJ, Wallace LJ (1996). Induction of locomotor activity by the glutamate antagonist DNQX injected into the ventral tegmental area. Brain Res., 728: 209-214.

Dawson Jr. R, Annau Z (1983). A behavioral assessment of arcuate nucleus damage after a single injection of monosodium glutamate, Neurobehav. Toxicol. Teratol., 5: 399-406.

Dubovický M, Skultétyová I, Jezová D (1999). Neonatal stress alters habituation of exploratory behavior in adult male but not female rats. Pharmacol. Biochem. Behav., 64(4): 681-686.

Dunn AJ, Webster EL, Nemeroff CB (1985). Neonatal treatment with monosodium glutamate does not alter grooming behavior induced by novelty or adrenocorticotropic hormone Behavioral and Neural Biology, 44(1): 80-89.

Gonzalez-Burgos I, Perez-Vega MI, Beas-Zarate C (2001). Neonatal exposure to monosodium glutamate induces cell death and dendritic hypotrophy in rat prefrontocortical pyramidal neurons. Neurosci. Lett., 297(2): 69-72.

Grimm EV, Frieder B (1985). Differential vulnerability of male and female rats to the timing of various perinatal insults. Int. J. Neurosci., 27: 155-164.

Hlinák Z, Gandalovicová D, Krejcí I (2005). Behavioral deficits in adult rats treated neonatally with glutamate. Neurotoxicol. Teratol., 27(3): 465-473.

Jedema HP, Moghddam B (1996). Characterization of excitatory amino acid modulation of dopamine release in the prefrontal cortex of conscious rats. J. Neurochem., 66: 1448-1453.

Kiss P, Hauser D, Tamás A, Lubics A, Rácz B, Horvath ZS, Farkas J, Zimmermann F, Stepien A, Lengvari I, Reglódi D (2007). Changes in open-field activity and novelty seeking behavior in periadolescent rats neonatally treated with monosodium glutamate. Neurotox. Res., 12(2): 85-93.

Leung AY, Foster S (2003). "Monosodium Glutamate". Encyclopedia of Common Natural Ingredients: Used in Food, Drugs, and Cosmetics (2nd Ed.). New York: Wiley. ISBN 978-0-471-47128-8, pp. 373-375.

Lucas DR, Newhouse JP (1957). The toxic effect of sodium L-glutamate on the inner layers of the retina. Arch. Ophthalmol., 58: 193-201.

Maragakis NJ, Rothstein JD (2001). Glutamate Transporters in Neurologic Disease. Arch. Neurol., 58: 365-370.

Martinez-Contreras A, Huerta M, Lopez-Perez S, Garcia-Estrada J, Luquin S, Beas-Zarate C (2002). Astrocytic and microglia cells reactivity induced by neonatal administration of glutamate in cerebral cortex of the adult rats. J. Neurosci. Res., 67(2): 200-210.

Narayanan SN, Kumar RS, Paval J, Nayak S (2010). Effect of ascorbic acid on the monosodium glutamate-induced neurobehavioral changes in periadolescent rats. Bratisl Lek Listy. 111(5): 247-252.

Ng T (2002). Re-evaluation of the Tasty Compound: MSG, Nutrition Bytes, 8: 1.

Park CH, Choi SH, Piaoa Y, Kim S, Lee Y, Kim, Jeong S, Rah J, Seo J, Lee J, Chang K, Jung Y, Suh Y (2000). Glutamate and aspartate impair memory retention and damage hypothalamic neurons in adult mice, Toxicol. Lett., 115(2): 117-125.

Sano C (2009). "History of glutamate production". Am. J. Clin. Nutr., p. 90.

Takahata R, Moghaddam B (1998). Glutamatergic regulation of basal and stimulus-activated dopamine release in the prefrontal cortex. J. Neurochem., 71: 1443-1449.

Walker R, Lupien JR (2000). The safety evaluation of Monosodium Glutamate J. Nutr., 30(4S):1049S-1052S.

Yanagisawa K, Nakamura T, Miyata K, Kameda T, Kitamura S, Ito K (1961). Nohon Seirigaku Zasshi J. Physiol. Soc. Japan, 23: 383-385.

Zomurski CF, Thio LL (1992). Properties of vertehrate glutamate receptors: Calcium mobilization and desentization. Prog. Neurobiol., 39: 295-336.

Evaluation of anxiolytic and novelty induced behaviours following bee-honey consumption in rats

O. A. Oyekunle[1]*, M. A. Akanmu[2] and T. P. Ogundeji[1]

[1]Department of Physiology, College of Health Sciences, Ladoke Akintola University of Technology, Ogbomoso, Nigeria.
[2]Department of Pharmacology, Faculty of Pharmacy, Obafemi Awolowo University, Ile-Ife, Nigeria.

Bee honey has been shown to have many trace elements. Antibacterial and antioxidant properties of bee honey have been reported and employed for therapeutic purposes. The present work evaluates the anxiolytic values and effect on novelty induced behaviours of bee honey consumption. Wistar rats of either sex were given different concentrations of bee honey (10, 20 and 40%) at the dose of 0.5 ml/100 g p.o. The control rats were allowed access to distilled water *ad lib*. Anxiolytic value was accessed in the Hole Board test while novelty induced behaviours were accessed in the Open-Field test. The result showed a significant dose dependent increase in exploratory activities of the experimental animals in the test groups when compared with the control (P<0.05) in the hole board test. In novelty induced behaviour tests, bee honey also produced a significant dose dependent increase in locomotor, rearing and grooming activities with the 40% concentration producing the highest level of significance when compared with the control (P<0.01). The results suggest that bee honey consumption mitigates anxiety and exerts excitatory effect on the central nervous system especially at the highest non-sedative dose.

Key words: Anxiolytic, locomotor, hole board, bee honey, rearing, grooming neurobehaviour, open-field.

INTRODUCTION

Honey is produced by honey bee (genus *Apis*) from nectar of flowers. Honey gets its sweetness from the monosaccharide fructose and glucose and has approximately the relative sweetness as that of granulated sugar (http//www.honey.com, 2008; http//www.food.oregonstate.edu/sugar, 2008). It contains essential trace elements which have been implicated in brain functions - Copper (Prohaska, 1987); Zinc (Dreosti, 1983; Prohaska, 1987; Sandstead 1985; Wallwork, 1987); Iron (Beard et al., 1993; Yehuda, 1990; Beard, 2003) and Manganese (Dreosti and Richard, 1985). Bee honey has also been reported to be rich in vitamins- Riboflavin, Naicin, Pantothenic acid, Folic acid and Ascorbic have been reported to have neuromodulatory role. Bee honey has a pH range of 3.2 to 4.5 (Al-Waili, 2004) and this corroborates its antibacterial activity (Wahdah, 1998). It appears to be effective in killing drug resistant biofilms which are implicated in chronic rhinosinusitis (Science Daily, 2008). Antioxidants in honey have been employed in the treatment of colitis (Bilsel et al., 2002) such claims are consistent with its uses in traditions of folk medicine (Molan, 1992).

Role of free radical has been suggested in pathogenesis of diseases including neurodegenerative disorders (Halliwell, 1994; Wulf, 2002). These free radicals are produced during normal cellular metabolic functions and include hydroxyl radical (OH^-), superoxide anion (O^{2-}), hydrogen peroxide (H_2O_2) and nitric oxide (NO) (Halliwell and Gutteridge, 1999; Frei, 1994). These reactive species have high chemical reactivity and the brain is highly susceptible to such oxidative damages, due to its high polyunsaturated fatty acid content and less balance is crucial in neurodegenerative/neuronal processes and antioxidant directly or indirectly protect cell from adverse effect of drugs, xenobiotics and toxic radical reactions (Halliwell, 1994; Wulf, 2002). In view of the above, this present study was designed to evaluate

*Corresponding author. E-mail: oalanre@gmail.com.

the possible involvement of trace elements and antioxidant constituents of bee honey in relieving anxiety and neurobehavioural characteristics.

MATERIALS AND METHODS

Bee honey

The pure bee honey was procured from LAUTECH VENTURES and produced by the University's apiary under the management of the faculty of agricultural sciences, Ladoke Akintola University of Technology, Ogbomoso.

Bee honey concentrations

Bee honey concentrations were prepared as follows:

For 10%:

0.5 ml of bee honey dissolved in 4.5 ml distilled water.

For 20%:

1 ml of bee honey dissolved in 4 ml distilled water.

For 40%:

2 ml of bee honey dissolved in 3 ml of distilled water.

Dose basis

0.5 ml/100 g body weight.

Animal

40 Wistar rats of both sexes and non-pregnant weighing 100 -120 g were used in this investigation. The rats were kept in plastic cages in the Animal house of Pharmacology Department, Faculty of Pharmacy, Obafemi Awolowo University (O.A.U), Ile-Ife, Osun State, with an unrestricted access to both food and water. After one week of habituation, animals were subjected to the experiments. For each of the experiment, each animal was tested only once. All tests were carried out between 8.30 am and 4.30 pm. The guidelines on Animal experiments were strictly followed.

Experimental protocol

Each experimental procedure consists of 4 groups with 5 rats in each group. Group1 (control group) was given water *ad lib* while groups 2-4 (treatment groups) were given 10, 20 and 40% bee honey concentration respectively with the aid of oral canula.

Hole board test

In this procedure, as described by Boissier and Simon (1960), one hour after the administration of bee honey concentration the animal was placed on a board (40 x 40 cm) with 16 holes (symmetrically distributed in four rows) for 5 min. The number of times the animal dips its head into the hole during the 6 min period was registered. The results obtained were expressed as mean total number of head dips (Lister, 1987).

Open-field test

For each test session, the animals were allowed to explore the testing environment, a quiet well-ventilated room, for at least 30 min. Spontaneous motor activity is monitored for 30 min in the modified Open-Field test as described by Eckeli et al. (2000). Briefly, the structure consist of a rectangular arena composed of a hard board floor (diameter 60 x 60 cm) with a surrounding wall of dimension 64 x 64 x 64 cm^3, both made of white painted wood. The floor was divided by permanent red marker into squares of 4.2 cm^2 at the bottom (on the external surface). One hour after oral administration of bee honey, each rat was introduced into the arena. Locomotor activity was evaluated by counting the number of floor unit crossed on the floor of the square with all paw (during 30-min period). Grooming activity was evaluated by counting the numbers of licking of the body and pubis with mouth and face washing actions. Rearing behaviour was evaluated by counting the number of times in which the animal stood on its hind limbs with its forearm against the wall of the observation cage or in the air during the 30 min period after oral administration of bee honey. Before introducing each animal into the arena, the arena was cleaned with methylated spirit to eliminate the possible bias due to the odour that could be left by the previous subject.

Statistical analysis of results

Results of the experiments and observations were expressed as mean ± standard error of mean (SEM). The significance of differences between groups was determined using one-way analysis of variance (ANOVA) followed by post-hoc Dunnett test. In all the observations, statistical significance was considered at $P < 0.05$.

RESULTS

Figure 1 showed the result obtained from the Hole Board test which is a model for anxiolytic investigation. It showed gradual increase in numbers of head dip obtained with increasing concentrations of bee honey. Only 20 and 40% concentrations of bee honey produced significant difference when compared with the control. Figures 2a-c showed the results obtained from the Open-Field test. There was concentration dependent increase in locomotor activities but only the 20 and 40% concentration produced significant difference ($P<0.05$) when compared with the control. In rearing behaviour only 40% bee honey concentration produced a significant difference ($P<0.05$) when compared with the control. In grooming activity, only 20 and 40% bee honey concentrations produced significant difference when compared with the control. In all the novelty induced behaviours, the most significant effects were observed at 40% bee honey concentration.

DISCUSSION

Nutritional factors such as lack of trace elements and vitamins in the diet can influence the neurobehavioural profile of the organism and precipitate anxiety-like syndrome. The neuronal changes mediating these

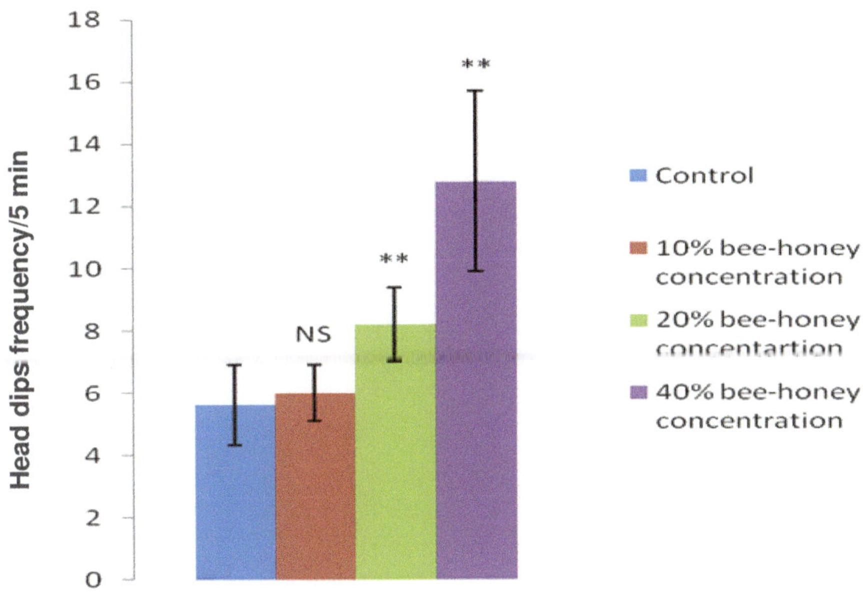

Figure 1. Effects of bee honey on Hole Board exploratory behaviour in rats. Each column and bar represents Mean ± SEM of number of head dips 1 hour after oral administration of water (control) and bee honey concentrations. ** P< 0.05 (N = 5).

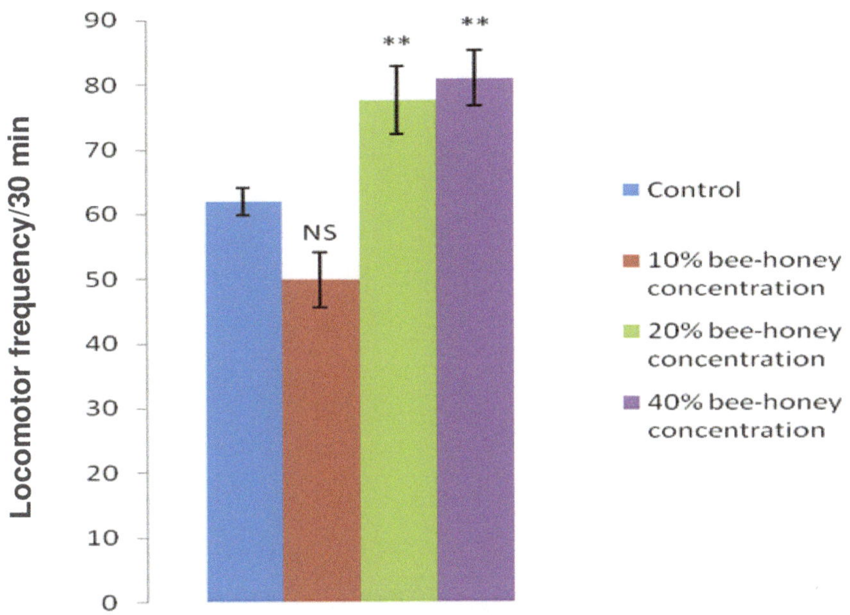

Figure 2a. Effects of bee honey on locomotor activities in rats after 30 min session. Each column and bar represents Mean ± SEM of frequency of locomotor activities 1 h after oral administration of water (control) and bee honey concentrations. **P<0.05 (N = 5).

behavioral deficits appear to be free radicals and the oxidative stress they generate (Cantuti-Castelvetri et al., 2000). Both Hole Board and Open Field tests have been effectively employed to access the neurobehavioural profile of animals under the influence of anxiogenic/anxiolytic agents. Drugs that reduced anxiety are known as anxiolytics and there is increased exploratory behaviour in novel situations (Bharttachanya and Statyan, 1997). The increased number of head dips and locomotor activities observed in Hole Board and Open field tests especially at 40% bee honey concentration are reliable indices of anxiolytic effects.

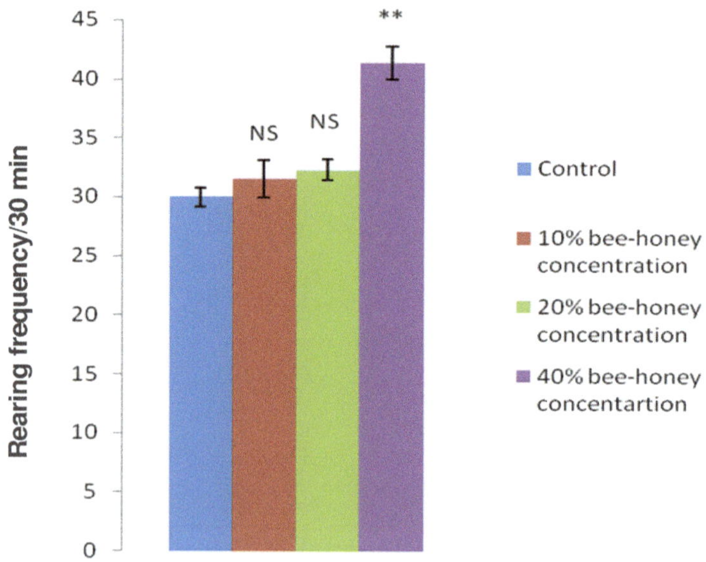

Figure 2b. Effects of bee honey concentrations on rearing behaviours in rats after 30 min session. Each column and bar represents Mean ± SEM of frequency of rearing behaviour 1 h after oral administration of water (control) and bee honey concentrations.**P<0.05 (N = 5).

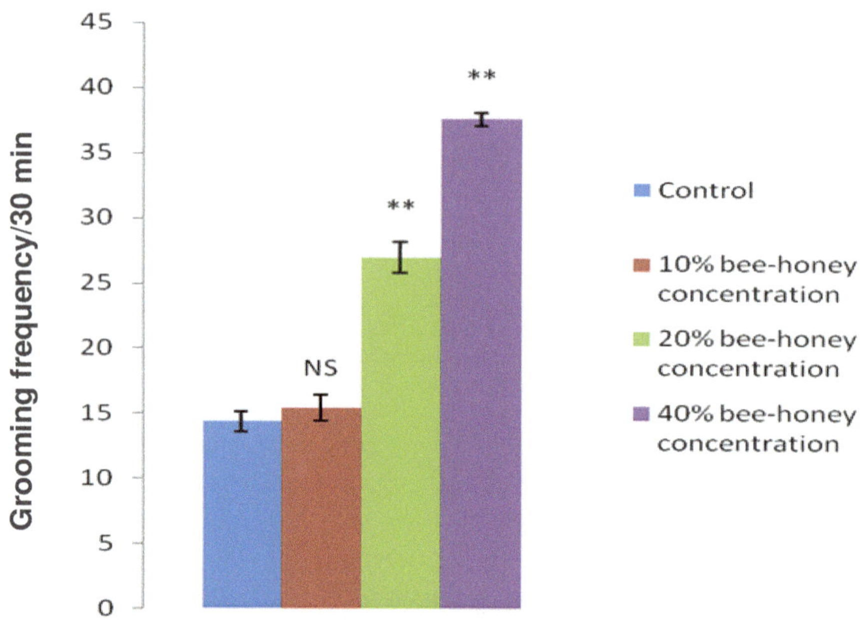

Figure 2c. Effects of bee honey on grooming behaviours in rats after 30 min session. Each column and bar represents Mean ± SEM of frequency of grooming activities 1 h after oral administration of water (control) and bee honey concentrations. **P<0.05 (N = 5).

Neuronal lesion are oftentimes associated with various degrees of behavioural impairments, and among the prime candidates responsible for producing the neuronal changes mediating these behavioral deficits appear to be free radicals and the oxidative stress they generate. Therefore, there have been a number of studies which have examined the putative positive benefits of antioxidants in altering these neuronal/behavioral decrements, with varying degrees of success (Morris et al., 2002; Sofic et al., 2002).

From the result, the presence of antioxidants (majorly vitamins) in bee honey tends to mop up free radical generated in the CNS thereby alleviating anxiety. Biochemically, serotonin and its receptors have long been viewed as neurotransmitter involved in behavioural changes (Iversen, 1984; Briley et al., 1990). Of the 14 or more mammalian serotonin receptors subtypes that have been described in literatures at least four have been implicated in anxiety in various animal models (Lucki, 1996). The role of iron in neurotransmitter metabolism has been investigated and reported, it is now known that iron is essential for a number of enzymes involved in neurotransmitter synthesis (Beard et al., 1993; Ashkenazi et al., 1982) including tryptophan hydroxylase (serotonin), tyrosine hydroxylase (norepinephrine (NE) and Dopamine). In addition, iron is a cofactor for ribonucleotide reductase and is essential for the functioning of a number of electron transfer reactions related to both lipid metabolism and brain-energy metabolism (Wigglesworth and Baum, 1988). Therefore, the behavioural modulatory activity of bee honey could be as a result of the presence of this essential micronutrient (iron) in its composition. It has been suggested that there is an involvement of mesolimbic dopamine system in the novelty induced grooming. Selective dopamine D1 and D5 receptors agonists elicit an intense grooming behaviour while dopamine D2 receptor agonists reduce this behaviour (Griebel et al., 1994). Bee honey consumption appears to influence novelty induced behaviours in the animals as observed in the results especially at 40% concentration. The increased excitatory activity in the central nervous system could be due to certain component of bee honey acting probably via D1 and D5 receptors. This observation could be linked with the fact confirming co-localization of iron with dopaminergic neurons throughout the brain (Yehuda, 1990; Wigglesworth and Baum, 1988). In conclusion, it could be said that pure bee honey possess behavioural modulating potentials and may be used as an anxiolytic agent and may also be used to stimulate the central nervous system (antidepressant). Pure bee honey can be used as supplement in special diet formulation for subjects with mood disorders.

ACKNOWLEDGEMENTS

Our sincere gratitude goes to Mr. E.O. Akinbolusere, Chief Technologist, Department of Physiology, Ladoke Akintola University of Technology, Ogbomoso. Technical staff of Department of Pharmacology, Obafemi Awolowo University, Ile-Ife.

REFERENCES

Al-Waili NS (2004). Investigating the antimicrobial activity of natural honey and its effect on the pathogenic bacterial infections of surgical wounds and conjunctiva. J. Med. Food, 7(2): 210-22.

Ashkenazi R, Ben-Shachar D, Youdim MBH (1982). Nutritional iron deficiency and dopamine binding sites in the rat brain. Pharmacol. Biochem. Behav., 17: 43–47.

Beard J (2003). Iron deficiency alters brain development and functioning. J. Nutr., 13: 1468S-1472S.

Beard JL, Connor JR, Jones BC (1993). Iron in the brain. Nutr. Rev., 51: 157-170.

Boissier JR, Simon P (1960). L' utilization du test de la traction, (Test de JULOU- COURVOISIER) pour l'etude des psycholeptiques. Therapie, 15: 1170-1174.

Bharttachanya SK, Statyan KS (1997). Experimental methods for the evaluation of psychotropic agents. Indian J. Exp Biol., 35: 565.

Bilsel Y, Bugra DS, Yamaner T, Bulut U, Turkoglu U (2002). Could honey have a place in colitis Therapy. Digestive Surgery 29: 306-312.

Briley M, Chopin P, Moret C (1990). Effect of serotonergic lesion on anxious behaviour measured in the elevated plus-maze test in the rat. Psychopharmacology, 101: 187-189.

Brocardo PS, Budni J, Pavesi E, Franco JL, Uliano-Silva M, Trevisan R, Terenzi MG, Dafre AL, Rodrigues AL (2010). Folic acid administration prevents ouabain-induced hyperlocomotion and alterations in oxidative stress markers in the rat brain. Bipolar Disord., 12(4): 414-24.

Cantuti-Castelvetri I, Shukitt-Hale B, Joseph JA (2000). Neurobehavioral aspects of antioxidants in aging. Int J. Dev. Neurosci., 18(4-5): 367-381.

Dreosti IE (1983). Zinc and the central nervous system. In: [IE Dreosti and RM Smith, eds]. Neurobiology of the Trace Elements, New Jersey: Humana Press, 1: 135-162.

Dreosti IE, Richard MS (editors) (1985). Neurobiology of the Trace Elements: Neurotoxicology and Neuropharmacology. Humana Press, pp. 175-176.

Eckeli AL, Dach F, Rodrigues (2000). Acute treatments with GMP produce antidepressant-like effect in mice. Neuroreport 11: 839-843.

Frei B (1994). Reactive oxygen species and antioxidant vitamins: Mechanism of action. Am. J. Med., 97: 5S.

Griebel G, Moreau JL, Jenck F, Misslin R, Martin JR (1994). Acute and chronic treatment with 5-TH reuptake inhibitors differentially modulate emotional responses in anxiety models in rodents. Psychopharmacology, 113: 463-470.

Halliwell B (1994). Free radicals, antioxidants and human diseases: Curiosity cause or consequences? The Lancet, 344: 721.

Halliwell B, Gutteridge JMC (1999). Free radicals in biology and medicine (Oxford Univ. Press, New York).

Hoane MR, Wolyniak JG, Akstulewicz SL (2005). Administration of riboflavin improves behavioral outcome and reduces edema formation and glial fibrillary acidic protein expression after traumatic brain injury. J. Neurotrauma, 22(10): 1112-22.

Iversen SD (1984). 5-HT and anxiety. Neuropharmacology, 23: 1553-1560.

Lister RG (1987). The use of a plus-maze to measure anxiety in the mouse. Psychopharmacology III, pp. 323-333.

Lucki I (1996). Serotonin receptors specificity in anxiety disorder. J. Clin. Psychiatry, 57(6): 5-7.

Molan PC (1992). Honey for treatment of infections: The New Zealand Bee keeper, 216: 19-20.

Morris MC, Evans DA, Bienias JL (2002). Vitamin e and Cognitive Decline in Older Persons. Arch Neurol. 59: 1125-1132.

National Honey Board (2008). "Carbohydrate and the sweetness of honey". Last accessed May 5. http//www.honey.com.

Oregon State University (2008). "Sugar Sweetness". Last accessed May 5. http//www.food.oregonstate.edu/sugar.

Prohaska JR (1987). Functions of trace elements in brain metabolism. Physiol. Rev., 67: 858-901.

Sandstead HH (1985). Zinc: essentiality for brain development and function. Nutr. Rev., 43: 129-37.

Science Daily (2008). Honey effective in killing bacteria that causes chronic sinusitis 71-73.

Sofic E, Rustembegovic A, Kroyer G, Cao G (2002). Serum Antioxidant Capacity in Neurological, Psychiatric, Renal Diseases and Cardiomyopathy J. Neural. Transm., 109: 711-719.

Wahdah H (1998). Causes of the antibacterial activity of honey. Infection, 26(1): 26-31.

Wallwork JC (1987). Zinc and the central nervous system. Progress in Food Nutr. Sci., 11: 203-247.

Wigglesworth JM, Baum H (1988). Iron dependent enzymes in the brain. In: Brain Iron: Neurochemical and Behavioural Aspects (Youdim, M. B. H., ed.), Taylor and Francis, New York, pp. 25-66.

Wulf D (2002). Free radical in the physiological control of cell function. Physiol. Rev., 82: 253.

Yehuda S (1990). Neurochemical basis of behavioral effects of brain iron deficiency in animals. In: Brain, Behavior, and Iron in the Infant Diet (Dobbing J., ed.) Springer-Verlag, London, pp. 83-106.

Attitudes of university students towards abortion in Nigeria

Olukunmi Lanre OLAITAN

Department of Human Kinetics and Health Education, University of Ilorin, Ilorin, Nigeria.
E-mail: lanreolives@yahoo.com, olaitan.ol@unilorin.edu.ng

The study examined the attitude of university students towards abortion in Nigeria. A total of nine hundred (900) respondents gave their opinions on a self structured questionnaire. The frequency counts and percentages were used to analyse the personal data of the respondents and means, standard deviation, t-test and analysis of variance (ANOVA) for analyzing the hypotheses at $\alpha = 0.05$ level of significance. Some students support abortion when it is on health condition of either the mother or the baby. Based on the findings, some of the recommendations made include proper reproductive health education and counseling should be given to young ladies and boys about unsafe abortion preventive method; Federal government as a matter of urgency should consider legalization of induced abortion to prevent the practice of clandestine abortion in the back street.

Key words: Attitude, university students, abortion, reproductive health, infertility, premarital sex, promiscuity.

INTRODUCTION

Abortion is the removal or expulsion of an embryo or foetus from the uterus, resulting in or causing its death. This can be spontaneously as miscarriage or artificially induced by chemical, surgical or other means. "Abortion" can refer to an induced procedure at any point during human pregnancy; it is sometimes medically defined as either miscarriage or induced termination before the point of variability. Through history, abortion has been induced by various methods and the moral and legal aspect of abortion is subject to intense debate in many parts of the world (Jones et al., 2004),

However, a clearer definition of abortion is the removal of a growing embryo or foetus from uterus to which it is attached. This general definition covers spontaneously abortion (miscarriage) and induced abortion but distinguished both from premature birth, live or still. Golden (2001) stated that certain authorities seem to complicate the issue by defining abortion as a termination expulsion or detachment of foetus or fertilized ovum before its time of viability. In general a foetus is not viable before the 28th weeks of gestation. The following medical terms are used to categorize abortion:

1. Spontaneous abortion (Miscarriage): Spontaneous abortion, according to Mules (2001) is the sudden termination or expulsion of the foetus/pregnancy. It is characterized by complaints of feeling of uneasiness before the on set of specific signs and symptoms, by the mother such as vaginal bleeding that is, brown spotting or bright red blood. Spontaneous abortion can be due to accidental trauma or natural causes; most miscarriages are due to uncorrected replication of chromosomes; they can also be caused by environmental factors.
2. Induced abortion: This is an abortion brought about by interference either by therapeutic or elective abortion as a result of deliberate human action (Roche, 2004).
3. Therapeutic abortion: An abortion performed either to:

a. Save the life of the pregnant woman.
b. Preserve the woman's physical or mental health.
c. Terminate pregnancy that would result in a child born with a congenital disorder that would be fatal or associated with significant morbidity.
d. Selectively reduce the number of foetus to lessen health risks associated with multiple pregnancies.

In United Kingdom, legal termination of pregnancy is a therapeutic procedure carried out under the terms of the 1967 abortion act (United Kingdom Abortion Act, 2011). Before this type of abortion can be carried out, 2 registered medical practitioners should be of the opinion that the pregnancy should be terminated and consent must be obtained from the husband and wife. The procedure is performed after an agreement must have been reached between the 2 doctors.

4. Elective abortion: This is an abortion performed at will by an individual in contravention of the *Abortion Act* (United Kingdom Abortion Act, 2011). This type of abortion is performed for any other reason; such procedures are illegal and punishable by imprisonment especially country like Nigeria.

It is attempted by unqualified, non-expert person or non medical (Quack) practitioner; it can also be done by patient herself by ingesting corrosive substance such as taking blue, potash, lime or excessive salt.

The world-wide legal status of abortion ranges from complete prohibition to elective procedures at the request of the pregnant women. Olaitan (2010) opined that in the wake of a growing awareness of population and environmental concerns, social-economic development and recognition of the right of women to control their own fertility and aided by technological innovational, abortion has gradually emerged from an aura of social ambivalence. However, abortion has continued ranging debates in political social, medical, theological and legal fields (Christian, 1999). To this end, two major camps have emerged namely:

1. The Pro-choice.
2. The pro-life.

The pro choice fights for the legalization of abortion and hence that a woman should have the right to decide whether or not to have her baby. To pro-life activists, on the other hand fight for the right, the unborn child to life and hence are vehemently opposed to the legalization of abortion (Christian, 1999).

Since we live in a free world, who would not favour the privilege of choice? But at the same time, looking at the issue from reasonable man's perspective, which would not be favorable? In resolving this controversial issue, its becomes imperative to conduct an individual opinion/survey strictly on abortion so as to be able to decide whether abortion should be legalized in Nigeria as in case of Britain, United State of America and other Western Countries. Thus, the university students appear to be the fertile area for this study since the modal societal impression is that this cohort is the most responsive to change of a traditional ideas and the adoption of what may be heuristically labeled as liberal political and social philosophy.

Purpose of the study

The purpose of this study is:

1. To examine the general attitudes of university students in south west Nigeria towards abortion.

2. To asses whether gender, religion, marital status, age, tribe and institution influence university students' attitudes towards abortion.

Research questions

To what extent do gender, religion, marital status, age, tribe and institution of students influence their attitudes toward abortion in south West Nigeria?

Research hypothesis

1. There is no significant difference in the attitudes of University students toward abortion on the basis of their gender.
2. There is no significant difference in the attitudes of University students toward abortion on the basis of their religion.
3. There is no significant difference in the attitudes of University students toward abortion on the basis of their marital status.
4. There is no significant difference in the attitudes of University students toward abortion on the basis of their age.
5. There is no significant difference in the attitudes of University students toward abortion on the basis of their tribe.
6. There is no significant difference in the attitudes of University students toward abortion on the basis of their institutions.

MATERIALS AND METHODS

The study area is located in south Western Nigeria. A cross-sectional survey design was adopted for the study. The population of the study area is a heterogeneous group of both gender, different age groups, religions, tribes, marital status and institutions. There are many universities from each state, but 6 universities located at the capital city of each state were purposively selected and 150 students from each of the institutions through a simple random sampling technique to make total of 900 students as the subjects.

A purposely designed structured validated questionnaire that was tested for reliability was distributed to the students by the researcher with the help of 12 trained research assistants who administered the questionnaire to the students in their various institutions to gather information about their attitudes towards abortion. The information provided on the questionnaire includes, gender, religion, martial status, age, tribe and institution of the respondents. Also general information about attitudes towards abortion was included. Data were analysed by using descriptive statistics of frequency count and percentage for the bio-data and inferential statistics of *t*- test and analysis of variance (ANOVA) were employed to test the hypotheses formulated at $\alpha = 0.05$ level of significance.

RESULTS AND DISCUSSION

Table 1 revealed that majority of the respondents 62%

Table 1. Bio-data of respondents in percentages (N = 900).

Variable		Freq.	%
Gender	Male	342	38.0
	Female	558	62.0
Religion	Christian	378	42.0
	Muslim	522	58.0
	Traditional	-	0.0
Marital status	Single	520	57.8
	Married	380	42.2
Age group	≤30 years	318	35.3
	≥31 years	582	64.7
Tribe	Yoruba	504	56.0
	Hausa	120	13.3
	Igbo	276	30.7
Institution	University of Lagos, Akoka, Lagos State, Nigeria (UNILAG)	150	16.7
	University of Agriiculture, Abeokuta, Ogun State, Nigeria (UNAAB)	150	16.7
	University of Ibadan, Ibadan, Oyo State, Nigeria (UI)	150	16.7
	Obafemi Awolwo University, Ile-Ife, Osun State, Nigeria (OAU)	150	16.7
	Federal University of Technology, Akure, Ondo State, Nigeria (FUTA)	150	16.7
	University of Ado-Ekiti, Ekiti State, Nigeria (UNAD)	150	16.7

were females while 38% were males. As much as 58.0% of the respondents were Muslims while 42.0% were Christians. Majority of the respondents 57.8% were single, while 42.2% were single.

Also, 35.3% of the respondents were less than or equal to 30 years old while 64.7% were greater than or equal to 31 years old. 56.0% of the respondents were Yorubas, 13.3% were Hausas, while 30.7% were Igbos. 150 (16.7%) each of the respondents were from UNILAG, UNAAB, UI, OAU, FUTA and UNAD respectively

Table 2 shows the *t*-test statistics for gender, religion, marital status and age group. Also, analysis of variance (ANOVA) statistics for tribe and institution were shown. The calculated *t*-values are 2.55, 2.10, 1.34 and 1.62 for gender religion marital status and age group respectively. Hence, the hypothesis that there is no significant difference in the attitudes of University students toward abortion on the basis of gender was accepted meaning that significant difference existed in the attitude of male and female students towards abortion. Male with the mean of 47.54 does not have a good attitude towards abortion as female with the mean score of 96.67. The result of this finding contrary to the finding of Adler (2001) that both male and female students have a liberal attitude towards abortion. In the same vein, the study concluded by Martin (2002) when students (males and females) were asked if they favoured or opposed abortion at anytime during the first three months of pregnancy. The results showed that two third (67%) of both male and female students questioned were in favour of abortion been legalized regardless of circumstances.

The finding obtained on religion revealed that, the hypothesis was rejected, which implies that significant difference existed in the attitudes of University students toward abortion on the basis of their religions. The mean value for Christian is 33.34 and so have negative attitudes towards abortion compared with Muslim with the mean of 59.28. The result of this finding was expressed by certain scholars in respect to abortion and religion. Moore (2004) and David (2003), who did an extensive examination of the statement by western religious scholar of diverse persuasions, came to the conclusion that Christianity religion according to Okagbue (1998) set its face sternly against abortion mainly because it regards it as high religious crime that a child should be killed. However, Islam's view on abortion is not precise. To them abortion is strictly prohibited after the foetus has acquired a life or soul of its own which is estimated to about 120 days. In a nut shell, Christians are totally against abortion, while the Muslim supports before formation of life (before 120 days) therefore, both religions have different views.

The result on marital status shows that the calculated value is greater than the table value. Therefore, the

Table 2. Results of hypotheses testing on differences in the attitudes of university students towards abortion on the basis of gender, religion, marital status, age, tribe and institution (N = 900).

S/N	Variable	Alternative	Ẍ	SD	Calculated value statistical test	Critical value	Decision on Ho
Ho 1	Gender	Male Female	47.54 96.67	7.98 16.54	*t*-test = 2.55	1.96	Rejected
Ho 2	Religion	Christianity Islamic	33.34 59.28	3.15 8.91	t-test = 2.10	1.96	Rejected
Ho 3	Marital status	Single Married	91.27 79.56	15.11 10.78	t-test -= 1.34	1.96	Accepted
Ho 4	Age group	≤ 30 years ≥ 31years	83.23 76.67	12.24 10.98	t-test = 1.62	1.96	Accepted
Ho 5	Tribe	Yoruba Hausa Igbo	59.92 51.65 56.67	8.44 7.99 8.21	F-test = 4.03	4.07	Accepted
Ho 6	Institution	Unilag UNAAB UI OAU FUTA UNAD	50.98 54.11 57.02 52.23 51.78 55.56	7.98 8.34 8.41 8.08 8.01 8.39	F-test = 2.98	3.69	Accepted

Ho: Hypothesis. P≤0.05.

hypothesis formulated that, there is no significant difference in the attitudes of university students towards abortion on the basis of marital status was accepted. That is, both single with mean of 91.27 and married with the mean of 79.67 have positive attitude towards abortion. The result of the findings tallied with the submission of Raphael (2001), whose findings revealed that both the single and married students have liberal attitudes toward abortion; over 679 of the students said abortion should be as available to the single as it is to the married students.

On tribes, however, the hypothesis was accepted, meaning that there was no significant difference between Yoruba (59.92), Hausa (51.65) and Igbo (56.67) on their attitudes towards abortion; they all have positive attitudes towards it. This finding corroborated with Olaitan (2010) who in his study on sociodemographic factors, said that the attitudes of Nigerians are more or less the same when it comes to reproductive health issues, regardless of the tribes.

As regards the institutions of the respondents with the following means (Ẍ), UNILAG (54.11), UNAAB (57.02), UI (52.23), FUTA (51.78) and UNAD (55.56); the ANOVA result showed that the hypothesis was accepted. Hence, regardless of the institutions, students have positive attitudes towards abortion. The result of this funding tallied with some of the reasons for abortion in some societies according to Potts et al. (2007) which included the following:

1. For the sake of the mother's health.
2. A pregnancy resulting from a crime like rape or child abuse
3. The child resulting to serious physical deformity, genetic problem and mental defects after delivery.
4. Poverty
5. Regulating population size, etc.

CONCLUSIONS AND RECOMENDAATIONS

Gender and religion have been seen to have significant influence on the attitudes of university students towards abortion; whereas, age, marital status, tribe and institutions have been seen as sociodemographic factors that do not have influence on the attitudes of university students towards abortion. They are of the opinion that abortion should be allowed when it on health conditions of either the mother or the baby to be given birth to, and that abortion should be legalized and people be educated on unsafe abortion.

Based on the findings of this study, the following recommendations were made:

1. The federal government as a matter of urgency should consider legalization of abortion to prevent the practice of abortion in the back street or corner by unqualified medical doctors or quacks.
2. Proper education should be given to young ladies and boys about preventive methods of unsafe abortion.
3. Reproductive health (sex and family life) education should be introduced at secondary and tertiary institutions in the country, for the students to be properly informed on issues such as abortion and other related areas in human sexuality.
5. Further researches should be carried out on areas of abortion and other areas relating reproductive health, sexuality, family life and sex education.

ACKNOWLEDGEMENTS

The author expressed his gratitude to Professor D. B. Parakoyi, the head, Department of Epidemiology and Community Health, University of Ilorin, Nigeria; Professor O. O. Obiyemi, Director of Institute of Education, University of Ilorin, Nigeria, and Professor E. A. Ogunsakin, the head, Department of Human Kinetics and Health Education, University of Ilorin, Nigeria for their valuable comments and suggestions. Also to Professor J. O. Odeyemi of the University of Ibadan for the data analysis and his research assistants, who are Postgraduate students of Public Health and Health Education, University of Ilorin, Nigeria for taking pains to go round the selected institutions for the distribution and collection of questionnaires.

REFERENCES

Adler NE (2001). Abortion: social and psychological perspective. J. Soc. Issues, 35: 100-119.

Christian G (1999). Their right to live: case against legalized abortion, UK law Press, pp. 1-2.

David HP (2003). Abortion policies. In E.S Hodgon (2001) Abortion and sterilization, medical and social aspect: Academic press, Grune and Staton, London.

Golden F (2001). All kind of family planning. Ibadan: African University Press.

Jones KI, Sheinberg IW, Byer AS (2004). Dimension a changing concept of health San Francisco Canfield Press.

Martin EC (2002). Comparing attitude of students towards issues in human sexuality. Int. Digest of Health Legislation, 40. 245-252.

Moore EC (2004). International inventory information and induced abortion. International Institute for the Study of Human Reproduction Columbia University, New York.

Mules SO (2001). The role of physician in post abortion family planning. Med. Pract., 32(516): 63-65.

Okagbue OC (1998). Abortion in Nigeria, Nigerian Med. Pract., 16(4): 135-137.

Olaitan OL (2010). Knowledge of female genital cutting among parents in south west Nigeria. Available online: http://www.transbiomedicne.com ISSN 21f72-0479. Translational Biomed. J., 1(2): 39-40.

Potts M, Diggory P, Peels J (2007). Abortion Cambridge: University Press Cambridge, pp. 12-16.

Raphael BA (2001). Pattern of Induced Abortion, In Kenya and Selected other African Countries P.A.. H.O. Scientific Publication Washington D.C., p. 306.

Roche NJF (2004). Attitudes of American teenagers towards abortion. Fam. Plann. Perspect., 7(3): 89-91.

United Kingdom Abortion Act (2011). United Kingdom abortion act of 1967 in the United Kingdom. Retrieved from: ukabotion.org/abortion act 1967/UK, 10th May, 2011.

APPENDIX

Questionnaire

Questionnaire on attitude of university students towards abortion (qausta) in south West Nigeria

Dear Respondent,
This questionnaire is designed for a sexuality education research in reproductive health research. The attempt is to find out the attitude of University students towards abortion.
Items in the questionnaire are therefore designed to collect information on the research title under study.
You are therefore requested to kindly provide your honest opinion to indicate your attitudes towards abortion. Any information supplied will be treated strictly confidentially.
Thanks for your anticipated co-operation.

Yours sincerely,
O. 'Lanre OLAITAN, *Ph.D.*
Reproductive and Family Health Specialist
University of Ilorin, Nigeria
(Researcher)

Section A: Bio-data

Instruction: Please tick [√] where applicable to you.
Gender: (A) Male [ ] (B) Female [ ]
Religion: (A) Christian [ ] (B) Muslim [ ] (C) Traditional [ ]
Marital status: (A) Single [ ] (B) Married [ ]
Age group: (A) ≤ 30 years [ ] (B) ≥ 31 years [ ]
Tribe: (A) Yoruba [ ] (B) Hausa [ ] (C) Igbo [ ]
Institution ....

Section B: Information on abortion

Instruction: Please tick [√] the following columns appropriately

S/N	Statement	SA	A	D	SD
1	Abortion is a method of birth control				
2	Abortion is good when it is on health condition				
3	Abortion should be done in case of rape				
4	Unmarried women should go for abortion in case of unwanted pregnancy				
5	Abortion is preferable than forced marriage when pregnancy occurred				
6	Abortion is an immoral act				
7	Abortion is a social problem of the society				
8	Abortion is the same thing as murder				
9	Legality of abortion in Nigeria is not effective				
10	Legalization of abortion reduces maternal mortality rates				
11	Infertility results from series of abortion				
12	Premature delivery usually cause series of abortion				
13	Emotional stress can be as a result of frequent abortion				
14	There should be serious enlightenment on abortion				
15	Abortion should be legalized without any restriction				
16	Abortion causes psychological trauma on people				
17	Married women should be engaged in abortion				
18	Abortion should not be forced on anybody				
19	Abortion should be a decision of the women concerned				
20	Abortion should be seen as part of reproductive health care				

Changes in oestrous cycle of adult female wistar rats treated with artemether

A. A. Abiodun[1], B. A. Falana[2] and I. P. Oyeyipo[2]

[1]Department of Anatomy and Cell Biology Obafemi Awolowo University, Ile-Ife, Nigeria.
[2]Department of Anatomy, College of Health Sciences, Osun State University, Osogbo, Nigeria.

Artemether is an ante malaria that has proved rapidly effective. It has replaced chloroquine and quinine is many parts of the world. This is an experimental study designed to examine the effects or artemether on oestrous cycle of lower primates since this drug is highly consumed by females in child bearing age. Twenty four cyclic female rats were randomly divided into three groups A, B and C all administered 10 mg/kg body weight of rat for 24, 48 and 96 h, respectively intramuscularly. Estrous cycles were established by vagina smears taken daily and smears examined under the light microscope. Results of this study show prolongation of various phases of the oestrous cycle in many of the rats. This was however reversible and dose dependent. It was concluded that arthemeter treatment altered estrous cycles in rats, thus distortion of menstrual cycle should be borne in mind in patients taking this drug.

Key words: Artemether, estrous cycle, vaginal smear, *Rattus norvegicus*.

INTRODUCTION

Artemether is a lipid soluble methylether of dihydroartemisinin. Artemisinin is a novel sesquiterpene lactone, extracted from the leaves of the shrub *Artemesia annua* and possesses an endoperoxide bridge which is a rare feature in natural products. The Endoperoxide Bridge is essential for its antimalarial activity.

Its chemical formula is 3R,5aS,6R,8aS,9R,10S,12R, 12aR)-Decahydro-10-methoxy-3,6,9-trimethyl-3,12-epoxy -12H-pyrano[4,3-j]-1,2-benzodioxepin. Its molecular formula is $C_{16}H_{26}O_5$ and its molecular weight is 298.4.

Clinical pharmacology

Artemether is active against all Plasmodia including those which may be resistant to other antimalarials.

Artemether has very rapid schizontocidal activity. The schizontocidal activity of artemether is mainly due to destruction of the asexual erythrocytic forms of *P. falciparum* and *P. vivax*.

Artemether is concentrated in the food vacuole. It then splits its endoperoxide bridge as it interacts with haem, blocking conversion to haemozoin, destroying existing haemozoin and releasing haem and a cluster of free radicals into the parasite. There is inhibition of protein synthesis during growth of trophozoites. There is no cross resistance with chloroquine.

Artemether is not active against hypnozoites, therefore, an 8- amino-quinoline derivative such as primaquine should be given sequentially after the combination in cases of mixed infections of *P. falciparum* and *P. vivax* to achieve hypnozoites eradication.

Artemether reduces gametocyte carriage. There is no rationale at present for using artemether for chemoprophylaxis.

Pharmacokinetics

The drug is slowly absorbed from intramuscular injection. Peak plasma concentrations have been achieved in about 6 h after intramuscular injection of artemether. Artemether is hydrolyzed after administration to a biologically active metabolite, dihydroartemisinin. Dihydroartemisinin accounts for most or all of clinical antimalarial activity.

Total protein binding is 95.4%. The drug is rapidly and extensively metabolised in the liver.

*Corresponding author. E-mail: benabiola@yahoo.com

In animal studies, unchanged artemether has not been detected in both faeces and urine due to its rapid and high first-pass metabolism, but several metabolites (unidentified) have been detected in both faeces and urine.

The elimination half-life is approximately 1 h, but following intramuscular administration, the elimination phase is prolonged because of continued absorption.

The elimination half life of dihydroartemisinin was approximately 2 h. Artemether has been reported to clear fever in severe falciparum malaria within 30 - 84 h.

Indications

Artemether injection is indicated for treatment of severe and complicated malaria caused by *P. falciparum* both in adults and children in areas where there is multidrug resistance.

Contraindications

Artemether is contraindicated in patients with hypersensitivity to artemether or other artemisinin compounds.

Artemether is not recommended in the first trimester of pregnancy because of limited data.

Intramuscular antemether and dihydroartemisin tablets have proved rapidly effective and they have replaced chloroquine and quinine in China and many parts of the world (LI-GQ, 1994). In a study artemether caused abortion in 4% and still births in 3% of kaven pregnant women in Thailand (McGready, 1998).

Ovarian activity is initiated by LH after which the subsequent LH stimulation does not alter or affect it (Lipner, 1973). Its activity begins about 4th -5th day of age (Uilenbroek and Van der Linden, 1983). It is initiated through follicular growth independent of gonadotrophins (Peter and Byskor, 1973). At this period, ovarian histology show non-growing oocytes in groups and surrounded by the closest stromal cells, destined to differentiate and form the first set of granulosa cells (Byskot and Lintern-Moors, 1973).

The mean oestrous cycle in 4.4 days (Abiodun, 2002) or 4.5 days (Blandau, 1955). Proestrus lasts for 12 - 14 h, Estrous 25 - 27, Metestrus 6 - 8 h and Diestrus 55 - 57 h.

MATERIALS AND METHODS

Twenty four rats weighing 150 - 180 g were acclimatized for one week in the animal house of the department of Anatomy and cell biology OAU Ile-Ife Nigeria.

Their oestrous cycles were established by daily vaginal smear taken with (Abiodun, 2002); Blandau (Blandau, 1955) Ashtwood separate pipettes containing physiological saline (0.9 Nacl). Under light microscope, smears were examined to determine the epithelia cells predominantly present in the vaginal lavage.

RESULTS

Treatment on proestrous

Three groups of rats were treated with 10 mg/kg body weight of artemether at 1000, 1400 and 1800 h proestrous, respectively. All continued into oestrous.the following day. Later there was prolongation of proestrous in many members administered 10 mg/kg body weight between 24 and 96 h (4 days).

Treatment on oestrous

Dose of 10 mg/kg body weight of the drug was administered for two consecutive days to members of this group. About half of the members of the group had normal oestrous cycle after the first dose while the remaining had prolonged diestrous II before entering proestrous and oestrous.

Treatment on diestrous I and II

10 mg/kg body weight of the drug was given to this group. It showed prolongation of Diestrous I in all the members varying from one to four days.

These photomicrographs are characteristic for early oestrous development after a period of anoestrus. The vaginal smear of control cases showed fewer cells than that shown in Figures 1 to 9.

Examination of vaginal smears in the rat administered arthemeter

Dioestrus: At this stage of the oestrous cycle there is little material to be collected, and it consists mainly of traces of secretory material with cellular debris. There are few intact cells to be found. Some parabasal and intermediary cells may be observed. There are usually few leucocytes, if any, to be seen (Figure 1).

Transition from dioestrus to pro-oestrus

There is considerably more mucus at this stage, often present as thick strands or discs. The histological picture is more complex and darker. Leucocytes are rarely seen in pro-oestrus. Most of the cells present are parabasal cells, often with an irregular or shrunken appearance, but intermediary cells may also be observed (Figure 2).

Early pro-oestrus: The smear becomes "cleaner", with less mucus. Parabasal cells appear more clearly, as do

Figure 1. showed the estrous cycle of rats treated with 10 mg/kg body weight arthemeter for 24 h, there is little material to be collected, and it consists mainly of traces of secretory material with cellular debris. There are few intact cells to be found. Some parabasal and intermediary cells were observed.

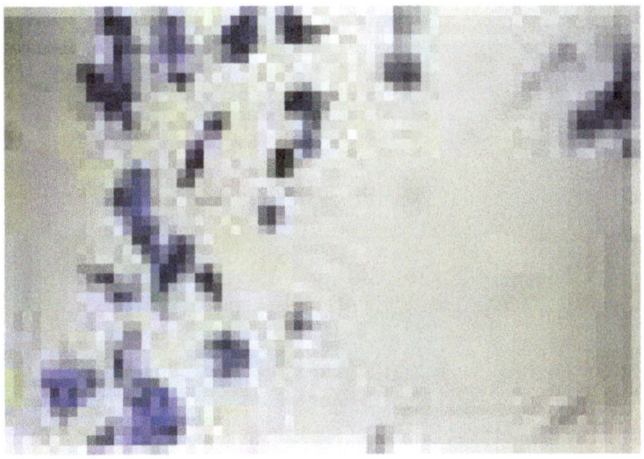

Figure 2. Showed photomicrograph of the proestrous stage of rats treated with 10 mg/kg body weight of arthemeter for 48 h, here, more mucus was observed at this stage, present as thick strands or discs. The histological picture is more complex and darker. Leucocytes. Most of the cells present are parabasal cells.

intermediary cells. Cell debris can still be observed.

Pro-oestrus: The smear is much lighter in colour and mucus is rarely seen. The cells are predominately intermediary cells, and parabasal cells are rare. Lecocytes are hardly ever observed (Figure 3).

The transition from pro-oestrus to oestrus

The smear is clear and dominated by cells. These consist of intermediary cells, superficial cells and anuclear (keratinised) cells.

Oestrus: The smear consists nearly entirely of keratinised superficial cells that lie singly in early oestrus.

Figure 3. This smear is much lighter in colour and mucus is rarely seen. The cells are predominately intermediary cells, and parabasal cells are now rare probably as a consequence of the treatment. Lecocytes were not observed.

Figure 4. Showed photomicrographs of rats treated with 10 mg/kg body weight of arthemeter for 72 h. A few intermediary cells with intact nuclei may occasionally be observed probably as a consequence the treatment and duration of administration.

They form groups as oestrus progresses and by the end of this stage of the cycle they can form large flakes (Figure 4). A few intermediary cells with intact nuclei may occasionally be observed.

The transition from oestrus to metoestrus

Although flakes of keratinised cells are still present, this stage is characterised by the presence of leucocytes and (to a lesser extent) intermediary cells.

Metoestrus: The picture at this stage of the cycle is dominated by leucocytes, often in large numbers, and intermediary cells (Figure 5).

As this stage progresses, more intermediary cells begin to appear. These are often small and dark. Parabasal cells can also be seen. However, larger intermediary cells and leucocytes are also present (Figure 6).

Figure 5. Photomicrograph of the smear of the metestrous stage rats treated with 10 mg/kg body weight arthemeter for 72 h leucocytes, are in large numbers, and intermediary cells.

Figure 6. As this stage progresses, more intermediary cells begin to appear. These are often small and dark. The figure showed smear of rats treated with 10 mg/kg body weight of arthemeter for 24 h, compared to figure 5 above, Parabasal cells were observed. However, larger intermediary cells and leucocytes are also present.

The transition from metoestrus to dioestrus

This stage is characterised by the reduction in cell numbers and the reappearance of mucus. Often in thin strands (Figure 7).

This picture shows a continuation of this process, as the mucus becomes progressively more apparent and cell numbers decline (Figure 8).

Anoestrus: The cellular picture at this stage resembles in many ways the transition from dioestrus to pro-oestrus, but the general picture is darker, the cells rarely appear intact and there is a lot of mucus and cellular debris. It is often at this stage that the rat's oestrous cycle may halt.

Figure 7. Photomicrograph of rats treated with 10 mg/kg arthemeter for this stage is characterized by the reduction in cell numbers and the reappearance of mucus. Often in thin strands.

Figure 8. Photomicrograph of rats treated with 10 mg/kg arthemeter for 48 h metestrous as compared to 72 h. This stage is characterized by mucus, and it becomes progressively more apparent and cell numbers decline.

Figure 9. Photomicrograph of rats treated with 10 mg/kg arthemeter for 48 h metestrous as compared to group of rays treated with arthemeter for 24 h.

The transition from pro-oestrus to oestrus

Figure 9 shows a characteristic early oestrous development after a period of anoestrus. The vaginal smear may in some cases show fewer cells than in this picture (Figure 9).

Figures 1 to 9 show the observed daily vaginal smear taken on rats treated with 10 mg/kg body weight arthemeter intramuscularly.

DISCUSSION

Oestrous cycle has been known to be disrupted by genetic, nutritional and endocrine factors. Several drugs affect oestrous cycle by acting at different levels of hypothalamic-pituitary axis or at ovarian level to inhibit ovulation (Astwood, 1939). In this present investigation, effect of artemether on oestrous cycle showed that it altered the oestrous cycle. His alteration is dose dependent and reversible thus when the drug is withdrawn the cycle returns back to normal. This is similar to observation on Halofanthrine studies (Psychopharmacology, 2000). Therefore distortion of menstrual cycle should be borne in mind in patient using it. Withdrawal of function thus causing delay in piestrous and metestrus. The drug should therefore be made in event of distortion. The delay in oestrous circle is probably due to the fact that arthemeter treatment inhibits the hormonal function probably while compromising cellular integrity and function. Influence of sex, estrous cycle, and drug-onset age on cocaine self-administration in rats (*Rattus norvegicus*). Kantak et al in their work investigated the influence of sex, phases of the estrous cycle, and age of drug onset on cocaine self-administration .Adult male, adult female, and adolescent male rats (*R. norvegicus*) were evaluated using low fixed-ratio (FR) schedules of drug delivery with a single fixed cocaine unit dose or a range of cocaine unit doses with a single FR schedule. Sex differences in adults were observed for mg/kg consumption of the 3.0 mg/kg unit dose, with consumption being significantly less in estrus females than in males. Over the estrous cycle, mg/kg consumption of this unit dose was significantly less during estrus than during metestrus-diestrus. Differences due to age of drug onset were also observed, with mg/kg consumption of the 3.0 mg/kg unit dose being significantly less in adolescent males than adult males or adult females during metestrus-diestrus. In contrast, these various groups did not have significantly different mg/kg intakes of cocaine unit doses <3.0 mg/kg, nor did they significantly differ in the rates and patterns of responding and number of infusions earned as a function of FR schedule or unit dose of cocaine available. The role of sex, estrus cycle, and drug-onset age on cocaine self-administration appears to be minimal under these experimental conditions. Experimental conditions that favor no sex or age differences in cocaine intake (1.0 mg/kg unit dose and low FR) may be useful for evaluating potential sex or age differences in the consequences of cocaine self-administration more reliably, as cocaine intake would not be an uncontrolled factor in comparison to this study, arthemeter administration was only observed in female wistar rats thus found to inhibit estrous cycle.

RECOMMENDATION

It was recommended that studies on age, sex and after effects of loading dose of arthemeter should be subjected for future studies including hematological parameters.

ACKNOWLEDGEMENT

Authors are grateful to Mr Gbela of the histopathology department of college of health sciences OAU Ile Ife Nigeria for the technical assistance.

REFERENCES

Abiodun AA (2002). Effects of halofanthrine on Oestrous cycle, Ovulation and microscopic structure of the Ovary: Biosci. Res. Comm., 14(1): 11-14.

Astwood EB (1939). Changes in weight and water content of uterus of the normal adult rat. Am. J. Physiol., 126: 162-170.

Blandau RJ (1955). Ovulation in the living albino rat. Fertil. Steril., 6: 391-404.

Byskot AG, Lintern – Moors S (1973): Follicle formation in the immature ovary; the role of the rete ovari J. Anat., 116: 207-217.

Li-G, Guo XB, Fu LC (1994). Clinical trials of artemisinin and its derivatives in the treatment of malaria in China. Trans. Royal Soc. Trop. Med. Hyg., 88(1): 55-56.

Lipner H (1973). Mechanism of mammalian ovulation. The handbook of Physoilogy, Endocrinology, 2(1): 409-437.

McGready R, Cho T, Cho JJ (1998). Artemisnin derivatives in the treatment of falciparum malarial in pregnancy, Trans. Royal Soc. Trop. Med. Hyg., 92: 430-433.

Peter SH, Byskor AG (1973). The effect of gonadotrophin and follicle growth initiation in neonatal mouse ovary. J. Reprod. Fertil., 35: 139-141.

Psychopharmacology (Berl) (2000). Effects of sex and the estrous cycle on regulation of intravenously self-administered cocaine in rats, 152(2): 132-139.

Uilenbroek J, Van DLR (1983). Changes in gonadotrophin binding to rat ovaries during sexual maturation. Acta Endocrinil. (Copenh), 103: 413-419.

28

Differential behavioral outcome of anxiety tests in runner rats treated with corticosterone

Suk-Yu Yau[1,2,3], Benson Wui-Man Lau[1,2], Tatia M. C. Lee[2,4,5,6] and Kwok-Fai So[1,2,3,7]*

[1]Department of Anatomy, Li Ka Shing Faculty of Medicine, University of Hong Kong, SAR, Hong Kong.
[2]State Key laboratory of Brain and Cognitive Science, Li Ka Shing Faculty of Medicine, University of Hong Kong, SAR, Hong Kong.
[3]Research Centre of Heart, Brain, Hormone and Health Aging, SAR, Li Ka Shing Faculty of Medicine, University of Hong Kong, SAR, Hong Kong.
[4]Laboratory of Neuropsychology, University of Hong Kong, SAR, Hong Kong.
[5]Institute of Clinical Neuropsychology, University of Hong Kong, SAR, Hong Kong.
[6]Laboratory of Cognitive Affective Neuroscience, University of Hong Kong, SAR, Hong Kong.
[7]JGHM Institute of CNS Regneration,Jinan University and The University of Hong Kong, Guangzhou, China

Both clinical and pre-clinical studies have suggested that physical exercise is beneficial for lowering anxiety. However, some animal studies fail to demonstrate the anxiolytic effect of physical exercise. The inconsistencies among studies may be due to differences in animal models and behavioral tests. Previously, injection of corticosterone (CORT) for 14 days induced depression-like behavior to varying based on was shown. Animal model was used to investigate whether CORT treatment induced anxiety-like behavior and to examine the anxiolytic effect of voluntary running using two behavioral measurements: open field test and elevated plus maze. Results indicated that running reduced anxiety-like behavior in vehicle-treated animals in both tests. Treatment with CORT showed a significant anxiogenic effect in the open field test regardless of the doses, but not in the elevated plus maze. Running reduced anxiety in theopen field test, but showed no effect in elevated plus maze in the CORT-treated rats. The data suggest the discrepancy of these two anxiety-related measures in the animal model of stress.

Key words: Corticosterone (CORT), stress, voluntary running, open field test, elevated plus maze, anxiety-like behavior.

INTRODUCTION

Hippocampus is not only involved in cognitive functions, but also plays an important role in emotional regulation (Mac, 1949) and anxiety state (Bannerman et al., 2004). In our daily life, we always face challenges that are anxiogenic, for example sitting for an examination, job interviews and public presentations. Anxiety is a normal response to a stressor that helps an individual to promptly cope with the demanding situation. Anxiety disorder presents as an excessive pathological form of fear consisting of a fear state with excessive reaction for the actual threat. Anxiety disorder frequently presents in clinical psychiatry with a 30% occurrence rate. In addition, patients with co-occurring symptoms of anxiety always show worsened severity of depression (Mineka et al., 1998).

In animal studies, it has been shown that exposure to acute uncontrollable stressors cause a variety of behaviors called learned helplessness such as exaggerated shock elicited freezing; deficits in shuttle box escape learning. These kinds of stress responses have been suggested to represent the animal analogs of human anxiety (Maier and Watkins, 1998). Physical exercise is known to reduce the signs and symptoms of anxiety disorder and depression with support from a number of human studies (Dun et al., 2001; Merali et al., 2003;

*Corresponding author. E-mail: hrmaskf@hku.hk.

Blumenthal et al., 2007). Recently, it has been reported that exercise could exert similar anxiolytic effect as antidepressant treatment in animals (Duman et al., 2008). Preventative and curative effects of physical exercise in depression- and anxiety-like behaviors in animal model have also been reported (Binder et al., 2004; Dulawa et al., 2004). In vehicle-treated rats, four or eight weeks of wheel running is able to alter anxiety behavior in the open field test, but not in the elevated plus maze (Burghardt et al., 2004). Chronic running (6-week) reduces anxiety-like behaviors in terms of exaggerated shock-elicited freezing and shuttle box escape deficits in rats exposed to uncontrollable stress (McKinney and Bunney, 1969). However, inconsistent effects of exercise in the animal models of anxiety have also been found in different studies in which animals with voluntary wheel running show anxiolytic effect (Duman et al., 2008; Salam et al., 2009), no effect (Chiang et al., 2010) or anxiogenic effect (Burghardt et al., 2004). The differences in animal models (normal or stressed animals), animal species, and behavioral tests may contribute to the inconsistencies among those studies.

Psychiatric patients suffering from depressive disorders are often associated with hyperactivation of hypothalamus-pituitary-adrenal axis (HPA axis) that leads to elevated plasma corticosteroids. Animal models with repeated stress have been widely used to study the neurobiological changes following stress exposure (Nestler et al., 2002). However, this model may increase the experimental variability since individual differences in the activation of HPA axis in response to stress exposure may result in different levels of CORT elevation among different individuals exposed to the same stressor. The alternative way is to use repeated exogenous CORT administration as a mean to mimic the effect of stress that associated with elevated CORT levels. This model could provide an effective control over the increases in blood CORT levels in the animals and increase depression-like behavior in rats in a dose-dependent manner (Yau et al., 2011b).

However, exogenous administration of CORT has been reported to both increase (Calvo et al., 1998) or decrease (Andreatini and Leite, 1994) the anxiety level in the elevated plus-maze. It is unclear whether the discrepancy is due to dose effect of CORT treatment. It has previously been reported that treatment with different doses of CORT for 14 days produced a graded increase in depression-like behavior and plasma CORT level (Yau et al., 2011b). Furthermore, wheel running or antidepressant treatment could counteract CORT-induced depression-like behavior and depression-impaired memory in the rats. Since there is no experimental data on measuring anxiety-like behavior in animals treated with different doses of CORT, in the present paper, we used different doses of CORT administrations to examine whether there was an increase in anxiety-like behavior in CORT-treated rats; and to characterize the effects of voluntary running on anxiety-related behaviors in the open field test and the elevated plus maze (the two behavioral paradigms that are commonly used in anxiety tests).

In vehicle-treated rats, the results showed that voluntary running reduced anxiety-like behaviors in the open field test and elevated plus maze. In the CORT-treated rats, the anxiety level was significantly increased by CORT treatment and decreased by running in the open field test. However, in the elevated plus maze, neither CORT treatment nor voluntary running affected the anxiety level in the CORT-treated rats. The data may indicate a discrepancy in measuring the anxiety-like behavior between the open field tests and elevated plus maze in the CORT-injected rat model of stress.

MATERIALS AND METHODS

Animal group and treatment

Adult Sprague Dawley (250 ± 20 g, 6 to 7 weeks old) male rats were obtained from the Laboratory Animal Unit, University of Hong Kong. All experimental procedures were approved and followed the guidelines of the Committee on the Use of Live Animals in Teaching and Research, University of Hong Kong. Rats were kept on a 12 h light-dark cycle with *ad libitum* access to food and water. The animals were divided into runner and non-runner groups and were treated with different doses of CORT (30, 40 and 50 mg/kg) or sesame oil for 14 days (n = 8 to 10/group). The day after the CORT treatment (day 15), the rats were subjected to the open field test and elevated plus maze to examine anxiety-like behavior.

Corticosterone (CORT) treatment

CORT (Sigma-Aldrich, USA) at different doses (30, 40 and 50 mg/kg) and sesame oil were prepared and injected subcutaneously according to the method of Hellsten et al. (2002). The dose of 40 mg/kg has been reported to elevete blood levels of CORT over a 24 h period (Sapolsky et al., 1985). A stock of CORT emulsion was prepared by suspending CORT in sesame oil, followed by vortex and sonication. Injection (0.8 ml/ rat) was made subcutaneously in the neck region daily at 4:00 p.m. The CORT treatment was started at the same time when the rats were allowed to run. The control rats received daily injections of sesame oil.

Voluntary wheel running

Runner rats were housed singly in polyethylene cages equipped with running wheels (diameter, 31.8 cm; width, 10 cm; Nalgene Nunc International, NY). Animals were allowed to familiarize with living condition with locked wheels for 3 days prior to the treatment. The locked wheels were then unlocked for 14 days in the runner groups or kept locked for the non-runner groups. Wheel revolutions were recorded by computer using VitalViewer software (Mini Mitter Company, Inc, OR). Non-runners were housed with locked running wheels in cages identical to that of runners.

Open field test

The behavioral test was conducted in a quiet and dimmed room with constant illumination; the test was performed from 2:00 to 4:00 p.m. After 2 h of habituation in the test room, each rat was individually placed into the center of the open field arena (90 × 90 cm with 40 cm-high side walls). The locomotor activity was recorded for 5 min by a video camera. The arena was then cleaned with 70% ethanol and dried with towel for each trial. Results were analyzed using the Smart Junior software (Panlab, Spain). The open field was broken into two zones for analysis: the peripheral and central zones. Anxiety-like behaviors were indicated by the time spent in the peripheral and central areas, while locomotor activity was indicated by average traveling speed and distance over 5 min in the arena.

Elevated plus maze

Each rat was tested in the elevated plus maze 2 h after the open field test in the same room under the same lighting condition. The elevated plus-maze consisted of four arms made of Plexiglas, elevated 50 cm above the floor. Two arms were open (0.5 cm high edges), while the other two arms were enclosed with 36 cm high wall. Each animal was placed onto the center of the apparatus facing an open arm and was then evaluated for 5 min test. The maze was wiped with 70% ethanol and dried between each trial. The behavior was recorded with a video camera and then analyzed using Smart Junior system (Panlab, Spain). Anxiety-like behavior was evaluated through percent time spent in open and closed arms.

Statistical analysis

Two-way analysis of variance (ANOVA) with CORT treatment and running as between-subject factors was performed with Fisher's LSD post-hoc test. A repeated measure ANOVA was applied for analyzing body weight change and running activity over the 14-day treatment period. Student's t-test was only applied for comparison between vehicle-treated non-runners and runners. The statistical difference was determined with P-value < 0.05. Data were presented as mean± standard error of mean (SEM).

RESULTS

Change of body weight and adrenal gland weight

Weight loss of the adrenal gland which occurs after CORT treatment indicates the efficacy of subcutaneous injections of CORT. Repeated measures of ANOVA revealed a significant change in body weight gain during the 14-day treatment period (Figure 1a and b), effect of day: $F_{3,57} = 19.2$, $P = 0.00090$). Significant interaction between day and CORT treatment on body weight change was also observed (day X CORT: $F_{3,57} = 44.9$; $P = 0.00053$). CORT treatment and running decreased body weight gain during the treatment (effect of CORT: $F_{3,57} = 57.2$, $P = 0.0077$; effect of running: $F_{1,57} = 7.7$, $P = 0.00050$). The adrenal gland weight was expressed as the ratio of adrenal gland weight to body weight. Two-way ANOVA indicated that the ratio of adrenal gland to body weight was significantly decreased by CORT treatment (effect of CORT: $F_{3,57}=142.7$, $P=0.00033$) (Figure 1c), but was not affected by running (effect of running, $F_{1,57} = 1.1$, $P = 0.300$).

Running activity of CORT-treated runners

Repeated measures ANOVA indicated that all rats increased their running activity during the treatment period (Figure 2: $F_{3,38} = 14.8$, $P = 0.00042$). The runners showed increased running activity during the treatment period (effect of day: $F_{3,38} = 5.8$, $P = 0.0060$). Runners with CORT treatment showed a relative higher running activity when compared to runners with vehicle treatment; however, there was no significant effect of CORT on increasing running activity (effect of CORT: $F_{3,38} = 1.4$, $P = 0.29$).

Running and CORT treatment did not affect locomotor activity in the rats

Results showed that neither CORT treatment nor running for 14 days affected traveling distance (Figure 3a: effect of running: $F_{1,50} = 1.0$, $P = 0.75$; effect of CORT: $F_{3,50} = 1.8$, $P = 0.16$) and travelling speed (Figure 3b: effect of running: $F_{1,50} = 1.4$, $P = 0.24$; effect of CORT: $F_{3,50} = 1.$, $P = 0.15$) in the open field test. This data suggests that the difference in anxiety-like behavior was not an artifact of altered locomotor activity following CORT treatments.

Anxiety behavior of the CORT-treated runners and non-runners in the open field test

Anxiety-like behavior of the rats was tested in the open field test and elevated plus maze following the 14-day treatment. In the open field test, CORT, nor running showed no significant effect on the time spent in the central area (Figure 3c: effect of CORT: $F_{3,56} = 0.8$, $P = 0.52$; effect of running: $F_{1,56} = 1.4$, $P = 0.25$). However, there was a relative increase in time spent in the central area in the vehicle-treated runners when compared with the vehicle-treated non-runners (student's t-test, $P < 0.05$), indicating running reduced anxiety level in the vehicle-treated rats.

Time spent in the peripheral area was increased by CORT (Figure 3d: effect of CORT: $F_{3,47} = 3.0$, $P = 0.042$). Post hoc analysis showed that the rats treated with 30 and 40 mg/kg CORT demonstrated a significant increase in time spent in the peripheral area when compared with the vehicle-treated rats ($P < 0.05$). The main effect of running was also observed (effect of running: $F_{1,47} = 16.7$, $P = 0.00021$), indicating running decreased anxiety level in CORT-treated rats in the open field test. There was a significant decrease in time spent in the peripheral area in the vehicle-treated runners when compared with the vehicle-treated non-runners (student's t-test, $P < 0.05$).

Effect of CORT and running on anxiety-like behavior in elevated plus maze

There was no significant effect of CORT and running on the locomotor behavior in the elevated plus maze (data not shown). Running and CORT treatment was ineffective

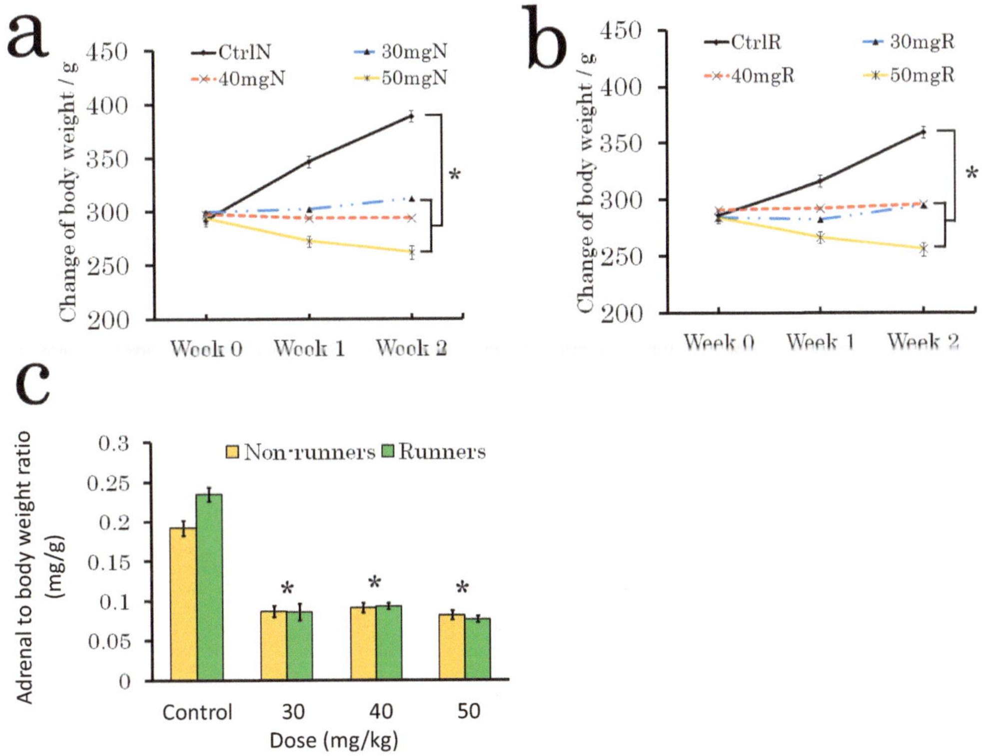

Figure 1. Change of body weight and adrenal weight of the CORT-treated runners and non-runners. (a and b) Body weight gain was significantly decreased by CORT treatments in the non-runners and runners. Running reduced body weight gain. (c) Adrenal to body weight ratio was an indicator for the efficacy of CORT administration. A significantly decreased adrenal weight was found in the CORT-treated rats when compared with the vehicle-treated rats. Ctrl: Vehicle treatment; 30, 40 and 50 mg: doses of CORT per body weight (kg). N: non-runners; R: runners. Value are respresented as mean±SEM. *P < 0.005 compared to the vehicle-treated group.

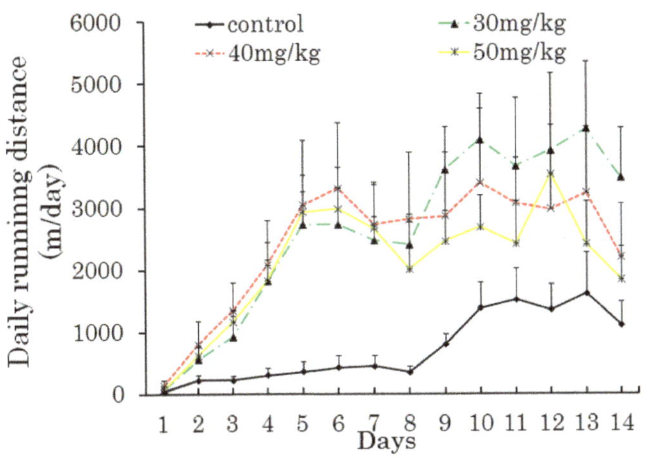

Figure 2. Voluntary running activity of the CORT- and vehicle-treated rats. The running activity was increased in the first week, and was then maintained at the level of 2 to 4 km/day. The rats treated with CORT showed a relatively higher running activity as compared to the vehicle-treated control. Data are expressed as daily mean running distance (m) per day mean ± SEM.

ineffective in altering the time spent in the open arms (Figure 4a: effect of running: $F_{1,51} = 0.1$, $P = 0.71$; effect of CORT: $F_{3,51} = 0.6$, $P = 0.63$) and in the closed arms (Figure 4b: effect of running: $F_{1,54} = 1.5$, $P = 0.23$; effect of CORT: $F_{3,51} = 0.4$, $P = 0.34$). The CORT-treated runners and non-runners did not show an increase or decrease in time spent in the open arms and closed arms, indicating that CORT treatment alone or running in CORT-treated rats did not exert effects on anxiety-like behavior in the elevated plus maze. Furthermore, CORT treatment showed no effect on time spent in the center (Figure 4c: effect of CORT: $F_{1,51} = 1.11$, $P = 0.35$). Conversely, running showed a main effect on time spent in the center (effect of running: $F_{1,51} = 6.06$, $P = 0.018$). Running showed an anxiolytic effect in the vehicle-treated runners as evidenced by relatively decreased percentage of time spent in the closed arms, and increased time spent in the open arms when compared with the vehicle-treated non-runners (student's t-test: $P < 0.05$).

DISCUSSION

In the present study, we used the open field test and elevated plus maze to examine: (1) whether different doses of repeated CORT treatment could induce anxiety-

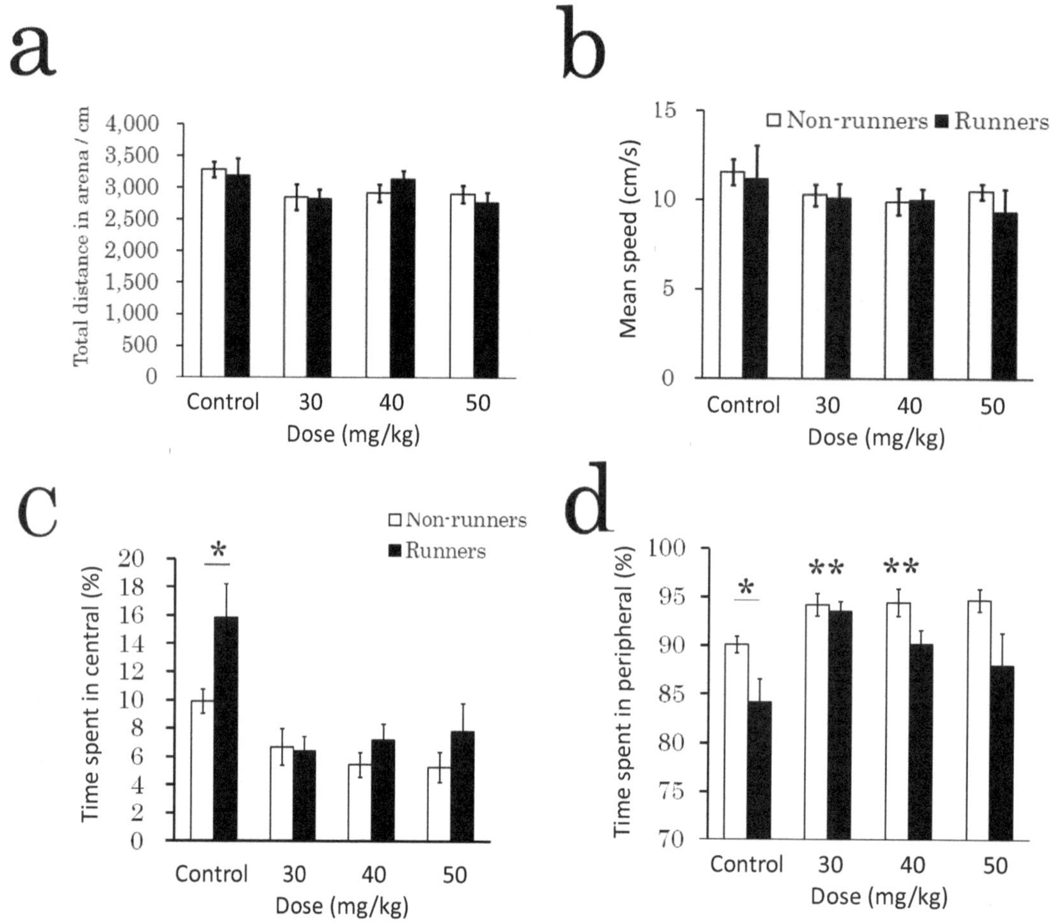

Figure 3. Locomotor activity and anxiety-like behavior of runners and non-runners in the open field test. (a) CORT treatment did not affect locomotor activity in the runners and non-runners. There was no significant difference in the mean speed of the CORT-treated runners and non-runners. (b) Total distance in the arena of the CORT-treated rats remained in the similar level as the vehicle-treated rats. (c) The CORT-treated rats showed no difference in time spent in the central area of the arena when compared with the vehicle-treated rats. However, running significantly increased the time spent in the central area in the vehicle-treated rats, but not the CORT-treated rats. (d) Rats treated with CORT showed increased time spent in the peripheral area. Runners showed a significant decrease in time spent in the peripheral area of the arena when compared to the non-runners. The vehicle-treated runners showed significantly decreased time spent in peripheral areas when compared with the vehicle-treated non-runners. Student's t-test: *$P < 0.05$ compared to the vehicle-treated non-runners. One-way ANOVA: **$P < 0.05$ compared to the vehicle-treated rats.

like behaviors; and (2) the counteractive effect of voluntary wheel running on CORT-induced anxiety-like behavior. The vehicle-treated runners showed an increase in time spent in the center of the open field test, in the open arm and the center of the elevated plus maze, respectively.

The findings confirmed that voluntary running for two weeks was associated with a reduced anxiety-like behavior as previously shown in the vehicle-treated rats by other group (Salam et al., 2009). However, CORT treatment increased anxiety level in the open field test, but not in the elevated plus maze. The results raise the question on the discrepancy between these behavioral tests for anxiety-like behavior in animal model of stress.

Although exercise has been shown to reduce anxiety in humans (Dunn et al., 2001; Manger and Motta, 2005) and in exercised animals (Binder et al., 2004), some studies fail to show the anxiolytic effect of exercise (Burghardt et al., 2004; Chiang et al., 2010). Contradictory results on the effects of exercise on anxiety behavior have been reported in some animal studies (Andreatini and Leite, 1994; Calvo et al., 1998). Contradictory results are also found in the open field test and elevated plus maze, for example, same mouse strain was defined as anxious in the elevated plus maze, but non-anxious in the open field test (Trullas and Skolnick, 1993, Rogers et al., 1999). Although these two tests are commonly applied to examine anxiety-like behavior in the animals, the differences in anxiogenic property of these two apparatuses have been reported. Carola et al. (2002) suggested that

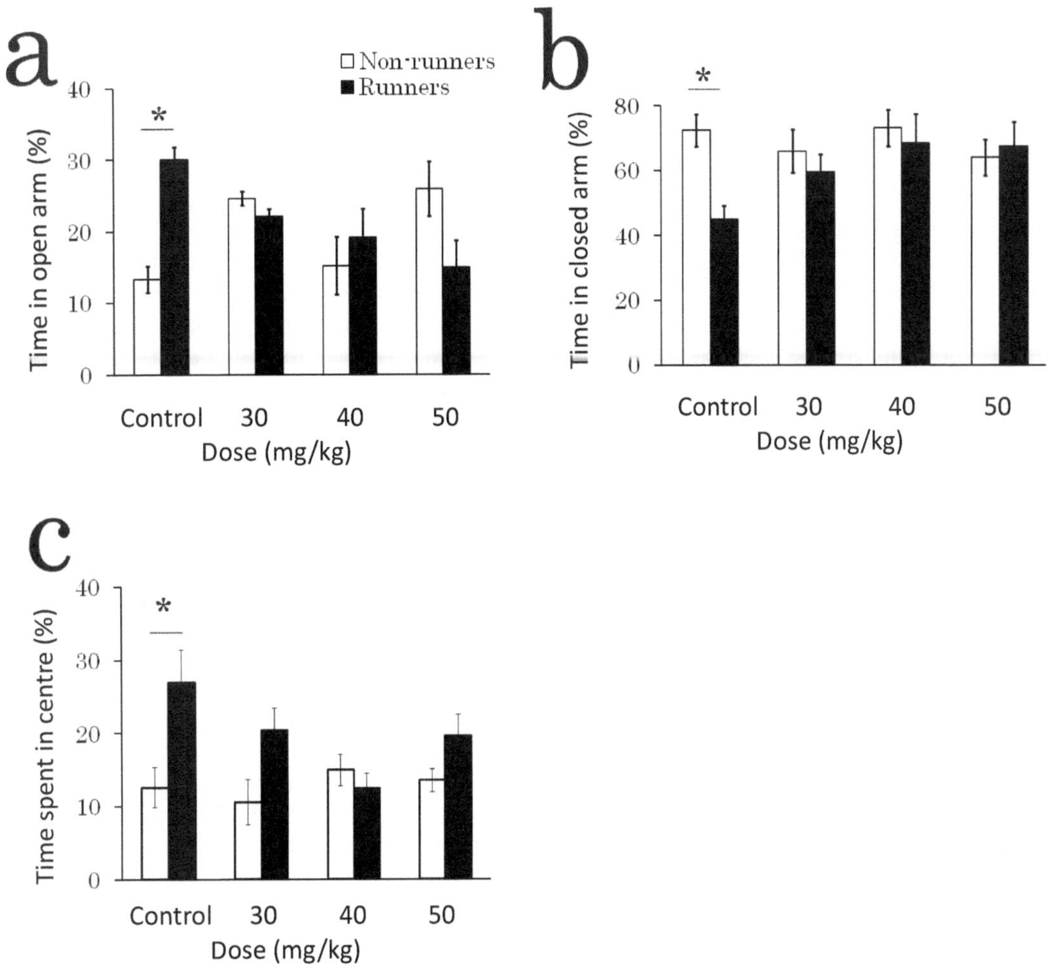

Figure 4. Running decreased anxiety-like behaviour in the vehicle-treated rats, but not CORT-treated rats in the elevated plus maze. Running and CORT treatment did not affect the percentage time spent in the open arms (a) and closed arms (b), respectively. Student's t-test revealed significant increases in time spent in open arms and center (c), and a decrease in time spent in closed arm in the vehicle-treated runners when compared to vehicle-treated non-runners. *P < 0.05 compared to runner counterpart by student's t-test.

discrepancies between these two tests may be due to differences in analyzing criteria among different studies or it is possible that the elevated plus maze may be more anxiogenic to experimental animals than the open field test.

Aversive stress in the open field test is mainly due to the novelty in a new environment, whereas aversive stress in the elevated plus maze is due to novelty and the height of the maze that comprise the behavior of risk assessment during the test, suggesting a stress coping to the animals during the test (Rodgers, 1997). In the elevated plus maze, the animals are placed in the centre of the plus maze as the starting point where animals initially engage in high level of risk assessment, therefore, the design of the elevated plus maze offers more choices and causes a higher level of stress to the animals as compared to the open field test. Nosek et al. (2008) conclude that the differences in the stressfulness between the open field test and elevated plus maze may contribute to the differential outcome. Nosek et al. (2008) suggested that the open field test would be a better measure of passive coping, while the elevated plus maze would be a more sensitive measure of active coping in response to stress.

A consistent result was observed in the vehicle-treated rats that running reduced anxiety level in both the elevated plus maze and open field test. The differential behavioral outcome between these two tests in the CORT-treated rats may suggest a differential stress response between these two tests in our CORT-injected rats. Pre-exposure to the open field test may contribute as a confounding effect since pre-exposure to different novel environment (e.g. the open field) immediately before testing in the elevated plus maze may alter the motor activity in the elevated plus maze and lead to a greater preference of entering the open arms of the maze

(Pellow et al., 1985). However, Walf and Frye (2007) reported that pre-exposure to other testing environment does not alter subsequent behavior of rats and mice in the elevated plus maze. To avoid any possibility of different experience or stressor exposure altering the behavior of rats in the elevated plus maze, the rats were left in the transport cages for 2 h before testing to ensure that the experimental rats have similar level of stress exposure before the behavioral test. Therefore, it is unlikely that the order effect will be a confounding variable to our study. Prut and Belzung (2003) suggested that the open field test is not a valid test for anxiety as it is not sensitive to some effective compounds (e.g. alprozolam and selective serotonin reuptake inhibitor (SSRI)) in treating anxiety disorders, they also concluded that the open field test may be a test for rodent model of normal anxiety.

Increased open field locomotion and decreased anxiety measures following wheel running have been found in the animals after 24 h of wheel running (Dishman et al., 1996; Burghardt et al., 2004). In this study, there was no difference in locomotor activity between the CORT-treated runners and non-runners as indicated by similar activity levels in the open field test and elevated plus maze, though there was a higher running activity in the CORT-treated rats as compared to the vehicle-treated rats.

The presented data shows that CORT treatment significantly increased anxiety-like behavior (increased time spent in peripheral) in the open field test regardless of the doses of CORT treatment, but not in the elevated plus maze. The counteractive effect of running on reducing anxiety-like behavior in CORT-treated rats was only observed in the open field test, but not in elevated plus maze. Gregus et al. (2005) reported that CORT (40 mg/kg) treatment for 21 days in non-running rats significantly increased immobility time in the forced swim test, but showed minimal effect on anxiety-like behavior in the open field test. The hippocampus has been known to play a crucial role in anxiety and depression. The dorsal and ventral hippocampi exhibit discrete functions in regulating learning and emotion, respectively. It has been reported that lesions of dorsal hippocampus led to relatively a weak anxiolytic-like effect, while lesions of ventral hippocampus produced a robust anxiolytic-like effect (Bertoglio et al., 2006; Pentkowski et al., 2006). Recently, it has been suggested that adult neurogenesis in the dorsal and ventral hippocampus might function in a dissociated way (Duncko et al., 2007) in which the dorsal hippocampus is likely specialized for memory functions, whereas the ventral hippocampus is dedicated to anxiety functions (Engin and Treit, 2007). Our previous study showed that physical exercise in terms of running wheel could protect the animals from detrimental effects of CORT via restoring adult neurogenesis and dendritic atrophy in the dorsal part of the hippocampus (Yau et al., 2011a). Several studies reported that a decrease in hippocampal neurogenesis is associated with an increase in anxiety-related behaviors (Ageta et al., 2008; Bergami et al., 2008; Revest et al., 2009). In particular, Revest et al. (2009) demonstrated an increased anxiety-like behavior in transgenic mice with an inducible reduction in neurogenesis throughout the rostro-caudal axis of the dentate gyrus. It is possible that depressive behavior and memory impairment is more dependent on the dorsal part of the hippocampus, while anxiety behavior is more dependent on the ventral part of the hippocampus.

We have previously reported that the dorsal hippocampal neurogenesis was increased in rats with two-week voluntary wheel running (Yau et al., 2011b). This study demonstrated that running decreased anxiety-like behavior in vehicle-treated rats; the promoting effect of running on adult neurogenesis and structural changes in the ventral hippocampus could possibly contribute to the observed effects of wheel running in our vehicle-treated rats. However, this speculation warrants further investigation with examination on the effects of specific blockade of ventral or dorsal hippocampal neurogenesis on emotional behavior.

In summary, these results have demonstrated that voluntary running reduced anxiety-like behaviors in the vehicle-treated rats in two behavioral paradigms: the open field test and the elevated plus maze. The CORT treatment increased anxiety level in the open field test, but showed an effect in the elevated plus maze. Running primarily reduced anxiety-like behavior in the open field test, but not in the elevated plus maze in the CORT-treated rats. The data indicated a differential anxiety-like behavior measured by these two tests in the CORT-treated rats. Extra attention should be given to the discrepancy of these two anxiety-related measures in animal model of stress since the physiological basis of anxiolytic effect of exercise will only be revealed with consistency of effects of exercise across the anxiety-related measures.

ACKNOWLEDGEMENTS

The authors thank Mr. Peter Ksiazek and Ms. Jennifer Graham for their help in proofreading the manuscript, and Mr. Bolton Chau for his comments on statistical analysis. This study was supported by funding from Jessie Ho Professorship in Neuroscience (The University of Hong Kong Foundation for Educational Development and Research Limited), the National Natural Science Foundation of China, the Areas of Excellence (AoE) Scheme established under the University Grants Committee of the Hong Kong and AoE Matching Fund from the University of Hong Kong and the Fundamental Research Fund for the central universities (21609101, KF SO).

REFERENCES

Ageta H, Murayama A, Migishima R, Kida S, Tsuchida K, Yokoyama M,

Inokuchi K (2008). Activin in the brain modulates anxiety-related behavior and adult neurogenesis. Plos One .3(4):e1869.
Andreatini R, Leite JR (1994). The effect of corticosterone in rats submitted to the elevated plus-maze and to to pentylenetetrazol-induced convulsions. Prog. Neuropsychopharmacol. Biol. Psychiatry 18:1333-1347.
Bannerman DM, Matthews P, Deacon RM, Rawlins JN (2004). Medial septal lesions mimic effects of both selective dorsal and ventral hippocampal lesions. Behav. Neurosci. 118:1033-1041.
Bergami M, Rimondini R, Santi S, Blum R, Gotz M, Canossa M (2008). Deletion of TrkB in adult progenitors alters newborn neuron integration into hippocampal circuits and increases anxiety-like behavior. Proc. Natl. Acad. Sci. USA. 105:15570-15575.
Bertoglio LJ, Joca SR, Guimaraes FS (2006). Further evidence that anxiety and memory are regionally dissociated within the hippocampus. Behav. Brain Res.175:183-188.
Binder E, Droste SK, Ohl F, Reul JM (2004). Regular voluntary exercise reduces anxiety-related behaviour and impulsiveness in mice. Behav. Brain Res. 155:197-206.
Blumenthal JA, Sherwood A, Rogers SD, Babyak MA, Doraiswamy PM, Watkins L, Hoffman BM, O'Connell C, Johnson JJ, Patidar SM, Waugh R, Hinderliter A (2007). Understanding prognostic benefits of exercise and antidepressant therapy for persons with depression and heart disease: the UPBEAT study--rationale, design, and methodological issues. Clin. Trials 4:548-559.
Burghardt PR, Fulk LJ, Hand GA, Wilson MA (2004). The effects of chronic treadmill and wheel running on behavior in rats. Brain Res. 1019:84-96.
Calvo N, Martijena ID, Molina VA, Volosin M (1998). Metyrapone pretreatment prevents the behavioral and neurochemical sequelae induced by stress. Brain Res. 800:227-235.
Carola V, D'Olimpio F, Brunamonti E, Mangia F, Renzi P (2002). Evaluation of the elevated plus-maze and open-field tests for the assessment of anxiety-related behaviour in inbred mice. Behav. Brain Res. 134:49-57.
Dishman RK, Dunn AL, Youngstedt SD, Davis JM, Burgess ML, Wilson SP, Wilson MA (1996). Increased open field locomotion and decreased striatal GABAA binding after activity wheel running. Physiol. Behav. 60:699-705.
Dulawa SC, Holick KA, Gundersen B, Hen R (2004). Effects of chronic fluoxetine in animal models of anxiety and depression. Neuropsychopharmacology 29:1321-1330.
Duman CH, Schlesinger L, Russell DS, Duman RS (2008). Voluntary exercise produces antidepressant and anxiolytic behavioral effects in mice. Brain Res. 1199:148-158.
Duncko R, Cornwell B, Cui L, Merikangas KR, Grillon C (2007). Acute exposure to stress improves performance in trace eyeblink conditioning and spatial learning tasks in healthy men. Neurobiol. Learn Mem. 14:329-335.
Dunn AL, Trivedi MH, O'Neal HA (2001). Physical activity dose-response effects on outcomes of depression and anxiety. Med. Sci. Sports Exerc. 33:S587-597; discussion 609-510.
Engin E, Treit D (2007). The role of hippocampus in anxiety: intracerebral infusion studies. Behav. Pharmacol. 18:365-374.
Gregus A, Wintink AJ, Davis AC, Kalynchuk LE (2005). Effect of repeated corticosterone injections and restraint stress on anxiety and depression-like behavior in male rats. Behav. Brain Res. 156:105-114.
Hellsten J, Wennstrom M, Mohapel P, Ekdahl CT, Bengzon J, Tingstrom A (2002). Electroconvulsive seizures increase hippocampal neurogenesis after chronic corticosterone treatment. Eur. J. Neurosci.16:283-290.
Mac LP (1949). Psychosomatic disease and the visceral brain; recent developments bearing on the Papez theory of emotion. Psychosom. Med. 11:338-353.
Maier SF, Watkins LR (1998). Cytokines for psychologists: implications of bidirectional immune-to-brain communication for understanding behavior, mood, and cognition. Psychol. Rev. 105:83-107.
Manger TA, Motta RW (2005). The impact of an exercise program on posttraumatic stress disorder, anxiety, and depression. Int. J. Emerg. Ment. Health 7:49-57.
McKinney WT, Jr., Bunney WE, Jr. (1969). Animal model of depression. I. Review of evidence: implications for research. Arch. Gen. Psychiatry 21:240-248.
Merali Z, Levac C, Anisman H (2003). Validation of a simple, ethologically relevant paradigm for assessing anxiety in mice. Biol. Psychiatry 54:552-565.
Mineka S, Watson D, Clark LA (1998). Comorbidity of anxiety and unipolar mood disorders. Annu. Rev. Psychol. 49:377-412.
Nestler EJ, Barrot M, DiLeone RJ, Eisch AJ, Gold SJ, Monteggia LM (2002). Neurobiology of depression. Neuron 34:13-25.
Nosek K, Dennis K, Andrus BM, Ahmadiyeh N, Baum AE, Solberg Woods LC, Redei EE (2008). Context and strain-dependent behavioral response to stress. Behav. Brain Funct. 4:23.
Pellow S, Chopin P, File SE, Briley M (1985). Validation of open:closed arm entries in an elevated plus-maze as a measure of anxiety in the rat. J Neurosci. Methods 14:149-167.
Pentkowski NS, Blanchard DC, Lever C, Litvin Y, Blanchard RJ (2006). Effects of lesions to the dorsal and ventral hippocampus on defensive behaviors in rats. Eur. J. Neurosci. 23:2185-2196.
Prut L, Belzung C (2003). The open field as a paradigm to measure the effects of drugs on anxiety-like behaviors: a review. Eur. J. Pharmacol. 463:3-33.
Revest JM, Dupret D, Koehl M, Funk-Reiter C, Grosjean N, Piazza PV, Abrous DN (2009). Adult hippocampal neurogenesis is involved in anxiety-related behaviors. Mol. Psychiatry 14:959-967.
Rodgers RJ (1997). Animal models of 'anxiety': where next? Behav. Pharmacol., 8:477-496; discussion 497-504.
Rogers DC, Jones DN, Nelson PR, Jones CM, Quilter CA, Robinson TL, Hagan JJ (1999). Use of SHIRPA and discriminant analysis to characterise marked differences in the behavioural phenotype of six inbred mouse strains. Behav. Brain Res. 105:207-217.
Salam JN, Fox JH, Detroy EM, Guignon MH, Wohl DF, Falls WA (2009). Voluntary exercise in C57 mice is anxiolytic across several measures of anxiety. Behav. Brain Res. 197:31-40.
Sapolsky RM, Krey LC, McEwen BS (1985). Prolonged glucocorticoid exposure reduces hippocampal neuron number: implications for aging. J. Neurosci. 5:1222-1227.
Trullas R, Skolnick P (1993). Differences in fear motivated behaviors among inbred mouse strains. Psychopharmacology 111:323-331.
Walf AA, Frye CA (2007). The use of the elevated plus maze as an assay of anxiety-related behavior in rodents. Nat. Protoc. 2:322-328.
Yau SY, Lau BW, So KF (2011a). Adult hippocampal neurogenesis: a possible way how physical exercise counteracts stress. Cell Transplant 20:99-111.
Yau SY, Lau BWM, Tong JB, Ching YP, Lee TMC, So KF (2011b). Hippocampal neurogenesis and dendritic plasticity support running-improved spatial learning and depression-like behaviour in stressed rats. PlosOne 6:1-15.

Anxiogenic potential of prulifloxacin in experimental animal model

S. Rekha*, S. Kavimani and K. V. Raman

Department of Pharmacology, Mother Theresa Post Graduate and Research Institute of Health Sciences, Puducherry - 605006, India.

Prulifloxacin, the prodrug of ulifloxacin, is a broad spectrum oral fluoroquinolones antibacterial agent. Fluoroquinolones have been used for the treatment of bacterial infection for many years. Although they were considered as relatively safe drugs, various adverse effects have recently been reported along with increase in the usage of new generation fluoroquinolones. In the present study, prulifloxacin 200 and 400 mg/kg were screened on anxiety parameter in mice. Our result suggested that prulifloxacin (200 and 400 mg/kg) exerted anxiety-like effect in the elevated plus maze, hole board apparatus and light/dark exploration test in mice.

Key words: Prulifloxacin, elevated plus maze, hole board apparatus, light/dark exploration test.

INTRODUCTION

Fluoroquinolones are one of the most widely prescribed classes of antimicrobial. Although generally tolerated, central nervous system effects are the second most common type (after gastrointestinal) of adverse drug reactions (ADR's) reported with fluoroquinolones. These include mild reactions including headache, confusion, dizziness, tiredness, insomnia, anxiety or more sever psychotic reactions, agitation, hallucinations, nightmare, restlessness, depression and seizures reported clinically. The severe reactions are rare, occurring in less than 0.5% (Cross, 2001). A variety of neurobehavioral adverse effects, other than seizures have been reported with fluoroquinolones. For example in a single case report, ciprofloxacin was associated with psychosis in women with no psychiatric history (Bharal et al., 2006). Similarly, levofloxacin produced anxiety like effects in rodent experimental models (Erden et al., 2001).

Prulifloxacin is one of the newer generations of fluoroquinolones. The neurobehavioral effects of fluoroquinolones have been reported experimentally as well as clinically for drugs like ciprofloxacin, norfloxacin, pefloxacin, ofloxacin etc. Sparfloxacin have been reported for insomnia, sleep disorders and convulsions (Erden et al., 2001). Prulifloxacin is a new thiazeto-quinolones antibacterial agent prodrug of the quinolone carboxylic acid ulifloxacin characterized by a potent and broad-spectrum antibacterial activity. It has been reported to produce nausea, dizziness, insomnia and agitation (Matera, 2006). Such anxiety effects have been reported with ciprofloxacin, norfloxacin, gatifloxacin, sparfloxacin and levofloxacin in experimental animals. The anxiogenic effect could well be related to inhibition of $GABA_A$ receptor complex (Johnstone et al., 2004). Quinolones have an inhibitory effect on the receptor binding of $GABA_A$, and may thus exert an inhibitory CNS stimulant action (Akahane et al., 1994). The adenosine or $GABA_A$ receptor has therefore been proposed as a possible target for quinolones, particularly with older agents like norfloxacin and ciprofloxacin, and less so with pefloxacin (Dodd et al., 1988). N-methyl-D-aspartate (NMDA) receptors present in the hippocampus may also be responsible for the anxiogenic property exhibited as side effects of fluoroquinolones (Sen et al., 2007). However, experimental evidence is still needed to study its neurobehavioral effects. In the present study, we investigated the neurobehavioral effects of prulifloxacin on experimental models of anxiety.

*Corresponding author. E-mail: rekhampharmcology@gmail.com.

Table 1. Effect of short term (7 days) administration of prulifloxacin on elevated plus maze.

Group no.	Dose and drug	Number of entries		Time spent by the animal (s)	
		Open arm	Closed arm	Open arm	Closed arm
I	Control	4 ± 2.08	8.6 ± 2.6	24.6 ± 15.16	275 ± 15.17
II	Prulifloxacin (200 mg/kg)	4 ± 0.57	7.3 ± 0.33	23.6 ± 9.3*	276 ± 9.4
III	Prulifloxacin (400 mg/kg)	2.6 ± 1.76	5 ± 2.3	24 ± 7.2*	275 ± 7.2

Values are expressed as mean ± SD. *Indicates statistical significance in comparison to the control treatment; * denote p < 0.01 respectively by student t pair test. n = 5.

Table 2. Effect of short term (7 days) administration of prulifloxacin on hole board apparatus.

Group no.	Treatment	Dose	Number of head poking during 5 min
I	Control	Saline	102 ± 7.79
II	Prulifloxacin	200 mg/kg	34 ± 2.3*
III	Prulifloxacin	400 mg/kg	17.6 ± 1.2*

Values are expressed as mean ± SD. * Indicates statistical significance in comparison to the control treatment; *denote p < 0.005 by student t pair test. n = 5.

MATERIALS AND METHODS

Both sexes of albino mice were used for this study. Animals were housed in groups of five in standard polypropylene laboratory cages at an ambient temperature of 25 ± 2°C and 45 to 55% relative humidity with reversed 12:12 h light/dark cycle. They had free access to rodent chow and tap water *ad libitum*. The animal studies were carried out after getting approval from the institution of animal ethical committee.

Prulifloxacin were freshly prepared dissolved in distilled water and administered intraperitonially in the morning for seven consecutive days. A dose of 200 and 400 mg/kg was chosen for the present study. The control animals were given the same volume of distilled water. Separate groups of mice were used for each behavioral test. Elevated plus maze, hole board apparatus, light/dark exploration test were employed in this test. Experiments were performed on the seventh day, 45 min after the drug administration.

Elevated plus maze

The elevates plus maze consisted of two opposite arms (50 cm × 10 cm) crossed with two opposite enclosed arms of the same dimension with 40 cm high walls. The arms were connected with a central square (10 cm × 10 cm) to give the apparatus a plus sign appearance. The maze was kept elevated 50 cm above the floor in a dimly-lit room. The mice were individually placed on the central square of the plus maze facing on enclosed arm. The time spent and numbers of entries made by the mice, during the next 5 min, on open and enclosed arms were recorded. An arm entry was defined when all the four limbs were on the arm (Sen, 2007).

Hole board test

The hole board apparatus consisted of a wooden box (40 × 40 × 25 cm^3) with 16 holes (each of diameter 3 cm) evenly distributed on the base of box. The apparatus was elevated to the height of 25 cm. Mice were treated with prulifloxacin 200 and 400 mg/kg before they were placed in the apparatus. The number of head pokes and the time of head dipping during a 5 min period were recorded (Barua et al., 2009).

Light/dark exploration test

The apparatus consisted of a dark compartment (13 × 22 × 26 cm^3) connected by a 5 × 5 cm^2 window to a bright compartment (illuminated, 600 lux, 23 × 22 × 26 cm^3). Mice were placed in the dark compartment and activity was measured for 5 min. The percent time spent in the bright compartment and number of entries into the bright compartment and number of entries into the bright compartment were used as an index of the anxiety state of mice (Suzuki et al., 2007).

RESULTS

The effects of prulifloxacin treatments on the behavior of mice in the elevated plus maze, hole board apparatus and light/dark exploration test shown in Tables 1, 2 and 3, and Figure 1, 2 and 3. In the elevated plus maze, prulifloxacin treated mice spent significantly more time and made more number of entries to the enclosed arms, and decreasing the time spent in open arms. The results of the ratio between open arm and enclosed arm time and entries also indicated that both doses of prulifloxacin caused significant anxiogenic behavior in mice. In hole board apparatus, both doses 200 and 400 mg/kg showed anxiogenic response by significantly reduced the number of head poking. Reduction of number of entries in the bright side and increase of time spent by the animal in dark side were observed in the light/dark exploration test.

DISCUSSION

Fluoroquinolones are widely prescribed antimicrobial

Table 3. Effect of short term (7 days) administration of Prulifloxacin on light/dark exploration test.

Group no.	Treatment and dose	Time spent (s)		No. of entries in bright side
		Bright side	Dark side	
I	Control	104 ± 40	195 ± 40	6.25 ± 0.91
II	Prulifloxacin (200 mg/kg)	101 ± 57	223 ± 36	2.25 ± 0.47*
III	Prulifloxacin (400 mg/kg)	65 ± 28.6	235 ± 37	2.3 ± 1.4**

Values are expressed as mean ± SD. * Indicates statistical significance in comparison to the control treatment; *denote $p < 0.005$ and ** denote $p < 0.025$ by student t pair test. n = 5.

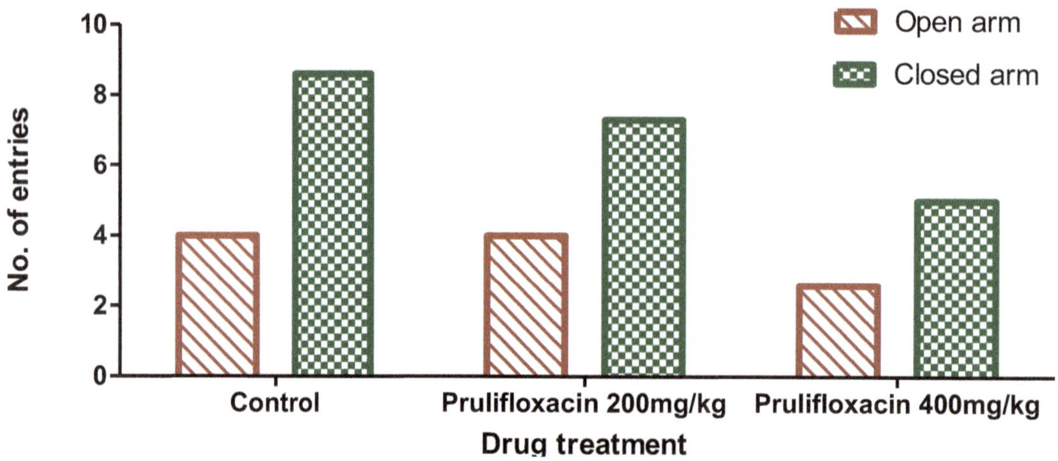

Figure 1. Effect of seven days administration of prulifloxacin on elevated plus maze.

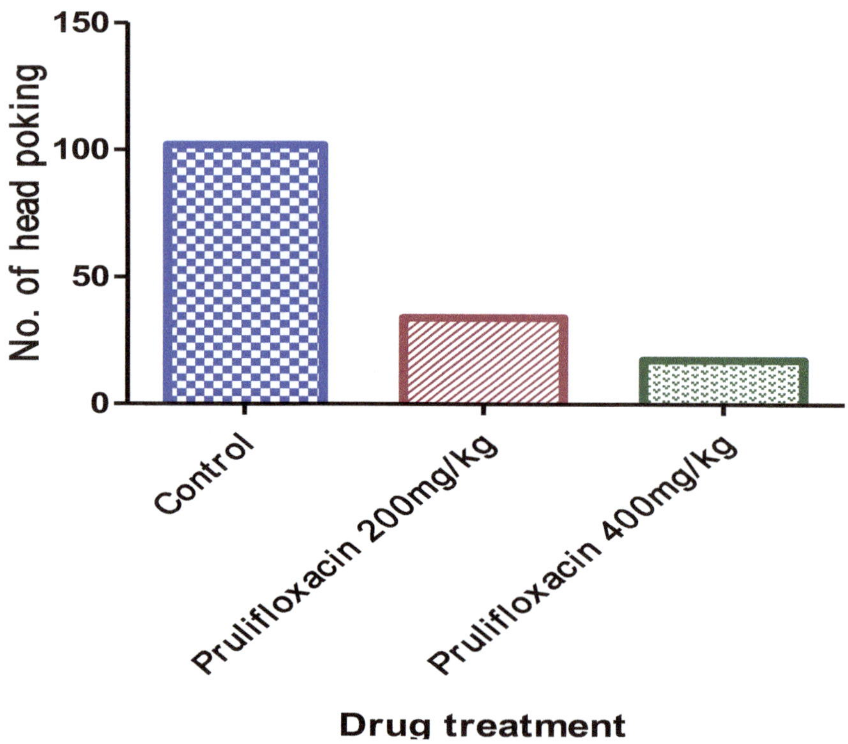

Figure 2. Effect of seven days administration of prulifloxacin on hole board apparatus.

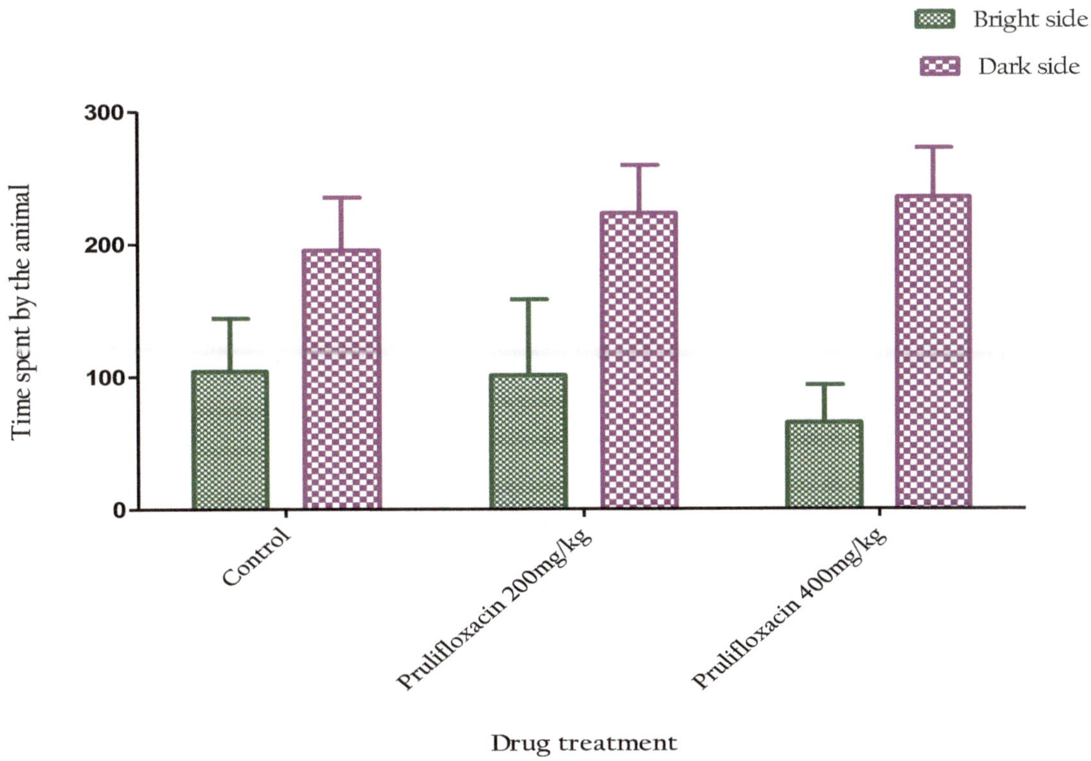

Figure 3. Effect of seven days administration of prulifloxacin on light/dark exploration test.

agents although convenient to administer, and have been reported to have some adverse drug reactions on the CNS during their clinical usage. The present study was conducted to investigate the neurobehavioral effects of prulifloxacin in mice. In 7 days administration study, the results indicate that prulifloxacin at 200 and 400mg/kg, i.p dose showed anxiogenic effects as indicated by decreased number of entries and time spent in closed arms. In hole board apparatus, they showed reduced the number of poking. In light/dark exploration test, they reduced the number of entries in bright side. Such anxiety effects have been reported with ciprofloxacin, norfloxacin, gatifloxacin, sparfloxacin and levofloxacin in experimental animals. More recently, however, an anxiolytic effect has been reported by modifying norfloxacin. The anxiogenic effect could well be related to inhibition of $GABA_A$ receptor complex (Johnstone et al., 2004).

The role of gamma-aminobutyric acid (GABA) in anxiety is well documented (Sen et al., 2007). Some studies indicate that fluoroquinolones function as GABA receptor antagonists (Unseld et al., 1990) and the epileptogenic action of quinolones has been proposed to be related to the GABA-like structure of ring substitutes. The central nervous system (CNS) effects of pefloxacin in clinical settings have been explained by some reported biochemical studies. Quinolones have an inhibitory effect on the receptor binding of $GABA_A$, and may thus exert an inhibitory CNS stimulant action (Akahane et al., 1994). The adenosine or $GABA_A$ receptor has therefore been proposed as a possible target for quinolones, particularly with older agents like norfloxacin and ciprofloxacin, and less so with pefloxacin (Dodd et al., 1988). The excitatory potentials of fluoroquinolones have been reported to be increased in a dose dependent manner in the electrophysiological studies of the field potentials in the CA 1 region of the rat hippocampus slice (Schmuck et al., 1998). N-methyl-D-aspartate (NMDA) receptors present in the hippocampus may also be responsible for the anxiogenic property exhibited as side effects of fluoroquinolones (Sen et al., 2007).

Conclusion

The present study indicates that prulifloxacin produces anxiogenic response at the dose of 200 and 400 mg/kg on experimental animal model.

REFERENCES

Akahane K, Tsutomi Y, Kimura Y, Kitano Y (1994). Levofloxacin, an optical isomer of ofloxacin, has attenuated epileptogenic activity in mice and inhibitory potency in GABA receptor binding. Chemotherapy, 40: 412-417.

Barua CC, Roy JD, Buragohain B, Barua AG, Borah P, Lahkar M (2009). Anxiolytic effect of hydroethanolic extract of Drymarai cordata

L wild. Indian J. Exp. Biol., 47: 969-973.
Bharal NK, Pillai K, Divya Vohora (2006). Effects of sparfloxacin on CNS functions and urinary hydroxyproline in mice. Pharmacol. Res., 54: 111-117.
Cross JT (2001). Fluoroquinolones. Semin. Pediatr. Infect. Dis., 12(3): 211-223.
Dodd PR, Davies LP, Watson WE, Nielsen B, Dyer JA, Wong LS, Johnston GA (1988). Neurochemical studies on quinolone antibiotics: effects on glutamate, GABA and adenosine systems in mammalian CNS. Pharmacol. Toxicol., 64: 404-411.
Erden BF, Ulak G, Yildiz F, Utkan T, Ozdemirci S, Gacar N (2001). Antidepressant, anxiogenic and antinociceptive properties of levofloxacin in rats and mice. Pharmacol. Biochem. Behav., 68: 435-41.
Johnstone TBC, Hogenkamp D J, Coyne L, Su J, Halliwell RF, Tran MB, Yoshimura RF, Li WY, Wang J, Gee KW (2004). Modifying quinolone antibiotics yields new anxiolytics. Nat. Med., 10: 31-32.
Matera MG (2006). Pharmacologic characteristics of Prulifloxacin. Pulmonary pharmacol. Therapeutics, 19: 20-29.
Schmuck G, Schürmann A, Schlüter G (1998). Determination of the excitatory potencies of fluoroquinolones in the central nervous system by an *in vitro* model. Antimicrob. Agents Chemother., 42: 1831-1836.
Sen S, Jaiswal AK, Yanpallewar S, Acharya SB (2007). Anxiogenic potential of ciprofloxacin and norfloxacin in rats. Singapore Med. J., 48(11): 1028-1032.
Suzuki T, Amata M, Sakaue G, Nishimura S, Inoue T, Shibata M, Masjimo T (2007). Experimental Neuropathy in mice is associated with delayed behavioral changes related to anxiety and depression. Int. Anesthesia Res. Soc., 104: 6.
Unseld E, Ziegler G, Gemerhardt A, Janssen U, Koltz U (1990). Possible interaction of fluoroquinolones with the benzodiazepine-$GABA_A$receptor complex. Br. J. Clin. Pharmacol., 30: 63-70.

The pattern of clinical presentation of epilepsy among adolescence Sudanese epileptic patients

Amira Sidig, Abbasher Hussein*, Faroug Yassien, Ahmed Hamad, Omer el-Adil, Mohmad Saad, Bedraldin Mubark and Mohmad Malk Aldar

Faculty of Medicine, University of Khartoum, Sudan, P. O. Box 102, Khartoum, Sudan.

The aim of this study is to describe the clinical presentation of epilepsy among adolescence. It is a cross-sectional hospital based study conducted at Elshaab Teaching Hospital and Sheik Mohammad Kheir neurological clinic (from August, 1999 to April, 2009). The study population included 480 epileptic patients (age 10 to 19 years). The clinical presentation was similar to that which was reported by other researchers worldwide except the fact that the percentage of epilepsy, following infections, increased among the groups used in this study. Epilepsy and its treatment have a direct bearing on major aspects of adolescence lifestyle such as education and employment prospects, driving ability, the use of alcohol and recreational drugs, relationships, contraception, pregnancy and parenthood.

Key word: Sudanese, adolescence, epilepsy.

INTRODUCTION

Epilepsy is a common chronic neurological disorder characterized by recurrent unprovoked seizures (Berkovic et al., 1996; Raymond et al., 1995). These seizures are transient signs and/or symptoms of abnormal, excessive or synchronous neuronal activity in the brain (Taylor et al., 1971). About 50 million people worldwide have epilepsy, with almost 90% of these people living in developing countries (Palmini et al., 1991). Epilepsy is more likely to occur in young children or people above the age of 65 years; however, it can occur at any time (King et al., 1996). On the other hand, over 30% of the people with epilepsy do not have seizure control even with the best available medications (Lüders et al., 1993; Lüders et al., 1998). Africa is a diverse continent and it represents people of different cultural backgrounds. There are approximately 3 to 4 million people living with epilepsy in Africa. There are various traditional beliefs pertaining to epilepsy, its causes and treatments. These beliefs, however, keep 80% of the epileptic patients in Africa from receiving proper treatment. The prevalence of epilepsy in Sudan varies from 0.7 to 4.8%, while in Nigeria, the prevalence of epilepsy varies from approximately 0.53 to 3.7%. The prevalence of epilepsy among African Americans is higher than that of Caucasians and Hispanics, while the prevalence rate is somewhere between 0.010 and 0.012% for African Americans, which is relatively high when compared with 0.007 and 0.009% for Whites and Hispanics, respectively. In addition, the risk of seizures during a lifetime is only 10% among Caucasians; whereas, it is 25% for African Americans.

Puberty involves complex physiologic changes. It is also a time of emotional transition with the development of the desire for independence from parental supervision, increased interaction with peers and emerging sexuality. Adolescence with epilepsy may be complicated by problems in adjusting to a chronic condition that is unpredictable and one that can affect social interactions. Also, they may have inaccurate perceptions about themselves and their seizure disorders, and in addition, fear ridicule and rejection, which in turn will make them withdraw socially. There is a general agreement that most seizure disorders are not altered by the onset of puberty (Engel, 1998; Placencia and Shorvon, 1992). Some researchers report a transient deterioration in seizure control, which is secondary to rapid growth and suboptimal antiepileptic drug (AEDs) levels (Placencia

*Corresponding author. E-mail: abbashar59@yahoo.com.

and Shorvon, 1992). Certain epileptic syndromes, such as juvenile myoclonic epilepsy and photosensitive epilepsy, characteristically develop around the onset of puberty (Cockrell et al., 1997), whereas other syndromes, such as childhood absence and benign rolandic epilepsy with centrotemporal spikes, tend to remit during adolescence. Catamenial epilepsy refers to seizure exacerbation related to the menstrual cycle. The most common pattern is an increased tendency for seizures just before or at the onset of menstruation. This increased frequency is noted in women with epilepsy who have idiopathic epilepsy and in those with symptomatic seizures. Menses-related seizure is one of the complications associated with reaching adolescent. Alcohol and drug abuse and destructive behaviors, common among adolescents, may have especially negative effects on teens with epilepsy (Woodbury and Woodbury, 1990; Berkovic et al., 1996). A driver's license is regarded by many adolescents as essential to freedom and independence. State laws vary, but adolescents with epilepsy may be denied this privilege unless their seizures are completely controlled. Health care providers may find medication adherence to be more dependable when obtaining a driver's license is the desired outcome. Sports, with the potential of head injury, should be undertaken with caution, since the risk of seizures increased. Adolescents can be encouraged to participate in less risky activities. However, activities that may result in injury if a seizure occurs should be carefully monitored, especially recreational activities involving water (Raymond et al., 1995; Taylor et al., 1971).

The aim of this work is to study the clinical presentation of epilepsy among adolescence Sudanese epileptic patients seen in Elshaab teaching hospital and Sheik Mohammad Kheir neurological clinic (Sudan).

METHODOLOGY

Study area

Subjects with epileptic seizures had been randomly recruited from Sheik Mohammad Khier Neurological Referral Clinic and El shaab Teaching Hospital (a 240 bedded hospital). The study population included 540 epileptic patients referred to the hospital from August, 1999 to April, 2009. The study was a descriptive cross sectional hospital based study and about 60 patients were dropped due to difficulty of follow up, while the rest of the patients were followed by the authors until the end of the study period.

Inclusion criteria

All the patients were Sudanese and their ages ranged between 10 and 19 years.

Exclusion criteria

Non-Sudanese patients were excluded from the study to include those below 10 years and those above 19 years. All the patients gave their verbal consent to participate in the study, and this was approved by the ethics committee. The diagnosis of epilepsy and its subtypes was made by a neurologist. A full detailed medical and personal history including the following factors: psychological (personality and behavior), social (home, school and education), medical (psychiatry, learning disability and physical symptoms and illness), work, personal environment and information on any traumatic life events (loss and bereavement), was followed by physical examinations.

The physical signs were grouped into general, systemic and neurological, while the following investigations such as: random blood sugar, total blood count, L.F.Ts, blood urea, serum sodium, serum calcium and serum magnesium, were done for each patient. All the patients had MRI of the brain and EEG. The diagnosis of the MRI of the brain was made by a neuroradiologist, while the diagnosis of the EEGs was done by a neurophysiologist. A stress was made on the regular monthly follow up of the patients on the following: (1) Whether the patients take their medication regularly or not; (2) whether they experienced an attack of convulsion or not; (3) whether or not a history of symptoms of drugs intoxication was taken and whether proper examination of each patient looking for signs of drug toxicity was done or not.

Data collection

Data were collected by self-administered questionnaires composed of personal data, full detailed history and examination.

Data analysis

All collected data were finally entered into the computer using the statistical package program for social science (SPSS) to analyze the data via simple descriptive statistics.

RESULTS

Out of the 480 patients, 260 were males (54.15%), while 240 were females (45.85%). A large number of the patients used for this study were from Khartoum (288) and they were mostly students. Regarding age distribution, 160 were between 10 and 15 years and 320 were between 16 and 19 years. Regarding the aetiology of epilepsy among the studied group 320 patients (66.7%) had no cause, while other causes included infections like meningitis and encephalitis. Other causes observed were mental retardation, brain tumors, down syndrome, tuberous sclerosis, microcephaly, Sturge Weber syndrome, past history of brain anoxia, infantile hemiplegia, past history of trauma, degenerative brain diseases and alcohol consumption (Table 1).

The study showed that 96 patients (20%) had a family history of epilepsy. It was found that 412 patients (86.4%) had generalized epilepsy, while 68 patients (13.6%) had focal epilepsy. Out of the 412 patients with generalized epilepsy, 68 had secondary generalized epilepsy; whereas in those that had partial epilepsy, 48 (9%) had complex partial seizure and 20 (4.6%) had simple partial seizure. It appeared that out of 412 patients with generalized convulsion, 360 showed no abnormality on clinical examination and out of the 68 patients with partial

Table 1. Showing the aetiology of epilepsy among 480 Sudanese patients.

Idiopathic		Trauma		Tumor		Infection		Cerebral anoxia		Infantile hemiplegia		Alcohol		Degenerative diseases		Mental retardation		Congenital	
No.	%	No.	%	No.	%	No.	%	No.	%	No.	%	No.	%	No.	%	No.	%	No.	%
320	66.7	20	4	20	4	56	12	12	2.5	8	1.8	8	1.8	12	2.5	24	5	5	4

Microcephaly		Down syndrome		Tuberous sclerosis		Sturge-Weber syndrome		Neurofibromatosis		
No.	%	No.	%	No.	%	No.	%	No.	%	%
8	1.8	4	0.9	4	0.9	4	0.9	4	0.9	2.5

Table 2. Showing incidence of abnormal neurological findings among 480 Sudanese epileptic patients.

Generalized epilepsy				Focal epilepsy			
No. of abnormal signs		Abnormal sign		No. of abnormal signs		Abnormal sign	
No.	%	No.	%	No.	%	No.	%
370	90	42	10	34	50	34	50

Table 3. Showing types of abnormal EEG among 480 Sudanese epileptic patients.

Generalize discharge		Focal discharge	
No.	%	No.	%
272	**86.4**	**44**	**13.6**

epilepsy, 34 showed abnormality on examination (Table 2).

Among the 480 epileptic patients, 312 had abnormal EEG, (Table 3) and thus showed a distribution of abnormal EEG.

The study showed that 370 patients with generalized epilepsy (90%) had a normal MRI of the brain, while 42 patients (10%) had abnormal MRI of the brain. In those that had focal epilepsy, 34 patients (50%) had abnormal MRI of the brain, while 34 patients (50%) had a normal MRI of the brain. The distribution of the 480 epileptic patients according to antiepileptic drugs they received was as follow: 180 patients received phenytoin, 168 received phenobarbitone, 140 received carbamazine and 152 patients received sodium valproate. Out of the 480 patients, 320 (66.6%) took one drug, while 160 (33.3%) received more than one drug. Acne, skin rash, hirsutism and coarse facial appearance were found to be the common idiosyncratic side effect of phenytoin, while the other side effects and dose related side effects can be seen in Tables 4 and 5, respectively.

Out of the 168 patients taking phenobarbitone, 16 had skin rash (idiosynchratic). Table 6 showed that depression and listlessness were the common dose related side effects.

The idiosynchratic adverse effects of carbamazebine were found as follow: 16 patients had skin rash, 4 had a granulocytosis and 4 had aplastic anaemia. However, nausea and vomiting were found to be the common dose related side effects of carbamazebine (Table 7). Out of the 140 patients taking sodium valproate, 4 had thrombocytopenic and 4 had encephalopathy. Weight gain, tremor and menstrual cycle disturbances were found to be the common dose related side effects (Table 8). Most of our patients had normal serum level of AEDs as seen in Table (9). The study showed that 248 patients (52%) became seizure-free during the period of

Table 4. Showing the adverse effects' incidence of phenytoin (indiosynchratic).

Side effects	Acne	Rash	Hirsutism	Coarse facial app	Blood dyscrasia	Lymph adenopathy
No.	20	16	16	16	4	1
Side effects (cid)	**SLE like syndrome**	**Hepato toxic effect**	**Stevens- Johnsons syndrome**	**Dupuytren contracture**	**Teratogencit**	
No.	1	1	4	4	-	

Table 5. Showing the adverse effects' incidence of dose related phenytoin.

Side effects	Nausea	Vomiting	Ataxia	Nystagmus	Gingival hypertrophy	Megalblastic anaemia	Drowziness
No.	16	16	3	12	16	4	16

Out of 180 patients taking phenobarbitone, 16 had skin rash (Idiosynchratic).

Table 6. Showing the adverse effects' incidence of phenbarbitone (dose related).

Side effects	Listlessness	Fatigue	Depression	Insomnia	Irritability	Drowsiness	Distractibility and hyperkinasia
No.	8	20	8	4	4	4	4

Table 7. Showing the adverse effects' incidence of carbamazebine (dose related).

Side effects	Nausea and vomiting	Steepness	Drowsiness	Neutropenia	Dizziness	Diplopia	Headache	Hyponatraemia	Arrhytmia	Orofacial dyskinesia
No. of patients	20	16	12	12	8	1	4	4	1	1

treatment, while 232 patients (48%) still had convulsions.

DISSCUSSION

The study showed that, males are affected more than females. It is a fact that, although epilepsydoes affect both sexes, males are more prone to the condition than females, though the reason for this is not known, but it seems that some of the risk factors, like trauma, are more common among males. Also, it may be due to the fact that diagnosis of epilepsy is a stigma in our society, both for the patient and his family, so female patients do not tend to appear before doctors. It appears that elderly ones are more affected than young people; this is similar to what was mentioned in the literature (Engel, 1998). The study showed that out of the 480 patients, only 96 (20%) had a family history of convulsion. This was similar to that which was mentioned in the literature, but some researchers have discovered that some forms of epilepsy can be linked to the

Table 8. Showing the adverse effects' incidence of sodium valproate (dose related).

Side effects	Tremor	Weight gain	Nausea and vomiting	Menstrual cycle disturbances	Alopecia	Peripheral oedema
No.	12	16	8	12	8	1

Table 9. Showing distribution of the serum level of AEDs.

AEDs	No. of patients with normal serum level of AEDs	No. of patients with abnormal serum level of AEDs
Phenytoin	120	20
Phenobarbitone	120	20
Carbamazebine	120	8
Sodium valproate	92	8

inheritance of specific genes which might help in part to explain why sometimes members of the same family are affected by the condition. However, for most people, there is no family history of the disease at all (Placencia and Shorvon, 1992; Cockrell et al., 1997).

The increased incidence of epilepsy among first degree relatives of epileptic patient may be due to genetic factors (Woodbury and Woodbury, 1990). Regarding the underlying causes of epilepsy in most of the patients, there are no obvious causes. The major risk factor in this study was found to be infection (Raymond et al., 1995), while other risk factors include trauma, brain anoxia, tumors, infantile hemiplegia, congenital abnormalities and degenerative diseases. These results were similar to that which was found in other places, but the percentage of epilepsy following infections increased in our country (14%). This was mostly due to the increased incidence of meningitis and encephalitis, which may scar the cortical mantle resulting in subsequent development of seizures. However, this supported the idea that African children have some of the highest rates of bacterial meningitis in the world. Bacterial meningitis in Africa is associated with a high case of fatality and frequent neuropsychological sequelae as reported by Ramakrishnan and his colleagues (Ramakrishnan et al., 2009). Twenty-four cases were reported to be associated with congenital abnormalities, and this included: microcephaly, down syndrome, tuberous sclerosis, sturge-webber syndrome and neurofibromatosis. Although the commonest type of epilepsy, according to the underlying causes, is idiopathic, this is common among children and elderly ones like that which was mentioned in the literature (Raymond et al., 1995). Most of the study's epileptic patients had generalized epilepsy, while few of them had focal epilepsy, and this was not similar to that which was reported by the UK National General Practice Study of Epilepsy (two thirds focal epilepsy and one third generalized epilepsy) (Taylor et al., 1971), but it approximates that which was reported by WHO about epilepsy in the African region (where the majority of the cases were tonic clonic epilepsy) (Taylor et al., 1971).

The discrimination, from the findings of the UK National General Practice Study of Epilepsy, may be due to the fact that grand mal epilepsy is dramatic in its presentation so that affected people are interested to seek for medical treatment, unlike partial seizures which may go unnoticed especially in the developing countries. However, this might be the same reason for its compatibility with the WHO report about epilepsy in the African region (Taylor et al., 1971). Grand mal epilepsy was found to be the commonest type, although some of the study's patients were presented with tonic epilepsy, myoclonic epilepsy and atypical absence. Most of those who came with partial epilepsy had a complex one which was similar to that which was mentioned in the literature (Palmini et al., 1991). The incidence of prodromal symptoms in patients with generalized convulsion (20%) is less than that in patients with partial epilepsy (45%), although most of the patients with prodromal symptoms have secondary generalized epilepsy rather than primary generalized epilepsy. Nevertheless, the abnormal neurological findings were common among patients with partial epilepsy than those with generalized epilepsy, and this was similar to that which was mentioned in the literature

(King et al., 1996; Lüders et al., 1993). From this study, it did appear that abnormal EEG in patients was 64.8%; although the study's finding did not differ much from that which was reported worldwide (Lüders et al., 1993). There was no real difference in gender distribution of abnormal EEGs, in that the lower number of females when compared with males (65:55) could be due to the stigmatization of epilepsy in denying female epileptics to seek medical advice or might be due to other factors.

Sleep deprivation EEG recording within 48 h of aseizure and seizure frequency of at least one attack per month are all known to increase the chances of finding epileptic disorders. The inability to have EEG recording within the first 48 h was due to practical difficulties, as quite a number of the study's patients were revered from distant Sudanese states and districts. It is thought that the prospect for the future is to do a second recording (during sleep) for every patient with a negative EEG. This hopefully will increase the chance of obtaining more positive EEGs. The study showed that most of the patients with generalized epilepsy had a normal MRI of the brain (90%) and only 10% had an abnormal MRI of the brain. However, most of the patients who had abnormal MRI of the brain had secondary generalized epilepsy rather than primary generalized epilepsy.

Also, a large number of them had late-onset epilepsy rather than early-onset epilepsy. This result is similar to studies done worldwide; at the same time, the incidence of abnormal MRI of the brain increased to 50% among patients with partial epilepsy, so MRI of the brain is indicated in those who have local epilepsy, late onset epilepsy and epilepsy with abnormal neurological findings (Lüders and Acharya, 1998). The study showed that, there is no clear-cut relation between the plasma concentration of AEDs, their effect and toxicity, and since the daily variation in plasma concentration is wide, routine monitoring may not be helpful unless it is correlated with the patients' clinical situation. The study showed that, 160 patients (33.1/3%) had seizures which are refractory to treatment with single antiepileptic drug, many of which have partial seizures or secondary generalized seizure due to an underlying anatomical lesion. Before long term treatment with more than one drug was undertaken, all reasonable options for monotherapy were exhausted. If one drug was ineffective, an alternative drug was introduced gradually, and if the patient responds well to the second drug, an attempt was made to withdraw the original drug. The two drugs were continued when the attempt was unsuccessful. Out of the 480 epileptic patients, 248 patients (52.7%) became seizure free for three years, while 232 patients (47.3) still have recurrent attacks of convulsions. More so, out of the 248 patients who are seizure-free for three years, 160 patients (66%) normally took one drug, while 88 patients (34%) normally took more than one drug. Many patients who received treatment with more than one drug showed an increased incidence of the central nervous system and other toxic effects. It is important to balance the adequacy of seizure control with the quality of life. Little is lost by gradually reducing the number of drugs and simplifying the dose schedules, and paradoxically, this approach often reduces the frequency of seizure. Even for healthy teenagers, coping with emerging adulthood is a major challenge.

A chronic disability such as epilepsy simply magnifies the problems of adolescence and the penalties for seizures at this time are far more severe than in childhood. Epilepsy and its treatment have a direct bearing on major aspects of lifestyle such as education and employment prospects, driving ability, the use of alcohol and recreational drugs, relationships, contraception, pregnancy and parenthood. Self consciousness is paramount and deviations from peer group norms assume great importance, in that epilepsy can be disastrous for an adolescent's self esteem and sense of identity. When anti-epileptic drugs are indicated, the ideal thing to do is to prescribe the lowest effective dose of a preparation that has possibly few side effects, and given once or twice daily. Compliance with drug treatment is a particular problem in adolescence. As at any age, the reasons include denial of epilepsy, over side effects and complacency about good seizure control. Side effects of AEDs are extremely important at this age since even mild cognitive dysfunction may permanently harm education and employment prospects. Cosmetic effects limit the usefulness of certain antiepileptic drugs (such as phenytoin) in young people. Several lifestyle issues merit discussion. Young women taking enzyme inducing antiepileptic drugs must be warned about potential failure of oral contraceptives. More importantly, all women of childbearing age taking antiepileptic drugs need to know of their possible teratogenicity. Complete abstinence from alcohol should be encouraged; while teenagers must recognize its potential for interacting with drugs, impairing the quality of sleep and thus provoking seizures. The risk of exposure to computer screens and flashing lights often concerns patients and parents. Photosensitive epilepsies may be present in teenage years, but such exposure is harmless to most teenagers. Epilepsy affects educational and employment prospects, with career choices being inevitably restricted by the diagnosis. Further restrictions imposed by parents and suggested by peers or initiated by the patient are sometimes inappropriate. Such restrictions can threaten independence, deny opportunities for friendship and encourage social isolation. A common sense approach is needed towards leisure and sports activities, in that both patient and parents often have to accept living with a degree of risk. The problems faced by teenagers with epilepsy often apply to a lesser extent across the range of patients with epilepsy. As the services for this vulnerable group are improved, the lessons learnt can only benefit people with epilepsy as a whole.

REFERENCES

Berkovic SF, McIntosh A, Howell R (1996). Familial temporal lobe epilepsy: A common disorder identified in twins. Ann. Neurol., 40: 227-235.

Cockrell OC, Johnson AL, Sander JWAS (1997). Prognosis of epilepsy: a review and further analysis of the first nine years of the British National General Practice Study of epilepsy, a prospective population based study. Epilepsia, 38: 31-46.

Engel J (1998). Classification of the international league against epilepsy: Time for reappraisal. Epilepsia, 39: 1014-1017.

King MA, Newton MR, Fitt GJ (1996). Epileptology of the first seizure: Study of 200 consecutive cases. Epilepsia, 37(5): 82.

Lüders H, Acharya J (1998). Baumgartner. Semiological seizure classification. Epilepsia, 39. 1000-1010.

Lüders HO, Burgess R, Noachtar S (1993). Expanding the international classification of seizures to provide localization information. Neurology, 43: 1650-1655.

Palmini A, Andermann F, Olivier A (1991). Focal neuronal migration disorders and intractable epilepsy: a study of 30 patients. Ann. Neurol., 30: 741-749.

Placencia M, Shorvon S, Paredes V, Bimos C, Sander JWAS, Suarez J, Cascante SM (1992). Epileptic seizures in an Andean region in equador: incidence and prevalence and regional variation. Brain, 115: 771-782.

Ramakrishnan M, Ulland AJ, Steinhardt LC, Moïsi JC, Were F, Levine OS (2009). Sequelae due to bacterial meningitis among African children: a systematic literature review. Sep. BMC Med., 14(7): 47.

Raymond AA, Fish DR, Sisodiya SM (1995). Abnormalities of gyration, heterotopias, tuberous sclerosis, focal cortical dysplasia, microdysgenesis, dysembryoplastic neuroepithelial tumour and dysgenesis of the archicortex in epilepsy. Brain, 118: 629-660.

Taylor DC, Falconer MA, Bruton CJ (1971). Focal dysplasia of the cerebral cortex in epilepsy. J. Neurol. Neurosurg. Psychiat., 34: 369-387.

Woodbury DM, Woodbury JW (1990). Effects of vagal stimulation on experimentally induces seizures in rats. Epilepsia, 31(2): S7-S9.

Risk factor profile among black stroke patients in Northeastern Nigeria

Watila M. M.[1]*, Nyandaiti Y. W.[1], Ibrahim A.[2], Balarabe S. A.[3], Gezawa I. D.[4], Bakki B.[1], Tahir A.[1], Sulaiman M. M.[1] and Bwala S. A.[1]

[1]University of Maiduguri Teaching hospital, P. M. B. 1414, Maiduguri, Borno State. Nigeria.
[2]Federal Medical Centre, Azare, Bauchi State, Nigeria.
[3]Usman Danfodio University Teaching Hospital Sokoto. Nigeria
[4]Aminu Kano Teaching Hospital, PMB 3011 Kano, Nigeria.

Few studies have evaluated risk factors among stroke patients in our population. This study is aimed at exploring risk factors among black stroke patients. A total of 524 stroke patients seen at University of Maiduguri Teaching Hospital between January 2005 and June 2011 were evaluated to ascertain risk factors. Prestroke risk factors were obtained from patient's medical history and hospital records. Risk factors such as hypertension were gotten from case history, with hypertension defined as blood pressure (BP) of ≥ 140/90 mmHg or features of long standing hypertension. History of smoking, alcohol intake, transient ischaemic attack (TIA) were also noted. Hypertension was the commonest risk factor, found in 87% of patients, followed by hypercholesterolaemia 15.1%, past history of stroke 11.5%, diabetes 10.1%, alcohol 8.8%, smoking 6.8%, TIA 5.3%, heart failure 2.4% and preeclampsia-eclampsia 2.0%, while 19.7% had more than one risk factor. About 53% had no prior knowledge of being hypertensive, and only about 10% had treatment for hypertension prior to having a stroke. Males had higher systolic BP. Alcohol consumption and smoking were commoner in males and the young. The younger patients were more likely to acquire basic education, nephrotic syndrome and HIV infection. Hypertension and hypercholesterolaemia were common among the middle age group, while past history of stroke and multiple risk factors were commoner among the elderly. Thirty-day fatality was 17.7% and higher in older patients. Hypertension was found to be the most important risk factor for stroke among our study population. Public enlightenment on the importance of early detection of hypertension and adherence to antihypertensive medications will go a long way in reducing the morbidity and mortality associated with stroke in our environment.

Key words: Risk factors, hypertension, stroke, blacks, Nigerians.

INTRODUCTION

Stroke is the second most common cause of death worldwide (Beaglehole and Yach, 2003) and a leading cause of disability in adults (Murray and Lopez, 1997). A large percentage of stroke deaths occur in low-income to middle-income countries (Strong et al., 2007). An estimate of the leading cause of death in developing countries reported that strokes account about 8% of total deaths (Beaglehole and Yach, 2003). The morbidity and mortality from stroke may continue to increase in sub-Saharan Africa even as it is decreasing in developed countries (Tolonen et al., 2002; Connor et al., 2007). Stroke mortality in Nigeria is high, with stroke reviews reporting a 30-day case fatality rate raging from 28 to 40% (Ogun et al., 2005; Wahab et al., 2007). Discrepancies occur in stroke presentation and outcome between blacks and Caucasians, which may be attributable to differences in risk factors. Hypertension is

*Corresponding author. E-mail: Watilamusa@yahoo.com.

Table 1. The Siriraj stroke scale.

$$Siriraj\ Stroke\ Score = (2.5 \times level\ of\ consciousness) + (2 \times vomiting) + (2 \times headache) + (0.1 \times DBP) - (3 \times atheroma\ marker) - 12$$

Consciousness: Alert = 0; drowsy, stupor = 1; coma = 2
Vomiting: no = 0; yes = 1
Atheroma markers: none = 0; yes = 1
Score of:
< - 1= Ischemic stoke
> +1= Hemorrhagic stroke
Between -1 and +1= Indeterminate stroke

the most important risk factor for stroke worldwide, and the risk of all stroke subtypes increase with increasing blood pressure (Leppala et al., 1999; WHO, 1997; Makino et al., 2000). Hypertension appears to be more prevalent in blacks; while diabetes mellitus, smoking, atrial fibrillation (AF) and myocardial infarctions (MI) are commoner in whites (Sacco et al., 1995; Hajat et al., 2004). Risk factors should influence practice and prevention, as large proportion of Nigerians are still living in poverty and it will be logical to focus our attention on stroke prevention strategies. This study was designed to evaluate various risk factors of stroke in Northeastern Nigeria.

METHODS

Our subjects were all black and resident in Nigeria. We recruited 524 patients who consented; Information about all patients admitted to the program was captured prospectively in an in-hospital stroke registry between January 2005 and May 2010 at the University of Maiduguri Teaching Hospital (UMTH), a tertiary hospital located in Northeastern Nigeria, with a bed capacity of 600. The study was approved by the Research and Ethics committee of the hospital.

Stroke was clinically defined in accordance with the World Health Organization criteria as "rapidly developing clinical sign of focal and/or global disturbance of cerebral function, with symptoms lasting twenty-four hours or longer or leading to death with no apparent cause other than of vascular origin". (WHO, 1988)

Data collected and recorded in a stroke proforma for each patient at the time of the presentation include: Age, sex, educational level, and residence in a rural or urban area. Educational level was categorized into those with at least a secondary education and those with less than a secondary education. The presence of stroke risk factors was determined from medical histories, clinical examination, diagnostic procedures, and their past medical records. Hypertension was defined as a previously recorded systolic blood pressure ≥ 140 mmHg or diastolic blood pressure ≥ 90 mmHg on two separate occasions or during the course of stroke admission; those aware of being hypertensive as told by a health professional; or subjects taking antihypertensive medications. Compliance with antihypertensive medications in those diagnosed hypertensive was noted.

Diabetes mellitus was defined as those who had a prior diagnosis of DM, on antidiabetic medications, or previous fasting blood glucose level ≥ 7 mmol/L or random plasma glucose of > 11 mmol/L (Sridharan et al., 2009). Transient ischaemic attacks (TIA) was defined as sudden onset of focal neurological deficit with complete recovery within 24 h. Atrial fibrillation (AF) and myocardial infarction (MI) were diagnosed by clinical examination and electrocardiography. Heart failure was diagnosed based on clinical examination. HIV infection was diagnosed using the enzyme linked immunosorbent assay (ELISA). Hypercholesterolaemia was defined as fasting cholesterol concentration of > 5.5 mmol/L (200 mg/dl) (Tolonen et al., 2005). Sickle cell disease was diagnosed from history and haemoglobin electrophoresis. Information on social habits such as alcohol intake and cigarette smoking were obtained; smokers were considered as those who had smoked consistently for more than a year inclusive of those who had stopped smoking less than 6 months in accordance with a study by Tuomilehto et al. (1996). Consistent cigarette smoking is defined as ≥ 1 cigarette/day for ≥ 1 year, and significant alcohol intake was estimated as ≥ 200 g/week for more than a year (Moroney et al., 1998).

Other less common causes of stroke, such as antiphospholipid antibody syndrome, giant cell arteritis, thyrotoxicosis were screened only when there was a clinical suspicion of such conditions.

A computerized tomography scan (CT) or magnetic resonance imaging (MRI) was used to distinguish between intracerebral haemorrhage (ICH), cerebral ischaemia (CI) and subarachnoid haemorrhage. Being a resource poor setting, a large percentage (78.6%) of our patients did not have a neuroimaging. In such patients, stroke subtype was distinguished using the Siriraj stroke scale (SSS) (Poungvarian et al., 1991). The SSS had been validated in our centre in a study by Nyandaiti and Bwala, (2008) and is useful in resource poor settings to clinically assist in differentiating between stroke types.

The score was computed for each patient using the formula shown in Table 1. We categorized patients risk factors based on age and sex.

Statistical analysis

Risk factor differences among stroke groups were based on age and gender; the student's t-test was used to compare differences in mean values, while the χ^2 tests was used to compare differences in percentages of risk factor.

RESULTS

During the study period, 590 patients were seen with suspected diagnosis of stroke. Sixty-six patients were

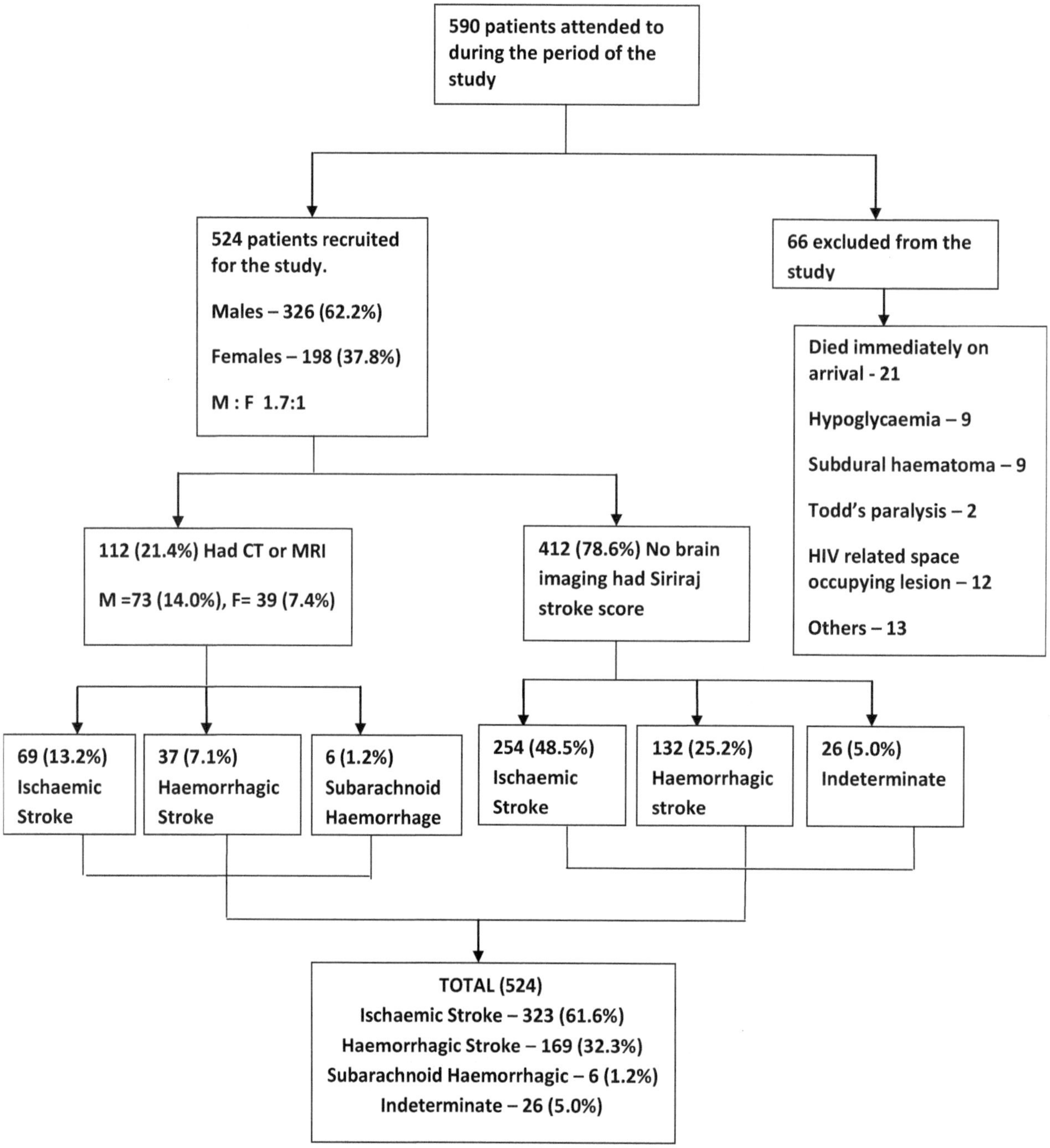

Figure 1. Flow chart showing the selection criteria and stroke subtype among the study subjects.

excluded from the study for various reasons (Figure 1). Therefore, 524 subjects were recruited for the study. The patients were all black Africans. The mean age of the patients was 56.4 ± 13.0 years, with 37.8% being females, with a male: Female ratio of 1.65:1. Less than one-third of the total subjects had basic formal education. Figure 2 summarizes the risk factors of the general population. The most frequent risk factors are hypertension 87%, hypercholesterolaemia 15.1%, past history of stroke 11.5%, diabetes mellitus 10.1%, alcohol 8.8%, smoking 6.8%, TIA 5.3%, heart failure 2.4%, preeclampsia-eclampsia 2.0% and 19.7% having more than one risk factor.

The main characteristics comparing men and women are presented in Table 2. Males were significantly older than females ($p = 0.001$). There were more females than males in the 26 to 35 years age group ($p = 0.001$). Females were more likely to have ischaemic stroke ($p = 0.002$), while males were more likely to have haemorrhagic stroke ($p = <0.001$). Females were less

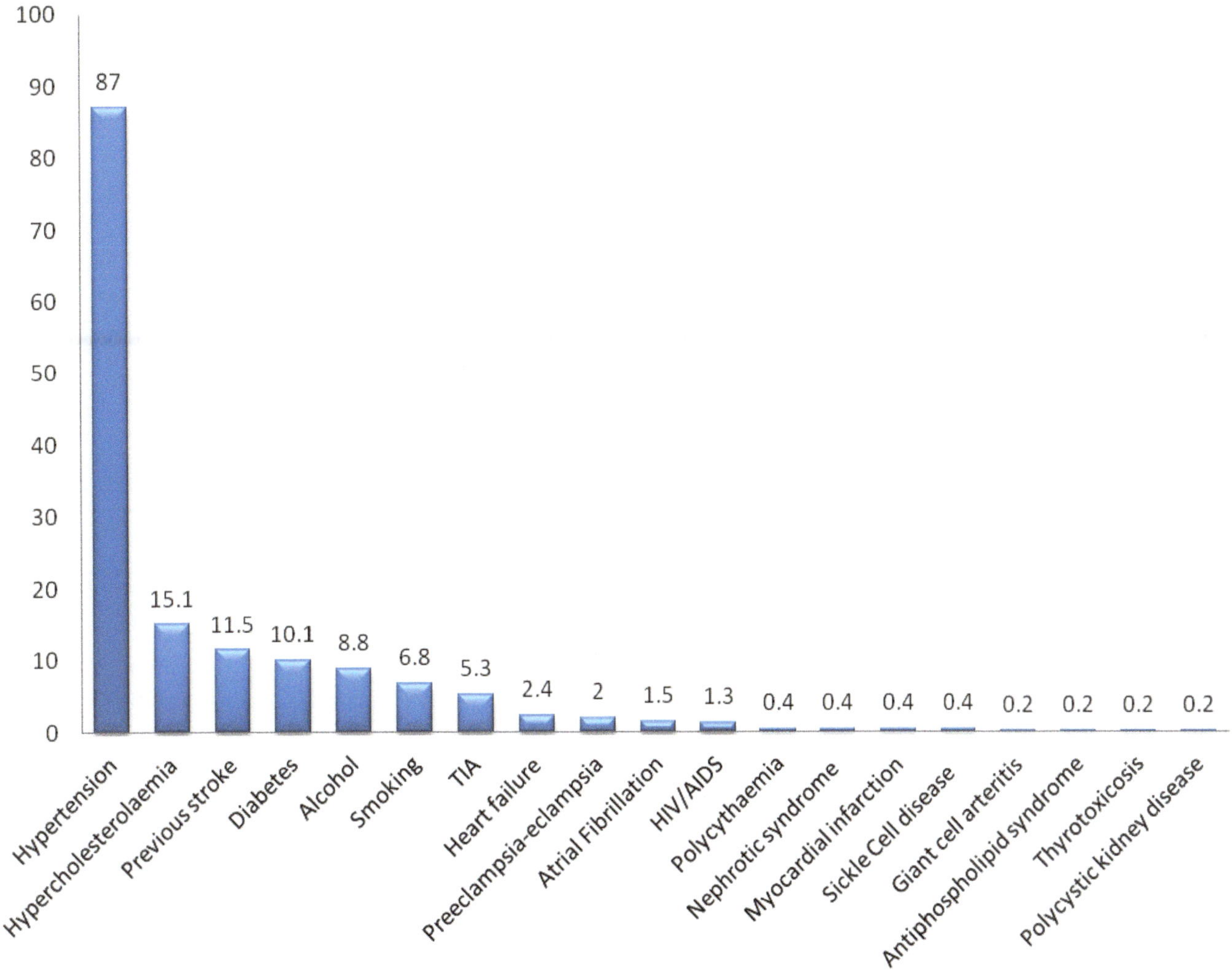

Figure 2. Distribution of stroke risk factors among the study subjects.

likely to have basic (postsecondary) education (p = <0.001). There was no significant gender difference in the frequency of hypertension as a risk factor. About 60.7% of males compared with 40.4% of females had a prestroke knowledge of being hypertensive (p = <0.001). Males were more likely to be on antihypertensive medication(s) (p = 0.036). Despite the aforementioned advantages in males, they still had a higher systolic blood pressure at presentation (p = 0.034). The proportion of those smoking or taking alcohol was higher among males than among females (p = <0.001); while females were more likely to have AF (p = 0.029). Preeclampsia and eclampsia is an important risk factor in females.

Table 3 shows the distribution of risk factor by age among the study subjects. The younger age group (<45 years) were more likely than the older ones to be formally educated (p = 0.002), to be current smokers (p = 0.018), to be infected with HIV (p = <0.001) and to have nephrotic syndrome (p = 0.007). In keeping with the age of reproduction, preeclampsia-eclampsia was more common in the younger age group (p = <0.001). The younger age were more likely not to have a discernable risk factor (p = <0.001). The middle age group (45 to 65 years) were more likely to be hypertensive (p = <0.001), to be diabetic (p = 0.023) and to have hypercholesterolaemia (p = 0.045). The older age group (>65 years) were more likely to have a past history of stroke (p = 0.045) and were more likely to have more than one risk factor (p = <0. 001). The overall 30-day stroke fatality was 17.7%, and these deaths were less likely to occur among the young (p = 0.01). No significant sex difference in 30-day fatality.

DISCUSSION

Most studies in Nigeria that looked at risk factors for stroke were mainly retrospective in design. Our study showed that stroke occurs at a relatively younger age, a finding that is in with keeping earlier reports (Gillum,

Table 2. Distribution of study subjects in relation to sex.

Variable	Male (n=326)	Female (n=198)	p-Value*	Total (N=524)
Mean age (years)	57.9 ± 12.4 (18-90)	53.9 ± 13.6(20-90)	0.001	56.4 ± 13.0 8-90)
Age group (years)				
<25	6 (1.8)	5 (2.5)	0.596	11(2.1)
26-35	8 (2.5)	17 (8.6)	0.001*	25(4.8)
36-45	39 (12.0)	32 (16.2)	0.173	71(13.5)
46-55	78 (23.9)	51 (25.8)	0.637	129(24.6)
56-65	108 (33.1)	58 (29.3)	0.360	166(31.7)
66-75	72 (22.1)	30 (15.2)	0.052	102(19.5)
76-85	12 (3.7)	4 (2.0)	0.284	16(3.1)
>86	3 (0.9)	1 (0.5)	0.596	4 (0.8)
Education				
No secondary	208 (63.8)	170 (85.9)	<0.001*	378 (72.1)
Secondary	118 (36.2)	28 (14.1)	146 (27.9)	
Rural dweller	81 (24.8)	52 (26.3)	0.718	133(25.4)
Urban dweller	245 (75.2)	146 (73.7)		391 (74.6)
Stroke type				
Ischaemia	184 (57.0)	139 (70.2)	0.002*	323 (61.6)
Haemorrhage	124 (38.0)	45 (22.7)	<0.001*	169 (32.3)
Indeterminate	15 (4.6)	11 (5.5)	0.637	26 (5.0)
SAH	5 (1.5)	1(0.5)	0.283	6 (1.2)
Hypertension	280 (85.9)	176 (88.9)	0.322	456 (87.0)
Previous stroke	33 (10.1)	27 (13.6)	0.221	60 (11.5)
Hypercholesterolaemia	47 (14.4)	32 (16.2)	0.588	79 (15.1)
Diabetes	31 (9.5)	22 (11.1)	0.555	53 (10.1)
Alcohol	44 (13.5)	2 (1.0)	<0.001*	46 (8.8)
Smoking	35 (10.7)	1 (0.5)	<0.001*	17 (5.2)
TIA	36 (6.8)	11 (5.5)	0.866	28 (5.3)
Preeclampsia-eclampsia	0 (0.0)	10(5.1)	<0.001*	10 (2.0)
Heart failure	5 (1.5)	8 (4.0)	0.074	13 (2.4)
Atrial fibrillation	2 (0.6)	6 (3.0)	0.029*`	8 (1.5)
HIV	4 (1.2)	3 (1.5)	0.781	7 (1.3)
Polycythaemia	2 (0.6)	0 (0.0)	0.269	2 (0.4)
Nephrotic syndrome	2 (0.6)	0 (0.0)	0.269	2 (0.4)
Myocardial infarction	2 (0.6)	0 (0.0)	0.269	2 (0.4)
Sickle cell disease	2 (0.6)	0 (0.0)	0.269	2 (0.0)
Giant cell arteritis	1 (0.3)	0 (0.0)	0.435	1 (0.2)
Antiphospholipid syndrome	1 (0.3)	0 (0.0)	0.435	1 (0.2)
Thyrotoxicosis	1 (0.3)	0 (0.0)	0.435	1 (0.2)
Polycystic kidney disease	1 (0.3)	0 (0.0)	0.435	1 (0.2)
More than one risk factor	59 (18.1)	44 (22.2)	0.249	103 (19.7)
No discernable risk	11 (3.4)	5 (2.5)	0.584	16 (3.1)
SBP (mmHg)	160.0 ± 35.4	153.6 ± 29.8	0.034*	157.6 ± 33.5
DBP (mmHg)	98.9 ± 20.6	95.5 ±17.1	0.052	97.6 ±19.4
Awareness of hypertension	198 (60.7)	80 (40.4)	<0.001*	278 (53.1)
Hypertensive medication	13 (6.6)	0.036*	53 (10.1)	40 (12.3)
30-day fatality	58 (17.8)	35 (17.7)	0.973	93 (17.7)

Students' t-test for continuous variable; χ^2, for categorical variable. *, p-value ≤ 0.05; SAH, subarachnoid haemorrhage, TIA, transient ischaemic attack; SBP, systolic blood pressure; DBP, diastolic blood pressure.

Table 3. Distribution of risk factors by age of subjects.

Risk factor	< 45 years (n=88)	45-65 years (n=314)	> 65 years (n=122)	p-Value
Level of education				
Less than secondary	46 (52.3)	202 (64.3)	92(75.4)	0.002*
Secondary education	42 (47.7)	112 (35.7)	30 (24.6)	
Hypertension	59 (67.1)	292 (93.0)	105 (86.1)	<0.001*
Previous stroke	4(4.5)	37 (11.8)	19 (15.6)	0.045*
Hypercholesterolaemia	14 (15.9)	56 (17.8)	9 (7.4)	0.023*
Diabetes	2 (2.3)	43 (13.7)	8 (6.6)	0.002*
Alcohol intake	9 (10.2)	31 (9.9)	6 (4.9)	0.226
Current smoking	12 (13.6)	19 (6.1)	5 (4.1)	0.018*
TIA	5 (5.7)	14 (4.5)	9 (7.4)	0.472
Preeclampsia-eclampsia	7 (8.0)	0 (0.0)	0 (0.0)	<0.001*
Heart failure	2 (2.3)	9 (2.9)	2 (1.6)	0.754
Atrial fibrillation	0 (0.0)	4 (1.3)	4 (3.3)	0.136
HIV/AIDS	6 (6.8)	1 (0.3)	0 (0.0)	<0.001*
Nephrotic syndrome	2 (2.3)	0 (0.0)	0 (0.0)	0.007*
Myocardial Infarction	0 (0.0)	1 (0.3)	1 (0.8)	0.611
Sickle cell disease	1 (1.1)	1 (0.3)	0 (0.0)	0.403
Antiphospholipid syndrome	1 (1.1)	0 (0.0)	0 (0.0)	0.084
Thyrotoxicosis	1 (1.1)	0 (0.0)	0 (0.0)	0.084
Giant cell arteritis	0 (0.0)	1 (0.3)	0 (0.0)	0.715
Polycystic kidney disease	1 (1.1)	0 (0.0)	0 (0.0)	0.084
More than one risk factor	10 (11.4)	40 (12.7)	53 (43.0)	<0.001*
No discernable risk factor	6 (6.8)	5 (1.6)	5 (4.1)	0.031*
30-day fatality	6 (6.8)	60 (19.1)	27 (22.1)	0.01*

χ^2, For categorical variables. *, p-value ≤ 0.05; TIA, transient ischaemic attack.

1998; Bravata et al., 2005). Men were older than females in this study; this is similar to an earlier study done in this centre (Watila et al., 2011), but at variance with studies done in whites (Bravata et al., 2005; Wadley et al., 2007).

More than two-third of our patients, especially women, had no basic education. Low educational attainment may probably translate into a low income. Stroke incidence appears to increase with lower educational attainment, social class and income (Bravata et al., 2005), but Chang et al. (2002) in a study among Africans reported contrasting findings. The relationship between high stroke incidence and low social class as found in this study, has not been fully elucidated, but may be related to inequalities in access to health care, as well as dietary factors (Chang et al., 2002; McFadden et al., 2009).

A variety of risk factor exists in this study, with hypertension being the most important regardless of age and sex. Hypertension is the most significant risk factor for stroke worldwide (Sacco et al., 1995; Feigin et al., 1998; Simons et al., 1998; McGruder et al., 2004; Smeeton et al., 2009; Andersen et al., 2010). The prevalence of hypertension in this study is similar to other Nigerian studies (Bwala, 1989; Amu et al., 2005) and similar to other epidemiological studies in Mozambique (Damasceno et al., 2010) and India (Sridharan et al., 2009). Studies done in whites show a much lower value when compared with blacks (Wadley et al., 2007; Hajat et al., 2001; Ohira et al., 2006). A study by McGruder et al. (2004) showed that blacks were 1.65 times more likely to be hypertensive than whites. Management of hypertension prevents strokes (Simons et al., 1998; Ohira et al., 2006) with studies showing that antihypertensive therapy reduces the risk of stroke by about 42% (MacMahon and Rogers, 1994; Bronner et al., 1995). A study by Zhang et al. (2004) reported that 50% or more of all strokes in Asians could be prevented if hypertension is controlled. We noted that more than half of our patients had no prior knowledge of being hypertensive and this lack of knowledge is more pronounced among females; nonetheless uncommon in some studies (Broderick, 1997; Samal et al., 2007). This trend may reflect poor public knowledge, poor health practices and access to healthcare. Even when blacks are treated for hypertension, they were less likely than whites to be compliant with medications and have their blood pressure controlled (Howard et al., 2006). A study by Woo et al. (2004) reported that women were more likely to have their hypertension treated than men, which is at variance with our study. Knowledge of risk factors for stroke is influenced by educational level (Samal et al., 2007).

Diabetes is an important risk factor for stroke (Tuomilehto et al., 1996; Andersen et al., 2010; Hu et al., 2005) and an independent risk factor for death (Tuomilehto et al., 1996). It has been noted that diabetes and hypertension have an additive effect on the risk of stroke (Hu et al., 2005; Iso et al., 1989). Studies have shown that blacks were more likely to be diabetic (Hajat et al., 2001, 2004; McGruder et al., 2004) but the percentage of our patients with diabetes was rather low when compared with those in whites (Hajat et al., 2001). A study has shown a preponderance of males being more likely to be diabetic (Andersen et al., 2010) but our study revealed no sex difference.

Hypercholesterolaemia appears to be an important risk factor for stroke in this study. High total cholesterol has been associated with stroke and stroke mortality (Iso et al., 1989) but another study reported a contrary view (Rhoads and Feinleib., 1983). The role of lipids in stroke patients in our environments needs further work in carefully selected stroke subjects. This finding may be important in this respect in our environment, as our populace now imbibe the western habit of eating high fatty foods and doing away with the indigenous high fiber diet.

Although blacks suffer less AF (Hajat et al., 2001) consistent with our study; it is still an important independent risk factor for stroke and also a predictor of early recurrence (Simons et al., 1998; Moroney et al., 1998). Anticoagulation is of use in preventing stroke recurrence especially in the elderly (Atrial Fibrillation Investigators, 1994), a treatment we do not commonly make use of.

Prior history of stroke is an important risk in our study; this is in keeping with a study by Simons et al. (1998) commonly due to lack of proper treatment of stroke risk factors. Other reasons for the high stroke recurrence in our study may be due to poor health care and education among our patients.

In sub-Saharan Africa, there is now an excess of stroke risk from HIV infection commonly in the young (Damasceno et al., 2010) as reported in this study. Viral pathogens have been linked to atherogenesis and vasculitis in cerebral vasculature (Lindsberg and Grau, 2003).

Alcohol intake and cigarette smoking are commoner in males and the young in this study; which is comparable to a study in black Caribbean patients (Smeeton et al., 2009). Smoking is a potential risk factor for stroke, and is more prevalent in males and the young (Ueshima et al., 2004) while the study by Andersen et al. (2010) reported an equal frequency of smoking in both genders. A high prevalence (49%) was reported in a study by Li et al. (2005). Smoking promotes atherosclerosis, platelet aggregation and vascular occlusion. Light alcohol intake is adjudged to be protective, but heavy alcohol intake significantly increases the risk of stroke; this increase of risk was more marked in hypertensive, suggesting a synergistic effect of alcohol and hypertension (Kiyohara et al., 1995). Women with preeclampsia-eclampsia have a significantly higher risk of stroke (both hemorrhagic and ischemic), and after delivery this risk remains significant at least 12 months for hemorrhagic stroke and 6 months for ischemic stroke (Tang et al., 2009). Preeclampsia-eclampsia is common in this part of the world due to poor antenatal care (Audu et al., 2002). Other factors that may contribute to pregnancy as a stroke risk are: Malnutrition, stress from pregnancy, increased risk of cardiac disease and haemostatic impairment (Qureshi et al., 1997; Zhang et al., 2009). Pregnancy-related causes of stroke may explain the significant switch in sex ratio in the age group 26 to 35 years of age; and may explain the relatively younger age of women in this study since they occur within the reproductive age group. Pregnancy-related strokes in our environment may be an area for further studies. The other risk factors in this study although important, contribute a smaller percentage to stroke risk in this environment, but should in no way be neglected. A multicentre study in Nigeria is imperative to assess various risk factors on a larger scale. The strength of the study is that it is a prospective study, and incorporating a large percentage of stroke admissions during the study period. Some of the weaknesses of this study include a relatively large percentage of patients not having a CT or MRI. Performing a brain scan for all patients would have increased the strength of the study, by assessing the relationship between risk factors and stroke subtype.

In conclusion, this study showed that hypertension is the most important risk factor. Hypertension is however a potentially preventable and treatable condition. We need to embark on public awareness towards regular BP checks and optimum BP control. We should also take time to educate our patients and insist on compliance. Nigerians must begin to understand the risk factors for strokes in order to reduce its incidence. Stroke is one condition in which the word "prevention is better than cure" stands true. Africa stands at a disadvantaged position with respect to stroke care. Although more neurologists are being trained albeit grossly insufficient and unevenly distributed, resources for stroke care are still grossly inadequate. Poverty combined with illiteracy is a major factor militating against the effective management of hypertension, which if achieved will significantly reduce stroke incidence in our environment. Preventive strategies are more cost effective than managing index cases. It is time to act towards risk factor modifications.

ACKNOWLEDGEMENT

We wish to acknowledge the contributions of the members of the radiology and chemical pathology departments.

REFERENCES

Amu E, Ogunrin O, Danesi M (2005). Re-Appraisal of risk factors for stroke in Nigerian Africans. A Prospective case - control study. Afr. J. Neurosc., 24:20-27.

Andersen KK, Andersen ZJ, Olsen TS (2010). Age- and Gender-Specific Prevalence of Cardiovascular Risk Factors in 40 102 Patients with First-Ever Ischemic Stroke. A Nationwide Danish Study. Stroke, 41: 2768-2774.

Atrial Fibrillation Investigators (1994). Risk factors for stroke and efficacy of antithrombotic therapy in atrial fibrillation: analysis of pooled data from five randomized controlled trials. Arch. Int. Med., 154:1449–1457.

Audu BM, Obed JY, Kyari O (2002). Review of factors predisposing to eclampsia and outcome. Trop. J. Obstet. Gynaecol., 19: 23.

Beaglehole R, Yach D (2003). Globalisation and the prevention and control of non-communicable disease: the neglected chronic diseases of adults. Lancet, 362:903–908.

Bravata DM, Wells CK, Gulanski B, Kernan WN, Brass LM, Long J, Concato J (2005). Racial Disparities in Stroke Risk Factors. The Impact of Socioeconomic Status. Stroke, 36: 1507-1511.

Broderick JP (1997). Logistics in acute stroke management. Drugs, 54(3): 109 –116.

Bronner LL, Kanter DS, Manson JE (1995). Primary prevention of stroke, N Engl. J. Med., 23: 1392–1400.

Bwala SA (1989). Stroke in sub-Saharan Nigerian hospital: A retrospective study. Tropical Doctor, 19: 11-14.

Chang CL, Shipley MJ, Marmot MG, Poulter NR (2002). Can cardiovascular risk factors explain the association between education and cardiovascular disease in young women? J. Clin. Epid, 55:749-755.

Connor MD, Walker R, Modi G, Warlow CP (2007). Burden of stroke in black populations in sub-Saharan Africa, Lancet Neurol., 6: 269–278.

Damasceno A, Gomes J, Azevedo A, Carrilho C, LoboV, Lopes H, Madede T, Pravinrai P, Silva-Matos C, Jalla S, Stewart S, Lunet N (2010). An Epidemiological Study of Stroke Hospitalizations in Maputo, Mozambique. High Burden of Disease in a Resource-Poor Country. Stroke, 41:2463-2469.

Feigin VL, Wiebers DO, Nikitin YP, O'Fallon WM, Whisnant JP (1998). Risk Factors for Ischemic Stroke in a Russian Community: A Population-Based Case-Control Study. Stroke, 29: 34-39.

Gillum RF (1998). Stroke in blacks. Stroke, 19: 1–9.

Hajat C, Tilling K, Stewart JA, Lemic-Stojcevic N, Wolfe CDA (2004). Ethnic Differences in Risk Factors for Ischemic Stroke. A European Case–Control Study. Stroke, 35:1562-1567.

Hajat C. Dundas R, Stewart JA, Lawrence E, Rudd AG, Howard R, Wolfe CDA (2001). Cerebrovascular Risk Factors and Stroke Subtypes Differences between Ethnic Groups. Stroke, 32:37-42.

Howard G, Prineas R, Moy C, Cushman M, Kellum M, Temple E, Graham A, Howard V (2006). Racial and Geographic Differences in Awareness, Treatment, and Control of Hypertension. The REasons for Geographic and Racial Differences in Stroke Study. Stroke, 37:1171-1178.

Hu G, Sarti C, Jousilahti P, Peltonen M, Qiao Q, Antikainen R, Tuomilehto J (2005). The Impact of History of Hypertension and Type 2 Diabetes at Baseline on the Incidence of Stroke and Stroke Mortality. Stroke, 36: 2538-2543.

Iso H, Jacobs DR, Wentworth D, Neaton JD, Cohen JD (1989). Serum cholesterol levels and six-year mortality from stroke in 350,977 men screened for the Multiple Risk Factor Intervention trial. N Engl. J. Med., 320: 904-910.

Kiyohara Y, Kato I, Iwamoto H, Nakayama K, Fujishima M (1995). The Impact of Alcohol and Hypertension on Stroke Incidence in a General Japanese Population. The Hisayama Study. Stroke 26: 368-372.

Leppala JM, Virtamo J, Fogelholm R, Albanes D, Heinonen OP (1999). Different Risk Factors for Different Stroke Subtypes: Association of Blood Pressure, Cholesterol, and Antioxidants. Stroke, 30: 2535-2540.

Li C, Engström G, Hedblad B, Berglund G, Janzon L (2005). Risk Factors for Stroke in Subjects with Normal Blood Pressure: A Prospective Cohort Study, Stroke, 36: 234-238.

Lindsberg PJ, Grau AJ (2003). Inflammation and Infections as Risk Factors for Ischemic Stroke. Stroke, 34: 2518-2532.

MacMahon S, Rogers A (1994). Epidemiological association between blood pressure and stroke. Implication for primary and secondary prevention. Hyper Res., 17: 523-532.

Makino Y, Kawano Y, Minami J, Yamaguchi T, Takishita S(2000). Risk of Stroke in Relation to Level of Blood Pressure and Other Risk Factors in Treated Hypertensive Patients. Stroke, 31:48-52.

McFadden E, Luben R, Wareham N, Bingham S, Khaw KT (2009). Social Class, Risk Factors, and Stroke Incidence in Men and Women. A Prospective Study in the European Prospective Investigation into Cancer in Norfolk Cohort. Stroke, 40: 1070-1077.

McGruder HF, Malarcher AM, Antoine TL, Greenlund KJ, Croft JB (2004). Racial and Ethnic Disparities in Cardiovascular Risk Factors among Stroke Survivors United States 1999 to 2001, Stroke, 35: 1557-1561.

Moroney JT, Bagiella E, Paik MC, Sacco RL, Desmond DW (1998). Risk Factors for Early Recurrence after Ischemic Stroke: The Role of Stroke Syndrome and Subtype. Stroke, 29: 2118-2124.

Murray CJL, Lopez AD (1997). Mortality by cause for eight regions of the world. The global burden of diseases study. Lancet, 349: 1269-1279.

Nyandaiti Y, Bwala SA (2008). Validation Study of Siriraj Stroke Score in North-eastern Nigeria. Niger J Clin. Pract., 11: 176-180.

Ogun SA, Ojini FI, Ogungbo B, Kolapo KO, Danesi MA (2005). Stroke in South West Nigeria. A 10-year review. Stroke, 36: 1120-1122.

Ohira T, Shahar E, Chambless LE, Rosamond WD, Mosley TH Jr, Folsom AR (2006). Risk Factors for Ischemic Stroke Subtypes: The Atherosclerosis Risk in Communities Study. Stroke, 37; 2493-2498.

Poungvarian N, Viriyavejakul A, Komotri C (1991). Siriraj Stroke score and the validation study to distinguish supratentorial intracerebral haemorrhage from infarction. BMJ., 302: 1565-1567.

Qureshi AI, Giles WH, Croft JB, Stern BJ (1997). Number of pregnancies and risk for stroke and stroke subtypes. Arch Neurol., 54: 203–206.

Rhoads GA, Feinleib M (1983). Serum triglyceride and risk of coronary heart disease, stroke and total mortality in Japanese-American men. Arterioscl., 3: 316-32.

Sacco RL, Kargmann DE, Zamanillo MC (1995). Race-ethnic differences in stroke risk factors among hospitalized patients with cerebral infarction: the Northern Manhattan Study. Neurol., 45: 659–663.

Samal D, Greisenegger S, Auff E, Lang W, Lalouschek W (2007). The Relation between Knowledge about Hypertension and Education in Hospitalized Patients with Stroke in Vienna. Stroke, 38: 1304-1308.

Simons LA, McCallum J, Friedlander Y, Simons J (1998). Risk Factors for Ischemic Stroke: Dubbo Study of the Elderly. Stroke, 29: 1341-1346.

Smeeton NC, Corbin DOC, Hennis AJ, Hambleton IR, Fraser HS, Wolfe CDA, Heuschmann PU (2009). Differences in Risk Factors between Black Caribbean Patients with Stroke in Barbados and South London. Stroke, 40: 640-643.

Sridharan SE, Unnikrishnan JP, Sukumaran S, Sylaja PN, Nayak SD, Sarma PS, Radhakrishnan K (2009). Incidence, Types, Risk Factors, and Outcome of Stroke in a Developing Country. The Trivandrum Stroke Registry. Stroke, 40: 1212-1218.

Strong K, Mathers C, Bonita R (2007). Preventing stroke: saving lives around the world. Lancet Neurol., 6: 182–187.

Tang CH, Wu CS, Lee TH, Hung ST, Yang CYC, Lee CH, Chu PH (2009). Preeclampsia-Eclampsia and the Risk of Stroke among Peripartum in Taiwan. Stroke, 40: 1162-1168.

Tolonen H, Keil U, Ferrario M, Evans A (2005). For the WHO MONICA Project. Prevalence, awareness and treatment of hypercholesterolaemia in 32 populations: results from the WHO MONICA Project. Int. J. Epidemiol., 34:181–192.

Tolonen H, Mähönen M, Asplund K, Rastenyte D, Kuulasmaa K, Vanuzzo D, Tuomilehto J (2002). For the WHO MONICA Project. Do Trends in Population Levels of Blood Pressure and Other Cardiovascular Risk Factors Explain Trends in Stroke Event Rates?

Comparisons of 15 Populations in 9 Countries Within the WHO MONICA Stroke Project. Stroke, 33: 2367-2375.

Tuomilehto J, Rastenyte D, Jousilahti P, Sarti C, Vartiainen E (1996). Diabetes Mellitus as a Risk Factor for Death From Stroke. Prospective Study of the Middle-aged Finnish Population. Stroke, 27: 210-215.

Ueshima H, Choudhury SR, Okayama A, Hayakawa T, Kita Y, Kadowaki T, Okamura T, Minowa M, Iimura O (2004). NIPPON DATA80 Research Group. Cigarette Smoking as a Risk Factor for Stroke Death in Japan: NIPPON DATA80. Stroke, 35: 1836-1841.

Wadley VG, McClure LA, Howard VJ, Unverzagt FW, Go RC, Moy CS, Crowther MR, Gomez CR, Howard G (2007). Cognitive Status, Stroke Symptom Reports, and Modifiable Risk Factors among Individuals with no Diagnosis of Stroke or Transient Ischemic Attack in the REasons for Geographic and Racial Differences in Stroke (REGARDS) Study. Stroke, 38: 1143-1147.

Wahab KW, Sani MU, Samaila AA, Gbadamosi A, Olokoba AB (2007). Stroke at a tertiary medical institution in Northern Nigeria: patient's profile and predictors of outcome. Sahel Med. J., 10: 6-10.

Watila MM, Nyandaiti YW, Bwala SA, Ibrahim A (2011). Gender variation in risk factors and clinical presentation of acute stroke, Northeastern Nigeria. J. Neurosc. Behav. Health, 3: 38-43.

WHO (1988). Monica project, Principal investigators. The World Health Organization Monica project (monitoring trends and determinants in cardiovascular disease) a major international collaboration. J. Clin. Epid., 41: 105-114.

WHO (1997). World Health Organization (WHO). The World Health Report, Conquering Suffering, Enriching Humanity. Geneva. 1-162.

Woo D, Haverbusch M, Sekar P, Kissela B, Khoury J, Schneider A, Kleindorfer D, Szaflarski J, Pancioli A, Jauch E, Moomaw C, Sauerbeck L, Gebel J, Broderick J (2004). Effect of Untreated Hypertension on Hemorrhagic Stroke. Stroke, 35: 1703-1708.

Zhang XF, Attia J, D'Este C, Yu XH (2004). Prevalence and Magnitude of Classical Risk Factors for Stroke in a Cohort of 5092 Chinese Steelworkers over 13.5 Years of Follow-up. Stroke, 35: 1052-1056.

Zhang X-O, Shu X, Gao Y-T, Yang G, Li H, Zheng W (2009). Pregnancy, Childrearing, and Risk of Stroke in Chinese Women. Stroke, 40: 2680-2684.

Effect of interaction between eye-hand dominance on dart skill

Rahil Razeghi, Parvaneh Shafie Nia, Nahid Shebab bushehri and Farzad Maleki*

Department of Sport Psychology, Faculty of Physical Education and Sport Science, Shahid Chamran University of Ahvaz, Iran.

The purpose of this research was surveying the effect of interaction between eye hand dominance on dart skill. Twenty healthy male subjects (age: 21.43±1.33) from University of Shahid Chamran were served as the participants for this study. Subjects were divided into two groups: unilateral (right eye and right hand or left eye and left hand) group (10 subjects) and cross lateral (right eye and left hand or left eye and right hand) group (10 subjects). Each group trained for 12 sessions in the same condition. The acquisition test was made after the last training session and the retention test was made 1 week later. The scores of pre-test, acquisition and retention were recorded. Subjects threw 60 darts in each training session. Porta (Roth, 2002) and Hole in the card test (Sage, 1984) was used to select eye dominance and Edinburgh questionnaire (Oldfield, 1971) was used to determine handedness. Values of $p<0.05$ were chosen as significant. The results of dependent t-test (paired t-test) analysis showed that there was a significant difference between the pre-test, acquisition and retention between two groups that showed both groups learn dart skill. On the other hand, the subjects of two groups improved significantly in acquisition and retention phases rather than pre-test phase. Moreover, the results of independent t-test showed that there was no significant difference between unilateral and cross lateral in acquisition and retention tests. Our findings revealed that interaction between hand and eye dominance does not affect dart skill.

Key words: Unilateral, cross lateral, dart.

INTRODUCTION

Most people tend to use one side of their bodies more easily, more frequently, and more dexterously than the other side and this is often characterized by left- or right-handedness by the dominant use of a left or right foot (Suttle et al., 2008).

Laterality is defined by the American Heritage Medical Dictionary as "preferential use of limbs of one side of body." Knowing one's laterality pattern (dominance of eye, hand, and foot) makes it possible to suggest situations adapted for learning skills more efficiently, to detect and guide young talents, to optimize the work of limbs for each side of the body and to achieve powerful coordination (Laborde et al., 2009).

It has been demonstrated that the ocular system is not an exception and that an individual will usually prefer to use one eye rather than the other for certain tasks. Ocular dominance is not correlated with other types of lateral body dominance, such as handedness (Suttle et al., 2008). This preference leads to numerous perceptual effects: subjects are more accurate using their dominant eye images which appear clearer and larger when viewed by the dominant eye and stabilized retinal images fade slower when viewed by the dominant eye (Shneor et al., 2006).

The concept of handedness has shaped most considerations of the functional asymmetry or laterality of the human movement system. To a significant degree, the privileged status of handedness has arisen because, more formally, a person`s preference for hand use can be assessed in straightforward ways by either a questionnaire or a battery of performance test (Balasubramania, 2000).

Ninety percent of people are right-handed, 80%

*Corresponding author. E-mail: Lihar000@yahoo.com.

right-foot, 70% right-eyed, about 60% are right-eared (Saudino et al., 1998) and about 35% of right-handers and 57% of left-handers are left-eye dominant (McManus et al., 1999).

People whose eye dominance and handedness are in the same side are named unilateral or uncross (right-hand and right-eye or left-eye and left-hand) lateral and people whose eye dominance and handedness are not same side are named cross lateral (right-eye and left-hand or left-eye and right-hand) (Payne et al., 2002).

It is clear that visual information is critical to performance sport skill. If the visual system does not receive messages accurately or quickly enough, performance may suffer. It is important for visual systems to be functioning at advanced levels because athletic performance can be one of the most rigorous activities for the visual system (Deborah, 2009). The dominant eye will focus directly toward external stimulus, such as an oncoming ball or the movement of the opponent. This suggests that the dominant eye should play a significant role in the development of sport skills, from aiming tasks, such as archery and golf-putting to faster-paced sports, such as tennis and soccer (Steinberg et al, 1999).

Considering sports like shooting, it seems that interaction between hand preference and eye dominance is an effective factor on performance. The uncrossed eye-hand pattern is distinctly more successful than the crossed eye-hand, given the features of activity, motionless target, and nonexistent time pressure. Moreover, to aim at the target, athletes have to align two points between eye and target. So, it is an advantage to use the arm corresponding to the sighting eye (unilateral eye hand pattern) (Deborah, 2009). However, the amount of this effect on different sport skills is significantly variable.

In addition, the vision requirements of each sport are different. The breakdown of visual skills by sport shows these differences and the relative importance of these skills to each sport (Gardner, 1995). For example, researches claimed that there is no significant difference between unilateral and cross lateral in baseball skill (Goss, 1995; Portal, 1998). But, novice unilateral (uncrossed lateral, right eye and right eye dominance) were better than novice crossed laterals (left eye and right hand dominance) in archery when they did not use sights (Laborde et al., 2009).

There is another fact about effect of interaction of eye-hand dominance on some sport skills. In task conditions characterizing duel sports, the dominant eye is requested and functionally connected via the lateral geniculate nucleus to the ipsilateral hemisphere. On the contrary, concerning manual responses, the responding hand is connected via its motor area with the contralateral hemisphere. Consequently, the functional connection between visual input and motor output involves only one hemisphere for subjects presenting a contralateral relationship between the dominant eye and the responding hand. These subjects, therefore, do not need such an interhemispheric transfer, relatively expensive in time. The result for them is an advantage in reaction times, compared to subjects with ipsilateral dominant eye and the responding hand (Azémar et al., 2008). Although dart needs accuracy more than speed, aiming at far targets, such as those in basketball or darts, appears to use a different form of visuo-motor control. Vickers's results provide support for an open-loop mode of control in dart. In open-loop models of control, vision on the target is used to organize the aiming commands prior to the final movement, which is run-off without any need for feedback. Open-loop models argue that since the aiming commands are set early during sustained fixation, there is no need to maintain vision on the target as the dart is thrown (Vickers et al., 2000). So, regarding these different results and differences which potentially exist in different sports, it can be said that the effect of relationship of eye-hand dominance with dart shows interesting results.

On the other hand, this subject can be beneficial in selecting an effective method to teach sport skills, like dart. Brain is an important component in determining how humans learn, but brain cannot learn by itself. Eyes, ears, hands, and feet are all mechanisms of information transportation to the brain. They provide stimulant information that brain can use to make appropriate decisions about learning. Although dominant preferences vary over time, ultimately, the right or left side of each of these senses will tend to dominate and function more efficiently than the other when it comes to learning (Deborah, 2009).

Moreover, the challenge is to find an appropriate system to determine learning strengths and weaknesses and this can be addressed through the use of dominant preferences (Deborah, 2009). The increasing diversity of students and the current standards reform movement are two additional developmental areas supporting the use of various learning styles. With increased diversity, students will have a wide variety of learning needs (Bellanca, 1998; Curry, 1999). Educators need to understand dominance profiles because the research suggests incongruities between learning preferences of teachers and preferences of the students they teach. Knowledge in this area can help physical educators determine best teaching practices and applications to enhance learning. Dominance profiles can give the teacher and/or student an understanding of how she/he learns best. This understanding can create an awareness of strengths and weaknesses in ones teaching approach so that all students are taught according to their inherent learning preferences. The standards reform movement also suggests that by understanding the variety of inherent learning styles in students, teachers can increase performance, hence meeting higher standards mandated by the reform initiatives (Deborah, 2009). So, it seems that interaction can be effective for some skills, for example, unilateral group learned rifle skill better than cross lateral (Jones et al., 1999).

This variability in eye dominance among the student population could play a key role in developing an appropriate individualized lesson plan; thus, its determination should be included in the lesson plan (Steinberg et al., 1999).

It seems that eye–hand dominance quality (unilateral and cross lateral) can affect the accuracy of performance in many sports but there are many results that show disagreeing results. On the other hand, more affective styles can be selected to teach some sport skills by recognizing lateral preferences; therefore, the aim of the present study is to compare unilateral and cross lateral in acquisition and retention phases in dart throwing skill.

METHODOLOGY

Subjects

One hundred male students (age 21.43±1.33 years) who studied in Shahid Chamran University of Ahvaz, Iran, in 2010, were randomly selected before the administration of the tests. All subjects completed the Edinburgh questionnaire (Oldfield, 1971) to determine handedness and did Porta (Roth, 2002) and Hole in the card test (Sage, 1984) to determine eye dominance. Subjects who had one of the following qualities were deleted from the study:

i. Subjects who used glass or lens
ii. Subjects who had experience in aiming skill especially in dart.
iii. Subjects who got a mark between -40 and +40 ($-40 < X < +40$) in Edinburgh questionnaire (subjects were ambidextrous)
iv. Subjects who could not see the target just by one eye (right or left) in both Porta and Hole in the card tests (in this part, there was tendency to delete people who had neither eye dominance nor weak eye dominance)

Finally, 10 subjects were selected as unilateral group (8 subjects were right-eye and right-hand, 2 subjects were left-eye and left-hand dominance) and 10 subjects were selected as cross lateral group (8 subjects were left-eye and right-hand, 2 subjects were right-eye and left-hand dominance).

Eye dominance

Hole in the card test

Each subject held a card (25 cm^2) with both hands stretched and extended straight forward to the target. There was a hole in the middle of the card (0.5 cm diameter) and subjects could see the target by this hole. Target was a black circle (with 1 cm diameter at 2 m distance) in white paper. When the target was sighted, the examiner covered alternately each of the subject's eyes, and asked if the target was still visible. The eye with which the subject viewed the target was the dominant sighting eye (Sage, 1984).

Porta test

The observer extended one arm and then with both eyes open, aligned the index finger with a distant object. The observer then alternated closing the eyes or slowly drew the thumb/finger back to the head to determine which eye was viewing the object (that is, the dominant eye) (Roth, 2002).

Methods

Dart-throwing accuracy was used as a performance measure in this study. In accordance with World Darts Federation rules, the dart board was used. The dart board was positioned 2.37 m from the foot line and uppermost edge at a height of 1.73 m.

Each subject performed 30 trials of throwing darts to warm up. The score of these hits were not recorded. These 30 trials were thrown in 5 blocks, subjects rested for 30 s after each block. After 2 min, subjects threw 30 darts like previous step but in this stage, the score of darts were recorded. The summation of scores of the first session was considered as the subjects' scores in the pre-test phase.

Experimental training was performed 4 weeks, 3 times per week (12 sessions). This experiment consisted of acquisition and retention. The scores in the last session were regarded as the acquisition scores. One week later, each subject threw 30 darts and the scores were recorded as retention. In this phase, there was no throwing as warm up.

Measurements

The dartboard was made up of three circles and the scoring was as follows:

a) 5 points for darts inside the bull's-eye;
b) 3 points for darts inside the triple-score circle (but not in the bull's-eye);
c) 1 point for darts inside the double-score (outer) circle (but not inside the triple-score circle).

Darts missing the dartboard were given 0 points (Bindarwish et al, 2006). Therefore, each participant's final score of trials could be ranged from 0 to 150 points.

Statically analysis

Dependent t-test was used to measure acquisition and retention in both unilateral and cross lateral groups. Also, independent t-test was used to compare retention and acquisition in dart skill between unilateral and cross lateral group. Values of $p<0.05$ were found significant. Statistical analyses were performed using the SPSS version 18 for Windows.

RESULTS

In order to assess differences between pre-test and retention phases of the study, dependent t-test (paired t-test) was used. The results are shown in Table 1.

As shown in Table 1, there is a significant difference between scores of pre-test and retention in unilateral ($p=0.001$, $t= 8.139$) and cross lateral ($p=0.001$, $t= 11.387$). So, the scores of subjects increased significantly in retention phase in comparison with pre-test values. This result shows that both groups learn dart skill.

In order to measure differences between pre-test and retention phases of study, dependent t-test (paired t-test) was used. The results are shown in Table 2.

As shown in Table 2, there is a significant difference between scores of pre-test and acquisition in unilateral ($p=0.001$, $t= 10.940$) and cross lateral ($p=0.001$,

Table 1. Results of dependent t-test to compare pre-test and acquisition in unilateral and cross lateral group.

Group	Pre-test		Acquisition		t	p
	M	SD	M	SD		
Unilateral	31.600	4.376	51.700	6.583	8.139	0.001
Cross lateral	32.100	4.840	54.00	6.055	11.387	0.001

Table 2. Results of dependent t-test to compare pre-test and retention in unilateral and cross lateral group.

Group	Pre-test		Retention		t	p
	M	SD	M	SD		
Unilateral	31.600	4.376	50.900	2.846	10.940	0.001
Cross lateral	32.100	4.840	53.300	3.368	14.236	0.001

Table 3. Results of independence t-test to compare acquisition and retention between unilateral and cross lateral groups.

Group	Unilateral		Cross lateral		t	p
	M	SD	M	SD		
Acquisition	51.700	6.583	54.00	6.055	- 0.813	0.427
Retention	50.900	2.846	53.300	3.368	- 1.721	0.102

t= 14.236). So, the scores of subject are increased significantly in acquisition phase in comparison with pre-test values. These results show that the learning of two groups was constant.

For assessing the comparison of comparing unilateral and cross lateral in acquisition and retention phases of study, independent t-test was used. The results are shown in Table 3.

Results showed that there are no significant differences in acquisition (p=0.427) and retention (P=0.102) phases. So, interaction between eye and hand dominance do not have any significant effect on dart skill. In other words, there is no difference between cross and lateral unilateral groups in dart throwing.

DISCUSSION

The present research aimed at surveying the effect of interaction between eye- hand dominance on dart throwing skill. In order to accomplish this, amateur males were divided in two groups; unilateral (right eye and right hand or left eye and left hand) and cross lateral (right eye and left hand or left eye and right hand). The results showed that all subjects of the two groups improved in dart throwing skill and their scores were better in acquisition and retention in comparison with scores in pre-test phase. However, there was no significant difference between unilateral and cross lateral, neither in acquisition nor retention phase. This identifies that interaction between eye and hand dominance does not affect dart skill.

When a person is required to make a discrete manual aiming movement to a stationary target, the eyes normally get fixed at the target before any movement preparation begins. This provides the control system with visual information about the position of the target and later, the hand moves toward the target (Binsted et al., 2001). So, according to this information, eyes identify movement of hand in skills like dart. Also, accuracy in darts was affected by the temporal control of quiet eye (QE) (in the dart throw, QE was defined as the final fixation on the target prior to the extension of the arm toward the target) fixation relative to the alignment, flexion, and extension phases of the throw. Hits occurred when QE was of longer duration and occurred during late alignment and early flexion (Vickers et al., 2000). So, it seems that surveying vision system can be beneficial.

Posner and Raichle (1994) describe three networks of visual attention (posterior orienting, anterior executive, and vigilance). They describe the posterior orienting network as being responsible for the control of the direction of gaze in space. This network, which is located in the parietal region, functions to direct visual attention to specific locations of interest and importance in a task. In the dart throw, this network may have been responsible for directing QE to the target during the alignment phase of each throw. The second network, the executive anterior network, may be responsible for the sustained concentration one sees during highly competitive games of darts. In the dart throw, this may have been responsible for the longer duration of QE, characteristic of higher levels of skill and accuracy. The anterior network imposes higher-order understanding on a task and allows the performer to control an action relative to specific goals. The vigilance network co-ordinates the functions of the posterior and anterior networks and prevents unwanted or distracting information from gaining access to both systems (Vickers et al., 2000). So, these networks are the same in healthy people and there are no differences between unilateral and cross lateral. So, effective nervous factors on accuracy in dart relate to special networks that are not different between two groups with different eye hand dominance.

Consequently, duration of gaze in dart can affect the level of skill and accuracy. Again, it can be found that success in dart in which accuracy is the most important factor for success, to a large extent, depends on duration of fixating eye, not interaction between eye-and hand. Interaction of eye-hand dominance does not have any effect on effective factors on dart performance.

Our results support the findings obtained from assessing the effect of ocular dominance on the performance of professional baseball players showed that hand-ocular dominance patterns do not have any effect on batting average (Laby et al., 1998).

In addition, a critical literature review was done on 4 articles (Adams, 1965; Goss, 1998; Portal, 1998) which are about the relationship of eye dominance and baseball batting showed that the overall reviewed studies do not suggest any effect of the eye dominance/batting side relationship on batting performance. It appears that other measures of visual system function, such as visual reaction time, eye movement skills, or dynamic stereoacuity are more likely to correlate with batting performance. The results of the present study agree with these results (Goss, 1998).

Unlike the result of the present study, unilateral eye-hand pattern is more successful in archery when the bow is used with no sights, but this effect of laterality seems to be eliminated in practitioners by their use of a specific accessory, the sight (Laborde et al., 2009).

There is disagreement between the study of archery and the present one. This contractor may result from protocol of both studies. Archery requires repetition of the same gesture many thousands of times, leading to automation. This may be based on complex cognitive changes in the central nervous system. The process of motor learning may perhaps be associated with changes in the laterality pattern (Laborde et al., 2009). But in this study, there were 12 sessions in 4 weeks to learn dart skill and subjects threw 720 darts. Also, there are potential differences between dart and archery that can make variety of results, like visual adjustability. Based on Gardner category (Gardner, 1995), this visual skill is the most important skill in archery while it has the lowest importance in success in dart skill.

Moreover, a study showed an association between eye dominance and training for rifle marksmanship (Jones et al., 1999). These findings showed that the subjects with unilateral had qualification scores that were significantly higher than subjects with crossed dominance to achieve rifle qualification. He approved that the earning of rifle marksmanship is influenced by eye dominance. Individuals who shoot right-handed and are left-eye dominant or who shoot left-handed and are right-eye dominant do not learn marksmanship skills as readily as individuals who have matched eye and hand dominance. These studies disagree with the present study.

It seems that the reason of conflict is that if you shoot off the right shoulder with strong left eye dominance and you have both open eyes during the act of shooting, you will experience "cross firing" and will shoot inconsistently as a result. In the cross firing, the eye that is above the rib must be the one that the shooter uses to make the correct target/barrel relationship. If it is not, the wrong eye will take over as the gun is brought to the point of aim and the barrels will be pointing in the wrong place as the shot is triggered. The right-shoulder, left-dominant-eyed shooter will shoot behind a left-to-right crossing target and in front of right-to-left (Blakeley, 2003). Every person has a dominant eye that processes and transmits information to the brain a few milliseconds faster than the other one. The dominant or sighting eye also guides the movement and fixations of the other eye (Knudson et al., 1997). So, maybe this is the reason for existence of differences between performances of unilateral and cross lateral in rifle and archery skills.

On the other side, cross laterals shoot off using the dominant shoulder and non-dominance eye set above the rib (Blakeley, 2003) since processing of visual input of dominant eye is more preferred in comparison with the other eye (Rice et al., 2008) and dominant eye processes and transmits information to the brain a few milliseconds faster than the other (knudson et al., 1997). So, as a result, it seems that brain directs movement of hand based on the input of eye dominance and since there is distance between two eyes, the information of eye dominance while target is seen by non-dominance (above the rib) cannot guide the hand for shooting. In dart throwing, there is no aiming by the special eye and usual movement of hand which is selected by information of eye dominance. So, these consistent results are related to potential differences between rifle, archery and dart. On the other hand, different quality of rifle, archery, and dart is the main reason of disagreeing results of the previous studies (Jones, 1996; Laborde, 2009) and this study.

Sugiyama showed that mean scores for right-eyed (unilateral) were higher than the mean scores for the left eyed (cross lateral) in Golf (Thain, 2002). This result is inconsistent with our results. There are some points that should be considered. First, he just selected right-handed subjects, while unilateral and cross lateral involve left hand-right eye and left-hand and left-eye people. In addition, right-handed subjects with right-eye dominance have better spatial orientation than right-handed subjects with left-eye dominance and the involvement of the frontal cortex in cognitive and motor processes is decreased in subjects with the left-eye dominance (Lazarev et al., 2007). Therefore, maybe differences between unilateral and cross lateral in putting Golf are not related to interaction between eye-hand dominance and these differences refer to difference of right-eye dominance and left-eye dominance. Also, the obtained data suggest that the role of the thalamic-frontal-medial cortical system of selective attention decreases in subjects with left-eye dominance (Lazarev et al., 2007). But in the present study, subjects with left-hand (right-eye, left-eye) and right-hand (right-eye, left-eye) were selected as well.

This result also indicated that putting performance was higher in the right eye condition (using only right eye) than the left eye condition (using only left eye) for either the right-eyed or the left-eyed subjects. It is suggested that the right eye may play a fairly important role in judging the direction and hitting the ball straight in putting than the left eye because the right eye is normally positioned behind the ball whereas the left eye is positioned between the ball and the cup (Thain, 2002).

Conclusion

In conclusion, the effect of interaction between eye and hand dominance on performance in each sport depends on the type of sports and visual skills which can affect performance in those sports. Thus, the results of this study approve that this factor does not affect dart throwing.

ACKNOWLEDGEMENTS

This study was supported by the Sport Psychology Department, Shahid Chamran University of Ahvaz, Iran. The authors also like to sincerely thank all participants in this study and the Physical Education and Sport Sciences faculty.

REFERENCES

Adams Gary L (1965). Effect of eye dominance on baseball batting. Res. Q., 36: 3-9.

Annet Marian (1998). Handedness and cerebral dominance: the right shift theory. neuropsychiatry.10: 459-469.

Azémar Stein G, Ripoll JFH (2008). Effects of ocular dominance on eye–hand coordination in sporting duels. Sci. Sports, 23: 263-277.

Balasubramaniam R, Turvey MT (2000). The handedness of postural fluctuations. Hum. Move. Sci., 19: 667-684.

Bellanca J (1998). Teaching for intelligences in the classroom. Alexandria VA: Association for Supervision and Curriculum Development.

Bindarwish Jamal, Gershon Tenenbaum (2006). Metamotivational and contextual effects on performance, self-efficacy and shifts in affective states. Psychol. Sport. Exercise., 7: 41–56.

Binsted G, Chua R, Helsen W, Elliot D (2001). Eye hand coordination in goal-direced aiming. J.Human. Movement. Sci., 20: 563-585.

Blakeley Peter F (2003). Successful shot gunning: how to build skill in the field and take more birds in competition. ISBN 0811700429. pp. 63-64.

Curry L (1999). Cognitive and learning styles in medical education. Acad. Med., 74: 409-413.

Dassonville Paul, Zhu Xiaho-Hong, Ugurbil Kamil, Kim Seong-GL, Ashe James (1997). Functional activation in motor cortex reflects the direction and the degree of handedness. The National Academy of Sciences. 94: 14015–14018.

Deborah Stevens-Smith (2009). Profile of dominance in physical education. Kinesiology 41:40-51

Zupan Michael F, Arata Alan W, Wile Alfred, Parker Ryan (2006). Visual adaptations to sports vision enhancement training. Clinical sport vision. 19: 43-48.

Gardner JJ, Sherman A (1995). Vision requirements in sport. In sports vision. Butter Worth Heinemann. pp. 22-37.

Goss David (1998). The relationship of eye dominance and baseball batting. Behav. Optom., 9: 87-91

Griffiths GW (2003). Eye Dominance in sport – a comparative study. Optometry Today. 43:16

Jones LF, Classe JG, Hester M, Harris K (1996). Association between eye dominance and training for rifle marksmanship: a pilot study . Am..Optom. Assoc., 67: 73-76.

Knudson Duane, Kluka Darlene A (1997). The impact of vision and vision training on sport performance. Physical Education.

Laborde Sylvain, Dosseville Fabrice EM, Pascale Leconte, Margas Nicolas (2009). Interaction of hand preference with eye dominance on accuracy in archery. J. Perceptual. Motor. Skills.,108: 558-564.

Laby Daniel M, Kirchen David G, Losenbaum Arthur L, Mellman Michael F (1998). The effect of ocular dominance on the performance of professional baseball players. Ophthalmology. 105: 0864-866.

Lazarev IE, Kirenskaya AV(2007). The Influence of Eye Dominance on Saccade Characteristics and Slow Presaccadic Potentials . Human. Physiol., 34: 150-160.

McManus IC, Porac Boucher C, Bryden RMP (1999). Eye-dominance, Writing Hand, and Throwing Hand. Laterality. 4: 173-192.

Oldfield RC (1971). The assessment and analysis of handedness: The Edinburgh inventory.Neuropsychol., 9: 97-113.

Payne Gregory V (2002). Human Motor Development. 398-399

Portal JM, Romano PE (1998). A review and study of athletic proficiency and eye-hand dominance in a collegiate baseball team. Binocular Vis Strabismus Q. 13(3): 165-166.

Psilantia Antonia, Hatzitakia Vassilia, Grouios George (2009). Lateralized effects of hand and eye on anticipatory postural adjustments in visually guided aiming movements. Neuroscience Letters. 462: 121–124.

Rice Melissa L, Leske A, Smestad David E, Smestad Christina E, Holmes M, Jonathan (2008). Results of ocular dominance testing depend on assessment method.American Association for Pediatric Ophthalmology and Strabismus.12: 365-369.

Roth HL, Lora AN, Heilman K M (2002). Effects of monocular viewing and eye dominance on spatial attention. Oxford. J. Med. Brain., 125: 2023–35.

Sage George H (1984). Motor ability; Motor learning and control: A neuropsychological approach. ISBN 0697000788.

Saudino K, Mc Manus IC (1998). Handedness, footedness, eyednessand earedness in the Colorado adoption project. Developmental psychology. 16: 167-174.

Shneor Einat, Hochstein Shaul (2006). Effects Eye dominance in feature search. Vision research. 46: 4258-4269.

Steinberg Gregg M, Parker Melissa (1999). The Benefits of Assessing Eye Dominance in Motor Skill Instruction. Physical Education, Recreation & Dance. 70: 20-21.

Suttle Catherine, Alexander Jack (2008). Sensory ocular dominance based on resolution acuity, contrast sensitivity and alignment sensitivity. compilation Optometrists Association Australia. 92: 2-8.

Thain Eric (2002). Science and Golf. ISBN 041528302-7. pp. 151-154.

Vickers Joan N, Rodrigues Sergio T, Gene Edworthy (2000). Quiet eye and accuracy in the dart throw. Int. J. Sports. Vision.,pp. 1-6.

Some effects of manganese dichloride administration on the body weight, Purkinje cell population, brain, and cerebellar weights of adult Wistar rats

Ajibade A. J.*, Fakunle P. B., Fatoba O. O. and Olayemi O. T.

Department of Anatomy, Ladoke Akintola University of Technology, Ogbomosho, Osun State, Nigeria.

Some effects of manganese dichloride an essential trace metal that is required for bone formation, brain development and metabolism of carbohydrate on the body weight, brain and cerebellar weights were investigated in adult Wistar rats. Twenty eight adult Wistar rats of both sexes weighing between 150 to 200 g were separated into four groups including controls, each containing seven rats. Treated rats in Groups A, B and C received $MnCl_2$ orally at a doses of 5, 15 and 25 mg/kg body weight respectively for 21 consecutive days. The rats in Group D (control) received volumes of distilled water equal to those in the treated groups. The rats were sacrificed by cervical dislocation on the 26th day of the treatment. The cerebellum of each rat was removed and-weighed before fixing in 10% formol saline for routine histological procedures. The body weights of the Wistar rats decreased significantly ($p < 0.05$) in the treated Groups B and C compared with the controls. The body weight of the treated Group A rats showed a nominal decrease that was not- statistically significant. The cerebellar Purkinje cell population decreased significantly ($p < 0.05$) for all treatment groups. Similarly, the total brain and cerebellar weight decreased significantly ($p < 0.05$) in Groups B and C compared with the controls; and Group A also demonstrated a statistically decrease in the total brain weights but not in the cerebellar weights. The observed decrease in cerebellar Purkinje cell population, the total brain and cerebellar weights suggest that brain functions may be adversely affected.

Key words: Manganese, brain, cerebellum, Purkinje cells, weight, decrease.

INTRODUCTION

Manganese is an essential trace metal that is involved in bone formation, brain development and in the metabolism of carbohydrates, cholesterol and amino acids (Keen, 1984). It is typically expected to enter the body either by ingestion or by inhalation. Mn^{2+} is thought to move by neuronal transport to the pallidum, thalamic nuclei and substantial nigra which are areas involved with motor control and movement (Aschner, 2005). At normal plasma level, Mn^{2+} enters the brain mainly across the capillary epithelium, at elevated level of Mn^{2+} in the blood, transport across the choroid plexus becomes more prominent (Aschner, 2005). Manganese exposure via the pulmonary route leads to more rapid absorption with higher efficiency and with greater transfer to the brain compared with other routes (Drown, 1986; Roels, 1997). Excessive exposure of humans to manganese by inhalation can result in a characteristic neurologic and psychological disorder called manganism (Lucchini, 1991). The brain is particularly susceptible to damage from high levels of manganese and accumulation associated with manganism is characterized by both central nervous system (CNS) abnormalities and neurobehavioral abnormalities (Santamaria et al., 2007). The cerebellum is the largest part of the hindbrain. It is made up of outer gray matter (cerebellar cortex) and an inner white matter (Singh, 1998). The cerebellar cortex is made up of neurons or cells arranged in three layers (Ganong, 2005). The molecular layer is the outermost layer, the granular layer is the innermost layer, while the Purkinje cell layer consisting of the Purkinje cells is

*Corresponding author. E-mail: adeshinaajibade@yahoo.co.uk.

Table 1. Mean ± SEM of the body weights of Wistar rats before and during the treatment.

Period (weeks)	Control group D (n = 7)	Treated group		
		Group A (n = 7)	Group B (n =7)	Group C (n = 7)
Zero	200.2 ± 26.1	152.4 ± 9.8	171.2 ± 10.9	215.40 ± 22.1
1st	219.8 ± 27.0	157.8 ± 9.7	173.0 ± 8.6	199.30 ± 19.7
2nd	234.1 ± 28.3	168.9 ± 11.2	160.4 ± 9.2	190.30 ± 17.0
3rd	282.0 ± 25.9	170.5 ± 9.1	153.1 ± 9.8*	179.90 ± 15.5*

*Values significantly different from corresponding control ($p < 0.05$).

sandwiched between the molecular and granular layers.

This paper focuses on the effect of manganese on the body weight, Purkinje cell population, brain and cerebellar weights in adults Wistar rats.

MATERIALS AND METHODS

Twenty eight adult Wistar rats of both sexes weighing between 150 and 200 g were used for this study. The rats were fed daily with normal rat chow purchased from Bovajay from mill (Ogbomoso, Nigeria) and water was given to the rats *ad libitum.* All the rats were routinely inspected, screened and confirmed to be healthy during the period of acclimatization. The animals were treated in accordance with the "Guide for the Care and Use of Laboratory Animals" prepared by the National Academy of Sciences and published by the National Institutes of Health (1985).

The rats were then separated randomly into four groups with each group containing seven rats. Group D served as the control and the rats received distilled water as contained in experimental doses during the period. Groups A, B and C received oral doses of $MnCl_2$ dissolved in distilled water at 5, 15, and 25 mg/kg body weight respectively for 21 consecutive days. The rats were sacrificed by cervical dislocation on the 26th day of the treatment. The cerebellum of each rat was carefully dissected out after sacrifice -weighed and fixed in 10% formol saline for routine tissue processing by light microscopy. Serial sections of 7 µm thick were obtained using a rotatory microtome and the sections were subjected to histological staining following the methods of Carleton (1967).

The body weights of the rats were taken before and during the treatment in order to monitor changes in their weights.

Cerebellar Purkinje cells were counted using a microscope containing a graduated ocular micrometer inserted to its eye piece. The population of Purkinje cells was determined by counting the cells found along the length of the monolayer of Purkinje cells at several microscopic fields.

RESULTS

The body weights, brain and cerebellar weights were found to be smaller in the treated rats compared with the controls as shown in Table 1 and 2.

Results in Table 1 demonstrate that the body weights of manganese treated rats in Groups B and C were significantly reduced ($p < 0.05$) compared with controls after 3 weeks of treatment. The rat weights were assessed after the rats have been given adequate care.

Results shown in Table 2 indicate that the total brain weights at all doses were significantly reduced ($p < 0.05$). Similarly, data in Table 2 shows significantly reduced ($p < 0.05$) population of the cerebellar Purkinje cells in the manganese -treated rats.

DISCUSSION

Brain weight, cerebellar and body weights

The results obtained from the brain and body weights that were measured showed significant differences between the manganese- treated rats and controls. The effects seemed to be dose and duration dependent in relation to the body and cerebellar weights. For instance, body weights were not significantly different statistically until Week 3 of the treatment indicating a typical repeated dose requirement at these levels. Also the absence of statistical significance in the low dose group for both body and cerebellar weights indicates a dose-response relationship. Furthermore, the Purkinje cell population parameter appears to be the sensitive indicator of a dose-response relationship. Adverse effects from exposure to manganese have been shown in some studies. Atrophy of the cerebellar cortex was previously observed in a monkey subjected to inhalation of MnO_2 (VanBogaert and Dallemagne, 1945). Extensive loss of neurons in the cerebrum, brainstem and cerebellum had been reported following manganese administration (Pentschew et al., 1963). Body weight decreased significantly in pups that were exposed to high doses of manganese in drinking water from conception until post-natal day 30 (Pappas et al., 1997). Similarly, significant decrease in maternal weight had been reported by Kontur and Fetcher (1985) following exposure to manganese chloride in drinking water. Exposure of some Chilean miners to manganese concentrations in air has resulted in neurological disorders (Ansola et al., 1994). Brain atrophy occurred over the vertex and lateral aspects in a patient following manganese exposure who subsequently died - 14 years after the onset of the symptoms (Canavan and Drinker, 1934). Accumulation of manganese has occurred in critical areas of the brain following exposure to excess manganese which resulted in changes in brain chemistry and neuronal degeneration in mice and rats

Table 2. Mean ± SEM of brain, cerebellar and relative cerebellar weights number(s) of intact Purkinje cells per unit area in the Purkinje cell layer (/μm^2) mag × 40 at the end of treatment.

Rat groups (7 rats in each group)	Brain parameters(grams)		Relative cerebellar weight (%)	Mean ± SEM Purkinje cells number(s) per unit area in the Purkinje cell layer (/μm^2)
	Average total brain weight	Average cerebellar weight		
Control group D	1.58 ± 0.03	0.32 ± 0.01	20.4 ± 0.7	6.00 ± 2.00
Experiment group A	1.41 ± 0.06*	0.29 ± 0.01	20.4 ± 0.3	3.00 ± 1.00*
Experiment group B	1.42 ± 0.03*	0.24 ± 0.01*	16.9 ± 0.9*	3.00 ±1.00*
Experiment group C	1.49 ± 0.03*	0.20 ± 0.02*	13.2 ± 1.2*	2.00 ±1.00*

Values are expressed as Mean ± S.E.M of 7 rats in each group and analyzed by student's t-test.*Values significantly different from corresponding control ($p < 0.05$).

(Miller et al., 1975; Chandra and Shukla, 1978). As one focuses on the brain as a target organ for manganese, one notes that regulation of brain water content and therefore the volume, is critical for maintaining the inter cranial pressure within tolerable limits (Johanson, 1995). Brain volume is intimately related to water content. And the water content of cells depends directly on the total amount of osmotically active solutes (Johanson, 1995). As brain tissue swells or shrinks as in acute hyponatremia or hypernatremia, the activity of the cellular transporters is a potentially modified by up-or down-regulation (Johanson, 1995). Reduced brain and cerebellar weights in the manganese treated rats might be due to pathologic changes resulting from neurotoxic effect of manganese chloride that caused loss of cellular components and vacuolizations of the brain sections in rats that were treated with $MnCl_2$. This hypothesis is supported by degeneration and loss of cellular components in the cerebellar cortex of Wistar following quinine exposure where it was reported in H and E sections of the cerebellar cortex (Ajibade et al., 2006). Thus chronic exposure of adult Wistar rats to manganese may adversely affect the body weights, as well as total brain and cerebellar weights resulting from pathologic changes of the brain tissue over time, these changes may consequently lead to brain and cerebellar dysfunctions.

Population of Purkinje cells

Extensive cell death in the central nervous system has resulted from neuronal degeneration and neurotoxins have been implicated as prime candidates that induce neuronal degeneration (Waters, 1994).

There was a significant reduction ($p < 0.05$) in the population of the Purkinje cells in manganese-treated rats. The remarkable reduced population of the Purkinje cells in the treated rats might be due to neurotoxic - effect of manganese on the Purkinje cells. A fast Purkinje cell death is reported to be induced by mechanical lesion of the cerebellum (Rossi et al., 1995). Furthermore, degeneration and loss of Purkinje cells in the cerebellar cortex similar to findings in this study were observed in Wistar rats when they were treated with quinine dichloride (Ajibade et al., 2008) Cell degeneration occurs by necrosis and apoptosis. Necrosis affects extensive cell population which involves cytoplasmic swelling, while apoptosis is an organized form of self destruction that is characterized by cell shrinkage (Whyllie et al., 1980). Apoptotic cell death could be induced by cytotoxic drugs or physical (example, mechanical) stimulation (Cinthya and Rafael, 2004). While either of these mechanisms is possible, the Purkinje and Granule cells have been identified as the most important targets in the cerebellum for toxic substances (Fonnum and Lock, 2000), which suggests a common link between the two. We hypothesize that:

The marked reduction in the brain and cerebellar weights of the manganese –treated rats may have resulted from neuronal degeneration and loss which became evident in Purkinje cells that were enumerated during the study. There some Limitations in this study compared to other studies in addition to extrapolation to human health. For instance the agent here is $MnCl_2$, a fairly soluble form as opposed to a manganese metal oxide (MnO_X) common in human inhalation exposure. Also these were oral dosing regimens which may not reflect occupational exposure where inhalation is the primary route. Despite these limitations, this study strongly suggests that chronic exposure to manganese at sufficient doses may adversely affect the body weight, brain and cerebellar weight with reduced Purkinje cell population -in Wistar rats, which may subsequently affect brain function. In addition the Purkinje cell population appears to be the most sensitive of these parameters in assessing possible adverse effect from manganese.

REFERENCES

Ajibade AJ, Adenowo TK, Fajemilehin ME, Caxton-Martins EA and Omotoso EO (2006). Some histological observations on the cerebellar cortex of adult wistar rats following quinine administration. Sci. Focus, 11(2): 97-100

Ajibade AJ, Adenowo TK, Caxton-Martins EA, Ekpo OE (2008). Effect of quinine administration on purkinje cells in the cerebelar cortex of adult Wistar rats. WJ. Med., 27: 37-39.

Ansola J, Uiberall E, Escudero E (1994). Intoxification by manganese in Chile (study of 64 cases) Environmental and etiological factors. Res. Med. Chile, 72: 222-228

Aschner J (2005). The determination of manganese in biological material by activation analysis with a note on the gamma spectrum of blood. J. Nucl. Energy, 3: 18-24.

Canavan MM, Drinker CK (1934). Chronic manganese poisoning. Report of a case with autopsy. Arch. Neurol. Psychiart., 32: 501-573.

Chandra SV, Shukla GS (1978). Manganese encephalophathy in growing rats. Environ. Res., 15: 28-37.

Cinthya AG, Rafael L (2004). Programmed cell deaths. Eur. J. Biochem., 271: 1638.

Drown V (1986). Pulmonary route for manganese absorption. Arch. Neurol-psychiot. 32: 501-513.

Fonnum F, Lock EA (2000). Cerebellum as a target for toxic substance. Toxicol. Letter 112-113:916.

Ganong WF (2005). Review of Medical Physiology 22nd Ed. McGraw-Hill, 12: 220-221

Johanson CE (1995). Stability of brain volume in: Neuroscrence in medicine. Michael Conn. JB Lipincott. Company, pp. 187-189.

Keen A (1984). Essential trace elements in man, manganese a study on homeostasis. J. Chron. Dis. 19: 545-571.

Kontur PJ, Fechter LD (1985). Brain manganese catecholamine turnover and the development of startle in rats prenatally exposed to manganese, Teratology, 32: 1-11.

Lucchini F (1991). Histopathology of the brain resulting from manganese poisoning les. Neurol. Phsychiatri. 154:62-76.

Miller ST, Cotzia GC, Ever HA (1975). Control of tissue manganese: Initial absence and sudden emergence of excretion in the neonatal mouse. Am. J. Physiol. 229: 1080–1084.

National Institute of Health (1985). National Institute of Health Guide for the Care andUse of Laboratory Animals: DHEW Publication (NIH), revised, Office of Science and Health Reports, DRR/NIH, Bethesda, USA.

Pappas BA, Zhang D, Davidson CM, Crowder T, Park JA, Fortin T (1997). Perinatal manganese exposure; behavioral, neurochemical and histopathological effects in the rats. Neurotoxicity Teratology, 19: 17-25

Pentschew A, Ebner FF, Kovatch RM (1963). Experimental manganese encephalopathy in monkeys. A preliminary report. J. Neuro. Pathol. Exp. Neurol. 22: 448-499.

Roels Z (1997). Pulmonary route for weight manganese absorption. Arch. Neurol. Psychiatr. 32: 501-513.

Rossi F, Jankovski A, Sotelo C (1995). Target Neuron controls the integrity of afferent axon phenotype. A study on the purkinje cell climbing fiber system in cerebellar mutant mice. J. Neurosci. 15(3): 20-40.

Singh J (1998). The cerebellum: textbook of human neurocanatomy. 5th edition, pp. 145-170.

Santamaria AB, Colleen AC, James MA, Brent LF, Fionna SM (2007). State of the Science Review, Does Manganese Exposure During Welding pose a Neurological risk? J. Tox. Environ. Health Part B, 10: 417-465.

VanBogaert L, Dallemagne MJ (1945). Approaches experimentales des troubles nervaux du mangnanisme. Monatsschr. Psychiat. Neurol. 111: 60.

Waters CM (1994). Glutamate induced apoptosis of striatal cells in rodent model for parkinsonisn. Neurosci. 63: 1-5.

Whyllie AH, Kerr JFR, Curried AR (1980). Cell death: the significance of apoptosis international version. Cytology, 68: 251-305.

Multiple sclerosis: An overview of the disease and current concepts of its pathophysiology

Bolaños-Jiménez R.[1]*, Arizmendi-Vargas J.[1], Carrillo-Ruiz J. D.[2,3], López-Lizárraga M. E.[4], Calderón Álvarez-Tostado J. L.[5], Martínez-Menchaca H.[6], Leyva Resendiz I.[7], Serrato-Ávila J. L.[1], Rendón-Molina A.[1] and Rivera-Silva G.[6]

[1]School of Medicine, Universidad Panamericana, Mexico City, Mexico.
[2]Neurosciences and Psycophysiology Department, Universidad Anáhuac, Mexico City, Mexico.
[3]Functional Neurosurgery and Radiosurgery Service, Hospital General de México, O.D., Mexico City, Mexico.
[4]School of Dentistry, Universidad Intercontinental, Mexico City, Mexico.
[5]Médica Sur Clinic and Foundation, Mexico City, Mexico.
[6]Tissue Engineering and Regenerative Medicine Laboratory, Department of Basic Sciences, School of Medicine, University of Monterrey (UDEM), San Pedro Garza García, NL, Mexico.
[7]School of Medicine,Universidad Nacional Autónoma De México. Mexico.

The oligodendrocytes, myelin-producing cells in the central nervous system (CNS), have an essential role in "multiple sclerosis". This disease is of unknown etiology, and thus, of a variable prognosis. The main pathologic feature is the injury to the myelin and loss of oligodendrocytes in the CNS. Studies of animal models, demonstrating that autoreactive T cells (CD4 or CD8) can result in inflammatory demyelination of the central nervous system, support the theory that multiple sclerosis is an immune-mediated disorder involving one or more antigens located in the myelin of central nervous system cells (neurons and glia). About the disorder´s pathology, important findings have been made regarding inflammation, adhesion-molecules, ion-channel alterations and the process of neurodegeneration in the progression of the multiple sclerosis plaque. The progress made so far in the pathogenesis of the disease will allow a better understanding of the mechanisms involved in its progression and so, more specific treatments can be developed to ensure a better quality of life of the affected patients.

Key words: Oligodendrocytes, multiple sclerosis, myelin, demyelination, plaque, immune response, autoimmunity, pathogenesis.

INTRODUCTION

Multiple sclerosis is a chronic disease, of unknown etiology, in which symptoms vary on each patient. This enigmatic, progressive and relapsing disorder of the white matter, continues to challenge researchers, who try to understand the pathogenesis of the disease and prevent its progression. Multiple sclerosis typically begins in early adulthood and has a variable course. Fifty percent of patients will need assistance to walk within the first fifteen years of the after onset of the disease. Both clinical and imaging manifestations of disease activity have been improved by new therapies, although the long-term benefit from these treatments requires further study (Noseworthy et al., 2000). Classically, multiple sclerosis has been known as an autoimmune disease. Recent literature and studies of *in vitro* and *in vivo* have

*Corresponding author. E-mail: rodrigoboji88@hotmail.com.

Table 1. Multiple sclerosis symptoms.

Multiple sclerosis	
Visual	Pain Blindness in one eye Double vision Green-red color distortion
Sensory	Emotionlessness Insensitivity
Motor	Clumsiness Painfulness Absence of coordination Limitation in their extremities
Others	Discomfort Lightheadedness Spinning feeling

demonstrated that there are other factors involved in the pathogenesis of the disease and there isn't one unique cause. In other words, multiple sclerosis is a multifactorial disease. The objective of the present review is to briefly present an overview of the disease, of normal immune response and the actual knowledge in the study of multiple sclerosis pathogenesis, which will allow changing the perspective and approach for its treatment.

Multiple sclerosis

Multiple sclerosis (MS), also known as disseminated sclerosis, is a chronic and disabling neurological disease, which develops in people between fifteen and forty years old and is characterized by a disturbance in myelination (Lucchinetti et al., 2001). Therefore, it will affect the conduction of nerve impulses and the integrity of signals. Clinically, it is characterized as alterations in movement and sensitivity. This will be further discussed. In MS, the brainstem is primarily altered zone in the central nervous system (CNS), followed by the spinal cord white matter.

Clinical manifestations of MS

Symptoms depend on the degree and area of involvement. The initial symptom of MS is often double vision, red-green color distortion, or even blindness in one eye. There may be different kinds of symptoms; sensory symptoms are among the most common presenting symptoms, sensitive symptoms, such as tingling in the skin, paresthesias, pain, Lhermitte's sign(temporary paresthesias in arms and legs while bending) and Uhthoff phenomenon electrical transmission of the nervous system or worsening of symptoms in demyelinating disorders when exposed to elevating temperatures). Initially these can consist of an absence of sensation or can involve positive, uncomfortable sensations including pain or tingling; motor symptoms, as motor dysfunction, unsteady gait, dysmetria, among others; vegetative symptoms, like bladder and sexual dysfunction, constipation or diarrhea, etc. as well as cognitive impairment and affective disorders (Table 1).

Natural evolution of the disease

In the natural evolution of the disease, it is necessary to recognize the clinical and prognostic presentations of MS, as each one of them has a different course. This has great implications in the patient's quality of life. So, it can be said that MS is a heterogeneous disease (Prat and Antel, 2005). These presentations are:

Relapsing-remitting multiple sclerosis

It is characterized by episodes of neurologic dysfunction with clinical recovery but each one leaves a neurologic deficit. Its duration is very variable; from days to months.

Benign multiple sclerosis

Symptoms are merely of sensorial kind. There is no worsening over time, and the clinical manifestations are not permanent.

Primary progressive multiple sclerosis

The symptoms will worsen over time slowly, there are no "episodes" of neurologic dysfunction, but its course is progressive and incipient. There may be little improvement (Weinshenker et al., 1989).

Secondary progressive multiple sclerosis

Since the beginning of the disease, the patients present a progressive deteriorating course, with episodes of acute dysfunction and later recovery, as a relapsing-remitting pattern (Rose and Carlson, 2007).

Prognostic factors

There are some factors that have a direct impact on the patient's prognosis.

Favorable factors

Favorable factors include an early onset of disease, feminine gender, the relapsing-remitting clinical course and sensitive symptoms or optic neuritis as initial manifestations.

Factors of worse prognosis

Factors of worse prognosis late onset of the disease (beyond the age of forty), masculine gender, motor or cerebellar symptoms as initial manifestations, frequent episodes during the first five years, a short lapse between the first and second episodes, progressive course of the disease. The death causes in these individuals are associated with the neurologic deficits and the mobility limitation. The respiratory infections and pulmonary thromboembolism are in the top of the list. However, in young people, suicide represents an important mortality cause (Riise et al., 2003).

Elements of the normal immune response

The human body is constantly exposed to injury by strange agents, either microorganisms, as bacteria, virus, fungi or parasites, or isolated macromolecules. However, there are several defense mechanisms to protect the body against these agents (Cudrici et al., 2006). These mechanisms are:

Natural defense mechanisms

Those in constant functioning, like skin which stands as an impermeable barrier that prevents the entrance of these agents to the body; secretions as saliva or tears, that contain the lysozyme enzyme which has some bactericide action; the acid environment in organs like the stomach or the vagina that inhibit the bacterian development, among others.

Inespecific defense mechanisms

When the invasive agent enters the body, the inespecific defense mechanisms act in charge of cells as macrophages and neutrophils, which attack indistinctly against any strange substance.

Specific defense mechanisms

The ones in charge of this defense mechanism are the *lymphocytes*. There are two types of lymphocytes which have structural and functional differences:

T lymphocytes: It represents the 60 to 70% of the lymphocytes in the blood stream. According to the differentiation molecules present in the cell membrane (CD from cluster differentiation), T lymphocytes are subdivided in; CD4 T lymphocytes or T helpers and CD8 T lymphocytes or cytotoxic lymphocytes.

B lymphocytes: It represents 10 to 20% of the total amount of lymphocytes. The CD4 T lymphocytes are the key cells to start the immune response; they activate when an antigen-presenting cell (macrophage) presents them the captured antigens during the unspecific defense response. Once activated, the CD4 T cells may stimulate the CD8 T cells, which multiply and attack in a direct and specific way the antigen that produced their stimulation. This is called the cellular immune response. On the other hand, the CD4 T cells may stimulate the B lymphocytes, which also multiply and differentiate to plasmatic cells, which produce specialized proteins called immunoglobulins or antibodies that attach to the antigen and destroy it (Rudick, 2001).

FACTORS INVOLVED IN MS DEVELOPMENT

Multiple sclerosis is a complex disease, with genetic predisposing factors that interact with environmental ones. It is known that it is more common in people of Caucasian race of northern Europe. In studies with monocigotic twins, there has been a genetic concordance of 15 to 50%, compared to a concordance of 3 to 5% in dicigotic twins, which reveals an important genetic participation. Also, there is a strong environmental influence as some patients present the disease while others do not. The risk of presenting MS increases 2 to 4% among people who have a family member with the disease, while in general population it is estimated in 0.1% (Rivera-Olmos, 2007).

Genetic factors

The most important genetic influence has to do with

major histocompatibility class II molecules, but it requires the interactions of various genes to be a susceptible genotype to MS (poligenicity). It has been identified in chromosome 6p21 the human leucocyte antigen (HLA) and the mayor histocompatibility complex (MHC). Recently, it has been considered other regions as the alpha-receptor of interleukin 7 (IL-7RA), the interferon 5-regulator factor gene and the alpha-receptor of interleukin 1 (IL-2RA) (Alcina et al., 2009; Balabanov et al., 2007).

Environmental factors

Some specific genes can influence in susceptibility of one person but not from other; therefore it requires environmental elements to "activate" them. Among these ones, it includes the "geographic region" where MS is more frequent; this is attributed to the poles, as those are regions with less amount of solar light. There are some studies that associate this feature with "vitamin D" synthesis and function. It has been documented that vitamin D interacts with the HLA-DRB1, influencing its expression. In MS, it has been demonstrated that patients have low levels of vitamin D. This can be explained as there is a further separation from the equator and less conversion and cutaneous activation of vitamin D. One of the environmental factors considered is tobacco consume; however, this has not been completely explained although there is a hypothesis which states that nicotine, as other substances from tobacco smoke, produces an immunotoxic effect and alters the cell T antigen-mediated signalization (Wekerle and Honifeld, 2003). In "dietary" aspects, during the 1950's decade, some studies documented certain protective effect against MS in subjects that consumed great amounts of fish; other investigators found that a big amount of calories from animal fats increased the risk. Moreover, it has been stated that linoleic acid consume is a protective factor against MS.

The viruses have been targeted as possible factors involved in MS pathogenesis (Forman et al., 2006; Sotelo et al., 2007). The measles, Rubella, Epstein-Barr, Herpes type 6 and Herpes-Zoster virus are most mentioned and associated with the origin of the disease. In a recent study made in Mexico, through real time PCR, Varicella-Zoster virus DNA was found in 95% of patients with MS during an exacerbation of the disease (Franklin and Nelson, 2003; Gronning et al., 1993).

INFLAMMATION AS THE PILLAR OF THE DISEASE

In multiple sclerosis, there is a whole cascade of events occurring in the central nervous system. There is an actual active inflammatory process occurring. The encephalon is one of the privileged sites in the human body, as it is protected by an anatomical and functional barrier, the "blood-brain barrier", which stands as a defense mechanism against microorganisms, toxins, etc. However, in multiple sclerosis, there is a disruption of this barrier, allowing lymphocytes and other cells and factors involved in inflammation to enter the central nervous system and start the inflammatory process. T and B lymphocytes, macrophages, plasma cells and others such as dendritic cells have been implicated in the pathogenesis of MS (Frohman et al., 2006). The regulation of these immune components, by either receptor activation or cytokine release, is what triggers the pathogenic process. Which antigen starts this response is an unknown matter up to now (Hemmer et al., 2002).

Humoral response

Some cells are directly implicated in damage to myelin or oligodendrocytes, while others have regulatory function or cause damage through indirect mechanisms, such as immunoglobulin production (Huseby et al., 2001). More specifically, antibodies against molecules expressed on the extracellular surface of myelin and oligodendrocytes, like glycolipids, are synthesized (Genain et al., 1999). In models of multiple sclerosis, such as experimental autoimmune encephalomyelitis (EAE), complement activation stimulates the creation of antibodies. The fact of finding elevated antibody levels and oligoclonal IgG bands in the cerebrospinal fluid, which are actually some of the most important tests for diagnosing MS, supports the involvement of humoral immunity in the pathogenesis of MS. Also, another key point for this argument is the actual recognition of ectopic lymphoid follicle-like structures with active germinal centers in the meninges that serve as a continuous source of B cells and their products (Husted, 2006).

Cellular response

Macrophages

Macrophages have their role in MS pathogenesis producing substances that cause direct tissue injury, such as proteases, lipases, cytotoxic cytokines, reactive oxygen species and nitric oxide radicals. The later ones have demonstrated to be an important part in damage to oligodendrocytes and axons. A mechanism of synthesis is through cell stress, provoked by mitochondrial injury and hypoxia. Other relevant molecule produced by macrophages is "osteopontin". It is highly expressed in MS and contributes to inflammation perpetuation. Its action mechanism; it stimulates monocyte recruitment (monocytes are macrophage immature forms), causes T-cell apoptosis inhibition (provoking tissue injury indirectly) and produces proinflammatory cytokines (Chang et al., 2002). Other factors contribute to oligodendrocyte toxicity, such as an excess of excitatory neurotransmitter (glutamate), T cell products (perforin/lymphotoxin), interaction of fas antigen with fas-ligand (implicated in apoptosis), etc.

Lymphocytes

CD8 T lymphocytes

CD8 cells have classically been implicated in damage to oligodendrocytes and their axons, because of their direct cytotoxic effect. This is achieved through recognition of class I peptide epitopes on the surfaces of axons. Among their effects observed in MS, CD8 cells can transect axons, induce oligodendrocyte death and promote vascular permeability (Blakemore, 2008).

CD4 T lymphocytes/T helpers

Besides the CD8+ T cells, the T helper cells are also involved in MS pathogenesis. As mentioned above, CD4 effector cells have the function of activating and directing other immune cells, and are particularly important in the immune system. There are two major subtypes of cells, known as Th1 and Th2, which have several differences between them, but the main one is the immune response promoted by each one of them. Th1 cells trigger the cellular immune system, while Th2 cells stimulate the humoral immune system. This polarization from CD4 lymphocytes depends on the exposure to certain types of interleukins (IL) (Imitola et al., 2006). It has been described that MS is primarily a Th1 cell-mediated disease, with proliferation of cytokines that up-regulate cytotoxic cells, including IL-2, □-IFN, and TNF-□. In spite of this, there has been demonstrated that Th2 cells can participate in autoimmune processes. Specifically, in MS there is formation of antibodies against myelin-oligodendrocyte glycoprotein (MOG) and myelin basic protein (MBP), important components of myelin covering. This contribution from Th2 cells aggravates the Th1 autoimmune process (Saikali et al., 2007). Subtypes of Th1 cells are the Th17 CD4 cells. Specifically, these cells are relevant in MS as they produce proinflammatory cytokines involved in myelin damage, such as IL-17, TNF-a and IL-6. It has been seen that IL-17 is expressed in MS lesions. IL-6 has the effect of inhibiting the negative regulation of Th17 cells, so it acts as a positive feedback to keep the inflammatory process active. Besides Th1 and Th2 derived cells from naïve CD4 lymphocytes, there is another type of cell that comes from these ones; the regulatory T cells (T reg).

T regs are in charge of regulating not only Th1/Th2 function, but also the activity of IL-17. Besides, it has been demonstrated that patients with MS have reduced T reg function.

Dendritic cells

Dendritic cells (DC) are antigen-presenting cells, which are the primary cells that recognize foreign antigens and induce cell differentiation by the release of certain cytokines. In MS, there is evidence that DC appears in the cerebral spinal fluid (CSF) circulation to survey inflamed CNS tissue and they remain in an active state. So, there is a constant synthesis, release of IL and cell induction and this may be the primary source of the disease pathogenesis. Specifically, TLR-9 (toll-like receptor 9) and MyD88 (myeloid differentiation factor 88) have been found to be essential mediators for the induction of EAE in experimental models.

Other relevant considerations

Another factor that may have to do with MS pathogenesis is the "progenitor cell pool". Oligodendrocytes appear to be reduced in active stages of disease and in sites of active local inflammation. However, in areas of remyelination or inactive inflammatory process, there seems to be a recovery in the number of these myelin producing cells. This may be attributed to progenitor cells which differentiate into mature oligodendrocytes. However, in sites of intense tissue destruction, at active sites of demyelination, there is absence not only of oligodendrocytes, but also of progenitor cells. This could be an interesting starting point of future study for new therapeutic approaches (Wolfgan, 2007). The difficulty in clinical recovery with each episode that occurs may be influenced by "axon destruction" and not only myelin disruption. This is supported by the evidence of *in vivo* studies that show reduced levels of N-acetyl-aspartate, a neuronal marker, in brain lesions in relapsing-remitting multiple sclerosis. It has been seen that duration of clinical active disease does not have to do with damage to the white matter, but the "background of active tissue inflammation", as there may be periods of clinical remission and still there is damage occurring at the same time or there may be more overt clinical manifestations but progression of the disease may delay more time. The main problem then may not be a lack of myelin repair, but the process of remyelination may be unstable as long as the inflammation remains active. This may be a reason why some patients have a different evolution within the natural history of the disease (Lassmann, 2008).

How does damage occur in MS?

If an individual younger than 15 years and genetically susceptible is exposed, for a minimum of two years and during periods of intense proliferation of oligodendrocytes, to an environmental factor, up to now no well defined (probably viral), he will develop a cross reaction between the environmental antigen "X" and the myelin components and/or their producing cells (oligodendrocytes) or even non-myelin proteins (alpha, beta, cristalin, phosphodiesterases, S-100 proteins). This leads to sensitization (permanent memory) of T cells, but are inactive against myelin and/or the oligodendrocytes, which have turned into auto-antigens due to the cross reaction. When the right antigen enters the body, it is phagocytized by the macrophages. Once in the surface of the antigen-presenting cells, the MHC-antigen complex is recognized by the receptor in the surface of the CD4+ cells. From this moment, T cells are turned into activated T helper cells (Th1) capable of crossing the brain-blood barrier. It has been described that MS is primarily a Th1 cell-mediated disease, with proliferation of cytokines that up-regulate cytotoxic cells, including IL-2, γ-IFN, and TNF-α. As Th1 cells, T lymphocytes induce a proinflammatory immune response characterized by: proliferation of T cells (clonal expansion), proinflammatory cytokines release (IL-2 stimulates the production of γ-IFN, IL-12, α-TNF, β-TNF and lymphotoxin), activation of B cells and macrophages by other proinflammatory cytokines (which intensifies the immune response), antibody production and release of anti-inflammatory cytokines (IL-1, IL-4, IL-10) through Th2 subtype (Kasper and Shoemaker, 2010).

The effect of the proinflammatory cytokines, together with the effect of local factors in the CNS (as metabolic stress), generates Th1 cell attraction to the vascular endothelium and amplification of the expression of the endothelial adhesion molecules receptors, of E-selectins and integrins. These allow cells to cross the blood-brain barrier. At the same time, proteases (as the matrix-metalloproteinase) degrade the extracellular matrix molecules of the endothelial cells, causing a break in the blood-brain barrier and favoring even more the cell migration. Within the CNS, the TH1 cells are reactivated by antigen-presenting cells, but this time the antigen is not exogenous, but an own antigen (as a myelin protein); this generates an "amplification of the immune response" whose components recognize the autoantigens of the CNS and cause demyelination. At this point, the autoimmunity process can be suppressed, or it can continue with the process of demyelination. Apparently, the suppression is secondary to the action of the Th2 cells which secrete anti-inflammatory lymphokines and the subsequent "cleaning" of the inflammatory infiltrate and edema remission. The autoimmune process stops without generating demyelination; however, if there was cytokine and immunoglobulin (IgG) secretion, as well as blood-brain barrier breakage, there will be clinical manifestations, but of reversible nature (Zhou et al., 2006). Demyelination is the characteristic that defines MS; it presents when the myelin destruction exceeds its production. It predominates in the optic nerves, periventricular white matter, brainstem, cerebellum, and spinal cord white matter. Regardless of the demyelination mechanism, the immediate consequence is the reversible blockage of the nerve conduction.

Sometimes, after demyelination, there is a remyelination process. This is characterized by being incomplete (aberrant) generally limited to active demyelination zones; but also it is possible to watch these in chronic lesions, as some conserve an important number of oligodendrocytes precursor cells. The axons are not the primary target in MS, but their damage or loss is the main cause of irreversible neurologic disability and the main determinant of the secondary progressive presentation of the disease (Kantarci et al., 1998). It is a continuum process due to the axon vulnerability to inflammatory response mediators. The process initiates from the earliest stages of the disease and continues in patients with a disease evolution greater than ten years, independently of the clinical course (Kuhlmann et al., 2002).

CONCLUSIONS

Multiple sclerosis is a chronic, heterogeneous and complex disease, in terms of origin, pathophysiology, illness course, progression mechanisms and treatment response. The main feature is the involvement of the myelin and loss of oligodendrocytes in the CNS due to an active inflammatory process. Its development is determined by the intervention of genetic and environmental factors. Within the genetic factors, there are multiple genes that predispose or increase the risk of developing the disease (genetic susceptibility), making it harder for investigators to determine the heritage pattern of expression. Among the environmental factors, it has been proposed several ones; however, there is no convincing evidence that one has a greater impact than other, although the viral theory has been the most solid one. From the population point of view, it has important consequences, as it affects young and economically active individuals and their quality of life. The advances in molecular biology will allow identifying more specific genes involved in the genetic susceptibility and in the development of the disease. And so, this will allow implementing more specific therapies. In future, this is promising, as it could not only affect the sick individual, but it would prevent its appearance in subjects with family risk.

REFERENCES

Alcina A, Fedetz M, Ndagire D, Fernandez O, Leyva L, Guerrero M, Abad MM, Arnal C, Delgado C, Lucas M, Izquierdo G, Matesanz F (2009). IL2RA/CD25 Gene Polymorphisms: Uneven Association with Multiple Sclerosis (MS) and Type 1 Diabetes (T1D). PLoS ONE 4: e4137.

Balabanov R, Strand K, Goswami R, McMahon E, Begolka W, Miller SD, Popko B (2007). Interferon-Gamma-Oligodendrocyte Interactions in the Regulation of Experimental Autoimmune Encephalomyelitis. J. Neurosci., 27: 2013-2024.

Blakemore WF (2008). Regeneration and repair in multiple sclerosis: The view of experimental pathology. J. Neurol. Sci., 265: 1-4.

Chang A, Tourtellotte WW, Rudick R, Trapp BD (2002). Premyelinating Oligodendrocytes in Chronic Lesions of Multiple Sclerosis. N. Engl. J. Med., 346: 165-173.

Cudrici C, Niculescu T, Niculescu F, Shin ML, Rus H (2006). Oligodendrocyte Cell Death in Pathogenesis of Multiple Sclerosis: Protection of Oligodendrocytes from Apoptosis by Complement. J. Rehabil. Res. Dev., 43: 123-132.

Forman EM, Racke MK, Raine CS (2006). Multiple Sclerosis – The plaque and its pathogenesis. N. Engl. J. Med., 354: 942-955.

Franklin GM, Nelson L (2003). Environmental risks factors in multiple sclerosis: Causes, triggers, and patient autonomy. Neurology, 61: 1032-1034.

Frohman EM, Racke MK, Raine CS (2006). Multiple Sclerosis — The Plaque and Its Pathogenesis. N. Engl. J. Med., 354: 942-955.

Genain CP, Cannella B, Hauser SL, Raine CS (1999). Identification of autoantibodies associated with myelin damage in multiple sclerosis. Nat. Med., 5: 170-175.

Gronning M, Riise T, Kvale G, Albrektsen G, Midgard R, Nyland H (1993). Infections in Childhood and Adolescence in Multiple Sclerosis. Neuroepidemiology, 12: 61-69.

Hemmer B, Cepok S, Nessler S, Sommer N (2002). Pathogenesis of multiple sclerosis: an update on immunology. Curr. Opin. Neurol., 15: 227–231.

Huseby ES, Liggitt D, Brabb T, Schnabel B, Ohlen C, Goverman J (2001). A pathogenic role for myelin-specific CD8 (+) T cells in a model for multiple sclerosis. J. Exp. Med., 194: 669-676.

Husted C (2006). Structural Insight into the Role of Myelin Basic Protein in Multiple Sclerosis. Proc. Natl. Acad. Sci., 12: 4339–4340.

Imitola J, Chitnis T, Khoury SJ (2006). Insights into the molecular pathogenesis of progression in multiple sclerosis. Potential implications for future therapies. Arch. Neurol., 63: 25-33.

Kantarci O, Silva A, Eraksoy M, Sutlas N, Agaoglu J (1998). Survival and predictors of disability in Turkish MS patients. Neurology, 51: 765-772.

Kasper LH, Shoemaker J (2010). Multiple sclerosis immunology. The healthy immune system vs the MS immune system. Neurology, 74: S2–S8.

Kuhlmann T, Lingfeld G, Bitsch A, Schuchardt J, Bruck W (2002). Acute axonal damage in multiple sclerosis is most extensive in early disease stages and decreases over time. Brain, 125: 2202-2212.

Lassmann H (2008). Models of multiple sclerosis: New insights into pathophysiology and repair. Curr. Opin. Neurol., 21: 242–247.

Lucchinetti C, Bruck W, Noseworthy J (2001). Multiple sclerosis: recent developments in neuropathology, pathogenesis, magnetic resonance imaging studies and treatment. Curr. Opin. Neurol., 14: 259–269.

Noseworthy JH, Lucchinetti C, Rodriguez M, Weinshenker BG (2000). Multiple Sclerosis. N. Engl. J. Med., 343: 938-952.

Prat A, Antel J (2005). Pathogenesis of multiple sclerosis. Curr. Opin. Neurol., 18: 225–230.

Riise T, Nortvedt MW, Ascherio A (2003). Smoking as a risk factor for multiple sclerosis. Neurology, 61: 1122-1124.

Rivera-Olmos VM (2007). La genética de la Esclerosis Múltiple. Aspectos regionales y raciales. In: Cuevas-García C (ed). Fronteras en la Esclerosis Múltiple. Mexico: PYDESA, pp. 15-24.

Rose JW, Carlson NG (2007). Pathogenesis of multiple sclerosis. Continuum Lifelong Learn. Neurol., 13: 35–62.

Rudick RA (2001). Evolving concepts in the pathogenesis of multiple sclerosis and their therapeutic Implications. J. Neuro-Ophthalmol., 21: 279–283.

Saikali P, Antel JP, Newcombe J, Chen Z, Freedman M, Blain M, Cayrol R, Prat A, Hall JA, Arbour N (2007). NKG2D-mediated Cytotoxicity toward Oligodendrocytes suggests a Mechanism for Tissue Injury in Multiple Sclerosis. J. Neurosci., 27: 1220-1228.

Sotelo J, Ordoñez G, Pineda B (2007). Varicella-zoster virus at relapses of multiple sclerosis. J. Neurol., 254: 493-500.

Weinshenker BG, Bass B, Rice GPA, Noseworthy J, Carriere W, Baskerville J, Ebers GC (1989). The natural history of multiple sclerosis: A geographically based study in clinical course and disability. Brain, 112: 133-146.

Wekerle H, Hohlfeld R (2003). Molecular mimicry in multiple sclerosis. N. Engl. J. Med., 349: 185-186.

Wolfgan B (2007). New insights into the pathology of multiple sclerosis: Towards a unified concept? J. Neurol., 254: I/3-I/9.

Zhou D, Srivastava R, Nessler S, Grummel V, Sommer N, Bruck W, Hartung HP, Stadelmann C (2006). Identification of a Pathogenic Antibody Response to Native Myelin Oligodendrocyte Glycoprotein in Multiple Sclerosis. Proc. Natl. Acad. Sci., 103: 19057-19062.

Brief aphasia evaluation (minimum verbal performance): Psychometric data in healthy participants from Argentina

Viglilecca Nora Silvana[1]*, Peñalva Marisa Carola[2], Castillo Jorge Antonio[2], Molina Silvia Cristina[2], Voos Javier Alfredo[3], Ortiz Maria Marta[4] and Ribichich Marialicia[5]

[1]Consejo Nacional de Investigaciones Científicas y Técnicas de la Argentina (CONICET); - Argentina. Servicio de Neurocirugía del Hospital Córdoba; Centro de Investigaciones de la Facultad de Filosofía y Humanidades- (CIFFyH). Universidad Nacional de Córdoba, Argentina.
[2]Centro de Investigaciones de la Facultad de Filosofía y Humanidades (CIFFyH). Universidad-Nacional de Córdoba, Argentina.
[3]Grupo de Ingeniería Clínica de la Universidad Tecnológica Nacional (UTN) Regional Córdoba, Argentina.
[4]Colegio de Fonoaudiólogos. Buenos Aires, Argentina.
[5]Consultorio Psicopedagógico Privado. Buenos Aires, Argentina.

Aphasia test psychometric studies are necessary, especially for brief instruments in Spanish. A test was designed to quickly detect the basic resources of verbal communication in aphasic patients. In a sample of healthy Spanish-speakers, it was studied: (a) their test performance according to demographic variables; (b) the inter-item-internal consistency; (c) the subtest-factor structure; (d) the test-retest reliability during an extended inter-test interval of 7 to 14 months; (e) the inter-rater reliability. Data were collected from 151 participants living in Cordoba or Buenos Aires, aged 6 to 80, 56% females, with an average 8-year education. Subsamples of 34 and 26 participants were evaluated for test-retest and inter-rater reliability studies. The total score was only affected by age. Age and education had a significant effect on the time required to perform the test. Satisfactory reliability coefficients were observed. An exploratory and unrestricted factor analysis indicated that 68% of the variance was explained by three factors. A one factor solution was also suitable. The test-score proved to be reliable, representative of a verbal homogeneous construct and sensitive to the effect of age. The administration of this test of free-distribution (with 72 items) required on average, between 11 and 17 min.

Key words: Aphasia screening test, minimum verbal performance, reliability, validity, norms, comparative city studies, age, education, gender, free-distribution tests.

INTRODUCTION

Background

Spanish is one of the most widely spoken languages in the world and Spanish-speaking populations are increasing worldwide. Therefore, developing valid and reliable psychological instruments for any Spanish-speaking community is necessary. Considering aphasia tests, although, there is a need to psychometric studies on these tests in general; Spanish instruments particularly lack these types of studies.

Healthy subject (HS) studies are crucial in

*Corresponding author. E-mail: nsviglilecca@hotmail.com.

psychometrics. Nevertheless, there are no aphasia tests for Spanish speakers which had shown, in their psychometric bases, the test-performance according to the demographic variables as well as the inter-rater reliability in HS. The comprehensive Boston Diagnostic Aphasia Examination (BDAE)-Spanish version (Goodglass and Kaplan, 1996) and the short Bedside Assessment of Language in Spanish (Sabe et al., 2008) did not provide any kind of HS data or inter-rater reliability indices in their original studies. As a way of completing the data provided in the English and the Spanish BDAE manuals, Davis (1993) reported inter-rater reliability studies on the original BDAE and Pineda et al. (2000) analyzed the HS performance and the effect of demographic variables on a Spanish version of this test.

Considering brief aphasia tests in any language, not only is the information pertaining to measurement properties and clinical utility limited (Salter et al., 2006) but also and most probably as a result of ceiling effect, HS-reliability studies are rare. Test-retest reliability throughout long-term periods in HS has never been studied and factor analysis has not been commonly carried out. Besides, the effect of demographic variables as part of the norm studies is not clear (Kostalova et al., 2008).

In the present exploratory study, a new aphasia test was analyzed trying to respond to some of the questions described earlier for HS. The Brief Aphasia Evaluation (BAE) was developed to mainly assess the minimum verbal performance (that is, the basic verbal functioning) of patients with aphasia so as to begin, after that with a more complete and better organized neuropsychological or language evaluations. By means of this technique the patient's performance was attempted to be explored through a more operative way, which is imperative for professionals who have to administer neuropsychological tests in difficult conditions, particularly in public hospitals.

By assessing the minimum verbal performance in HS rather than just the impairment in patients, the patients' dysfunction was mainly inferred by the discrepancy observed with respect to HS. However, other comparisons are also needed for validation (see below).

In this laboratory, the presence and magnitude of a general verbal deficit (including the presence and magnitude of its symptoms or components) are considered more useful for the patient's diagnosis and treatment than try to find a perfect archetype for each combination of symptoms (Vigliecca, 2010). In spite of that, we do not intend to replace the theoretical and technical perspective of the professional involved, but simply to complement it.

Neuropsychological techniques are proposed to reach through psychological tests, an appropriate diagnosis of brain functions both in their quality and magnitude. Studies from our laboratory have demonstrated the concurrent validity of this test to differentiate between patients with left cerebral lesions (that is, patients injured in the verbal dominant hemisphere) and patients with right cerebral lesions, as well as patients with left cerebral lesions and HS (Vigliecca et al., 2011).

Factor-structure studies

Salter affirmed (Salter et al., 2006) that screening tools are useful to detect the presence or absence of a particular condition of construct. However, there are almost no studies which have verified through factor analysis, the structure of the components of the aphasia screening tests according to the expected construct. As far as we know, the factor structure of a brief aphasia test has only been studied in the Reitan-Indiana Aphasia Screening Examination (ASE) (Williams and Shane, 1986).

Regarding the BAE, the underlying or theoretically expected construct is the minimum verbal performance, which is shared by patients and HS. An unrestricted factor analysis carried out in a sample of patients and HS (Vigliecca et al., 2011) indicated that, all its subtests (with loadings of 0.65 or above) grouped in one verbal factor which explained 78% of the variance. The same pattern was observed in the sample of patients alone. However, as only 38 HS participated of that study, factor analysis could not be accomplished in the control group since some subtests showed no variance.

Reliability studies

Satisfactory reliability coefficients have been reported for the Western Aphasia Battery (WAB) (Shewan and Kertesz, 1980) and the BDAE (Goodglass and Kaplan, 1996) although; both studies have been performed just on aphasic patients.

Inter-rater reliability coefficients of 0.75 or above have been reported for the BDAE (Davis, 1993). The BDAE original manual does not provide test-retest reliability data. Shewan and Kertesz (1980) reported test-retest reliability coefficients of 0.88 or above for the WAB subtests only in a group of chronic aphasic patients; however, this test is worldwide used (many times as the gold standard) not only for chronic patients. Test-retest coefficients were studied by these authors during an extended inter-test interval of at least 6 months but the statistical significance of the changes observed between test and retest was not reported.

As regards brief aphasia tests, reliability studies have also been performed on patients. Test-retest and inter-rater reliability coefficients of 0.70 or above have been reported for the Acute Aphasia Screening Protocol and the Frenchay Aphasia Screening Test (FAST) (Salter et al., 2006; Crary et al., 1989; Enderby et al., 1987).

Theodoros et al. (2008) reported intra and inter-rater reliability coefficients of 0.59 or above for the short form of the BDAE which was assessed via an internet-based videoconferencing system. For Spanish language, Sabe et al. (2008) reported test-retest and internal-consistency coefficients of 0.62 or above in aphasic patients. Although, the time since onset of disease was not reported by these authors (Sabe et al. (2008), the changes observed between test and retest (46% of variation) were highly significant.

Aphasia versus language stability

In spite of the earlier said, the aphasic condition is not expected to be stable; great fluctuations can be observed in aphasic patients even overnight. On the contrary, it is the underlying verbal ability of non-brain-damaged participants which is expected to be stable thus, allowing the establishment of a normative performance against which to judge the aphasic performance.

A significant performance improvement has consistently been reported for aphasic patients when several weeks or months elapsed since onset of condition (Sabe et al., 2008; Shewan, 1986; Wade et al., 1986). Therefore, a reliable aphasia test should show a corresponding stability in HS during those several weeks or months. Otherwise, learning curves would be necessary for patient and control groups.

Effect of demographic variables

Considering the comprehensive BDAE in its Spanish version, Pineda et al. (2000) observed, in a sample of healthy Colombian workers living in Medellin, that gender and age had a significant effect on reading and writing subtests, while education had a significant impact on most of the BDAE subtests. In fact, a stepwise regression model showed that education was the best predictor of the variance in the BDAE scores.

Regarding the HS-effect of demographic variables in brief aphasia tests, Kostalova et al. (2008) reported an effect of education on the Mississippi Aphasia Screening Test- Czech version (MASTcz), which was coincident with the original MAST (Nakase-Thompson et al., 2005) and the ASE (Williams and Shane, 1986). Although, no effects of age (range 14 to 87) or gender were reported (Kostalova et al., 2008), an interaction between age and education was observed when age was coded below and above 60 years old. The lack of effects of age and gender (Kostalova et al., 2008) was not coincident with the original MAST (Nakase-Thompson et al., 2005). Meanwhile an inverse relationship between age (range 21to81) and score was observed for the FAST (Salter et al., 2006).

Minimum verbal performance, HS-variance and ceiling effect

These demographic contradictory results are interesting because a minimum verbal performance test involving over learned verbal tasks should supposedly be less prone to be affected by demographic variables in HS. Actually, a minimum neuropsychological performance which as a whole can be reached by all or almost all HS (but not by all brain-injured patients) is the rationale which underlies the very widespread mini mental test of Folstein, for example (Folstein et al., 1975). Nevertheless, not only should the poor variance but also the effect of demographic variables be corroborated in HS, before analyzing the factors which contribute to determine the variance among brain injured patients. As far as we know, the effect of demographic variables on brief aphasia tests has never been studied in Spanish-speaker samples.

On the other hand, ceiling effect (if it really exists in HS) is almost a necessary condition to be studied in this kind of tests considering that it represents both a superior limit and a control parameter for the patients' performance. As a consequence, it should be specifically analyzed, not avoided or assumed *a priori.*

Research questions

The BAE is part of a bigger research project which attempts to develop culture-free (or easily adaptable to different languages) tests under a multicenter approach. So, the BAE items were specially designed for this purpose. The words were selected in view of their high frequency of use and cultural or geographical dependent words or phonemes were excluded. The underlying and general scientific proposal of such research, aims at developing efficient tests, that is, brief and/or easy to apply neuropsychological techniques without neglecting the goals of accuracy and validity.

In the present study, we specifically wanted to analyze the performance which can be expected in different groups of HS according to the demographic variables as a way of getting a preliminary standardized reference (a norm) for the patients' performance interpretation. In order to analyze the effect of the recruitment place, a small subsample belonging to an additional city was evaluated.

With the aim of analyzing whether the different parts of the BAE can be considered as components of the same verbal construct (conceptual validity), an exploratory subtest-factor analysis was carried out in this bigger and more variable sample of HS than the one recruited in a previous study (Viglieca et al., 2011).

Regarding the reliability indices, not only the internal consistency of the items which measure the same concept was deemed to be estimated, but also the stability and the objectivity.

In this exploratory research, no specific hypotheses were formulated in view of the lack of enough or consistent antecedents. However, and in addition to the need of exploring the HS psychometric properties and the test efficiency, it was expected that the test resulted as resistant as possible to the effect of demographic variables and (as any other norm referenced test) useful to be applied in health institutions belonging to the places from which the samples were recruited.

Additionally, the present methodological approach may represent a step forward (not a perfect one) in the difficult process of getting satisfactory psychometric properties in short tests.

Objectives

To study in a sample of healthy Spanish speakers; (a) their performance in the BAE according to demographic variables; (b) the inter-item-internal consistency; (c) the subtest-factor structure and, in a subgroup of those HS; (d) the test-retest reliability during an extended inter-test interval of 7 to 14 months, as well as (e) the inter-rater reliability.

By simultaneously analyzing several indices of HS performance, a better control parameter for the patients' performance may be obtained.

MATERIALS AND METHODS

Materials

The present test, which was freely offered by its authors in paper, informatics and English versions, (http://neurotests.frc.utn.edu.ar) was designed to bed-side and quickly detect the basic resources of verbal communication in aphasic patients. This aphasia instrument is part of the battery of "Neuropsychological Tests Abbreviated and Adapted for Spanish-Speakers" (Vigliecca, 2004; Vigliecca and Aleman, 2009) and it was composed of 72 items scored from 0 to 3 (maximum score 216). This test was developed ten years ago (Vigliecca, 2000), independently of the proposed in other aphasia screening tests.

The main functions to be studied with the test were: Comprehension, expression, naming, repetition, reading, writing, attention (phonemic analysis and synthesis), memory and praxia. All the tasks were verbal except maybe for praxia (see below).

Comprehension included items such as salutation, questions to be answered with a gesture, questions to be answered with "Yes/No" or "I don't know" and "point at" questions; *expression* explored the interviewee's ability to describe his/her own disease, as part of the spontaneous speech and it also involved saying the numbers from 1 to 10 and saying the alphabet (until the letter "l"), as part of verbal automatisms; naming included the tasks of saying the names of single objects and completing sentences which were started by the interviewer; repetition included the tasks of saying the same words, word series and sentences which were uttered by the interviewer; reading involved the visual discrimination of numbers, letters and words which were said by the interviewer, the execution of written commands, the comprehension of written expressions by confrontation with pictures and reading aloud; writing included items such as writing the name, the numbers from 1 to 10 and the alphabet until the letter "l", writing numbers, letters, words and sentences by dictation, as well as writing spontaneously a sentence; attention was based on the tasks of phonemic discrimination (selection of a target among several options), phonemic synthesis (recognition of a spelled word), spelling (phonemic analysis) and reversed spelling; memory involved a delayed repetition (that is, the recall of words which had been previously said by the interviewer); praxia involved the imitation of a mouth movement made by the interviewer.

The first six functions (specially the first four and complementarily, reading and writing) are classically assumed as the main factors which determine the variance among brain injured patients, thus, hypothetically discriminating aphasia types. The remaining three functions were incorporated with exploratory purposes. Other conditions such as visual agnosia, visual field defects, orientation, prosody, gesture- comprehension and expression, etc. are also complementarily explored by this test, but they were not analyzed in the present work.

Subjects

Participants were community-dwelling Argentinean volunteers without any known neurological or psychiatric disease, adapted to their daily life demands. They were recruited from academic, cultural, recreational and retirement centers from Córdoba (77%) and Buenos Aires (23%). The centers were intentionally selected trying to get heterogeneity in the socioeconomic background. The institution authorities were interviewed and the research objectives as well as the characteristics required for the participants were explained. A list of potential volunteers was prepared. The test did not pose any risk to the participants who, on the contrary, were cognitively stimulated. We had the informed consent of the participants or the caregivers. The institutions and individuals who participated in the research remained anonymous. They were asked for other potential participants thus, trying to create a network of volunteers.

In order to include a subject in the sample, we also took into consideration the information provided by the initial interview of the neuropsychological battery. This interview evaluated risk factors, background and their probable incidence on cognition and behavior. We asked questions about genetic neurological or psychiatric disorders; hypoxia during labor; significant diseases; head trauma with loss of consciousness; seizures; tumors; hypertension; heart disease; faints; consumption (previous and current) of: drugs, alcohol, cigarettes, medicines, etc.; malnutrition; contact with toxic agents (frequency and duration); school performance (failures and merits); development (language, motor skills, sphincter control); relevant changes in: feeding behavior, sexual behavior, sphincter control, sleep-wake cycle, mood or character; presence of: unexpected responses, odd sensations, delusions, hallucinations, alterations in perception (illusions, distortions), etc.; memory, speaking, verbal comprehension, attention, orientation (personal, place and time), reading, and writing problems; sensory difficulties, etc. For younger than 11 year-old-subjects the interview questions were answered by the parents or caregivers.

We excluded subjects who showed symptoms of neurological or psychiatric disorders, psychotropic drug consumption including excessive alcohol, risk of neurological damage by disease or accident, any kind of medical illness which could affect neuropsychological performance or sensory or motor difficulties which prevented them from carrying out the tests fluently. Students who had done some academic year twice were also excluded. In case of any doubt from any member of the research team regarding the intervening variables, participants were excluded.

The effect of demographic variables, the internal consistency and the factor structure were studied in a sample of 151 HS, aged 6 to 80 (mean ± SD: 31.30 ± 24.25); 56% females and 44% males; 59% with a background of elementary education, 22% with a background of high school (secondary) education and 18% with a college or university background (education years: 7.81 ± 5.56). Only eight subjects were not right-handed (ambidextrous or left-handed). Only eight six-year-old children (6YOC), 3 girls and 5 boys attending the first grade of the elementary school, were in the process of acquiring the basic reading and writing skills. The rest of the subjects had at least completed one year of education.

From this total sample, a sub group of 31 right-handed subjects was re-evaluated for the test-retest reliability study. In this subsample of 7 to 80 years old (50.23 ± 24.03), there were 47% females and 53% males, of whom 35% had an elementary level, 33% a high school level and 32% a higher level of education (education years: 11.06 ± 5.74). The range of the inter-test interval was 7 to 14 months (10.85 ± 2.16).

From this subsample, another group was re-evaluated for the inter-rater reliability study. In order to carry out this study, two trained interviewers acting independently evaluated the same interviewee. The consistency between the two interviewers' evaluations was analyzed by means of both the interview recorded on an audiotape (in which written answers could not be seen) and the interviewee's written answers during the written subtests. For the audio-register, only those subjects who had either agreed to be recorded or had favorable recording conditions in their environments were studied. This subsample was made up of 26 HS of 7 to 80 years old (51.92 ± 25.12), 57% females and 42% males; 38% with elementary level of education, 31% with secondary level and 31% with higher level (education years: 10.61 ± 6.03).

Alternatively, the interpretation that the second rater made from the first rater's administration protocol was also analyzed. Such interpretation was done independent of the explicit interviewee's behaviors, that is, by just looking at the first rater's written-administration registers (evaluations, crosses, marks, comments, etc.) about the interviewee. For this paper register, the sample of the previously described 31 HS was studied.

Statistical analysis

When the effect of demographic variables was analyzed, the total score and the duration of the test were the dependent variables. The total score was the main variable of study because the verbal performance is primarily expressed by this index. The test duration was incorporated just as complementary information. Both variables were analyzed by a gender x education x age ANOVA (age-range: 12 to 80; age-intervals: 24 years). For younger than 12 year-old-subjects (age-range: 6 to 11) only a gender x age ANOVA was carried out since all these subjects only attended elementary school; besides, years of study were correlative to years of age for this group. One-way ANOVAs were carried out for those analyses in which only one independent variable was involved.

The dependent variables were quantitative; the adequacy of the underlying model for the ANOVAs was checked by the residual analysis (the primary tool for checking normality was the residual histogram (plots shown)); the plots of the residual versus the predicted values was mainly used for checking the equality of variances (plots not shown)); in case of inadequacy, data were reevaluated by their ranks to check consistency (results not shown). In case of inconsistency, data were reevaluated by nonparametric statistics (main effects only, results not shown). The coefficients of variation (CV) were also taken into account in the analysis of ANOVAs assumptions.

The internal consistency was analyzed by the standardized Cronbach's alpha coefficient (Vogt, 2005) and the rest of the reliability indices by the intra-class correlation coefficient (ICC), whereby the order of administration is randomized. Differences between test and retest and differences between both raters were analyzed by the dependent sample-Student t-test. An exploratory factor analysis (by using the principal component-method and the varimax raw-rotation) was carried out with the nine subtests of this instrument. The variance involved in each successive factor was analyzed (that is, the explained variance) and only factors with Eigen values greater than 1 (Kaisser criterion) were retained; factor loadings were shown as descriptive data.

RESULTS

Effect of demographic variables

Participants from Córdoba and Buenos Aires did not differ either in the total score or in the time required to perform the test (score (F (1, 149) = 0.78, $p < 0.38$: Buenos Aires: 210.23 ± 11.58, Córdoba: 211.89 ± 9.17, total sample 211.51 ± 9.77; test duration (F (1, 149) = 1.76, $p < 0.19$: Buenos Aires: 13.11 ± 5.23, Córdoba: 14.23 ± 4.07, total sample 13.97 ± 4.38). Participants of these two cities were also similar in their demographic characteristics (years of age and education (F (1, 149) ≤ 0.19, $p \geq 0.66$; gender and manual preference ($\chi^2 \leq 0.97$; df: 1; $p \geq 0.32$). Therefore, both samples were considered as a single one.

The score of non-right handed subjects was not significantly different from the score of right-handed subjects (F (1, 149) = 0.53, $p < 0.47$). As a consequence, manual preference was not considered a criterion to exclude subjects in the analysis of demographic variables. On the contrary, a significant difference was observed between the 6YOC and the rest of the sample (F (1, 149) = 225.38, $p < 0.001$: 6YOC: 179.62 ± 24.78; rest of the sample: 213.33 ± 3.13). (The 6YOC were also different from both the rest of the children and the seven-year-old children (results not shown)). As a consequence, we excluded the 6YOC from the analysis of demographic variables except otherwise indicated. The remaining sample was distributed according to age-categories in thefollowing way: <11: 31%; 12 to 35: 29%; 36 to 59: 19%; >60: 20% (N = 143).

For the total score, the gender x education x age ANOVA for older than 12-year-old subjects indicated only a significant main age effect (Table 1). In general terms, the oldest subjects showed a poorer performance than the younger ones (Figure 1). By pooling subjects with secondary and higher levels of education, results did not change (Table 1). The gender x age ANOVA for younger than 12-year-old subjects indicated that, girls showed a

Table 1. Score: Effect-summary of gender x education x age ANOVA.

Total score (part a)							Total score (part b)						
ANOVA: 1-Gender, 2- education (three levels), 3- age							ANOVA: 1-Gender, 2- education (two levels), 3- age						
	df Effect	MS Effect	df Error	MS Error	F	p-level		df Effect	MS Effect	df Error	MS Error	F	p-level
1	1	2.06	80	6.74	0.31	0.582	1	1	2.61	86	6.75	0.39	0.536
2	2	7.17	80	6.74	1.06	0.350	2	1	7.07	86	6.75	1.05	0.309
3	2	59.82	80	6.74	8.87	0.000 *	3	2	93.13	86	6.75	13.80	0.000 *
12	2	3.10	80	6.74	0.46	0.633	12	1	0.62	86	6.75	0.09	0.762
13	2	12.58	80	6.74	1.87	0.161	13	2	11.26	86	6.75	1.67	0.195
23	4	3.29	80	6.74	0.49	0.745	23	2	2.79	86	6.75	0.41	0.663
123	4	9.85	80	6.74	1.46	0.222	123	2	2.90	86	6.75	0.43	0.652

Part a: 1st, 2nd and 3rd education levels. Part b: 2nd and 3rd levels were pooled.* Significant effect.

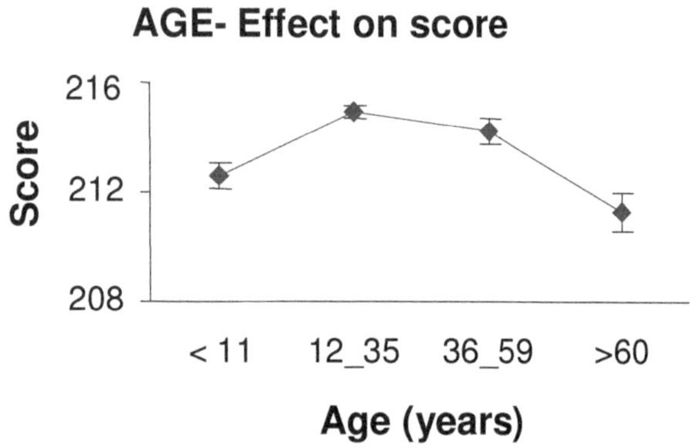

Figure 1. Score mean ± SE according to age-category, p < 0.001 (ANOVA).

trend to have a better performance than boys (results not shown) but, again, only a significant main effect of age was observed (gender: $F(1, 41) = 3.01$, $p < 0.09$; age: $F(1, 41) = 5.73$, $p < 0.02$; gender x age interaction: $F(1, 41) = 1.09$, $p < 0.30$). As expected for children, in this case the younger subjects showed a poorer performance than the older ones. Considering that both children and older subjects showed equivalent results, the two samples were pooled. Figure 1 shows the effect of age (alone) on score ($F(3, 139) = 11.37$, $p < 0.001$) for 7-to-80-year-old subjects. The average change between the age-category with the best performance and the age-category with the worst performance was less than 4 points, indicating less than 2% of variation.

Interestingly, by including the 6YOC, results did not change and the gender x age ANOVA also indicated just a main effect of age (gender: $F(1, 143) = 0.75$, $p < 0.39$; age: $F(3, 143) = 5.97$, $p < 0.001$; gender x age interaction: $F(3, 143) = 1.82$, $p < 0.15$). In this case, the mean score for <11-year-old subjects was 207.62 ± 15.30.

Just for informative purposes, when the test duration (see below) was incorporated as a covariate, none of the score-outputs changed (results not shown). Considering the test duration, the gender x education x age ANOVA for older than 12-year-old subjects indicated a significant main effect of both education and age without interaction among factors (Table 2). By pooling subjects with secondary and higher levels of education, results did not change (Table 2). Figure 2 shows the effect of age x education for 12-to-80-year-old subjects. As can be seen, older subjects showed a poorer performance (a longer test duration) than younger subjects and less educated subjects showed a poorer performance than more educated subjects. Nevertheless, the average change between the category with the best performance and the category with the worst performance was less than 4 min, indicating less than 4% of variation.

The gender x age ANOVA for younger than 12-year-old subjects in the test duration indicated neither main effects of gender or age nor interaction between factors (gender: $F(1, 41) = 0.27$, $p < 0.61$; age: $F(1, 41) = 2.37$, $p < 0.13$; gender x age interaction: $F(1, 41) = 0.02$, $p < 0.87$). The average time for the whole group of children was 15.19 ± 4.60 min, which was similar to the value observed in subjects with elementary level of education in the 12 to 80-year-old sample ($F(3, 78) = 1.21$, $p < 0.31$). By including the 6YOC in the sample of children, a significant age effect emerged (gender: $F(1, 49) = 0.05$, $p<0.82$; age: $F(1, 49) = 6.11$, $p<0.02$; gender x age interaction: $F(1, 49) = 0.22$, $p<0.64$). In this case, the average test-duration for 9-11-year-old children was 14.09 ± 4.32 minutes, while the average test-duration for <9-year-old children was 17.37 ± 4.91 minutes.

The histograms for the original three-way ANOVAs (Figures 3 and 4) indicated that, the residuals were fairly adjusted to normality (normality was shown by a curve). On the contrary, the plot of the residual versus the

Table 2. Test-duration: Effect-summary of gender x education x age ANOVA.

Test-duration (part a)							Test-duration (part b)						
ANOVA: 1-Gender, 2- education (three levels), 3- age							ANOVA: 1-Gender, 2- education (two levels), 3- age						
	df Effect	MS Effect	df Error	MS Error	F	p-level		df Effect	MS Effect	df Error	MS Error	F	p-level
1	1	3.72	80	4.63	0.80	0.373	1	1	2.31	86	4.47	0.52	0.474
2	2	43.58	80	4.63	9.42	0.000 *	2	1	76.51	86	4.47	17.13	0.000 *
3	2	35.90	80	4.63	7.75	0.001 *	3	2	34.20	86	4.47	7.66	0.001 *
12	2	0.36	80	4.63	0.08	0.925	12	1	0.29	86	4.47	0.06	0.799
13	2	7.97	80	4.63	1.72	0.185	13	2	7.40	86	4.47	1.66	0.197
23	4	1.17	80	4.63	0.25	0.907	23	2	2.94	86	4.47	0.66	0.520
123	4	1.66	80	4.63	0.36	0.837	123	2	3.20	86	4.47	0.72	0.492

Part a: 1st, 2nd and 3rd education levels. Part b: 2nd and 3rd levels were pooled. * Significant effect.

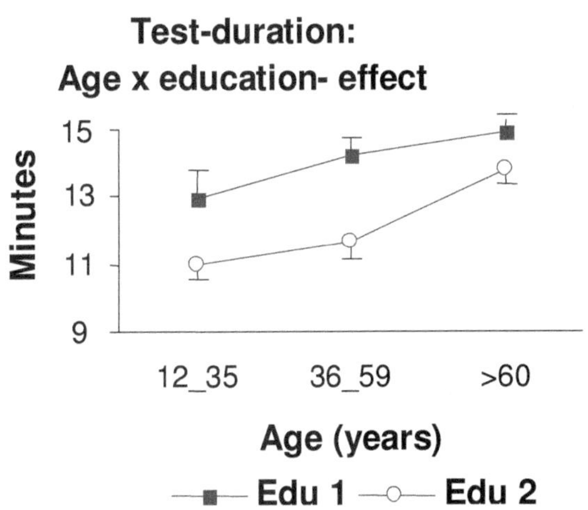

Figure 2. Time-mean ± SE according to age-category and education-level (Edu 1: First level, Edu 2: second and third level). ANOVA: Age effect: $p < 0.001$, education effect: $p < 0.001$. Age x education interaction: $p < 0.520$.

predicted values indicated a tendency for the variance of the residuals to decrease as the scores increased. The same plot did not reveal anything problematic for the test duration. The CVs were < 2% for the total score and 15% for the test duration which were considered satisfactory. Anyway, all the statistical analyses brought about identical outputs (results available upon request).

Additional information

Considering the total score, the 10th, 50th and 90th percentiles for the whole sample were 208, 214 and 216 respectively and by excluding the 6YOC, those percentiles were 209, 214 and 216.

Considering the test duration, the 10th, 50th and 90th percentiles for the whole sample were 10, 14 and 19 respectively and by excluding the 6YOC, those percent-tiles were 9, 14 and 17. (More information is available upon request).

Internal consistency and factor structure

By excluding items with zero variance, the Cronbach´s alpha coefficient indicated an internal consistency of 0.93. An unrestricted factor analysis indicated that, 68% of the variance was explained by three factors. Six of the verbal tests showed loadings of 0.50 or above in the first factor; naming and memory (with loadings of 0.72 and 0.74, respectively) grouped in the second factor, while *praxia* emerged as an independent third factor with a loading of 0.96. An internal consistency of 0.87 was observed among the subtests of the first factor, while in the rest of the factors the Cronbach´s alpha coefficient could not be calculated due to ceiling effect. A one factor solution was also acceptable with a subtest-internal consistency of 0.77 and an explained variance of 48%. Under this model, all the verbal subtests showed factor loadings of 0.22 or above.

Test-retest and inter-rater reliability

As regards the test stability, a satisfactory consistency between test and retest was observed for the total score without significant differences between both measures according to the Student t-test (Table 3). The average change between test and retest for the total score was 0.12 points, indicating a variation close to 0%. Consistency was lower for the test duration and a significant decrease in this measure was observed from the 1st to the 2nd administration. Nevertheless, the

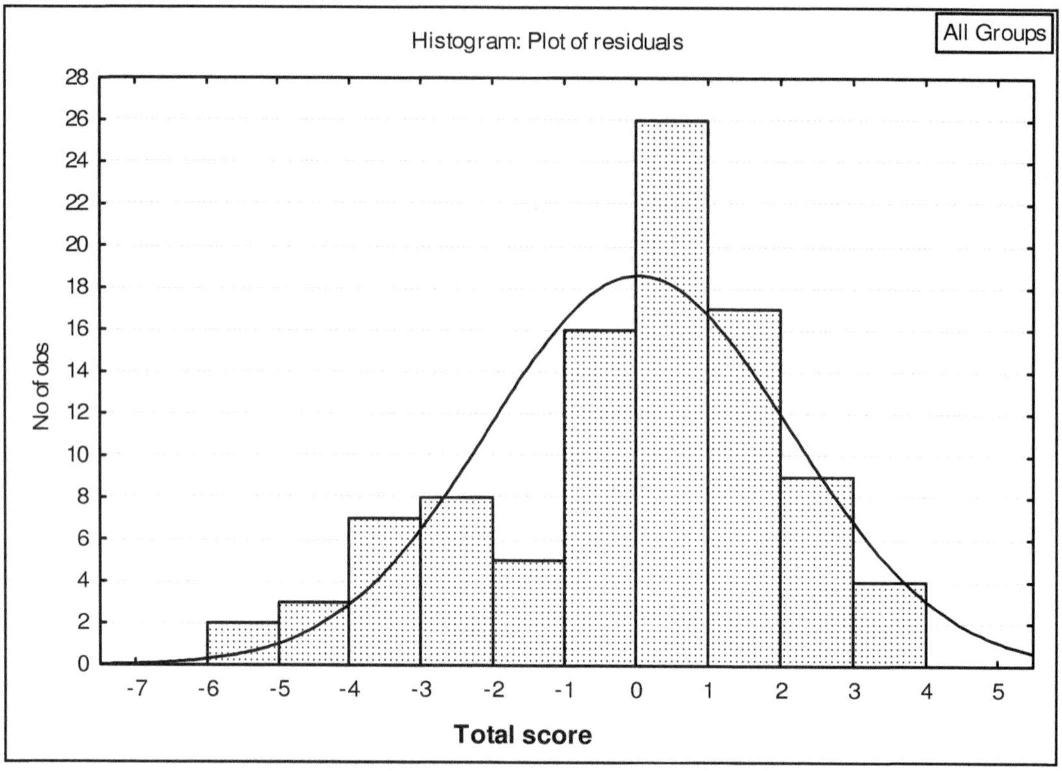

Figure 3. Histogram of the residuals for the gender x education x age ANOVA (Total score).

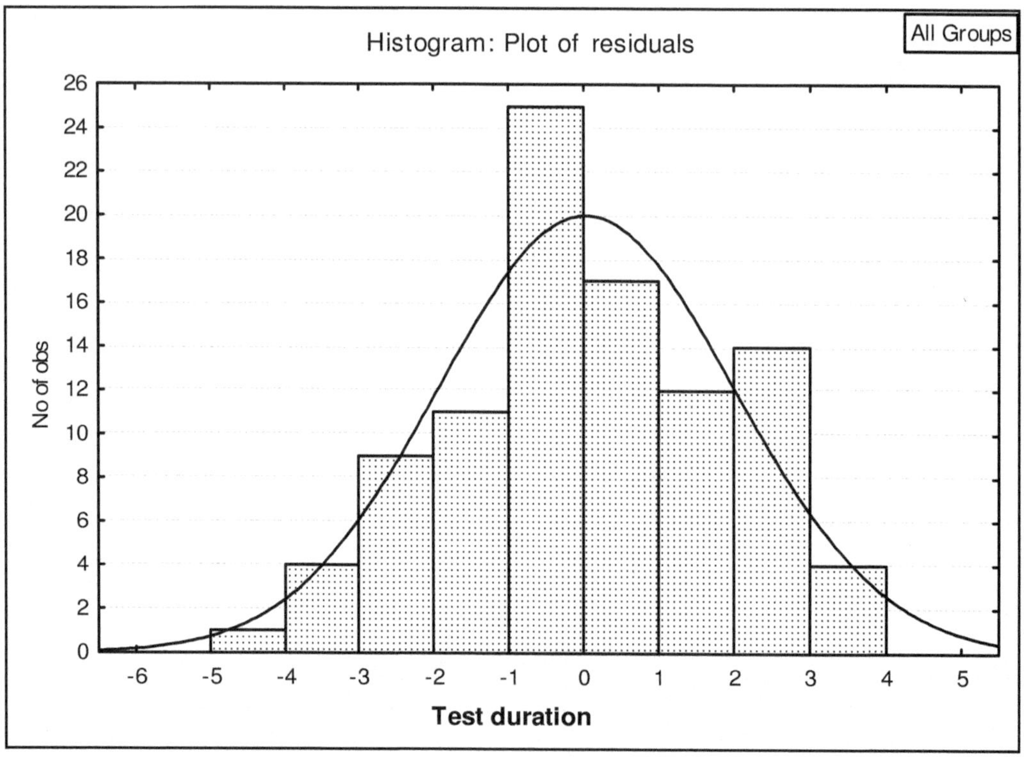

Figure 4. Histogram of the residuals for the gender x education x age ANOVA (Test-duration).

Table 3. Test-retest reliability.

	Test [(1)]	Retest [(1)]	ICC	Difference
Score	213.29 ± 2.61	213.18 ± 2.76	0.78	t = 0.40, df: 33, p < 0.689
Test-duration	13.03 ± 3.11	12.18 ± 3.27	0.74	t = 2.30, df: 33, p < 0.028 *

[(1)] Mean ± SD; * Significant effect.

Table 4. Inter-rater reliability.

Interpretation of the written and audio-taped interviewee's answers				
	Rater 1 [(1)]	**Rater 2 [(1)]**	**ICC**	**Difference**
Score	212.88 ± 2.76	212.69 ± 3.07	0.96	t = 1.31, df:25, p < 0.20
Time	12.73 ± 3.35	13.15 ± 3.74	0.93	t = -1.69, df:25, p < 0.11
Interpretation of the first rater's registers				
	Rater 1 [(1)]	Rater 2 [(1)]	ICC	Difference
Score	213.17 ± 2.76	213.15 ± 2.74	0.99	t = 0.44, df: 33, p < 0.66
Time	12.18 ± 3.27	12.21 ± 3.30	0.99	t = -1.00, df: 33, p < 0.32

[(1)] Mean ± SD.

average change between test and retest for the test duration was less than one minute. As regards the inter-rater reliability, a high consistency was observed among all the measures analyzed (that is, the second rater's interpretation of the interviewee's answers, and the second rater's interpretation of the first rater's registers in both the total score and the test duration). Significant differences between the two raters were not observed for any of the evaluations (Table 4).

DISCUSSION

The present age effect on score was coincident with the FAST (Enderby et al., 1987) and the original MAST studies (Nakase-Thompson et al., 2005). Nevertheless, the average change between the age-category with the best performance and the age-category with the worst performance in this work was less than 4 points, indicating less than 2% of variation.

Unlike the MASTcz (Kostalova et al., 2008), the MAST (Nakase-Thompson et al., 2005), the ASE (Williams and Shane, 1986) and even the extensive BDAE in its Spanish version (Pineda et al., 2000), we did not observe an effect of education on the present test score which surely had to do with the over learned tasks chosen for testing. This finding could be seen as an advantage for these kinds of tests which intentionally attempt to get a superior level of reference as resistant as possible to the effect of confounding factors. However, we did observe an effect of education on the test duration.

In previous aphasia test studies carried out on aphasic patients, the effect of demographic variables did not seem to be apparently a factor of interest. In the present HS-study, the coefficients obtained from the internal consistency and inter-rater reliability analyses were excellent, in agreement with previous aphasia test studies (Crary et al., 1989; Davis, 1993; Enderby et al., 1987; Goodglass and Kaplan, 1996; Sabe et al., 2008; Shewan and Kertesz, 1980). The score-test-retest ICC can also be considered satisfactory because the mean inter-test time was close to one year and as demonstrated with demographic variables, the scores of the most extreme age-categories tended to go in opposite directions throughout a year. The average change between test and retest for the total score indicated a variation close to 0%. Shewan and Kertesz (1980) observed a variation of 10% in chronic aphasic patients and Sabe et al. (2008) observed a variation close to 50% in apparently, non-chronic aphasic patients. In any case, present results set a precedent for the common and implicit assumption that healthy subject aphasia test scores do not significantly change during extended intervals. On the contrary, a significant decrease was observed between test and retest in the test duration, thus, surely representing an index of the effect of practice in this longitudinal design.

The subtest factor structure of the present test essentially showed one or two major verbal factors which clearly included eight of the nine subtests except for *praxia,* which apparently emerged as a non-verbal factor. Nevertheless, as this isolated subtest assesses an oral praxia related to verbal phonation (which is usually affected in aphasic patients), when the test was administered to patients, such subtest grouped with the rest of the verbal subtests (Vigliecca et al. 2011). Williams and Shane (1986) reported two major factors for the ASE; general language abilities factors band a sensorimotor coordination factor. However, the ASE intentionally includes non-verbal tasks.

Conclusions

Present results demonstrated that this test of minimum verbal performance (in its scored expression) can be considered a reliable instrument, representative of a homogeneous construct and in spite of dealing with over learned verbal tasks, sensitive to the effect of age in healthy subjects. According to the age factor, the inverted U-shaped figure obtained in the present study is consistent with most studies on long-term cognitive evolution. The poor variance observed on score also guarantees that a bigger number of cases are not necessary to confirm that pattern.

In general terms, the time required to administer the test was short according to the purpose of the test. In the older than 12-year-old sample, this time was affected by age and education but even considering the most extreme values achieved by the different groups, the time ranged on average between 11 and 15 min approximately. For children, this time was a little longer (between 14 and 17 min approximately). The test turned out to be efficient (valid, reliable and brief) although, it is well-known that comprehensive and extensive scales usually have better psychometric properties than brief scales. If a more subtle assessment of the aphasic symptoms is needed, a more complete language evaluation will have to be administered.

All the figures described in the present work shed light on the performance which can be expected from the different groups of HS analyzed, including children, adults, elderly people and to a certain extent, illiterates. As expected, most of the present subjects got a score near the maximum because this test was specially designed to detect pathology (not ability).

In principle, the test can be considered useful to be applied in Cordoba and Buenos Aires. The lack of effect of the recruitment place can be seen as a positive finding in the attempt of attenuating the strong impact that the different cultures usually have on verbal language tests. Further research would be necessary to see if the present results can be corroborated (or generalized to other samples and situations) considering that the study was carried out with an accidental sample of Spanish speakers.

If the usual cautions for norm referenced tests are taken into account (Haynes and Pindzola, 2008), the present psychometric studies and the methodological approach employed may represent helpful options to get better inferences in the aphasia topic.

ACKNOWLEDGEMENTS

This study was supported by funds from the National Council of Scientific and Technological Research in Argentina (CONICET) and the Ministry of Science and Technology of Cordoba Province. We are grateful to Cecilia Actis for her English assistance.

Abbreviations: BAE, Brief aphasia evaluation; **BDAE,** Boston diagnostic aphasia examination; **HS,** healthy subject; **ASE,** aphasia screening examination; **WAB,** western aphasia battery; **FAST,** frenchay aphasia screening test; **MASTcz,** Mississippi aphasia screening test- Czech version; **MAST,** Mississippiaphasia screening test; **6YOC,** six-year-old children; **ICC,** intra-class correlation coefficient; **SD,** standard deviation; **ANOVA,** analysis of variance; **df,** degrees of freedom; **CV,** coefficients of variation.

REFERENCES

Crary MA, Haak NJ, Malinsky AE (1989). Preliminary psychometric evaluation of an acute aphasia screening protocol. Aphasiol., 3: 611-618.

Davis GA (1993). A survey of adult aphasia and related language disorders (2nd edition). Englewood Cliffs, New Jersey: Prentice Hall Inc.

Enderby PM, Wood VA, Wade DT, Hewer RL (1987). The Frenchay Aphasia Screening Test: a short, simple test for aphasia appropriate for non-specialists. Int Rehabil Med., 8: 166-170.

Folstein MF, Folstein SE, McHugh PR (1975). "Mini-mental state". A practical method for grading the cognitive state of patients for the clinician. J. Psychiatr. Res. 12: 189-198.

Goodglass H, Kaplan E (1996). Evaluación de la afasia y trastornos relacionados. Adaptación española. Madrid: Panamericana.

Haynes WO, Pindzola RH (2008). Diagnosis and Evaluation in Speech Pathology (7th edition). Boston: Allyn and Bacon.

Kostálová M, Bártková E, Sajgalíková K, Dolenská A, Dusek L, Bednarík JA (2008) Standardization study of the Czech version of the Mississippi Aphasia Screening Test (MASTcz) in stroke patients and control subjects. Brain. Inj., 22: 793-801.

Nakase-Thompson R, Manning E, Sherer M, Yablon SA, Gontkovsky SLT, Vickery C (2005). Brief assessment of severe language impairments: Initial validation of the Mississippi aphasia screening test. Brain. Inj., 19: 685-691.

Pineda DA, Rosselli M, Ardila A, Mejia SE, Romero MG, Perez C (2000). The Boston Diagnostic Aphasia Examination-Spanish version: the influence of demographic variables. J. Int. Neuropsychol. Soc., 6: 802-814.

Sabe L, Courtis MJ, Saavedra MM, Prodan V, de Luján-Calcagno M, Melián S (2008). Desarrollo y validación de una batería corta de evaluación de la afasia: '*bedside* de lenguaje'. Utilización en un centro de rehabilitación. Rev. Neurol., 46: 454-460.

Salter K, Jutai J, Foley N, Hellings C and Teasell R (2006). Identification of aphasia post stroke: a review of screening assessment tools. Brain. Inj., 20: 559-568.

Shewan CM and Kertesz A (1980). Reliability and validity characteristics of the Western Aphasia Battery (WAB). J. Speech. Hear. Disord., 45: 308-324.

Shewan CM (1986). The Language Quotient (LQ): a new measure for the Western Aphasia Battery. J. Commun. Disord., 19: 427-439.

Theodoros D, Hill A, Russell T, Ward E, Wootton R (2008). Assessing acquired language disorders in adults via the Internet. Telemed J. E.

Health, 14: 552-559.
Vigliecca NS (2004). Neuropsychological tests abbreviated and adapted to Spanish speakers: Review of previous findings and validity studies for the discrimination of patients with anterior vs. posterior lesions. Rev. Neurol., 39: 205-212.
Vigliecca NS (2000). Towards a more agile and operative aphasia evaluation. Rev Neurol Arg. 25 (Suppl. Section Neuropsychol., p.52.
Viglieсса NS, Aleman GP (2010). A novel neuropsychological assessment to discriminate between ischemic and nonischemic dementia, J. Pharmacol. Toxicol. Methods., 61: 38-43.
Viglieсса NS, Peñalva MC, Molina SC, Voos JA (2011). Brief Aphasia Evaluation (minimum verbal performance): Concurrent and Conceptual Validity Study in Patients with Unilateral Cerebral Lesions. Brain Inj. 25: 394-400 (doi:10.3109/02699052.2011.556106).
Viglieсса NS (2010). Aphasia: what are we measuring? Revista de Neuropsiquiatría y Neurociencia Cognitiva. 9: 54-55. (See also http://www.saneurociencias.org.ar/descargas/Libro_Congreso_de_Neurociencia_IIRCN.pdf, 234-235, accessed Feb 23, 2011).
Vogt WP (2005). Dictionary of statistics and methodology: a nontechnical guide for the social sciences (3rd edition). Thousand Oaks, California: Sage Publications, Inc.
Wade DT, Hewer RL, David RM, Enderby PM (1986). Aphasia afterstroke: natural history and associated deficits. J. Neurol. Neurosurg. Psychiatry, 49: 11-16.
Williams JM, Shane B (1986). The Reitan-Indiana Aphasia Screening Test: scoring and factor analysis. J. Clin. Psychol., 42: 156-160.

Efficacy of oxcarbazepine add on therapy on intractable seizures in Children

Azita Tavassoli[1]*, Mohamad Ghofrani[2], Mohsen Rouzrokh[3] and Eznollah Azargashb[4]

[1]Department of Pediatric Neurology, Ali Asghar Children Hospital, Iran University of Medical Science, Tehran, Iran.
[2]Department of Pediatric Neurology, Mofid Children Hospital, Shahid Beheshti University of Medical Science, Tehran, Iran.
[3]Department of pediatric surgery, Mofid Children Hospital, Shahid Beheshti University of Medical Science, Tehran, Iran.
[4]Department of Health and Social Medicine, Shahid Beheshti University of Medical Science, Tehran, Iran.

Almost 50 million people in the world, a third of whom children, suffer from epilepsy. Up to 30% of them develop refractory epilepsy. In this group, there is a need for more efficacious antiepileptic drugs. This study was undertaken to evaluate the efficacy and safety of oxcarbazepine a new antiepileptic drug, as an adjunction therapy in children with refractory epilepsy. From February, 2004 until September 2006, 30 patients with refractory epilepsy aged between 4 and 14 years, were evaluated in a before and after type (pre-post) study in the department of neurology of Mofid children's hospital. Patients had at least one seizure per month to over 10 seizures daily and none of them had used oxcarbazepine previously. They received oxcarbazepine with a maximum dose 50 mg/kg/day orally in combination with their current antiepileptic drugs. The parents kept seizure diaries and the patients were regularly assessed for seizure frequency and side effects. The follow-up period was for 10 months. We compared the daily seizure frequency before and after starting the new medication. After 10 months of oxcarbazepine adjunction therapy, 10% of the patients became seizure-free, 36.6% experienced more than 50% reduction in seizure frequency and 13.3% had increasing seizures. The drug was especially effective in the patients with partial seizures. Within the first days of treatment, brief and transient adverse effects including somnolence, dizziness and headache were seen in 36.6% of the patients which disappeared with continuation of treatment. In one patient with history of hypersensitivity to carbamazepine, skin rash occurred and resulted in withdrawal of the drug. Wilcoxon signed ranks test showed that oxcarbazepine was effective in the treatment of refractory seizures in children (P = 0.003) and as shown by Fisher's exact test, it is more effective in partial seizures. (P = 0.0043).The results showed that Oxcarbazepine is a useful medication in the treatment of refractory epilepsy especially partial type in children.

Key words: Add-on therapy, children, intractable epilepsy, oxcarbazepine, side effect.

INTRODUCTION

Epilepsy is one of the most common neurologic diseases (Kalis, 2001). Mean incidence of epilepsy in childhood (from birth to 16 years of age) is approximately 40 in 100,000 children in each year (Peter et al., 2006).

Antiepileptic drugs (AED) generally used are associated with side effects and drug interactions; however, in many epileptic patients, epilepsy is controlled after using one of these antiepileptic agents. On the other hand, up to 30% of the patients develop refractory epilepsy which is frequently common in the patients with partial seizures (Castillo et al., 2000).

When the patient is resistant to the medication or cannot

*Corresponding author. E-mail: Azita_Tavasoli@yahoo.com.

tolerate the treatment due to the drug's adverse effects, more efficacious or better tolerable medications are needed (Connock et al., 2006).

One of these newly introduced medications is Oxcarbazepine (OXCBZ) which has been approved by Food and Drug Administration (FDA) (Malphrus and Wilfong, 2007).

Many studies have shown OXCBZ to be a valuable medication in treatment of partial seizures in children and adults both in monotherapeutic or adjunctive settings (Schimdt et al., 2001; Flesch, 2004; Bang, 2004; Arroyo, 2001; Schmidt and Elger, 2004). OXCBZ is chemically similar to carbamazepine (CBZ) but with a different metabolism (May et al., 2003). Its antiepileptic effect is due to blockade of voltage-dependant sodium channels and modulating calcium channels (Schmidt and Elger, 2004; Flesch, 2004), it is safer, is tolerated much better, has less drug reactions and the risk of over dose is extremely low in comparison with CBZ. No significant side effects has been reported for OXCBZ (Horga and Horga, 2006).

This study was performed to evaluate the efficacy and safety of OXCBZ in an adjunctive therapeutic setting in pediatric patients with resistant epilepsy.

METHODS

In this before and after type study, 30 children between 4 and 14 years of age with refractory epilepsy including partial seizures with or without secondary generalization generalized tonic-colonic seizures and mixed type seizures, seeking treatment in department of pediatric neurology were recruited to be subjects of the study. None of these patients had ever used OXCBZ previously and the seizure frequency of them was from once a month to more than 10 times per day, before the commencement of the trial. We explained advantages and probable side effects of OXCBZ to the patient's parents and informed consent was obtained from them. The diagnosis of refractory epilepsy was made according to the definition of Berg and Shiner (2001) that defined intractability as "lack of seizure control while the patient had received at least 2 first-line antiepileptic medications, having more than 1 seizure per month in an 18- month period. Also, the patients should not be seizure free for more than 3 consecutive months" (Peter et al., 2006). We prescribed OXCBZ concomitantly with other AEDs that the patients were receiving. In the period of treatment with OXCBZ other AEDs were not added but the dosage of current AEDs could be changed. The dosage of OXCBZ was 30 mg/kg/day for first week, 40 mg/kg/day for second week and 50 mg/kg/day for third week. This maintenance dose was then continued for 10 months. The parents kept seizure diaries (in view of frequency, duration and type of seizure) and the patients were regularly (every two weeks) assessed in the neurology clinic for seizure frequency and side effects of the new medication. The follow-up period was for 10 months and we compared daily seizure frequency before and after starting the new medication. Clinical responses to OXCBZ treatment was defined as: seizure-free status or complete control the seizures, improvement or more than 50% decrease in seizures frequency, unchanged or less than 50% decrease and worsening or more than 50% increase in seizure frequency.

Laboratory investigations (CBC, BUN, Cr, Na, K, Ca, P, ALT, AST, U/A) were done in the beginning of the study and checked monthly. If any significant hematologic, renal, hepatic or systemic side effect was seen, the treatment with OXCBZ was stopped and the patient was excluded.

The statistical analysis was performed using SPSS version 11.5 (SPSS; Chicago, IL, USA). Wilcoxon signed Rank and Fisher's exact tests were used to evaluate the efficacy of OXCBZ in the treatment of refractory epilepsy in children.

RESULTS

Thirty patients with intractable epilepsy were enrolled in this before and after type study. Mean age was 7.7 ± 2.9 years range 4 - 14 years and the group included 20 boys and 10 girls. The patients had received an average of nine AEDs before starting treatment with OXCBZ, but their seizures were not controlled satisfactorily. During the period of treatment with OXCBZ, 18 patients (60%) received 1, 10 patient (33.3%) received 2 and 2 patients (6.66%) received 3 AEDs concomitantly. In patients with control of seizures after OXCBZ therapy, 9 patients had received one and 6 had received two concomitant AEDs.

Nineteen patients (63.3%) had mixed type seizures, nine (30%) had partial seizures with or without secondary generalization and two (6.6%) had generalized tonic colonic seizures. Table 1 shows patient information.

The effects of OXCBZ add-on therapy on intractable epilepsy is shown in Table 2. OXCBZ was effective in controlling intractable seizure in children (P = 0.003). The best response was seen in patients with partial epilepsy (77.7%) (P = 0.0043) and the patients with mixed-type seizures showed the least response to the drug. The average dose to control seizure was 45 mg/kg/day. No case of status epilepticus was reported during this period.

In one patient, the occurrence of extensive skin rash led to discontinuation of the medication. Retrospectively, we found that a history of skin reaction to CBZ was present in this patient. In another patient, increasing dose of OXCBZ led to diplopia and dizziness that disappeared with reduction of the drug dose. The other side effects include asymptomatic transient hyponatremia (Na = 130 - 132), drowsiness, headache, nausea and vomiting, ataxia and agitation (each in 1 patient). All of these side effects were seen in the initiation of treatment and disappeared after a few days. Overall, transient side effects were seen in 11 patients (36.6%) and in 1 patient (3.3%) we had to discontinue the drug because of adverse event (skin rash). Serious complications including bone marrow depression and hepatic or renal involvement were not detected in any of our patients.

DISCUSSION

OXCBZ is a new medication similar to CBZ which has a favorable profile. It is rapidly absorbed and has a rapid and complete reductive metabolism to form active 10-

Table 1. Comparison between efficacies of OXCBZ in different types of refractory epilepsy.

Seizure type \ Response		Complete control	Improvement	Unchanged	Worsening	Total
Partial onset	Number	3	5	1	0	9
	Percent	33.3	55.5	11.1	0	100
Generalized tonic clonic	Number	0	1	1	0	2
	Percent	0	50	50	0	100
Mixed type	Number	0	6	9	4	19
	Percent	0	31.5	47.3	21.05	100

Table 2. Total evaluation of treatment response to OXCBZ.

Response	Number	Percent
Seizure-Free	3	10
Improvement	12	36.6
Unchanged	11	40
Worsening	4	13.3
Total	30	100

monohydroxy derivative (MHD) which is glucorunidated and excreted in the urine, with minimal involvement of the hepatic cytochrome P450- dependent enzymes. Oxcarbazepine has no auto induction and has minimal interaction with other antiepileptic medications (Glasuer, 2001). It is quite efficient in the treatment of partial seizures in children when administered both alone and in combination with other antiepileptic medications (Bang and Goa, 2003).

According to our results, in 46.6% of the patients, the seizures were completely controlled or a minimum of 50% reduction in seizure frequency was obtained. In the study of Gaily and coworkers, a minimal 50% reduction in the frequency of seizures was detected during the treatment with OXCBZ in 50% of the patients with localization related epilepsy and in 40% of patients with generalized epilepsy (Gaily et al., 1998). In the studies by Rufo-Campas et al and Freidel and colleagues, similar results were obtained (Rupo-Campos et al., 2006; Freidel et al., 2007). In a study assessing the efficacy of OXCBZ in an adjunctive setting (with median dose of 31.4 mg/kg/day), patients with partial seizures were evaluated. A 35% reduction in the frequency of seizures was detected, whereas, this rate was 9% in the placebo group (Bang and Goa, 2003).

In our study, the best result was seen among the patients with partial seizures (22.2% seizure-free rate and 55% reduction in the frequency of seizure), which is in accordance with other studies (Kalis, 2001; Gaily et al., 1998; Glauser et al., 2000; Wellington and Goa 2001).

Adverse effects of drug appeared in 40% of our patients. Most common side effects of OXCBZ are nausea, vomiting, dizziness, fatigue, diplopia and somnolence (Kalis, 2001; Arroyo, 2001; Horga and Horga, 2006; Wellington and Goa 2001).

Usually these side effects are transient and disappear with dose decrease (Arroyo, 2001). OXCBZ shows better tolerability and safety than CBZ which is due to absence of 10 - 11 epoximetabolites of CBZ, less drug interaction with other antiepileptic, less risk of overdose for the patient and no severe hematologic, renal, hepatic or nervous system side effects (Peter et al., 2006; Horga and Horga, 2006). In 3% of the patients (regardless of child or adult), asymptomatic hyponatremia is detected, most frequently in the patients predisposed to hyponatremia (because of diseases or medications such as diuretics or non steroidal anti inflammatory drugs) (Schmidt et al., 2001; Arroyo, 2001).

Hyponatremia generally improves a few days after discontinuation of the medication (Rene and Richard, 2002). Therefore measurement of the baseline serum sodium level is not necessary except for the conditions previously mentioned. When the patient is on the maintenance therapy with OXCBZ, serum level of sodium should also be measured when the symptoms of hyponatremia develop (Schmidt et al., 2001). The risk of symptomatic hyponatremia is greater when the child has an infection or the seizure is prolonged (Rene and Richard, 2002). In our study one patient (3.33%) developed asymptomatic hyponatremia in the first week of treatment.

Allergic skin reactions are rare and develop mostly within the 3 first months of the treatment (Rene and Richard, 2002). Cross reactivity is also detected in 25% of the patients who are hypersensitive to CBZ (Dam, 1994). In our study one patient (3.33%) developed skin rash in the first week of treatment. She has the history of skin rash to CBZ previously. The uncommon side effects of OXCBZ include abdominal pain, acne, alopecia, apathy, diarrhea, gum hyperplasia, tremor and weight gain (Rene and Richard, 2002). None of these side effects were seen in our patients. Based on other researches done so far, in patients with mild to moderate hepatic dysfunction, no adjustment in the dose of OXCBZ is needed (Flesch, 2004; Schmidt and Sachdeo 2000).

Conclusion

OXCBZ is a favorable medication in treatment of epilepsy especially partial seizures in children. We observed some advantages of drug including rapid titration, low rate of drug-drug interaction, low rate of serious side effect and good tolerability and safety. Also based on other research done so far, there is no need for monitoring of the laboratory findings of the patients.

ACKNOWLEDGMENTS

We gratefully acknowledge Shahid Beheshti University of Medical Science for the financial support. We thank Mrs. F. Abdollah Gorji for technical support.

REFERENCES

Arroyo S (2001). Oxcarbazepine. Neurologia, 16: 370-375.

Bang L, Goa K (2003). Oxcarbazepine: a review of its use in children with epilepsy. Pediatr. Drugs, 5: 557-573.

Bang LM, Goa KL (2004). Spotlight on oxcarbazepine in epilepsy. CNS Drugs, 18: 57-61.

Castillo S, Schmidt DB, White S (2000). Oxcarbazine add-on for drug-Resistant partial epilepsy. Cochrane Database Syst. Rev., 3: CDoo 2028.

Connock M, Frew E, Evans BW, Bryan S, Cummins C, Fry-Smith A, Po ALW, Sandercock J (2006). The clinical effectiveness and cost-effectiveness of newer druges for children with epilepsy. A systematic review. Health Technol. Asses., 10(3) 9-118.

Dam M (1994). Practical aspects of oxcarbazepine treatment Epilepsia, 35: 523-525.

Flesch G (2004). Overiew of the clinical pharmacokinetics of oxcarbazepine. Clin. Drug Invest., 24: 185-203.

Freidel M, Krause E, Kuhn K, Peper R, Vogel H (2007). Oxcarbazepine in the treatment of epilepsy. Fortschr. Neurol. Psychiatr., 75: 100-106.

Gaily E, Granstrom ML, Liukkonen E (1998). Oxcarbazepine in the treatment of epilepsy in children and adolescents with intellectual disability. J. Intellect Disabil. Res., 42(1): 41-45.

Gaily E, Granstrom ML, Liukonen E (1997). Oxcarbazepine in the treatment of early childhood epilepsy. J. Child Neurol., 12: 496-498.

Glasuer TA (2001). Oxcarbazepine in the treatment of epilepsy. Pharmacotherapy, 21: 904-919.

Glauser TA, Nigro M, Sachdeo R, Pasteris LA, Weinstein S, Abou-Khalil B, Frank LM, Grinspan A, Guarino T, Bettis D, Kerrigan J, Geoffroy G, Mandelbaum D, Jacobs T, Mesenbrink P, Kramer L, D'Souza J (2000). Adjunctive therapy with oxcarbazepine in children with partial seizures. The Oxcarbazepine Pediatric Study Group. Neurology, 27: 2237-2244.

Horga de la Parte IF, Horga A (2006). Oxcarbazepine in the treatment of epilepsy. A review and update. Rev. Neurol., 42: 95-113.

Kalis MM, Huff NA (2001). Oxcarbazepine, an antiepileptic agent. Clin. Ther., 23: 680-700.

Malphrus AD, Wilfong AA (2007). Use of the newer antiepileptic drugs in pediatric epilepsies. Curr treat options Neurol., 9: 256-267.

May TW, Korn-Merker E, Rambeck B (2003). Clinical pharmacokinetics of oxcarbazpine. Clin Pharmacokinet, 42: 1023-1042.

Peter RC, Carol S (2006). Camfield, pediatric epilepsy: An overview in : Swaiman KF, pediatric Neurology principles and practice, mosby, 4th edition pp. 981-989.

Rene HL, Richard H (2002). mattson; Anti epileptic Drugs, Lippincott Williams and Wilkins, 5th edition, pp. 449-458.

Rupo-Campos M, cases-Fernandez C, Martinez-Bermejo-A (2006). long term use of oxcorbazepine oral suspension in childhood epilepsy: Open-label study. J. Child Neurol., 21: 480-485.

Schimdt D, Arroy S, Baulac M, Schmidt D, Arroyo S, Baulac M, Dam M, Dulac O, Friis ML, Kälviäinen R, Krämer G, Van Parys J, Pedersen B, Sachdeo R (2001). Recommendations on the clinical use of oxcarbazepine in the treatment of epilepsy: a consensus view. Acta Neurol. Scand., 104: 167-17.

Schmidt D, Elger CE (2004). How is oxcarbazepine different from carbamazepine? Nervenarzt, 75: 153-160.

Schmidt D, Sachdeo R (2000). Oxcarbazepine for treatment of partial epilepsy: A Review and Recommendations for clinical use. Epilepsy Behav, 1: 396-405.

Wellington K, Goa KL (2001). Oxcarbazepine: an update of its efficacy in the management of epilepsy. CNS Drugs, 15: 137-163.

Medical students' beliefs about treatment and rehabilitation of persons with mental illness

F. Olatunji. Aina[1*], F. Tajudeen Suleiman[2], O. Yewande Oshodi[1] and Derin O. Olorunshola[1]

[1]Department of Psychiatry, College of Medicine of the University of Lagos, Idi-Araba, Lagos State, Nigeria.
[2]Department of Psychiatry, Lagos University Teaching Hospital, Nigeria.

Advances in treatment and rehabilitation of persons with mental illness (PWMI) have generally improved their well-being. However, some people most especially the lay public and no-psychiatric health workers still hold a lot of reservation about the effectiveness of such management interventions. Thus, this study set out to explore medical students' beliefs about treatment and rehabilitation of PWMI. A descriptive and cross-sectional study carried out among medical students of the College of Medicine of the University of Lagos (CMUL), Lagos, Nigeria. Subjects were selected through multistage and systematic random sampling techniques, with age and sex-matched controls selected among dental students. They were evaluated with a Questionnaire adapted from an instrument earlier used by Sechrest et al. (1973) on cross-cultural study of attitude to mental illness among university students. A total of 130 medical students (subjects) and 57 controls (dental students) were studied. The mean age of subjects was 23.2 ± 3.0 years. Varying beliefs about mental illness (MI) were expressed by both subjects and controls. One hundred and seventeen (90%) of subjects and 46 (80.7%) of controls believed PWMI can be effectively treated and most of them believed orthodox treatment to be the important one. On rehabilitation, 8 (6.2%) of subjects and 3 (5.3%) of controls believed treated PWMI should not be allowed to marry (X^2 =9.28, DF=4, p=0.05*). Ninety eight (75.4%) of subjects and 40 (70.2%) of controls believed treated PWMI should have chance of securing jobs. When stratified to pre-clinical and clinical levels of study, 68 (65.4%) of preclinical and 24 (10.9%) clinical students believed PWMI should be kept away from the community (X^2 =24.90, DF=4, p<0.01*). The study has found varying beliefs of the subjects about treatment and rehabilitation of PWMI, most of which are favorable. However, there is still need to emphasize on anti-stigma education on the subjects over their perceived negative beliefs about psychiatry.

Key words: Beliefs, treatment and rehabilitation, mental illness, medical students, Nigeria.

INTRODUCTION

Treatment and rehabilitation in psychiatric practice have witnessed a lot of advances in the past few decades. The discovery of antipsychotic drugs including the more recent second generation types, electro-convulsive therapy (ECT) and effective rehabilitation techniques among other things have led to movement away from institutional care towards greater involvement in the community (Amering et al., 2005; Macpherson et al., 2005; Ahanotu and Onyeizugbo, 2007). This heightened interest in deinstitutionalized system of care for persons with mental illness (PWMI) necessitated increased need for their social and occupational rehabilitation (National Advisory Mental Health Council, 1993; Lyons and McLoughlin, 2002; Glozier et al., 2006). As an important aspect of mental health care, rehabilitation is to enable treated patients recover their previous social and occupational skills and to help the disabled and handicapped to achieve maximum good health, occupational and social integration and quality of life (Hafner, 1996).

In Nigeria, orthodox mental health practice is characterized by paucity of facilities and mental health professionals, with concentration of care in the relatively few available psychiatric hospitals and psychiatric units of

*Corresponding author. E-mail: ainafran@yahoo.com.

some general and teaching hospitals (Odejide and Ohaeri, 1997; Aina et al., 2007). However, increasing awareness among the general public leading to increased patronization of the few psychiatric facilities has led to overstretching the available services most especially in patient facilities (Osibogun, 2004; Boroffka, 1995 -1996). This has led to recent calls in the country for de-emphasis on institutionalization in favor of de-institutionalization as practiced in the Western countries (Gureje et al., 1995; Ladapo et al., 2008). However, an identified potential problem of deinstitutionalized care in Nigeria is the general negative attitudes of the public towards PWMI (Kabir et al., 2004; Gureje et al., 2005). Across various cultures of the world, PWMI have been found to suffer from varying degrees of insidious discrimination which leads to strained social interactions, compromised quality of life, low self esteem, unemployment and loss of income (Link BG and Phelan, 2006). For example, from Canada, studies have shown that elderly people aged 60 years and above tend to keep social distance from patients with schizophrenia when compared with their younger counterparts (Stuart and Arboleda-Florez, 2001). Also in the United Kingdom, varying levels of stigmatizing attitudes were found to be expressed to different types of mental illness; high stigma to persons with substance dependent problem but relatively more positive attitudes to those with depression (Link BG and Phelan, 2006)

Compared to these UK findings, Fernando et al (2009), in a recent study found Sri Lankan doctors and medical students to express higher levels of stigma towards subjects with depression and those with substance dependence problems; but less stigmatized attitude towards schizophrenia (Fernando et al., 2009). Furthermore, the Sri Lankan medical students showed more negative attitudes than the doctors (Fernando et al., 2009). On treatment for PWMI, many studies have also shown that lay respondents as well as health workers believe in the effectiveness of orthodox treatment (Jorm et al., 199; Lauber et al., 2005), even in developing countries (Kirmayer, 1989; Makanjuola, 2006). However, despite the belief in the effectiveness of orthodox treatment for mental illness, it is generally found that health workers / professionals maintain negative attitudes towards PWMI (Fleming and Szmukler 1992; Glozier et al., 2006). Thus, it has been suggested for interventions aimed at modifying negative attitudes towards PWMI to be put in place; and one of the suggestions was for medical students to have contact with recovering patients in community psychiatric settings (Fernando et al., 2009).

Again, the dearth of available practicing psychiatrists in the country which necessitates the involvement of non-psychiatric clinicians in the care of their patients with co-morbid psychiatric disorders (Mbakwem and Aina, 2008) and the suggestion that medical education is a major component of attitude change against mental health care (Singh et al., 1998) prompted this study.

METHODS

A descriptive and cross sectional study carried out in the College of Medicine, University of Lagos (CMUL). (The college shares the same compound with Lagos University Teaching Hospital (LUTH) in Idi-Araba, Surulere, Lagos. It is the second medical college to be established in Nigeria and took off as a medical school in 1962 but transformed into CMUL via a decree in 1967. The college provides training for medical, dental, physiotherapy and radiography students among others (Ogunnowo et al., 2004; Historical Background in Prospectus 2006-2008).

The study was carried out on medical students that gave verbal consent using a multi-stage sampling method to select the subjects for study. The first stage was to stratify them to pre-clinical (100 - 300 levels) and clinical students (400 -600 levels) groups. The clinical students were those who have had four weeks clinical rotation through psychiatry (usually in year one or two clinical). In each level of study, systematic random sampling was used to select the subjects for inclusion. Age and sex-matched students of dentistry acted as controls. Unlike their medical students' counterparts (subjects), the dental students (controls) do not undergo rotation through psychiatric posting in the course of their training.

A questionnaire made up of two parts was administered: section one to elicit necessary socio-demographic data of the subjects and the second section to elicit their attitudes to PWMI with emphasis on their beliefs as regards treatment and rehabilitation of PWMI. This main section (2) of the instrument is a 25 item questionnaire adapted from that of cross-cultural study of attitude to mental disorders among university students in USA, Pakistan and Philippines by Sechrest et al (1973). Confidentiality and anonymity were guaranteed on the information obtained from the subjects. Data obtained was entered and analyzed using version 16 of Statistical Package for Social Sciences (SPSS-16). Where necessary, percentages and mean were obtained and cross tabulations done. For the categorical variables, differences were obtained using chi-squared statistics with significant level set at $p \leq 0.05$.

RESULTS

Socio-demography

A total of one hundred and eighty seven (187) persons made up of 130 medical students (subjects) and 57 controls (dental students) were studied. The mean age was 23.2 ± 3.0 years and made up of 137 (73.3%) males and 50 (26.7%) females and this is a reflection of the usual gender distribution of medical students in Nigeria. There were 104 (55.6%) pre-clinical (100 - 300 level) and 83 clinical (400 - 600 level) students.

General knowledge about Mental Illness

Nearly equal proportion of subjects (73.6%, n = 130) and controls (73.7%, n = 57) believed mental illnesses are common in the country and consequently 96.6% of subjects would want psychiatry to be strongly entrenched in the curriculum of medical undergraduate training. Ninety seven (74.6%) of the subjects and 35 (61.4%) of controls claimed psychiatric illness seen in the country are mainly psychotic disorders. However, in term of levels of study, 66.3% (n=104) of the pre-clinical students agreed with the concept of psychiatric illness as mainly psychoses as against nearly 75% (n=83) of clinical students but the differences were not statistically significant.

One hundred and six (81.5%) of the subjects believed a normal person can suddenly become mentally ill and no one is immune from developing the illness as against 38 (66.7%) of controls. In the same vein, 76 (73.1%) of pre-clinical and 68 (81.9%) of clinical students held this view. The differences were not significant. Sixty four (49.2%) of the subjects as against 26 (45.6%) of controls believed only very few of PWMI would do anything to harm others. Similarly, 46 (44.2%) of pre-clinical and 44 (53.0%) of clinical students respectively held this belief. The differences were not significant. Only fourteen (10.8%) of subjects and four (7.0%) of controls believed psychiatric illness was due to punishment for sins committed in the past. While 8 (7.7%) pre-clinical and 10 (12.0%) of clinical students respectively held this belief; and the differences were non-significant.

Thirty nine (30%) of subjects and 10 (17.5%) of controls believed "evil spirits" have nothing to do with mental illness, while 25 (24.0%) of preclinical and 24 (28.9%) of clinical students held this belief. The differences were not significant.

Beliefs about treatment and rehabilitation of PWMI

One hundred and seventeen (90%) of the subjects and 46 (80.7%) of controls believed PWMI can be effectively treated to become normal again. Ninety two (88.5%) of pre-clinical and 71 (85.5%) of clinical students believed this. The differences were not significant. One hundred and twelve (86.2%) of subjects and 47 (82.5%) of controls believed orthodox care is the best form of treatment for mental illness. Similarly, 87 (83.7%) of pre-clinical and 72 (86.7%) of clinical students agreed with this. The differences were not significant. Furthermore, more of controls compared with very few subjects (medical students) believed PWMI taken to psychiatric hospitals would end up been institutionalized; the difference was significant (X^2=11.73, DF=4, p=0.04*). In the same vein, 42 (32.3%) of subjects and 6 (10.5%) of controls believed PWMI are best treated in their home environment than been institutionalized with significant difference (X^2=11.6, DF=4, p=0.03*).

Similarly, 14 (11.5%) pre-clinical and 34 (41.0%) of clinical students believed in home care respectively also with significant difference (X^2=22.74, DF=4, p<0.01*). Forty eight (36.9%) of the subjects and 24 (42.1%) of control believed PWMI would require being tied and locked up in special rooms sometimes in their lives to respond to treatment, the difference was not significant. However, 47 (45.2%) of pre clinical and 25 (30.1%) clinical students respectively believed in this with significant difference (X^2=11.64, DF=4 and p=0.02*).

In terms of rehabilitation, 8 (6.2%) of subjects and 3 (5.3%) of controls believed recovered PWMI should not be allowed to marry and the difference was significant (X^2=9.28, DF=4 and p=0.05*). Ten (9.6%) pre-clinical and 1(1.2%) clinical students respectively held this believe but the difference was not significant. Ninety eight (75.4%) of subjects and 40 (70.2%) of controls believed recovered PWMI should have equal chances of securing jobs as those who have never been mentally ill. Seventy nine (76.0%) of pre-clinical and 59 (71.1%) of clinical students believed this. The differences were however not significant.

Sixty one (46.9%) of subjects and 31 (54.4%) of controls believed PWMI should be kept away from the community so as not to harm others but the differences was not significant. Sixty eighth (65.4%) of pre-clinical and 24 (10.9%) clinical students held this belief and the difference was statically significant (X^2=24.90, DF=4, p=0.00*).

DISCUSSION

The non-psychiatric clinicians are becoming more involved in the care of PWMI due to large numbers of patients in general hospitals setting who have serious co-morbid psychiatric disorders (Reiser et al., 1982-1986; Keane, 1990). Yet studies have shown that doctors have negative opinions about PWMI and find it difficult to talk to them (Mukherjee et al., 2002). One of the major areas of concern is their doubt about the response to treatment and rehabilitation of PWMI (Reiser et al., 1982-1986). In Nigeria where there is a dearth of mental health clinicians, a study of this nature for the future medical doctors that would be involved in care of PWMI at one time or the other in the course of their professional career is imperative. In our study, large percentages of our subjects and even the controls have good general knowledge of mental illness. Perhaps their exposure to medical education could have largely contributed to this finding. As seen from the Table 1, the subjects' belief that the major types of MI seen in Nigeria are psychotic cases was probably borne out of the fact that psychotic disorders are the commonest MI presenting for treatment in tertiary health institutions of their medical training (Aina et al., 2007; Gureje et al., 1995).

In Africa, studies have shown that majority of Africans irrespective of their educational attainment still hold to spiritual causation of mental illness and even some physical illnesses that defy simple methods of treatment (Gureje et al., 2005; Odejide et al., 1989). However, contrary to this belief, the majority of medical students and even the controls in our study seemed not to share the view of spiritual causes of MI such as punishments for sins committed and evil spirits. This could probably be

Table 1. Beliefs about mi and treatment/rehabilitation of PWMI.

		Subjects n = 130 (%)	Controls n = 51 (%)	Significance X^2	df	p	Pre-clinical students n = 104 (%)	Clinical students n = 83 (%)	Significance X^2	df	p
General knowledge of MI											
*MI is common in Nigeria	Yes	97 (74.6)	42(73.7)	1.36	4	0.71	72(69.2)	67(80.7)	6	4	0.20
	No	33(25.4)	15(26.3)				32(30.8)	16(19.3)			
*Main MI seen in Nigeria	Yes	97(74.6)	35(61.4)	3.83	4	0.43	69(66.3)	62(74.7)	7.72	4	0.10
are psychotic disorders	No	33(25.4)	22(38.6)				35(33.7)	21(25.3)			
*No one is immuned from	Yes	106(81.5)	38(66.7)	2.06	4	0.72	76(73.1)	68(81.9)	8.81	4	0.01*
having MI	No	24(18.5)	19(33.3)				28(26.9)	15(18.1)			
*Only few of PWMI would	Yes	64(49.2)	26(45.6)	3.85	4	0.43	46(44.2)	44(53.0)	2.57	4	0.63
harm others	No	66(50.8)	31(54.4)				58(55.8)	39(47.0)			
*MI is due to punishment	Yes	14(10.8)	4(7.0)	1.93	4	0.74	8(7.7)	10(12)	2.10	4	0.72
for sins committed	No	116(89.2)	53(93.0)				96(92.3)	73(88.0)			
*Evil spirits have nothing	Yes	39(30.0)	10(17.5)	3.46	4	0.48	25(24.0)	24(28.9)	0.94	4	0.92
to do with MI	No	91(70.0)	47(82.5)				79(76.0)	59(71.1)			
Treatment of PWMI											
*PWMI can be treated to	Yes	117(90.0)	46(80.7)	4.98	4	0.29	92(88.5)	71(85.5)	2.64	4	0.62
become normal again	No	13(10.0)	11(19.3)				12(11.5)	12(14.5)			
*Orthodox care is the best	Yes	112(86.2)	47(82.5)	1.78	4	0.78	87(83.7)	72(85.5)	1.34	4	0.86
treatment of MI	No	18(13.8)	10(17.5)				17(16.3)	11(14.5)			
*PWMI taken to Psychiatric Hospitals eventually	Yes	10(7.7)	4(7.0)	11.73	4	.04**	8(7.7)	6(7.2)	11.80	4	0.38
get institutionalized	No	120(92.3)	53(93.0)				96(92.3)	77(92.8)			
*PWMI is best treated at home	Yes	42(32.3)	6(10.5)	11.16	4	.03**	14(13.5)	34(41.0)	22.74	4	.00**
	No	88(67.7)	51(89.5)				90(86.5)	49(59.0)			
*PWMI requires to be tied and locked up	Yes	48(36.9)	24(42.1)	6.65	4	0.16	47(45.2)	25(30.1)	11.6	4	0.02**
	No	82(63.1)	33(57.9)				57(54.8)	58(69.9)			
Rehabilitation of PWMI											
*Recovered PWMI can not marry	Yes	8(6.2)	3(5.3)	9.28	4	.05**	10(9.6)	1(1.2)	8.31	4	0.08
	No	122(93.8)	54(94.7)				94(90.4)	82(98.8)			
*Recovered PWMI should be employable	Yes	98(75.4)	40(70.2)	2.80	4	0.67	79(76.0)	59(71.1)	0.79	4	0.94
as those without MI	No	32(24.6)	17(29.8)				25(24.0)	24(28.9)			
*PWMI should be kept away so as not to harm	Yes	61(46.9)	31(54.4)	3.55	4	0.47	68(65.4)	24(28.9)	24.9	4	0.00*
others	No	69(53.1)	26(45.6)				36(34.6)	59(71.1)			

due to the suggestions that medical education is seen as the major component of attitude change against mental illness (Singh et al., 1998; Olley et al., 2007). In term of treatment, very large percentages or our subjects and controls, cutting across both pre-clinical and clinical levels of training believed PWMI can be treated to become normal again and orthodox psychiatric care being the best form of treatment. Our findings are similar to those from studies on medical students and doctors in Britain (Mukherjee et al., 2002) and Pakistan (Naeem et al., 2006). But contrary to findings in USA (Reitel et al., 1999), Australia (Malhi et al., 2002) and back home (Nigeria) (Olotu and Osahon, 2001) where medical students that were previously studied perceived psychiatric treatment as some less effective and PWMI hardly get better.

In line with de-institutionalization concept, some of our subjects (32.3%) and controls (10.5%) believed PWMI are best treated in their home environment and PWMI taken to psychiatric facilities for treatment would not necessarily be institutionalized. These findings are relevant to psychiatric practice in Nigeria because the high percentages of subjects and controls who do not share this belief of home care for the mentally ill in a way tactfully approved institutional care which obviously could overstretch the few psychiatric facilities and professionals available in the country. Rehabilitation is a major issue in psychiatric practice with the principal aims of social re-integration, gainful employment and improved quality of life (Lehman, 1983; Browne, 1999; Naber et al., 2002).

In our study, majority of subjects and controls cutting across pre-clinical and clinical levels of training favored PWMI to have equal chance of employment with those that have never suffered from mental illness. On the other hand, majority of subjects and controls would want PWMI to remain unmarried and prefer them (PWMI) to be kept away from the community for institutional care so as not to harm others. Thus, taking into cognizance these beliefs, majority of our subjects and controls seem not to support effective psycho-social rehabilitation plan for PWMI. This has implication on psychiatric aspect of medical education in the country. Thus, there is need to lay more emphasis on psychiatric rehabilitation and anti-stigma contents of psychiatric teachings in the medical curriculum.

REFERENCES

Amering M, Stastny P, Hopper K (2005). Psychiatric advance directives: qualitative study of informed deliberations by mental health services users. Brit. J. Psychiatry 186: 247–252.

Macpherson R, Dix R, Morgan S (2005). A growing evidence base for management guidelines. Advances in Psychiatric Treatment 11: 404–415.

Ahanotu CA, Onyeizugbo EU (2007). The practice of psychiatry in Nigeria: A call for a paradigim shift. Niger. J. Psychiatry 5(1): 42-44.

National Advisory Mental Health Council (1993). Health care reform for Americans with severe mental illness. Am. J. Psychiatry 150: 1447-1465.

Lyons D, McLoughlin DM (2002). Recent advances in psychiatry. Brit. Med. J. West Afr. Edition 5; 1: 11-14.

Glozier N, Hough C, Henderson M, Holland-Elliot K (2006). Attitudes of Nursing staff towards co-workers returning from psychiatric and physical illnesses 52: 525–534.

Hafner H (1996). Psychiatric rehabilitation: general issues. Eur Psychiatry 11: 39s–50s.

Odejide AO, Ohaeri JU (1997). The existing mental health facilities in Nigeria. Niger. J. Psychiatry 1(4): 235-248.

Aina OF, Ladapo HTO, Lawal RA, Owoeye OA (2007). Community–oriented services in a psychiatric hospital. Efforts to reduce stigmatization. Niger. J. Psychiatry 5(1): 19-25.

Osibogun A (2004). Crisis and challenges in the Nigerian health sector. J. Community Med. and Primary Health Care 16(2): 1-7.

Boroffka A (1996). Psychiatric care in Nigeria. Psychopathologie Africaine XXVII: 27–36.

Gureje O, Odejide OA, and Acha RA. Pathways to psychiatric care in Ibadan, Nigeria. Tropical and Geographical Medicine 1995; 47: 125–129.

Ladapo HTO, Aina OF, Lawal RA, Adebiyi OP, Olomu SO, Aina RB (2008). Long stay patients in a psychiatric hospital in Lagos, Nigeria. Afr. J. Psychiatry 11: 128-132.

Kabir M, Iliyasu Z, Abubakar IS, Aliyu MH (2004). Perception and beliefs about mental illness among adults in Karfi village, northern Nigeria. BMC International Health Human Rights 20(4): 1-2.

Gureje O, Lasebikan VO, Ephraim–Oluwanuga O, Olley BO, Kola L (2005). Community study of knowledge and attitude to mental illness in Nigeria. Brit. J. Psychiatry 186: 436–441.

Link BG, Phelan JC (2006). Stigma and its public health implications. The Lancet 367: 528-529.

Stuart H, Arboleda-Florez J (2001). Community attitudes towards people with schizophrenia. Canadian J. Psychiatry 46: 245-252.

Fernando SM, Deane FP, McLeod HJ (2009). Sri Lankan doctors' and medical undergraduates' attitudes towards mental illness. Social Psychiatry and Psychiatric Epidemiology published online 18 August 2009. Assessed (Abstract): 30/11/2009. www.springer.com/medicine/psychiatry/journal/127

Jorm AF, Korten AE, Jacomb PA, Christensen H, Henderson S (1988). Attitudes towards people with a mental disorder: a survey of the Australian public and health professionals. Aust. New Zea. J. Psychiatry 33: 77-83.

Lauber C, Carlos N, Wulf R (2005). Lay beliefs about treatments for people with mental illness and their implications for antistigma strategies. The Canadian J. Psychiatry 50: 745-752.

Kirmayer L (1989). Cultural variations in the response to psychiatric disorder and emotional distress. Social Science and Medicine 29: 327-329.

Makanjuola AB (2006). Public stigma towards psychiatric patients in a southwestern Nigerian town. Niger. Postgrad. Med. J. 13; 3: 210-215.

Fleming J, Szmukler GI (1992). Attitudes of medical professionals towards patients with eating disorders. Aust. New Zea. J. Psychiatry 26: 436-443.

Glozier N, Hough C, Henderson M, Holland-Elliot K (2006). Attitude of nursing staff towards co-workers returning from psychiatric and physical illnesses. Int. J. Soc. Psychiatry 52: 525-534.

Mbakwem AC, Aina OF (2008). Co-morbid psychiatric disorders among subjects in stable state of heart failure in a West African Teaching Hospital. Brit. J. Cardiol. 15(6): 322–325.

Singh SP, Baxter H, Standen P, Duggan C (1998). Changing the attitudes of tomorrow's doctors towards mental illness and psychiatry: a comparison of two teaching methods. Medical Education 32(2): 115-120.

Ogunnowo BE, Odeyemi KA, Iyamabo VA (2004). Needs assessment for health services for young adult students of the College of Medicine of the University of Lagos. J. Clin. Sc. 4(1): 1-4.

College of Medicine of the University of Lagos. Historical Background In Prospectus (2008). Session. College of Medicine Press, Medilag Ventures Ltd., Idi-Araba, Lagos pp. 2–3.

Sechrest LT, Fay SB, Zaidi GR, Flores HA (1973). Attitudes towards mental illness among college students in the US, Pakistan and the Phillipines. J. Cross-Cultural Psychol. 3: 341-359.

Statistical Package for Social Sciences (SPSS) (2007). 16.0 SPSS Inc., 233 South Wacker Drive, 11th Floor, Chicago, IL 606066412.

Reiser L, Sledge W, Edelson M 1988. Four-year evaluation of a psychiatric clerkship: 1982–1986. Am. J. Psychiatry 145: 1122–1126.

Keane M (1990). Contemporary beliefs about mental illness among medical students: Implications for Education and Practice. Academic psychiatry 14; 4: 172-177.

Mukherjee R, Fialho A, Wijetunge A, Checinski K, Surgenor T (2002). The stigmatization of psychiatric illness: the attitudes of medical students and doctors in a London Teaching Hospital. Psychiatric Bulletin 26: 178-181.

Odejide AO, Oyewumi LK, Ohaeri JU (1989). Psychiatry in Africa: An overview. Am. J. Psychiatry 146: 708-716.

Olley BO (2007). Changes in attitudes towards mental illness after exposure to a course in abnormal psychology among students of a Nigerian University. Niger. J. Psychiatry 5(1): 30–41.

Naeem F, Ayub M, Javed Z, Irfan M, Haral F, Kingdon D (2006). Stigma and psychiatric illness. A survey of attitude of medical students and doctors in Lahore, Pakistan. J Ayub Med Coll Abbottabad 18(3): 46–49.

Reitel D, Moutier CY, Swerdlow NR (1999). Attitudes towards psychiatry as a prospective career among students entering medical school. Am. J. Psychiatry 156: 1397-1402.

Malhi GS, Parker GB, Parker K, Kirkby KC, Boyce P, Yellowlees P (2002). Shrinking away from psychiatry? A survey of Australian medical students' interest in psychiatry. Aust. N. Z. J. Psychiatry 36: 416-423.

Olotu OS, Osahon PO (2001). The effects of clinical posting in psychiatry on the beliefs and attitudes of medical students towards the discipline. Niger. J. Psychiatry 1(5): 305-314.

Lehman W (1983). The well-being of chronic mental patients: assessing their quality of life. Arch. Gen. Psychiatry 40: 369-373.

Browne S (1999). Rehabilitation programmes and quality of life in severe mental illness. Int. J. Soc. Psychiatry 45: 302–309.

Naber D, Karow A, Lambert M (2002). Psychosocial outcomes in patients with schizophrenia: quality of life and reintegration. Current Opinion in Psychiatry 15: 31-36.

Permissions

All chapters in this book were first published in JNBH, by Academic Journals; hereby published with permission under the Creative Commons Attribution License or equivalent. Every chapter published in this book has been scrutinized by our experts. Their significance has been extensively debated. The topics covered herein carry significant findings which will fuel the growth of the discipline. They may even be implemented as practical applications or may be referred to as a beginning point for another development.

The contributors of this book come from diverse backgrounds, making this book a truly international effort. This book will bring forth new frontiers with its revolutionizing research information and detailed analysis of the nascent developments around the world.

We would like to thank all the contributing authors for lending their expertise to make the book truly unique. They have played a crucial role in the development of this book. Without their invaluable contributions this book wouldn't have been possible. They have made vital efforts to compile up to date information on the varied aspects of this subject to make this book a valuable addition to the collection of many professionals and students.

This book was conceptualized with the vision of imparting up-to-date information and advanced data in this field. To ensure the same, a matchless editorial board was set up. Every individual on the board went through rigorous rounds of assessment to prove their worth. After which they invested a large part of their time researching and compiling the most relevant data for our readers.

The editorial board has been involved in producing this book since its inception. They have spent rigorous hours researching and exploring the diverse topics which have resulted in the successful publishing of this book. They have passed on their knowledge of decades through this book. To expedite this challenging task, the publisher supported the team at every step. A small team of assistant editors was also appointed to further simplify the editing procedure and attain best results for the readers.

Apart from the editorial board, the designing team has also invested a significant amount of their time in understanding the subject and creating the most relevant covers. They scrutinized every image to scout for the most suitable representation of the subject and create an appropriate cover for the book.

The publishing team has been an ardent support to the editorial, designing and production team. Their endless efforts to recruit the best for this project, has resulted in the accomplishment of this book. They are a veteran in the field of academics and their pool of knowledge is as vast as their experience in printing. Their expertise and guidance has proved useful at every step. Their uncompromising quality standards have made this book an exceptional effort. Their encouragement from time to time has been an inspiration for everyone.

The publisher and the editorial board hope that this book will prove to be a valuable piece of knowledge for researchers, students, practitioners and scholars across the globe.

List of Contributors

Rafiqul Islam
Department of Population Science and HRD, University of Rajshahi, Rajshahi-6205, Bangladesh

Mosharaf Hossain
Department of Population Science and HRD, University of Rajshahi, Rajshahi-6205, Bangladesh

Moshiur Rahman
Department of Population Science and HRD, University of Rajshahi, Rajshahi-6205, Bangladesh

Fakoya Francis Adelade
Department of Anatomy and Cell Biology, Faculty of Basic Medical Sciences, Obafemi Awolowo University,Ile-Ife, Nigeria
Department of Anatomical Sciences, St. George's University School of Medicine, True Blue, St. George's Grenada,The Caribbean

Osoniyi Omolaja
Department of Biochemistry, Faculty of Science, Obafemi Awolowo University, Ile-Ife, Nigeria

Obuotor Efere Martins
Department of Biochemistry, Faculty of Science, Obafemi Awolowo University, Ile-Ife, Nigeria

Siamak Khodarahimi
Islamic Azad University-Eghlid Branch, Iran

Ali Rasti
Islamic Azad University-Arsanjan Branch, Iran

Kedra Wallace
Department of Obstetrics and Gynecology, University of MS Medical Center, 2500 N. State St., Jackson, MS 39216, USA

Jennifer Horgan
Department of Pharmacology, University of MS Medical Center, 2500 N. State St., Jackson, MS 39216, USA

William A Bennett
Department of Obstetrics and Gynecology, University of MS Medical Center, 2500 N. State St., Jackson, MS 39216, USA

Tamás Fischer
Körvasút str. 75/B, H-1158 Budapest, Hungary

Narongsak Noosorn
Faculty of Public Health, Naresuan University, Mueang, Phitsanulok 65000, Thailand

Rung Wongwat
Sukhothai Provincial Public Health Office, Mueang, Sukhothai 64000, Thailand

T Ogundeji
Department of Veterinary Physiology, Faculty of Veterinary Medicine, Ahmadu Bello University, Zaria, Nigeria

J. O Ayo
Department of Veterinary Physiology, Faculty of Veterinary Medicine, Ahmadu Bello University, Zaria, Nigeria

T Aluwong
Department of Veterinary Physiology, Faculty of Veterinary Medicine, Ahmadu Bello University, Zaria, Nigeria

A. Mohammed
Department of Human Physiology, Faculty of Human Medicine, Ahmadu Bello University, Zaria, Nigeria

Ahmed Rady
Department of Psychiatry, Alexandria University, P. O. Box 518, Alexandria 21511, Egypt

Adel Elsheshai
Department of Psychiatry, Alexandria University, P. O. Box 518, Alexandria 21511, Egypt

Osama Elkholy
Department of Psychiatry, Alexandria University, P. O. Box 518, Alexandria 21511, Egypt

Heba Abou el Wafa
Department of Psychiatry, Alexandria University, P. O. Box 518, Alexandria 21511, Egypt

Mahmoud Hakamizanjai
Department of Physical Education, Zanjan University of Medical Sciences and Heath Service, Iran

Abolfazele Ghoreyshi
Psychiatric Department, Zanjan University of Medical Sciences and Heath Service, Iran

Nooraddin Mosavinasab
Department of Social Medicine, Zanjan University of Medical Sciences and Heath Service, Iran

Davood Sohrabi
Department of Histology, Zanjan University of Medical Sciences and Heath Service, Iran

A. J Ajibade
Department Anatomy, Ladoke Akintola University of Technology Ogbomoso, Nigeria

T. K Adenowo
Department of Anatomy, Bowen University, Iwo, Nigeria

O. W Akintunde
Department Anatomy, Ladoke Akintola University of Technology Ogbomoso, Nigeria

P. B Fakunle
Department Anatomy, Ladoke Akintola University of Technology Ogbomoso, Nigeria

O. O Oyewo
Department Anatomy, Ladoke Akintola University of Technology Ogbomoso, Nigeria

E. A Ashamu
Department Anatomy, Ladoke Akintola University of Technology Ogbomoso, Nigeria

A. Y Onaolapo
Department Anatomy, Ladoke Akintola University of Technology Ogbomoso, Nigeria

Rolando Romero Dávalos
Laboratorios BioSim©; Área de Desarrollo e Investigación Científica, México

P. Fermín Pacheco-Moisés
Departamento de Química, Centro Universitario de Ciencias Exactas e Ingenierías. Universidad de Guadalajara.Guadalajara, Jalisco, México

Armida Miranda-Riestra
Laboratorio de Estrés Oxidativo, División de Neurociencias,Centro de Investigación Biomédica de Occidente, Instituto Mexicano del Seguro Social, Guadalajara, Jalisco, México

Carmen Barajas-Martínez
Departamento de Química, Centro Universitario de Ciencias Exactas e Ingenierías. Universidad de Guadalajara.Guadalajara, Jalisco, México

Ariana Navarro-Meléndez
Departamento de Química, Centro Universitario de Ciencias Exactas e Ingenierías. Universidad de Guadalajara.Guadalajara, Jalisco, México

Sergio Rodríguez-Reynoso
División de Investigación Quirúrgica, Centro de Investigación Biomédica de Occidente, Instituto Mexicano del Seguro Social, Guadalajara, Jalisco, México

Irma E.Velázquez-Brizuela
OPD Instituto Jalisciense de Cancerología, Guadalajara, Jalisco, México

J. A. Cruz-Ramos
Laboratorio de Estrés Oxidativo, División de Neurociencias,Centro de Investigación Biomédica de Occidente, Instituto Mexicano del Seguro Social, Guadalajara, Jalisco, México

Genaro Gabriel Ortiz
Laboratorio de Estrés Oxidativo, División de Neurociencias,Centro de Investigación Biomédica de Occidente, Instituto Mexicano del Seguro Social, Guadalajara, Jalisco, México

Jiamjit Saengsuwan
Faculty of Nursing, Khon Kaen University, Khon Kaen, 40002, Thailand

Suwanna Boonyaleepan
Faculty of Nursing, Khon Kaen University, Khon Kaen, 40002, Thailand

Jitpinan Srijakkot
Faculty of Nursing, Khon Kaen University, Khon Kaen, 40002, Thailand

Kittisak Sawanyawisuth
Department of Medicine, Faculty of Medicine, Khon Kaen University, Khon Kaen, 40002, Thailand

Somsak Tiamkao
Department of Medicine, Faculty of Medicine, Khon Kaen University, Khon Kaen, 40002, Thailand

N. Auevitchayapat
Srinagarind Epilepsy Research Group, Srinagarind, Thailand

S. Arunpongpaisal
Srinagarind Epilepsy Research Group, Srinagarind, Thailand

A.Chaiyakum
Srinagarind Epilepsy Research Group, Srinagarind, Thailand

S. Jitpimolmard
Srinagarind Epilepsy Research Group, Srinagarind, Thailand

S. Lertsinudom
Srinagarind Epilepsy Research Group, Srinagarind, Thailand

W. Phuttharak
Srinagarind Epilepsy Research Group, Srinagarind, Thailand

K. Phunikhom
Srinagarind Epilepsy Research Group, Srinagarind, Thailand

Tiamkao Si
Srinagarind Epilepsy Research Group, Srinagarind, Thailand

S. Vannaprasaht
Srinagarind Epilepsy Research Group, Srinagarind, Thailand

M. M Watila
University of Maiduguri Teaching hospital, P. M. B. 1414, Maiduguri, Borno State, Nigeria

Y. W Nyandaiti
University of Maiduguri Teaching hospital, P. M. B. 1414, Maiduguri, Borno State, Nigeria

S. A Bwala
University of Maiduguri Teaching hospital, P. M. B. 1414, Maiduguri, Borno State, Nigeria

A Ibrahim
Federal Medical Centre, Azare, Bauchi State, Nigeria

P. D. Shallie
Department of Anatomy, Obafemi Awolowo College of Health Sciences Olabisi Onabanjo University,Ago-Iwoye, Ogun State, Nigeria

A. K. Adefule
Department of Anatomy, Obafemi Awolowo College of Health Sciences Olabisi Onabanjo University,Ago-Iwoye, Ogun State, Nigeria

H. B. Akpan
Department of Anatomy, Obafemi Awolowo College of Health Sciences Olabisi Onabanjo University,Ago-Iwoye, Ogun State, Nigeria

O. O. Olubiyi
Department of Biochemistry, Obafemi Awolowo College of Health Sciences, Olabisi Onabanjo University, Ago-Iwoye.Ogun State, Nigeria

P. B. Fakunle
Department of Anatomy, Ladoke Akintola University, Ogbomosho, Oyo State, Nigeria

E. N. Adejumo
Department of Chemical Pathology, Obafemi Awolowo College of Health Sciences, Olabisi Onabanjo University,Ago-Iwoye, Ogun State, Nigeria

Yalçin Yetkin
Department of Physiology, Medical Faculty, Yüzüncü Yil University, 65 200, Van, Turkey

Koksal Erman
Department of Biology, Science Faculty, Atatürk University, 25 240, Erzurum, Turkey

Camila Batista dos Santos
Hospital das Clínicas's - Department of Neurology of São Paulo Medical School (HC-FMUSP), Brazil

Maria Fernanda Gouveia da Silva
Hospital das Clínicas's Development and Qualification Center (HC-FMUSP), São Paulo, Brazil

Paulo Henrique Pires de Aguiar
Hospital das Clínicas's - Department of Neurology of São Paulo Medical School (HC-FMUSP), Brazil

Sureyya Talay, Derih Ay
Department of Cardiovascular Surgery, Erzurum Regional Training and Research Hospital Erzurum, Turkey

Ozgur Dag
Department of Cardiovascular Surgery, Erzurum Regional Training and Research Hospital Erzurum, Turkey

Mehmet Ali Kaygin
Department of Cardiovascular Surgery, Erzurum Regional Training and Research Hospital Erzurum, Turkey

Bilgehan Erkut
Department of Cardiovascular Surgery, Erzurum Regional Training and Research Hospital Erzurum, Turkey

Sameer Dhingra
nstitute of Pharmacy and Emerging Sciences, Baddi University of Emerging Sciences and Technology, Baddi,Himachal Pradesh, India
Pharmacology Division, Department of Pharmaceutical Sciences, Guru Jambheshwar University of Science and Technology, Hisar, Haryana, India

Milind Parle
Pharmacology Division, Department of Pharmaceutical Sciences, Guru Jambheshwar University of Science and Technology, Hisar, Haryana, India

M Ijomone Omamuyovwi
Department of Anatomy and Cell Biology, Obafemi Awolowo University, Ile-Ife, Osun State, Nigeria

U Nwoha Polycarp
Department of Anatomy and Cell Biology, Obafemi Awolowo University, Ile-Ife, Osun State, Nigeria

U Obi Augustine
Department of Anatomy and Cell Biology, Obafemi Awolowo University, Ile-Ife, Osun State, Nigeria

O Alese Magaret
Department of Anatomy and Cell Biology, Obafemi Awolowo University, Ile-Ife, Osun State, Nigeria

R .S. Jaggi
Department of Neurosurgery, Rajiv Gandhi Cancer Institute and Research Centre, Sector V, Rohini, New Delhi, India

S. Mehta
Department of Plastic surgery, Rajiv Gandhi Cancer Institute and Research Centre, Sector V, Rohini, New Delhi, India

S. Pasricha
Department of Pathology, Rajiv Gandhi Cancer Institute and Research Centre, Sector V, Rohini, New Delhi, India

Nitin Joseph
Department of Community Medicine, Kasturba Medical College, Mangalore, Manipal University, India

Ananya Ray

Department of Community Medicine, Kasturba Medical College, Mangalore, Manipal University, India

B. K Reshma
Department of Community Medicine, Kasturba Medical College, Mangalore, Manipal University, India

Shruthi Bhat
Department of Community Medicine, Kasturba Medical College, Mangalore, Manipal University, India

Madhumitha Herady
Department of Community Medicine, Kasturba Medical College, Mangalore, Manipal University, India

Ashith Kumar
Department of Community Medicine, Kasturba Medical College, Mangalore, Manipal University, India

K Shri Kiran
Department of Community Medicine, Kasturba Medical College, Mangalore, Manipal University, India

Archaniotis I. Vasilios
Primary Health Care Course Program, Medical School, University of Thessaly, Mezourlo, Larissa, Greece

Wozniak Greta
Department of Medicine, University of Thessaly, Mezourlo, Larissa, Greece

Zoe Roupa
Department of Medicine, University of Thessaly, Mezourlo, Larissa, Greece

Mouzas D. Odysseas
Department of Psychiatry, Medical School, University of Thessaly, Mezourlo, Larissa, Greece

Constantinos Tsipras
Endocrinologist, Outwards Patients, Athens, Greece

Olu Malomo
College of Food Science, Bells University of Technology, P.M.B. 1015, Ota, Ogun State, Nigeria

O. A. B Ogunmoyela
College of Food Science, Bells University of Technology, P.M.B. 1015, Ota, Ogun State, Nigeria

S. O Oluwajoba
College of Food Science, Bells University of Technology, P.M.B. 1015, Ota, Ogun State, Nigeria

Daniel 'Toyosi
College of Food Science, Bells University of Technology, P.M.B. 1015, Ota, Ogun State, Nigeria

Shakya Dhana Ratna
Department of Psychiatry, B P Koirala Institute of Health Sciences, Nepal

M Ijomone Omamuyovwi
Department of Anatomy and Cell Biology, Obafemi Awolowo University, Ile-Ife, Nigeria

U Nwoha Polycarp
Department of Anatomy and Cell Biology, Obafemi Awolowo University, Ile-Ife, Nigeria

K Olaibi Olayemi
Department of Anatomy and Cell Biology, Obafemi Awolowo University, Ile-Ife, Nigeria

U Obi Augustine
Department of Anatomy and Cell Biology, Obafemi Awolowo University, Ile-Ife, Nigeria

Alese Magaret O
Department of Anatomy and Cell Biology, Obafemi Awolowo University, Ile-Ife, Nigeria

Onaolapo, Olakunle James
Department of Pharmacology, Faculty of Basic Medical Sciences, College of Health Sciences, Ladoke Akintola University, Ogbomoso Oyo State, Nigeria

Onaolapo, Adejoke Yetunde
Department of Human Anatomy, Faculty of Basic Medical Sciences, College of Health Sciences, Ladoke Akintola University, Ogbomoso, Oyo State, Nigeria

O. A. Oyekunle
Department of Physiology, College of Health Sciences, Ladoke Akintola University of Technology, Ogbomoso, Nigeria

M. A. Akanmu
Department of Pharmacology, Faculty of Pharmacy, Obafemi Awolowo University, Ile-Ife, Nigeria

T. P. Ogundeji
Department of Physiology, College of Health Sciences, Ladoke Akintola University of Technology, Ogbomoso, Nigeria

Olukunmi Lanre OLAITAN
Department of Human Kinetics and Health Education, University of Ilorin, Ilorin, Nigeria

A. A. Abiodun
Department of Anatomy and Cell Biology Obafemi Awolowo University, Ile-Ife, Nigeria

B. A. Falana
Department of Anatomy, College of Health Sciences, Osun State University, Osogbo, Nigeria

I. P. Oyeyipo
Department of Anatomy, College of Health Sciences, Osun State University, Osogbo, Nigeria

Suk-Yu Yau
Department of Anatomy, Li Ka Shing Faculty of Medicine, University of Hong Kong, SAR, Hong Kong.State Key laboratory of Brain and Cognitive Science, Li Ka Shing Faculty of Medicine, University of Hong Kong, SAR, Hong Kong
Research Centre of Heart, Brain, Hormone and Health Aging, SAR, Li Ka Shing Faculty of Medicine, University of Hong Kong, SAR, Hong Kong

Benson Wui-Man Lau
Department of Anatomy, Li Ka Shing Faculty of Medicine, University of Hong Kong, SAR, Hong Kong
State Key laboratory of Brain and Cognitive Science, Li Ka Shing Faculty of Medicine, University of Hong Kong, SAR, Hong Kong

Tatia M. C. Lee
State Key laboratory of Brain and Cognitive Science, Li Ka Shing Faculty of Medicine, University of Hong Kong, SAR, Hong Kong
Laboratory of Neuropsychology, University of Hong Kong, SAR, Hong Kong
Institute of Clinical Neuropsychology, University of Hong Kong, SAR, Hong Kong
Laboratory of Cognitive Affective Neuroscience, University of Hong Kong, SAR, Hong Kong

Kwok-Fai So
Department of Anatomy, Li Ka Shing Faculty of Medicine, University of Hong Kong, SAR, Hong Kong
State Key laboratory of Brain and Cognitive Science, Li Ka Shing Faculty of Medicine, University of Hong Kong, SAR, Hong Kong
Research Centre of Heart, Brain, Hormone and Health Aging, SAR, Li Ka Shing Faculty of Medicine, University of Hong Kong, SAR, Hong Kong
JGHM Institute of CNS Regneration,Jinan University and The University of Hong Kong, Guangzhou, China

S. Rekha
Department of Pharmacology, Mother Theresa Post Graduate and Research Institute of Health Sciences, Puducherry - 605006, India

S. Kavimani
Department of Pharmacology, Mother Theresa Post Graduate and Research Institute of Health Sciences, Puducherry - 605006, India

K. V. Raman
Department of Pharmacology, Mother Theresa Post Graduate and Research Institute of Health Sciences, Puducherry - 605006, India

Amira Sidig, Abbasher Hussein
Faculty of Medicine, University of Khartoum, Sudan, P. O. Box 102, Khartoum, Sudan

Faroug Yassien
Faculty of Medicine, University of Khartoum, Sudan, P. O. Box 102, Khartoum, Sudan

Ahmed Hamad
Faculty of Medicine, University of Khartoum, Sudan, P. O. Box 102, Khartoum, Sudan

Omer el-Adil
Faculty of Medicine, University of Khartoum, Sudan, P. O. Box 102, Khartoum, Sudan

Mohmad Saad
Faculty of Medicine, University of Khartoum, Sudan, P. O. Box 102, Khartoum, Sudan

Bedraldin Mubark
Faculty of Medicine, University of Khartoum, Sudan, P. O. Box 102, Khartoum, Sudan

Mohmad Malk Aldar
Faculty of Medicine, University of Khartoum, Sudan, P. O. Box 102, Khartoum, Sudan

M. M Watila
University of Maiduguri Teaching hospital, P. M. B. 1414, Maiduguri, Borno State. Nigeria

Y. W Nyandaiti
University of Maiduguri Teaching hospital, P. M. B. 1414, Maiduguri, Borno State. Nigeria

A Ibrahim
Federal Medical Centre, Azare, Bauchi State, Nigeria

S. A Balarabe
Usman Danfodio University Teaching Hospital Sokoto. Nigeria

I. D Gezawa
Aminu Kano Teaching Hospital, PMB 3011 Kano, Nigeria

B Bakki
University of Maiduguri Teaching hospital, P. M. B. 1414, Maiduguri, Borno State. Nigeria

A Tahir
University of Maiduguri Teaching hospital, P. M. B. 1414, Maiduguri, Borno State. Nigeria

M. M Sulaiman
University of Maiduguri Teaching hospital, P. M. B. 1414, Maiduguri, Borno State. Nigeria

S. A Bwala
University of Maiduguri Teaching hospital, P. M. B. 1414, Maiduguri, Borno State. Nigeria

Rahil Razeghi
Department of Sport Psychology, Faculty of Physical Education and Sport Science, Shahid Chamran University of Ahvaz, Iran

Parvaneh Shafie Nia
Department of Sport Psychology, Faculty of Physical Education and Sport Science, Shahid Chamran University of Ahvaz, Iran

Nahid Shebab bushehri
Department of Sport Psychology, Faculty of Physical Education and Sport Science, Shahid Chamran University of Ahvaz, Iran

Farzad Maleki
Department of Sport Psychology, Faculty of Physical Education and Sport Science, Shahid Chamran University of Ahvaz, Iran

A. J Ajibade
Department of Anatomy, Ladoke Akintola University of Technology, Ogbomosho, Osun State, Nigeria

P. B Fakunle
Department of Anatomy, Ladoke Akintola University of Technology, Ogbomosho, Osun State, Nigeria

O. O Fatoba
Department of Anatomy, Ladoke Akintola University of Technology, Ogbomosho, Osun State, Nigeria

O. T Olayemi
Department of Anatomy, Ladoke Akintola University of Technology, Ogbomosho, Osun State, Nigeria

R Bolaños-Jiménez
School of Medicine, Universidad Panamericana, Mexico City, Mexico

J Arizmendi-Vargas
School of Medicine, Universidad Panamericana, Mexico City, Mexico

J. D Carrillo-Ruiz
Neurosciences and Psycophysiology Department, Universidad Anáhuac, Mexico City, Mexico
Functional Neurosurgery and Radiosurgery Service, Hospital General de México, O.D., Mexico City, Mexico

M. E López-Lizárraga
School of Dentistry, Universidad Intercontinental, Mexico City, Mexico

J. L Calderón Álvarez-Tostado
Médica Sur Clinic and Foundation, Mexico City, Mexico

H Martínez-Menchaca
Tissue Engineering and Regenerative Medicine Laboratory, Department of Basic Sciences, School of Medicine,University of Monterrey (UDEM), San Pedro Garza García, NL, Mexico

Leyva Resendiz I
School of Medicine,Universidad Nacional Autónoma De México. Mexico

J. L Serrato-Ávila
School of Medicine, Universidad Panamericana, Mexico City, Mexico

A Rendón-Molina
School of Medicine, Universidad Panamericana, Mexico City, Mexico

G Rivera-Silva
Tissue Engineering and Regenerative Medicine Laboratory, Department of Basic Sciences, School of Medicine

Vigliecca Nora Silvana
Consejo Nacional de Investigaciones Científicas y Técnicas de la Argentina (CONICET); - Argentina. Servicio de Neurocirugía del Hospital Córdoba; Centro de Investigaciones de la Facultad de Filosofía y Humanidades-(CIFFyH). Universidad Nacional de Córdoba, Argentina

Peñalva Marisa Carola
Centro de Investigaciones de la Facultad de Filosofía y Humanidades (CIFFyH). Universidad-Nacional de Córdoba,Argentina

Castillo Jorge Antonio
Centro de Investigaciones de la Facultad de Filosofía y Humanidades (CIFFyH). Universidad-Nacional de Córdoba,Argentina

Molina Silvia Cristina
Centro de Investigaciones de la Facultad de Filosofía y Humanidades (CIFFyH). Universidad-Nacional de Córdoba,Argentina

Voos Javier Alfredo
Grupo de Ingeniería Clínica de la Universidad Tecnológica Nacional (UTN) Regional Córdoba, Argentina

Ortiz Maria Marta
Colegio de Fonoaudiólogos. Buenos Aires, Argentina

Ribichich Marialicia
Consultorio Psicopedagógico Privado. Buenos Aires, Argentina

Azita Tavassoli
Department of Pediatric Neurology, Ali Asghar Children Hospital, Iran University of Medical Science, Tehran, Iran

Mohamad Ghofrani
Department of Pediatric Neurology, Mofid Children Hospital, Shahid Beheshti University of Medical Science,Tehran, Iran

Mohsen Rouzrokh
Department of pediatric surgery, Mofid Children Hospital, Shahid Beheshti University of Medical Science, Tehran, Iran

Eznollah Azargashb
Department of Health and Social Medicine, Shahid Beheshti University of Medical Science, Tehran, Iran

F. Olatunji. Aina
Department of Psychiatry, College of Medicine of the University of Lagos, Idi-Araba, Lagos State, Nigeria

F. Tajudeen Suleiman
Department of Psychiatry, Lagos University Teaching Hospital, Nigeria

O. Yewande Oshodi
Department of Psychiatry, College of Medicine of the University of Lagos, Idi-Araba, Lagos State, Nigeria

Derin O. Olorunshola
Department of Psychiatry, College of Medicine of the University of Lagos, Idi-Araba, Lagos State, Nigeria